History of Israel

1000 Years of
Biblical Adventure

James E. Smith, Ph.D.

Dedicated to

Susan Sydor
And the memory of
Dan Sydor

A cheerful heart is good medicine
Proverbs 17:22

ISBN
978-1-105-75923-9

PREFACE

There are various ways of studying biblical history, but probably the chronological method is the most practical. That is the method followed in this survey. The so-called twelve books of history in the English Bible follow roughly a chronological sequence with notable exceptions. The last six chapters of Judges probably describe events that occurred shortly after the death of Joshua. The Book of Ruth should probably be assigned to the judgeship of Jair. Some of the events in the early chapters of 1 Samuel chronologically precede or parallel the judgeship of Samson. Several events in 2 Samuel are not related in chronological order. During the Sister Kingdom period the author of Kings "walks" through the history by picking up the history of Judah, advancing it beyond the last narrated event in the history of Israel, then repeating the process for the opposite kingdom. The events in the Book of Esther fit chronologically in the middle of the Book of Ezra.

My earlier work *The Books of History* (College Press, 1995) related events in the order they appear in the twelve books. While that arrangement facilitated a study of the individual books, it made things awkward for teachers of the history of Israel to make reading assignments without having the students jump all over the book. I have taken that material here and revamped it to facilitate the use as a textbook in a college-level history of Israel.

The events narrated in Joshua through Nehemiah cover roughly a thousand years, from about 1400 BC to 400 BC. I have discussed that material in forty-two chapters, about three chapters a week for a standard college semester.

This is primarily a survey of the biblical text of Joshua through Nehemiah. Though it is not a book on biblical archaeology, I have included references to some of the more important discoveries relating to this history. As noted above, I have tried to arrange the material in chronological order following the most recent studies in that area. Students should be aware, however, that there are many competing systems of biblical chronology. Dates are less certain prior to David, more certain in the period of Israel's kings, and very precise in the postexilic era.

The Apostle Paul commended the study of biblical history when he wrote, "Now these things happened to them as an example, and they were written for our instruction, upon whom the ends of the ages have come" (1 Corinthians 10:11).

James E. Smith
Florida Christian College

Contents

Sister Kingdom Period
930-722 BC

OVERVIEW

All things must be fulfilled which are written in the law of Moses, and in the prophets, and in the psalms, concerning me. Then he opened their understanding, that they might understand the scriptures. Luke 24:44-45.

Chart 1	
Overview of Israel's History	
PERIOD 7 Periods	BIBLICAL SOURCES 12 Books
1. Conquest	Joshua + Judges chapters
2. Judges	Judges + 1 Samuel 1-7
3. Single Kingdom	1 Samuel 8-1 Kings 11 + Chronicles chaps.
4. Sister Kingdoms	1 Kings 12-2 Kings17 + Chronicles chaps.
5. Assyrian Period	2 Kings 18-23 + Chronicles chaps
6. Babylonian Period	2 Kings 24-25 + Chronicles chaps
7. Persian Period	Ezra, Nehemiah, Esther
1000 YEARS	

CONQUEST PERIOD
Victory of Faith

Biblical Location: Book of Joshua + Judges chapters

Beginning: Crossed Jordan River (1406 BC)

Conclusion: Conquered by Cushan (1378 BC)

Duration: 28 years

Key Players: Joshua, Caleb, Rahab

Key Events: Battles, Allotments, Commitment, "Konfusion"

Scriptural Theme:
He [the Lord] overthrew seven nations in Canaan and gave their land to his people as their inheritance (Acts 13:19 NIV).

Christian Application:
For if Joshua had given them rest, God would not have spoken later about another day. There remains, then, a Sabbath-rest for the people of God (Hebrews 4:8-9 NIV).

Chart 2
PREACH THE WORD
"Fearless Confidence"

Text: Joshua 1:6-9 *Be strong and courageous!*
YOU can have fearless confidence IF...

   A. You Claim God's Promises (1:6).
   B. You Obey God's Commands (1:7)
   C. You Master God's Word (1:8)
   D. You walk in God's Company (1:9)

1
PREPARATION FOR CONQUEST
Joshua 1-5

Chapter Chronology

		Nisan 15
	15 Days in Mar/Apr 1406 BC	
Nisan 1		

Our main biblical source for the Period of Conquest is the Book of Joshua. The book is anonymous; but it seems to have been written by an eyewitness of the events narrated. Jewish tradition is probably right to assign the authorship to the person who is also the leading figure in the book, viz. Joshua the son of Nun.

JOSHUA COMMISSIONED
Joshua 1

Date: ca. 1406 BC; Nisan 1-2 (Mar/Apr)

As the Book of Joshua opens, the people of Israel are poised to push into Cis-jordan, the heart of the land promised to Abraham, Isaac, and Jacob. The plan of God revealed by Moses required the armies of Israel to cross the Jordan and dislodge those who were occupying the territory which was Israel's by divine decree. That would not be an easy task. Canaanite cities were well fortified; their armies were well equipped. In theory at least Canaan at this period was under Egyptian hegemony. The Pharaoh's assistance to his vassal clients was always a possibility. Even with his limited military experience Joshua must have realized that, humanly speaking, his forces faced incredible odds against success beyond the Jordan.

The Book of Joshua opens and closes with exhortation. The first chapter consists of three hortatory utterances: 1) Yahweh to Joshua, 2) Joshua to the tribes, and 3) the people to Joshua.

Yahweh to Joshua
Joshua 1:1-9

11

At about the age of ninety Joshua must have been filled with apprehension about succeeding Moses. The very fact that God would speak directly to him (1:1) was of itself a significant encouragement to this aging man of God. Previously the Lord had spoken only to Moses, *the servant of Yahweh*. Joshua had been only Moses' servant, a position of honor and apprenticeship (cf. Numbers 27:15-23; Deuteronomy 1:38; 3:21f), but nonetheless a secondary position. Now Joshua was to be the intermediary for divine revelation to Israel. That God broke the silence was the first of several steps taken by the Lord to bolster the confidence of Joshua and to magnify him in the eyes of the people. In his message the Lord first brought encouragement and then he offered exhortation to Joshua.

A. Encouragement (Joshua 1:2-5)

1. Assurance to Joshua (1:2a): The encouragement took several forms. First, Yahweh assured Joshua that the plan to conquer Canaan had not been altered by the death of Moses. Joshua and the people were to arise and pass over Jordan. Earlier the Lord had told Joshua that he would lead Israel into the Promised Land (Deuteronomy 31:7, 23). Now he was being encouraged to assume that leadership role. Second, Yahweh reassured Joshua that he was about to give them (a participle implying imminent action) the land.

2. Assurance to the people (1:3): In the third and fourth words of encouragement God is addressing the entire nation through Joshua. This is indicated by the switch from the singular to the plural second person pronoun in the Hebrew. The Lord declared that he already had given (perfect form of the verb) every place within that territory where they had the faith to tread. The gift was to be in proportion to the faith which they exercised in marching through the land. God always rewards courageous faith!

3. Painting a picture (1:4): To magnify the promise just made, the Lord gave a verbal sketch of the broad contours of the territory he intended to give Israel. Their territory stretched from the wilderness to the Lebanon Mountains and Euphrates River in the north, and from the territory they already occupied in the east to the Great (Mediterranean) Sea in the west. The Lord specifically indicates that *all the land of the Hittites* will be theirs. The Hittites had in recent years been an international power which controlled territory in Syria and northern Palestine.

4. *More assurance to Joshua (1:5):* Fifth, God assured Joshua—the pronoun now reverts to singular—that, though Israel faced resistance, anyone who tried to defend the land would not be able to stand before him. Sixth, the Lord repeated what Moses already had told Joshua (cf. Deuteronomy 31:8), that he could count on the same divine assistance which Moses had received during his tenure as leader. With his own eyes Joshua had seen the supernatural intervention with which the Lord had come to the aid of Moses in crisis after crisis.

B. Exhortation (Joshua 1:6-9)

The promises just made to Joshua were conditional. Joshua was commanded three times to *be strong and courageous.* He must manifest a fearless confidence in God's ability to fulfill what he had sworn to do for his people. Joshua must believe that he would lead his people to *inherit* their land.[1] If he would enjoy success in his work he must manifest that same fearless confidence in executing exactly what Moses had commanded in the Law regarding the Conquest. Joshua's *way*—his life and leadership—would be prosperous if he were careful to obey the stipulations of God's word. Finally, God commanded fearless confidence because that is the only appropriate disposition for one who has God as a traveling companion. Fear and anxiety are tantamount to unbelief.

Joshua to the Tribes
Joshua 1:10-15

Bolstered by the encouraging revelation from the Lord, Joshua immediately began to exercise his authority over the people. He spoke first to the officers, and then to the eastern tribes.

A. Commandment to the Officers (Joshua 1:10-11)

A chain of command within Israel was recognized. The tribal officers were to pass on to the people a command, an explanation and a promise. The command was to prepare *provisions* (NASB), i.e., to

---

[1]The verb *inherit* and the derived noun are important words in Joshua. They appear in 11:23; 14:13; 16:4; 17:6. Cf. also Deuteronomy 1:38; 12:10. The word argues for Israel's legitimate claim to the land. The concept has been carried over into the New Testament to speak of kingdom blessings which are inherited by the believer (e.g., 1 Peter 1:4).

gather up all supplies they might need to sustain them until they were established in Canaan. The explanation for the command was that within three days they will cross over Jordan to possess their inheritance. The promise was that God will give them that land as their own possession.

B. Conversation with Tribes (Joshua 1:12-15)

Joshua immediately sought out the leaders of the two and a half tribes which were intending to settle in Transjordan. He reminded them that Moses already had given them their rest—their inheritance (cf. Numbers 32:16-32). That gift, however, had been made conditionally. The Reubenites, Gadites and half tribe of Manasseh were to leave their families in Transjordan and lead the way across the Jordan *in battle array* (NASB) or *fully armed* (NIV). They were to help their brothers until they had been given rest, i.e., the cessation of hostilities, and had possessed their inheritance. Joshua understood that in the wars of the Lord God's people must be united. The issue which Joshua explored with these tribes was that of leadership. Would they honor their word to Moses? Would they recognize Joshua as Moses' legitimate successor?

People to Joshua
Joshua 1:16-18

1. Commitment to Joshua (1:16-17a, 18a): The leaders of the eastern tribes immediately recognized the authority of Joshua. *All that you have commanded us we will do.* They will leave their families behind and march together with their brothers until victory was achieved. They were willing to go wherever Joshua wished to send them. The eastern tribes agreed to render to Joshua the same cheerful obedience that they had given to his predecessor. Furthermore, they will regard as treason any rebellion against the authority of Joshua. The death penalty will be executed against any that refused to obey the voice of the new leader (cf. Deuteronomy 17:12).

2. Hope for Joshua (1:17b, 18b): The speech of the Transjordan leaders contains provisos that are certainly wishes and may be prayers. Both are introduced by the word *only.* First, they expressed the hope (condition?) that God would be with Joshua as he had been with Moses. These men realized that divine intervention would be necessary if the campaign in Canaan was to be successful. Second,

14

the easterners prayed that Joshua might *be strong and courageous.* They knew that without courageous leadership the mission had no chance of success.

SPYING OUT THE LAND
Joshua 2:1-24

Date: ca. 1406 BC; Nisan 3-5 (Mar/Apr)

Jericho was the first objective beyond the river. Joshua needed to know what he was up against there. Perhaps he anticipated receiving information that would bolster troop morale on the eve of the river crossing. In any case, the dispatching of the two spies is evidence of Joshua's foresight as a general.

Mission of the Spies
Joshua 2:1-7

A. Spies Dispatched (Joshua 2:1)

Joshua secretly dispatched two men from Shittim to spy out Canaan, especially Jericho. Why secretly? Did he not wish his own people to know what he had done? Did he think that such a move might imply that his faith was not strong? Or was the stealth necessary to avoid Canaanite patrols on the western bank of the Jordan? The text offers no clue. Nor does the account describe what must have been a harrowing adventure for these two men in crossing that rampaging, flood-swollen river.

B. House of Rahab (Joshua 2:2-3)

The spies proceeded immediately to Jericho. They found lodging in the house of a harlot named Rahab. Perhaps they chose this house of ill repute because they thought that fewer questions might be asked of them there. Even so, the men were quickly spotted, recognized as Israelites, and reported to the king of the city. Messengers were sent to Rahab ordering her to bring out the men who had entered her house. If Rahab was a sacred prostitute connected with one of the temples of the city that might explain why the authorities did not simply barge into the house and seize the strangers.

C. Actions of Rahab (Joshua 2:4-6)

1. *She hid the spies (2:4a):* Rahab was not too sure that the sanctuary of her house would be respected by the king's men. She took the precaution of hiding her guests among stalks of flax on the flat roof of her house.

2. *She misled the soldiers (2:4b-7):* As it turned out, hiding the spies was unnecessary. Rahab was able to convince the soldiers that the strangers had indeed come, but they had left about sundown when the city gate was closed. She feigned concern that the soldiers pursue immediately after these men so that they might overtake them. The soldiers followed the woman's advice. They searched every road leading to the Jordan. Though a sizable search party must have been sent out of the city, precautions were taken to shut the gate after their departure. Fear gripped the city that the Israelites might launch a surprise attack even during the night.

Covenant of the Spies
Joshua 2:8-21

After the soldiers left, Rahab went immediately to the roof to converse with her two guests.

A. Rahab's Confession (Joshua 2:8-11)

At the door of her home Rahab had taken a stand. She had renounced her country and its gods. Now she enthusiastically embraced Yahweh as *God in heaven above and earth beneath.* She confessed her faith in the program of God: *I know that Yahweh has given you the land.* Her conviction grew out of personal observation and prior testimony. Rahab personally had observed that the Canaanites already had lost their land because they were too terrified to offer effective resistance. This fear grew because of reports of what Yahweh had done for Israel over the past forty years. Through traveling merchants the Canaanites knew of the crossing of the Red Sea on dry land. Within the past few months fugitives from the Amorite kingdoms of Sihon and Og had reported how Israel had put their nations under the curse (□□□□□□) of total destruction. These reports led to two results: fear and faith. For most Canaanites it was only fear; for Rahab, both fear and faith.

B. Rahab's Request (Joshua 2:12-14)

16

Rahab not only believed in the power of Yahweh, she must have also believed in his mercy. For this reason she pled with the spies to enter into a covenant with her that she and her household might be spared in the day of attack. On condition that she tell no one about their mission the two spies pledged on their lives that Israel would deal *in covenant loyalty and faithfulness,* i.e., they would honor the covenant with Rahab.

C. Rahab's Advice (Joshua 2:15-16)

In the overcrowded city of Jericho Rahab's house had been built upon the wall. When the men descended by rope from the window of her house they would be outside the walls. Rahab urged the men to head west toward the nearby mountains which are honeycombed with caves. If they waited there for three days it would be safe for them to return to their camp east of Jordan.

D. Conditions of Salvation (Joshua 2:17-21)

Before leaving the scene the spies underscored again the conditions of the oath that they had just made to spare Rahab and her house. The oath would not be binding if these conditions were not met. First, she must tie *this cord*—apparently the rope upon which they had descended—in her window. This rope was made of bright scarlet thread woven together; it would be easily recognizable in the day of battle. (At this point the men assumed Jericho would fall by battle). Second, she was responsible for gathering her family into the designated house. The spies refused to guarantee the safety of anyone outside the house. Third, they underscored again the necessity of absolute secrecy. Rahab agreed to those conditions. She put the scarlet cord in her window apparently that very night.

Report of the Spies
Joshua 2:22-24

The spies disappeared into the night. They followed the advice of Rahab and headed for the hills, exactly the opposite direction of the way the pursuers assumed they had taken. There they hid for three days. Then they returned to camp by the route they had come. They reported to Joshua that the Canaanites had melted away in fear before Israel. Their concluded: *Surely Yahweh has given all the land into our hands.* This is now the fifth utterance of this glorious truth. The Lord said it to Joshua (1:2, 3), Joshua said it to the officers and the Transjordan tribes (1:11, 15), Rahab said it to the spies (2:9) and now the spies said these words to Joshua.

CROSSING JORDAN
Joshua 3:1-4:18

Date: ca. 1406 BC; Nisan 7-10? (Mar/Apr)

Before undertaking the Conquest one formidable challenge had to be met. The Jordan River was in flood (3:5). Though two robust spies had navigated that river, now an army of thousands, not to mention women, children and livestock, would have to cross.

Approaching Jordan
Joshua 3:1

After three days of breaking camp (1:11), Joshua led the Israelites to a position closer to the Jordan. No hint had yet been given as to how they would be able to negotiate that raging river. The distance from Shittim east of Jordan to Gilgal on the western bank was not more than six miles. Those miles, however, were potentially the most difficult and terrifying traveled thus far by Israel. Yet if there was to be a Conquest at all, Joshua had to reposition his forces in a staging area west of the river. For three days they awaited further instructions.

Further Instructions
Joshua 3:2-13

After three days the plan for crossing Jordan began to take shape. Instructions were passed from the Lord to Joshua, and from Joshua and the officers to the people.

A. Instructions of the Officers (Joshua 3:2-4)

The plan was for the people to follow the Ark of the Covenant as it was carried by the Levitical priests. Because of the vast number of people, the ark was to be 2000 cubits (3000 feet or over half a mile) in front of the group. That way every Israelite would know that Yahweh was leading them forward. The rationale for letting the Lord lead is as valid for the believer today as for the Israelites then: *You have not passed this way before.* The officers mentioned nothing of a

18

miraculous crossing on dry land. That, apparently, had not yet been revealed. They simply were trusting God to provide a way through an impassable barrier.

B. Initial Instructions of Joshua (Joshua 3:5-6)
Joshua addressed first the people and then the priests.
1. For the people (3:5): He urged the people to *consecrate* themselves. He challenged them to believe that on the morrow they would see Yahweh *do wonders* among them. He did not state, however, what those wonders would be. Perhaps his words brought to their minds what had happened at the Red Sea some forty years earlier.
2. For the priests (3:6): Joshua then spoke to the priests,[2] directing them to take up the ark and move forward ahead of the people. They immediately obeyed. What great faith was being demonstrated by these men of God! God's people can only do the impossible when the leaders of the faith are willing to be out in front.

C. Instructions of the Lord (Joshua 3:7-8)
Yahweh revealed a bit more of the plan to Joshua. He was first assured that the events of that day would exalt him in the eyes of his people. They would realize that Joshua enjoyed the divine blessing upon his work as much as Moses had before. What God had promised in his commission (1:5, 9) would now be fulfilled. The great miracle would be initiated by the courage of the priests. Joshua was to command those men to wade out into the river and stand there. The Lord needed to say no more. Joshua got the picture. He hastened to pass his vision on to the people.

D. Final Instructions by Joshua (Joshua 3:9-13)
1. Confidence of victory (3:9-10): Joshua introduced his final pre-crossing directive to the people as *the words of Yahweh.* This suggests that Joshua received more direct information from the Lord than has been recorded in the text in 3:7-8. The miracle of the crossing would lead to experiential knowledge of two key

---

[2]Literally, *the priests, the Levites.* Normally the Levites of the clan of Kohath carried the ark. On special occasions, however, the priests carried the ark. See e.g., Deuteronomy 31:9; 1 Kings 8:3, 6. They are called Levitical priests, not to distinguish them from other priests but to underscore the honor bestowed upon their tribe through its priestly members in leading the procession into the Promised Land.

propositions of faith. First, what happened at the river would prove that the *living God* was among his people. Second, the river crossing would be a pledge that all the "ites"—the seven ethnic groups which occupied Canaan—would be dispossessed by the invading Israelites.

2. *Prediction of miracle (3:11-13):* Joshua pointed out that the ark was already moving forward. He ordered that one man from each of the twelve tribes be designated. Presumably they were to follow the priests into the river. Joshua then indicated that at the moment those priestly feet entered the river the Jordan would stop flowing south. That Joshua was able to *predict* the miracle adds to the wonder of the event. God may have used natural means to produce the path across the river, but the timing of that action requires that the event be regarded as thoroughly supernatural.

Crossing Jordan
Joshua 3:14-4:18

A. River Miracle (Joshua 3:14-17)

The remaining verses of Joshua 3 in typical Hebrew style relate in detail how the predictions of Joshua came to pass. When the priests carrying the ark dipped their feet into the river, the flow of water was cut off *a great distance away at Adam.* The priests stood on dry ground in the middle of the river bed while all the people passed over on dry ground.

B. Commemorating the Crossing (Joshua 4:1-9)

1. *Stones from the river (4:1-8):* After the crossing, Yahweh spoke directly to Joshua for the third time. The function of the twelve men previously designated (3:12) was now indicated. These men were to pick up twelve stones from the place where the priests had stood in the midst of the riverbed. They were to carry these stones to the lodging place on the western bank and erect them as a monument. The stones were to be a *sign* or monument to provoke inquiries from future generations. Adults were to rehearse in the ears of the children the wondrous act of covenant faithfulness which God had performed for them through his ark.

2. *Stones in the river (4:9):* Joshua himself erected a twelve-stone monument in the riverbed where the feet of the priests had stood. Those stones still protruded above the waters of the river at the time the Book of Joshua was written, about twenty years later.

C. Conclusion of the Crossing (Joshua 4:10-18)

1. Emphasis on obedience (4:10): The conclusion of the crossing account stresses the obedience of all those who participated. Joshua faithfully had carried out all that the Lord had spoken to him in the past through Moses and more recently in direct communication. The priests had also done exactly as Joshua had commanded them. The people cooperated by hurrying across the dry riverbed.

2. Order of march (4:11-13): When the crossing ended the ark of God again moved to the lead position in the marching formation. The Transjordan contingent—forty thousand strong—followed the ark. Again the emphasis is on the obedience of these warriors to the instruction which Moses had given them.

3. Exaltation of Joshua (4:14): Yahweh honored his own word that day. He had promised to exalt Joshua in the eyes of the people. That is exactly what he did. The people came to revere Joshua all the days of his life just as they had revered his predecessor.

4. Return of the water (4:15-18): The description of the ark's departure out of the Jordan is every bit as dramatic as that of the ark's approach to the river. The priests left the riverbed at Joshua's command which was issued in obedience to the directive of the Lord. As soon as their feet touched the western bank a raging wall of water came down the riverbed. The water again overflowed its banks as before. The timing of the return of the waters was just as much a miracle as the crossing had been a few hours earlier.

GILGAL ENCAMPMENT
Joshua 4:19-5:12

Date: ca. 1406 BC; Nisan 10-22 (Mar/Apr)

After crossing the river the people camped at Gilgal (location uncertain). The event is so important that the date was long remembered. Israel camped in Canaan for the first time on the tenth day of the first month in the forty-first year after leaving Egypt (4:19). While encamped there the children of Israel made spiritual preparation for the long struggle to follow.

Covenant Faithfulness Recalled
Joshua 4:19-5:1

21

A. Joshua's Speech (Joshua 4:19-24)

Under Joshua's direction the twelve stones taken from the midst of the Jordan were set up in Gilgal. The establishment of this memorial was accompanied by a brief speech by Joshua. As he had previously indicated (4:6f), those stones were to have a pedagogical purpose. Children over the years would be inclined to ask what those twelve huge stones, obviously stacked by human hands, meant. Adults then were to recount the glorious story of the crossing. The crossing of the Jordan is linked by Joshua to the crossing of the Red Sea. Both miracles were designed to teach all peoples that Yahweh is indeed mighty. At the same time, both miracles were designed to underscore God's special relationship with Israel. Such mighty acts should have made Israel reverence Yahweh their God forever.

B. Canaanite Fear (Joshua 5:1)

Rahab had alluded to the Red Sea crossing and the effect of that miracle on the peoples in Canaan who had heard about it. The author now indicates the effect of the Jordan crossing upon those same people. Not just the common people, but even the kings of the region melted in fear at the news that Israel had crossed the Jordan on dry ground. The kings knew that they would now be compelled to face the armies of the Living God, the God of heaven and earth.

Covenant Sign Renewed
Joshua 5:2-9

A. A Memorial Rite (Joshua 5:2-8)

In the fifth direct divine communication with Joshua, the Lord ordered a renewal of the rite of circumcision. This very basic covenant rite (Genesis 17:11) had been suspended during the years of desert punishment, but for what reason is a matter of conjecture. In any case, Joshua was ordered to make flint knives and circumcise that second generation of Israelites who had never received the sign of the Abrahamic covenant in their flesh. The place where the surgery was performed was called *Gibeath-haaraloth,* the hill of the foreskins. The men were forced to remain in camp until all were healed.

B. A Memorial Name (Joshua 5:9)

A declaration of the Lord to Joshua—the sixth divine communication to him—provided the name for that first camping spot. Now that Israel had been brought into the land flowing with milk and honey, and through circumcision had recommitted themselves to the covenant of the fathers, *the reproach of Egypt* had been rolled away. The Egyptians had heaped ridicule on the people of God with their dreams of a homeland. This was especially the case when the Israelites had been forced to wander so many years in the desert. Merchants and desert nomads kept the Egyptians informed of the whereabouts of this nation of former slaves. While Israel wandered in circles in the desert they must have been the butt of many a joke in Egypt. But no more. The God who had brought them out of Egypt had now brought them into Canaan. So they called that first camping spot Gilgal, *rolling,* to commemorate the fact that God had rolled away their reproach.

Covenant Meal Revived
Joshua 5:10-12

A. Record of Passover Observance
The first Passover was observed in Egypt the night of the death plague against the firstborn of the land. The second Passover was observed while Israel was camped at Mount Sinai. So far as the record goes, the third observance of this great festival took place at Gilgal. Henceforth the Passover celebration would not only commemorate the "going out" (Exodus), it would also commemorate the "entering in."

B. Significance of this Passover (Joshua 5:10)
Like circumcision, Passover seems to have been suspended during the period of wilderness wandering. In fact, no uncircumcised person was permitted to participate in the Passover ritual (Exodus 12:48). Therefore, as the years of wandering progressed, an ever increasing percentage of Israelites would have been disqualified from observing the feast. Now that barrier had been removed. On the fourteenth day of Nisan, four days after the circumcision (cf. 4:19), the nation observed the first of hundreds of Passovers in the Promised Land. Most of the males were still quite sore from the surgery which had been performed upon them. Nonetheless, the celebration must have been joyous indeed.

C. Special Feature of this Passover (Joshua 5:11-12)

A special feature of this Passover was the eating for the first time of the *produce of the land*. They ate *parched grain* along with the unleavened bread which was normally eaten at Passover. Once they were able to feed upon the fruits of Canaan, God no longer miraculously provided for them the manna that he had supplied over the past forty years.

Conclusion

In preparing for victory God's people had to overcome four great obstacles: 1) the death of Moses (chapter 1); 2) the morale of the troops (chapter 2); 3) the raging waters of Jordan (chapters 3-4); and 4) the spiritual condition of the people (chapter 5). The first obstacle was surmounted by words of encouragement and exhortation; the second, by information derived from reconnaissance; the third, by dramatic manifestation of the power of God; and the fourth, by renewal of basic ceremonies which marked Israel as the special people of God.

Chart 2 *Victorious Faith: A Comparison*		
Hebrews 11:30		**Galatians 3:26-27**
The Walls of Jericho Fell Down	**WHAT**	You are all the Children of God
by Faith	**HOW**	by Faith
after they had been Compassed about Seven Days	**WHEN**	for as many of you as have been baptized into Christ have put on Christ
TO SAY THAT WE ARE SAVED BY FAITH WITHOUT OBEDIENCE IN BAPTISM IS TO SAY THE WALLS OF JERICHO WOULD HAVE FALLEN WITHOUT MARCHING		

2
CONQUEST OF
CENTRAL CANAAN
Joshua 6-8

Chapter Chronology

	1405
One Year +	
1406	

In the initial engagements of the Canaan campaign the Israelites encountered three very different types of enemies. At Jericho the enemy was holed up within their fortifications. At Ai the enemy was bolder, venturing beyond their walls to attack the Israelites. The Hivites who dwelled in Gibeon resorted to trickery to avoid a military confrontation with Israel.

CONQUEST OF JERICHO
Joshua 5:13-6:27

Date: ca. 1406 BC; Nisan 17-29

Joshua and his commanders knew that Jericho had to be the first objective in the central Canaan campaign The Jericho campaign was important militarily, for the city was located at the convergence of major valleys that led up into the highlands of Canaan. Psychologically Jericho was important because this was going to be the first battle in Canaan proper. Jericho was one of the oldest cities on earth, and a very prestigious city too. Spiritually this battle was important because here the Israelites would see a dramatic demonstration of the power of God who promised to be with them throughout their campaign to conquer Canaan.

Faith Instructed
Joshua 5:13-6:5

A parenthetical note (6:1) makes clear the condition of the first enemy which Israel faced. The city gates were tightly shut. No one was entering and leaving the city. Israel was unskilled in siege warfare. The situation was hopeless from a military standpoint.

Thus far the author has indicated six occasions when Yahweh spoke directly to Joshua. The seventh divine communication came in a theophany—a visible manifestation of God. The captain of Yahweh's host revealed to Joshua the battle plan for the first campaign in Canaan.

A. Encounter with Deity (Joshua 5:13-15)

1. Joshua's challenge (5:13): Joshua had assumed even before the river crossing that Jericho would be the first objective in Canaan. From a distance he reconnoitered the city and contemplated what strategies might give Israel access to those walls with the least amount of causalities. Joshua thought he was alone with his thoughts. As he lifted up his eyes, however, he was shocked to see *a man* standing before him with a drawn sword, i.e., ready for combat. The scene was full of ambiguity. Joshua drew near with a question: *Are you for us or for our adversaries?*

2. Captain's response (5:14-15): The stranger responded that he was not a mere soldier fighting on either side. Rather he was the commander of the host of Yahweh. Joshua immediately bowed to the ground in respect to this one who was his military superior. He indicated that he was prepared to receive any orders which the captain might have for him. The captain let Joshua know that mere respect such as one officer might have for a superior was not sufficient. He, like Moses at the burning bush, was standing on holy ground. He needed to remove his sandals. This was a symbol of the removal of impurity and a token of respect for the holy presence of God. Joshua immediately complied.

3. Identity of the Captain: Clearly a superhuman presence is depicted here. This person was undoubtedly the same as the angel of the Lord who appeared at various points in Patriarchal history, a visible manifestation of God's presence. The drawn sword conveyed the thought that God himself would fight for Israel.

B. Strategy at Jericho (Joshua 6:2-5)

1. Jericho a gift (6:2): In the person of the captain of Yahweh's host the Lord assured Joshua that *I have given Jericho into your hands.* The king of the city and all his valiant warriors will fall into Joshua's hands. Chapter 6 of the Book of Joshua celebrates the most outstanding instance of God's "giving" of the land to Israel. God always has a better plan. The fall of Jericho was to be an act of faith (Hebrews 11:30) as well as an act of God. What a relief those words must have been to Joshua.

2. *A simple plan (6:3-5):* The plan was simple. The Israelite army was to march around the walls of Jericho every day for six days. Seven priests carrying ram's horn trumpets were to escort the ark in that procession. On the seventh day the Israelite troops were to march seven times around the walls. The number seven is obviously symbolical, recalling God's works of creation. Then the priests were to blow their trumpets, and the people were to shout with a great shout. At that moment, God promised, the walls would *fall down flat.* At whatever point in the procession an Israelite soldier might find himself, he will be able to move straight ahead into the city. The protective walls of Jericho will virtually melt away.

C. Chronological Note

After the appearance of the commander of the Lord's army to Joshua on Nisan 17 there is a period of unknown duration. Perhaps Joshua waited until the completion of the seven days of Unleavened Bread following Passover before beginning the Jericho campaign.

Faith Triumphant
Joshua 6:6-7:1

The Hebrew narrative skillfully employs repetition to underscore what the author considered important in the account. His style emphasizes the exact compliance with the directives of the captain of Yahweh's host.

A. Plan Presented (Joshua 6:6-10)

Joshua immediately passed on the instructions of the Lord.

1. *Order of march (6:6-7):* Joshua first explained the role of the priests. He then told the people about the march around the city. A unit dressed in full battle array preceded the ark. This may be a reference to the forty thousand Transjordan contingent of 4:13. The advanced guard was followed by the priests who marched *before Yahweh* i.e., the ark which symbolized Yahweh's presence. Another military contingent—the rear guard—was to follow the ark.

Chart 3				
March Around Jericho				
Joshua 6				
1.	**2.**	**3.**	**4.**	**5.**
Soldiers	**Priests**	**Ark**	**Soldiers**	**People**
v. 9	**vv. 6, 8, 13**	**vv. 5, 8, 13**	**v. 9**	**v. 7**

2. Acceptance of the plan (6:8-10): Apparently the strange plan for the conquest of Jericho was accepted without question. Both the people and the priests fulfilled their respective roles in the strategy. A final detail of the plan was that the procession was to march in silence. Not one word was to be spoken until Joshua gave the signal.

B. Plan Executed (Joshua 6:11-15)
1. First day's march (6:11): As soon as the Feast of Unleavened Bread was over the Israelites began their march around the walls. Given the known size of ancient Jericho—about thirteen acres—a trip around the walls would have only taken about an hour. The text gives the impression that the first day's march took place late in the day. When the ark—the emphasis on the ark should be noted—had made its trip around the walls the first day the soldiers returned to the camp at Gilgal where they spent the night.

2. Six more marching days (6:12-15): The march was repeated on each of the next five days. On the seventh day the procession marched around the wall seven times as God had ordained.

C. Ban Applied (Joshua 6:16-25)
1. Victory shout (6:16): On the seventh circuit of the seventh day the priests gave a special blast on the trumpets. Joshua signaled for the shout of victory. Standing before those towering walls which as yet had shown no signs of weakening Joshua made a great proclamation of faith: *Yahweh has given you the city!*

2. Skeptic explanations: Skeptics through the years have tried to explain away the miraculous collapse of Jericho's walls. According to one theory an earthquake brought down the walls. But earthquakes do not happen on cue. Furthermore, nearby Gilgal was not affected. Another theory is that the blast of the trumpets created sound waves that knocked the walls down. But assuming that sound waves would be powerful enough to do the job, would not the walls have fallen inward? Another view is that the rhythmic marching of thousands of feet created shock waves that brought down the walls.

3. Ban ordered (6:17-19): At this point the text records Joshua's orders regarding the ban (*cherem*) which was to be placed on the city. He probably had given these orders to tribal officers earlier in the camp, but they are placed here in the account because they were about to be executed. The concept of the ban was simple: everything within the city belonged to God either to be used in his worship or destroyed. In this case all metallic objects were to be considered holy, i.e., set apart for God, and therefore placed in the treasury of the Lord. No captives were to be taken. All human inhabitants and animals were to be slain. To confiscate for private use anything within the city would bring a curse on the camp. The only exception to these general rules was Rahab. Since she had hidden the Israelites spies, Rahab and her family were to be spared.

4. Ban executed (6:20-21): When the trumpets blew and the people shouted with a great shout, the walls of Jericho *fell down flat,* i.e., crumbled before them. The Israelite soldiers surged forward and took the city, apparently with some resistance on the part of the inhabitants (cf. Joshua 24:11). Every living thing in the city was utterly destroyed with the edge of the sword. The exception was Rahab and her family.

5. Rescue of Rahab (6:22-25): Joshua assigned the task of protecting Rahab's family to the two spies who had stayed in her home. Apparently one portion of the wall had been left standing, viz., the portion where Rahab's house was located. The converted harlot and her relatives were brought out safely. Since they were Gentiles and inhabitants of a city under God's curse they were ceremonially unclean (Leviticus 13:46; Deuteronomy 23:3). They were therefore compelled to live for a time outside the camp of Israel. After certain days, Rahab lived in the midst of Israel. Eventually she even married an Israelite man. She was still living in the midst of Israel at the time the Book of Joshua was written. Israel was a community of faith. Purely racial components never have defined "Israel."

So the population at Jericho was executed, except Rahab; but Rahab shows that any *believer* could be saved. The problem was that the Canaanites were hardened in unbelief.

D. Concluding Notes (Joshua 6:26-7:1)

1. *Oath regarding Jericho (6:26):* Joshua made the children of Israel take an oath that Jericho would never be refortified. Anyone who violated that oath would be cursed before Yahweh. In the process of trying to rebuild the walls and gates of the place the violator would lose his own sons in death. See 1 Kings 16:3 for a fulfillment of Joshua's *curse* or negative prediction.

2. *Fulfillment of a promise (6:27):* What happened at Jericho is a magnificent example of the divine assistance promised at the outset of the campaign. Because Yahweh was with him, the fame of Joshua spread throughout the region.

3. *Violation of the ban (7:1):* The account of the glorious triumph at Jericho is marked by one sour note. The terms of the ban were not strictly observed by everyone. Achan of the tribe of Judah took for his personal use some objects that were under the ban and belonged to God. Although only one man was the offender, the entire people were viewed as having *acted unfaithfully.* God considered Israel an organic unity. A sin by one brought guilt upon all. Achan's sin caused the anger of the Lord to burn against the sons of Israel. Corporate guilt and individual responsibility go hand in hand in Joshua 7. Thus the author prepares the reader for the account of the first setback experienced by Israel in their inheritance campaign.

FAITH FALTERING
Joshua 7:2-26

Date: 1406 BC Iyyar 10-17 (Apr/May)

Following the great victory at Jericho, Joshua was determined to press his advantage. His strategy was to knife up into the mountains and dissect the land separating the powerful Canaanite forces in the northern part of the land from those in the south. Joshua soon learned that not all the enemy would cower within walled cities. He learned too that on the road to ultimate victory Israel would have to cope with setbacks.

First Attack on Ai
Joshua 7:2-5

A. Spy Report (Joshua 7:2-3)

Joshua determined that Ai would be the next objective of the campaign. Ai was a military outpost in the mountains which guarded the approach to the larger city of Bethel. Ai is said to have been near to Beth-aven (location uncertain). Following the same strategy he had used at Jericho, Joshua dispatched some men to reconnoiter Ai. These men returned with the report that Ai was not heavily defended. Two or three thousand men should be sufficient to capture the place. The entire armed forces need not make the toilsome trip up into the mountains.

B. Israel's Defeat (Joshua 7:4-5)

1. Israel's defeat (7:4): Joshua dispatched three thousand troops to attack Ai. The defenders launched a counterattack which caught the overconfident Israelites off guard. Joshua's troops *fled from before the men of Ai.* Thirty-six Israelites died on the mountain slopes, the first to taste death in the inheritance campaign.

2. Israel's fear (7:5): This setback rekindled fear in the hearts of the people of Israel. *The heart of the people melted and became like water.* In their first attempt to take a city of Canaan by military means they had failed. God was not going to hand them Canaan on a silver platter. They would have to fight for their inheritance, and in the process of that fighting many would die. Likewise, from time to time there will be Jerichos in the life of Christian soldiers; but ordinarily we will have to fight and sacrifice and die to advance the cause of Christ.

Distress in the Camp
Joshua 7:6-15

A. Joshua's Discouragement (Joshua 7:6)

Joshua was distraught by this experience of defeat. He tore his clothes and fell to the earth on his face before the Ark of the Covenant. Both he and the elders put dust on their heads as a symbol of mourning. The leaders remained prone before the ark until that evening.

B. Joshua's Prayer (Joshua 7:7-9)

1. A complaint (7:7-8): Out of his despondency Joshua voiced a pathetic prayer. He began with the word *Alas!* by which he expressed deep pain and perplexity. Second, Joshua requested light in the present darkness. *Why did you, Lord, bring this people over the Jordan only to deliver us into the hands of the Amorites?* How prone are believers in times of discouragement to blame God for life's setbacks.

2. *A wish (7:9a):* Third, Joshua actually expressed the wish that the entire nation had remained on the eastern side of Jordan. Fourth, he used narrative prayer to describe to God the tragedy which so concerned him: *Israel has turned their backs before their enemies.* The anticipated result of this was that the inhabitants of Canaan would be emboldened by this news. They would surround and exterminate Israel at Gilgal.

3. *A request (7:9b):* Finally, Joshua made an oblique request in the form of a question: *Then what will you do for your great name?* Yahweh's reputation was linked with the people who worshiped him. If Israel disappeared, so would any reputation that Yahweh might have among the Gentiles. Thus Joshua was appealing for help. He was suggesting that helping Israel was in God's own self-interest.

C. Yahweh's Response (Joshua 7:10-15)

1. *Identification of the problem (7:10-12):* The Lord rebuked Joshua for lingering in this prayer of discouragement. He should have known when God did not aid his people at Ai that there must be sin in the camp. After all, Joshua had just warned Israel that if they violated the ban at Jericho they would bring trouble to the camp (6:18). That was exactly what had happened. Israel had sinned in regard to the things which were put under the ban at Jericho. The contraband objects were still in the camp. Thus a curse rested upon the camp. Until those objects were destroyed God would no longer be with his people. The sons of Israel would continue to flee before their enemies.

2. *Procedure going forward (7:13-15):* So what must be done? First, God told Joshua to *rise up.* Prayer must never be a substitute for action! Second, he was to order the people to *consecrate* themselves. Third, he was to announce to the people what most would be horrified to hear: *Things under the ban are in your midst.* Fourth, he was to indicate the results of the presence of this forbidden material within the camp: *You cannot stand before your enemies.*

Fifth, he was to outline a process by which the guilty party could be identified. Tribes, clans, families, households and finally individuals were to *come near* presumably to the Ark of the Covenant. There by lot God would indicate where the guilt lay. Sixth, he was to stipulate the punishment for the guilty party. The violator and all which belonged to him were to be burned (following execution by stoning) because of the magnitude of the sin committed. The guilty party had *transgressed* and committed a *shameful thing* in Israel.

Judgment on the Sinner
Joshua 7:16-26

Early the next morning Joshua did exactly what God had told him to do.

A. Exposure of the Sinner (Joshua 7:16-21)
1. Procedure (7:16-18): In the lengthy process of finding the culprit first the tribe of Judah was taken, then the clan of the Zerahites, and finally the family of Zabdi. When Zabdi brought his family near the ark the lot fell on Achan. Why did not the Lord simply reveal the name of the trespasser to Joshua? Why this time-consuming identification process? Probably the intention was to give the guilty party opportunity to repent. By refusing to come forth earlier in the process Achan revealed his hardened and defiant heart.
2. Admission (7:19-21): Joshua pled with Achan to acknowledge his guilt. Though it was too late for forgiveness, his admission would at least bear witness to the omniscience of God in pointing him out. Now that the finger of accusation pointed straight at him, Achan admitted what he had done. He confessed to stealing from the contraband 1) a beautiful garment from Shinar (Babylon), 2) two hundred shekels of silver (about 6.5 lbs.), and 3) a wedge of gold weighing fifty shekels (about 1.1 lbs.). The irony of his sin is that he never received any benefit at all from what he had stolen. In his own words, he *saw, coveted, took* and *concealed* what he had taken in the soil beneath his tent.

B. Execution of the Sinner (Joshua 7:22-26)
1. Verification (7:22-23): Messengers were dispatched immediately to the tent of Achan. There they found the contraband just where Achan had said. These items were brought to Joshua and the congregation. They were then *poured out before Yahweh* in

acknowledgment that the Lord was the true owner. None of these items, however, could be placed in the treasury. The taint of Achan's sin required their destruction.

2. *Stoning and burning (7:24-25):* Joshua and all Israel took Achan, the items he had stolen, and all his possessions and brought them to a valley which after this event was named *Achor* ("trouble"). Before the execution Joshua pointed out the appropriateness of what was taking place. Achan had troubled Israel; now he was to be troubled. All Israel then stoned Achan and his children. The fact that the children (Achan seems to have been a widower) were also stoned suggests that they were accessories after the fact (if not actual accomplices) to the transgression. The bodies of the guilty were then burned along with all the possessions of the man.

3. *Monument (7:26):* A great heap of stones—the third thus far—was raised up over the charred carcass of Achan to bear witness through the years to the necessity of rendering unto God his due. Thus was the fierce anger of the Lord, which had come against Israel because of Achan's transgression (7:1), now turned away.

Faith Rebounding
Joshua 8:1-29

A. Instructions from the Lord (Joshua 8:1-2)

1. *Promise of victory (8:1):* Once the camp had been purged, the time had come to get back on the victory trail. After the Ai debacle Joshua needed special encouragement if he was to continue in his mission. He did not dare renew the Conquest without an express word from the Lord. In his ninth direct revelation to Joshua the Lord commanded his captain to take all the army and proceed to Ai. This directive contains an oblique rebuke to Joshua for having misjudged the enemy strength earlier. At the same time it was a reminder that the Conquest was to be a united effort of all the people. God promised that he will now give Ai into the hands of the Israelites.

2. *Rules of engagement (8:2):* The rules of engagement were a bit different. First, like Jericho, Ai was to be completely destroyed. All the inhabitants of the place were to be executed. Second, permission was granted for the spoils and livestock to be taken as plunder by the Israelites. This was the standard procedure both before (Deuteronomy 2:34f; 3:6f) and after Jericho. Third, the Lord briefly

revealed how Joshua was to organize the attack against Ai. The method of victory this time was to be a military stratagem.

B. Deployment of Troops (Joshua 8:3-9, 12)

1. Detachment of troops (8:3-9): Joshua sent forth 30,000 valiant warriors by night to become part of an elaborate ambush at Ai. The plan was for the main body of troops to lure the soldiers out of Ai by feigning a rout. The ambushment then was to seize the city and burn it. Joshua assured the men that the strategy came from the Lord. If they followed that strategy they would be victorious over Ai. With these words of reassurance the thirty thousand immediately departed and assumed their position *between Bethel and Ai* on the west of Ai.

2. Second detachment (8:12): Joshua and the elders led the main body of troops to Ai early the next morning. He pitched camp on the north side of Ai in a valley. Joshua dispatched another five thousand men to serve as a rear guard still further to the west of where the ambushment had been deployed the previous night. These men were probably guarding against any attempted intervention from Bethel.[3]

C. Engagement with the Enemy (Joshua 8:10-23)

1. Israelite rouse (8:10-18): The strategy at Ai worked to perfection. The king of Ai saw Joshua and some of his men deployed in the valley. A sortie was sent forth to test the attackers. Then Joshua feigned a rout. The king of Ai ordered a total mobilization to pursue the Israelites. No one was left behind to guard Ai or Bethel. At this point the Lord took direct control of the operation. He ordered Joshua to give the signal to begin the full attack on Ai. This tenth direct divine communication with Joshua concluded with the encouraging words *I have given it into your hands*.

2. Total defeat of Ai (8:19-24): When they saw Joshua raise his javelin, the ambushment arose, entered Ai, and set the town ablaze. This fire was probably intended as the signal for the retreating Israelite forces to turn and press the attack toward the city. When the men of Ai looked behind them they knew they were trapped *in the midst of Israel*. Every soldier of Ai was cut down. Only the king was

---

[3]Either the defenders of Bethel had reinforced the garrison at Ai before the arrival of Joshua, or some communication system existed between the two sister towns. The Book of Joshua, which gives only an outline of the Conquest struggles, does not mention the capture of Bethel. The king of Bethel, however, is named among those slain by Joshua (12:16).

spared and brought to Joshua. Once the field army was destroyed the troops returned to the burning city and put the rest of the inhabitants to the sword.

D. Aftermath of Battle (Joshua 8:25-29)

Twelve thousand inhabitants of Ai died that day, the entire population. The Israelites took the spoils of Ai as their own. Ai was left *a heap,* i.e., a total ruin. The king of Ai was killed (cf. 10:26) and then his corpse was impaled on a tree until evening. This disgrace demonstrated the curse of God upon those who resisted the movement of God's people. The body of the king was then buried beneath a heap of stones in front of the gate of Ai. This is now the fourth heap of stones erected by Joshua during the conquest of Canaan.

FAITH RENEWED
Joshua 8:30-35

Date: 1405 BC; Nisan 1-7 (Mar/Apr)
Sacrifices
Joshua 8:30-31

A. March to Shechem

Now that resistance in central Canaan had been neutralized, Joshua was able to carry out a directive of Moses (Deuteronomy 11:29; 27:2-8). He led the tribes to the area of Shechem, right in the center of Canaan. Six hundred years earlier Abraham had built an altar in Shechem; Jacob has once resided there as well. So the place was one of sacred associations.

B. Altar Built (Joshua 8:30-31)

At Mount Ebal Joshua built an altar of uncut stones in order to avoid even the slightest hint of the *graven images* forbidden in the Ten Commandments. There the Israelites offered burnt offerings (symbolic of complete commitment) and peace offerings (symbolic of unbroken fellowship) before the Lord.

Ceremonies of Commitment
Joshua 8:32-35

A. Inscription (Joshua 8:32)

On plaster covered stones (cf. Deuteronomy 27:1-8) Joshua wrote the Law of Moses in the presence of the sons of Israel. How much of the law was written on the stones is not indicated. This monument of stones—the fifth to be erected by the Israelites—proclaimed the sovereignty of Yahweh over the entire land.

B. Formal Commitment (Joshua 8:33-35)

Something else took place at the twin mountains. The new generation of Israelites formally accepted Yahweh as their king by accepting the terms of his law. Joshua positioned the tribes, half on Mount Ebal and half on Mount Gerizim just as Moses had commanded. The Levitical priests who carried the Ark of the Covenant were positioned in the valley between the two mountains. Joshua read aloud the blessings and the curses of the law. The people responded by saying *Amen* (cf. Deuteronomy 27:11-26). All Israelites, including women and children, recommitted themselves to observe the Law of Moses. Mount Gerizim was the mount of blessings; Mount Ebal the mount of cursing.

The importance of the covenant renewal ceremony at the twin mountains cannot be overstated. The passage is a key for understanding the Book of Joshua. The main point is that possession of the land was granted those who voluntarily chose to place themselves under the authority of God as revealed in the Sinai covenant. The ceremony also served to formally recognize Joshua as Moses' successor.

Bones of Joseph
Joshua 24:32

The Israelites buried the bones of Joseph which they had brought up from the land of Egypt. The burial plot was a piece of ground which Jacob had purchased from the local inhabitants some five centuries earlier (Genesis 33:19). That piece of ground had now at long last become part of the inheritance of the sons of Joseph. This burial probably took place after the covenant renewal ceremonies narrated above. The report is delayed until the conclusion of the Book of Joshua in order to serve as a kind of climax to the conquest narrative. Before Joseph died he had expressed his faith in the fulfillment of God's land promise (Genesis 50:25). Now Joseph's faith in God's promise had been vindicated.

37

3
DEFEAT OF
CANAANITE COALITIONS
Joshua 9-11

Chapter Chronology

	1400
6 Years	
1405	

The enemies we face in our spiritual warfare are in all different kinds of circumstances. Some, like the Jericho Canaanites, are entranced behind massive fortifications. Others like the Ai citizens coming charging right at us. In this chapter we meet two new kinds of enemies. The first—the Gibeonites—resort to deception to throw us off our mission. Others like the coalitions of south and north Canaan join in powerful alliances to withstand the impact of gospel evangelism.

GIBEONITE DECEPTION
Faith Endangered
Joshua 9:1-27

Date: 1404 BC; Iyyar (Apr/May)
Canaanite Reaction
Joshua 9:1-3

Among the inhabitants west of Jordan two reactions to Joshua's initial successes manifested themselves. Most of the city states determined to band together to withstand the advance of the Israelites. The inhabitants of Gibeon, however, *acted craftily*. They determined that they would try to trick the Israelites into a solemn nonaggression treaty.

Gibeonite Plan

Joshua 9:4-6

A. Elaborate Deception (Joshua 9:4-6)

The Gibeonite plan was simple. They sent envoys to Joshua who pretended to be from a distant land. These men were dressed in tattered clothes; they carried worn-out sacks and mended wineskins. Even their bread was dry and crumbled. From their home in the mountains these envoys traveled the nineteen miles to Gilgal to which Israel had returned after the covenant renewal ceremony at Mount Ebal.

B. Alternatives

Was this the only alternative the Gibeonites had to save themselves from certain destruction? Joshua had been instructed not to make a league with the peoples of the land (Exodus 23:32; 34:12; Numbers 33:55; Deuteronomy 7:2); but what about Rahab? Note the contrast: Rahab feared, trusted, and was saved. The Gibeonites feared, showed no trust, and became slaves. God never rejects the sinner who throws himself upon divine mercy!

Gibeonite Success
Joshua 9:7-15

A. Story of the Gibeonites (Joshua 9:7-13)

Though the Israelites suspected a ruse, the Gibeonite envoys nonetheless convinced them that they had come from a distant land. They claimed that the fame of Yahweh had caused them to seek out Joshua. They had heard of what the Lord had done for his people in Egypt and in Transjordan. They were too cunning to mention the more recent news of the fall of Jericho and Ai since news of these victories would not yet have reached a distant land. The elders of Gibeon had dispatched these envoys with instructions to seek a peace treaty with Israel.

B. Suspicions of the Israelites (Joshua 9:14-15)

Because they were suspicious, the men of Israel checked the provisions in the knapsacks of the travelers. Everything seemed to be as the envoys claimed. Therefore, the men of Israel *took some of their provisions* (NASB). Here, however, the leaders of Israel were making a tragic mistake. They trusted their senses. *They did not ask counsel of Yahweh.* Joshua made *peace* and a *covenant* with the Gibeonites. The leaders of Israel bound themselves to the covenant with a solemn oath.

Aftermath of the Deception
Joshua 9:16-27

A. Israelite Anger (Joshua 9:16-18)

Three days after the covenant had been negotiated the Israelites discovered that these envoys were Hivites who came from a city within the territorial limits that Yahweh had assigned to Israel. The Israelites immediately marched toward Gibeon to demand an account. No doubt the Gibeonites met them at the border to remind them of the covenant and to point out that the terms of that covenant also applied to three neighboring villages under Gibeon's jurisdiction. The advance troops refused to attack because of the oath which the Israelite leaders had taken. Though they honored the oath, the whole congregation grumbled against the leaders.

B. Leaders Take a Stand (Joshua 9:19-21)

The leaders explained to the people that an oath taken in the name of God could not be broken even if that oath had been negotiated under false pretenses. Israel would incur the wrath of God should they slay any of these Hivites. No believer has a right to break a promise because it suits him (Matthew 5:37). If we have made a mistake, we should pray that we may glorify God in our mistake. The terms of the covenant, however, did not prohibit other kinds of action against the Hivites. The plan was to subject the Hivites to rigorous and humiliating servitude.

C. Gibeonites Punished (Joshua 9:22-27)

1. *Gibeonites rebuked (9:22-25):* Joshua summoned the Hivite leaders to report the decision to them. He first reproached the Hivites for their deception. He then announced that these people were under a perpetual curse as slaves to Israel. The Hivites attempted to explain their actions. They had heard that Yahweh had commanded Moses to give the land of Canaan to Israel and to destroy all the inhabitants of the land. *We feared greatly,* the Hivites admitted. They seemed to be very grateful to accept whatever fate short of death that the Israelites might assign them.

2. *Gibeonites reduced to servitude (9:26-27):* So Joshua prevented the Hivites from being killed. He made them, however, lowly servants from that day forth. Their twofold task was to serve as hewers of wood and drawers of water for the congregation in non-religious activities and for the worship center as well. Since the Lord had not yet indicated where his sanctuary was to be, the text does not name the place where the Gibeonites were to serve.

Conclusion

With the conquest of Jericho and Ai and the capitulation of Gibeon Joshua was the master of central Canaan. The remaining city states of the area were resolved to band together to resist the Israelite invaders. Unfortunately, from their point of view, Joshua had driven a wedge through the midst of their territories. Nonetheless, two major coalitions did emerge, one in southern Canaan, the other in the north.

SOUTHERN CAMPAIGN
Joshua 10:1-43

Date: 1403 BC; Sivan (May/Jun)

Adoni-Zedek king of Jerusalem was concerned about the destruction of Ai and the capitulation of Gibeon. Ai was a relatively small village. Gibeon, however, was "a great city." Historians theorize that Gibeon was within the jurisdiction of the king of Jerusalem. Therefore Gibeon's treaty with Israel was a renunciation of its allegiance to Jerusalem.

Occasion for the Campaign
Joshua 10:1-8

A. Attack on Gibeon (Joshua 10:1-5)
Adoni-Zedek invited four other kings of the region to join him in an attack against Gibeon. By military pressure the coalition planned to punish Gibeon for having taken the part of the Israelites. So the five kings went up, camped against Gibeon and initiated the hostilities. This assault was the first serious effort on the part of the Canaanite kings to resist the invasion of the Israelites.

Chart 4	
Southern Coalition	
King	City
Adoni-Zedek	Jerusalem
Hoham	Hebron
Piram	Jarmuth
Japhia	Lachish
Debir	Eglon

B. Appeal to Joshua (Joshua 10:6)
The Gibeonites reported what had happened to Joshua. They requested immediate help against the hill country coalition. Probably the covenant that the Israelites had signed with the Gibeonites provided for such military support.

C. Israelite Response (Joshua 10:7-8)
Joshua immediately mobilized his troops. He took not only the elite troops (*valiant warriors*) but all the rest of the army as well. In his eleventh direct communication to Joshua, Yahweh urged his general not to be afraid. He promised to deliver the enemy into the hand of Joshua. Not one of the enemy troops will stand before the army of Israel.

43

Battle of Beth-horon
Joshua 10:9-15

Joshua 10 clearly reveals again the principle which has appeared again and again in the Book of Joshua, viz., that God *gives*, and Israel *takes*. The narrative alternates between the actions of Joshua's army and the supernatural acts of God.

A. Initial Clash (Joshua 10:9-10)
By means of a night march up steep terrain Joshua was able to position his troops for an attack upon the southern coalition. The forced march caught the enemy by surprise. The summary of the great battle is first stated, and then the details are added. Four statements are made about the outcome.

- *Yahweh confounded* the enemy before Israel. Whether the enemy was confounded by the surprise attack or by the hailstorm which followed is not clear.
- Yahweh *slew them* with a great slaughter at Gibeon.
- When the enemy fled via the road leading to Beth-horon, Israel pursued them. The Canaanites fled in a westerly direction toward the coastal plain. The slopes above the road gave the Israelites excellent opportunity to continue to bombard the fleeing remnants of the enemy army.
- Yahweh continued to strike down the enemy as far south as Azekah and Makkedah.

B. Hailstorm (Joshua 10:11)
Yahweh used a hailstorm to smite down the enemy troops as they tried to escape from the Gibeon area. The *great stones* continued to fall upon them from the *ascent of Beth-horon* as far as Azekah. More died in the hailstorm than died by the sword of the Israelites.

C. Miracle in the Heavens (Joshua 10:12-15)

1. Joshua prayed publicly (10:12a): The narrator has established that the Lord fought for Israel in the battle of Beth-horon after the initial rout of the enemy at Gibeon. Next he explains how the divine intervention came about. *Then Joshua spoke unto Yahweh,* i.e., he prayed. When? After the hailstorm? Not necessarily. *Then* in Hebrew does not necessarily imply sequence. It is an indefinite indication of time. The prayer *may* have come before the great hailstorm. In any case, the prayer was *in the sight of Israel.* Perhaps Joshua assumed some posture which the Israelites immediately associated with prayer. He must have uttered his words audibly with Israel as eyewitness.

2. Joshua's prayer request (10:12b): Joshua's prayer was that the sun might *stand still* at Gibeon and the moon over the valley of Aijalon. The verb used here (*damam*) literally means "to be still, dumb or silent." Why did Joshua utter such a prayer? Three positions have been taken by the commentators.

- The oldest interpretation is that Joshua wished to prolong the sunlight so that the enemy might be completely destroyed before darkness provided an opportunity to escape.
- Some have suggested that Joshua was praying for relief from the heat of the day so that his troops could press the attack more effectively.
- Others have proposed that Joshua wished to maintain the advantage of darkness as he attacked the enemy in the earliest part of the day.

In the first and third views Joshua's objective was virtually to make time stand still.

3. Joshua's prayer answered (10:13a): The inspired writer next describes how Joshua's prayer was answered. The sun *stood still* (another form of the verb *damam*) and the moon *stopped* (*'amad*). Did the heavenly bodies cease in their motion or did they cease in their function? Joshua 10:13 could be understood to declare that either the daylight or the darkness was prolonged. If the sun stopped, or appeared to stop, in its *motion,* then daylight would be prolonged. If the sun stopped in its function, then darkness would be prolonged.

In the midst of (lit., "in the half of") the heavens does not necessarily mean, in the middle of the heavens. The Hebrew verb translated *go (bo')* does not necessarily refer to sundown. It can refer to a sunrise or to a sunset. Is the text saying that there was no sunset that day or that there was no sunrise? In any case, this unusual day continued until *the nation avenged themselves of their enemies.*

4. *Book of Jashar (10:13b):* In what he has reported thus far about the battle of Beth-horon the author of the Book of Joshua has been citing the Book of Jashar (lit., "upright, just"). Holy Spirit inspiration does not mandate originality, only accuracy and truthfulness. The Holy Spirit often guided biblical writers to cite resource material. The Book of Jashar is mentioned one other time in the Old Testament (2 Samuel 1:18). It appears to have been a poetic composition describing the wars of Yahweh. The original Book of Jashar is not extant. It is not properly speaking "a lost book of the Bible." Had God intended for it to be part of the sacred collection the book providentially would have been preserved. A spurious edition of the Book of Jashar is available, but it is worthless for any serious historical investigation.

5. *Writer's confirmation (10:13c):* Some commentators attempt to explain away the miracle of Joshua 10 as poetic exaggeration. The Israelites supposedly accomplished as much in one day as they would normally accomplish in two. This approach to the text is entirely unacceptable. Though it is true that Joshua's prayer is cited in poetic form, the sacred historian himself verifies that a miracle actually happened in the heavens in response to that prayer. *The sun stopped* [or ceased] *in the midst of the sky.* The sun *did not hasten to go down* [or come] *for about a whole day.* The report of what happened, like the prayer which called it forth, is ambiguous. The Hebrew verbs

could just as easily be taken to refer to a prolonged night as to a prolonged day.

6. *Inspired assessment (10:14):* Whatever happened that day in the sky over Gibeon was a miracle wrought in answer to Joshua's prayer. Never before or since had the Lord listened to the voice of a man to alter the normal routine of the heavenly bodies. By answering Joshua's prayer Yahweh *fought for Israel.* This phrase used in verse 14 in connection with the sun *standing still* recalls the language of verses 10-11 where the Lord caused great hailstones to fall on the enemy. When the Lord caused the sun to *stand still* he created the weather conditions that produced the hailstones of verses 10-11. A rapid cooling of moisture laden air is the natural cause of hail. Joshua's prayer was answered when God caused the sun to cease producing light. This may have been done by means of a cloud. The sudden change in temperature produced the hailstorm. Fleeing down the ascent of Beth-horon the Canaanites were pelted by the huge hailstones.

D. Return to Camp (Joshua10:15)

At the conclusion of the great victory over the armies of the southern coalition Joshua and his troops returned to the camp at Gilgal. To the western reader 10:15 seems out of place. It signals the end of the story whereas it is clear from what follows that another dramatic incident occurred on that same day. The verse serves to mark the conclusion of phase one of the conquest in the south, viz., the defeat of the enemy host. Now having related the striking defeat of the armies of the southern coalition, the author relates another incident which occurred later that same day—the capture and execution of the five kings.

Execution of the Kings
Joshua 10:16-27

A. Five Kings in a Cave (Joshua 10:16-19):

During the flight from the battle of Beth-horon, the five kings had hidden themselves in *the cave at Makkedah*. After an unspecified period of time, the Israelites found the kings. Their whereabouts was reported to Joshua. The general issued an order that the cave be sealed and guarded. The troops were to continue to press the remnants of the southern coalition. Every effort was to be made to prevent these Canaanites from returning to their cities.

B. Battle Concluded (Joshua 10:20-21):
How long the battle with the southern coalition lasted is not stated in the text. After the southern Canaanites were completely crushed and the few survivors had entered their cities, the Israelites returned to the camp which Joshua had established at Makkedah. No one dared challenge Israel or even utter a negative word against them in view of the smashing success which they had experienced.

C. Victory Ceremony (Joshua 10:22-25)
Joshua then ordered the cave of Makkedah opened and the five kings brought out. He ordered that the military officers who were with him on this campaign come near and put their feet upon the necks of the captive kings. This act symbolized what God will do to all the enemies of Israel. Therefore, Joshua urged his subordinates to *be strong and courageous*. These words had previously been spoken to Joshua by Moses, the Lord and the people (e.g., 1:6, 18). Now Joshua for the first time uses these words to encourage his subordinates.

D. Execution of the Kings (Joshua 10:26-27)
The Canaanite kings were then executed, and impaled on five *trees* or posts until evening. One who hung on a tree was considered cursed of God (Deuteronomy 21:23; Galatians 3:13). In compliance with the Law of Moses (Deuteronomy 21:23), before sunset Joshua ordered the corpses taken down. They were thrown in the cave in which earlier the kings had taken

refuge. Huge stones were then placed over the entrance of the cave to serve as another stone monument, the sixth in the book.

Capture of Southern Cities
Joshua 10:28-43

A. Enumeration of Cities (Joshua 10:28-39)

At this point the author lists a number of cities in southern Canaan—the future territory of Judah—that were captured by Joshua. The passage is characterized by a certain monotony of repetition. It emphasizes the role of Yahweh in *giving* these cities into the hands of Israel. In each case the ban was applied. All the inhabitants were executed including the king. Six southern cities are listed: 1) Makkedah (10:28); 2) Libnah (10:29-30); 3) Lachish (10:31-32); 4) Eglon (10:34-35); 5) Hebron (10:36-37); and 6) Debir (10:38-39).

Three of these cities were mentioned earlier in the chapter as part of the southern coalition. While the author presents a stereotypical description of the capture of each of these cities, certain individual variations in the reports are present.

- In four of the six reports the execution of the king is mentioned. No mention is made of the fate of the kings of Lachish and Eglon.

- The language used to describe the movements of Joshua's army is different depending on the geographical circumstances of each particular city. So Joshua *passed on* or *went up* or simply *returned* (NASB).

- The city of Lachish received aid from the king of Gezer delaying the capture of that city by one day. The army from Gezer was crushed (10:33).

- Both Debir and Hebron had to be recaptured at a later period.

- The mention of the execution of the king of Hebron in 10:37 is interesting in the light of 10:23 in which he was executed on the day of the smashing victory. The conquests reported in 10:28-39 must have stretched over considerable time. The citizens of Hebron had replaced their fallen king.

B. Regional Summary (Joshua 10:40-43)

1. Geographical areas (10:40a): The author of the Book of Joshua next gives a description of the territory controlled by Israel at this point in the Conquest. First, he describes the four natural regions which had fallen into Israelite hands: 1) the hill country; 2) the Negev; 3) the lowland; and 4) the slopes. The hill country and the lowland (Shephelah) were mentioned in 9:1-2 as areas in which the kings were alarmed over the success of Joshua. The Negev ("dry area") is the region roughly south of the Gaza-Beersheba road. The southern border of the Negev merges into the highlands of the Sinai Peninsula. This region of about 4,500 square miles is nearly half the area of the modern state of Israel. The "slopes" mentioned here lie between the Judean Mountains and the Shephelah.

2. Ban inflicted (10:40b): Second, the author indicates that Joshua applied the ban to all inhabitants within the area conquered. This was done, the reader is again reminded, at the command of Yahweh. In the light of verses to follow (15:14f, 63) it is clear that some inhabitants of these cities did escape. The text therefore means that no one was deliberately spared by Joshua's forces. In no case does the text state that any of the southern cities were burned.

3. Territorial dimensions (10:41): Third, the author gives the dimensions of the territory thus far conquered in terms of terminal points in four directions. Kadesh-barnea marked the southernmost point of Conquest. This is the oasis in the wilderness of Zin where the Israelites had faltered in their faith some forty years before (Numbers 13). On the west the Israelites had taken Gaza. They controlled all the land of Goshen. This was a border region between the Judean Mountains and the Negev. It is not to be confused with the famous land of Goshen in Egypt. The northern extremity of the Conquest at this point was Gibeon.

4. Other details (10:42-43): Fourth, the southern region had all been captured *at one time,* i.e., in one campaign. The author does not indicate how long the campaign lasted. It probably extended over several months. Fifth, the author again inserts a reminder that all the victories in the south had been made possible *because Yahweh, the God of Israel, fought for Israel.* Finally, when all the united effort in the south concluded, Joshua and the army returned to the camp at Gilgal.

NORTHERN CAMPAIGN
Joshua 11:1-23

Date: ca. 1400 BC; Tammuz (Jun/July)

The text does not indicate how much time elapsed between the southern and northern campaigns. The entire united effort of the tribes lasted over seven years. Thus it is clear that only the highlights of the Conquest are recorded in the Book of Joshua.

Northern Coalition
Joshua 11:1-5

A. Formation of the Coalition (Joshua 11:1-3)

1. Leader: Hazor was the leading city in northern Canaan. Jabin, the king of Hazor, heard of the successes of Joshua in southern Canaan. He realized that the only chance his region stood of remaining free of Israelite domination was for city states to band together.

2. Allies: So Jabin formed an alliance with several neighboring kings. Only one is named, viz., Jobab king of Madon. Two other cities are specifically mentioned—Shimron and Achshaph. Also included in the coalition were the kings of four geographical areas: 1) the hill country to the north of Hazor; 2) the Arabah (Plain) south of Chinneroth (Sea of Galilee); 3) the lowland; and 4) the heights of Dor to the west.

The alliance included six ethnic groups, normally at odds with one another, united in order to thwart the advance of the people of God.

B. Strength of the Coalition (Joshua 11:4-5)

The northern coalition was powerful. Using Near Eastern hyperbole to underscore this point, the author indicates that the armies of the northern kings were as numerous as *the sand that is on the seashore*. They also had superior weaponry. Because of the terrain in northern Canaan chariots could be employed for the first time against Israel. This powerful force assembled at the waters of Merom to the north of the Sea of Galilee to make their stand against Israel.

Battle at Merom
Joshua 11:6-9

A. Encouragement from Yahweh (Joshua 11:6)

Once again prior to the battle the Lord spoke words of encouragement to Joshua. This was now the twelfth recorded time when Yahweh spoke directly to Joshua. First, the Lord urged Joshua not to be afraid. Without doubt the general already knew through reconnaissance the strength of the enemy forces. Second, there was the gift promise: *I will give all of them as slain before Israel*. Third, Yahweh gave new instructions. Joshua was to hamstring their horses and burn their chariots. To hamstring a horse—cutting the tendons at the hoof or knee—renders the animal unsuitable for further military usage.

B. Israelite Attack (Joshua 11:7-9)

The next day the Israelite army swooped down *suddenly* upon the northern kings near the waters of Merom. True to his word, the Lord gave the northern army into the hand of Israel. The coalition broke apart. Every contingent fled for its own territory. The Israelite forces chased them in three different directions. No survivor was left to the Canaanite forces. Following the battle Joshua carried out exactly the orders he had been given by the Lord. He hamstrung their horses and burned their chariots.

Capture of Cities
Joshua 11:10-15

A. Hazor (Joshua 11:10-11)

Once the main force of the enemy had been routed, Joshua turned his attention to capturing the various cities in the north. Hazor, *the head of all those kingdoms* is mentioned first. The king—presumably Jabin had escaped to the safety of his walls—was put to the edge of the sword. All the inhabitants of the city were destroyed. For the first time since Jericho and Ai Joshua ordered the city burned. Because Hazor had held the leading position among the northern cities it received a special exemplary punishment.

B. Other Northern Cities (Joshua 11:12-15)

All the other cities of the northern coalition were captured. Their kings and populations were executed, utterly destroyed, just as Moses the servant of the Lord had commanded. However, no city in the north was burned except Hazor. Apparently the Israelites took possession of these cities, thus fulfilling the promise of Deuteronomy 6:10. The plunder of the cities belonged to Israel, but the inhabitants were executed. That standing order had originated with the Lord. It was passed down to Moses, and from Moses to Joshua. The author is anxious to emphasize that Joshua carried out exactly what he had been instructed to do.

4
DIVISION OF THE LAND
Joshua 12-21

Chapter Chronology

	1398
2+ Years	
1400	

Joshua had broken the back of the unified Canaanite resistance. There were individual pockets of Canaanites that still needed to be removed; but in general it can be said that *the land had rest* (Joshua 11:23). Following the account of the southern and northern campaigns the author presents an overview of the entire campaign.

OBSERVATIONS REGARDING
THE CONQUEST
Joshua 11:16-13:6

Geography of the Conquest
Joshua 11:16-17

The author of the Book of Joshua loved to paint verbal pictures of the extent to which the Israelites had been successful in the Conquest. He first states a generalization: *Joshua took all that land.* The author emphasized that point by enumerating the various regions which comprised *that land:* 1) the hill country; 2) the Negev; 3) *all that land of Goshen;* 4) the lowland; 5) the Arabah or plain; 6) the hill country of Israel; and 7) the lowland of Israel.

To be more precise, the area conquered by the united effort of the tribes extended from Mount Halak in the south to the Mount Hermon in the north. Baal-gad at the foot of Mount Hermon is the northernmost site mentioned. In this entire region the kings were all executed.

Chronology of the Conquest

At this point Joshua is said to have *made war a long time with all those kings* (Joshua 11:18). The length of the *long time* can be computed by the following steps:

- Caleb was 40 when he spied out the land (Joshua 14:7).
- Israelites wandered 38 years in the wilderness (Deuteronomy 2:14).
- Therefore Caleb must have been 78 when the Israelites entered the land.
- Caleb was 85 when he conquered his lot shortly after the united tribal effort ended (Joshua 14:10).
- Therefore, 85 minus 78 years = 7+ years for the campaign by the united tribes to conquer Canaan.

Theology of the Conquest
Joshua 11:15, 19-20

Not one city attempted to make peace with Israel with the exception of the Gibeonites who used deception to secure a peace treaty (cf. Joshua 9). All of the territory acquired by Israel was won on the battlefield; but why did none of the city states sue for peace? *It was of Yahweh to harden their hearts, to meet Israel in battle* (Joshua 11:20). The destruction of the Canaanites was a judicial act of God. His will was that the Canaanites should be completely destroyed. They were to receive no mercy. The divine will regarding the Canaanites was first revealed to Moses, and Moses laid the burden of execution on Joshua.

Yet it is a fact that one Canaanite begged for mercy and received it (cf. Joshua 2). All the Canaanites knew of the mighty acts of God on behalf of his people. Only one was willing to renounce idolatry and embrace the Living God. God is said to harden a heart when an individual has rejected all prior efforts to effect moral change. The hardening of the heart is a withdrawal of further efforts to soften the heart; it is an introduction of circumstances which tend to make the wicked become ever more belligerent.[4] In the case of the Conquest, the more territory Israel captured the more determined the Canaanites were to withstand their advance.

---

[4]On the hardening of heart, see Exodus 7:3; 14:4; Isaiah 6:10; Matthew 13:13-15; Romans 9:17f.

Climax of the Conquest
Joshua 11:21-22

No mention has been made heretofore in the book about those dreaded Anakites, the ones that had so terrified the ten spies in the initial reconnaissance of the land (Numbers 13:33). This was a giant race of people that made the Israelites feel like grasshoppers. Anakites were encountered at various locations in the hill country of Judah and in the hill country of Israel. Joshua utterly destroyed them with their cities. No Anakites were left in the land of Israel. Only in three locations in the Philistine plain did any of this race survive. The author surely withheld any information to this point about the Anakites to suggest that in defeating these giants a climax in the Conquest had been reached.

Concluding Summary
Joshua 11:23

To his account of the united conquest the author adds a concluding summary. In it he states first that Joshua took the whole land. In so doing he fulfilled the promises regarding the Promised Land which God had made to Moses. The conquered territory was then divided up as an inheritance to the tribes of Israel. The details of how that was done will be recounted in the following chapters.

Thus the land had rest from war. This note must be understood in a limited sense. The author refers to the massive confrontations of armies and bloody sieges of cities. Certainly he does not mean that once the territory was divided there was no more conflict, for that would contradict what he relates in subsequent chapters. He means that the enemy's chief resistance was now broken. The united effort of *all Israel* was now over. From this point on each tribe the responsibility to remove remaining pockets of Canaanites from their inheritance.

Exclamation Point
Joshua 12:1-24

To the narrative account of the Conquest the author has appended a systematic listing of thirty-three kings defeated by the Israelites.

This boring list is in reality a song of praise for the triumph of the King of Kings over the kings of this world. The author speaks first of the conquests under Moses east of Jordan, and then of the more recent conquests under Joshua west of Jordan.

A. Transjordan Conquests (Joshua 12:1-6)

1. Geographical extent (12:1): The geographical extent of the territory conquered by Israel east of Jordan is first given. This may have been done for three reasons: 1) to draw another parallel between Moses and Joshua; 2) to stress the unity of Israel; and 3) to underscore that the Transjordan area was now considered part of the Promised Land. The Arnon river valley marked the southern boundary, the foothills of Mount Hermon, the northern boundary. This territory included all the Arabah or plain of the Jordan east of the river.

2. King Sihon (12:2-3): King Sihon was the first to be conquered when Israel emerged from the desert (Numbers 21:21-35). His capital was Heshbon. This Amorite kingdom stretched from the Arnon River to the Jabbok River. It included all the valuable Arabah (Plain) between the Sea of Chinneroth (Galilee) and the Salt (Dead) Sea.

3. King Og (12:4-5): The second territory conquered east of Jordan was that of Og who ruled the region north of the Jabbok known as Bashan. Og was a remnant of the Rephaim, a giant race of people. He had two capitals, one at Ashtaroth, the other at Edrei.

4. Distribution of land (12:6): Both Sihon and Og were defeated by Israel under the leadership of Moses. This territory was then given to the tribes of Reuben, Gad and half of the tribe of Manasseh. Twice in this verse Moses is called *the servant of Yahweh*, perhaps to underscore the legitimacy of Israel's claim to the Transjordan territory.

B. Cis-jordan Conquests (Joshua 12:7-24)

1. Geographical extent (12:7-8): The author next lists the kings conquered by Joshua west of the Jordan. These kings had ruled collectively a large territory extending from Baal-gad at the foot of Mount Hermon to Mount Halak in the south. This territory embraced several distinct geographical regions: 1) hill country, 2) lowlands, 3) Arabah, 4) slopes, 5) wilderness and 6) Negev. Several different ethnic groups lived in this region: 1) Hittite, 2) Amorite, 3) Canaanite,

4) Perizzite, 5) Hivite and 6) Jebusite. Within this territory Joshua conquered thirty-one kings whose cities are now enumerated without comment. Perhaps this list was intended to be recited from time to time to remind the Israelites of the glorious victories that had been theirs when they experienced tribal unity under Joshua's leadership. Three observations regarding this list are in order.

- The list of defeated kings follows roughly the order in which events have been narrated in the preceding chapters.
- Half of the names on the list have not been mentioned in the Conquest narratives. Most of the new names are of cities in central and northern Canaan, where the narratives were extremely sketchy.
- From subsequent narratives it becomes clear that the Canaanites were not permanently driven out of all of these towns. Some even had to be re-conquered.

The most puzzling name on the list is the thirtieth—the king of Goiim in Gilgal. Goiim could be translated *nations*. Here, however, it is probably the name of a small tribe. Obviously the *Gilgal* here is not the camping spot near Jericho. This seems to have been a Gilgal in the region of Galilee. In fact, the Septuagint here reads *Galilee* which may well be the most ancient reading.

C. Reasons for Israelite Success

Of course Yahweh was with his people, assisting them at every step in the conquest of Canaan. Over and over again the author of the Book of Joshua emphasizes that Yahweh *gave* the land to Israel; but in addition there were other factors that contributed to the successful conquest of the land.

- Work of the hornet (Exodus 23:28; Deuteronomy 7:20). Probably an allusion to the armies of Pharaoh Tutmose I who invaded Canaan shortly before the arrival of the Israelites.
- Lack of unity among the city-states of Canaan is revealed in the Amarna letters written to the Pharaoh requesting assistance against the *Habiru* (Hebrews).
- Terrain for the most part neutralized the Canaanite chariots.
- Few Canaanites actually lived in the hill country.
- None of the great powers were in a position to interfere.

59

- Canaanite society was decadent; they lacked the will to organize effective resistance.
- Canaanites had heard of the marvelous works of God on behalf of his people, and they were terrified.
- Israelites were driven by religious zeal stirred by the miracles they had witnessed in earlier battles.
- Israelites were numerically powerfully.
- Israelites had a wise and energetic leader in Joshua.

DISTRIBUTION OF THE LAND
Joshua 13:1-19:51

Date: ca. 1400 BC; Iyyar (Apr/May)

Joshua was now approaching a hundred years of age. He is described as *old and advanced in years* (13:1). Joshua still had one major part of his commission to carry out. The land that had previously been conquered needed to be parceled out to the various tribes. This long unit begins by citing the revelation which Joshua received mandating the distribution of the land. The author then describes the allotment east and west of Jordan. The unit concludes with a discussion of the cities of refuge and the Levitical cities.

Divine Command
Joshua 13:1-7

A. Unconquered Areas (Joshua 13:1-6)

1. A puzzling statement (13:1): The thirteenth divine communication to Joshua began with a recitation of the lands which were yet to be controlled by Israel. At this point *very much of the land* remained to be possessed. This statement, however, seems to be at variance with what chapter 11 declared: *Joshua took the whole land.... Thus the land had rest from war* (Joshua 11:23). The victories that Joshua had won gave Israel the possession of the land in principle. No Canaanite forces were left which were capable of presenting any effective resistance to Israel. Occupation in principle, however, is not the same as possession of the land. Pockets of Canaanite resistance remained here and there. These areas are now identified by the author.

2. Unconquered territories (13:2-6a):

- Territory of the Philistines and allied Geshurites along the southwest coast of Canaan (13:3).
- The *whole land of the Canaanite* along the Phoenician coast as far as Aphek some twenty-three miles north of modern Beirut (13:4).
- The land of the Gebalite and *all of Lebanon* eastward (13:5).
- The mountain regions from Lebanon to Mesrephoth-maim which was located just south of the so-called Ladder of Tyre on the Mediterranean coast. This area is said to be occupied by the Sidonians (13:6a).

3. Promise and faith (13:6b-7): God promised that he would drive out all the remaining inhabitants of the area. In this statement the principle is again operative, God gives, but Israel must take. Even though some of the land was not yet fully possessed, it was to be divided among the nine and a half tribes as an *inheritance.* Thus, not all of the land assigned to the various tribes actually was under effective Israelite control at this time. The very act of assigning that territory was an act of faith.

B. Precedent for Tribal Allotments (Joshua 13:8-33)

1. General statement (13:8-12): The tribes of Reuben, Gad and half of Manasseh had received their inheritance east of Jordan. The boundaries that had been worked out for each tribe by Moses *the servant of the Lord* are now set forth.

2. Footnotes (13:13-14): To this general geographical description of Transjordan the author appends two notes. First, he notes that the children of Israel did not dispossess the Geshurites or Maacathites who lived in the vicinity of the Sea of Galilee. Second, he notes that no inheritance was given to the Levites in Transjordan. The offerings made by fire to the Lord were their inheritance. The reference is to the portions of various sacrifices which were designated for the Levitical priests.

3. Verbal map (13:15-31): Having introduced the Transjordan allotments the author verbally maps out the areas assigned to the two and a half tribes. The territory was assigned essentially in the order it was conquered. From the Arnon River north to Sihon's old capital at Heshbon was given to Reuben. The territory between Heshbon and Ramoth-Gilead—virtually the entire Jordan Valley east of the river—belonged to Gad. Manasseh occupied Bashan, the territory formerly ruled by King Og.

4. Concluding note (13:32-33): The description of the Transjordan allotments concludes with a note that 1) stresses the authority by which these tribal assignments were made; and 2) underscores again that no land inheritance was given to Levi because of the greater spiritual inheritance enjoyed by that tribe.

Gilgal Distribution
Joshua 14:1-14

While the territory east of Jordan was apportioned by Moses, that west of Jordan was done by committee. Joshua, Eleazar the high priest, and the tribal leaders shared in the decision (14:1). Nine and a half tribes were given territories west of Jordan. All together then, counting the two and a half territories east of Jordan, twelve tribal areas were assigned. The descendants of Joseph received two portions, for Joseph's two sons had become full-fledged tribes in Israel. The Levites, the author continues to emphasize, did not receive a tribal allotment. They did, however, receive cities scattered throughout the tribes. All of these arrangements were exactly what Moses had stipulated (14:3-5).

A. Tribe of Judah (Joshua 14:6-15:63)
The discussion of the allotment to Judah emphasizes the role of Caleb in the settlement of that tribal area. Caleb's faith and courage are held up as a model for what God expected from all of the tribal units. The request of Caleb for an inheritance is followed by a verbal description of the geography of Judah, a note about the early successful efforts of Caleb and Othniel, and a list of the cities that were in this tribal area.

1. Caleb's history (14:6-10): Caleb led a delegation to Joshua at Gilgal and reminded him of the commitments that had been made to him in the wilderness (cf. Numbers 14:24, 30). In making his claim Caleb rehearses the history of how he had been sent from Kadesh-barnea to spy out Canaan. Because Caleb had been fully committed to the Lord, Moses swore that he would have his own personal inheritance in the Promised Land. Now some forty-five years later Caleb at age eighty-five claimed his inheritance. In the wilderness Caleb had risked his life to bring to his countrymen a positive report

4: Division of the Land

regarding Canaan. Now Caleb's land inheritance is placed at the head of all the allotments in Cis-jordan.

2. Caleb's request (14:11-15): In spite of his age, Caleb was not inclined to seek retirement. He felt he was as strong as ever. Therefore he requested as his inheritance the hill country where the Anakites—the giants—were located. Apparently some of the Anakites who had escaped Joshua's initial conquest (11:21f) had returned to the area. Caleb believed that the Lord would honor his word (cf. 13:6) and drive those Anakites from the land. Thus Caleb was modeling the faith that God desired all his people to have at this stage of the Conquest. This is how Caleb received Hebron and environs as his inheritance. The city, once named Kiriath-arba after Arba the greatest of the Anakites, was now renamed Hebron. Following the conquest of Hebron *the land had rest from war* at least for a time. The cessation of hostilities made possible the further distribution of the land.

3. Verbal map of Judah (15:1-12): The author meticulously traces the tribal borders of Judah. Each tribe's territory was designated by lot by which divine guidance was assured. The phrase *according to their families* suggests that tribal areas where broken down into smaller portions. Mercifully the Holy Spirit has spared modern readers the details of the family assignments. For the Israelites such lists had a legal purpose. Perhaps these boundary lists were also recited in worship liturgy to celebrate the faithfulness of God in keeping his covenant promises. Since many of the places listed in tribal areas were still in Canaanite hands, the boundary lists also served the purpose of establishing a program of expansion for each of the tribes. The overriding spiritual truth in all this is that God has a place in his kingdom for every one of his children.

4. Caleb's settlement model (15:13-19): The author relates how Caleb was successful in driving out from Kiriath-arba (Hebron) the three giant sons of Anak. Caleb then proceeded to attack Kiriath-sepher (Debir), another city previously conquered (10:36-39) but reoccupied by Canaanites. He offered his daughter Achsah in marriage to the man who could conquer this town. Othniel, his brother or half-brother, captured Hebron and thereby won the hand of Achsah. This young lady was very insightful and determined. She knew that land without water was worthless. So she persuaded her husband to allow her to ask Caleb for some nearby springs of water as a wedding present. Pleased with the pluck of his daughter, Caleb gave her *the upper and the lower springs*.

5. *Cities of Judah (15:20-62):* The text next lists 114 cities along with some villages which were not reckoned as "cities." The cities are listed in four major regions:

- Negev (15:20-32).
- Lowlands (15:33-47).
- Hill country (15:48-60).
- Desert (15:61-62).

Some of these cities were later taken from Judah and given to the tribe of Dan.

6. *Status of Jerusalem (15:63):* A most significant note comes at the conclusion of the long city catalog. Judah was unable to drive the Jebusites out of Jerusalem. Not until the time of David did the city finally and permanently come under Israelite control.

B. Tribe of Ephraim (Joshua 16:1-10)

1. *Joseph tribes (16:1-4):* The descendants of the two sons of Joseph, Ephraim and Manasseh, were reckoned as two separate tribes in Israel. The author first presents a general picture of the lot that fell to the Joseph tribes. He then discusses individually these two tribes.

2. *Verbal map of Ephraim (16:5-9).*

3. *Status of Gezer (16:10):* To the outline of Ephraim's boundaries the author adds an important note. The tribe of Ephraim did not drive out the Canaanites that lived in Gezer. They could have, but they did not. Instead the Ephraimites chose to make forced laborers out of these Canaanites. So the Ephraimites thought they had a better plan than that of the Lord which called for extermination of the Canaanites.

C. Tribe of Manasseh (Joshua 17:1-13)

1. *Zelophehad tracts (17:1-6):* Part of the tribe of Manasseh already had been given an allotment east of Jordan. The rest of the tribe received ten portions of land in an area west of the Jordan. Five of those tracts were given to the daughters of Zelophehad. Zelophehad had died in the wilderness. He had no sons. In the plains of Moab his five daughters had come to Moses requesting that they be recognized as the rightful descendants of their father. The young

ladies won their case. As long as they did not marry outside their tribe they would each be entitled to a portion in the Promised Land (Numbers 27:1-11; 36:5-9). Joshua honored the word of the Lord as spoken through Moses regarding these women.

   2.   Verbal map of Manasseh (17:7-10):

   3.   Manasseh's failure (17:11-13): Because the area contained few cities, Manasseh was assigned six cities in neighboring tribal areas. Unfortunately Manasseh was not able to take control of all these cities. When the Israelites became strong, however, they put the Canaanites to forced labor.

D.   Complaint of the Joseph Tribes (Joshua 17:14-18)

   1.   Their problem (17:14-15): The Joseph tribes complained to Joshua about the size of their portion. In point of fact at least three other tribes were more numerous. Joshua, however, did not argue with them. He challenged them to carve out a settlement in *the forest* which covered a considerable portion on the northwest of their allotment. Of course there they would have to tangle with the Perizzites and Rephaim.

   2.   Their whining (17:16): Joshua's answer did not satisfy the Joseph tribes. They felt the hill country was not large enough. The Canaanites who lived in the valley of Jezreel possessed *chariots of iron.* Perhaps the Josephites expected some kind of favoritism from Joshua since he was of the tribe of Ephraim. Joshua, however, would not budge.

   3.   Joshua's challenge (17:17-18): Joshua repeated the boasts of the Ephraimites to them. They were a numerous people. They needed more land. So take the hill country, he charged, and drive the Canaanites out. If they would only assert themselves they would have all the land they needed in spite of the iron chariots of their enemies.

Shiloh Distribution
Joshua 18:1-19:48

   Shiloh was the site where the final allotment was made. The tent of meeting was set up there once the main Canaanite resistance had been removed. By some revelation God had designated that spot as the site of his earthly palace (cf. Deuteronomy 12:11; Jeremiah 7:12). The site was ideal for a sanctuary because of its central location among the tribes (18:1). The complaint of the Josephites had indicated that tribal self-interest threatened national unity. The relocation of the tabernacle at this point in the tribal area of Ephraim was intended to counter this trend. The Shiloh distribution probably took place in 1398 BC, the month of Iyyar (Apr/May).

After describing how the Shiloh distribution was organized, the author proceeds to describe the territories of the tribes that had not yet received their inheritance. The tribal distribution chapters conclude with a note concerning a special portion given to Joshua.

A. Organization of the Distribution (Joshua 18:1-10)

1. Joshua's rebuke (18:2-7): At this point seven tribes had not yet received their inheritance. Joshua chided these tribes for not entering their respective areas to take possession of them. Three men from each of these tribes were organized into a survey team. They were to go through the land, write a description of the prospective areas, and divide the remaining territory into seven areas. Then Joshua promised to cast lots *before Yahweh our God* to determine how the seven allotments were to be assigned. Joshua used this public speech to do what he did at every opportunity, viz., underscore the national unity of the twelve tribes. He did this by alluding to the Transjordan tribes, the two and a half tribes already assigned territory in Cis-jordan, and the Levites who had the priesthood as their portion.

Chart 5			
Distribution to the Seven Tribes			
Tribe	Scripture	Sq. Miles	Est. Population
Benjamin	Josh 18:11-28	200	182,000
Simeon	Josh 19:1-9	1,000	88,800
Zebulun	Josh 19:10-16	300	242,000
Issachar	Josh 19:17-23	400	257,000
Asher	Josh 19:24-31	200	213,600
Naphtali	Josh 19:32-39	800	181,600
Dan	Josh 19:40-48	500	257,600

2. Completion of survey work (18:8-10): The twenty-one man survey team completed their work. Probably a good portion of what is recorded in Joshua 13-19 is the result of their work. They described the land *by cities in seven divisions in a book.* Joshua cast lots for them before the Lord in Shiloh. Through the lot (equivalent to drawing straws) the Lord assigned each tribe to the area of the land where he intended for them to reside.

B. Notes on the Tribal Allotments (Joshua 18:11-19:48)

The lot fell in the following order: Benjamin (18:11-28), Simeon (19:1-9), Zebulun (19:10-16), Issachar (19:17-23), Asher (19:24-31), Naphtali (19:32-39), and Dan (19:40-48). Discussion of the multitude of geographical details in this unit is beyond the scope of this survey. Concerning these allotments, however, the following observations are in order:

- The lot of Benjamin is the most carefully described. It consists of both border stations and a city list of twenty-six entries.
- The lot of Simeon was taken from within the tribal area of Judah because the portion of Judah was *too large for them.*
- A portion of the tribe of Dan migrated to the north beyond the territory assigned to any tribe. The details of this tribal migration are reported in Judges 18.[5]

C. Joshua's Inheritance (Joshua 19:49-51)

The discussion of the tribal allotments west of Jordan began with the reference to the area assigned to Caleb. The same unit ends with a reference to the personal allotment of Joshua. Caleb and Joshua had risked their lives by bringing a good report regarding the land when Israel was camped at Kadesh-barnea (Numbers 14:6-10). How appropriate then that the author has used the inheritance of these two men as a frame around the allotment chapters.

1. Request of Joshua (19:49-50): In compliance with the commandment of the Lord, *the sons of Israel* gave Joshua an inheritance in their midst. The exact command regarding Joshua's inheritance is not recorded, but the idea may be implied in Numbers 14:30. He asked for and received the city of Timnath-serah in the hill country of Ephraim about sixteen miles southwest of Shechem. Joshua is said to have *built* (i.e., rebuilt) this city and settled it.

2. Conclusion of allocations (19:51): With the allocation of Timnath-serah to Joshua the western tribal allotment came to an end. Eleazar, Joshua and the tribal leaders had fulfilled their responsibility.

---

[5]This event probably took place after the time of Joshua. If that is the case, an editor of the Book of Joshua has placed this brief note here in order to round out his account of the allotment of Dan.

The final phase of the allotment was performed at Shiloh *before Yahweh* at the door of the tent of meeting.

Designation of Special Cities
Joshua 20:1-21:45

Appended to the descriptions of the various tribal areas are two lists of important towns, viz., the cities of refuge and the Levitical cities. Actually all six cities of refuge were also Levitical cities that served a special function in the judicial system.

A. Cities of Refuge (Joshua 20:1-9)

In the fourteenth direct address to Joshua[6] Yahweh directed that cities of refuge be appointed.

1. Principles of asylum (20:1-6): In this communication the Lord repeated the principles by which this system of asylum was to operate (cf. Deuteronomy 19:1-13). Cities of refuge were sanctuaries for those who had committed manslaughter. The *avenger of blood* could not execute the manslayer as long as he resided within the walls of one of these cities. Some commentators think the avenger of blood was a kinsman of the person who had been killed. Another view is that the avenger was a title for a government functionary whose job it was to execute those that had committed murder.

The elders of the city of refuge decided who was eligible for the sanctuary within their walls. The sanctuary could be temporary, i.e., until a formal trial could be conducted, or indefinite where unintentional manslaughter had been determined. In the latter case the manslayer had to remain in the city until the death of the high priest.[7] Then he was free to return to his own city.

2. Three new cities (20:7-9): Three cities of refuge already had been appointed by Moses east of Jordan: Bezer in Reuben, Ramoth in

---

[6]In 20:1 the Hebrew uses the verb *dabhar* ("spoke") rather than *'amar* ("said") which was used in the previous instances of direct divine communication to Joshua. For this reason Jewish tradition regards this as merely passing on to Israel what the Lord had previously said to Moses.

[7]Scriptures do not state why the death of the high priest meant release for the manslayer. These theories have been offered: 1) the death of the high priest had a kind of atoning effect since he had been anointed with oil. 2) Since the high priest was the head of the tribe of Levi, his death released the hold of the Levitical city (city of refuge) over the manslayer. 3) The death of the high priest signaled the end of an era and thus a general amnesty was declared.

68

4: Division of the Land

Gad and Golan in Manasseh. Now Joshua and his advisers appointed three additional cities west of Jordan: Kedesh in Naphtali, Shechem in Ephraim and Hebron in Judah.

B. Levitical Cities (Joshua 21:1-45)

Under Moses' leadership the decision had been made that Levites would be given cities throughout the tribal areas of Israel (Numbers 35:1-8). Chapter 21 relates how each of the three major branches of Levites received by lot its own cities. Thus the Levites occupied their towns by divine appointment.

The Levites approached Eleazer and Joshua at Shiloh to request that they might be given cities in which to settle. Forty-eight cities were assigned to them. Apparently these teachers of the law and religious leaders were to be readily available to all of the people of God. The descendants of Aaron were situated in the tribal areas of Judah, Simeon, and Benjamin. Thus the priests were located relatively close to Jerusalem which God later would designate as the site for his temple.

Chart 6 Levitical Cities		
Levitical Clans	**Location of Cities**	**Number**
Family of Aaron	Judah-Simeon (9) Benjamin (4)	13
Other Kohathites	Ephraim (4) Dan (4) Manasseh West (2)	10
Gershonites	Issachar (4) Asher (4) Naphtali (3) Manasseh East (2)	13
Merarites	Zebulun (4) Reuben (4) Gad (4)	12
Total Levitical Cities		**48**

70

5
DEPARTURE OF AN
OLD WARRIOR
Joshua 22:1-Judges 2:6

Chapter Chronology

	1385
About 12 Years	
1397	

The concluding verses of Joshua 21 present succinctly the view of the biblical historian regarding Israel's possession of the Promised Land. Yahweh *gave* Israel all the land: as he had sworn to their fathers (21:43). He *gave* them rest on every side: as he had sworn to their fathers (21:44). Yahweh *gave* all their enemies into their hand (21:44). Then comes this important verse: *Not one of the good promises that the Lord had made to the house of Israel failed: all came to pass* (Joshua 21:45).

DISPUTE AMONG THE TRIBES
Joshua 22:1-34

Date: 1397 BC; Nisan 22-29 (Mar/Apr)

Joshua 22 indicates how the national unity which Joshua had cultivated during his years of leadership was nearly broken by foolish actions of the tribal leaders.

Tribal Unity Praised
Joshua 22:1-8

After the years of united tribal warfare, Joshua summoned to Shiloh the military contingent from the two and a half Transjordan tribes. This group which crossed the Jordan seven years earlier forty thousand strong had served faithfully. They had honored the word that they had given to Moses about fighting with their brethren. They had obeyed every command that Joshua had issued during the campaign. Now that the Cis-jordan tribes had achieved their *rest* it

71

was time for these valiant soldiers to return to the possession that Moses had appointed them on the other side of the Jordan.

A. Parting Admonition (Joshua 22:1-5)

Joshua had a parting admonition for the Transjordan warriors. He urged them carefully to observe the Law of Moses. This involved loving the Lord, walking in all his ways, keeping his commandments, holding fast to him and serving him *with all your heart and with all your soul.* Only then would they be able to enjoy their rest in Transjordan.

B. Parting Blessing (Joshua 22:6-8)

With these words of commendation and admonition Joshua *blessed* the troops and sent them away. The *blessing* took the form of an imperative. He encouraged them to share with their tribal brothers all the spoils that they had captured in battle. These spoils are called *great riches.* They consisted of livestock, silver, gold, bronze, iron and *very many clothes.*

Tribal Unity Threatened
Joshua 22:9-20

A. Cause of the Problem (Joshua 22:9-12)

1. Controversial altar (22:9-10): The Reubenites, Gadites and half-tribe of Manasseh departed for the land of Gilead. In the vicinity of the Jordan River they decided to build a large altar. When the other tribes heard of this, they gathered together at Shiloh to go into Gilead and make war against their brethren.

2. Explanation (22:11-12): From a distance it appeared that the eastern tribes were attempting to introduce an altar to rival the one authorized altar at the Tabernacle. A second place of worship constituted a serious violation the Law of Moses. Fortunately cooler heads prevailed. A committee consisting of ten tribal leaders led by Phinehas, the son of the high priest, was dispatched to Transjordan to challenge the construction of the altar. Phinehas' zeal for Yahweh already had been demonstrated in the incident that had taken place at Baal-Peor (Numbers 25:7).

B. Accusations (Joshua 22:13-20)

The committee was harshly accusatory with the eastern tribes. They accused their brethren of an *unfaithful act* or *turning away from following Yahweh*. By building the altar the eastern tribes had committed a trespass on the magnitude of what had transpired at Peor in the last days of Moses. The committee seemed most afraid that the altar transgression would bring God's wrath on the entire nation. The committee reminded the eastern tribes that they were welcome to cross the river and take up residence among the nine and a half tribes. By building the altar, however, they were rebelling both against Yahweh and their brothers. The committee closed its presentation with the ominous reminder of what happened when Achan had acted unfaithfully. The entire congregation had been punished for the sin of one man. Thus the other tribes had a legitimate concern about the purpose of this altar near the Jordan.

C. Tribal Unity Preserved (Joshua 22:21-34)

1. Explanation by the easterners (22:21-29): The eastern tribes responded to the broadside of the committee of tribal leaders with shock and humility. They had not built their altar in an act of rebellion. Their altar was not intended for sacrificial purposes. Rather it was a monument to the unity of the nation. A future generation west of Jordan might wish to disown the eastern tribes and cut them off from participation in Tabernacle worship. In such an event the altar near the Jordan would be a reminder of the fact that the eastern tribes had fought alongside their brothers in the conquest of Canaan. Thus the newly constructed "altar" was really a monument celebrating the spiritual unity that bound the tribes on both sides of the Jordan into one nation. The large altar had even been modeled after the altar of the Tabernacle and thus was another expression of their loyalty to Yahweh. The eastern tribes were horrified at the thought that their actions were misconstrued as rebellion against the Lord.

2. Reaction of the western tribes (22:30-33): The response from the Transjordan tribes pleased the investigative committee. A serious threat had been averted. No illegal act had been committed. Therefore there was no reason to think that Israel would experience the hand of divine wrath. God was still in their midst. Phinehas and his ten committee members returned from the land of Gilead in Transjordan and reported their findings. The report pleased the congregation. All talk of war against the eastern tribes ceased.

3. *Application:* Misunderstanding between brethren arises when one group launches into some activity without seeking approval from the congregational leadership and without explaining intentions. Often brothers jump to conclusions about motives without first carefully investigating the situation. Joshua 22 contains several lessons which can be helpful in maintaining the unity of the spirit in the bond of peace.

4. *Concluding note (22:34):* This account concludes with a note that the eastern tribes named the Jordan altar "Witness." The altar was intended to bear witness that Yahweh is God.

FINAL WORDS OF JOSHUA
Joshua 23:1-24:28

Date: 1392 BC; Nisan 15 (Mar/Apr) & 1390 BC; Iyyar (Apr/May)

Joshua 23-24 contain Joshua's last words to the people he had served throughout his lifetime. The tone of these chapters is hortatory. Thus the Book of Joshua ends as it began with words of exhortation. Though the two chapters have a great deal in common, certain differences are clear. Chapter 23 is oriented toward what God will do in the future, whereas chapter 24 focuses on what God had done in the past. The location of the two meetings probably was different. Also the scope of the assembly in chapter 24 seems to be larger (*all the tribes of Israel*) than that in chapter 23.

Joshua's Farewell Speech
Joshua 23:1-16

Joshua's farewell address was delivered when he was *old and advanced in years*. Since this same language is used in 13:1 at the time of the land apportionment, it is impossible to determine how much time, if any, had elapsed since that event. Joshua summoned all Israel, but to what place is not indicated. The likely possibilities include Shiloh, Shechem and Timnath-serah. *All Israel* was represented in the person of its elders, heads, judges and officers. The address consists of three calls to covenant obedience each of which is preceded by a recitation of past favors bestowed by the Lord.

A. Call to Covenant Faithfulness (Joshua 23:2b-8)

1. Joshua's confidence (23:2b-5): Joshua began his speech by calling attention to his great age. He was approaching 110. Joshua apparently intended his words to be regarded as a kind of last will and testament. He spends very little time rehearsing the victories of the Conquest period. Joshua first gives credit to the Lord for what was accomplished on the battlefields of Canaan. He then explained that he had given Israel as an inheritance two kinds of land: the land of nations that had been *cut off;* and the land of nations that yet remained. Joshua could make these allocations because he was fully confident that Yahweh would fulfill his promises and drive the remaining nations out of the inheritance he had given to Israel.

2. Appeal for faithfulness (23:6-8): Joshua urged these leaders of Israel to *be very firm* (lit., be strong) to observe the commandments of Moses. Specifically, Joshua was referring to the Mosaic commands regarding absolute separation between the people of God and the peoples remaining in the land. Israel was not to *associate* with them. To do so would result in gradually making mention of the names of their gods. This certainly includes prayer to those gods. That in turn leads to taking oaths in the names of their gods, and even worse, the worship of those non-existing deities. To be successful in their inheritance Israel needed to continue to *cling* to Yahweh.

B. Second Call for Faithfulness (Joshua 23:9-13)

Based on their recent experience there was every reason to remain faithful to Yahweh. The Lord had driven out mighty nations before Israel. No man had been able to stand before their armies. Because the Lord fought for Israel, one Israelite soldier had been able to put to flight a thousand of the enemy. The Lord had kept his word in a marvelous way.

Israel must not assume that such divine aid as they had recently experienced would automatically continue. The Lord's help was conditional. Israel must continue to love Yahweh, and love for him was an exclusive thing. In Canaan constantly they will be tempted to *go back* (i.e., commit apostasy) and *cling* to surrounding nations. They will be tempted to give the same kind of loyalty to these pagans that they should be giving to the Lord. Intermarriage is one example of what Joshua meant by clinging to the nations. In the event of such apostasy, God would abandon Israel. No longer would he drive out those nations before Israel. Those heathen nations would become a snare and a trap. They would torment Israel producing pain like that of a whip upon the back or thorns poking into an eye. Ultimately the heathen influence would cause Israel to *perish from off this good land* that they had just received from the Lord.

C. Third Call for Faithfulness (Joshua 23:14-16)

Joshua reminded his audience of his impending death: *I am going the way of all the earth.* Both Joshua and these leaders had observed that every promise that God had made had been fulfilled. Not one word of promises had failed. The same God who kept his positive promises to Israel will also keep his threats. He would in fact destroy them from off that land if they did not continue to cling to him. Faithfulness to the covenant was the key. If Israel began to take up with other gods, the Lord would *burn* against them. Israel would then *quickly perish* off the good land that their God had just given them.

Covenant Renewal
Joshua 24:1-28

Because of its ancient Patriarchal connections, Joshua chose Shechem as the site for the final covenant renewal ceremony of his life. *All the tribes* were present, at least in the person of their representatives. The elders, heads, officers and judges presented themselves *before God.* Joshua then addressed the assembly (Joshua 24:1).

A. Basis of the Appeal (Joshua 24:2-13)

1. Review of history (24:2-7): Joshua began his covenant renewal speech by reviewing the history of God's dealings with Israel, beginning with Abraham. He mentioned Abraham's journey to Canaan, the birth of Isaac, the descent of Jacob and his sons into Egypt. He spoke of the plagues against Egypt, the crossing of the sea, the destruction of the Egyptian army and the preservation of Israel in the wilderness *for a long time.* Most of this was ancient history for the audience of Joshua.

2. Review of recent events (24:8-13): Joshua then began to speak of events with which his audience was personally acquainted. He mentioned the defeat of the Transjordan Amorites, and the reversal of the curses of Balaam (Numbers 22-24). He reminded them of the battle at Jericho and the long campaign against all the ethnic groups that inhabited the land of Canaan. God sent *the hornet*[8] before

Israel that drove out *the two kings of the Amorites*. At this very moment, because of God's unspeakable blessing, Israel was living in cities they had not built, and eating from vineyards and groves they had not planted.

B. Exhortation and Response (Joshua 24:14-24)

1. Remove false gods (24:14-15): All that Joshua had been saying was building up to a challenge. *Now therefore, fear Yahweh and serve him in sincerity and truth.* This entailed two specific actions, one negative and the other positive. 1) They must put away the gods that their fathers served beyond the Euphrates River and in Egypt; and 2) they must serve Yahweh. Service (i.e., worship) to Yahweh is exclusive. If they did not wish to serve Yahweh, then they should choose what gods they would serve, either the old gods of Mesopotamia or the newer gods that they had encountered in Canaan. In any case, Joshua let the assembly know what his choice was: *As for me and my house, we will serve Yahweh.*

2. Initial commitment (24:16-18): The assembly responded in a forceful way. To forsake Yahweh and serve other gods was a horrifying thought. After all, it was Yahweh who brought up *us* and *our fathers* out of the *house of bondage,* i.e., Egypt. Yahweh is the God who performed great signs in *our sight.* Yahweh had preserved this people in whatever hostile circumstances they had found themselves over the years. He had driven out the Amorites, i.e., inhabitants of Canaan before Israel. Since Yahweh had demonstrated himself to be their God, the Israelites formally committed themselves anew to serving him.

3. Commitment bar raised (24:19-20): Joshua then raised the bar of commitment to a higher level. He reminded his audience that Yahweh was a holy God. He was *a jealous* God who would not merely ignore their dalliance with *strange* deities. If they turned from serving Yahweh to serve the foreign gods, Yahweh would turn against them and consume them as a nation. Disobedience turns covenant blessings into covenant curses.

---

[8]The *hornet* is difficult to identify. Is a plague of insects intended? Others have taken the *hornet* to be a symbol for the stinging, paralyzing fear that seized the Canaanites before the arrival of Israel (cf. 2:9; 5:1). Still others think the reference is to Palestinian campaigns of certain Pharaohs one of whom used a bee or hornet as his symbol.

4. *Intensified commitment (24:21-22):* Once again, and doubtless even more vociferously, the people declared their intention to serve Yahweh. Then Joshua coaxed yet another statement of commitment from them. The people declared that they were witnesses against themselves that they had chosen to serve Yahweh in full knowledge of what the consequences would be if they lapsed into pagan religion. The people affirmed: *We are witnesses.* By setting forth the voluntary acceptance of covenant obligation on the part of Israel, the author is making clear that any later calamities which befell Israel for covenant unfaithfulness cannot be blamed upon God.

5. *Ultimate challenge (24:23-24):* After these several verbal declarations of devotion to Yahweh, Joshua put the people to the true test of sincerity. *Put away the foreign gods that are in your midst.* Such an act would demonstrate that their hearts were inclined to Yahweh. For the fourth time the people declared their intention to serve Yahweh. They added, *And we will obey his voice.* Presumably they were referring to the commandments regarding recognizing other gods or making graven images.

C. Covenant Documentation (Joshua 24:25-28)

1. *Covenant written (24:25-26a):* All that had just transpired is described as *a covenant.* That covenant became the law of the land. Joshua wrote down these words in the Book of the Law of God. Presumably the reference is to the writings of Moses. What Joshua wrote was the nucleus of the present Book of Joshua. The fact that Joshua was permitted to add words of any kind to the book already deemed sacred indicates that the people regarded him as a prophet inspired of God. What Joshua wrote was immediately regarded as Scripture.

2. *Covenant spot marked (24:26b-28):* To mark the spot of this covenant renewal, Joshua erected a large stone and set it under the oak that was *near the holy place of Yahweh* (NIV). The sanctity of that spot near Shechem went back to the time of Abraham (Genesis 12:6). The stone had been a silent witness to the words of the Lord that Joshua had just spoken. The gracious acts of the Lord that Joshua had rehearsed before Israel at Shechem would testify against them should they ever be unfaithful to the covenant. Having made provision for the stone of witness, Joshua dismissed the tribes, each to its own inheritance.

DEATH OF JOSHUA
Joshua 24:29-30

Joshua died at the age of 110 (ca. 1387 BC). His age at death was the same as that of Joseph whose final burial is mentioned in the following verses. In this concluding note about him Joshua is given for the first time the title Moses had worn: *servant of Yahweh.* Joshua was buried in his own inheritance of Timnath-serah in the hill country of Ephraim.

TRIBAL CONQUESTS
AND FAILURES
Judges 1:1-2:5

Date: 1387-1385 BC
The Book of Judges is not arranged in strict chronological order. Some of the episodes in this lesson may have transpired before the death of Joshua. In respect to the chronological placement of the tribal conquests related in Judges three views are represented in the literature.

- During the lifetime of Joshua. But what about Judges 1:1?
- After the death of Joshua. But what about the fact that some of these events were recorded earlier in the Book of Joshua?
- Judges 1:1-2:5 contains a summary account of the tribal conquests including some episodes from before the death of Joshua and some from after his death.

Request for Guidance
Judges 1:1-2

The Book of Judges begins on a positive note. The death of Joshua about 1387 BC triggered a renewed interest in driving the Canaanites from the land. The Israelites, however, were hesitant to begin the program without some direction from the Lord. So the *sons of Israel* in the person of their leaders assembled to *inquire of the Lord.* They wished to know what tribe should initiate the hostilities with the Canaanites. Doubtless they approached Eleazer the high priest. Through the priestly oracle (the Urim and Thummim) Eleazar

79

answered their question. So far as the record goes this is the first time the Israelites asked advice from the Lord in this way.

Why the tribes felt they needed to have one tribe lead out in the tribal conquest is not stated. Perhaps there was a doubt whether the Lord would continue to drive out the Canaanites now that Joshua was dead. One tribe will "test the waters" for the others. The success of that tribe will signal all the others to launch their own campaigns. In spite of the uncertainties in the opening verses of Judges, two positive developments were triggered by Joshua's death: 1) interest in tribal conquest was rekindled; and 2) the tribal leaders were concerned to seek God's direction about the campaign.

The response of the Lord indicated that the tribes were right to renew the conquest and right to seek his will. The Lord indicated that Judah should go up first against the Canaanites. The Lord assured this tribe that he would give the land into their hand.

Substantial Progress in the South
Judges 1:3-21

Judah invited the tribe of Simeon to *come up* to the Judean hill country to fight the Canaanites. Judah pledged to return the favor and subsequently aid the Simeonites in their territory. This was appropriate since the territory of Simeon was entirely within the territory of Judah (Judges 1:3). The allied tribes first attacked Bezek, then Jerusalem and other cities in the hill country, and finally the Negev and the coastal areas.

A. At Bezek (Judges 1:4-7)

1. Punishment of Adoni-Bezek (1:4-6): First objective in the Judah-Simeon campaign was Bezek, the location of which is uncertain. The Canaanite king Adoni-Bezek ("Lord of Bezek") was able to field an army of ten thousand, a considerable force for this small city state. Nonetheless, Yahweh gave his combined force of Canaanites and Perizzites into the hands of the two Israelite tribes. The king fled the scene; but he was pursued and apprehended. In just vengeance for his cruel reign of terror in the area the Israelites cut off his thumbs and big toes.

2. Confession of Adoni-Bezek (1:7): Adoni-Bezek recognized the justice of what had befallen him. He himself had maimed seventy other kings over the years by cutting off their thumbs and toes. He

80

had further humiliated his victims by making them gather scraps under his table like a pack of wild dogs. This cruel and proud king finally got a dose of his own medicine. Adoni-Bezek was taken to Jerusalem where he subsequently died.

B. At Jerusalem (Judges 1:8)

Technically Jerusalem was not part of the tribal inheritance of Judah. The city, however, was right on the border with Benjamin. Therefore, the Judahites, perhaps in concert with the Benjamites, captured Jerusalem, put its inhabitants to the sword, and then burned the city.

C. At Hebron (Judges 1:9-10)

Judah next undertook a campaign against Hebron, formerly known as Kiriath-arba. The author of the Book of Joshua was concerned to emphasize the individual role of Caleb in this campaign (15:13f). The writer here sees it as an illustration of tribal success. Both accounts are true. Caleb certainly did not defeat the Anakites there single-handedly. In 1:20 Judges gives Caleb due credit for what was accomplished at Hebron.

C. At Debir (Judges 1:11-15)

1. Leadership of Othniel (1:11-13): Likewise Judges considers the conquest of Kiriath-sepher ("Booktown"), later called Debir, as a tribal victory. Yet Othniel was the hero of the battle. He had been challenged to undertake the campaign out of romantic considerations. Caleb had promised to give his daughter to the man who could capture the city. Othniel, Caleb's younger brother, won the prize, presumably not without the acquiescence of Achsah. Uncle-niece marriages were not one of the forbidden categories of marriage under the Law of Moses. This account serves to set the stage for the judgeship of Othniel in chapter 3. The man was already a military hero in Israel before he was called to be Israel's first Judge.

2. Pluck of Achsah (1:14-15): The author of Judges appreciated the pluck of the women of Israel. Achsah is the first woman to appear in the book. She was not merely chattel, a possession gained by bloody fighting. She was a shrewd, determined, and far-sighted woman. When Achsah *came to him* in marriage she persuaded her husband to request a field in addition to the city of Debir itself. She is the one who immediately pressed the request, with or without the permission of her husband. She pointed out to her father that a town in the Negev needed a water supply. So Caleb gave his daughter a *blessing* or wedding gift of two springs near Debir.

3. *Application:* Aside from the author's interest in portraying women in a positive light, what might have been the purpose for the inclusion of this rather private and inconsequential event in Holy Scripture? This is a question which may not be conclusively answered. Certainly at the least it illustrates the principle, "Ask and you shall receive."

D. Other Campaigns (Judges 1:16-18)

1. *Relocation of Kenites (1:16):* The success of Judah in the Negev is indicated by the fact that the Kenites left the region of Jericho (*city of palms*) and went to live among the Judahites in the wilderness area south of Arad. The Kenites were a Midianite tribe skilled in working with metals. Moses' in-laws were Kenites. Hobab, Moses' brother-in-law, had apparently accepted Moses' offer to accompany the Israelites to the Promised Land (cf. Numbers 10:29).

2. *Conquest of Zephath (1:17):* The Judah-Simeon coalition next undertook the conquest of Zephath, a city allotted to Simeon. The city was *utterly destroyed* and thus was given the name Hormah ("Destruction"). Some twenty years earlier the Israelites had done the same thing to the cities of this region (cf. Numbers 21:1-3).

3. *Coastal cities (1:18):* In the Mediterranean coastal area the Judahites were able to take the Philistine cities of Gaza, Ashkelon, and Ekron and surrounding territories. Unfortunately these cities did not remain under Israelite possession for very long.

E. Status Report on the South (Judges 1:19-21)

1. *Efforts of Judah (1:19-20):* Whatever success Judah had in clearing the hill country of Canaanites was due to the presence of Yahweh. The Judahites, however, did not fare well against the inhabitants of the lowlands to the west because they had *iron chariots*. Why was Yahweh unable to help them in the lowlands? The problem was that 1) Judah did not press the initial advantage in the lowlands; and 2) failed to settle the areas which had been conquered.

2. *Efforts of Benjamin (1:21):* Benjamin did even worse. They did not follow up on the initial Judahite victory over Jerusalem. The Jebusites returned, and the Benjamites made no effort to drive them

out. At the time the Book of Judges was written the Jebusites were still living *with the sons of Benjamin* in Jerusalem.

Uneven Progress in the North
Judges 1:22-36

The author now paints a picture of the progressive failure of the northern tribes to dispossess the Canaanites. The campaigns started well enough, but then tribal efforts slacked off. Finally the Canaanites got the upper hand in one area and forced the relocation of the tribe of Dan.

A. Initial Success (Judges 1:22-26)
1. Spies at Bethel (1:22-23): The house of Joseph (the tribes of Ephraim and Manasseh) followed the example of Judah and launched a campaign to clean the Canaanites out of their territory. Bethel, which was initially conquered by Joshua (Joshua 12:16), was their first target. *The Lord was with them* in this effort.
2. Traitor at Bethel (1:24-26): Israelite pies spotted a man coming out of the city. They requested that he show them *the entrance* of the place. City entrances in this period had various configurations ranging from very simple to extremely complex zigzag affairs. To storm the entrance without having some advance knowledge of its construction meant needless death to many soldiers. Like Rahab the Bethelite apparently was sympathetic to the Israelite cause. Upon a promise of kind treatment from the attackers, the man diagrammed the entrance to the city. Bethel was subsequently smitten with the sword, i.e., put to the ban. The informer, however, was released. Unlike Rahab, this unnamed man chose not to join the people of God. He moved north outside of Canaan to the land of the Hittites. There he built a city that he named Luz after the original name of Bethel.

B. Failures of the Joseph Tribes (Judges 1:27-29)
1. Failures of Manasseh (1:27-28): Manasseh had been assigned certain cities from the tribes of Issachar and Asher (Joshua 17:11). Four of these towns were in the Esdraelon Valley, and one was on the coast. Manasseh *did not* take possession of these cities. They could have, but they did not. If fear was the initial reason for inaction, it did not continue to be a factor. The problem was not tribal

83

strength, for at some point *Israel became strong.* Still the Canaanites were not driven from the land. They were only put to forced labor. One can only speculate as to the possible reasons for Manasseh's failure.

2. *Failures of Ephraim (1:29):* The Ephraimites made the same mistake as their brethren the Manassehites by not driving out the inhabitants of Gezer. Again, the text does not say that Ephraim *could not* drive out the enemy. They simply left this strategic city in Canaanites hands.

C. Failures of the Other Tribes (Judges 1:30-36)

1. *Failures of Zebulun (1:30):* Zebulun left two cities in the hands of the Canaanites. Zebulun was strong enough, however, to subject the Canaanites to forced labor.

2. *Failures of Asher and Naphtali (1:31-33):* Asher and Naphtali *lived among the Canaanites.* This language suggests that at some point these tribes were actually at the mercy of the natives who lived in their territories.

3. *Failures of Dan (1:34-36):* In the case of Dan, the Amorites forced a retreat back into the hill country of Ephraim. The Danites never were able to gain the upper hand.

D. Assessment of Tribal Efforts

And so the litany of failure concludes. Seven times in these verses the sad words appear: *did not drive out.* Certainly there were good reasons to have carried out God's initial orders to drive the Canaanites from this land. Some of the sites left in Canaanite hands were geographically strategic. The danger from Canaanite enclaves, however, was fundamentally spiritual, not military or economic. Toleration led to association and then to accommodation. Yahweh came to be regarded as just another deity, one among many, that needed appeasement from time to time. Here in Judges 1 are the roots of the apostasy so prevalent later in the book: failure to obey the primary command of God to expel the Canaanites.

From the standpoint of the author of Judges—a true preacher—the record of tribal activity in the north was one of dismal failure. The text, however, acknowledges that the Israelites did come eventually to dominate their Canaanite neighbors militarily and economically. Four times (vv. 28, 30, 33, 35) he stresses that the Canaanites were put to forced labor. Thus the accusation here is not that Israel could not because of lack of faith drive out the Canaanites. Rather the charge is that Israel *deliberately disobeyed* the commandment of God. Israel *chose* to live side by side with Canaanites. Thus the text suggests that success may be measured by many yardsticks. Judged physically, Israel's occupation of Canaan was a success. Judged spiritually, Israel had miserably failed.

Divine Rebuke & Warning
Judges 2:1-6

When the tribal efforts to expel the Canaanites ceased, the angel of Yahweh, whose directives launched the Conquest at Jericho (cf. Joshua 5:13-15), appeared again. His message now was one of rebuke and warning.

A. Angel's Appearance (Judges 2:1a)

1. Identity of the angel: The terminology *angel of Yahweh* is never used of a human messenger or prophet in the historical books. The angel of Yahweh is a theophany, a visible manifestation of Yahweh. This appearance should be dated sometime between the death of the faithful elders who outlived Joshua ca. 1380 BC and the rise of the first foreign oppressor ca. 1378 BC.

2. Location of the appearance: The angel of Yahweh *went up* from Gilgal in the Jordan valley to Bochim. The location of Bochim is unknown, but apparently some prominent place in the hill country is meant. Since the passage indicates that the place received the name Bochim ("Weepers") from what transpired in this passage, the site must have been known by another name before this event. Since the text indicates that the "angel" spoke to *all Israel* some place of national assembly must be intended. Two places appear possibilities: Shechem where Joshua led Israel in covenant renewal, and Shiloh where the Tabernacle was located.

3. Significance of the appearance: Why does the text speak of going up from "Gilgal"? The "angel" did not physically follow a road from the one site to the other. The text only means to say that the same divine person who issued the initial battle plan at Gilgal now appeared at Bochim. At Gilgal the reproach of God's people had been rolled away. There the covenant feast and covenant sign had been renewed after thirty-eight years of suspension. At Gilgal Israel learned the power of obedient faith; at Bochim the dismay of disobedience. Thus the phrase "from Gilgal to Bochim" expresses the decline of Israel from spiritually lofty heights to the pit of spiritual despair.

B. Angel's Message (Judges 2:1b-3)

   1. Reminder of past assistance (2:1b): The "angel" did not introduce his speech with a messenger formula (*thus says Yahweh*) because the "angel" is Yahweh. What he said is something that only Yahweh can say. The message began with a reminder of three things. First, the "angel" reminded Israel of his gracious acts, how he had brought them out of Egypt; how he had brought them into the land that he had sworn to give to their fathers. Thus he is the God of dramatic power and faithful promise.

   2. Other reminders (2:1c-2a): Second, he reminded Israel of his gracious commitment. Yahweh had promised never to break the covenant with Israel. Third, he reminded Israel of covenant obligations. Israel was not to make a covenant with the inhabitants of Canaan. This reminder suggests that formal covenants had been made with the native population promising to spare their lives (cf. Joshua 9). Furthermore, Israel was to destroy all Canaanite altars and symbols of worship.

   3. Accusation of disobedience (2:2b): Following the reminder, the "angel" brought an accusation against Israel in the form of a direct statement and a question. *You have not obeyed me.* Nothing could be more plain and forceful than this terse statement (three words in the Hebrew). The question (*What is this you have done?*) is designed to underscore the shocking nature of such flagrant and deliberate disobedience to the Lord.

   4. Warning (2:3): Finally, the "angel" uttered a threat against Israel. It is couched in language previously used by the Lord in the days of Moses (Numbers 33:55) and in the days of Joshua (Joshua 23:13). First, Yahweh threatens not to drive the Canaanites out before Israel. Second, these nations will become like thorns in the side of Israel, i.e., they will oppress them. Third, the Canaanite gods will be snares to entrap and finally destroy Israel. Israel will be infected by the cancer of Canaanite idolatry. Thus will Israel be ensnared in its own folly.

C. Reaction to the Angel (Judges 2:4-5)

In reaction to the appearance and message of the angel of Yahweh the people did three things. First, they lifted up their voice and wept. They were not yet so hardened as to be unmoved by the reminder of their spiritual failings. Second, they named the place Bochim ("Weepers"). Third, they sacrificed to the Lord. Yet the text does not indicate that there followed any concerted effort to drive the Canaanites from the land. The tears of Bochim were those of remorse, but not real repentance.

END OF
THE JOSHUA ERA
Joshua 24:31, 33

The sacred historian reports that Israel served Yahweh all the days of Joshua and all the days of the elders who outlived Joshua. This probably represents a period of seven years or so. By that time most if not all of the elders who had seen the mighty acts of God in the wilderness and in Canaan had passed from the scene.

The Book of Joshua concludes with a note on the passing of Eleazar the son of Aaron who was Joshua's lieutenant during the Conquest. The author may be suggesting that Eleazar's death (ca. 1380 BC) marked the end of the period of the elders who outlived Joshua.

Chart 7
PREACH THE WORD
Commendation Day

Text: Joshua 22:1-4

When we stand before our Captain in the final day may it be said that…

    A. We have been Faithful to God's Word (22:2a)

    B. We have Listened to our godly Leaders (22:2b)

    C. We have been Loyal to our Brethren (22:3)

    D. We May Enter Our Promised Possession (22:4).

6
ROOTS AND FRUITS
OF APOSTASY
Judges 17-21

Chapter Chronology

	1378
7+ Years	
1385	

Judges is a book about apostasy. The opening paragraphs of the book trace the roots of that apostasy to the failures of the tribes to carry out the orders of God in their dealings with the Canaanites. The Book of Judges concludes with a five-chapter appendix that illustrates how bad conditions became in Israel after the death of Joshua because the tribes failed to drive the Canaanites out of the land. These chapters have been included in the book in order to illustrate the apostasy, lawlessness, immorality, disunity and legalism which characterized most of the period of the Judges.

DANITE MIGRATION
Judges 17-18

Date: ca. 1385 BC

Did the Danite migration occur shortly after the division of the land during the days of Joshua (Joshua 19:47), shortly after the death of Joshua (Judges 1:34) or at the very end of the period of the Judges (Judges 18)?

- Judges 1:1 *after the death of Joshua* hints (but does not prove conclusively) that this event occurred after Joshua was dead.
- Comparison of Judges 18:12 and 13:25 seems to indicate that the Danite migration took place prior to the time of Samson. (Mahaneh Dan got its name *after* the Danite migration.)
- Reference to Moses' grandson in 18:30 (not Manasseh's grandson as in KJV). Since Moses' son was born *before* the

89

Exodus (ca. 1470) it would be most unlikely that a grandson would live after 1300 BC.

- **Conclusion:** The Danite migration took place after the death of Joshua and before the period of the Judges.

Apostasy Illustrated
Judges 17:1-13

In chapter 17 the author of Judges illustrates what chronologically must have been the first blatant indulgence in idolatry during the Israelite occupation of the land (cf. Judges 2:11-23). Idolatry had always been part of the under-culture; but now it came out of the closet. The account revolves around an Ephraimite named Micah and his relationship to his mother, his shrine and a certain Levite.

A. Micah and his Mother (Judges 17:1-3)

1. Curse upon a thief (17:1-2a): Micah, which means "Who is like Yahweh," had stolen eleven hundred pieces of silver from his mother. Without realizing that her son was the thief, the mother pronounced a curse on the one who stole her money. When the renegade son returned the silver his mother sought to reverse the curse with a blessing. She then dedicated the money to Yahweh *for her son.* By this action she was probably attempting to remove the dangers that were associated with the initial curse.

2. Attempt to undo the curse (17:2b-3): The mother apparently thought she would be performing an act of devotion by providing *a graven image and a molten image* to assist in the worship of Yahweh. This is the technical language of Deuteronomy 27:15 where a curse is pronounced against anyone who would make such an object. Thus again the author is pressing home his consecrated sarcasm. Micah's mother was attempting to negate a human curse by bringing her son under a divine curse!

B. Micah and his Shrine (Judges 17:4-6)

1. Images fashioned (17:4): Two hundred shekels of the silver were given to a silversmith who fashioned the desired images. These images were kept in the house of Micah in the hill country of Ephraim. That a man with the orthodox name Micah would be cited as the first after the entry into Canaan to represent the invisible God by means of cultic objects is an irony the author surely intends his readers to note.

2. Shrine established (17:5-6): Little by little Micah's illegal worship expanded. He built a shrine for his gods. He made an ephod, an upper garment worn by those in priestly service. He constructed *household idols* in addition to the images constructed with his mother's silver. To preside over his shrine Micah consecrated one of his sons as priest. The author of Judges explains that this idolatrous cancer was tolerated because *there was no king in Israel; every man did what was right in his own eyes.* The right kind of king would have been loyal to the covenant. He would have squelched this incipient idolatry.

C. Micah and his Levite (Judges 17:7-13)

1. Levite enticed (17:7-10): An itinerant Levite provided Micah the opportunity to add to the prestige of his idolatrous shrine. This young man from Bethlehem Judah was traveling through Ephraim when he happened to spend the night at Micah's house. When Micah learned that this Levite was attached to no particular sanctuary, he offered him employment. Micah agreed to pay the young man ten silver pieces per year, furnish him with a new suit of clothes, and provide his maintenance if the Levite would be *a father,* i.e., spiritual advisor, *and a priest* at his shrine.

2. Levite service (17:11-13): The Levite sinned when he accepted the offer to be Micah's priest. He lived in Micah's house. As time went on this sacerdotal employee was treated more like a son. Micah was overjoyed with his good fortune at having secured a man from the priestly tribe to serve at his idolatrous shrine. He actually thought Yahweh would smile upon him and bring him prosperity now that a Levite officiated at all the worship activities in his house.

3. Application: For Micah worship was private business. He wanted to do his own thing. He bought into the philosophy that as long as one is sincere strict compliance to God's word was not necessary. Though he did not totally abandon Yahweh, he borrowed worship forms from his pagan neighbors to "enrich" his own approach to God. Though modern man may not make a graven image, he still displays much of the same attitude about worship that guided Micah down a dead end street. Biblical worship is God-centered, not man-centered. To please God must be the ultimate obsession of the worshiper. God cannot be pleased when his specific commands about worship are either violated or ignored.

Lawlessness Illustrated
Judges 18:1-31

The account of the illicit worship in the hill country of Ephraim is continued in chapter 18 but with a new element. The chapter illustrates the lawlessness which was prevalent in Israel during the decades prior to the monarchy. The action centers about certain families in the tribe of Dan.

A. A Spy Mission (Judges 18:1-10)
   1. Spies dispatched (18:1-2): To this point in time—shortly after the death of Joshua—the Danites had not been able to control their original allotment. So the tribal elders dispatched five men to search for a location which might be suitable for a tribal inheritance.
   2. Spies and the Levite (18:3-6): Apparently the spies turned aside at the house of Micah because they recognized, even at a distance, the voice of the Levite. They seem to have been most surprised to encounter him there in the hill country of Ephraim. When the Levite explained that he was now serving as a Micah's priest, the Danites requested that he inquire of God as to the success of their mission. The Levite assured them that *Yahweh* approved of the way they were going.
   3. Spies at Laish (18:7): The five Danites proceeded on to the town of Laish (Leshem in Joshua 19:47) north of the Sea of Galilee. This was a Phoenician city loosely associated with Sidon. Because of the considerable distance from Sidon, Laish was basically independent. It had no strong army to protect it.
   4. Spies report (18:8-10): The five spies reported back to their brethren what they had found. The tribe made the decision immediately to move against Laish. This spacious region of abundance would easily fall into the hands of these fierce fighters.

B. A Tribal Migration (Judges 18:11-26)
   1. Danite march (18:11-14): Six hundred armed Danites set out with their families toward Laish. En route they passed through the hill country of Ephraim. As the Danites approached the house of Micah, the five spies told their brethren about the religious paraphernalia

which was there. The armed men determined that they would take these objects with them to Laish, and they would invite the Levite to go with them as well.

2. *Danite theft (18:15-20):* Backed by the small army, the five spies entered into the shrine. They gathered up the images and ephod. They offered the Levite the position of *father and priest* to the Danites. Much better, they argued, to be the priest of a tribe than the priest of one man. The Levite was overjoyed with this "call" to a larger pulpit. He himself supervised the theft of the religious objects. Then he joined the group for the march to Laish.

3. *Explanation:* The religious decline of the nation is clearly illustrated in this passage. Contrary to the design of the Law of Moses, Israelites had developed a strong desire for local shrines. They apparently believed that the mere possession of sacred objects guaranteed success in their ventures. Character counted for nothing in religious figures if they could demonstrate some measure of genealogical legitimacy. In these new attitudes the influence of Canaanite paganism is in evidence.

4. *Micah's confrontation with the Danites (18:21-24):* The Danites anticipated some violent response when Micah learned of the theft of his religious objects and the pirating of his personal clergyman. They arranged their column so that the little ones and valuables were in front. The six hundred armed men acted as a rear guard. As expected, Micah assembled the men of the community, and they overtook the Danites. Micah accused the Danites of having taken his *gods* and his priest. In these verses the author underscores the folly of idolatry. A god that can be carried off is a non-god. The author has made Micah, the first idolater of the settlement period, to testify to the ultimate stupidity of idolatry.

5. *Danite threat (18:25-26):* The Danites, unable to refute the accusation, responded belligerently. Micah had best keep his complaints to himself or he and the men with him will come under attack by *hot-tempered* (NIV) or *fierce* (NASB) men. The Danites apparently held to the philosophy that "might makes right." Micah realized that he and his ill-equipped force were no match for the Danites, and so he turned back to his own house. Thus Micah who had stolen from his mother was now repaid by a theft of what he revered. The author wishes his readers to note that the sanctuary at Dan had its origin in a double theft.

C. Capture of a City (Judges 18:27-29)

1. Action of the Danites (18:27-29): Following the confrontation with Micah, the Danites and their new priest continued their migration to Laish. They struck the quiet town with the edge of the sword, and burned down the place. The remoteness of the town made rescue by the city of Sidon impossible. Why the city was put to the torch is not clear. Perhaps they were motivated by some superstitious fear that they might be harassed by the guardian spirit of the dwellings. In any case, after totally destroying the place, the Danites rebuilt Laish and named the place Dan after their tribal ancestor. This town became the northernmost settlement of the children of Israel in the land of Canaan.

2. Analysis: Did the Danites have the right to attack Laish? The city was within the boundaries of the Promised Land. Certainly Israelites had the right to conquer the place. Laish, however, was within the tribal limits of Naphtali. The Danites were acting in a cowardly way by failure to press the attack within their own allotment. The peaceful inhabitants of Laish were no military challenge to the Danites. Furthermore, the Danites did not follow the general principle of Deuteronomy 20:10-15 by first offering peace to the inhabitants of the place.

The author depicts the Danites in the worst possible light. They stole what belonged to another man. They had as their spiritual head a priest who could be bought. They pounced on a defenseless city. They established a shrine that was the rival of the house of Yahweh at Shiloh.

D. A Cult Established (Judges 18:30-31)

1. A surprising twist (18:30a): The Danites established their own religious shrine in the newly built city. They installed therein the graven image that they had confiscated from Micah back in the hill country of Ephraim. The wandering Levite who was consecrated to be the priest of that shrine is at last identified. His name was Jonathan. He was a grandson or great grandson of Moses.[9] This fact provides a

---

[9]Apparently the Hebrew text originally read *Moses* in Judges 18:30. Later scribes could not accept the fact that a grandson of Moses would have agreed to serve as priest at an idolatrous shrine. They assumed that the original reading was *Manasseh* rather than *Moses*. The difference between the two names in the Hebrew text is a single consonant. In some Hebrew manuscripts the scribes have "restored" the missing letter by inserting above the line of writing a small letter *nun* at the

chronological framework for the first appendix to Judges. The involvement of Moses' grandson (or great grandson) dates the Danite migration shortly after the death of Joshua.

2. Duration of the cult (18:30b-31): The prestigious Levitical family continued to serve at the illegal and idolatrous shrine until *the captivity of the land.* The reference is probably not to the Assyrian captivity of Israel which did not begin until about 745 BC. Most likely the reference is to the Philistine captivity of the land, when the ark of God was captured and Shiloh was destroyed (1 Samuel 4-5). A date of 1080 BC probably would not be far off. This explanation of the *captivity of the land* fits well with the note with which the first appendix to Judges closes. Micah's graven image continued to be worshiped *all the time that the house of God* (i.e., tabernacle) *was at Shiloh.* The point seems to be that the idolatrous shrine in Dan was a rival of the legitimate worship center in Shiloh until the latter was destroyed.

WAR AGAINST BENJAMIN
Judges 19-21

Date: ca. 1379 BC

Judges 19 illustrates a third dimension of the moral mess which characterized the years immediately following the death of Joshua. Again a Levite is involved, and he is portrayed in a less than favorable light. The account opens with the reminder that *in those days Israel had no king* (19:1). This note seems intended to link chronologically the events of the two previous chapters to those about to be narrated. At the same time the author intends to warn his readers that he is about to relate shocking events, events which would never have transpired had there been a strong, god-fearing king in those days.

Immorality Illustrated
Judges 19:1-21

A. A Trip to Bethlehem (Judges 19:1-9)

1. Marital problems (19:1-2): The Levite, who lived in the remote part of Ephraim's hill country, had taken a concubine from

appropriate place.

Bethlehem in Judah. She, however, had *played the harlot* against him. She deserted her husband and returned to the house of her father.

2. Reconciliation (19:3-9): After four months of painful separation the Levite set out for Bethlehem with a servant and a pair of donkeys. He went after his concubine to *speak tenderly* (lit., speak upon her heart) in order to persuade her to return with him to their home. He must have mended the relationship, for she brought him into her father's house. The Levite's father-in-law was glad to see his daughter's husband. For three days the men feasted. The overly gracious father-in-law persuaded the Levite to spend a fourth day and night in Bethlehem. Not until afternoon of the fifth day was the Levite able to depart for his home in Ephraim.

B. A Stopover in Gibeah (Judges 19:10-21)

1. Bypassing Jebus (19:10-13): By the time the travelers had gone six miles or so it was late in the afternoon. The Levite's servant proposed that his master turn aside for the night into the Jebusite city of Jebus (Jerusalem). The Levite, however, refused to lodge in a city occupied by *foreigners*. He was determined to press on for Gibeah or Ramah.

2. Hospitality by an Ephraimite (19:14-21): By the time the threesome reached Gibeah the sun already had set. They entered the city and sat down in the public square. Normally citizens would provide lodging for weary travelers. Gibeah, however, was most inhospitable. Finally an old man, who was an Ephraimite living in Gibeah, came in from the field. When he learned that the Levite was an Ephraimite, he was most cordial. The Levite assured the old man that he would provide the food for himself, his concubine, servant and donkeys. He would not be a burden. The old man, however, insisted that the travelers come into his home and accept his provisions. The Levite quickly accepted the invitation.

C. Attack by the Locals (Judges 19:22-26)

1. Moral perversion (19:22-24): The joyous evening meal was interrupted by a pounding on the door. The men of the city, certain *sons of Belial* (worthless fellows), had surrounded the house. They demanded that the old man surrender the Levite to them that they might *know* (i.e., have carnal relations with) him. This unnatural lust (cf. Romans 1:27) shows how corrupt the men of Gibeah had become. The old man pled with his neighbors not to contemplate such

96

foolishness. To dramatize the magnitude of the sin of homosexual rape, the old man offered to surrender to the mob his own virgin daughter and the concubine of his guest. The mob could ravish these women and do with them as they pleased if only they would cease attempting to rape the Levite.

2. *Moral insensitivity:* The moral perversity of the Benjamites was only matched by the moral insensitivity of the old man. He regarded a heterosexual rape even of a virgin, bad as that might be, as far less of a crime than a homosexual rape. Granted, under the code of the east, he had a responsibility to protect his guest from danger. The end, however, does not justify the means. That the men in this account have a very low estimation of the value of women is rather clear. One should remember, however, that the very purpose of this story is to illustrate the disgusting immorality which was sweeping the land in the days just after the death of Joshua. Certainly biblical *teaching* does not support the notion that the rape of a woman is a lesser offense than the rape of a man, or that heterosexual immorality is less serious than homosexual immorality.

3. *Moral brutality (19:25-26):* The Levite was as morally perverse and insensitive as the old man and the mob. When he saw that the mob refused to listen to the old man, he seized his concubine and shoved her out the door. Accepting this sacrifice to their perverted lust, the men of Gibeah showed no further interest in the old man or his guest. They raped the woman and abused her all night long. At the approach of dawn they released her. She staggered to the door of the house, and fell. There she breathed her last breath.

D. Reaction to the Atrocity (Judges 19:27-30)

1. *National shock (19:27-30):* Early in the morning the Levite arose to continue his journey. He saw the crumpled body of his concubine at the doorway. When she did not respond to his cold command to arise, the Levite realized that she was dead. He placed her on his donkey and continued on toward the hill country of Ephraim. At his house the Levite took a knife and dismembered the corpse. The man had as little respect for his spouse in death as he had had for her in life. He sent the pieces of her body throughout the territory of Israel. The entire nation was shocked at the sordid tale of the sin of the Benjamites. Nothing like that had ever happened in Israel since the day that the children of Israel had come up from Egypt.

2. *Application:* The crime at Gibeah illustrates the depths of the moral depravity into which many of the Israelites quickly had fallen after the death of Joshua and the elders of his generation. Hosea regarded this outrageous sin as the standard by which to measure all other depraved acts (Hosea 9:9); he saw in this narrative the initial act of apostasy after Israel entered Canaan (Hosea 10:9). This chapter, taken together with the one which follows, however, also illustrates the divine law of sowing and reaping. The woman who played the harlot died by being sexually abused. The Levite who sacrificed his spouse to save his honor lost her altogether. The men of Gibeah, along with thousands in their tribe who condoned their actions, died in a war of retribution.

Disunity Illustrated
Judges 20:1-48

The moral perversity of the men of Gibeah set in motion a chain of events that drove a wedge between the tribes. The internecine bloodshed that was narrowly averted in the days of Joshua (cf. Joshua 22) became a bloody reality shortly after his death.

A. National Assembly (Judges 20:1-10)

1. *Missing tribe (20:1-3a):* From Dan to Beersheba and from Gilead as well the sons of Israel assembled at Mizpah. The tribal chiefs took their stand in the assembly of the people. Some 400,000 swordsmen were present. The author is much impressed with the unity of the tribes. Three times he states that they gathered *as one man.* Yet one tribe—Benjamin—was not represented. By failing to appear the Benjamites were signaling that they were siding with the men of Gibeah. So the unity of Israel here is directed against one of their own tribes. Three times the author seems to lament the tragedy of the whole situation by noting that the united tribes and the Benjamites were *brothers.*

2. *Levite's address (20:3b-7):* The assembly requested from the Levite a firsthand report of what had happened that night in Gibeah. The Levite rehearsed the dreadful details of the event, being careful to place his own despicable conduct in the best possible light. He alleged that the men of Gibeah intended to kill him. Though the narrative of the previous chapter does not state this explicitly, the Levite is probably not exaggerating when he states that his life was in

jeopardy. His gruesome butchery of the woman's corpse was justified by the magnitude of the sin committed against her by the Benjamites. They had committed *a lewd and disgraceful act* in Israel. The word *lewd* denotes a sin so vile that the perpetrator must be *cut off* from the nation (cf. Leviticus 18:17, 29). The word translated *shameful act* is the same term used by the old man when he appealed to the men of Gibeah to abandon their sinful course (cf. Judges 19:23).

The shocking dismemberment of the corpse had accomplished exactly what it was intended to accomplish, viz., the massing of the national assembly. Now the Levite called upon those assembled to give advice and counsel regarding the incident.

3. Commitment to holy war (20:8-10): Those assembled pledged not to return to their homes until a military campaign had been launched against Benjamin. Following the holy war traditions, they cast lots to set aside ten percent of their number to serve as a quartermaster corps to provide food for the army. The others marched against Gibeah of Benjamin.

B. Positions of the Two Sides (Judges 20:11-17)

1. Benjamites (20:11-16): Messengers were dispatched throughout the tribe of Benjamin to demand the surrender of the *sons of Belial* in Gibeah. Only the death of those rapists and murderers could remove the wicked blot from Israel. The Benjamites refused to join the national effort to punish the atrocity at Gibeah. On the contrary, an army of 26,000 swordsmen rushed to Gibeah to bolster the defense of the town. Among the Benjamite defenders were 700 left-handed slingers who could sling a stone at a hair and not miss. By taking the side of their tribesmen the Benjamites came to share the guilt of the murderers. They too came under the ban that had been imposed on Gibeah.

2. United tribes (20:17): The united tribes numbered their swordsmen at 400,000. This constituted an advantage of almost fifteen to one. That this vast army did not immediately crush the Benjamites and in fact suffered heavy casualties at their hands suggests that Yahweh was punishing the united tribes as well as Benjamin in this account.

C. Battles (Judges 20:18-35)

Over the next several days the united tribes clashed with the Benjamites three times. In the first two battles Benjamin was victorious. In the third clash the united tribes virtually wiped out the Benjamites.

1. First attack against Gibeah (20:18-21). Representatives of the eleven tribes went to Bethel to seek by priestly oracle direction concerning the war with Benjamin. The text makes no mention of any request for divine wisdom or even divine help for that matter. Nor is there any record of offerings being brought in worship. Their only question was: Which tribe will lead the campaign against Benjamin? The same question was asked in reference to the warfare against the Canaanites in Judges 1:1. The response there and here is that Judah should lead the tribes into battle. The next day as the men of Israel approached Gibeah, the Benjamites came out to meet their attackers. Some 22,000 men of Israel became casualties in the first clash of the war.

2. Seeking God's face (20:22-23): The united tribes were discouraged by their heavy losses, but they were not yet ready to relinquish the effort to punish the lawless Benjamites. Again they arrayed themselves for battle in the same position which they had held on the previous day. Representatives of the eleven tribes again *went up before Yahweh* (at Bethel?). Until evening time they wept and inquired of the Lord. Should they renew hostilities with Benjamin? Their tears were not those of real repentance. They were attempting to coerce Yahweh to be sympathetic to their cause. The priestly oracle directed them to resume the attack. The oracle, however, offered no assurance of victory.

3. Second attack against Gibeah (20:24-25): The results of the second battle were similar to those of the first clash. The Benjamites again came out against the united tribes and cut down 18,000 swordsmen. Thus far Israel had received the favor of divine guidance but not divine aid in the battle itself. Yet the significance of this should not be overlooked. In spite of all that was wrong in Israel, the Israelites still had access to divine guidance through the high priest. This Benjamin did not have.

4. Seeking God's face (20:26-28). In the two disastrous defeats the Israelites had learned that victory was not going to come through their military might, but only through empowerment by the Spirit of God. They dared not go forward with their campaign against Benjamin until they were assured that the Lord would give them victory. So all of the people went up to Bethel to inquire of the Lord. Phinehas, the grandson of Aaron, stood before the ark and ministered there. The Israelites fasted and wept, and offered various sacrifices before the Lord. They again asked if they should go up against Benjamin. This time, however, they added the words *or not.* They were now willing to break off the attack if that be the will of Yahweh. No longer were they presuming that their plan to punish Benjamin was within the will of God. Again the priestly oracle directed the united tribes to attack Gibeah a third time. This time victory was assured.

5. New strategy (20:29-35): A new strategy was employed by the united tribes in the third attack against Gibeah. They set men in ambush around the city with the obvious intention of catching the Benjamites in a pincher movement. The main body began the attack then feigned retreat. The Benjamites, overconfident because of their previous victories, began to pursue the retreating men of Israel. The maneuver worked. The Benjamites where lured out into the open where they were attacked from three directions. The battle was fierce. The Benjamites did not suspect that their army was about to be decimated.

D. Explanation of Victory (Judges 20:36-48)

1. Gibeah burned (20:36-43): Having given a thumbnail sketch of the third clash, the author now explains how that victory was possible. One contingent of the ambush rushed the city itself. When they saw the smoke rising from Gibeah, the Benjamites lost their will to fight. They attempted to flee toward the wilderness. The battle, however, overtook them. The Lord struck the Benjamites before Israel.[10]

2. Benjamite losses (20:44-48): The Benjamite casualties in that third day of battle were staggering. The total is said to be 25,100 swordsmen (verse 35). A band of 600 Benjamites made it to the rock of Rimmon where they remained for four months. Having crushed the army of Benjamin, the united tribes turned back against the territory of Benjamin. The non-combatants were struck with the edge of the sword, the cattle were destroyed and the cities burned. The entire tribe

---

[10]The exact count of casualties on the third day of battle is said to be 25,100 (v. 35). This is rounded off to 25,000 in verse 46. The number of Benjamite casualties added to the 600 survivors falls 1,000 short of the figure given for the Benjamite forces at the beginning of the war. The text is silent about any Benjamite casualties in the first two clashes. The 1,000 unaccounted for in the casualty figures from the third clash may have been lost in the first two clashes.

was under the ban of total destruction since it had taken the side of the men of Gibeah.

Legalism Illustrated
Judges 21:1-25

In their shock over the behavior of the Benjamites, the men of Israel had taken a rash vow before the war. They had sworn in solemn oath that they would not give their daughters in marriage to Benjamites. Now they realized that an entire tribe was about to be lost. The leaders of Israel consequently devised a scheme whereby they could technically keep the terms of their sacred oath, and at the same time provide wives for the surviving Benjamites. In this kind of hypocritical legal fiction the Israelites became skilled with the passing of years. The scribes of Jesus' day were experts in knowing how to keep the letter of the law while at the same time breaking the spirit of that law.

A. Virgins of Jabesh (Judges 21:1-14)
1. Lamentation (21:1-4): The prospect of losing one of the tribes entirely was a matter of great concern. Again the people went to Bethel where they expressed their grief all day before the Lord. In their zeal to punish the atrocity of Gibeah they had entered into a rash vow. Now they bemoaned the consequences of their own stupidity. Sacrifices were offered in an attempt to move the Lord to heal the breach in their nation.
2. Potential solution (21:5-9): After a day of lamentation and worship, a potential solution occurred to some of the leaders. When the national assembly had been called to Mizpah (20:1-11), another oath had been taken. This oath obligated them to put to death soldiers who failed to assemble before the Lord. A roll call of the army indicated that no contingent from Jabesh-gilead had aided in the war against Benjamin.
3. Attack on Jabesh (21:10-11): The assembly determined to put Jabesh-gilead under the ban. A contingent of twelve thousand men was dispatched with orders to put to death the inhabitants of the place. Thus human logic determined to resort to massacre of their countrymen in order to undo the results of the massacre of other countrymen. Only the young virgins were to be spared. Since virgins wore distinctive clothing in ancient cultures, they easily would be

identified by the attacking forces. The original oath, however, must either have applied only to the men of military age, or to the entire population of towns which sent no support to the war effort. The sparing of the virgins was completely arbitrary. The desperate effort here was to undo the effects of one rash vow by the selective implementation of another.

4. *Jabesh virgins (21:12-14):* Four hundred virgins were found among the inhabitants of Jabesh-gilead. These girls were brought back to Shiloh, the site of the tabernacle. Then a peace offering was sent to the six hundred Benjamites at the rock of Rimmon. They left their stronghold in the wilderness, came to Shiloh, and claimed as brides the four hundred virgins from Jabesh. Still, however, two hundred of the Benjamites did not have wives.

B. Daughters of Shiloh (Judges 21:15-25)

1. *Bizarre plan (21:15-22):* More wives were needed. Another solution occurred to some of the rulers. Though not as violent, it was equally bizarre. During the annual feast at Shiloh the Benjamites who still needed wives were to conceal themselves in the vineyards. When the daughters of Shiloh came out to join in the dancing, the Benjamites were to rush forth from the vineyards and seize wives. Should fathers or brothers complain to the leaders, they would be assured that they were innocent of any violation of the oath. They had not actually *given* their daughters or sisters to the Benjamites. No one seems to have cared that a festival of the Lord was being used for this chicanery.

2. *Kidnapping wives (21:23-25):* The Benjamites did as they were told. Each single man captured one of the dancing daughters of Shiloh and carried her off, cave-man style, to be his wife. A more despicable desecration of marriage can hardly be imagined. The Benjamites then returned to their tribal inheritance with their new brides to rebuild and occupy their towns. The national assembly of the eleven tribes, having served its purpose, also dissolved. The men of Israel returned to the territories of their respective tribes and clans. The narrative concludes with a final reminder of how such unpleasant episodes could have taken place. There was no central government during the days of the Judges. Everybody simply did what he thought was right.

END OF THE CONQUEST PERIOD
We have now Covered 28 Years of Bible History

JUDGES PERIOD
Israel's Dark Ages

Biblical Location: Judges 3-16 + Ruth + 1 Samuel 1-7

Beginning Point: Cushan Invasion (1378 BC)

Ending Point: Saul Crowned (1048 BC)

Duration: 330 Years

Key Players: Deborah, Gideon, Samson, Samuel

Key Events: Sisera victory, Midian victory, Samson exploits, Samuel's call, Ark captured

Scriptural Theme:
After this, God gave them judges until the time of Samuel the prophet (Acts 13:20 NIV).

Christian Application:
I do not have time to tell about Gideon, Barak, Samson, Jephthah, David, Samuel and the prophets, who through faith conquered kingdoms, administered justice, and gained what was promised; who shut the mouths of lions, quenched the fury of the flames, and escaped the edge of the sword; whose weakness was turned to strength; and who became powerful in battle and routed foreign armies (Hebrews 11:32-34 NIV).

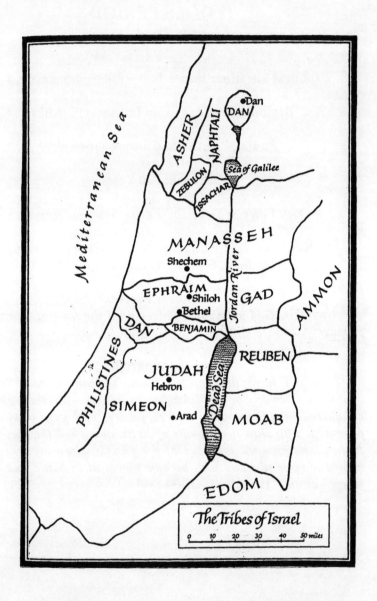

The Tribes of Israel

0   10   20   30   40   50 miles

7
A STRANGE SALVATION
Judges 3-5

Chapter Chronology

Oppress. 1378	Othniel 1371	Oppress. 1332	Ehud 1315	Oppress. 1236	1178 Deborah 1217
200 Years					

The focus of Judges 3-16 is on the glory of God's salvation. The author has selected several stories of sin, supplication and salvation in order that his readers might appreciate God's salvation even more.

Since God refused to drive out the native population any longer, the Israelites had no alternative except to live among the Canaanites. Thus at the outset of the period of the Judges, Israel was living at peace with people who should have been their enemies. Toleration of pagan ways led to accommodation, integration and finally apostasy, Israel's distinct identity was thus compromised. Israelites married Canaanite women and served their gods (3:5-6). The warning from the Angel of Yahweh (2:1-5) obviously went unheeded.

The first four oppressions and deliverances of Israel in the Book of Judges fell roughly within the period 1378-1178 BC. The oppressors during this period were Cushan, Eglon, the Philistines and Jabin. The deliverers were Othniel, Ehud, Shamgar and Deborah. These deliverances arose from unexpected quarters. Thus a certain strangeness characterized the salvation of God's people.

SALVATION THROUGH
AN OLD MAN
Judges 3:7-11

Date: 1378-1332 BC

The account of the first oppression and deliverance sets a literary pattern for those which follow in the Book of Judges. Though Othniel was the tool used by the Lord in this situation, the spotlight is really on God throughout. The text speaks of the anger, grace, action and gift of God.

Anger of God
Judges 3:7-8

A. Path to Oppression (Judges 3:7)

The author outlines in three steps the circumstances that led to the first oppression of Israel by an external power. These steps move from the general to the specific. First, Israel *did what was evil in the sight of Yahweh.* Second, Israel forgot Yahweh their God, i.e., forgot his claims, his commands, his character, and his mighty acts on behalf of the nation. Third, Israel served the various Baal gods of the Canaanites along with their female counterparts, the Asheroth.

B. Agent of Oppression (Judges 3:8)

1. Introduced: The apostasy of Israel triggered the anger of Yahweh. His anger is a jealous anger that refuses to let go of his people. He will not allow them to be comfortable in their sin. God *sold them* into the hands of Cushan-rishathaim king of Aram Naharaim (NIV)—"Aram of the two rivers." *Rishathaim* was a nickname bestowed upon this oppressor by the Israelites. It means "double wicked." Thus the Israelites called their oppressor "Double trouble from twin rivers."

2. Identified: The name "Cushan" appears to be Hittite. Cushan may have been a king of the kingdom of Mitanni who was a vassal of the powerful Hittite empire. He was probably attempting to extend his kingdom southward into Canaan. Apparently the entire land of Canaan was subject to him. For eight years (c.1378-1371 BC) Israel *served* this king. Presumably this meant that the Israelites paid tribute to Cushan. Throughout Old Testament history God frequently gave expression to his anger against unfaithfulness by empowering a Gentile ruler against his people.

Grace of God
Judges 3:9

The Israelites *cried[11] unto Yahweh.* God was moved by those tears to raise up for his people a *deliverer.* To *raise up* means to call,

---

[11]The dominant connotation of the Hebrew word translated *cried* is desperation. When repentance is included another word is added for clarity. Therefore the cries for

commission and empower a person to do a certain job. In this case, the job was to deliver Israel from the oppression of Cushan. The author has previously introduced this deliverer. He was Othniel ("lion of God"), Caleb's younger brother. Many years earlier Othniel had established his credentials as a warrior in the capture of Debir. If he were as much as twenty years younger than Caleb he would have been about eighty-six at this point. The "lion of God" was indeed a harmless old lion. Even so, he had the spirit of his more famous brother who at the same age looked for giants to conquer! Othniel was the most prominent representative of that older generation that had witnessed God's mighty deeds in the conquest of Canaan.

Action of God
Judges 3:10

God used Othniel for great things. *The Spirit of Yahweh* came upon him. By that Spirit he was enabled to *judge* Israel. The function of the Judge was to set right what was wrong in the land. In this case, the wrong was the heartless oppression of Cushan. So *judging* Israel eventually meant going to war with Cushan. No details of the crucial battle are recorded. The text simply states that the Lord *gave* Cushan the double wicked into the hands of Othniel. The result was that Othniel *prevailed* over Cushan.

Gift of God
Judges 3:11

The land of Israel had *rest* for forty years after the expulsion of Cushan. *Rest* does not merely mean the absence of war. The term has a more positive side to it. To have *rest* means to have peace, happiness and well-being.

The text mentions the death of Othniel after the forty years of rest. This is probably not to be taken to mean that Othniel lived through that entire forty years. If so he would have been amazingly old—about 125—at the time of his death. Whereas in early Old Testament history some lived to this age and beyond, in this period people were not living such long lives. Surely note would have been taken of the fact had Othniel lived so much beyond the century mark.

---

help in Judges do not necessarily imply real repentance.

Most likely, then, the *rest* achieved by Othniel on the battlefield continued long after his death. This rest is probably to be dated about 1371-1332 BC.

SALVATION
THROUGH A LEFTY
Judges 3:12-31

Date: 1332-1236 BC

The Book of Judges goes into more detail concerning the second oppression and deliverance. The text speaks of the oppressor, the deliverer, the assassination of the oppressor and the victory over his forces.

Oppressor
Judges 3:12-14

A. Israel's Evil (Judges 3:12)

Israel again began to do evil immediately after the death of Othniel and probably during the forty years of *rest*. Thus even while enjoying the blessing of Yahweh the people again did what was contrary to his will. A new generation had grown up after the oppression by Cushan. They ignored the lessons of their history and turned again to the paths of apostasy that their fathers had trod. At the conclusion of the forty years of *rest* God punished his people a second time by means of a foreign adversary. He *strengthened* Eglon, king of Moab, against Israel.

B. Eglon's Invasion (Judges 3:13-14)

Eglon with his allies the Ammonites and Amalekites invaded and defeated Israel in some decisive battle. The forces of the king occupied *the city of palm trees* in the general vicinity of old Jericho. From that headquarters Eglon was able to wield authority over the Israelites for eighteen years.

Deliverer
Judges 3:15-16

A. Personal Information (Judges 3:15a,b)

110

1. A Benjamite (3:15a): Yahweh was moved again by the agonizing cries that his people directed unto him. The Lord therefore *raised up* Israel's second deliverer. Concerning Ehud the text relates the following. First, he was the son of Gera. What significance may be attached to the mention of his father is not indicated. Second, Ehud was a Benjamite. Chronologically, the civil war which almost wiped out the tribe of Benjamin (Judges 19-21) probably already had taken place. Ehud was one generation removed from that time when his tribe narrowly escaped extinction. Because of that bloody civil war *Benjamite* must have been in this period a designation of contempt.

2. Left-handed (3:15b): What is more, Ehud was left-handed. Left-handedness in the ancient world was considered a stigma. The fact that Ehud was left-handed does not necessarily mean that his right arm was useless. In a right-handed world the left-handed enjoyed certain military advantages. Some who trained to be warriors would have their right hand bound to their side throughout their youth so that they might become skilled in the use of their left hand. Within the tribe of Benjamin at the time of the civil war there were six hundred such warriors (Judges 20:16). Ehud may have been descended from one of them.

C. Ehud's Plan (Judges 3:15c-16)

1. His position (3:15c): Ehud seems to have been designated as leader of the groups that annually carried the tribute to Eglon. Whether or not this was deemed an honor is questionable. Ehud probably had been in or led that delegation several times during the eighteen years of Moabite oppression. He saw clearly what action must be taken if Israel were to be liberated from these oppressors.

2. His weapon (3:16): Apparently without telling anyone of his intentions, Ehud fashioned a two-edged sword a cubit (18 inches) in length. This weapon he strapped on his right thigh under his garment. He had observed that the guards always checked the left side of those who sought an audience with the king. They (rightly) assumed that a right-handed man would draw his sword from his left side. Since he was left-handed Ehud planned to smuggle his weapon into the presence of Eglon. The weapon probably had no crosspiece on it and thus would have been easier to conceal under the long flowing robes.

Assassination
Judges 3:17-22

A. Circumstances (Judges 3:17-19)

Ehud had the assassination of Eglon carefully planned. First, he presented the tribute to the obese king as he had doubtless done many times before. Then he made sure his companions got safely through the Moabite perimeter in the Jericho region. He went with them as far as the *idols*[12] at Gilgal. There he turned back toward Eglon's headquarters. He was readmitted to the king's presence by announcing that he had *a secret message* for the king. Eglon may have thought that Ehud was about to reveal some secret Israelite plan to rebel against him. In any case, it is clear that Eglon trusted Ehud. He ordered all attendants from the room.

B. Smiting the King (Judges 3:20-22)

In the cool roof chamber of the headquarters building, Ehud approached the king. He explained as he did so that his secret message was from God. Pagan people had no problem embracing many gods. Eglon probably believed that Israel's God Yahweh was to be respected in this land. So he rose, out of respect for the God from whom he believed he would receive a message. At this point Ehud reached for his sword. Before the king could take evasive action or even cry out for help, the sword was buried in his fat belly. Ehud struck the king with such force that even the handle of the razor-sharp blade entered the body of the king. Ehud did not attempt to withdraw the sword. The king's entrails came out around the gaping wound.

C. Assessment

Some have voiced great concern over the ethics of Ehud's actions. These points need to be stressed: First, Ehud was raised up by God. His calling as a Judge required him to rid the land of those who were causing oppression. Second, Ehud did not act out of base motives of selfishness or personal vengeance. Third, the Bible does not explicitly nor implicitly condemn Ehud for the course he followed.

Escape

---

[12]The *idols* may refer to the twelve stones erected at Gilgal by Joshua when Israel crossed the Jordan. Others think the idols were Moabite and the Gilgal is not the famous site by that name, but the place mentioned in Joshua 15:7 which was southwest of Jericho on the road to Jerusalem.

Judges 3:23-26

A. Bolting the Doors (Judges 3:23-24)

The details of Ehud's escape from the scene of the assassination are not dear. Somehow he was able to lock the doors to the upper room where the king had died. One view is that he used a key taken from the person of the dead king to lock the doors from without. Another view is that he bolted the doors from the inside and then fled through a back door or window, or possibly even through the toilet shaft. It is not clear whether or not the king's servants actually noticed Ehud leave. When they attempted to return to their stations in the upper room, they found the door locked. The locked door plus the odor that must have been generated by the rupture of the king's anal sphincter led the courtiers to conclude that the king was defecating (lit., "covering his feet") in the upper chamber. No doubt Israelites told this story over the years with a chuckle over the stupidity of the Moabite soldiers.

B. Discovery of the Corpse (Judges 3:25-26)

The royal guards waited until they became anxious. They then secured the key and opened up the upper room. There they were shocked (*behold!*) to find their master lying on the floor dead. Meanwhile Ehud had escaped to Seirah, an otherwise unknown location in the hill country.

Victory
Judges 3:27-30

A. Strategy (Judges 3:27-29)

Ehud blew the trumpet throughout the hill country of Ephraim. After explaining what he had done, the Israelites followed him back down toward the Jordan. He assured the hastily assembled troops that Yahweh had given their enemies into their hand. The Israelite hosts seized the Jordan fords leading to Moab. None of the enemy was allowed to escape. About ten thousand Moabites were killed in the struggle.

B. Significance (Judges 3:30)

The defeat of the Moabite army at the Jordan eliminated the threat from that quarter for a number of years. *Moab was subdued*

113

that day under the hand of Israel. Consequently that part of the land was undisturbed for eighty years.

SALVATION
THROUGH A GENTILE
Judges 3:31

A. Shamgar's Identity

Only one verse describes the career of Shamgar. The name is not Hebrew. For that reason scholars think he probably was a Gentile. He is called *the son of Anath.* Anath was the name of a female goddess of sex and war among the Canaanites. This may be the intended meaning here, but other possible explanations have been proposed. A note in chapter 5 (5:6) suggests that Shamgar was a man of considerable influence for some time. Though little is recorded about him in the Bible he must have been a legend in his own time.

B. Shamgar's Deliverance

God used Shamgar to deliver Israel from a new threat from the west. Shamgar's exploits against the Philistines should be dated about 1300 BC or shortly thereafter. Shamgar was able to strike down six hundred Philistines using as his weapon an ox goad, a sharp-pointed stick used to prod oxen. The strangeness of God's salvation is indicated by the odd instruments that the deliverers used against the enemy. Ehud used a homemade dagger, Jael a hammer and peg. Now Shamgar is said to have used an ox goad. God can win great victories with whatever is in the hand of a willing servant.

SALVATION
THROUGH A WOMAN
Judges 4:1-5:31

Date: 1236-1178 BC

The author of Judges appreciated godly women. Already he has given a cameo of Achsah, Caleb's lovely and clever daughter (1:13-15). In the fourth deliverance account of Judges the author introduces two women totally different in personality and station, but equally committed to the kingdom of God.

Need for Salvation
Judges 4:1-3

A. Israel's Sin (Judges 4:1)

The text does not actually relate when Ehud died. Most likely he did not live to the conclusion of the eighty years of *rest* which followed his victory over the Moabites. A suggested date would be 1281 BC. In any case, when he died *the sons of Israel again did evil in the sight of Yahweh.* Commitment that depends on some external force (e.g., Ehud) is not real commitment. Sin is soberingly repetitious. This apostasy most likely began in the northern tribes where the influence of Ehud's work had been felt the least.

B. Israel's Servitude (Judges 4:2-3)

1. Jabin (4:2): The Lord *sold them* into the hand of a Canaanite king named Jabin whose capital was in Hazor. This is not the same Jabin who ruled Hazor in the days of Joshua almost a century and a half earlier (Joshua 11:10-13). *Jabin* may have been a dynastic title for all the rulers of this city. Perhaps while Israel was occupied with the oppressions by Cushan and Eglon, this Canaanite city gradually had risen to power.

*2. Sisera (*Judges *4:3):* The commander of Jabin's army was Sisera whose military headquarters was in Harosheth-hagoyim (location unknown). The main source of Sisera's power was a unit of nine hundred iron chariots. For twenty years (c. 1236-1217 BC) he was able to dominate northern Israel.

Tools of Salvation
Judges 4:4-11

A. Deborah (Judges 4:4-5)

Deborah differed from all the other Judges who appear in the book in four respects. First, she was a woman, *the wife of Lappidoth.* Women in positions of political or spiritual leadership during Old Testament history were rare. Second, unlike the other Judges who began their careers in response to a foreign oppression, Deborah seems to have been active for some time prior to the deliverance from Sisera. She was *judging Israel at that time.* Third, Deborah is described as *a prophetess.* She received direct revelation from the Lord that enabled her to interpret the past, give direction in the present and announce the future. Fourth, Deborah had a regular spot from which she judged Israel. Under a palm tree between Ramah and Bethel in the hill country of Ephraim Deborah held court. The sons of Israel came there to her for *judgment.* Life in the heart of Israelite territory could proceed as usual. Jabin's influence had not spread much further south than the valley of Esdraelon.

B. Barak (Judges 4:6-7)

1. His commission (4:6-7): How long Deborah ministered prior to the great deliverance is not stated. At some point she summoned Barak from Kadesh in the tribal area of Naphtali. Kadesh was farther north than Hazor. Undoubtedly Deborah was following divine direction when she summoned this man. Barak came from the tribe that had suffered the most under the Canaanite oppression. Deborah shared with him a prophetic revelation that directed him to assemble ten thousand men and march them to Mount Tabor overlooking the valley of Esdraelon. He was to secure his troops from the tribes of Naphtali and Zebulun. God promised to *draw out* (lit., pull or drag out) Sisera to the River Kishon which flowed through the valley. He promised to give Sisera into the hand of Barak.

2. His reluctance (4:8-9): Barak agreed to carry out this divinely ordained mission if Deborah would accompany him. Was Barak showing cowardice? Was his faith wavering in spite of the assurances that Deborah had given? Not necessarily. He may simply have wanted Deborah to be present for the value of her prophetic advice. In any case, Deborah was quite willing to go with Barak. She warned Barak, however, that the honor associated with a victorious campaign will not belong to him. She predicted that the Lord will *deliver Sisera into the hands of a woman.* That prediction was fulfilled in an amazing manner later in the chapter (4:8-9).

3. His army (4:10): Encouraged by Deborah's agreement to go to Kadesh with him, Barak raised his army of ten thousand men. These men came from the two tribes most affected by Jabin's oppression, Naphtali and Zebulun. Other tribes, however, contributed to the effort (cf. 5:14). Deborah kept her word and went up to Kadesh with Barak.

C. Jael (Judges 4:11)

A parenthetical note introduces another aspect of the strangeness of God's salvation. Heber separated himself from the Kenites who

116

had migrated to the southern part of Judah (cf. Judges 1:16). He moved north to the general region of Kadesh. Jael, Heber's wife, will be yet another tool used by God in the deliverance from Sisera Thus the author of Judges wants his readers to reflect on the providence of God that led a family to relocate and thus position itself to be the agent of God's salvation.

Day of Salvation
Judges 4:12-16

A. Sisera's Actions (Judges 4:12-13)

The movement of ten thousand men from Kadesh to Mount Tabor could not be kept secret, nor did the Israelites wish to keep it so. Sisera heard that this army had positioned itself on Tabor. He therefore massed his nine hundred chariots and supporting infantry. He slowly began to move his forces from his headquarters to the Kishon River in the valley of Esdraelon. Sisera probably thought this show of force would intimidate the Israelites as it had done many times before. The position of the Israelites atop Mount Tabor was a strong one, but they could not stay there forever. As soon as the Israelites dared to come down into the valley of Esdraelon Sisera aimed to destroy them.

B. Prediction of Deborah (Judges 4:14)

Deborah the prophetess was not intimidated. She urged Barak to launch the attack. She predicted that this day Yahweh will deliver Sisera into the hand of Barak. *Behold,* she said cryptically, *Yahweh has gone out before you.* His faith strengthened by the words of the prophetess, Barak led the charge down the slopes of Mount Tabor.

C. Victory of Barak (Judges 4:15-16)

The Lord *routed* (lit., threw into confusion) Sisera and his army *with the edge of the sword* before Barak. That, however, was not the whole story. Apparently a driving rainstorm made the floor of the valley impossible terrain for the chariot forces (cf. 5:20f). When Sisera saw that the battle was lost he fled on foot. Meanwhile Barak pursued the chariots and infantry back to their headquarters at Harosheth-hagoyim. Not one of the enemy troops survived the onslaught by Barak's men.

Completeness of Salvation
Judges 4:17-24

A. Sisera's Refuge (Judges 4:17-20)

While his army fled west, Sisera on foot fled north and east. At Zaanamim he came upon the tent of Heber. As he approached, Jael went out to meet him. She invited him to come into her tent. She urged him not to be afraid. Since there was peace between King Jabin and the Kenites, Sisera thought he might find sanctuary within Jael's tent. She then *covered him with a rug.* The general requested a drink of water. Jael gave him goat's milk instead. Sisera requested that Jael stand in the doorway of the tent to divert possible pursuers.

B. Sisera's Death (Judges 4:21-22)

When Sisera fell asleep, Jael seized the opportunity to strike a blow for freedom. She took a tent peg and hammer. These were items she knew well how to use, for among the desert peoples the pitching of the tent was the work of the women. She cautiously approached the sleeping general. Sisera, however, was so exhausted by his flight that he was fast asleep. Jael drove the tent peg through his temple. The tyrant of the past twenty years was dead. As Barak approached her tent, Jael came out to meet him. She invited him into the tent to see *the man whom you are seeking.* There Barak saw Sisera lying in a pool of blood with a tent peg in his temple.

C. End of Canaanite Oppression (Judges 4:23-24)

With his army totally annihilated it was only a matter of time before King Jabin himself fell before Israel. *The hand of the sons of Israel pressed heavier and heavier upon Jabin.* Finally he was destroyed, just as Joshua had destroyed the earlier Jabin who had ruled Hazor.

Song of Salvation
Judges 5:1-31

Deliverance from a ruthless adversary demands celebration. Judges 5 is a song sung by Deborah and Barak on the day of the great victory over Sisera (5:1). This ancient piece of Hebrew poetry is difficult to translate. Popular English versions of the Bible reflect a

118

wide range of possible renderings of this chapter. Nonetheless, this poem is regarded as one of the masterpieces of world literature.

A. Savior (Judges 5:2-11)

1. Praise for Yahweh (5:2-5): The poem begins with praise for Yahweh. First, the Lord is praised because the leaders led and the people volunteered to follow them. Without courageous leaders and loyal followers God's work cannot be accomplished. Second, the poem praises Yahweh for his awesome presence. Yahweh is depicted going out *from Seir* or Edom. As he marched forth the ground trembled, the heavens dripped water. At Sinai the mountains quaked at the presence of Yahweh. This same God who with such awesome power appeared at Sinai had now come to the aid of his people against Sisera.

2. Need for salvation (5:6-9): The presence of God among his people was much needed. The situation in Israel had been desperate in the days of Shamgar and Jael. Major highways controlled by the Canaanites in the north and the Philistines in the south were deserted. New gods were being worshiped. Though war threatened their cities Israel had no courage to take up shield or spear in defense of the land. Forty thousand could have been hurled against Sisera, but no one would fight in those desperate days before Deborah arose. She inspired confidence in the troops. Deborah realized, however, that she would not have been able to gain the victory without the aid of valiant commanders. For them she praised the Lord.

3. Celebration of salvation (5:10-11): All segments of society are called upon to join the song of joy now that some normalcy had been restored. The ruling class (*who ride* on *white donkeys*), the merchants (*who travel on the road*) and the shepherds all have reason to celebrate *the righteous deeds of Yahweh.*

B. Summons (Judges 5:12-18)

1. Response to summons (5:12-15a): Next the poem recalls how the people of Israel responded to the appeal to rise up against their enemies. Barak responded first to the challenge to take captives of the enemy. Then those who had survived the twenty years of oppression responded. *The people of Yahweh came down to me* [Deborah] *as warriors.* Leaders from the tribes of Ephraim, Benjamin, Machir (west Manasseh), Zebulun and Issachar joined Deborah for the rebellion. They followed Barak into the valley of Esdraelon.

2. *Failure to respond (5:15b-17):* Not all the tribes were interested in fighting against Sisera for the freedom of God's people. The Reubenites had *great resolves of heart,* i.e., good intentions. They talked about joining the fray. They searched their heart. Finally, however, the Reubenites decided that they were just too busy with their sheep. The Gileadites (the tribes of east Manasseh and Gad) also remained safely on the other side of Jordan. West of Jordan no help was offered by Dan and Asher. These two coastal tribes were caught up in a profitable maritime trade. Those who rest while their brothers fight the battle nearby stand condemned by the Lord.

3. *Special commendation (5:18):* If there were tribes that refused to fight for freedom, there were two in particular that merited special praise. Zebulun was *a people who despised their lives even to death.* They courageously threw themselves into the struggle without considering the fact that they might lose their lives in the battle. The same was true of Naphtali.

C. Struggle (Judges 5:19-23)

1. *Yahweh's intervention (5:19-22):* The kings of Canaan—those who were allies with Jabin—sent their armies to fight the insurgents. At Taanach near the waters of Megiddo in the Valley of Esdraelon the two armies clashed. The Canaanites were not able this time to take plunder. *The stars fought from heaven* against Sisera. This is a poetic way of speaking of how the Lord intervened in the battle. A terrific rainstorm caused the normally placid Kishon River to become a raging torrent. The horses mightily struggled to pull their chariots through the morass, but to no avail.

2. *Curse on Meroz (5:23):* The third unit of the poem closes with a reference to the failure of another group of Israelites to assist in the battle. Through Deborah the *angel of Yahweh* put a curse on Meroz *because they did not come to the help of Yahweh* in the struggle against the enemy warriors. This city was near to the scene of the battle. Even after the battle had been won these Israelites did not help in the pursuit.

D. Slaying (Judges 5:24-27)

The fourth unit of the poem celebrates Jael's contribution to the struggle for freedom. Her blessing stands in sharp contrast to the curse on Meroz. She is called *most blessed of women.* Jael was an ordinary woman of a tent-dwelling tribe. She normally attended to duties about *the tent.* Jael, however, is celebrated for her cleverness, courage and strength. Sisera asked for water which might refresh him. She cleverly gave him milk instead. This hastened his sleep. Jael took her life in her hand as she approached the sleeping general. She used all of her strength to pound that tent peg through the temple of the sleeping tyrant.

E. Sorrow (Judges 5:29-30)

1. A mother's worry (5:28): While there is jubilation in Israel, Deborah paints a sad picture of the sorrow that filled at least one heart. As a mother Deborah could understand the pain that one woman was feeling. Every Sisera has a mother, someone who loves him in spite of his cruelty. So Deborah imagines how it must have been that day for Sisera's mother. In typical motherly concern Sisera's mother paced in the palace, looking out the window from time to time to see if she could see any evidence that the troops were returning from the battle. She could not understand the delay that day.

2. Attempts to console (5:29-30): Those about Sisera's mother—*her wise princesses*—attempted to console her by suggesting various explanations for the inordinate delay. Perhaps the division of the spoil captured from the Israelites was so great that it was taking longer than usual to divide it among the soldiers. Perhaps females had been captured as a result of the battle and the soldiers were having their way with them. In any case, Sisera would return shortly bringing wonderful garments for his mother and others in the palace.

Sisera's mother heard these suggestions, and even convinced herself that they were correct. She repeated them to herself. She knew not that another mother had engineered the defeat of her son on the battlefield. She had no idea that even while she was anticipating sharing the spoils of the battle, her son lay dead at the feet of a humble tent woman.

F. Supplication (Judges 5:31)

1. Petition regarding enemies (5:31a): Deborah was not a hard woman. She could appreciate the pain that the death of a Sisera might have on another mother. At the same time Deborah was not guided by feminine sentimentality. She loved the Lord and the people of the Lord more than life itself. So Deborah prayed, *Thus let all your enemies perish, O Yahweh.* The prophetess regarded Sisera as one of the enemies of the Lord. Wicked oppressors frequently respond to no inducement to moderate their ways. They respond only to force. In essence Deborah prayed that God's kingdom might be established on earth as it is in heaven. She longed for the day when God's people will enjoy permanent *rest* because the last of their oppressors has been destroyed.

2. *Petition for God's people (5:31b):* Deborah also prayed that those who love the Lord might be *like the rising of the sun in its might.* God's people are meant to be a light in this world which dispels the power of darkness.

3. *Concluding note (5:31c):* The account of Deborah concludes with a note that the land had rest for forty years. The rest can be dated to about 1217-1178 BC.

8
STRENGTH IN WEAKNESS
Judges 6-9

Chapter Chronology

			1131
Oppression 1178	1172	GIDEON	Abimelech 1133
		47 Years	

The first four instruments used by Yahweh in the period of the Judges illustrate the strangeness of God's salvation. The fifth—Gideon—illustrates how God demonstrates his strength through human weakness. God delights in using the weak things of this world to confound the wise.

GIDEON AND HIS 300
Judges 6:1-8:35

Date: 1178-1133 BC

Need for Salvation
Judges 6:1-6

A. Oppressors (Judges 6:1)

At some point during the forty years of rest after the deliverance from Jabin, the Israelites again *did evil in the sight of Yahweh*. About 1178 BC the Lord *gave them* into the hands of the Midianites for seven years. This desert people were descended from Abraham through his concubine Keturah (Genesis 25:2). Because the Midianites were distant relatives of the Israelites this oppression was particularly onerous.

B. Oppression (Judges 6:2-6)

Each year at harvest the Midianites, along with their allies, swept in from the desert, crossed the Jordan, proceeded up the Esdraelon Valley, the bread basket of Canaan, and then south through the coastal plain. They confiscated all the grain that they could carry away with them. The Midianites brought their camels with them in such numbers that an accurate count was impossible. Like a locust plague they stripped the land. The invaders left virtually no means of sustenance for the people of Israel or their animals. The Israelites salvaged what they could in mountain caves and dens.

Prophetic Explanation
Judges 6:7-10

A. Appearance of a Prophet (Judges 6:7-8a)

The Midianite incursions brought the Israelites low. They cried to the Lord. The answer to their prayer came in a strange way. God sent a prophet to them. That Israel should understand the present predicament was more important than the immediate deliverance from their oppressors. God gave them what they really needed, not what they wanted. Understanding a problem may be more important than eliminating the problem. The word of God is the key to such understanding.

B. Message of the Prophet (Judges 6:8b-10)

1. God's past assistance (6:8b-9): The unnamed prophet began with a messenger formula: *Thus says Yahweh.* This is a claim that what the prophet said was directly spoken by *the God of Israel.* First, the Lord reminded his apostate people of his gracious acts in the past. He had brought them out of slavery in Egypt. He had delivered them from the hands of the Egyptians at the Red Sea. Those *oppressors* who stood in Israel's path en route to Canaan (e.g., Sihon and Og) were dispossessed before the people of God. The Lord gave to his people the land of all their enemies.

2. God's relationship to Israel (6:10a): Second, the prophet stressed the relationship which existed between God and Israel, a relationship which had been initiated by the Lord himself. Often God had declared Israel to be his people. He had bound himself to them by covenant.

3. God's demand repeated (6:10b): Third, the prophet repeated the basic demand of Yahweh's covenant: Israel must not *fear* (i.e., worship or serve) the gods of the Amorites in whose land they were dwelling.

4. God's accusation (6:10c): Finally, after these various reminders, the Lord through his prophet made this charge: *You have not obeyed me.* The word of the Lord exposes and rebukes human failings. How gracious God is to bring his word of judgment to bear upon the lives of his wayward people!

5. *Response:* The text does not indicate directly what effect the preaching of the prophet throughout the land might have had. The purpose of his coming was to bring the nation to repentance and thereby prepare them for the deliverance from Midian. When the prophet had finished his work, the Angel of Yahweh himself appeared in the land.

Call of a Deliverer
Judges 6:11-40

More is known about the call of Gideon than of any of the other Judges. His call involved three types of divine revelation. In the first the Lord appeared directly to Gideon. In the second, God spoke verbally to Gideon. The third revelation involved supernatural deeds of God. These three types of revelations were designed to equip Gideon spiritually and psychologically for the great work he was about to do.

A. Theophonic Revelation (Judges 6:11-26)

In a theophany God appeared directly to individuals in the Old Testament period. When he assumed human-like form the theophany is called the Angel of Yahweh. That Angel who last appeared at Bochim at the conclusion of the Conquest period (Judges 2:1-5), now made his first appearance during the Judges period.

1. *Angel's greeting (6:11):* The Angel sat down under a well-known oak tree on the property of Joash who was of the Abiezrite clan of the tribe of Manasseh. Joash's son Gideon was nearby beating out wheat in a wine press. By threshing his wheat in this unlikely place Gideon hoped to preserve a portion of the harvest from the Midianites. The Angel made himself known to Gideon through an abrupt greeting: *May Yahweh be with you.* This was a common greeting in the days of the Judges (cf. Ruth 2:4). The Angel addressed Gideon as *valiant warrior.* Gideon was in no mood for pleasantries.

2. *Gideon's response (6:12-13):* Gideon challenged the assumption that Yahweh was with any Israelite. If Yahweh were with us—the shift to plural is noteworthy—then *why has all this happened to us?* The unstated premise upon which this question rests is that God would not allow such unpleasant circumstances if he were really with his people. He surely could not look askance while his people

125

suffered. He would surely perform some mighty act on their behalf. Where were all the miracles which Yahweh was said to have performed in former generations? Since he had seen no evidence of miraculous intervention, Gideon could only conclude that Yahweh had abandoned his people. He had given them over to the power of Midian.

3. *Gideon's commission (6:14):* God answered Gideon's objections by revealing more of himself to the man. The Angel of Yahweh (who now is identified simply as Yahweh) faced Gideon. Gideon could see that the stranger was not making light of him. He was in dead earnest. Then came the commission: *Go in this your strength and deliver Israel from the hand of Midian.* The *strength* to which the Angel alluded was the power that God supplies to those he calls to do his bidding. The question *Have I not sent you?* calls attention to that divine source of power.

4. *Gideon's response (6:15):* Gideon was beginning to realize that the one with whom he was speaking was no ordinary person. He questioned, not the power of God, but the wisdom of God's choice: *How shall I deliver Israel?* Gideon saw his family as being the least in the tribe of Manasseh. He was the youngest in his family. He was lacking two essential ingredients of leadership: influence and maturity.

5. *Gideon's reassurance (6:16):* Yahweh bolstered the self-confidence of Gideon by reiterating the words of the greeting with which the conversation had begun. What was first stated as a mild wish now became a solid promise. *Surely I will be with you.* God's presence will enable Gideon to smite the entire Midianite army as though he were smiting only one man.

B. Credentials Offered (Judges 6:17-24)

1. *Gideon's request (6:17-18):* Gideon wanted proof that it really was the Angel of Yahweh who was speaking to him. He requested a *sign,* (i.e., supernatural verification) of the identity of this stranger. Gideon wished to present an offering to the stranger, as Abraham had done so many years before (Genesis 18:5-8). Gideon specified no particular miracle. He must have assumed that an *offering* would give the Lord opportunity to show his power in some manner. The Angel agreed to remain until the offering was presented.

2. *Offering presented (6:19-21):* Gideon prepared an elaborate meal to present as an offering to his guest—a young goat and a

tremendous quantity of unleavened bread. He put the meat in a basket and its broth in a pot and brought it to the Angel who was waiting patiently beneath the oak tree. The Angel directed him to place the goat and the unleavened bread on a rock which became a makeshift altar. The broth he was to pour out, perhaps on the offering. The Angel then put out the end of his staff and touched the offering. Fire sprang up from the rock and consumed the goat and the unleavened bread. At the same time the Angel vanished from Gideon's sight.

3. Gideon's reaction (6:22): Gideon now was certain that he had been conversing with the Angel of Yahweh, a manifestation of God himself. He was immediately struck with fear. *Alas* signifies the deepest agony. Gideon apparently felt that to look upon the Angel of Yahweh face to face meant death. What irony! Gideon needed assurance of Yahweh's promise (v. 16), but when the assurance came he was intimidated, not emboldened.

4. Gideon's altar (6:23-24): God spoke to Gideon, no doubt in an audible voice. He urged him not to be afraid. He will not die. Gideon immediately built an altar to Yahweh to mark the spot of this manifestation. He named that altar *Yahweh is Peace* to celebrate the fact that he had seen the Angel face to face without tasting death. At the time the Book of Judges was written that altar was still present in Ophrah.

C. Verbal Revelation (Judges 6:25-32)

In the theophonic revelation Yahweh had indicated that he was committed to Gideon. That very night in a verbal revelation Yahweh demanded that Gideon demonstrate his commitment to his God.

1. Requirements of Gideon's God (6:25-27): Gideon was directed to destroy his father's Baal altar and the Asherah pole beside it. Those who are to be leaders of God's people must first set in order the affairs of their own house. Gideon was then to build an altar to Yahweh *on top of this stronghold.* The two altars could not exist side by side. One cannot serve both Yahweh and Baal.

Gideon was to use the wood of the Asherah pole for kindling. Then he was to offer up to Yahweh the seven-year old bull. The deliberate mention of the bull's age may be an allusion to the fact that Midian had oppressed Israel for seven years. Offering up the bull may symbolize national rededication after seven years of oppression. Be that as it may, Gideon took ten men of his servants and carried out the instructions of the Lord. Because he anticipated interference from his

127

father's household and the men of the city, he destroyed the Baal altar by night.

2. Reactions of Gideon's neighbors (6:28-30): The men of the city discovered the next day that the Baal altar and Asherah had been destroyed. A new altar of the fashion used in Yahweh worship had been constructed. They could tell that the new altar had been used during the night for sacrificial purposes. Diligent inquiry revealed that Gideon was guilty. The town leaders demanded that Gideon be handed over by his father to be executed for the sacrilege.

3. Response of Gideon's father (6:31-32): Joash refused to hand over Gideon. He argued in effect that Baal, if he really were a god, could take care of himself. Here Gideon's father seems to be taking a decisive stand against Baal and his worshipers. Growing out of this incident Gideon received the nickname *Jerubbaal,* "Let Baal Contend against Him." This passage makes crystal clear that the struggle against foreign oppression and the struggle against foreign gods were inextricably linked.

D. Action Revelations (Judges 6:33-40)

Gideon heard no further from the Lord until the Midianites swept into the land on their annual raid. Then he received a new revelation, not in words, but in actions. These new revelations equipped him for his mission and confirmed him in it.

1. Equipping revelation (6:33-35): At the time the Midianites and their allies came up into the Valley of Jezreel, the Spirit of God *came upon Gideon* (lit., clothed himself with Gideon). He was empowered to assume leadership. He blew a trumpet in the area of his clan, and the Abiezrites came together to follow Gideon into battle. Messengers were sent throughout the tribe of Manasseh and neighboring tribes. Thousands responded and joined Gideon and his nucleus of Abiezrites .

2. Confirming revelation (6:36-40): Gideon still needed reassurance that God was about to deliver Israel. This is cautious faith, but it certainly is not unbelief. Gideon thus put out his fleece on a threshing floor. He requested that the fleece be wet the next day, and the ground about it dry. That miracle will indicate that the Lord was about to use Gideon to deliver Israel. The next morning Gideon found the fleece soaking wet. Still he needed reassurance. He put the same fleece out and requested that it remain dry while the ground round about was wet. Since wool has a tendency to absorb moisture, the fleece could only remain dry by supernatural intervention. The next morning the fleece was dry. Gideon was now ready to lead his troops against the Midianites.

The Lord granted both signs to Gideon because his request was not a demand made in unbelief, or an arbitrary test of God's faithfulness. A double sign was appropriate because Gideon will shortly experience a double testing of his faith. God delights in strengthening fragile faith. Far better to admit weakness and ask for strengthening than to go into battle with a cocky faith.

Methods of Faith
Judges 7:1-18

The account of the deliverance by Gideon reveals clearly the methods of faith. God delights in teaching his people absolute dependence on him. Hence in this unit the narrator discusses the reduction of Gideon's army, the concessions that God made to Gideon's weakness, and the preparations for the battle.

A. Reduction of the Force (Judges 7:1-8)

1. Gideon's army too large (7:1-2): Gideon may have been ready for confrontation with the Midianites, but God was not. Gideon had positioned his troops at the spring of Harod. The Midianites were encamped beneath in the Valley of Jezreel. The Lord spoke to Gideon there on the eve of battle. Gideon's army was too large to be an effective tool of God. If the battle were won using such a large force, the Israelites would attribute victory to their own power. God's people have a propensity for glorifying their own efforts, for stealing the praise that belongs to the Lord.

2. First reduction step (7:3): Gideon was instructed to use a provision of the Law of Moses (cf. Deuteronomy 20:8) and dismiss all those who were afraid when they looked down upon the Midianite camp. Twenty-two thousand men left the army. Gideon now had but ten thousand men to face the hordes below.

3. Second reduction step (7:4-8): Gideon must have been a bit apprehensive as he saw two-thirds of his troops walk away. Again the Lord declared, *The people are still too many.* Gideon was directed to bring his remaining forces down to the water so that God might test them there. Only those who passed the water test were to be permitted to go with Gideon into battle. At the water Gideon was told to

129

segregate those who lapped water as a dog from those who knelt down to drink. The "lappers" scooped up water in the hand and drank while standing. They refused to break ranks. These numbered three hundred. The 9,700 who knelt down to drink were dismissed. The three hundred men apparently took the provisions of those who left including their trumpets.

The major question regarding the river episode is whether the "lappers" were intrinsically better soldiers than those who knelt to drink. Those who preach on this passage usually affirm that the "lappers" were more vigilant, more disciplined than the others. Commentators are divided on the question. Many feel that God simply used the drinking exercise as a mechanism for further reducing the force to "faith size." Certainly the text is silent about any military superiority of the "lappers" over the "kneelers."

B. Concession to Weakness (Judges 7:9-14)

1. Gideon's dispatched (7:9-12): That night the Lord again spoke to Gideon. If he had the least bit of fear regarding his mission, he was to go to the enemy camp. If he was afraid to go alone, he was authorized to take with him his personal servant Purah. God wanted Gideon to eavesdrop on a conversation in the Midianite camp to *strengthen* his hands, i.e., give him confidence. What a concession to human frailty! God knows how scared circumstances can make his servants.

Gideon did not feign courage. He was not the stereotypical hero with ice water in his veins. He had no concern to maintain his macho image, not with God at least. He was doubly afraid—afraid to take on the Midianites with three hundred men, and afraid to attempt to penetrate their camp alone. So Gideon took Purah and descended into the valley to one of the outposts of the vast Midianite camp.

2. Gideon convinced (7:13-14): When Gideon and his servant got within listening distance of the outpost they heard a strange thing. One Midianite soldier was relating a dream to a companion. A loaf of barley bread was tumbling into the camp of Midian smashing a tent before it. His companion interpreted that dream without a moment's hesitation. Since the Israelites were grain farmers, the barley loaf represented the sword of Gideon. God had given Midian and the camp into the hand of Gideon. From this it is clear that the Midianites had heard of the resistance movement headed by Gideon. They must have heard some rumors about a divine visitor who had dispatched

130

Gideon on this mission. Finally, Gideon concluded from what he heard that the rank and file of the Midianite army were terrified at the prospects of having to face the Israelites in battle.

C. Preparation for Battle (Judges 7:15-18)

1. Inspiring the men (7:15): When he heard the dream in the Midianite camp, Gideon bowed and worshiped God on the spot. Having had his own morale lifted, Gideon returned to his camp and inspired his men with the assurance that Yahweh had given the Midianite camp into their hands.

2. Equipping the men (7:16): In preparing his three hundred men for battle, Gideon took advantage of what he had heard in the camp. His plan was to provoke panic within the enemy camp by feigning an all-out attack on three sides by three hundred *companies* of men. No thought was ever given to defeating the Midianite camp by force of arms. Gideon divided his men into three companies. Each man was equipped with a trumpet, a pitcher and a torch, the light of which was shielded by the pitcher.

3. Instructing the men (7:17-18): All were to look to Gideon's company for the cue as to what to do. He will lead his company to the outskirts of the Midianite camp, perhaps to the very spot where he and Purah had been earlier that night. When those who were with Gideon blew their trumpets all the others were to do the same. Then they were to shout the battle cry: *For Yahweh and for Gideon!*

Defeat of Midian
Judges 7:19-8:28

The account of the defeat of the Midianites is difficult because it is abbreviated and because it contains geographical references which are hard to identify. Therefore the movements of the two forces are not always easy to decipher. Four key developments are clear: 1) the initial rout of the enemy; 2) the involvement of the reserve forces; 3) the pursuit of the Midianites; and 4) the return from the battle.

A. Initial Rout (Judges 7:19-22)

The plan worked to perfection. Gideon's company approached the outskirts of the camp at the beginning of the middle watch just after the new guards had been posted. At Gideon's signal the three companies blew their trumpets, smashed their pitchers, held their torches high above them, and shouted the battle cry. While the Israelites each stood in their places around the Midianite camp, the enemy began to panic. They thought they were being attacked from all directions by three hundred companies. The Midianites fled down the Jezreel Valley toward the Jordan River. Later prophets regarded this victory as one of the greatest in the history of Israel (cf. Isaiah 9:4).

B. Involvement of Reserve Troops (Judges 7:23-8:3)

1. Involvement of Ephraimites (7:24-25): Once the Midianites were put to flight, Gideon summoned the stand-by army—those men who previously had been dismissed—to take up the pursuit. The Ephraimites, who had no part in the original mobilization, were encouraged to seize the Jordan River crossings, thus thwarting the Midianite escape. Since Ephraim bordered the Jordan this made good sense. The Ephraimites responded in a positive way. They were able to capture two Midianite princes, Oreb and Zeeb. The Ephraimites brought the heads of these two princes to Gideon *across the Jordan*. Gideon and his men had been the first to reach and cross the river in hot pursuit of the enemy.

2. Complaint of Ephraimites (8:1-3): The Ephraimites were very angry that they had not been included in the original battle against Midian. Perhaps they felt that they were going to miss out on the spoils of war. On the other hand, perhaps the exclusion had wounded the ego of the temperamental Ephraimites. In any case, Gideon had to deal with this difficulty. He "smoothed their ruffled feathers" by lauding them for the capture and execution of Oreb and Zeeb. Whereas it was true that Gideon and his men had been permitted to reap the harvest, i.e., strike the initial blow, in this case the *gleanings* were more important. Capturing the Midianite princes was more important than anything that Gideon had achieved that night. Furthermore, since God had given the victory to Israel there was no room for boasting by any man. By these wise and disciplined words Gideon put to rest the Ephraimite anger. Sometimes keeping peace in the camp is more of a challenge than chasing the enemy!

C. Pursuit of the Midianites (Judges 8:4-12)

1. Rejected at Succoth (8:4-7): Gideon and his three hundred continued the pursuit of the Midianites deep into Transjordan. At the Israelite city of Succoth, located where the Jabbok River empties into

132

the Jordan, he requested some provisions for the troops. The leaders of Succoth were still cautious. Zebah and Zalmunna, the Midianite kings, still had not been captured. As a city close to the desert Succoth would suffer severely if the Midianites were able to counterattack. Prudence—or was it cowardice—demanded that they reject Gideon's request. They even *taunted* (cf. v. 15) Gideon, i.e., mocked or insulted him. They sided with the enemy and acted like the enemy, so Gideon treated them like the enemy. He warned the leaders of Succoth that when he returned from the pursuit of the Midianite kings he will *thrash* their naked flesh with *thorns of the wilderness and with briers.*

2. *Rejected at Peniel (8:8-9):* At Peniel a bit further east on the Jabbok River, Gideon received a similar response to his request for aid. There he threatened to tear down the tower of the city when he returned.

3. *Midianite last stand (8:10-12):* Zebah and Zalmunna attempted to reassemble what was left of their forces at Karkor. The exact location of Karkor is unknown, but it is thought to have been near Rabbah, the modern Amman Jordan, far to the southeast of Penuel. Only 15,000 of an original force of 120,000 were still intact. Gideon tracked down these forces. The Midianites were no doubt demoralized. Both the size of their remaining force and the distance from the original battlefield perhaps contributed to lack of military discipline. In any case, Gideon was able to launch another surprise attack. The Midianite army again was routed. Zebah and Zalmunna fled. Gideon, however, was able to capture them.

The final defeat of the Midianites was achieved basically without the enthusiastic support of God's people. The Ephraimites were more concerned about their tribal status than about smashing the enemy. The Transjordan towns of Succoth and Penuel chose neutrality rather than jeopardize their security. Everyone wants to join the victory parade. Few are willing to hazard their lives in the heat of battle. A wise warrior will expect disappointment from God's people. He will, nonetheless, press on to victory.

D. Punishment of Two Cities (Judges 8:13-17)

1. *Punishment of Succoth (8:13-16):* Gideon returned to Succoth to make good on the threat he had made before the final battle with Midian. A captured youth revealed the names of the seventy-seven leading men of the city. Gideon showed them the two captured

Midianite kings. Then he disciplined the elders of the city with the thorns and briers, i.e., he administered corporal punishment.

2. Punishment of Peniel (8:17): From there he proceeded to Penuel where he tore down the tower, as he had threatened, and executed the men in the city. Why Penuel received the harsher punishment is not clear. Both towns, however, had been guilty of treason. Both paid the price for failing to come to the aid of their countrymen in a time of national peril.

E. Execution of Two Kings (Judges 8:18-21)

1. Crimes of the kings (8:18-19): After returning to Ophrah Gideon confronted Zebah and Zalmunna with one of their crimes against the Israelites. He reminded them of a massacre which they had ordered at Tabor. There, it turned out, those two kings had killed the blood brothers of Gideon. The implication is that Gideon's brothers had been treacherously murdered under the orders of these two kings rather than killed in fair combat. If only they had showed mercy to his brothers, Gideon would have spared their lives.

2. Jether's reluctance (8:20): Gideon turned to his firstborn son Jether and ordered him to slay the kings. Perhaps the point here was to inflict humiliation upon the kings by having them slain by an inexperienced youth. On the other hand, maybe Gideon was giving Jether a chance to show his manhood. In any case, Jether refused to draw his sword *because he was still a youth.*

3. Death of the kings (8:21): The two kings then requested that Gideon himself wield the sword of execution. He was strong enough to slay them with one blow. Gideon compiled with their request. As a trophy of his defeat of Zebah and Zalmunna Gideon took the crescent ornaments that were on the necks of their camels.

F. Gideon Honored (Judges 8:22-26)

The men of Israel were overwhelmed with gratitude for what Gideon had done for the nation. They were willing to make him their ruler on the spot. While they refrained from using the word *king,* they clearly have in mind a hereditary regime. Gideon declined their offer insisting *Yahweh shall reign over you.* Gideon, however, did suggest that the troops could show their gratitude by each contributing one earring from his spoil. Since the adversaries were *Ishmaelites* each had an earring. The earrings had been taken from the corpses of the slain. The weight of the gold contributed to Gideon came to 1,700 shekels (about 43 lbs.). With this contribution plus the other valuable items that were taken from the two Midianite kings, Gideon became a wealthy man.

Closing Note about Gideon
Judges 8:27-35

A. Last Rest (Judges 8:28)

Following the victory over Midian the land had rest for forty years (8:28). This is the last time in the Book of Judges that such a declaration is made. The forty years ended about 1133 BC. Thereafter the land seems to have suffered constant war. The gift of *rest* was no longer granted to a people who so many times before had abused it.

B. Gideon's Ephod (Judges 8:27)

1. Making the ephod (8:27a): The last days of Gideon were disappointing. His gold shekels were *fashioned into a ephod.* An ephod was the upper garment worn by the high priest at the Tabernacle. The ephod described in Exodus 28 and 39 was very ornate and costly. It was woven with gold thread and contained numerous jewels. To what extent Gideon's ephod resembled that worn by the high priest cannot be ascertained. Nonetheless, it is clear that to make a proper ephod required considerable gold. Gideon placed his new ephod in his city of Ophrah.

2. Abuse of the ephod (8:27b): Perhaps the narrator was pained to recount all the details regarding this ephod. In the Old Testament the ephod with its breastpiece is associated with divine revelation. Several times before the battle Gideon had received direct communication from the Lord. Perhaps the ephod was an attempt to continue to receive divine guidance. Did Gideon himself attempt to function as a priest? Was he attempting to establish an alternative channel of divine communication? Did he feel that the normal means of revelation were not adequate? These are questions that cannot be answered. This much the text does clearly state: *All Israel played the harlot with it there.* That ephod became a snare to Gideon and his household. These words suggest that some kind of illegitimate worship centered around the ephod at Ophrah.

Gideon became a religious innovator rather than a reformer bent on bringing Israel back to the old paths. Believers must be careful about ephod-making—of attempting to solicit direction from God in ways that he has not authorized. In Scripture God already has provided all that the believer needs for his growth and direction.

C. Gideon's Lifestyle (Judges 8:29-32)

1. His women (8:29-30): Another disappointing fact about Gideon is that he took many wives. He had concubines in various cities. All together Gideon had seventy sons who were his direct descendants. God had warned that Israel's kings should not multiply wives (cf. Deuteronomy 17:17). How much more this would apply to those who were not kings.

2. His son (8:31): A third disappointing fact is related about Gideon. He named the son of one of his concubines *Abimelech* which means "My father is king." The narrator has introduced this fact to point out the contradiction between what Gideon said about kingship in 8:23 and the way he acted. Gideon, it seems, refused to be a king. Nonetheless, he wanted to live like a king. Like many believers he had a hard time bringing his walk into harmony with his talk. His theology was correct. God alone should be king. His psychology was imperfect. He regarded himself as a king.

3. His death (8:32): The closing words regarding Gideon's life remind believers that even the greatest champions of the faith can be brought low by avarice, lust and pride. Gideon died *at a ripe old age* (NASB) and was buried in the tomb of his father in Ophrah.

EXPERIMENT IN KINGSHIP
Judges 9:1-57

Date: 1133-1131 BC

Gideon's son Abimelech, though of lowly birth (cf. 8:31), had grandiose ambitions. He wanted the kingship that his father had declined. Abimelech was not a Judge. If anything he was an oppressor of Israel. Israel's unfaithfulness was punished, not by some foreign foe, but by internal discord and bloody civil strife. Chapter 9 should not be viewed merely as an appendix to the story of Gideon. The chapter serves to underscore the political implications of Baal worship. It portrays the terrible decline that set in after Gideon's death. It illustrates how God frequently brings about the demise of wicked men by turning them against one another. It represents another level in the social, moral and spiritual decline of the nation.

Sinful Ambition Unleashed
Judges 9:1-6

A. Appeal to Shechem (Judges 9:1-5)
1. Abimelech's argument (9:1-2): Abimelech anticipated that the seventy sons of Gideon were going to share the rule over Israel after their father was dead. He therefore contacted relatives in his native town of Shechem. He urged them to press the city leaders to recognize him, their own flesh and bone, as their sole ruler. The text offers no evidence that the sons of Gideon had any plan to rule Israel as an oligarchy. Abimelech appears to have been using scare tactics to get what he wanted from the men of Shechem.

2. Shechem's acceptance (9:3-5): The leaders of Shechem were inclined to follow Abimelech because he was related to them through his mother. They even gave him silver from their temple—the house of Baal-berith—to aid him in his bid for power. Abimelech hired some thugs and took them to Ophrah. There he rounded up his brothers and killed them *on one stone.* Only one, the youngest of the seventy sons of Gideon, escaped.

B. Abimelech's Coronation (Judges 9:6)
Having ruthlessly removed his potential rivals, Abimelech returned to Shechem. There the men of Shechem and all Beth-millo—an independent part of the city of Shechem—assembled for his coronation. The ceremony was held by the oak of the pillar which was in Shechem. This was the very spot where Joshua (cf. Joshua 24:26-27) many years earlier had called upon Israel to be faithful to God's covenant.

Sinful Ambition Exposed
Judges 9:7-21

A. Jotham's Fable (Judges 9:7-15)
Jotham, the surviving brother of Abimelech, went to Shechem. From a safe distance on an outcropping of Mount Gerizim he interrupted the coronation with a shout. He then delivered a fable to the men of Shechem that they might realize the stupidity of what they were doing. In the fable the trees were looking for a king. Various noble trees—the olive, fig, the vine—all declined the invitation. Only the worthless bramble agreed to become king. The bramble even

threatened to burn the rest of the forest if they did not anoint him as king. The basic point of the fable is that Abimelech, a man of ruthless temperament, is the least qualified to serve as king. How often God's people are attracted to the leadership of the men least qualified to lead!

B. Jotham's Reminder (Judges 9:16-20)

Jotham then began to remind the Shechemites of all that Jerubbaal (Gideon) had done for the nation. He had risked his life to deliver the land from Midian. Now the Shechemites had joined a plot to wipe out all of his sons. Was this deed done *in truth and integrity?* If so, then a happy relationship should exist between Shechem and their new "king." But if not, then Jotham predicted that the "king" and his subjects would destroy one another. His point is that a friendship based on ambition, ingratitude, disloyalty, and bloodshed could only have disastrous consequences for both sides.

C. Jotham's Flight (Judges 9:21)

Having finished his speech Jotham fled. He took refuge in Beer (location unknown) and remained there because of the danger from the ruthless Abimelech.

Sinful Ambition Thwarted
Judges 9:22-29

A. Treachery at Shechem (Judges 9:23-25)

1. Evil spirit from Yahweh (9:23-24): Abimelech claimed to rule all Israel. In truth his "reign" was limited to the region around Shechem. After three years the prophecy of Jotham began to come to pass. God sent *an evil spirit* between Abimelech and the men of Shechem. Even the evil spirits are subject to the will of the Creator. What God permits, he is said in the Old Testament to have done. One of the ways God destroys evil men is by turning them against each other. That is exactly what happened in Judges 9. The men of Shechem began to deal *treacherously,* i.e., to be disloyal, to Abimelech.

2. Shechemite ambushes (9:25): The Shechemites set ambushes along the busy road which passed through their city. Merchants and travelers were robbed and abused. Such actions were designed to discredit the "reign" of Abimelech, to make it appear that the new king was totally incapable of maintaining civil order. The sin of murdering the seventy sons of Gideon was now about to be visited on Abimelech. At the same time, God punished the Shechemites for their supportive role in the murders of Gideon's sons.

B. Abimelech's Rival (Judges 9:26-29)
1. Gaal's subversion (9:26): At this point another ambitious and vain man entered the picture. Gaal the son of Ebed and his relatives moved into Shechem. He quickly gained the confidence of the men of Shechem who were looking for someone who could protect them from Abimelech. The Shechemites put their trust in Gaal. Now they could openly break with Abimelech.
2. Gaal''s bluster (9:27-29): When the grape harvest was complete, the town celebrated in a drunken feast in the temple of their god. Emboldened by their drink, the men cursed Abimelech. Gaal in drunken bluster challenged Abimelech to gather his army and come out for a showdown.

Sinful Ambition Punished
Judges 9:30-57

God punished the sinful ambition of Abimelech and simultaneously the wickedness of the citizens of Shechem and their new leader Gaal. The events unfolded in four stages.

A. Judgment on Gaal (Judges 9:30-41)
1. Report on Gaal (9:30-33): Abimelech still had at least one loyal friend in the city, Zebul the mayor. Perhaps he had been appointed to his position by Abimelech. Be that as it may, Zebul was enraged at the treasonous talk of Gaal. He sent word to Abimelech *deceitfully,* i.e., secretly, appraising him of the situation. Zebul urged Abimelech to bring his army that night and position it about the city. At sunrise he should rush upon Gaal and his supporters.
2. Attack by Abimelech (9:34-38): Abimelech moved that night. He positioned his soldiers in four companies about Shechem. Gaal and his men went out of the city in the morning. Perhaps they were going on a raid, or maybe they were intending to protect the workers in the fields. In any case, Abimelech launched the attack prematurely. Gaal thought he saw something moving down from the mountains. Zebul, stalling for time, convinced Gaal at first that he was seeing

139

only shadows. A few minutes later, however, Gaal realized that he was coming under attack from several directions. Zebul now threw Gaal's boasts of the previous day back into his face and challenged him to go out and fight Abimelech.

3. *Defeat of Gaal (9:39-41):* So Gaal, the rebellious leader of Shechem, went out to face Abimelech. The skirmish was no contest. Gaal fled. Most of his supporters were slain. At the same time Zebul drove out all the relatives of Gaal so that they could no longer live in Shechem.

B. Judgment on Shechem (Judges 9:42-45)

The next day the Shechemites assumed that all was back to normal. Gaal and his supporters were gone. Abimelech appeared to have withdrawn from the area. The people, therefore, left the safety of their walls and went out into the fields to work. Abimelech, however, had not yet vented his anger on the city for tolerating rebellion against him. His troops were strategically placed in three places about the city. One company seized the city gate; the other two attacked the workers in the field. Abimelech waged war the whole day against Shechem. One by one he conquered each quarter of the city. The inhabitants were all slain. The city was razed. Then as a symbolic gesture of eternal desolation, Abimelech sprinkled salt upon the ruins.

C. Destruction of the Fortress (Judges 9:46-49)

A number of the leaders of Shechem happened to be in the tower fortress part of the city when Abimelech's attack began. They hurriedly took refuge in the inner chamber of the temple of El-berith. This appears to have been a subterranean chamber. Abimelech took his men to the nearby woods and cut large branches. These were set afire over the entrance to the inner chamber. The thousand men and women who had taken refuge there were either burned alive inside or forced by the smoke to come out and face the swords of Abimelech's men.

D. Attack on Thebez (Judges 9:50-55)

Abimelech then marched to nearby Thebez about six miles north of Shechem. This city also was in rebellion against him. He easily captured the city itself, but the fortress tower in the center of the city was a different matter. Abimelech attempted to burn the entrance of the tower. A certain woman, however, threw an upper millstone on

Abimelech's head mortally wounding him. He quickly called for his armorbearer to thrust him through lest it be said that he had been slain by a woman. The armorbearer obliged his master. Thus ended the brief and turbulent career of Israel's first "king." When Abimelech's supporters saw that he was dead, each departed for his home.

A Prophetic Explanation
Judges 9:56-57

The long account of Abimelech ends with a solemn appraisal of what has just been narrated. In the conflict between Abimelech and Shechem God was at work. Abimelech was being punished for the murder of his brothers. The Shechemites were being punished for *all their wickedness* which included blatant idolatry, violence, and support for the ruthless Abimelech. The curse of Jotham, the youngest son of Gideon, came upon the lot of these gangsters.

9
ISRAEL'S
CRITICAL CONDITION
Judges 10-11 + Ruth 1-4

Chapter Chronology

		1083
Tola	Jair	Jephthah
1131	1109	1088

The author of the Book of Judges has presented the history of a nation whose spiritual health deteriorated from ill, to seriously ill, to critically ill. In the present unit Israel has reached the third stage in this ugly process. Here the oppressions were more ruthless, the deliverances less dramatic, and the deliverers less noble. Above all, in this unit Israel no longer enjoyed periodic seasons of God-given rest.

TRAGEDY MITIGATED
Judges 10:1-5

Two minor Judges followed Abimelech. They are only minor in the sense that the sacred historian has not seen fit to supply any more than the barest of information about them. Here there is no catastrophic oppression, no desperate cry, and no divine call of a deliverer. At the same time, no "rest" is mentioned. These were not days of decisive battles but of constant turmoil. The brief notes about Tola and Jair suggest that the glory days of Ehud, Deborah and Gideon were part of Israel's past.

Judgeship of Tola
Judges 10:1-2

Not much is known about Tola. His lineage (*son of Puah, the son of Dodo*) is cited, perhaps indicating that he came from an outstanding family. He was of the tribe of Issachar, yet he lived in Shamir in the hill country of Ephraim. This suggests that his leadership was accepted by his own tribe. That he judged Israel for twenty years (c. 1131-1109 BC) suggests that he provided a stable and helpful leadership for the people. Though Abimelech comes between Gideon and Tola, it is reasonable to assume that Tola must have been the divinely ordained successor of Gideon.

The most important thing said about Tola is that he *arose to save Israel* after the death of Abimelech. The author seems to have regarded Abimelech as equivalent to an oppressor. The influence of this thug, and his cooperation with the idolaters at Shechem, created an environment throughout the land from which Israel needed deliverance. Tola apparently did what he could to curtail the negative influence that Abimelech had exerted on the nation.

Judgeship of Jair
Judges 10:3-5

The seventh Judge of Israel was a Gileadite, i.e., he hailed from the region beyond the Jordan known as Gilead. Presumably that is where he also exercised his judgeship for twenty-two years (c. 1109-1088 BC). Jair had thirty sons, which is good evidence that he had multiple wives. Gideon apparently had established a precedent. The sons rode on thirty donkeys which in that age was a mark of importance. Each son administered a city in Gilead. These towns were called Havvoth-jair ("Villages of Jair") even in the day that the Book of Judges was written.

SPOTLIGHT ON FAMILY LIFE
Ruth 1:1-4:22

Date: 1109-1088 BC

The events reported in the little Book of Ruth took place in the time of the Judges (Ruth 1:1), but the particular Judge who was on the scene is not indicated. Jewish tradition identifies the Judge as Jair.

The Book of Ruth originally was an appendix to the Book of Judges. It served to give a positive conclusion to the darkness of the Book of Judges. The story suggests that while the political and religious outlooks of Israel were bleak, God was still working quietly through godly individuals to bring about his ultimate purpose, viz., the coming of Messiah. Sometime in the first century before Christ the Jews put this material in a separate scroll so it could be read more conveniently at the Passover feast.

Faith Encompassed By Tragedy
Ruth 1:1-22

The focus in Ruth 1 is on the family of Elimelech ("My God is King"), an "Ephrathite" from Bethlehem Judah. Elimelech's wife Naomi ("Pleasant") is one of two leading characters in the book. Her sons Mahlon ("Sickness") and Chilion ("Vanishing") may have been given their names because of the sad plight of the nation during the dark days of the Judges.

A. Leaving Bethlehem (Ruth 1:1-5)

1. A famine (1:1a): The land of Judah experienced a famine in the days of Jair. Although famines were common in the days of the Patriarchs some eight hundred years earlier (cf. Genesis 12:10; 26:1; 43:1), this is the first recorded famine encountered by Israel since entering the land of Canaan.

2. A migration (1:1b-3): Elimelech decided to move his family to the land of Moab east of the Dead Sea to wait out the famine. Because of this decision Elimelech is vilified in rabbinical exegesis as an arrogant and evil man. His death in Moab is viewed by the rabbis as just punishment for having left the Promised Land. Naomi *was left* (lit., she remained) with her two sons in the land of Moab. Again rabbinical exegesis sees Naomi as defying the divine warning of the death of her husband by choosing to remain on foreign soil. Nothing in the text, however, suggests that Elimelech sinned by moving his family to Moab. Nothing suggests that his death was anything more than coincidental with his abiding in that foreign land. The passage does suggest, however, that godly people do experience unexpected tragedies, and sometimes in rapid succession.

3. Marriages (1:4): After the death of Elimelech, the two sons took Moabite wives. They thus, in the eyes of Jewish commentators, sinned more grievously than their father. If this passage is intended to be a protest against religious intermarriage it certainly is a mild one. That the women converted to the worship of the Living God before the marriages is not inconceivable. Technically, the marriage to Moabite women was not illegal. The law only forbade Moabite *males* from joining the assembly of the Lord (cf. Deuteronomy 23:3).

4. *More death (1:5):* For about ten years the Israelite men and their wives Orpah and Ruth lived in Moab. They had apparently given up all thought of returning to Bethlehem. The widow Naomi remained with her sons. In those days a widow was almost totally dependent upon her sons for support. As matters turned out, however, Naomi was shortly left destitute. Her two sons both died.

B. Contemplating Return (Ruth 1:6-18)

1. *Famine removed (1:6-7):* Through travelers Naomi learned that conditions in Judah had improved. Yahweh had *visited his people,* i.e., had intervened on their behalf, to provide food. Naomi considered her chances of surviving without a male provider to be greater in her native land than in Moab. Following eastern customs, her two daughters-in-law accompanied her for some distance on the road to Judah.

2. *Dialogue with daughters (1:8-9):* One of the unusual features of the Book of Ruth is that fifty-five of the eighty-five verses in the book are dialogue. At some point along the road Naomi urged her two daughters-in-law each to return to her mother's house.[13] She then pronounced a blessing upon them in the name of Yahweh. She prayed that the Lord would be as kind to these two Moabite women as they had been kind to their dead husbands and to Naomi. She further prayed that Yahweh would help each to find *a resting place*[14] each in the house of her husband. The term *resting place* carries the meaning of both peace and happiness. The term summarizes all the qualities of an ideal marriage in which a godly woman can find strength, security, material well-being and love. Naomi then kissed Orpah and Ruth. At this point the three could restrain their emotions no longer. They lifted up their voices and wept.

3. *Departure of Orpah (1:10-14):* The young women expressed determination to accompany Naomi all the way to Bethlehem. Naomi,

---

[13]Since Ruth's father was still living (Ruth 2:11), the reference to *mother's house* is puzzling. Jewish commentators suggest it is because "a proselyte has no legal father." Others have suggested that females lived in the mother's tent. Still others have pointed out that among the ancient Arabs a trace of matriarchal organization can be documented in which the tent was actually the property of the wife.
[14]The term *resting place* is used in the Old Testament of a camping place for the ark and people of God (Numbers 10:33), of the Promised Land (Deuteronomy 12:9; 1 Kings 8:56; Psalm 95:11) and of Zion as the residence of Yahweh (Psalm 132:8, 14). Any place God dwells is a resting place for his people. The term also has a military significance meaning a place free of strife (e.g., Judges 20:43).

146

however, insisted that they go back to their country. She could not provide husbands for them. Knowing that she must be deprived of the companionship of the two fine daughters-in-law made Naomi's burden even harder to bear. She had lost both her husband and sons to death. Now she was about to lose the last dear ones she had on earth through separation. All of this misfortune Naomi attributed to the actions of Yahweh. This frank and logical analysis of the situation caused the women again to burst into tears. Orpah yielded to Naomi's logic and submitted to her directions. She kissed her mother-in-law and departed for her home. Ruth, however, *clung* to Naomi and refused to leave.

4. *Naomi's challenge (1:15):* After some time passed Naomi began to urge Ruth to follow the example of her sister-in-law. Orpah had returned to her people and *to her gods.* If the women had embraced Yahweh when they married the Israelite men, Naomi knew that it would be impossible for Orpah to remain faithful to the Lord while surrounded by Moabite idolatry. Orpah's gods would doubtless include the god Chemosh who demanded child sacrifice from his devotees. Perhaps Naomi's words to Ruth should not so much be interpreted as a directive but as an invitation to declare her complete allegiance to Yahweh.

5. *Ruth's commitment (1:16-16):* Ruth could not bear the thought of returning to the heathen environment in which she had grown up. If she had not fully repudiated the gods of Moab before, Ruth does so at this point. She will hear no more of Naomi's urging to return to Moab. On the contrary, Ruth committed herself for better or worse to Naomi, Naomi's people, and Naomi's God. She did not even desire to return to her native Moab for burial. Nothing but death will separate her from Naomi. This commitment she sealed by a self-malediction or curse in which she used the name of Yahweh: *Thus may Yahweh do to me, and worse, if anything but death parts you and me.* The use of Yahweh's name exclusively in this oath again suggests a complete conversion on Ruth's part. When Naomi saw that Ruth was determined to go on to Bethlehem with her, she ceased urging her to return to Moab.

C. Returning to Bethlehem (Ruth 1:19-22)

1. *Naomi's bitterness (1:19):* The entire village of Bethlehem was a stir when Naomi and Ruth arrived. The sight of two women traveling alone toward the city was unusual. As they drew near the

147

women of Bethlehem thought they recognized Naomi, and inquired if the traveler were she. Naomi responded: *Do not call me Naomi* (i.e., "Pleasant") *but call me Mara* (i.e., "Bitter")." By this Naomi signaled that the decade in Moab had taken its toll in more ways than one.

2. Naomi's explanation (1:20-21): Naomi blamed her misfortune on the Lord. Shaddai, the Almighty, had afflicted her, or so she thought. When she had left Bethlehem she had been living a full life. She had a fine husband and two fine sons. Yahweh, however, had brought her back empty. By bringing this misfortune upon her Yahweh had witnessed against Naomi, i.e., had shown her to be a terrible sinner undeserving of his blessing. Instead of using his power to protect this woman, Shaddai had turned his power against her.

If Naomi referred to the permissive will of the Lord, her theology was impeccable. Her words, however, seem to blame all her misfortune directly on the Lord. God may have permitted her misfortune. To deny this would be to deny the omnipotence of God. That God initiated or directly caused Naomi all the pain she had experienced is never suggested in the text. Here is an example of that theology which so often rears its ugly head, viz., that calamity in one's life means that one is being punished for some sin. This theology decisively is laid to rest in the Book of Job.

3. Summary of the return (1:22): The dialogue between Naomi and the women of Bethlehem underscores dramatically the theme of the first chapter of the book, viz., the terrible ordeal of Naomi. The narrative of the homecoming concludes by emphasizing 1) the loneliness of the return—only the two women without their loved ones; 2) the sacrifice of the return—Ruth was a Moabitess who was forsaking all for her commitment to Yahweh's people; 3) the wisdom of the return—they came from Moab, a land where Chemosh was honored, to Bethlehem Judah in the Promised Land; and 4) the time of the return—at the beginning of the barley harvest. In April the barley crop ripened and was ready for harvest.

A Providential Meeting
Ruth 2:1-23

Ruth 2 begins with the introduction of the third leading character of the book. Boaz is described as 1) an acquaintance (NASB margin) of Elimelech; 2) a man of great wealth; and 3) a member of the family of Elimelech. The exact relationship between Elimelech and Boaz is left unclear. The rabbinical thesis that Boaz was a cousin of the dead man is without foundation. Another tradition makes Boaz Naomi's nephew by marriage.

A. Polite Requests (Ruth 2:2-7)

1. Ruth's request of Naomi (2:2): Ruth was an industrious woman. She was not afraid to work. She politely requested permission from her mother-in-law to go out into the fields where the barley was being harvested. Perhaps there she could find a friendly landowner who would allow her to follow behind the harvesters picking up the stalks that they left lying on the ground. Mosaic Law stipulated that the gleanings of the field were to be left for the poor, for strangers and for widows and orphans. Either this custom prevailed also in Moab, or Ruth had learned of it from local women, perhaps as she drew water at the public well. In any case, Naomi granted permission for Ruth to proceed with her plan.

2. Boaz comes to the field (2:3-4): At some point in her forays into the harvest fields Ruth happened upon the field of a wealthy farmer named Boaz. Providence must have brought her to that place because Boaz was from the same tribe as Elimelech. That Boaz was a godly man is stressed from the moment he is introduced in the account. When he came out from Bethlehem to inspect the harvest he greeted his reapers in the name of Yahweh. They responded in kind. Where both labor and management share the same faith in the Lord, peace and satisfaction will reign supreme.

3. Boaz inquires about Ruth (2:5-7): Noticing Ruth walking behind the reapers, Boaz inquired of the foreman about the stranger. The foreman introduced Ruth as *the Moabite woman who returned with Naomi from the land of Moab* (NASB). She had requested permission to glean after the reapers in the field, and the foreman had granted that request. Ruth had been hard at work in the field since early morning, except for a brief respite in the hut which was used by the reapers for rest and refreshment.

B. Gracious Offer (Ruth 2:8-13)

1. Boaz's first words to Ruth (2:8-9): Boaz addressed Ruth in a most courteous manner. Since he was considerably older than the Moabitess, he calls her *my daughter.* He invited her to join the women who were working for him. Ruth could follow them from field to field during the harvest. Boaz had given strict orders to his male servants not to touch or in any way hinder the efforts of Ruth. He further invited Ruth to help herself from the water jars which the servants might draw from some nearby well.

2. Commendation of Ruth (2:10-11): Ruth was overwhelmed by this display of kindness by the Israelite. In typical Oriental exaggerated respect, she bowed her face to the ground. She could not help but ask why she, a foreigner, should have found favor in his sight. Boaz explained that he had heard of all that Ruth had done for her mother-in-law after the death of her husband. Boaz had been particularly impressed by Ruth's willingness to leave her mother and father and the land of her birth to stay with Naomi in a strange land.

3. Blessing on Ruth (2:12): Boaz then pronounced a blessing on Ruth in the name of Yahweh. He prayed that the Lord might continue to bless the work of Ruth, that he might provide for her *a full reward* (BV) for all she had done. The Gentile had sought refuge under the *wings* of Yahweh, and therefore was entitled to his blessing. The language here is obviously metaphorical. Perhaps the reference is to the wings of the cherubim that were spread out over the Ark of the Covenant in the Tabernacle. In any case, the language here definitely confirms what was suggested in the previous chapter, viz., that Ruth had given her heart to the Lord.

4. Ruth's response (2:13): Ruth responded to this spiritual blessing with gratitude and humility. She did not consider herself equal to any one of Boaz's maidservants. Nonetheless, the farmer had bestowed favor upon her. This *comforted* or touched the heart of Ruth.

C. Generous Provision (Ruth 2:14-17)

1. More provisions for Ruth (2:14-16): At mealtime Boaz again was gracious to Ruth. He invited her to come and eat with the reapers. The meal of bread, with a special dip, and roasted grain was typical of that region. Ruth had more than enough to eat. As she arose to resume her labor, Boaz issued three orders to his servants. First, Ruth was now to be allowed to glean among the tied sheaves which the harvesters placed upright on the ground. Here the grains were more numerous. In addition, the servants were told to *drop some heads for her on purpose* (BV). Finally, no servant was to rebuke Ruth as she gleaned.

2. Success for the day (2:17): Ruth continued to glean in Boaz's field until evening. Then she beat out what she had gleaned. The

150

kernels of grain were knocked loose from the stalk with a stick. The Moabitess was able to carry home that day an ephah of barley, enough to last the two widows for a number of weeks.

D. Grateful Acknowledgment (Ruth 2:18-23)

1. Blessing on Boaz (2:18-20): Ruth returned to the city with the fruit of her labor. She shared with Naomi what remained of the bountiful lunch that Boaz had provided for her in the field. Naomi was amazed at the good fortune of her daughter-in-law. She pronounced a blessing on the benefactor, and then inquired as to his name. When she learned that it was Boaz, she again pronounced a blessing. Boaz, as it turned out, was a close relative, a kinsman-redeemer, in the family of Elimelech.

2. Kinsman-redeemer duties. In the Old Testament social structure the kinsman-redeemer had three responsibilities: 1) He had the duty to recover forfeited property of a kinsman (Leviticus 25:25). 2) If one had fallen into slavery, the kinsman-redeemer was to purchase his freedom (Leviticus 25:47-49). 3) Should a brother die leaving no male heir, the kinsman-redeemer was to marry the widow to raise up seed in the name of the dead relative (Deuteronomy 25:5-10; Genesis 38:8-10). Some think the kinsman-redeemer also had the responsibility to avenge the murder of a family member (Numbers 35:19).

3. More good news (2:21-22): With great excitement Ruth informed Naomi that Boaz had invited her to stay with his servants until the harvest was finished. Naomi was very pleased with this news. She knew that righteous Boaz would not allow any harm to come to the young widow while she worked in his fields.

4. Beneficial relationship (2:23): For the next several weeks Ruth stayed close by the maids of Boaz in order to glean. When the barley harvest was complete she continued in this relationship into the wheat harvest as well. All the while she continued to live with her mother-in-law.

A Dramatic Proposal
Ruth 3:1-18

Ruth 3 begins and ends with dialogue between Ruth and Naomi. These dialogue scenes introduce and evaluate the major scene of the chapter which depicts a late night meeting between Ruth and Boaz at the threshing floor.

A. Introductory Dialogue (Ruth 3:1-5)

1. Naomi's intentions (3:1): The introductory dialogue between Ruth and Naomi is essential to a correct perspective of the principal scene that follows. While Ruth took the initiative in chapter 2, here it is Naomi who proposes a bold move. Ruth only acts in this chapter on orders from Naomi. On her part, Naomi appears to be compelled by what she considers her moral obligation to seek for her daughter-in-law *a resting place,* i.e., marriage. Ruth did not belong in the fields with the hired hands. A woman of her worth deserved to be the queen of a home. Naomi recognized that when a godly woman marries a godly man, and both are committed to building their home upon divine principles, matrimony is a *rest* as much as anything on earth can be so called. Only in such a situation could Ruth *prosper* (BV), i.e., fulfill the deepest longings of her soul.

2. Naomi's instructions (3:2-4): Naomi knew that Boaz would be winnowing barley on the threshing floor that night. He would then sleep there to protect his crop from thieves. Naomi directed Ruth to bathe, anoint herself with fragrant oils, and put on her best clothes. Ruth should go down to the threshing floor. She should conceal herself until after Boaz had finished his evening meal. After the man had gone to sleep, Ruth should uncover his feet and lie down there. Boaz then would tell her what she was to do.

3. Explanation (3:5): Naomi's directions and Ruth's willingness to comply therewith must be judged by the standards of the times in which those women lived. On her part, Naomi had confidence in the good behavior and resolute chastity of her daughter-in-law. She knew that Boaz was a deeply religious man who would recognize immediately that he was being nudged ever so gently to perform his duty to his dead kinsman by marrying Ruth. On her part, Ruth trusted her mother-in-law's judgment and knowledge of local customs. She believed she was fulfilling a duty of love to her dead husband by approaching Boaz to remind him of his kinsman obligations.

B. A Marriage Proposal (Ruth 3:6-15)

1. Ruth at Boaz's feet (3:6-7): Ruth did exactly as Naomi had directed. After his meal Boaz's *heart was merry.* From the shadows

Ruth watched him lie down at the end of the heap of grain. Then she quietly approached him, uncovered his feet, and lay down.

2. *Ruth's proposal (3:8-9):* A midnight Boaz was startled to feel something soft and warm at his feet. He instinctively bent forward and discovered Ruth. In the dark he did not recognize her. Ruth identified herself. She then asked that he *spread* his *wing* over her since he was a kinsman-redeemer. The reference here is to the placing of the corner of the garment over a maiden as a token of marriage.

3. *Boaz's response (3:10-13):* Boaz responded to the marriage proposal with a blessing on Ruth. Her desire to marry a kinsman of her dead husband was commendable, especially since Boaz was considerably older than Ruth. Boaz urged Ruth not to fear. The Moabitess had the reputation of being a virtuous woman. He would be glad to do as she suggested. A problem, however, did exist. Whereas Boaz was a kinsman-redeemer, there was another who was closer than he. This anonymous relative first will have to relinquish his legal rights to *redeem* Ruth. If this nearer kinsman were unwilling to perform the function of the kinsman-redeemer, then Boaz assured Ruth by oath that he would do it.

4. *Boaz's concern (3:14-15):* Boaz invited Ruth to remain with him on the threshing floor that night. Concern for Ruth's reputation caused both to arise before sunrise. Boaz urged Ruth not to publicize that she had been to the threshing floor. As an added precaution, Boaz measured out to Ruth six measures of barley and laid it on her, i.e., put it on her head. If someone should spot her that morning it would appear that she had merely gotten an early start on the day's work by transporting this sizable allotment of grain from the threshing floor to her quarters. Ruth then departed for the city.

C. Concluding Dialogue (Ruth 3:16-18)

When Ruth approached the house, Naomi inquired, *Who are you, my daughter?* The early morning darkness may have obscured the identity of Ruth. More likely, however, Naomi's question meant: Are you one dishonored by rejection or one protected as a wife? She wanted to know if the plan had worked! Ruth then told her mother-in-law all that had taken place. The generous gift of the barley signaled Boaz's favorable disposition toward the two women. Naomi counseled Ruth to be patient. She was confident that Boaz will not rest until he had settled the matter with the nearer kinsman.

A Significant Marriage
Faith Finding Rest
Ruth 4:1-22

In the early morning Boaz went to the city gate. In ancient cities the gate complex was the center of social life. Legal judgments were rendered there. Before Boaz was able to function as the kinsman-redeemer of Naomi and Ruth, a legal proceeding was required.

A. A Legal Proceeding (Ruth 4:1-12)

1. Arrangements (4:1-2): When the nearer kinsman passed by, Boaz called him to turn aside and sit down. At the same time Boaz asked ten of the elders of the city to sit down to witness the proceedings. The nearer kinsman is called *friend.* Probably the author of Judges deliberately has suppressed his name to spare him embarrassment for refusing to perform his family duty. Apparently the right of the *go'el* was exercised according to an order of kinship priority which is found in Leviticus 25:49. The order is: the paternal uncle, his son, then other relatives.

2. Notification (4:3-6): Boaz formerly notified the closest kinsman that Naomi had to put her husband's property up for sale. The closest kinsman had the right of purchase. Boaz hints that he might be willing to purchase the property, but he has no legal right to do so. The closest kinsman was quite willing to make the purchase. Apparently he thought that the property belonged solely to Naomi, and that his duty ended with the purchase of the field from her. When he learned, however, that the transaction included marriage with Ruth, he withdrew. He felt that marriage to Ruth will in some way jeopardize his own inheritance.

3. Acquisition (4:7-10a): Transfer of the legal rights of the *go'el* was symbolized by the removal of a sandal. Presumably it was the closest relative who gave the sandal to Boaz in the presence of the witnesses. Boaz then acknowledged before the witnesses and *all the people* that he had *acquired* from Naomi all that once had belonged to her husband and sons. In addition, Boaz proudly claimed that he had also *acquired* Ruth as his wife. The legal terminology is the same with regard to the acquisition of the property and the wife. There, however, the similarity ended. Boaz clearly distinguishes between the acquisition of the property and the marriage to Ruth. In biblical teaching a wife is never regarded as property, but as a full partner in

154

the sacred task of building a home. Apparently the ceremony had attracted many of the townspeople of Bethlehem. They were most happy to see the plight of the two impoverished women alleviated by the legal intervention of the wealthy Boaz.

4. *Benediction (4:10b-12):* Unlike the closer kinsman, Boaz announced before the witnesses that he was most happy to perform the responsibility of the Levirate marriage to raise up a descendant for Mahlon. All the people in the gate responded to Boaz's announcement with the proper legal formula: *We are witnesses.* Then they spontaneously pronounced a blessing first on Ruth, then on Boaz. They prayed that Yahweh would make her as fruitful as Rachel and Leah from whom the whole house of Israel sprang. Regarding Boaz the people prayed for wealth and fame. They prayed that his household will be like that of Perez the son of Judah (Genesis 38). Why Perez? Probably because he was the offspring of Levirate marriage similar to that of Ruth and Boaz. Perez was the progenitor of one of the clans of the tribe of Judah (Numbers 26:21).

B. A Joyous Blessing (Ruth 4:13-17)

1. *Blessing of a marriage (4:13):* True to his public commitment, Boaz *took,* i.e., married, Ruth. He *went in unto her,* i.e., had sexual relations with her, that he might fulfill the responsibilities of a Levirate husband. Not long after the marriage the Lord *gave her conception.* She who had not been able to conceive by her young husband Mahlon, was enabled by God to conceive by the much older Boaz.

2. *Blessing of a birth (4:14-15a):* One of the themes of the Book of Ruth is the bitterness of Naomi. She left Bethlehem *full,* i.e., finding fulfillment in her family. She returned to Bethlehem *empty,* i.e., having lost both her husband and sons (1:21). With the birth of a grandson, however, she experiences anew the satisfaction and security afforded by male offspring. The women of Bethlehem blessed the Lord in joyous praise. The newborn son will assume the responsibilities of the nearest kinsman toward both his mother and grandmother. The women pray that he may become a famous man in Israel. They pray that he may be to Naomi a *restorer of life,* i.e., one who gives new meaning to living. The women also pray that the child will one day sustain Naomi in her old age. The fear of every woman in Israel was to grow old without a male provider.

3. *Blessing of a daughter (4:15b):* The women of Bethlehem considered Naomi blessed, not only because of the newborn child, but because she had a daughter-in-law who loved her *more than seven sons.* A mother of many sons in the Old Testament world was a happy mother. As long as she had no descendant, Naomi was so bitter that she could not really appreciate the blessing that Ruth represented in her life. Now that the stigma of childlessness had been removed, Naomi could come to appreciate how blessed she really was. Her life was indeed *full* of God's blessing.

4. *Blessing of a purpose (4:16-17):* Naomi took the child and laid him in her lap. She became his *nurse,* i.e., she raised the child. The action here appears to be some kind of formal ceremony in which guardianship of the child was assumed. The child hereafter was recognized as the son of Naomi as well as the son of Ruth. Certainly the neighbor women recognized this to be the case. They even were given the honor of naming the lad. They chose the name *Obed*, one who serves. Obed became the father of Jesse, and the grandfather of David.

Concluding Genealogy
Ruth 4:18-22

The concluding genealogy indicates the purpose and meaning of the entire Book of Ruth. The author aims to demonstrate that David came from solid Israelite stock even though he had Moabite blood in his veins.

Meanwhile, in the nation as a whole the polygamous marriages and the nepotism of Judge Jair hint at a further degeneration in the concept of judgeship. When Jair died he was buried in Kamon (Judges 10:5). The location of Kamon is unknown.

BIRTH & BOYHOOD
OF SAMUEL
1 Samuel 1:1-2:26

Date: 1105-1100 BC

We can only guess at a date for the birth of Samuel, except for two parameters. He was born during the high priesthood of Eli who began to judge Israel in 1099 BC. Eli, however, must have been high priest for a considerable time prior to that date. We know that Eli was

156

born about 1157 BC (1 Samuel 4:15). He began his priestly ministry at age thirty in 1127 BC. How long after that he became high priest cannot be determined. Another clue is that Samuel is depicted as an old man in 1048 BC when the elders requested that he select a king for Israel (1 Samuel 8). A date of about 1105 BC is thus appropriate for the birth of Samuel. That would make Samuel fifty-seven at the time of Saul's anointing. That age would not be considered "old" today; but similar language is used of Solomon who did not live to be sixty (1 Kings 11:4).

Dedication of a Child
1 Samuel 1:1-2:10

While the conditions in the period of the Judges continued to deteriorate, God was preparing to write the next chapter in the thrilling story of redemption. In the sinful darkness of those days God found a godly woman through whom he would bring a great reformer into the world.

A. Hannah's Plight (1 Samuel 1:1-8)
1. Family problems (1:1-2): Elkanah was a Levite who lived in Ramathaim-zophim (Ramah) in the hill country of Ephraim. While basically a godly man, he had taken two wives. The notation that Hannah had no children suggests that her infertility had driven Elkanah to marry a woman (Peninnah) who could produce an heir.
2. Family pilgrimage (1:3-8): Elkanah took his family each year to the annual feast at the Shiloh tabernacle some eighteen miles north of Jerusalem. The trips were most painful for Hannah. Her husband showed his greater love for her by giving her an extra portion at the sacrificial meal. Peninnah, however, made life miserable for Hannah, using her fertility to lord it over her rival (cf. Genesis 16:4; 30:1-24). Year after year the scene replayed itself. Peninnah provoked her rival; Hannah then became so emotionally upset that she could not eat. Elkanah attempted to comfort his beloved wife: *Am I not better than ten sons?* While intending to cheer his wife, these words only made this desperate woman feel her emptiness all the more.

B. Hannah's Petition (1 Samuel 1:9-19a)
1. Earnest prayer (1:9-13): While at Shiloh on one occasion Hannah finished the ritual meal. Near the entrance to the temple she

157

wept and poured out her heart to *Yahweh of hosts*. She approached him reverently as can be seen in her threefold reference to herself as *handmaid* of the Lord. She vowed that if the Lord would give her a son, she would dedicate him all the days of his life as a Nazirite. As she continued praying before the Lord, Eli the high priest, who was sitting by the doorpost of the temple, took note of her. Because Hannah was praying silently and only her lips were moving, Eli thought she was drunk. Tragic it is when a leader of God's people cannot recognize true piety when he sees it.

2. *Falsely accused (1:14-18):* Since it was his high priestly duty to guard the courts of the sanctuary from desecration, Eli rebuked Hannah. He ordered her to *put away* her wine. Hannah replied firmly but politely. She had not been drinking wine. She was not *a worthless woman,* i.e., a woman without respect for sacred things. Rather she was oppressed in spirit; she was pouring out her heart to the Lord. Eli then dismissed Hannah with a blessing: *May the God of Israel grant your petition.* Hannah then returned to her meal. Because she was now confident that God would hear her petition, her face was sad no longer.

3. *Conclusion of the trip (1:19a):* The eventful trip to Shiloh ended with a final time of worship. Then Elkanah took his family and returned to Ramah.

C. Hannah's Presentation (1 Samuel 1:19b-28)

1. *Birth of Samuel (1:19b-20):* Elkanah *knew* his wife, i.e., had marital relations with her. The Lord *remembered* Hannah, i.e., granted her petition. She conceived and bore a son. Hannah named the child *Samuel, "name of God."* She knew that this baby was truly an answer to prayer.

2. *Deferring the vow (1:21-23):* At the next annual sacrifice Elkanah was prepared to offer *his vow.* Unless repudiated by the husband, the vow of a wife became an obligation upon her husband. Hannah elected not to go to the sanctuary until she had weaned the child and could present him to the Lord. Under the Mosaic Law a woman was not obligated to attend the annual festivals. Elkanah agreed that this was the wisest course. He expressed aloud his prayer that the Lord would *confirm his word,* i.e., Yahweh would bring Hannah's vow to fruition.

3. *Samuel presented (1:24-28):* Eastern women nursed their babies up to three years. When the child was weaned, Hannah took

158

him and a generous offering to the sanctuary. The family first offered sacrifice. Then Hannah presented the young boy to Eli. She reminded the priest of the incident some three years earlier when he had mistaken her earnest petition as drunken gibberish. Since God had answered her prayer, Hannah dedicated the lad to the Lord for as long as he lived. In gratitude Eli bowed in worship.

D. Hannah's Prayer (1 Samuel 2:1-10)

When Hannah presented her son to Eli, she burst forth in a magnificent hymn-prayer inspired by the Holy Spirit. Yahweh is the central figure in this beautiful poem. Hannah began on a most positive note.

1. Rejoicing in her good fortune (2:1-8): Hannah identified the sources of her joy.

- She rejoiced in the personal deliverance from a life of misery that she recently had experienced (2:1).
- She rejoiced in the person of God—his holiness, his strength, and his knowledge (2:2-3). He is the Judge who weighs actions.
- She rejoiced in the government of God (2:4-8).

Hannah pointed out that often those who are rich, powerful and blessed are humbled. At the same time those who are poor, weak and dishonorable are suddenly exalted. The Lord *brings low and exalts.* Over the long haul life has a way of evening out. Hannah's own experience is a prime example of this principle.

2. Rejoicing in her hope (2:9-10): The righteous are under the watch care of God; the wicked, however, are swallowed up in darkness when God withdraws the light of his grace. At this point Hannah's poem becomes predictive. She announces that ultimately God will 1) judge the whole world, 2) give strength to his king, and 3) exalt the horn or power of his anointed. The context here of universal judgment suggests that the prophecy points to the Coming One, the Messiah.

Boyhood of Samuel
1 Samuel 2:11-26

Following the presentation of Samuel at the tabernacle, Elkanah and his family returned to their home in Ramah. The lad Samuel, however, remained at Shiloh ministering to the Lord under the supervision of Eli the high priest (1 Samuel 2:11). The narrator draws a stark contrast between the degeneracy of Eli's sons, and the spiritual growth of the young lad Samuel.

A. Sins of the Priests (1 Samuel 2:12-17)

The sons of Eli were *sons of Belial,* i.e., worthless men. Though they were priests of God, *they did not know Yahweh* in the experiential sense. Their brazen disregard for sacred ritual manifested itself in several ways. For example, they sent their servant to fish out of boiling cauldrons the priest's portion before the Lord had received his portion. Those who insisted that the Lord's portion should first be burned on the altar were threatened with violence. Thus these priests were treating the offerings of the Lord with contempt.

B. Faithfulness of Samuel (1 Samuel 2:18-21)

The boy Samuel was quite a contrast to the sons of Eli. He wore a linen ephod and ministered before the Lord. Each year his mother made him a little robe and took it to Shiloh. Eli pronounced a blessing on Hannah for having given Samuel to the Lord. Hannah's fertility continued. She bore three more sons and two daughters.

C. Failure of Eli (1 Samuel 2:22-26)

When Eli learned that his sons were having sexual relations with the women who served at the tabernacle, he tried to deal with them. He warned them that a sin against God was far more serious than a sin against man. The young men refused to listen to the voice of their father. The sacred historian explains their intransigence as due to the fact Yahweh desired to put them to death. Meanwhile Samuel was maturing and gaining favor with both the Lord and with men.

TRAGIC APOSTASY
Judges 10:6-16

From what has been related about the town of Shechem, Abimelech and the Judges who followed him, one can conclude that the unfaithfulness of Israel had reached a new low. That conclusion is confirmed by the author Judges who now paints the worst picture yet of the apostasy of the nation. The unit begins with words that have become by this time familiar to the reader of Judges: *Then the sons of Israel again did evil in the sight of Yahweh.* The author then gives a rapid-fire presentation of the accusations against Israel.

A. Intensified Idolatry (Judges 10:6)

Not only were the Israelites worshiping the Baals and Ashtaroth of the native Canaanites, they were embracing the gods of other peoples as well. From north of Canaan they embraced the gods of Aram and Sidon. From east of Jordan they were attracted to the gods of Moab and Ammon. The gods of the Philistines to the west also attracted them. This plethora of gods caused Israel to *forget Yahweh.* This does not mean that they forgot about him. They forgot him in the sense of failing to practice their faith, to walk by his law, to confess his exclusive claims to divinity. Failing to serve the Lord exclusively is forgetting him.

B. Intensified Oppression (Judges 10:7-10)

1. Israelite resistance crumbles (10:7-8a): The degradation of Israel called forth for the first time a double-barreled oppression. West of Jordan the Philistines were the oppressors while east of Jordan (mainly) the Ammonites were the enemy. Israel was *crushed* by these two enemies *that year,* probably c. 1088 BC. This suggests that the resistance of Israel crumbled in the same year the oppression started.

2. Ammonite expansion (10:8b-9): At some point during the eighteen years the Ammonites trampled Transjordan, they crossed the Jordan to harass the tribes of Judah, Benjamin and Ephraim. Caught as they were between two mighty enemies, it is no wonder that the author of Judges says that *Israel was greatly distressed.* The author discusses first the Ammonite oppression (ch. 11) and then that of the Philistines (chapters 13-16).

3. Supplication (10:10): Israel cried out unto Yahweh. This time the *cry* is accompanied by a confession of sin which appears here for the first time in the book. The confession admits to the twin sins of 1) having forsaken Yahweh 2) to serve the Baal gods.

C. Rebuke by a Prophet (Judges 10:11-16)

1. Yahweh's record of assistance (10:11-12): In response to the cry and confession, Yahweh spoke to his people, most likely through

161

a prophet (cf. Judges 6:8-10). His words suggest that the Israelite confession of sin was not completely sincere. In order to make Israel realize the depth of the sin, Yahweh lists several of the times he had rescued them from their enemies, beginning as always with the deliverance from Egypt. Under Joshua he had kept his people from being crushed by massive Amorite armies. The current enemies—the Ammonites and Philistines—had been the oppressors of Israel once before, but Yahweh had delivered his people. The Lord mentioned the deliverances from the Sidonians, the Amalekites and the Maonites, none of which are specifically mentioned in the sketchy narrative of the Book of Judges.

2. *Israel's record of transgression (10:13-14):* In each case of oppression the Israelites had cried unto Yahweh and he had orchestrated their deliverance. In spite of these repeated acts of God's grace the Israelites continued to forsake Yahweh and serve other gods. He will deliver t hem no more. Let them cry to the gods they had chosen to serve. Let those gods deliver Israel out of distress if they could.

3. *Israel's response (10:15-16):* Again the children of Israel confessed their sins. They placed themselves in the hands of God, resigned to face whatever fate he deemed appropriate. Yet they pled with him to deliver them from the oppressors. This prayer was accompanied by the removal of the foreign gods from among them. When they began to serve Yahweh, he could no longer endure their misery.

GILEADITE WAR
WITH AMMON
Judges 10:17-40

Date: ca. 1087 BC

A Tragic Figure
Judges 10:17-11:11

A. Need for a Leader (Judges 10:17-18)

About 1088 BC the Ammonites brought a host into Gilead and camped there. The Israelites gathered an army to Mizpah to block the Ammonite advance. Faced with a spirited resistance, the Ammonites delayed the attack. Meanwhile, the leaders of the Gileadites found themselves with no one qualified to lead the defense of the land. They

162

were so desperate that they offered to make the head of the army the ruler of all Gilead. The deliverer in this crisis was not raised up by God. Rather he was selected by the leaders of Gilead.

B. Summons of Jephthah (Judges 11:1-11)

1. Background of Jephthah (11:1-3): The obvious choice for leadership of the army was Jephthah. He was a valiant warrior; but he had no social standing. He was the son of a harlot. His half-brothers had driven him out of the family so that he had no claim in the family inheritance. Jephthah had fled from his brothers to the land of Tob. There a gang of *worthless fellows* gathered about him. Jephthah was virtually an outlaw leader.

2. Negotiations with Jephthah (11:4-7): Faced with the Ammonite invasion, the elders of Gilead went to Tob to ask Jephthah to lead the army. These elders had sanctioned the expulsion of Jephthah from the land. He made them eat the proverbial humble pie when they came to him with this emergency request.

3. Commitment to Jephthah (11:8-11): Jephthah let the elders squirm for a bit. He made them repeat the offer to make him ruler over Gilead if he should defeat the Ammonites. The leadership offer was confirmed by the elders with a solemn oath. Thus reassured, Jephthah returned with the elders. He was made leader of the Gileadites in a solemn ceremony *(before Yahweh)* there at Mizpah.

Tragic Stubbornness
Judges 11:12-28

A. Claims of the Ammonites (Judges 11:12-13)

Jephthah was a peace loving man. He first attempted to settle the dispute with the king of Ammon through negotiation. His messengers inquired of the Ammonite what quarrel he had with Israel that he had brought an army into Israelite territory. The king in his response accused the Israelites of having taken his land when they came out of Egypt. He was therefore expecting all the territory between the Arnon and Jabbok rivers to be returned to him.

B. Claims of the Israelites (Judges 11:14-26)

1. Historical argument (11:14-22): Jephthah then sent a second group of messengers to the king of Ammon. Through them he presented a marvelous defense of the Israelite claim to the territory in

Transjordan. First, he offered an argument based on history. When the Israelites emerged from the wilderness back in the days of Moses they did not seek military confrontation with any kings of the area. They circumvented Edom and Moab when they were refused permission to pass through those territories. The Amorites were then controlling the Transjordan territory. Israel requested permission from their king Sihon to pass through that territory. Sihon, however, gathered his armies and fought against Israel. Yahweh gave Sihon and all his people into the hand of Israel. That was how Israel came to possess the land of the Amorites which now the king of Ammon was claiming.

2. Theological argument (11:23-24): Jephthah next raised a theological argument. Yahweh the God of Israel had driven the Amorites from the land before his people. He had in effect deeded the land to Israel. What right then did the king of Ammon have to claim that territory? The land ruled by the king of Ammon is what Chemosh had given his people.

3. Precedent argument (11:25-26): Jephthah's third argument was based on precedent. Balak the king of Moab never disputed Israel's claim to the Transjordan lands back in the days of Moses (Numbers 22:6). He never tried to drive them from that land. Nor had any king of Ammon ever disputed the claim to this territory in the three hundred years Israel had lived there.

4. Conclusion (11:27-28): On the basis of these arguments Jephthah concluded that Israel had not *sinned* against Ammon, but rather vice versa. Yahweh, the ultimate Judge, will determine which people had just claim to the land. Jephthah correctly anticipated that the king of Ammon would reject any overtures towards a peaceful settlement of the dispute. The stage was thus set for a military showdown.

A Tragic Vow
Judges 11:29-40

A. Circumstances of the Vow (Judges 11:29-33)

1. Empowerment of Jephthah (11:29): Though God did not raise up this Judge as he had done in previous deliverances, he did equip Jephthah for leadership. This was tantamount to having endorsed the selection of Jephthah by the Gileadites. Under the influence of God's Spirit Jephthah first marched through Gilead and Manasseh (the land north of the Jabbok River). Presumably he was organizing his forces. With his reinforcements he then returned to the camp at Mizpah.

2. Terms of the vow (11:30-31): Before leading his troops into battle Jephthah made a vow to Yahweh, a vow he lived to regret. He pledged that if the Lord would give him a victory over the Ammonites, he would give to Yahweh *whatever comes out of the doors of my house to meet me when I return.* His exact words were *it shall be Yahweh's, and I will offer it up as a burnt offering.*

3. Battle outcome (11:32-33): Only a modicum of information is presented about the battle with the Ammonites. Jephthah initiated the hostilities *and Yahweh gave them into his hand.* He struck them with a very great slaughter all the way back to Ammon. A lengthy pursuit followed the battle. Twenty cities that had been occupied by Ammonites were retaken. The Ammonites were forced to retreat within their own borders.

Significantly the text does not say the land had rest after Jephthah's victory. Chronological considerations indicate that the Ammonites continued to harass the people of the Gilead area until ca. 1071 BC when they crossed the Jordan River and joined the Philistines in harassing some of the western tribes.

B. Compliance with the Vow (Judges 11:34-40)

1. A fateful meeting (11:34-35): When Jephthah returned to his home at Mizpah his daughter came out to meet him with tambourines and with dancing in celebration of the victory. She was his only child, the apple of her daddy's eye. He obviously did not expect that she would be the first to come out to meet him. He screamed his agony, and tore his clothes while he explained his vow to her. Jephthah had a lot of faults, but lack of integrity was not one of them. *I have given my word to Yahweh, and I cannot take it back.*

2. Heroic submission (11:36-38): Jephthah's daughter heroically accepted her fate. She recognized that her father could not renege on a vow made in the name of Yahweh. She did request, however, that she be given two months to go to the mountains to mourn her virginity with her companions. Marriage and motherhood, the essence of life for an Israelite girl, were never be hers to experience. Her father was perfectly willing to comply with this last request of his daughter before she became the Lord's.

3. Annual commemoration (11:39-40): At the end of two months Jephthah's daughter returned to her father. He *did with her according to the vow which he had made.* She was given to Yahweh. Then the note is added: *And she had no relations with a man.* Obviously the writer wished to underscore that this young lady was given to the Lord in a state of virginity. Four days each year the daughters of Israel went (to the tabernacle?) to commemorate the daughter of Jephthah. They recalled the willing sacrifice which she made in order that her father might fulfill his vow.

4. *Jephthah's sacrifice.* Jephthah certainly gave his daughter to the Lord. Did he also offer her up as a burnt offering? Scholars are divided. The text does not actually say that she was slain and then immolated. For this reason some scholars have proposed that Jephthah gave up his daughter to a celibate life of service at the tabernacle. At least two passages speak of females who had ministry responsibilities at the tabernacle (Exodus 38:8; 1 Samuel 2:22).

Human sacrifice was illegal under the Law of Moses. A person vowed to God could be redeemed by the payment of a stipulated amount (Leviticus 27); but obviously in this case no redemption money was paid. The question of human sacrifice here is mute. Good arguments can be made for and against that interpretation of the text. This much is certain: If Jephthah actually sacrificed his daughter he sinned in a grievous manner. No vow should be kept if the keeping of that vow involves a greater sin than the breaking of that vow.

10
ELI AND HIS
CONTEMPORARIES
Judges 12-13; 1 Samuel 2-3

Chapter Chronology

				1060
		ELI	Samson Birth 1069	
1099				
Jephthah	Ibzan		Elon	Abdon
	1083		1077	1068

Chronologically Eli was the eighth Judge (1 Samuel 4:18). He judged Israel for forty years (1099-1060 BC). His judgeship overlapped that of Jephthah, Ibzan, Elon, Abdon, and Samson.

SENTENCE
AGAINST THE PRIESTS
1 Samuel 2:27-36

Date: ca. 1098 BC

Sins in the Priesthood
1 Samuel 2:27-29

An unnamed *man of God* or prophet came to Eli with an unpleasant message. He first reminded Eli of the tremendous privilege that was his to be a priest of God. The Lord had revealed himself to Aaron even before the Exodus. He had chosen the family of Aaron for the priestly honor. Eli, however, was responsible for the disrespect that was being shown for God's sacrifice at Shiloh. The priests at Shiloh were getting fat with the choicest pieces of the sacrificial offerings. Eli had honored his sons more than the Lord. As chief religious officer, Eli was ultimately responsible for all the evil that was being tolerated at Shiloh.

Removal from the Priesthood
1 Samuel 2:30-34

God indeed had promised the priesthood (*walk before me*) to the house of Eli and to Eli's father's house (the Aaronides). God, however, will only honor those who honor him. Thus fidelity is the implied condition attached to every promise God makes. So in the case of Eli, God announced punishment. First, God would *cut off the strength* of the priestly house, i.e. the sons of that family will die before old age. Three times in the prophecy this point is stressed. Second, Eli will live to see the distress of God's dwelling, the tabernacle, i.e., the destruction of the place. Third, the priestly family will lose altar rights. Fourth, as a *sign* that the long range aspects of this prophecy will be fulfilled, Eli's two sons will both die on the same day.

The Faithful Priest
1 Samuel 2:35-36

A. Announcement (1 Samuel 2:35-36)

To replace the Aaronide priesthood once it was cut off Yahweh will raise up a faithful priest. This future priest will carry out the will of God perfectly. To acknowledge his faithfulness, Yahweh will build the faithful priest *an enduring house* or family, i.e., an eternal priesthood. Commentators generally conclude that the faithful priest was Samuel or Zadok. Samuel, however, if he was a priest in any sense, certainly did not have an enduring house. The slaughter of the priests at Nob (1 Samuel 22:11-23) and Solomon's banishment of Abiathar, the last representative of the house of Eli, certainly fulfilled a portion of the prophecy made to Eli (cf. 1 Kings 2:27). The anonymous prophet, however, predicted that the house of Eli's father (contextually, Aaron) will also be removed from office. Since Zadok was of the family of Aaron (cf. 1 Chronicles 6:1ff, 50ff), he certainly did not fulfill that portion of the prophecy. The Aaronide priesthood was not totally removed from priestly office until the destruction of Jerusalem in AD 70. The faithful priest, then, was neither Samuel nor Zadok.

B. Identity of the Faithful Priest

Who is the faithful priest of 1 Samuel 2:35? The prophecy is best interpreted messianically. The faithful priest is Jesus, God's anointed. For him God built an enduring house, the royal priesthood of 1 Peter 2:9. Before the Faithful Priest, a *house* or priestly family will *walk* or

168

minister.[15] Members of the old Aaronic priesthood will have to bow before God's anointed, Messiah, if they are to occupy a place of priestly service. When many of the Aaronide priests became obedient to the faith (Acts 6:7) this passage found ultimate fulfillment.

CALL OF SAMUEL
1 Samuel 3:1-18

Date: ca. 1097 BC

During the days when the sanctuary of Yahweh was at Shiloh prophetic revelations, whether auditory or visionary, were rare. For this reason the narrative goes into some detail about the first revelatory experience of Samuel. The narrator reports that Eli was nearly blind, perhaps explaining why Eli did not see what Samuel saw that night. Eli and the lad Samuel had retired for the night. Only the fading light of the lamp of God from within the Holy Place gave any illumination to the area where Samuel was sleeping (1 Samuel 3:1-3).

Appearance of God
1 Samuel 3:4-14

A. First Three Calls (1 Samuel 3:4-9)

Three times in the darkness Samuel heard the voice of God but mistook it for the voice of Eli. The narrator excuses this mistake by saying that Samuel did not yet know Yahweh experientially, nor had he received any revelation. Three times Samuel rushed to the side of the old man. Finally Eli recognized that God was calling the boy. He instructed his protégé to respond to any further call of his name by saying: *Speak, O Yahweh, for your servant is listening.*

B. Fourth Call (1 Samuel 3:10-14)

1. Description (3:10): Yahweh came to Samuel a fourth time *and stood and called* as at other times. The lad was experiencing what theologians call a theophany, a visual and auditory manifestation of

---

[15]What walks before God's anointed in 1 Samuel 2:35 is not the Faithful Priest, but his *house.* The latter is the nearest antecedent to the third person masculine pronoun. To *walk before* means to serve or minister as in 1 Samuel 2:30. Hence, the *house* of the Faithful Priest ministers or serves under his scrutiny or supervision. For a detailed discussion of the messianic interpretation of the passage, see James E. Smith, *What the Bible Says about the Promised Messiah* (Joplin: College Press, 1984), pp. 78-82.

169

the deity. Samuel responded on this occasion as Eli had instructed him.

2. Content (3:11-14): What Samuel heard from the Lord was basically what the man of God had told Eli earlier. What God was about to do will make the ears of all who hear of it *tingle.* The family of the old priest will fall under divine judgment because his sons had made themselves contemptible and Eli had failed to rebuke them. The Lord assured the house of Eli by oath that no sacrifice could atone for the sins they had committed.

Result
1 Samuel 3:15-4:1a

A. Report to Eli (1 Samuel 3:15-18)
Samuel lay down until the morning. He performed his usual chores, all the time trying to avoid a confrontation with Eli. He was afraid of hurting his beloved mentor should he be forced to divulge what he had learned during the night. Finally Eli sent for the lad and put him under a solemn curse if he withheld any part of the revelation. So Samuel told him everything. Eli accepted the disconcerting news with godly resignation. He knew Yahweh had revealed his will to Samuel. He believed Yahweh does only what was right. Therefore, he resigned himself to accept the verdict of God.

B. Fame of Samuel (1 Samuel 3:19-4:1a)
As Samuel grew to physical maturity, Yahweh was with him. The Lord let none of his words *fall to the ground,* i.e., go unfulfilled. His fame spread throughout the land, from Dan in the far north, to Beersheba on the edge of the Negev in the south. Because his prophecies were constantly being fulfilled, the people recognized that he was confirmed as a prophet. Yahweh continued to *appear* at Shiloh to Samuel. He revealed himself again and again *by the word of Yahweh.* What a sharp contrast there is here between the fully accredited Samuel on the one hand, and the very old Eli and his wicked sons on the other.

C. Philistine Oppression (Judges 10:7-9)
Jephthah had been able to win a decisive battle over the Ammonites (ca. 1088 BC). The Ammonites bounced back to harasses the tribes east of the Jordan for a total of eighteen years. In 1071 BC

they crossed the Jordan to support the Philistines in dominating the western tribes. All together the Philistines dominated the Israelites for forty years, until about 1049 BC. Thus the last oppression in the Book of Judges is twice as long as the next longest. From this oppression Judges records no deliverance, only a bit of periodic relief through the instrumentality of Samson.

BIRTH OF SAMSON
Judges 13:1-25

Date: ca. 1089 BC

Whereas other Judges were raised up in times of crisis to deliver God's people, Samson was dedicated to his task before his birth. Of the twenty-three references to the Angel of Yahweh in the Book of Judges, thirteen are found in the account of Samson's birth. Samson is the only deliverer in the Book of Judges about whose birth anything is related. The birth announcement demonstrated 1) the painstaking steps that Yahweh took to provide his people with a Judge; and 2) the truth that deliverance could only come through a special work of God. God's people were so powerless they could only receive deliverance as a gracious gift from Yahweh.

First Appearance of the Angel
Judges 13:1-7

A. Circumstances (Judges 13:1)

Something is missing in the account of Samson. The narrator begins by announcing another apostasy on the part of Israel and the judgment that followed it. He then tells the story of the birth of the man who was to become Israel's deliverer. He does not, however, mention any cry to Yahweh, either out of repentance or sheer misery. Sin is like that. Sin crushes and beats down until people have no will to change their circumstances however miserable. Yet here the glorious truth stands out that God begins his great work of deliverance even though his people do not have the good sense to cry out to him. Thank God that he does not give help to his people only when they pray!

Over a century had elapsed since the Angel of Yahweh appeared to Gideon at a winepress near Ophrah. About 1069 BC the Angel appeared again to the wife of a Danite named Manoah. This woman was barren—a shameful condition in those days. What is more, she is nameless in the text. Nonetheless, Manoah's wife is portrayed as a woman of great faith and calm assurance. She is another of the great feminine faces to appear in the Book of Judges. This woman underscores the blessed truth that God delights in working through anonymity and powerlessness to accomplish his purpose.

B. Announcement (Judges 13:2-5)
The stranger began by revealing his knowledge of the circumstances in the life of this godly wife. She was barren. That, however, was about to change. She will conceive and give birth to a son. In preparation for the birth of this son the woman was to be careful not to drink any strong drink or eat any unclean thing. The son was to be a Nazirite to God from the womb. God planned to use this consecrated man to *begin* to deliver Israel from the hands of the Philistines.

C. Report (Judges 13:6-7)
The woman reported the incident to her husband. She described her visitor as *a man of God*. This was terminology commonly applied to prophets. Nonetheless, she gave a description of the visitor that made clear to her husband that this man was no ordinary prophet. His appearance was *like the angel of God, very awesome* (NASB). Intimidated as she was by this appearance, the woman had not asked the stranger where he was from. Nor had the stranger volunteered to tell her his name. Then she repeated to her husband the instructions and the prophecy that the Angel of Yahweh had given her.

Second Appearance of the Angel
Judges 13:8-23

A. Manoah's Prayer (Judges 13:8-10)
Manoah believed his wife, but he felt he needed more information regarding the birth of the son. So he prayed that the man of God might come again to teach Manoah and his wife what needed to be done in regard to the boy. God heard that prayer. Again the Angel appeared to the woman. She ran quickly to inform her husband.

B. Manoah's Questions (Judges 13:11-18)

1. Question about the boy (13:11-14): After verifying that this man indeed had visited his wife earlier, Manoah asked the question that was uppermost in his mind. When the prophecy was fulfilled (note that Manoah had no doubt) what was to be the rule for the boy's life and work? The Angel responded that the woman should obey all his previous instructions. Those instructions were then repeated in the presence of Manoah. Though God answers the prayers of believers, he also places limits upon their actions. If one is to be used to accomplish anything for God he must follow directions.

2. Manoah's proposal (13:15-16): Manoah still thought at this point that he was dealing with a prophet of God. Wanting to be hospitable, he offered to prepare a meal for his guest. The Angel said he did not wish to eat a meal; but he promised to wait if Manoah cared to offer a burnt offering to Yahweh. Manoah recognized the clue here. His guest was much more than a prophet. Since he was not a human being, he wanted an offering rather than a meal.

3. Question about the name (13:17-18): Manoah then inquired as to the name of the Angel. The Angel refused to answer except to say that his name was "wonderful," i.e., beyond comprehension. For this reason Manoah was not to inquire about the name of the guest. While a person may know God, he cannot know God perfectly. Man must learn to be content with those things that God has revealed about himself. God is mysterious beyond human understanding. Those who deal with the things of God on a regular basis must never lose their sense of awe.

C. Manoah's Offering (Judges 13:19-21)

Manoah prepared the offering and laid it on the rock that served as an altar. Then Yahweh performed wonders while Manoah and his wife looked on. As the flame began to ascend from the sacrifice, the Angel of Yahweh ascended in the flame and disappeared. The two witnesses fell on their faces to the ground in reverence. Manoah was convinced then of what he probably suspected earlier, viz., that he had been conversing with the Angel of Yahweh.

D. Manoah's Panic (Judges 13:22-23)

Manoah panicked in the stress of the moment. He believed that he and his wife would die because they had seen God. Mrs. Manoah is portrayed as much more calm, logical and confident. If God had intended to slay them he would not have 1) accepted the sacrifice, 2) performed wonders, or 3) revealed good tidings. Here again, as frequently in Judges, the godly wisdom of a woman outshines that of the man in her life.

Birth and Growth of the Child
Judges 13:24-25

As predicted, the woman gave birth to a son. She named him Samson which means "sunshine" or perhaps "sunny" for short. His birth meant the dawn of a new day in the house of Manoah and for Israel. The childhood of Samson is passed over in silence. The text simply says that *the child grew up and Yahweh blessed him.* As he came into his adult years *the Spirit of Yahweh* began to *stir* him in *Mahaneh-dan* (lit., camp of Dan), a nearby place in Judah. This was the first of many times when Samson received overpowering impulses from the Spirit of God that drove him on and enabled him to perform amazing feats of strength.

CIVIL WAR WITH EPHRAIM
Judges 12:1-6

Date: ca.1087 BC

Cause of the War
Judges 12:1-4

A. Complaint to Jephthah (Judges 12:1-3)
1. Ephraimite threat (12:1): At some point the Ephraimites had been summoned to send troops to aid in Jephthah's war against Ammon. They arrived just after the battle and rebuked Jephthah for having gone into battle without them. In their blustering the Ephraimites threatened to burn down Jephthah's house in retaliation for bruising their egos.
2. Jephthah's response (12:2-3): Jephthah explained that he had summoned the Ephraimites before the battle. He waited as long as he dared, but the Ephraimite contingent never showed up. He therefore was forced to undertake the battle with only the forces he had mustered in Transjordan. Yahweh graciously had given the Gileadites the victory over Ammon. There was no reason for the Ephraimites to be showing hostility toward Jephthah.

B. Escalating Rhetoric (Judges 12:4)

The Ephraimites accused the Gileadites of being *renegades of Ephraim* (NIV). Perhaps the suggestion is that Gilead, which is situated between the big tribes of Manasseh and Ephraim, was so insignificant that it had no right to go to war on its own. At the least this was an ethnic slur; but it may also have hinted of Ephraimite desires to annex the territory of Gilead. In any case, the Gileadites were threatened by these words. They were willing to go to war against the Ephraimites.

Slaughter at the River
Judges 12:5-6

Jephthah re-gathered his troops and fought Ephraim. The Gileadites captured the fords of the Jordan opposite Ephraim. Any individual attempting to cross the Jordan at that point was challenged to pronounce the word *Shibboleth*. Apparently the Ephraimites could not pronounce the "sh" sound. Chronologically this was the second civil war during the period of the Judges, the third if one counts the Abimelech strife with Shechem. Some 42,000 Ephraimites fell in this civil war.

Evaluation of Jephthah
Judges 12:7

Jephthah's judgeship was comparatively short. It lasted only six years. When he died he was buried in *one of the cities of Gilead*. The great victory that he won over the Ammonites was overshadowed by the tragic vow that he made, the tragic stubbornness of the Ammonite king and the tragic civil war that erupted because of the pride of Ephraim.

TRAGEDY MITIGATED
Judges 12:8-15

Three minor Judges followed Jephthah. Not much is known about these men. Certain clues, however, do exist that they represent a further deterioration of the office of Judge. Things may have appeared to be normal on the surface. After Gideon, however, there is no reference to the God-given rest that is mentioned in connection with the earlier Judges. If the chronology adopted for this study is correct, Ibzan, Elon and Abdon were all Judges in their respective tribal areas while the Philistines were oppressing Israel in the south.

Judgeship of Ibzan
Judges 12:8-10

Ibzan was from Bethlehem, but probably not the famous village of that name in Judah. More likely he was from Bethlehem in Zebulun (cf. Joshua 19:15). Ibzan had thirty sons and thirty daughters. Thus he must have been married to several wives. He gave his daughters in marriage to those *outside,* and took thirty wives for his sons from those *outside.* The reference is probably to intermarriage with non-Israelites. Ibzan may have had an ecumenical spirit, but he was violating one of the most fundamental of God's laws of separation (12:8-9).

Daughters are mentioned in connection with only Jephthah and Ibzan. Jephthah had but one, and was forced by his foolish vow to surrender her while she was still a virgin. Ibzan had thirty daughters, all married, and thirty married sons as well. The fullness of Ibzan serves to underscore the barrenness of his predecessor in consequence of his vow.

Ibzan's judgeship was probably limited to Zebulun and tribal areas bordering on Zebulun. After serving seven years Ibzan died. He was buried at in his hometown. His judgeship can be dated to about 1083-1077 BC.

Judgeship of Elon
Judges 12:11-12

Elon from the tribe of Zebulun judged Israel for ten years. That is all that is said about him. Like a lot of church leaders, Elon merely held a title. He did not accomplish anything worth noting during his years of leadership. He was buried at Aijalon (location unknown) in the land of Zebulun. His judgeship can be dated to about 1077-1068 BC.

Judgeship of Abdon
Judges 12:13-15

Abdon is called the Pirathonite, i.e., he was from the town of Pirathon in the hill country of Ephraim. During his judgeship no doubt Ephraim regained some of the tribal prestige that had been lost in the humiliating defeat by the Gileadites (12:6). Like Gideon, Ibzan and Jair, Abdon was a polygamist. He had forty sons and thirty grandsons who rode about on seventy donkeys. That was a symbol of affluence and authority. One senses here a bit of pomp, arrogance and nepotism.

Abdon was buried at Pirathon in the land of Ephraim, *in the hill country of the Amalekites.* This note suggests that an enclave of the Amalekites had become entrenched in territory belonging to Ephraim. Apparently Abdon had not been very successful in reclaiming this territory for Israel. Perhaps he never even tried. The judgeship of Abdon can be dated to about 1068-1061 BC.

11
PHILISTINE BATTLES
Judges 14-15; 1 Samuel 4-6

Chapter Chronology

		1049
	SAMSON	
1060		

CAPTURE OF THE ARK
1 Samuel 4:1-6:21

Date: ca. 1060 BC

Arguably one of the darkest days in Israel's history was the day that the sacred Ark of God was captured by the Philistines. This triggered twenty years of low ebb existence for Israel. It was during this twenty years that the Lord used a strong man named Samson to inflict blows against the Philistines.

Defeat of Israel
1 Samuel 4:1b-11

A. First Defeat at Aphek (1 Samuel 4:1b-2)

In the days of Eli the Israelites attempted to put an end to Philistine incursions into the land. When these enemies camped at Aphek, the Israelites formed their ranks nearby at Ebenezer about two miles east of Aphek. In the ensuing battle some four thousand[16] Israelites were slain *in the field.* These last words suggest that the Israelites had held their ground in spite of the losses.

B. Second Defeat at Aphek (1 Samuel 4:3-11)

---

[16]Some understand the word *eleph*, usually translated "thousand," to be a technical name for a military unit of undetermined size. If an *eleph* consisted of thirty troops, for example, the losses here would be four times thirty or 120 men. While this approach to the battle figures in the Old Testament is possible in some passages, the methodology is not capable of consistent application to all the large numbers in the Old Testament.

1. *Erroneous conclusion (4:3-4):* In the camp that night the Israelites concluded that the Lord had delivered them into the hands of the Philistines because the sacred ark had been left at Shiloh. So they sent to Shiloh for the ark. Hophni and Phinehas accompanied the ark back to the Israelite encampment.

2. *Pre-mature celebration (4:5-9):* The Israelite army greeted the arrival of the ark with thunderous jubilation. The Philistines soon learned the reason for the shouting, and they became fearful. They recognized the sacred box as guaranteeing the presence of God. These pagans knew the traditions of how the "gods" of the Israelites—the Philistines assumed the Israelites were polytheists—had smitten the mighty Egyptians with plagues. They feared lest now the lowly *Hebrews* would gain the advantage over them and make them slaves. Therefore, with desperate determination they urged one another to fight all the harder.

3. *Battle result (4:10-11):* Again the Philistines defeated Israel, this time inflicting over seven times the number of casualties (30,000) experienced in the first engagement. What was worse, the ark was captured, and the two sons of Eli were slain.

Death of Eli
1 Samuel 4:12-22

A. Report to Eli (1 Samuel 4:10-18)

A disheveled messenger brought the grim message to Shiloh from the battlefield some eighteen miles distant. The aged Eli, now ninety-eight, was sitting on a stool beside the road awaiting the results of the battle. He feared for the safety of the ark. When Eli heard the tumultuous outcry of the city, he inquired as to its cause. The messenger ran to the blind old man and blurted out the news with four hammer-like blows: 1) the Israelites had deserted the field; 2) the army had experienced heavy losses; 3) Eli's two sons had been killed; and 4) the ark had been captured. When he heard that the ark had been captured, Eli fainted or experienced a stroke. He fell backward off the stool, falling in such a way that his neck was broken. In this inglorious way the forty year judgeship of Eli came to an end.

B. Birth of a Child (1 Samuel 4:19-22)

The trauma of that day hastened the labor of Phinehas' wife. Through great difficulty she gave birth to a son. The neighbor women

180

tried to calm the terrified woman with the news that she had given birth to a son. She, however, could only think of the great loss that both she and the nation had experienced that day. The high priest was dead. Her husband was dead. Israel had been humiliated by enemies. Worse still, the ark of God had fallen into pagan hands. With her last breath she whispered the name of the baby: *Ichabod* (lit., "glory has gone into captivity"). Ever after the name of this child recalled the day when the ark of God had departed from Israel.

Defeat of Dagon
1 Samuel 5:1-12

Though the Philistines had defeated Israel twice on the field of battle, a confrontation on a different level was about to take place. Israel's God now showed himself superior to the chief god of the Philistines.

A. Dagon Humiliated (1 Samuel 5:1-5)

The ark of God was deposited in the temple of Dagon in Ashdod (cf. Judges 16:23). In the morning the priests of Dagon discovered that the statue of their god had fallen on its face to the ground before the ark of God. So the priests set Dagon in his place again. The second morning the priests rose *early*—they must have been concerned for the welfare of their god—to find the statue of their god in the same position. This time the head and hands of the image had broken off at the threshold of the shrine. Dagon was reduced to a stump without a head for thinking or hands for acting. For that reason no one thereafter wanted to step on the threshold of that temple lest they defile the place where pieces of the statue of Dagon had lain. The main point here is that Yahweh defeated Dagon in his own temple. The memory of that humiliation was perpetuated in this religious superstition for generations.

B. Philistines Afflicted (1 Samuel 5:6-12)

The hand of Yahweh (i.e., his power) was heavy against any Philistine city where the ark lodged. The Lord *ravaged* (NASB) or *brought devastation on them* (NIV). The same verb is used for the destruction of vines and fig trees in Hosea 2:12.

1. In Ashdod (5:6-7): The Lord smote the men of Ashdod with tumors. Because of the connection of the tumors with rodents (cf. 6:4-

5, 17-18), many scholars think that some form of bubonic plague spread throughout the land.

2. In Gath and Ekron (5:8-12): When the Ashdodites complained to the lords of the Philistines, they were directed to take the ark to Gath. Again Yahweh smote the men of the city, both the young and the old, with the tumors. When the ark approached Ekron, the citizens of that place feared for their lives. The deadly plague broke out there just as in Ashdod and Gath earlier. Many died. Those who did not die suffered with tumors. The Ekronites were panic stricken. They petitioned the lords of the land to return the ark to Israel. At the same time the agonizing cry of the city *went up to heaven.* This narrative underscores the point that Yahweh was master even in Philistine territory.

Disaster at Beth Shemesh
1 Samuel 6:1-7:2

A. Philistine Reparations (1 Samuel 6:1-6)

After seven months of tumult, the Philistines had had enough of the ark. They consulted their diviners as to the proper method of returning the ark to its rightful place in Israel. If the plague was to be removed, the Philistines needed to send a guilt offering along with the ark as reparation to appease the God whose anger had been unleashed against them. Five golden *tumors* would magically grant relief from the terrible disease which plagued the land. They should be accompanied by five golden mice, in the likeness of the mice that ravished the land. By so doing the Philistines were giving glory to God and thereby making it possible for him to withdraw his hand from them. The diviners urged the lords of the Philistines not to be more hardened of heart than Pharaoh who eventually allowed Israel to depart from his land. Ancient peoples often feared the gods of other peoples, even those of their enemies.

B. Philistine Test (1 Samuel 6:6-12)

The pagan diviners suggested a method by which the lords of the Philistines could determine whether their national misfortune was simply a natural disaster, or was due to the judgment of God. Two cows were separated from their calves and hitched to a cart, a *new* cart that had not been defiled by secular labor. The ark was placed on the cart. Alongside the ark was a box containing the guilt offering of

182

golden tumors and mice. They then put the cart on the road to the nearest Israelite town of Beth-Shemesh. Rather than turn back to their calves, the cows went straight down the road lowing as they went under divine compulsion away from their calves. They turned neither to the right nor to the left. The lords of the Philistines followed the cart to the borders of Beth Shemesh, some ten miles east of Ekron. This guaranteed that no one tamper in any way with the experiment. The unnatural behavior of the cows convinced them that the disaster that had befallen their land was not mere chance. The hand of Yahweh had smitten the Philistines. Ironically the test proposed by the Philistine diviners only gave Yahweh another opportunity to demonstrate his power.

C. Israelite Reception (1 Samuel 6:13-21)

1. A sacrifice in the field (6:13-18): The farmers of the Levitical village of Beth Shemesh rejoiced when they saw the ark. The cows stopped near a large stone in the field of one named Joshua. The Levites removed the ark and placed it on the large stone. A fire was built with the wood of the cart. The cows were slaughtered and offered to Yahweh as burnt offerings. Other sacrifices apparently were also offered. From a distance the lords of the Philistines looked on as the box containing their guilt offering was opened. There the Israelites found five golden mice and five golden tumors representing the Philistine Pentapolis: Ashdod, Gaza, Ashkelon, Gath and Ekron. The large stone where the ark had been placed became a kind of national monument, a witness to the day the when the ark came home.

2. A mistake in exuberance (6:19-21): At this point the narrative takes a surprising turn. In their exuberance over the return of the ark, the men of Beth Shemesh made a serious mistake. They looked into the ark. Their motives may have been innocent enough. They probably wished to see if the Philistines had removed any of the memorial objects that were contained in the ark. Nonetheless, looking into the ark with profane curiosity was strictly forbidden (cf. Numbers 4:20). So Yahweh smote the people of the area with a great slaughter. The leaders of Beth Shemesh quickly sent to Kiriath Jearim to ask them to come and take away the ark.

3. Problem with the numbers. The number of people affected by the plague at Beth Shemesh is in dispute. Actually the Hebrew text contains two numbers side by side, seventy and fifty thousand. NIV chooses the smaller figure, apparently regarding the fifty thousand as a gloss. NASB follows the Septuagint in combining these numbers into one figure, 50,070.[17]

C. Low Ebb for Israel (1 Samuel 7:1-2)

Kiriath Jearim was ten miles northeast of Beth Shemesh and nine miles west of Jerusalem. The men of this village showed great faith and reverence by coming and removing the ark. The sacred chest was housed on the property of Abinadab. Eleazar, the son of Abinadab, was consecrated to care for the ark. For twenty years the Israelites lamented after Yahweh.

The ark remained in Kiriath Jearim for several decades. Probably it was not returned to Shiloh because that place had been defiled if not destroyed by the Philistines. As far as the record is concerned the ark disappeared from national life. Even when the tabernacle was reconstructed and located at Nob, the ark remained at Kiriath Jearim. The extent to which the ark played any role in the religious life of Israel cannot be determined. Only after David had established Jerusalem as his capital did the ark surface again as an important object in Israelite worship.

EXPLOITS OF SAMSON
Judges 14:1-16:3

Date: ca. 1060-1049 BC
Samson's Marriage
Judges 14:1-15:8

The key word in Judges 14 is the verb *go down*. Judges 14 focuses on several trips—the exact number is unclear—that Samson made into Philistine territory. Each of these journeys centers around a secret stated or implied in the text.

---

[17]In his *Encyclopedia of Biblical Difficulties,* Gleason Archer argued for the smaller number as the original reading of the passage. He points out that 1) the customary Hebrew word order is not used in expressing the figure 50,070; 2) Josephus (*Ant.* VI.i.4) refers to the loss of life at Beth Shemesh as only seventy, with no mention whatever of the fifty thousand; 3) a few Hebrew manuscripts entirely omit the fifty thousand; and 4) given the size of the village of Beth Shemesh the lower figure is probably the original. No one, however, has given a credible explanation of how the fifty thousand figure crept into the text.

A. Attraction Trip (Judges 14:1-4)

1. Trip to Timnah (14:1-3): First, Samson *went down* to nearby Timnah. The reason for his trip is not stated. There Samson saw a Philistine woman who attracted him. He returned to his home and requested that his parents arrange a marriage with this woman. Samson's parents tried to dissuade him. Could he not find a suitable mate among the Israelite women? Physical attraction, however, prevailed over wisdom and parental objection. *Get her for me,* Samson said, *for she looks good to me!* The lust of the flesh is a foundation of sand upon which to build the temple of marriage.

2. God's secret (14:4): The first secret in Judges 14 belonged to God. Neither Samson himself nor his parents realized that God's providence was at work. God was seeking an occasion to inflict upon the Philistines blows of judgment. Israel as a whole was too crushed to fight for liberty. God planned to bring devastation and death upon the oppressors through the personal grievance of Samson. The marriage to the Philistine woman was the first step in stirring up Samson to anger against the enemies of God's people. While the readers of Judges 14 know God's secret, the main characters in the chapter do not.

B. Arrangement Trip (Judges 14:5-7)

1. Samson's strength tested (14:5-6): The second trip down to Timnah was for the purpose of making marriage arrangements. Samson's parents accompanied him, for they would be involved in the marriage negotiations customary in that time. On this trip Samson turned aside into some vineyards. There he was attacked by a young lion. For the first time *the Spirit of Yahweh* came mightily upon him. He tore the lion with his bare hands as one might tear a kid. Now Samson had a secret. He did not tell his parents what he had done perhaps because touching something dead was a violation of his Nazirite vow. Here for the first time Samson had occasion to test his own strength.

2. Marriage arrangements (14:7): The marriage negotiations and "courtship," such as it was, went well. After talking with the woman, Samson still found himself attracted to this Philistine.

C. Celebration Trip (Judges 14:8-18)

1. Honey from a carcass (14:8-9): When Samson returned to take his bride he turned aside to see the carcass of the lion he had

185

slain on the earlier trip. There he found a swarm of bees and honey. He scooped up the honey in his hands and ate it as he walked along. When he caught up to his parents he gave them some as well, but he did not tell them where he had secured the honey. Again Samson had a secret, and his parents were in the dark.

2. *Drinking feast (14:10-11):* Following the custom of the time, Samson gave a marriage feast. Apparently his father helped in the arrangements. The family of his bride brought together thirty companions to be a part of the week-long celebration. The Hebrew word implies it was a drinking feast. In eating honey from the carcass of the lion Samson had violated the Nazirite rule about touching something that was dead. Now he appears to have violated the rule against drinking the fruit of the vine. In sports metaphor, this was strike two against Samson.

3. *A riddle to impress (14:12-14):* To impress the snobbish friends of his bride, Samson proposed a challenge to his Philistine guests. He propound a riddle. If the guests could solve the riddle during the seven days of the feast Samson promised to give to them thirty changes of garments including underwear. If, however, they were unable to solve the riddle then each of them would provide for him a similar change of garments. The Philistines agreed to the challenge not believing that any Israelite hillbilly could outwit the sophisticated men from the plains. So Samson put forth a two line rhyming riddle: *Out of the eater, something to eat; out of the strong, something sweet.*

4. *A confidence betrayed (14:15-17):* By the third day the Philistines still had not solved the riddle. On the fourth day they approached Samson's bride. If she did not coax the answer from him before the seventh day, they threatened to burn her and her father's house. They did not intend to be financially disadvantaged because they had agreed to attend a wedding feast honoring her husband.

Samson's wife turned on the tears at this point. She accused Samson of hating her, of not trusting her with his secret. Samson responded that he had not told his parents the riddle, so why would he tell her, a woman he hardly knew even though she was his wife. The woman, however, continued to plead for Samson to tell her the riddle. On the seventh day the pressure became so intense that Samson gave in. She went immediately and told the wedding guests.

5. *A riddle solved (14:18):* Before sunset on the seventh day the Philistines explained the riddle. What is sweeter than honey? What is

stronger than a lion? Samson knew immediately that they had secured this answer from his wife. He spoke another poetic couplet as he stormed out of the place: *If you had not plowed with my heifer, you would not have found out my riddle.*

D. Vengeance Trip (Judges 14:19-20)

1. Wager paid (14:19): For the second time the Spirit of Yahweh came mightily upon Samson. Empowered by God's Spirit, Samson began to fulfill his destiny. Samson went down to Ashkelon and killed thirty Philistines. He took the garments from these men back to Timnah and threw them down in front of those who had solved his riddle. This was the beginning of deliverance from the Philistine oppression. Yahweh's secret (v. 4) was starting to be revealed. The Lord does not always sanitize his deliverances. They are sometimes messy. Bloodshed is often the only means of breaking the yoke of tyrants.

2. Wife given to another (14:20): With his anger still burning over the Philistine conniving, Samson *went up* to this father's house. Even as he was at home trying to regain his composure, actions were being taken in Timnah that were to trigger round two in the pummeling of the Philistines. While he was away, Samson's wife was given in marriage to *his friend,* i.e., his best man, who also was a Philistine.

Mighty in His Vengeance
Judges 15:1-20

Judges 15 contains three examples of the kind of blows that Samson was able to inflict against the Philistines during his twenty year career. Each Philistine provocation was met with swift and devastating vengeance. The chapter concludes with Samson at the point of death, crying out to God for deliverance.

A. First Provocation (Judges 15:1-6a)

1. The wife issue (15:1-3): After a time Samson's anger cooled. During wheat harvest, a time of great celebration, he visited his wife in Timnah with a young goat. He was thereby proposing a reconciliation feast. The woman was still living in her father's house even though she had been given in marriage to a Philistine. Her father prevented Samson from entering his wife's room. He explained that

187

he thought Samson had deserted his wife for good, and that he therefore had given the woman to Samson's best man. The desperate father tried to assuage the anger of Samson by offering to him his younger daughter. The father considered her even more beautiful than her older sister. Apparently Samson did not agree. As he again left that house in anger Samson shouted for all to hear that he now had a right to get even with the Philistines for what they had done to him.

2. *Burning grain fields (15:4-6a):* Samson then rounded up three hundred foxes (or jackals). By twos he tied the tails of the foxes to a burning torch. The terrified animals drug the torches hither and yon through the grain fields and vineyards of Philistia. A good portion of the crop was totally destroyed.

B. Second Provocation (Judges 15:6b-8)
1. *Philistine retaliation (15:6b):* The Philistines soon ascertained the name of the culprit who had burned their fields and the reason he had created this devastation. Unable immediately to get their hands on Samson, a group of angry Philistines went to Timnah and torched Samson's wife and her father.

2. *Samson's vendetta (15:7-8):* The death of his wife at Philistine hands caused Samson to launch another vendetta against the enemies of God's people. Details of the confrontation have been omitted. The text simply states that Samson struck them ruthlessly with a great slaughter. Then he went down to live in a cave at the rock of Etam. Perhaps he was still grieving over the death of his wife. Perhaps he had grown weary of the slaughter.

C. Third Provocation (Judges 15:9-17)
1. *Philistine invasion (15:9-10):* At this point the Philistines launched a mass attack against Israel with the prime objective being the capture and death of Samson. The men of Judah wished no hostilities with the Philistines. They were perplexed by this incursion. When they learned that the objective of the invasion was the binding of Samson, the men of Judah, cowards that they were, agreed to hand Samson over to his enemies.

2. *Samson confronted (15:11):* Three thousand men of Judah went down to the cave where Samson was holed up. With two biting questions they challenged his wisdom and love for his countrymen. Was Samson so stupid that he did not know that the Philistines were rulers over Israel? Why would he provoke these enemies and thus

trigger an invasion by them? Samson responded that he was living by the iron rule: As they have done to me, so I have done to them. Samson does not seem to have grasped the significance of his role as Israel's deliverer. He was motivated strictly by personal revenge. Samson made no effort to mobilize the Israelites for a decisive battle against the Philistines. That was not his style. Perhaps he knew that, given the attitude of his people, military resistance would be impossible to organize.

3. *Samson surrendered (15:12-13):* Samson agreed to surrender peacefully to his countrymen if they would swear not to kill him. The Judahites agreed only to bind him and hand him over to the Philistines. They must have known that a fate worse than death awaited Samson should the Philistines get their hands on him. Nonetheless, they bound him with two new ropes and brought him up from the rock at Etam.

4. *Jawbone massacre (15:14-17):* The Philistines shouted triumphantly as they saw Samson being led into their camp at Lehi. Then, however, for the third time the Spirit of Yahweh came mightily upon Samson. He snapped the ropes that bound him as if they were charred flax. He grabbed a new donkey's jawbone from the ground. Using that as his weapon he was able to slay a thousand Philistines. Some think this feat was accomplished with the help of the Judahites who were emboldened by his actions. In any case the remainder of the Philistine force fled in panic back to their territory. Samson celebrated his victory with a poetic verse. He then named the spot *Ramath-lehi*, i.e., the high place of the jawbone.

D. A Personal Crisis (Judges 15:18-20)

1. *Samson's prayer (15:18):* The heat of battle, which must have lasted the better part of the day, had taken a physical toll on Samson. He was very thirsty, yet there was no source of water immediately available. For the first time the narrator mentions that Samson sought the Lord. His prayer recognized the fact that God had given the victory over the Philistines through him. Yet now he was in danger of dying from thirst. If that should happen his body would fall into the hands of the uncircumcised Philistines for mutilation.

2. *Yahweh's response (15:19):* The Lord heard that prayer. God *split the hollow place* that was in Lehi so that water came forth. The fresh water revived Samson. He named the spot where God provided the water "Spring of the Caller."

Cornered in Gaza
Judges 16:1-3

Judges 16 sketches the pitiful details of the downfall of Samson. Chapters 14-15 contain three references to the overpowering of Samson by the Spirit of God. No such reference appears in chapter 16. The author seems to be placing in juxtaposition two contrasting portraits of Samson, the first with the Spirit (chs. 14-15), and the second without the Spirit. Here Samson is self-sufficient and out of control.

A. Trapped in a Harlot's House (Judges 16:1-2)
For some unexplained reason Samson journeyed to the Philistine city of Gaza. There he met a harlot and went into her. When the men of Gaza heard that Samson had come to their city they surrounded the harlot's house. They intended at first light of day to slay their Israelite nemesis.

B. Humiliating the Philistines (Judges 16:3)
Somehow Samson learned that his enemies were prepared to ambush him in the morning. At midnight he slipped out of the house and passed the sentries. He went down to the city gates. They had been bolted shut for the night. He ripped the doors of the gate off their hinges. Along with the posts and bars of the gate, Samson carried the doors on his shoulders to the top of a hill near Hebron. Thus in the heartland of Judah Samson left tangible evidence of his latest humiliating blow against the Philistines.

190

12
LAST OF THE JUDGES
Judges 16; 1 Samuel 7-8

Chapter Chronology

	1048
Two Years	
1049	

The judgeship of Samuel is largely a blank. Clearly his judgeship overlapped that of Samson. The Philistines captured the Ark of God in 1060 BC, the same year that Samson got married. Once the ark was returned to Israel it remained in the out of the way village of Kiriath Jearim. At the end of those twenty years Samson died and Samuel led the nation in a great spiritual awakening.

DEATH OF SAMSON
Judges 16:4-31

Date: ca. 1049 BC

Entrapment
Judges 16:4-20

A. **Temptress** (Judges 16:4-5)
   1. Samson loved Delilah (16:4): Samson could not resist Philistine women. Even after his fiasco at Timnah, and his near escape from the house of the harlot in Gaza, Samson became involved with yet another Philistine woman, the infamous Delilah. Tradition says that she was the younger sister who had been spurned by Samson a few years earlier. Samson *loved* Delilah. He never suspected for a moment that she would bring about his downfall.
   2. Philistine payment (16:5): The Philistine lords took note of the attraction that Samson had for Delilah. Each promised to pay the vixen eleven hundred pieces of silver if she could discover the secret of Samson's strength. Their intention was to overpower Samson, and then afflict him. Revenge is a motive devoid of scruples. These Philistines stopped at nothing.

B. Temptation (Judges 16:6-20)

1. Initial resistance (16:6-12): To his credit Samson resisted the feminine wiles of Delilah for a time. He lied to her three times about the secret of his strength. Had he been as tough mentally as he was physically Samson would have refused to discuss the matter with her. He seemed to sense that she could not be trusted, but he could not resist her charms. Samson first told Delilah that if he were bound with seven fresh cords he would be as weak as other men. Next Samson told Delilah that if he were bound with new ropes he would lose his supernatural strength. In both cases when the woman aroused Samson with the shout that the Philistines were upon him, he snapped the restraints as if they were mere thread.

2. Samson weakening (16:13-14): Even when it became obvious that Delilah was laying a trap for him, Samson still was unable to resist her seduction. He walked into her temptations with open eyes. Delilah increased the pressure, and Samson told a third lie. If one were to weave the seven locks of his hair into the web of the loom and fasten it with a pin he would become weak like other men. Delilah's cry brought Samson to his feet. He pulled out the pin which tied his hair to the loom. Still the secret of his strength was intact.

3. Samson reveals his secret (16:15-20): Delilah continued to press Samson on a daily basis to reveal to her the secret of his strength. The man's soul *was annoyed to death* (NASB). Finally he told her that he had been Nazirite to God from birth. The secret of his strength was in his unshorn hair that was the outward symbol of the Nazirite vow. Delilah could sense that her man had now revealed the truth. She summoned the Philistine lords and received her wages of betrayal. Then she put Samson to sleep on her lap. A servant came in and cut the seven locks of his hair. When she aroused him, Samson again jumped to his feet. He thought that he would *shake himself free* from any attackers as on previous occasions. *But he did not know that Yahweh had departed from him.*

Bound in Prison
Judges 16:21-22

The Philistines seized Samson with little resistance. They gouged out his eyes to render him permanently harmless. He was then taken to Gaza, bound with bronze chains. There he was made to serve as a grain grinder, a job normally performed by oxen. It involved pushing

192

a large round grinding stone in a circle over stalks of grain. How humiliating! Even as he performed this exhausting labor, however, his hair was beginning to grow back. The Philistines failed to notice. Of course there was nothing magical about Samson's hair. His strength came from the Spirit of God. Yet the hair was the symbol of his strength. The sincere repentance that grew in the sightless darkness of the mill chamber positioned Samson for one last heroic act in the drama of redemption.

Mocked in a Temple
Judges 16:23-30

A. Samson on Display (Judges 16:23-25)

The lords of the Philistines assembled to offer a great sacrifice to Dagon their god. Little did they realize that they were setting the stage for the greatest feat of Samson. The assembly was filled with joy. When they saw Samson the people praised Dagon for delivering Samson into their hands. When they were in *high spirits* the crowd demanded that Samson be brought forth into the temple to amuse them. For a time they entertained themselves by playing a cruel game of blind man's bluff with the helpless Israelite.

B. Samson Positioning himself (Judges 16:26-27)

Three thousand jeering Philistine men and women joined their leaders in heaping their abuse upon the once formidable enemy. They were sitting on a balcony overlooking a courtyard where Samson was being tormented. When Samson sensed that he was standing near the main pillars of the structure, a plan formed within his mind. He asked the lad who was leading him by the hand to let him lean against the great pillars upon which the house rested.

C. Samson's Last Feat (Judges 16:28-30)

In his desperation Samson cried out to the Lord. He asked for one last infusion of divine strength that he might be avenged of the Philistines for the loss of his two eyes. He then braced himself between the two main pillars, with his right hand on the one and the left hand on the other. After praying that he might die with the Philistines, Samson pushed with all his might against the pillars. The author seems to delight in the irony that he who was brought into that building as an entertainer literally brought the house down upon the

193

revelers. In this final act of defiance, Samson slew more of the Philistines than he had slain during his lifetime. At the same time, this final blow wiped out the entire leadership of the Philistine people.

At the conclusion of Judges 14-15 Samson was at the point of death after the slaughter of the thousand. He cried out to Yahweh, and the Lord intervened with a miraculous supply of water. The climax of chapter 16 is likewise the prayer of Samson. He asked God for vindication and for death. Both requests were granted. Surely the author is stressing the principle that man's extremity is God's opportunity. Prayer is the key that brings to bear on desperate circumstances the powerful resources of heaven. One cannot escape the conclusion that if the Lord hears the prayers of a backslidden philanderer like Samson, he will surely hear the fervent prayer of a righteous man.

Epilogue
Judges 16:31

Samson's family came down to Gaza to retrieve the lifeless body of Israel's great hero. They buried him in the tomb of his father Manoah. Samson had judged Israel for twenty years, roughly 1060-1049 BC.

Assessment of Samson

Samson judged Israel *during* the Philistine oppression. He was not a military leader like Gideon or Jephthah. He used his own strength to inflict devastating blows upon the oppressors. Samson, however, was never able to free the land from the power of the Philistines. That remained for Samuel, the man of prayer, to accomplish.

Though Samson was extraordinary in many ways, he does not appear to have been a zealous servant of the Lord. Nor does the text supply evidence of any close bond between Samson and his countrymen. On the contrary, Samson was very friendly with the Philistines. He seemed particularly attracted to Philistine women. He was a man of impulse who was controlled by sensual desires. Revenge dominated his thinking, even in his prayers.

In retrospect one might ask how God could choose to use an unfaithful and immoral man like Samson. Here is a man who violated his vows and abused his gifts. Samson's physical prowess was not matched by his moral strength. Who can explain the sovereign choices of the Almighty? The tools that God employed during the entire period of the Judges are certainly not those who might be selected as leaders of God's people today. In Samson's defense only this can be said. He was willing to fight when no one else was. He knew who the enemy was, and he inflicted countless blows against them.

DELIVERANCE FROM
PHILISTINE OPPRESSION
1 Samuel 7:3-17

Date: ca. 1049 BC

Samuel's Revival
1 Samuel 7:3-9

A. Evidence of Repentance (1 Samuel 7:3-4)

After twenty years of spiritual malaise, Samuel sensed the time was right for revival. He called upon his people to return to Yahweh with all of their heart. If they removed the foreign gods including the popular female idols of Ashtaroth, and if they served Yahweh alone, the Lord would deliver them from the hand of the Philistines. Samuel's message struck a responsive chord. The Israelites removed the Baals and their female counterparts. They devoted themselves exclusively to Yahweh.

B. Mizpah Assembly (1 Samuel 7:5-6)

When he sensed the time was right Samuel called for all Israel to assemble at Mizpah where he promised to pray for them. The Mizpah meeting, some eight miles north of Jerusalem, was one of the great revivals in biblical history. The people fasted that day. To symbolize the surrender of their entire beings, they drew water and poured it out before the Lord. They confessed their sins. They recognized the authority of Samuel by allowing him to *judge* them.

C. Israelite Fear (1 Samuel 7:7-9)

The lords of the Philistines regarded this show of national unity in Israel as a threat to their hegemony. They came out against Israel in full force. The news of the Philistine approach struck terror in the

History of Israel

hearts of the Israelites. They begged Samuel to keep on crying to Yahweh on their behalf that he might save them. Samuel immediately offered up a lamb as a whole burnt offering to Yahweh. The sacrifice was accompanied by earnest petition which Yahweh immediately answered.

Defeat of the Philistines
1 Samuel 7:10-14

A. Yahweh's Intervention (1 Samuel 7:10-11)

As Samuel was offering his sacrifice, the Philistines were forming their battle lines. Yahweh thundered against the attackers with a great thunder. The Philistines were thrown into confusion. They fled before the men of Israel. The Israelites pursued and struck the enemy all the way to Beth-car.

B. Victory Commemoration (1 Samuel 7:12-14)

To commemorate the victory over the Philistines Samuel erected a monument between Mizpah and Shen. The stone was named Ebenezer, "stone of help." That victory marked the beginning of Israelite resurgence. All the days of Samuel the Philistines never again were successful in invading the territory of Israel *for the hand of Yahweh* was against them. Cities that had been lost to the Philistines were recovered. The ascendancy of Israel also caused the Amorites who lived within the borders of Israel to cease their hostilities.

Summary of
Samuel's Judgeship
1 Samuel 7:15-17

Thus, Samuel the man of prayer was able to accomplish what Samson the man of strength could not accomplish. The prophet judged all Israel all the days of his life. His judicial circuit, however, was limited to a relatively small area of central Palestine. He moved about in a circuit from Bethel to Gilgal to Mizpah and back to his home at Ramah. In these places he *judged* Israel. At Ramah Samuel built an altar to Yahweh. The text thus hints that Ramah became the center of national worship.

196

REQUEST FOR A KING
1 Samuel 8:1-22

Date: 1048 BC

According to Josephus, Samuel presided over the people alone twelve years after the death of the high priest Eli, and with King Saul eighteen years (*Antiquities* 6.294). This means that the anointing of Saul took place in the year 1048 BC. The Mizpah revival and subsequent victory over the Philistines in the previous year (1 Samuel 7) were the highlights of Samuel's long judgeship.

Initial Request by the Elders
1 Samuel 8:1-6

A. Catalyst (1 Samuel 8:1-3)

As Samuel grew older he made a tragic mistake. He appointed his two sons, Joel and Abijah, to judgeships in Beersheba some fifty miles southwest of Jerusalem. Apparently Samuel was trying to make the office of Judge hereditary. Samuel's sons, however, did not walk in the righteous path of their father. Out from under his watchful eye they turned aside after dishonest gain, and took bribes to pervert judgments.

B. Request (1 Samuel 8:4-6)

The elders of Israel used Samuel's sons as a pretext for demanding a king. They came to Ramah to request that Samuel appoint for them a king *like all the nations.* God had promised to give his people kings (Genesis 17:16; 35:11). The Law of Moses anticipated the day when Israel would have a king (Deuteronomy 17:14-20). Nevertheless, the request offended the prophet. He interpreted it as a rejection of his life and ministry. So Samuel did what all wounded souls should do. He went to the Lord in prayer.

Response of the Lord
1 Samuel 8:7-18

A. Instructions for Samuel (1 Samuel 8:7-9)

Yahweh instructed Samuel to listen to the voice of the people. They had not rejected the judgeship of Samuel, but the kingship of God (cf. Judges 8:22-23). This was but another example of the

197

spiritual rebellion manifested by Israel ever since God had brought them out of Egypt. While Samuel was to yield to the request for a king, he was first to go on record with a warning of what kingship would mean in Israel.

B. Warning for the People (1 Samuel 8:10-18)

Samuel spoke all the words of Yahweh to the people. He warned them of what they could expect from their king, viz., military conscription, property seizure, etc. Ultimately all Israelites will be servants of the crown. Then, Samuel warned, the people will cry to Yahweh for relief because of the king that they were now demanding. The Lord, however, will not respond to their prayer in that day.

Insistence of the People
1 Samuel 8:19-22

In spite of the very negative portrayal of kingship, the people insisted that a king be appointed to rule over them as in surrounding nations. They wanted their king to be a Judge and a leader in battle as well. Samuel repeated all the words of the people to the Lord. Yahweh authorized Samuel to appoint a king for Israel. After assuring the people that they will get their king, Samuel dismissed the assembly to their respective cities.

END OF THE JUDGES PERIOD
We have now covered 358 Years of Bible History

SINGLE
KINGDOM PERIOD
National Greatness

Biblical Location: 1 Samuel 8-1 Kings 11 + Chronicles Chapters

Beginning Point: Saul Crowned (1048 BC)

Ending Point: Kingdom Split (930 BC)

Duration: 118 Years

Key Players: Samuel, Saul, David, Solomon

Key Events: Saul Disobeys, Goliath Defeated, David's Danger, Saul's Death, David's Anointing, David's Adultery, Absalom's Attack, Solomon's Temple

Scriptural Theme:
He [Solomon] sent the people to their homes, joyful and glad in heart for the good things the LORD had done for David and Solomon and for his people Israel (2 Chronicles 7:10 NIV).

Christian Application:
The Queen of the South will rise at the judgment with the men of this generation and condemn them; for she came from the ends of the earth to listen to Solomon's wisdom, and now one greater than Solomon is here (Luke 11:31 NIV).

13
ESTABLISHMENT OF
THE MONARCHY
1 Samuel 9-12

Chapter Chronology

	1047
2 Years	
1048	

Though the people indicated the kind of king they desired, they left the appointment of the candidate up to God's prophet. The choice was Saul the son of Kish. He became king of Israel in four stages:

- Private announcement: in Ramah.
- Public anointing: in Mizpah.
- Military achievement: at Jabesh.
- National acceptance: at Gilgal

PRIVATE ANOINTING
1 Samuel 9:1-10:16

Date: 1048 BC

Introduction to Saul
1 Samuel 9:1-2

The biblical text next introduces the man whom God had selected as Israel's first king. First, Saul was from Benjamin, smallest of the tribes. Leaders of the larger tribes no doubt viewed this selection as a happy compromise designed to eliminate tribal jealousies. Second, Saul was from a prominent family. This is indicated by the inclusion of a brief genealogical record in the text. Third, Saul's father Kish was *a mighty man of valor*. The reference is not so much to his physical strength as to the power that comes through wealth or influence. Fourth, Saul had outstanding physical attributes. He was handsome and he was tall, in fact taller than any of the people. The elders desired a king like all the nations. In ancient pictures of royalty the king is usually depicted as taller than any of his subjects.

Background
1 Samuel 9:3-17

A. Search for Donkeys (1 Samuel 9:3-10)

A curious set of circumstances resulted in the initial contact between Samuel and Saul. Kish had dispatched his son from Gibeah, three miles north of Jerusalem, to search for some lost donkeys. A wide-ranging search through several districts in central Palestine did not locate the lost animals. Saul was ready to give up the search lest his father become anxious over his whereabouts. His servant, however, suggested that Saul consult the local *man of God* about the donkeys. This man of God had a reputation for accurate prediction. Saul thought the servant's suggestion was a good one. He pointed out, however, a problem. The provisions were exhausted. There was nothing suitable to serve as the customary offering—an interview fee—to the man of God for his services. Fortunately, the servant had a fourth of a shekel of silver. Since coins were not used until much later in Israel's history, this quarter shekel was a weight. For that amount the man of God would be willing to give prophetic advice. Saul and his servant then set out for nearby Ramah, the city of Samuel.

B. Visit to Ramah (1 Samuel 9:11-17)

1. Information from young women (9:11-14): As they approached the city the two travelers met some young women going out to draw water. They learned that Samuel was scheduled to officiate at a sacrificial meal that very day. The people were waiting on him to arrive, for they would not begin the festivities without his blessing. The women advised the two men to intercept the prophet on his way to the *high place* where only invited guests were permitted to assemble. As Saul and his servant proceeded toward the city, they met Samuel on his way up to the *high place*.

2. Revelation to Samuel (9:15-17): Yahweh prepared Samuel for his meeting with Saul. The previous day the Lord had revealed (lit., uncovered his ear) that within twenty-four hours he was going to send to Samuel *a man from the land of Benjamin*. This man was to be anointed *prince* and be given the commission to save the people from the Philistines. When the prophet saw Saul, Yahweh made the identification even more specific. This was the man who would rule over (lit., keep within bounds) God's people.

Initial Indications of Choice
1 Samuel 9:18-25

A. Royal Invitation (1 Samuel 9:18-21)

Saul approached Samuel to inquire where the seer lived. Obviously he had never met the prophet before. Samuel identified himself. He then invited Saul to the *high place* as his personal guest. Before Saul had an opportunity to mention the problem of the lost donkeys, the prophet assured him that they had been found. Samuel thus demonstrated to Saul his supernatural knowledge. Then he asked two cryptic questions to pique the curiosity of Saul. *To whom is all the desire of Israel? Is it not to you and to all the house of your father?* The meaning is simple. Saul was the person who fulfilled Israel's desire for a king. He was the chosen one. Saul sensed that some great honor was being announced. However, he could not understand why Samuel spoke to him in this manner. He was from Benjamin, the smallest tribe, and even within that tribe his father's family had little standing.

B. Royal Treatment (1 Samuel 9:22-25)

The communal meal over which Samuel presided that day functioned as an anticipation of a coronation banquet. Saul was treated royally. He was seated in the most honored place at the head of the thirty invited guests. Then a choice portion of meat was set before him. Samuel told him that this portion had been reserved for him since the day this special feast had been announced. Samuel hinted that the whole purpose of the meal was to honor Saul! That night Saul was a guest at Samuel's home. All of this was designed to prepare Saul for the great announcement to be made the following day.

Anointing of Saul
1 Samuel 9:26-10:8

A. Action (1 Samuel 9:26-10:1)

Early in the morning, Samuel aroused Saul from his sleep on the flat roof of the prophet's home. He walked with Saul and his servant to the edge of the city. There the servant was dismissed, so that Samuel might declare the word of God to Saul privately. The prophet then took a flask of oil and poured in on Saul's head, kissed him on the cheek, and explained these actions with a rhetorical question: *Is it not so that Yahweh has anointed you as a prince over his inheritance?* The term *prince* (*naghid*) in this context probably means something like "crown prince" or "king designate."

B. Signs (1 Samuel 10:2-7)

Three supernatural signs were to confirm that Saul's anointing indeed had been ordained by Yahweh. First, Saul will encounter two men near Rachel's tomb who report that the donkeys had been found and that Saul's father was worried about his whereabouts. Second, Saul will meet three men at the oak of Tabor who were on their way to worship at Bethel. They will be carrying various items to be offered as sacrifice. One of these strangers will greet Saul, and give him two of the three loaves of bread he was carrying. Third, at the hill of God where a Philistine garrison was stationed Saul will meet a group of prophets coming down from a *high place,* playing their musical instruments and *prophesying.* In their presence Saul will be overwhelmed by the Spirit of Yahweh. His whole personality will change and he too will join in the vigorous prophetic praise of God. These three signs will assure Saul that God was with him in a special way.

C. Instructions (1 Samuel 10:8)

Guided by God, Saul was to do for himself what the occasion required. The reference most likely is to the Philistine menace, for this seems to form the background for the demand for a king (cf. 9:16). One restriction was placed on Saul as he exercised his God-guided military leadership. Before he initiated hostilities against the Philistines, he was to go down to Gilgal in the Jordan valley and wait seven days for Samuel. The prophet intended to do two things: 1) to offer sacrifices; and 2) show Saul what he should do. The campaign to deal with the Philistines must be launched with divine blessing and prophetic guidance.

D. Confirmation (1 Samuel 10:9-13)

As Saul turned to leave Samuel, *God changed his heart.* The three signs announced by Samuel came about that very day. The Spirit of God rushed upon him thus indicating that Saul was a deliverer like the Judges before him (cf. Judges 11:29; 14:6 etc.). The quiet country boy became a vigorous public proclaimer of praise to Yahweh, and that right in the shadow of a Philistine garrison (cf. v. 5). People who previously knew Saul were astonished that one so shy was now drawn to a band of religious enthusiasts. A bystander rebuked the shocked observers by means of the question, *Who is their father?* The question suggests that one is not born a prophet. God's Spirit is what compelled men to join the prophetic band.[18]

E. Silence (1 Samuel 10:14-16)

When Saul reached home, his uncle questioned him about his long absence. In the light of the context of 1 Samuel this uncle was most likely Abner who later became the general of Israel's army. Saul briefly rehearsed the events of the past few days, but he did not volunteer information about the matter of the kingdom.

Saul Presented Publicly
1 Samuel 10:17-27

A. Brief Speech (1 Samuel 10:17-19)

One may assume that Samuel called for the people to *gather to Yahweh at Mizpah* very soon after the private anointing at Ramah. The old prophet opened the assembly with a brief speech in which he reminded the audience of all that God had done for them in the deliverance from Egyptian bondage and oppressions by neighboring nations. By taking the initiative in demanding a king, the people had rejected the God who had delivered them from all their past calamities. Nevertheless, Samuel ordered the people to present themselves before Yahweh by their tribes and clans.

B. Sacred Lot (1 Samuel 10:20-22)

---

[18]The question *Who is their father?* has been interpreted in a variety of ways. Some think the sense is that the prophets have no father and hence are a disreputable band with which Saul should have nothing to do. Others think the term *father* refers to the leader and interpreter of the group, *viz.,* Samuel. Hence the thought is, Why criticize Saul for joining the prophetic band when their *father* is none other than Samuel?

Though the mechanics of the sacred lot in Old Testament times are not known, certainly the process was controlled by Yahweh. In the person of their representatives, all the tribes of Israel one by one drew near to Samuel. Presumably the tribe of Benjamin, descended from the youngest of Jacob's twelve sons, was last. The lot indicated that Yahweh had chosen this tribe. Then the representatives of the clans of Benjamin drew near to Samuel and the Matrite clan was chosen. At this point the names of all the heads of families within the Matrite clan where perhaps placed on potsherds. By lot Saul the son of Kish was selected. When they looked for Saul, however, he could not be found. Further inquiry of Yahweh through the prophet Samuel revealed that Saul was hiding by the baggage.

C. Saul Introduced (1 Samuel 10:23-24)

Leaders hastened to bring Saul from his hiding place. When Saul stood among the people he was head and shoulders taller than any of his countrymen. Physically Saul qualified to be the kind of king Israel wanted. Samuel made sure that the audience understood that the unusual proceedings of that day were Yahweh's means of making known his selection for Israel's king. The people ratified the appointment by shouting the traditional *Long live the king*.

D. Kingdom Document (1 Samuel 10:25)

Samuel then set forth *the judgment of the kingdom,* i.e., the constitutional, historical and spiritual basis for the monarchy in Israel. This material was written by the prophet in *the scroll*. The reference may be to the scroll of Scripture which Samuel was now expanding. The scroll was then placed *before Yahweh,* i.e., in a sacred shrine, perhaps even before the ark of God. This act recognized that the written words of Samuel possessed divine authority like Moses and Joshua before him.

E. Mixed Response (1 Samuel 10:26-27)

When Samuel dismissed the people from Mizpah, Saul returned to Gibeah. Some valiant men *whose hearts God had touched* went with him. Certain *sons of Belial,* i.e., worthless men, mocked the appointment of the timid farmer from Gibeah. They despised him and brought him no gift in token of submission to his authority. Saul wisely refused to take action against his critics. He knew that he would have the opportunity soon enough to prove his mettle.

206

RESCUE OF JABESH
1 Samuel 11:1-11

Date: 1047 BC

Background
1 Samuel 11:1-3

A. Attack by Nahash (1 Samuel 11:1-2)

The test for Saul's leadership unexpectedly came, not from the Philistines to the west, but from the Ammonites across the Jordan. Nahash besieged the Israelite outpost of Jabesh in the region of Gilead.[19] Realizing that they had no chance of successfully resisting the siege, the men of Jabesh expressed willingness to become vassals of the Ammonite. Nahash, however, was not willing to settle for this type of submission. He wanted to inflict a humiliating defeat upon this Israelite town. Only if the men of Jabesh allowed Nahash to gouge out their right eyes would he be willing to enter into a covenant with them. Nahash wanted to make Jabesh *a reproach* in all Israel.

B. Appeal of Jabesh (1 Samuel 11:3)

When they realized that Nahash was in no mood to negotiate, the elders of Jabesh requested a seven-day reprieve so that they might seek deliverance from other tribes. Nahash was so confident of the political disarray of Israel that he actually granted the request of the elders. Even if other tribes should respond to the plea of Jabesh, Nahash was confident that he would be able to defeat the Israelites.

The messengers headed straight for Saul's town of Gibeah. Apparently few, if any, of the trappings of royalty marked the earliest days of the monarchy in Israel. Saul was out working with his oxen in the fields when the messengers arrived. The people of Gibeah lamented loudly when they heard the news from Jabesh.

---

[19]On the basis of one of the Dead Sea scrolls (4Q Sam^a) NRSV "restores" material that may have fallen out of the standard text of Samuel in the process of copying. This "missing" text relates how Nahash had been oppressing the Transjordan tribes for some time, gouging out the right eyes of all who fell into his hands. Seven thousand who had escaped from his hand had entered into Jabesh-gilead. About a month after they took refuge there, Nahash came against the city. The argument for regarding this material as part of the original text of Samuel is far from convincing.

207

Saul's Decisive Actions
1 Samuel 11:4-10

A. Threatening Message (1 Samuel 11:4-7)

When Saul learned of the brutal demands of Nahash, *the Spirit of God* rushed upon him. As a result he was filled with righteous anger. Whereas in other contexts the blowing of a horn mustered the tribes for a holy war, Saul determined that more dramatic action was necessary. He dismembered a yoke of oxen and sent the pieces throughout the territory of Israel by messengers, perhaps the same messengers who had come from Jabesh. The chunks of meat were to be visual aids to reinforce the first royal edict. If any man failed to report for military duty to follow Saul and Samuel, his oxen would be slaughtered (cf. Judges 19:29-30). Mentioning Samuel's name in this call to arms indicates the insecurity that Saul felt in his royal rank at this time.

B. Numbering Troops (1 Samuel 11:8)

Saul's dramatic action put the fear of Yahweh in the men of Israel. They assembled as one man to Bezek, the town near the Jordan that had been designated as the staging area for the Jabesh operation. There Saul numbered and organized his men. From Judah 30,000 men had responded, and from the other tribes 300,000.

C. Misinformation (1 Samuel 11:9-10)

The messengers from Jabesh were sent back with the glad news that deliverance was at hand. By the time the sun got hot the next day, the army of Israel planned to be there to rescue them. The men of Jabesh immediately sent word to Nahash that they were willing to surrender themselves to him the following day. He could then do with them whatever he had determined to do. This report no doubt lulled Nahash into a false sense of security. He most likely took no ordinary military precautions to prevent a surprise attack.

Defeat of the Ammonites
1 Samuel 11:11-13

A. Strategy (1 Samuel 11:11)

During the night the Israelite forces drew near. Saul organized his troops into three units, probably to facilitate a pinchers movement

208

against the enemy. During the morning watch (2 AM to 6 AM), the attack was launched. The battle turned out to be a slaughter of Ammonites. Only a few stragglers survived.

B. Saul's New Status (1 Samuel 11:12-15)

The brilliant and decisive defeat of the Ammonites convinced everyone that Saul indeed was the right choice for king. The people came to Samuel—he apparently had accompanied the troops to Jabesh—to urge that those who had vocally opposed Saul's anointing now be executed. Saul, however, would have none of that. Yahweh had granted deliverance in Israel. This was no day for recrimination, but for celebration. Samuel agreed.

Capitalizing on the current enthusiasm, Samuel urged the people to assemble at the ancient shrine of Gilgal to *renew the kingdom,* i.e., to give everyone an opportunity to express their support for Saul. So the people went to Gilgal and *made Saul king* before Yahweh. Burnt offerings and peace offerings were presented to the Lord. Unlike the Mizpah meeting that ended in mixed opinion about Saul a few months (?) earlier, at the Gilgal assembly Saul and all the men of Israel rejoiced together greatly.

Samuel's Valedictory
1 Samuel 12:1-25

At the Gilgal assembly Samuel delivered his valedictory. In so doing he resigned, in effect, from the office of Judge. The speech is interspersed with responses from the people and the description of a manifestation of God, a theophany.

A. Charges against Israel (1 Samuel 12:1-12)

1. Lifetime of faithful service (12:1-2): In the prologue to his speech, Samuel elicited from the people an acknowledgement that the integrity of his leadership had not been compromised. First, he mentioned the fact that he had done what they had asked him to do, viz., he had appointed a king for them. Their king was now *walking before* them, i.e., installed in office. Second, Samuel refers to himself as *old and gray,* perhaps suggesting that it was time for him to step down from his role of political leader. Third, Samuel made reference to his sons who are *with you.* Perhaps this was a father's way of admitting the painful truth that his sons were not in fact worthy of succeeding their father in the office of Judge (cf. 1 Samuel 8:3, 5). Fourth, Samuel reminds them of his lengthy service to the nation *from my youth even to this day.* Samuel had *walked before* them, i.e., he had been a public figure his entire life.

2. *Challenge to name his transgressions (12:3-5):* Samuel then challenged the audience to bear witness against him if they knew of any situation in which he had abused his power as Judge by taking bribes or defrauding citizens. The assembly unanimously agreed that Samuel had never abused his office in any way. Then Samuel in effect made the people swear before Yahweh and his anointed Saul that they could find no ill-gotten gain in his hand.

3. *What God had done for them (12:6-9):* Samuel devoted a major part of his address to demonstrating the many *righteous acts* that Yahweh had performed for his people. When the Israelites cried out in the midst of Egyptian bondage, Yahweh raised up Moses and Aaron to bring them out of the land of oppression. The Lord settled his people in Canaan. When, however, they proved time and again to be unfaithful to him, Yahweh delivered them into the hands of oppressing nations. In each of those oppressions the people cried out to Yahweh, confessing their sins and begging for deliverance. The Lord responded by sending Jerubbaal (Gideon), Bedan (Barak?), Jephthah and Samuel to deliver Israel from the hand of their foreign oppressors.

4. *Their ingratitude (12:10-12):* The request for a king had been triggered by the oppression of Nahash the Ammonite. Instead of trusting God to supply deliverance, the people had resolved to find their own solution. They insisted on having a king like all the nations even though the Lord had never failed them in so far as they were faithful to him. Thus history bore testimony that God faithfully had performed the royal office. The request for a king had been premature, unnecessary, and insulting to the Lord.

B. Conditions for God's Blessing (1 Samuel 12:13-15)

Samuel next addressed the present realities. Israel had now formally chosen as king the man God had ordained. Hence *Yahweh has set a king over you.* The requirement of Israel was to fear Yahweh, i.e., to serve and obey him. Following the Lord will lead to national blessing. On the other hand, the path of disobedience will bring the hand of Yahweh against them just as it had been against their fathers in times of their spiritual rebellion.

C. Confirmatory Sign (1 Samuel 12:16-18)

A miraculous sign was needed to underscore in the minds of the people the gravity of their sin in requesting a king. Samuel called attention to the time of the year. Wheat harvest was in progress. This was the dry season when rain scarcely ever falls in Palestine. Yet Samuel announced that he will call upon Yahweh to sent thunder and rain. One wonders if this announcement was greeted with skepticism by the assembly. Be that as it may, when the old prophet prayed, the thunder and rain came. Then the people greatly feared Yahweh and his servant Samuel.

D. Encouragement and Warning (1 Samuel 12:19-25)

1. Request for intercession (12:19): The ferocious thunderstorm got the message across. The people feared for their lives. They sensed the enormity of their sin against Yahweh. They immediately pled for Samuel to make intercession for them that they might not die.

2. Exhortation (12:20-21): Samuel calmed their fears. Yet he used the occasion to press for future strict and heartfelt obedience to Yahweh. If they ceased to serve Yahweh, they would inevitably follow after *futile things,* i.e., idols. Such *gods* were of no benefit to any nation since they could not deliver from danger.

3. Declaration of God's faithfulness (12:22): Yahweh, on the other hand, had chosen Israel as his own people. His divine name (honor, reputation) was bound up in the fate of this nation. Therefore he will not abandon Israel even though the nation had committed a grievous sin against him.

4. Pledge of continued leadership (12:23): Even though he was stepping down as Judge, Samuel did not relinquish his office of prophet. His prophetic responsibilities under the monarchy were twofold: 1) prayer and 2) instruction. Under no circumstances will Samuel sin against Yahweh by ceasing to pray for Israel. Intercessory prayer was a fundamental attribute of a prophet (cf. Genesis 20:7, 17). In addition to his prayers for Israel, Samuel will continue to instruct them *in the good and right way.*

5. Warning (12:24-25): Samuel's valedictory concluded with an admonition for Israel to *fear Yahweh and serve him in truth.* Heartfelt and cheerful obedience were the only proper responses to all the great things Yahweh had done for his people. On the other hand, if Israel

211

arrogantly insisted upon its own way, both the people and their king would be swept away.

14
REJECTION OF SAUL
1 Samuel 13-15

Chapter Chronology

	1029
18 Years of Saul's Reign	
1046	

Two important pieces of chronological data are missing in 13:1: the age of Saul when he began to reign; and the length of Saul's reign. The English translators have supplied in italics figures that represent an intelligent guess. Saul was probably between thirty and forty at the time he was anointed king. The length of his reign was something like thirty-two years. For some reason in the ancient transcription of the text of Samuel these figures dropped out.

The purpose of 1 Samuel 13-17 seems to be to document the deterioration of the reign of Saul. The author speaks of Saul's sinful impatience, foolish zeal, blatant rebellion, and faltering leadership. In three steps the rejection of Saul is made clear. First, Samuel announced that Saul will have no lasting dynasty. Second, Samuel declared that Saul personally had been rejected by the Lord. Third, Samuel went to Bethlehem to anoint one who was to be Saul's replacement in kingship.

GILGAL INCIDENT
1 Samuel 13:2-22

Date: ca. 1041 BC
Background
1 Samuel 13:2-7

Once the reins of government had been turned over to him, Saul devoted himself to the priority of his reign, viz., rescuing his people from the Philistines (cf. 1 Samuel 9:16).

A. Standing Army (1 Samuel 13:2)

213

How much time elapsed between the defeat of Nahash and the events of 1 Samuel 13 is not stated. Probably Saul wanted to capitalize on the zeal that the people manifested for his reign at the reaffirmation ceremony in chapter 12. Be that as it may, at some point Saul began to organize a standing army. As a nucleus he chose for himself 3,000 men. Of these, a thousand stayed with Saul at Michmash, while another thousand under the direct authority of the king were stationed near Bethel. The third thousand was with Saul's son Jonathan at Gibeah of Benjamin. The rest of the people were sent home.

B. Outbreak of Hostilities (1 Samuel 13:3-4)

Hostilities with the Philistines were triggered by the actions of Jonathan. He and his men attacked the Philistine garrison at Geba. Whether Jonathan acted on orders from his father or on his own initiative cannot be determined. In any case, this action made the Israelites odious to the Philistines. Anticipating a retaliatory invasion by the Philistines, Saul had the trumpet blown throughout the land. He alerted the *Hebrews,* those Israelites and kindred souls who had been mercenaries of the Philistines. Then he summoned the people of Israel to Gilgal.

C. Philistine Invasion (1 Samuel 13:5-7)

The Philistines assembled a massive army to invade Israel: 30,000 chariots, 6,000 horsemen, and infantry without number. This force camped at Michmash, Saul's former headquarters. The men of Israel had no will to resist such a vast host. They began to desert, taking refuge in terrain that they thought was inaccessible to the Philistines. Some of the Hebrews even fled across the Jordan. Though Saul and his troops remained in Gilgal, they were trembling at the prospects of having to do battle with the Philistines.

Sin at Gilgal
1 Samuel 13:8-14

A. Saul's Impatient Wait (1 Samuel 13:8-10)

Saul waited seven days for Samuel to appear in Gilgal. Each day more of his troops were deserting. Finally Saul ordered burnt offerings and peace offerings to be prepared. He himself seems to have officiated at the sacrifice. Just as Saul finished offering the burnt offering, Samuel appeared. Saul went out to greet him as though nothing were amiss.

B. Saul called to Account (1 Samuel 13:11-12)

Samuel demanded an explanation for Saul's action. The king defended himself with three arguments. First, he blamed his actions on the people. They were scattering, and he needed to do something to boost morale. Second, he blamed Samuel: *You* (the pronoun is emphatic in the Hebrew) did not appear within the appointed days. Third, he blamed the Philistines. They were assembling at Michmash for an all-out attack on Israel. Saul was convinced that the Philistines were about to attack him at Gilgal. Offering sacrifices before a holy war was customary. Therefore, the king said: *I forced myself* to offer the burnt offering.

C. Punishment Announced (1 Samuel 13:13-14)

Samuel did not bother to answer any of Saul's excuses. He simply stated a twofold assessment of the king's actions. First, Saul had acted foolishly; and second, he had disobeyed the commandment of Yahweh. Had he been obedient Saul would have been the founder of a long-lived dynasty. Now, however, the divine sentence is that Saul's dynasty will not endure. Yahweh already had sought out for himself *a man after his own heart.* This unnamed man will become the ruler of God's people because Saul had not done what the Lord had commanded him.

Saul's Predicament
1 Samuel 13:15-23

A. His Forces (1 Samuel 13:15-18)

Saul was now in quite a predicament. Samuel deserted him. He had left Gilgal bound for Gibeah of Benjamin. Saul no longer had the benefit of prophetic guidance. Then Saul numbered *the people* and found only six hundred still with him. With this little band Saul took up defensive positions near Geba of Benjamin. He was helpless to deal with the raiding parties dispatched to the north, to the south and to the west from the Philistine base camp at Michmash. Yet he was determined to defend his own tribal area of Benjamin.

B. His Weaponry (1 Samuel 13:19-22)

Lack of proper weaponry exacerbated Saul's predicament. The Philistines had removed all the blacksmiths from Israel, thus thwarting the manufacture of swords and spears. Israelites were forced to travel down to the Philistine plain to get their agricultural implements sharpened. Since the Philistines had a monopoly on the smelting and working of iron, they charged exorbitant prices—two thirds of a shekel—just to sharpen or repair Israelite tools. Such prices made weapons unaffordable to the average Israelite. All of this the author relates so that his readers may understand why it was that only Saul and Jonathan had proper spears and swords on the eve of battle. The rank and file was armed with clubs, slings and perhaps other weapons made of bronze.

C. Philistine Movement (1 Samuel 13:23)
The showdown with the Philistine invaders began when the enemy base camp moved south toward the pass of Michmash. The courage of Saul in facing this force with only six hundred under armed soldiers is to be commended.

VICTORY
OVER THE PHILISTINES
1 Samuel 14:1-46

Date: 1041 BC
Courageous Action at Micmash
1 Samuel 14:1-23

Early in his reign Saul decided to challenge the Philistine domination of Israel. The initial effort against this formidable foe was successful almost in spite of Saul. The king here is depicted as pious, though his piety seemed to paralyze rather than energize the effort. Yet through the courageous faith of Jonathan and the awesome power of Yahweh the Philistines were put to flight. In the previous chapter Saul lost the hope of dynastic succession. Here the author portrays the sterling qualities of Jonathan, the man who might have been king.

A. Background (1 Samuel 14:1-3)
For a time Saul failed to take any action against the Philistines. Once again (cf. 13:3) Jonathan decided to initiate the battle by attacking an outpost guarding the pass between Michmash and Geba.

His courageous faith stands out in bold relief against the background of Saul's paralysis. The king had only six hundred men in his encampment on the outskirts of Gibeah. Saul's force was small, yet the high priest was there wearing the ephod and the ark of God was also there (v. 18). Perhaps the author intends to say that Saul's situation was desperate, but not hopeless.

B. Attack at Michmash (1 Samuel 14:4-15)

1. Jonathan's challenge (14:4-7): Jonathan attempted to bolster the confidence of his young armorbearer by reminding him of two things. First, the enemy was *uncircumcised.* This was a kind of ethnic slur used to mock the enemy and thus express confidence in victory (cf. 1 Samuel 17:26, 36). Second, Jonathan stressed that Yahweh is capable of giving victories to the few as well as to the many. Yet Jonathan did not presume that his action automatically would fall within the will of God. *Perhaps,* he said to his armorbearer, *Yahweh will work for us.* The armorbearer pledged to stand with Jonathan no matter what decision he made.

2. Jonathan's plan (14:8-10): Jonathan and his armorbearer were to reveal themselves to the Philistines who controlled the heights above. If the enemy ordered them to halt they would not ascend the height. If the Philistines challenged them to climb up, Jonathan would regard that as a sign that Yahweh would give a victory. Such a challenge by the Philistines would indicate overconfidence, even carelessness. Since this fight with the Philistines was a holy war ordered by a prophet (10:8) and consecrated by sacrifices, Jonathan believed God would make his will clear.

3. Jonathan's victory (14:11-15): When the Philistines spotted Jonathan and his armorbearer, they assumed that they were *Hebrews* coming out of hiding. They therefore challenged the two to climb up to their camp. Jonathan then began to make the precipitous climb confident that the victory was his. When they reached the top Jonathan and his armorbearer slew twenty of the enemy in a very small area. Before the main force of the Philistines could come to the aid of their outpost, a tremendous earthquake shook the ground. The enemy was thrown into panic and began to flee back toward their homeland.

C. Saul's Response (1 Samuel 14:16-17)

1. *Aborted priestly oracle (14:16-20a):* Israelite lookouts observed great confusion in the Philistine camp. Saul suspected that some of his men had attacked the enemy. A quick numbering of his troops revealed the absence of Jonathan and his armorbearer. Saul ordered the high priest to bring the ark of God forward. Saul was making inquiry through the priestly oracle about his next move. Before the priest could complete the ritual inquiry, however, it became obvious that the Philistine camp was engaged in battle. Saul rallied his troops to join the fray.

2. *Philistine rout (14:20b-23):* As they approached the battlefield Saul witnessed the total confusion of the enemy. The Hebrew mercenaries within the Philistine army had rebelled. The Philistines were in full retreat. News of the rout of the Philistines spread like wildfire. Israelites that had hidden away in the mountains came forth to join the pursuit. The battle spread beyond Beth-aven. So Yahweh delivered Israel that day.

Saul's Rash Curse
1 Samuel 14:24-46

A. Imposition of the Curse (1 Samuel 14:24)

After reporting the glorious victory, the author focuses on a rash curse that nearly turned victory into calamity. Anxious that his men not lose the advantage over the Philistines, Saul placed a curse on anyone who stopped during the day to eat. The well-being of his men was of no concern to Saul *until I take vengeance on my enemies.* These words suggest selfishness on Saul's part, even fanatical zeal. He had lost the sense that the Philistines were Yahweh's enemies, and he was fighting Yahweh's battle. Not only did Saul's foolish oath work a hardship on his soldiers; other terrible consequences followed as well.

B. Violation of the Curse (1 Samuel 14:25-30)

Pursuing the enemy through a forest, the Israelite soldiers spotted an abandoned honeycomb that was oozing wild honey. None of the soldiers dared to touch that tempting treat because they feared the curse of their king. Jonathan, however, knew nothing of the oath. Therefore as he continued the pursuit, he dipped the end of his staff in the honeycomb and put it to his mouth. Immediately *his eyes brightened,* i.e., he experienced a sudden surge of energy. When informed about his father's oath Jonathan was discouraged. He called attention to the difference in his energy level and that of the men. An even greater victory over the Philistines would have been possible had Saul not *troubled the land* with his foolish oath. Perhaps Jonathan should not have spoken so critically of his father in front of the troops.

C. Defilement of the Troops (1 Samuel 14:31-35)

1. Eating improper meat (14:31-32): Another direct result of Saul's curse occurred at the end of the day. The Israelites had chased the Philistines as far as Aijalon some twenty miles west of where the battle was first joined. The troops now were faint from lack of food. As soon as the sun set, they pounced on the spoil of livestock. The animals were slaughtered on the ground. No provision was made for the proper drainage of blood (cf. Leviticus 19:26; Deuteronomy 12:16). The meat was eaten *with the blood,* which was a violation of Mosaic Law.

2. Saul's response (14:33-35): Saul was soon told that his troops were sinning against Yahweh by eating *with the blood.* Saul referred to what his men had done as *treachery.* He ordered a stone rolled to the spot. Officers circulated among the troops ordering them to bring their livestock to the central stone for slaughter. The stone was considered an altar, the first altar that Saul erected.

D. Transgression Discovered (1 Samuel 14:36-45)

1. Silent oracle (14:36-37): After the men had eaten, Saul determined that it was a good idea to press the attack against the Philistines into the night. The officers agreed, but the priest (Ahijah) suggested that it might be wise to *draw near to God,* i.e., seek an oracle regarding the proposed pursuit. So Saul inquired of God about the matter, but God did not answer him on that day through the Urim and Thummim of the high priest. By this silence Yahweh rebuked the rash piety of Saul in taking the oath in the first place.

2. Saul's second rash oath (14:37-39): Saul realized that there must be sin in the camp. He called upon his officers to investigate and report how the sin occurred. Then Saul took another oath. Even if the guilty party were prince Jonathan, he would still die for having violated the solemn curse of the king. Though it was generally known through the ranks that Jonathan had violated his father's curse, no one ventured to point the finger of accusation at him.

3. *Jeopardy of Jonathan (14:40-42).* Since no one would report any violation of the royal curse, Saul determined to find the guilty party in another manner. He cast lots. The first lot was between the royal family (Saul and Jonathan) and the troops. The king prayed for the Lord to give a perfect lot. Saul must have been shocked when the lot indicated that the guilt was in the royal family. A second lot was cast between Saul and his son. The lot indicated Jonathan.

4. *Jonathan interrogated (14:43-44):* Saul then interrogated Jonathan. The prince confessed to tasting a little honey during the midst of the battle. Now that Saul had bound himself by an oath to execute the guilty party, Jonathan was fully prepared to accept his fate. Then Saul took a third oath that reinforced the second. Jonathan must surely die.

5. *Intervention of the troops (14:45):* At this point the troops intervened. These soldiers gave the credit for the victory over the Philistines to Jonathan. He could only have accomplished what he had accomplished if he had *worked with God.* Therefore Jonathan should not die. The troops took an oath that not one hair of Jonathan's head would fall to the ground. Thus the oath of the many took precedence over the oath of the one, even if the one was the king. In this case Saul must have been very relieved that his troops overruled him.[20]

E. End of the Battle (1 Samuel 14:46)

Since his troops in effect had mutinied against him, any further pursuit of the Philistines became impossible. Saul and his men returned home. The Philistines withdrew from Israelite territory. They planned to return to fight another day.

AMALEK INCIDENT
1 Samuel 15:1-35

Date: ca. 1029 BC

Chapter 15 is devoted completely to events surrounding Saul's war with the Amalekites. Saul's dynasty was rejected in chapter 13.

---

[20]The text says that the troops *redeemed* (*padah*) Jonathan. This may mean they rescued him by insisting on his release. On the other hand, if the word "redeem" is used in its legal sense some price may have been paid for Jonathan's redemption, either money (Exodus 21:30; Numbers 3:46-51), or an animal substitute (Exodus 13:13, 15; 34:20). Some modern writers have even proposed that another man died in the place of Jonathan.

220

Here the king personally is rejected for disobedience to a direct command of Yahweh. The text supplies no information that allows a calculation of the time interval between chapters 14 and 15.

Background
1 Samuel 15:1-6

A. Commission of Saul (1 Samuel 15:1-3)

As Yahweh's anointed, Saul had an obligation to listen to what Yahweh said through his prophet Samuel. The Lord determined to punish Amalek for the obstruction that they had been to Israel at the time of the Exodus (Exodus 17:8-16; Deuteronomy 25:17-19). Though some four centuries had elapsed, Yahweh had not forgotten the threat that he had made concerning the Amalekites. Since in the intervening centuries Amalek had shown no signs of national repentance, that nation was now to be put under the ban, i.e., totally destroyed (Deuteronomy 7:2; 20:17). Nothing was to be spared.

B. Movements of Saul's Army (1 Samuel 15:4-6)

1. Numbering (15:4): Saul promptly summoned the people for a holy war against Amalek. He numbered his troops at the staging area of Telaim in the Negev of Judah some thirty miles south of Hebron. His large force—200,000 from Israel, and 10,000 from Judah—was necessary to chase the Amalekites across the sprawling desert. The point is that Saul had enough forces to carry out his mandate.

2. Warning to Kenites (15:5-6): Before going to war against the Amalekites, Saul warned the Kenites to leave the area lest they be caught up in the fighting. The Kenites were old allies of Israel dating back to the days of the Exodus.

Saul's Disobedience
1 Samuel 15:7-29

A. Nature of his Sin (1 Samuel 15:7-9)

While Saul concentrated on *the city of Amalek,* contingents of his army chased down the Amalekites from Havilah (northwest Arabia) to the borders of Egypt. Saul executed every Amalekite he could get hands on with one exception. He spared their king Agag. He and his troops were also unwilling to destroy the best of the livestock. Hence

221

Saul failed to put Amalek under the ban as ordered. In effect he committed the same sin as Achan had committed during the conquest.

B. Confrontation with Samuel (1 Samuel 15:10-21)

1. Revelation to Samuel (15:10-11): By revelation Samuel learned the sad truth about Saul. The king's actions caused Yahweh to be sorry that he had ever made Saul king. Saul had been warned that only if he honored God through obedience would he be blessed, and if he did not he would be rejected. Thus Yahweh's change of attitude toward Saul was not a change of purpose. For God to be unchanging in his purpose, he had to now change his attitude toward Saul. Samuel felt great distress over the matter. He cried out all that night in prayer to the Lord.

2. Meeting at Gilgal (15:12-13): Early in the morning Samuel set out to find Saul. He learned from travelers that Saul had returned to Carmel, a town seven miles south of Hebron. There Saul had erected a monument to celebrate his victory over Amalek. From there Saul was going to Gilgal. As Samuel approached Saul gave him a warm greeting in which he enthusiastically declared that he had carried out the commandment of Yahweh. Either Saul was bluffing, or he was part of that group in every age who think that partial obedience is acceptable to the Lord.

3. Saul called to account (15:14-15): Samuel cut short the blustering of the king. He called attention to the noise being made by the numerous livestock spared by Saul. The king then blamed *the people,* i.e., his troops, for sparing the best of the animals so that they might offer sacrifices to Yahweh. Saul was making two grave leadership mistakes. First, he was attempting to shift the blame to others. Even if true these excuses would be tantamount to an admission that Saul had no control over his troops. Second, he attempted to use a religious pretext as an excuse for disobedience. His words suggest that religious sincerity is a valid substitute for obedience to God. Besides this, in the peace offering most of the sacrificial animal was eaten by the worshipers. Had Saul really wished to give those animals to God he would have slain them as ordered in the first place.

4. Saul rebuked (15:16-19): "Stop" (NIV) Samuel said. "Enough of your excuses! Hear what Yahweh revealed to me last night." Saul agreed to listen. A rhetorical question reminded Saul that Yahweh had elevated him to kingship even when he in his own eyes was unworthy of such honor. He also reminded Saul of the precise words of the recent commission. The Amalekites were sinners. He had been commissioned to fight against them until they were exterminated. Why then, Samuel asked, did Saul commit evil by disobeying the voice of Yahweh? Samuel rejected any distinction between what Saul had done and what the troops had done. He placed total responsibility on the king.

5. *More excuses (15:20-21):* Saul strongly rejected Samuel's accusation that he had disobeyed the Lord. He had spared only Agag. The people had spared the choicest livestock to sacrifice to Yahweh *your* God at Gilgal. Saul ignored the fact that the Amalekite livestock already had been devoted to God by being placed under the ban. They therefore could not legitimately be presented to God as sacrifice (Leviticus 27:29; Deuteronomy 13:16).

Rejection by the Lord
1 Samuel 15:22-31

A. Samuel's Announcement (1 Samuel 15:22-23)

Samuel forcefully rejected Saul's contention that religious intention justifies selective obedience. *To obey is better than sacrifice.* No amount of religious ritual can substitute for doing what God commands. To be valid, external religious observance must reflect internal faith and piety. Rebellion and insubordination are sins equivalent in seriousness to divination and idolatry. Conscious disobedience is like idolatry in that one makes an idol out of the human will. The punishment suited the crime. Saul had rejected the word of Yahweh; therefore *Yahweh has rejected you from being king!*

B. Saul's Contrition (1 Samuel 15:24-25)

Samuel's announcement knocked the bluster out of Saul. He now realized the seriousness of what he had done. In humble contrition Saul confessed his transgression in listening to the voice of the people rather than to the words of Yahweh and his prophet. He begged that he might be pardoned, that Samuel might join him in public worship.

C. Penalty Repeated (1 Samuel 15:26-29)

Samuel at this point refused to join Saul in worship. The king might interpret his presence as tantamount to forgiveness of the transgression. Saul had been rejected as king and therefore Samuel

223

could not any longer give him public support. With that parting word Samuel turned to leave. In desperation Saul seized Samuel's robe. This constituted a final act of supplication on his part. The robe tore. The prophet used the torn robe to illustrate his announcement. Yahweh had torn the kingdom out of the hands of Saul and had given that kingdom to someone more worthy of it. Furthermore, Samuel added, *the Glory of Israel,* i.e., Yahweh, does not lie. He will not change his mind about the kingdom.

D. Saul's Request (1 Samuel 15:30-31)

For the second time, Saul acknowledged his sin and accepted his fate. He made one last request of the prophet. He asked Samuel to honor him before the elders and people by accompanying him back to Gilgal. This time Saul's request was not accompanied by a request for pardon. Since the king would not misunderstand his presence, Samuel followed him back to Gilgal. There Saul worshiped Yahweh, i.e., offered sacrifices to him. Samuel's presence acknowledged that the sinful king retained his office for the time being.

Execution of Agag
1 Samuel 15:32-33

After the worship ceremony concluded, Samuel demanded that Agag be brought to him. Agag came to him *cheerfully* (NASB) or *confidently* (NIV). The joyous worship celebration had convinced him that his life was no more in danger. Samuel, however, was of a different mind. He first pronounced sentence on the Amalekite. Agag's sword had made many women childless, so now his own mother would be childless. With those words of judgment Samuel hewed Agag to pieces *before Yahweh,* i.e., before Yahweh's altar at Gilgal. By slaying Agag, Samuel was executing the death sentence that the Lord already had pronounced against this king and his people.

Estrangement from Saul
1 Samuel 15:34-35

After the episode at Gilgal, both Samuel and Saul returned to their respective homes at Ramah and Gibeah. Samuel did not see Saul again in his advisory capacity until the day he died. During Samuel's last days he grieved over Saul. Yahweh also *regretted that he had made Saul king,* i.e., Yahweh grieved over the tragic fall of Saul as well.

FOOTNOTES
ON SAUL'S REIGN
1 Samuel 14:47-52

A. Military Accomplishments (1 Samuel 14:47-48)

The author now interjects a brief summary of other accomplishments of Saul's reign. Saul was successful in campaigns against Moab and Ammon to the east, Edom to the south, Zobah to the north, and the Philistines to the west. Saul was credited with defeating the Amalekites and other marauding desert tribes who *plundered* Israel from time to time. Thus Saul was doing what Israel's judges had done before him (cf. Judges 2:16).

B. Family (1 Samuel 14:49-51)

By his wife Ahinoam Saul had three sons and two daughters. The sons were Jonathan, Ishvi and Malchishua. The daughters were Merab and Michal. The captain of Saul's army was his uncle Abner.[21]

C. Negative Note (1 Samuel 14:52)

Chapter 14 closes with one other negative note about the king. Saul's recruiting policy marked a major shift from the emergency tribal levy that had served Israel to this point. Any men capable of military leadership were pressed into service on the royal staff. Such a policy became necessary because of the uninterrupted nature of the conflict with the Philistines.

---

[21]The *uncle* in 14:50 could have been either Ner or Abner as its antecedent. Whether Abner was Saul's uncle or cousin is unclear. Supporting the first interpretation are 1 Chronicles 8:33 and 9:39. According to this interpretation Ner has been omitted between Kish and Abiel in 1 Samuel 9:1. The second view sees Ner and Kish as brothers, sons of Abiel (1 Chronicles 9:36). This interpretation requires that one emend the word "son" to "sons" in 1 Samuel 14:51.

Chart 8 *Saul's Sons*		
1 Samuel 14:49	**1 Samuel 21:1**	**1 Chronicles 8:33**
Sons	Sons	Sons
(1) Jonathan	(1) Jonathan	(1) Jonathan
(2) Ishvi	(2) Ishvi	(2) Malchishua
(3) Malchishua	(3) Malchishua	(3) Abinadab
Daughters		(4) Esh-baal
(1) Merab		
(2) Michal		
Ishvi may have died young or Ishvi and Abinadab may be two names for the same son.		

15
RISE OF DAVID
1 Samuel 16-18

Chapter Chronology

	1019
10 Years of Saul's Reign	
1029	

The text does not indicate how many people knew that Saul had been rejected as king. Perhaps the matter was private, just between Samuel and Saul. When Samuel no longer appeared at the royal court, the people became uneasy. They must have suspected that all was not well between the prophet and the king.

DAVID THE CHOSEN
1 Samuel 16:1-23

Date: ca. 1029 BC

Chosen by God
1 Samuel 16:1-13

A. Samuel's Trip to Bethlehem (1 Samuel 16:1-5)

1. Samuel's fear (16:1-2a): Samuel's continued mourning over the downfall of Saul was deemed inappropriate because *Yahweh* had rejected him. The prophet was commanded to take his horn of oil to the house of Jesse in Bethlehem. Yahweh had selected a new *king* (not *prince* as in 9:16) from among the sons of Jesse. Samuel feared for his life, and for the life of anyone he might anoint. Furthermore, anointing a new king might trigger a civil war. These considerations explain Samuel's reticence to carry out his instructions.

2. Yahweh's instructions (16:2b-3): Yahweh directed Samuel to take with him a heifer to use as a sacrificial animal in Bethlehem. The animal was not a subterfuge, but a means of verifying his sacrificial intentions should he be challenged by Saul's agents. Jesse's family was to be invited to the sacrifice. At that time God promised to show Samuel what he should do. To anyone who inquired about his trip, Samuel was to tell the truth, but not the whole truth. He was to tell them he had come to sacrifice. Withholding the whole truth from those who have no right to know it is not unethical.

3. Samuel's explanation (16:4-5): So Samuel went to Bethlehem. The distance he traveled ranges from 10 to 25 miles, depending on which of four locations is identified as the home of Samuel. Since it was unusual for the prophet to be in their area, the elders feared the worst. They undoubtedly knew of the rift between the prophet and the king, and they did not wish to get involved. Samuel indicated that he had come in peace to offer a sacrifice. He told the elders to consecrate themselves for the service. He specifically invited Jesse and his sons.

B. David's Anointing (1 Samuel 16:6-13)
1. Wrong evaluation (16:6-7): Apparently after the public sacrifice, Samuel retired to the house of Jesse to partake of the sacrificial meal. As each of Jesse's sons entered the room for the sacrificial meal, Samuel sized them up. When he saw Jesse's firstborn Eliab he thought surely this was *Yahweh's anointed.* Yahweh, however, told the prophet not to look on the outward appearance. Yahweh looks on the heart.

2. An eighth son (16:8-11): All seven of Jesse's sons passed before Samuel, but in each case Yahweh rejected the candidate. Through inquiry Samuel learned of an eighth son who had been left to tend the sheep. Samuel directed Jesse to send for his youngest son. The family was not to sit down to eat of the fellowship meal until David had been brought in.

3. David anointed (16:12-13): David finally arrived. He made a pleasing appearance. He was *ruddy,* i.e., with reddish tint of hair and even skin. He had beautiful eyes and handsome features. He had an even more beautiful heart. Samuel was told to anoint this son. This he did *in the midst of his brothers.* From that day forward the Spirit of Yahweh rushed upon David. After the anointing Samuel departed for Ramah. The next time he saw David the young man was in flight from Saul.

Chosen by Saul
1 Samuel 16:14-23

A. Saul's Deterioration (1 Samuel 16:14-18)

228

1. An evil spirit (16:14): The same equipping Spirit that came upon David left Saul. He no longer had the resources to administer the kingdom. His own mental health deteriorated. An evil spirit from Yahweh, i.e., permitted by Yahweh, terrorized the man. This may have been a demonic spirit that Yahweh permitted to invade the mind of the king. On the other hand, the evil spirit may have been a psychological state sent on Saul as a divine judgment.

2. A suggestion by attendants (16:15-18); Saul's servants suggested that soothing music might help alleviate the panic caused by the evil spirit. So Saul authorized his servants to seek out a skilled harp player. Someone immediately thought of David who had a reputation as a skilled musician. David also possessed all the other attributes that Saul prized in his courtiers. He was prudent in speech, handsome, a warrior and *a mighty man of valor,* i.e., he was from a family of standing (cf. 1 Samuel 9:1). By slaying ferocious wild animals (cf. 17:34-35) David probably got the reputation of being a warrior.

B. David Enters Saul's Service (1 Samuel 16:19-23)

1. David drafted (16:19-20): Saul sent a draft notice to Jesse demanding that David be sent to the royal court. Jesse complied with the king's demand. Along with David, Jesse sent a donkey loaded down with gifts for the king.

2. King's armorbearer (16:21-22): David began to attend Saul. The king developed a special affection for him. Eventually David was given the high honor of being named armorbearer to the king. Saul sent a message to Jesse indicating that he had made David part of his permanent staff.

3. David's music (16:23): David's main function during this period was to play his harp whenever Saul was troubled by the evil spirit. This procedure worked well. Saul was refreshed by the music, and the evil spirit temporarily departed from him.

DAVID THE CHAMPION
1 Samuel 17:1-58

Date: ca. 1021 BC

Background
1 Samuel 17:1-23

An invasion by the Philistines demonstrated that Saul was faltering in his leadership. The Philistines brought with them a giant who single-handedly intimidated the entire army of Israel including King Saul. On the other hand, the Philistine-Israelite standoff in the valley of Elah was David's first opportunity publicly to demonstrate his courage and commitment to Yahweh.

A. Challenge (1 Samuel 17:1-11)

1. Philistine invasion (17:1-3): Periodically the Philistines invaded the territory of Israel. Chapter 17 reports one occasion when they penetrated as far as Socoh, about fourteen miles west of Bethlehem. They camped at Ephes-dammim in the vicinity of Socoh. Saul countered by calling up the army. The Israelites camped on a height overlooking a ravine (the valley of Elah) to block any further advance by the enemy. On the elevation across the valley the Philistines pitched their camp.

2. Philistine champion (17:4-7): Each day a *champion* named Goliath came forth from the Philistine camp to taunt the Israelites. His size was intimidating: six cubits and a span (over nine feet tall).[22] Goliath was a descendant of the tall Anakim race, the remnants of which had settled in the Philistine plain after the Israelite invasion under Joshua (Joshua 11:22). He wore a helmet and shin guards of bronze. His body armor weighed five thousand shekels (125 lbs.). He was armed both with a bronze javelin thrown over his shoulder and a spear. The shaft of that spear was as thick as a weaver's beam (part of a large loom), its head weighed six hundred shekels of iron (15 lbs.). As if that were not enough, the warrior had a shield bearer who walked before him.

3. Philistine taunting (17:8-11): Whenever the Israelites drew up in battle formation Goliath would propose that single combat replace fighting between armies. If some Israelite warrior could kill Goliath, the Philistines agreed to become servants of the Israelites. The opposite would be true if the Philistine should prevail. This daily winner-take-all challenge dismayed and intimidated Saul and all Israel. For forty days the daily challenge continued. Neither army moved during that period.

B. David's Mission (1 Samuel 17:12-19)

---

[22]Other manuscripts read "four cubits and a span," just under seven feet.

The three older sons of Jesse were part of Saul's army. Evidently David was no longer serving in Saul's court. As the youngest member of the family, David's job was to carry supplies to his brothers in the field. Apparently families were expected to supply provisions to their men in the field. During the standoff at the valley of Elah, Jesse dispatched David with food for his brothers and their commander. He was to check on the welfare of his brothers and bring back *their pledge,* i.e., some token that confirmed the delivery of the food and the well-being of the brothers.

C. Goliath's Intimidation (1 Samuel 17:20-23)

As David approached the perimeter of the Israelite camp the troops were moving into battle positions shouting the battle cry as they did. The Philistine army across the valley was going through the same exercise. David left his supplies with the quartermaster corps and hastened to the battle line to greet his brothers. While he was there Goliath made his daily appearance.

Defeat of Goliath
1 Samuel 17:24-51

A. David Volunteers (1 Samuel 17:24-40)

1. Discussion among the troops (17:24-25): Again the men of Israel *fled* from Goliath, i.e., they refused to move forward. David heard the troops talking among themselves of the tremendous rewards that Saul promised to any man who killed Goliath. The king promised to enrich that man, give his daughter to him in marriage, and exempt his father's house from taxation.

2. David's questions (17:26-30): David could not believe that no one took up the challenge of this *uncircumcised Philistine.* He grew increasing interested in the promised reward that he overheard the troops discussing. By questioning several men, David verified the truth of the reward rumor. When Eliab, David's oldest brother, heard these discussions, his anger burned against David. He wrongly rebuked David for abandoning his responsibilities of tending a small flock of sheep. He falsely accused David of having a perverse interest in watching the battle that was about to take place. David's response was typical of younger brothers throughout the centuries: *Was it not just a question?* David turned away from Eliab and began to question other men at the front.

B. Preparation for Battle (1 Samuel 17:31-40)

1. David's confidence (17:31-37): Saul soon heard about the brash young man who showed no fear of the Philistine. David lost none of his confidence in the presence of the king. He even volunteered to fight Goliath. Saul scoffed at this suggestion. Goliath had been trained as a warrior; David was but a youth. David, however, defended his fighting credentials. He had slain a lion and a bear in defense of his sheep. Goliath had taunted the armies of the living God. David therefore was confident Yahweh would deliver him from the hand of Philistine just as he had delivered him earlier from the paw of the lion and bear. Saul was convinced. He prayed Yahweh's blessing upon David's efforts.

2. David's weapons (17:38-40): Saul tried to clothe David in his personal armor. David tried on the royal armor, but felt so uncomfortable that he removed it. Since he had never *proved* or *tested* this armor in battle, he felt it would be more of a hindrance than a help. Rather he took his shepherd's stick (to help him negotiate his way down the steep ravine) and his sling. As he moved toward Goliath he paused at a wadi (dry stream bed) in the valley and picked up five smooth stones.

C. Victory over the Philistine (1 Samuel 17:41-53)

1. Attempted intimidation (17:41-44): Goliath came out to meet his challenger. When he saw that he was a youth and that he had no armor or sword, Goliath cursed David in the names of his gods. He considered it a personal insult that the Israelites had sent an unworthy opponent to fight him. Goliath mocked David's boyish appearance. He tried to verbally intimidate David by threatening to give his flesh to the birds and beasts.

2. David's courage (17:45-47): David continued to advance toward Goliath. The giant had never faced such bravado before. David employed his own version of psychological warfare. *You come at me with a sword, spear and javelin; but I come to you in the name of Yahweh of hosts, the God of the armies of Israel, whom you have taunted. This day Yahweh will deliver you into my hands.* David boasted that he will decapitate Goliath and give the bodies of the Philistine to the birds and beasts. Through this victory all the earth will know that there was a God in Israel. Those present on the battlefield will come to know that Yahweh does not deliver by sword or spear. *The battle is Yahweh's, and he will give you into our hands.*

3. *David's triumph (17:48-51a):* As Goliath rose and moved ponderously toward him, David began to run right at him. As he did so he loaded his sling and let fly a missile. The stone struck the one place where the giant had no armor. Goliath fell stunned to the ground. David ran forward, took the giant's own sword, slew him, and cut off his head.

4. *Philistine rout (17:51b-53):* When the Philistines saw that their champion had fallen, they broke ranks and fled. Saul's army pursued them to the very gates of their cities, about seven miles from the valley of Elah. As they returned to their own borders, the Israelites plundered the Philistine camps.

Epilogue
1 Samuel 17:54-58

A. David's Trophies (1 Samuel 17:54)

David took Goliath's head and showed it to the Jebusites and Israelites who jointly occupied Jerusalem[23] as a testimony to the greatness of Israel's God. David put Goliath's weapons in his own tent. Later, however, the sword was deposited in the tabernacle (cf. 1 Samuel 21:9).

B. Saul's Puzzling Question (1 Samuel 17:55-58)

Commentators are perplexed about the conversation between Saul and Abner that took place as David was going out to face the Philistine. In the light of the fact that David had served for a time in Saul's court, that Saul loved him, and had even made him the royal armorbearer, how could it be that neither he nor Abner recognized David? Various solutions have been offered. First, David may have matured considerably during his absence from the court. Second, in his disturbed state Saul may have paid little attention to the features of David as he played his harp. Third, the account of David serving in Saul's court may be chronologically later than the Goliath episode.

---

[23]Israelites took up residence in Jerusalem during the days of the conquest under Joshua (Joshua 15:63). The tribe of Judah was also able to conquer at least a part of Jerusalem (Judges 1:8). The fortress on Mount Zion, however, remained in the hands of the Jebusites until it was conquered by David (2 Samuel 5:6).

Actually the text does not say that Abner and Saul did not recognize David. The identity of David's father is the point at issue. This information would be necessary if Saul were to fulfill his pledge to make the father's house free of tax obligations. When David returned from killing Goliath, Abner brought him before Saul. David still had the Philistine's head in his hand. The king asked David about his father, and David proudly identified Jesse the Bethlehemite as his father.

In the victory over Goliath David proved himself to be a worthy leader of men. From that point on his fortunes were on the rise, while King Saul continued to decline both in popularity with the people and in his capacity to rule. David was about twenty at this time.

DAVID IN
SAUL'S COURT
1 Samuel 18:1-4

The events of chapter 18 follow immediately those of chapter 17. Saul did not allow David to return to his home. From this point on David was a national figure.

Friendship of Jonathan
1 Samuel 18:1-4

Jonathan, the son of Saul, became the closest of friends with David following the Goliath episode. His soul *was knit* (lit., chained itself) to the soul of David. He came to love David as he loved himself. Jonathan entered into a covenant of brotherhood with David and symbolized the same by bestowing on David his robe and armor. Many in recent years have viewed this "male bonding" between David and Jonathan as some kind of homosexual covenant. Nothing could be farther from the truth. Both men were married and had children. David was later lured in an adulterous act by the sight of a naked woman. This is hardly conduct typical of homosexuals.

Military Achievement
1 Samuel 18:5-9

A. Army Commander (1 Samuel 18:5)

During those early days in the court David continued to impress the king. He carried out whatever orders he was given. Eventually Saul made David a commander in the army. This move met with the approval of the people in general and Saul's advisors in particular.

B. Songs of the Women (1 Samuel 18:6-9)

Saul's jealousy was triggered by the adoration bestowed on David by the women when the troops returned from battles with the Philistines. To the accompaniment of musical instruments the women chanted: *Saul has slain thousands, but David his tens of thousands.* Saul believed that this popular adulation would catapult David to the throne itself. Therefore, from that day forward he viewed David with suspicion.

Hostility of Saul
1 Samuel 18:10-16

A. Attempts on David's Life (1 Samuel 18:10-11)

The *evil spirit from God* continued to trouble Saul from time to time. David played the harp in an attempt to bring peace to the king. On two occasions when Saul was raving under the influence of the evil spirit, he tried to slay David with his spear.

B. Captain of a Thousand (1 Samuel 18:12-16)

Saul was afraid of David. He saw that Yahweh was with the Bethlehemite. Saul himself no longer sensed the direction of God's Spirit. Therefore Saul made David a captain of a thousand to get him out of the court. Yet with Yahweh's blessing, David continued to prosper. This only fueled Saul's resentment. Yet the people of both Israel and Judah loved David.

David and Saul's Daughters
1 Samuel 18:17-30

A. Merab Offer (1 Samuel 18:17-19)

Saul schemed to bring about the death of David. He offered him the hand of Merab, his oldest daughter, if he would engage the Philistines in battle. David felt unworthy to be son-in-law to the king. On the day Merab was to become David's bride, Saul found some pretext to give her to another. This, no doubt, was intended to humiliate David.

B. Michal Offer (1 Samuel 18:20-25)

1.   Required dowry (18:20-25): Saul's second daughter loved David. When the king discovered this he again plotted against his rival. David had no wealth to pay a dowry suitable for a king's daughter. Saul, however, sent word that he desired as a dowry a hundred foreskins of slain Philistines. In this vulgar stipulation Saul was following the custom of other peoples of the ancient Near East who cut off the genitals of enemy soldiers as a trophy of victory. Again Saul was hoping that David would fall by the hands of Israel's enemies.

2.   David's compliance (18:26-29): David was happy to become the king's son-in-law on the terms stipulated. He and his men slew twice the requisite number of Philistines and brought their foreskins to Saul. The king this time honored his word and gave Michal to David. When he saw that his daughter really loved his rival, Saul was even more afraid of David. As son-in-law to the king, David now had established a possible claim to the throne. Saul became David's implacable enemy.

3.   David's recognition (18:30): Chapter 18 closes with a note that even the Philistine commanders began to take note of David. He behaved himself more wisely than any of Saul's officers, i.e., his tactical skills were superior to any other commander.

16
DAVID'S FLIGHT
FROM SAUL
1 Samuel 19-22

1019	4 Years	1015

ATTEMPTS ON DAVID'S LIFE
1 Samuel 19:1-24

Date: ca. 1019 BC

Jealousy of Saul
1 Samuel 19:1-17

A. Orders to Slay David (1 Samuel 19:1-7)

1. Saul's announcement (19:1-3): Finally Saul made public in his court what he had been thinking in his heart for some time. He wanted David dead! Jonathan warned David. He promised to signal his friend if he could not persuade his father to cancel the death warrant.

2. Jonathan's appeal (19:4-7): Jonathan gave an impassioned plea on behalf of David. He reminded his father that David had never committed any sin against him. On the contrary, David's activities had only benefited Saul, and that at great risk to his own life. On this occasion Saul listened to reason. He vowed not to put David to death. Jonathan immediately went and brought David back to the court.

B. Efforts to Slay David (1 Samuel 19:8-14)

1. David flees danger (19:8-12): New military accomplishments by David triggered the jealous spirit within Saul. Again while David was playing for the king, Saul tried to pin David to the wall with his spear. David escaped unharmed. Saul then dispatched assassins to wait outside David's house to slay him in the morning. Michal warned her husband that he must flee that night if he wanted to save his life. Michal helped David escape out a back window. Then she fixed up a decoy that was designed to buy some time for her husband.

237

She took a teraphim (household god) and put it in bed. She fixed the life-size statue to resemble a human figure. When Saul's agents came looking for David, Michal told them he was sick. Perhaps she allowed them to peek into the bedroom from a distance. In the dim light the teraphim looked the part of a sick man.

2. *Michal lies to Saul (19:15-17):* Saul ordered his agents to bring David to him on his sick bed so he could kill him. Only then did the agents discover that they had been tricked. They took Michal with them instead. Saul rebuked his daughter for aiding his enemy. To get back in the good graces of her father Michal lied. She only had aided David because he had threatened her life. This lie, of course, only fueled Saul's hatred of David.

David's Flight to Samuel
1 Samuel 19:18-24

At this point David was forced to become a fugitive. He was aided during the next several weeks by a number of individuals.

A. **Intervention by God** (1 Samuel 19:18-21)
David went first to Ramah to meet with Samuel. For a short time he resided in Naioth, the little community of prophetic students that was located near Ramah. When Saul heard where he was residing, he dispatched agents to arrest David. As they entered the area where the prophets were prophesying under the direction of Samuel, the Spirit of God came upon Saul's agents and they also prophesied. The same thing happened to a second and a third group of agents. Thus divine intervention prevented the capture of David at this point.

B. **Saul "Slain" by the Spirit** (1 Samuel 19:22-24)
Finally Saul decided to go to Ramah. While en route to his destination the Spirit of God came upon Saul and he also prophesied. When he arrived at Naioth Saul continued to prophesy before Samuel. He stripped off his outer garments and lay down *naked,* i.e., without his outer robes, all that day and even through the night. People were stunned once again by the religious devotion of Saul.

By the great manifestation of the Spirit of God at Naioth, Yahweh was demonstrating how he could disarm the most determined foe. God rebuked Saul's anger and gave David opportunity to escape again.

238

Last Efforts to
Rejoin Saul's Court
1 Samuel 20:1-42

A. David Appeals to Jonathan (1 Samuel 20:1-3)

David next sought out his friend Jonathan. The prince knew nothing of any new death warrant on David, and Saul always discussed his intentions with his son. David explained that Saul was now withholding such information from Jonathan because he knew of their friendship. In reality, David said, *there is but a step between me and death.*

B. A Plan to Test Saul (1 Samuel 20:4-11)

David asked Jonathan to ascertain whether Saul was still determined to kill him. At the New Moon celebration if Saul asked about his absence, Jonathan should tell his father that David had gone to Bethlehem for the annual family sacrifice. If Saul became angry about this excuse that would signal that Saul still harbored murderous thoughts toward David. The problem, however, was how the information could be communicated to David if the disposition of the king was still hostile.

C. A Covenant between Friends (1 Samuel 20:12-17)

Jonathan agreed to convey the information to David whether the news was good or bad. The prince asked his friend to enter into a covenant that he would not cut off Jonathan's house in the day that Yahweh gave David victory over his enemies. Thus Jonathan recognized that David would be the next king of Israel. David gladly entered that covenant with Jonathan.

D. Communication Plan (1 Samuel 20:18-23)

The plan for conveying the disposition of Saul to David was now worked out. David was to hide himself in the spot where he previously had hidden. Jonathan would shoot three arrows. As the servant went to retrieve the arrows, Jonathan would say *the arrows are beyond you* or *the arrows are on this side of you.* The first would indicate danger, the second, that everything was all right with Saul.

E. Saul's Outrage (1 Samuel 20:24-34)

239

1. Verbal attack on Jonathan (20:24-31): On the second day of the New Moon celebration Saul inquired about the absence of David. Jonathan gave the prearranged excuse. Saul exploded with anger, hurling a vicious epithet at his son, one in which he made disparaging comments about Jonathan's mother. Because of his friendship Jonathan had brought shame to *his mother's nakedness.* He asserted that the kingdom would never be Jonathan's as long as David lived. Saul ordered his son to bring David to him so that he might die.

2. Physical attack on Jonathan (20:32-34): Jonathan tried to reason with his father as he had done a few weeks before. Saul, however, hurled his spear, narrowly missing his son. Jonathan knew now that David would never again be safe in Saul's presence. He left the room in anger because of the way his mother and his best friend had been treated by Saul. Jonathan fasted in grief over the treatment of David.

F. Parting of Friends (1 Samuel 20:35-42)

The next morning under the pretext of practicing archery Jonathan went out into the field to keep his appointment with David. A little lad accompanied him. Jonathan carried out the prearranged signal with David because he feared that he might be watched. After the danger signal had been given, however, Jonathan threw caution to the wind. He gave his bow and quiver to the lad and sent him back to the city. David then came out of hiding. Both friends thought that this was the last time they would ever see one another. David expressed gratitude to Jonathan by bowing three times to the ground. In eastern style the friends kissed one another and wept. Jonathan reminded his friend of the covenant that had been made between them earlier. Then David and Jonathan went their separate ways.

DAVID'S FLIGHT
1 Samuel 21:1-22:5

Date: ca. 1016 BC

David was about twenty-three when he fled from Saul's court never to return.

David and Ahimelech
1 Samuel 21:1-9

A. David's Request (1 Samuel 21:1-5)

1. Need for food (21:1-3): David proceeded immediately to Nob, a couple of miles away on the northern outskirts of Jerusalem. The tabernacle was now located there. Ahimelech the high priest came trembling to meet David. He must have known of Saul's hatred of David. That David was traveling alone was a clue that he was no longer employed in government service. David told the priest he was on a secret royal mission. His entourage was to meet him at a designated spot. David requested five loaves or any food that Ahimelech had at the sanctuary.

2. Holy bread available (21:4-5): Ahimelech told David that the only bread in the place was holy. This bread was eaten by priests each Sabbath day (Leviticus 24:9). The priest determined that he could release that bread if David and his men were consecrated as soldiers normally were when they fought in a holy war. Abstinence from sexual relations was apparently a minimal requirement of consecration. If David's men had kept themselves from women, Ahimelech could share the consecrated bread with them. David assured the priest that 1) both he and his men had indeed abstained from sexual relations; and 2) their *vessels* (NASB), i.e., their clothing and/or bodies were *holy,* i.e., ritually clean.

B. Ahimelech's Provision (1 Samuel 21:6-9)

1. Hostile observer (21:6-7): Having been thus reassured, Ahimelech gave David the consecrated bread of the Presence that had just recently been replaced with freshly baked bread. Unfortunately, one of Saul's loyal servants was at the tabernacle that day. Doeg the Edomite, the overseer of Saul's herdsmen, *was detained before Yahweh,* probably on some ceremonial impurity.

2. Goliath's sword (21:8-9): David then asked the priest if he had available a weapon of some kind. He explained that the urgency of the king's business had prevented him from securing his own weapon. Ahimelech reminded David that the sword of Goliath was now housed in the tabernacle. He was welcome to that sword should he want it. *Give it to me,* David said, *for there is none like it.*

David and Achish
1 Samuel 21:10-15

241

A. Reception in Gath (1 Samuel 21:10-11)

David determined that the only way to escape Saul was to leave his kingdom. For this reason he went over to the Philistine city of Gath. King Achish apparently welcomed the defection of David. His servants, however, were suspicious. They reminded their king that David was virtually *king of the land,* and that he had the reputation of having slain even more Philistines than Saul.

B. Escape from Gath (1 Samuel 21:12-15)

Sensing that he was in danger, David began to feign madness. He *scribbled* (NASB), i.e., *made marks* (NIV) on the doors of the gate. He allowed his spittle to run down into his beard. A normal person would never have permitted such an indignity to himself. Achish was convinced. He wanted nothing to do with such a madman. The Philistines observed the code of the east which regarded the insane as possessed of the gods, and therefore sacrosanct. The fugitive was safe for the moment.

David and the Four Hundred
1 Samuel 22:1-2

David departed from Achish in peace. He returned to Judah, to the cave of Adullam about ten miles from Gath and about twelve miles west of Bethlehem. There his relatives joined him. All those who were not prospering in Saul's kingdom joined David at Adullam. David became the captain of some four hundred men.

David and the King of Moab
1 Samuel 22:3-5

A. Concern for his Parents (1 Samuel 22:3-4)

How long David remained at Adullam is not stated. From there he traveled south around the Dead Sea to Mizpah of Moab. He requested that the king of Moab allow his mother and father to stay in his land *until I know what God will do for me.* As long as David was in the *stronghold* his parents remained in Moab.

B. Concern of Gad (1 Samuel 22:5)

The prophet Gad was among those who followed David. He advised David to depart from the *stronghold* and return to the land of

Judah. Gad was probably thinking that David's claim to the throne might be jeopardized by remaining out of the country. David followed Gad's advice and entered the forest of Hereth in the Judean wilderness.

SLAUGHTER
OF THE PRIESTS
1 Samuel 22:6-23

Date: ca. 1015 BC

Now that David was back in Israel, his capture became the priority of Saul's reign. Five times David narrowly escaped from his determined father-in-law.

Saul's Court
1 Samuel 22:6-13

A. Purpose (1 Samuel 22:6)

1. Appeal for loyalty (22:6): Saul finally got word about David's whereabouts. He summoned his servants to a war council. Saul's court was simple. He sat under a tamarisk tree on a hill in Gibeah. Saul's spear served as his scepter. All his Benjamite courtiers stood in front of him. Saul appealed for the loyalty of his servants.

2. Argument of Saul (22:7-8): By means of two rhetorical questions Saul affirmed that he, not *the son of Jesse,* had given them property and appointed them to military commands. Yet none of these servants had kept Saul informed about the covenant between Jonathan and *the son of Jesse.* None of the servants felt sorry that Saul's son had stirred up *my servant* (David) against the king. No one seemed concerned that the son of Jesse was lying in ambush against Saul at that very moment. Of course Saul had it wrong. Jonathan had nothing to do with stirring up David against his father. In fact there was no evidence that David was hostile in any way to Saul, much less that he was setting an ambush for the king.

B. Condemnation (1 Samuel 22:9-15)

1. Priests summoned (22:9-13): Doeg the Edomite was standing by the servants of Saul. He now stepped forward to report what he had seen at Nob a few weeks before. Saul immediately summoned all the priests from Nob. He began to harangue against Ahimelech. He accused the priest of conspiring with *the son of Jesse* against the crown by inquiring of God for him and giving him bread and a weapon. Thus Ahimelech was responsible for the ambush that David allegedly had set for Saul in the wilderness.

2. *Ahimelech's defense (22:14-15):* Ahimelech eloquently defended himself. First, he argued that David was as faithful a servant as Saul had. Second, it was not unusual for the priest to inquire of God on behalf of David. Third, he pled ignorance of *this whole affair,* i.e., any conspiracy against the king.

C. Execution (1 Samuel 22:16-23)

1. *Carried out by Doeg (22:16-19):* Saul refused to listen. In his mind there was a conspiracy against him, and the priests were part of that conspiracy. Saul, therefore, ordered his servants to slay the priests. His servants, however, refused to put forth their hands against the holy men. The king then ordered Doeg to do the deed. He slew eighty-five members of the priestly family that day. He also smote the city of Nob, utterly destroying the place and all who lived there. Thus Saul enforced against the innocent populace of Nob the ban that he refused to execute against the Amalekite sinners.

2. *Sole survivor (22:20-23):* Only one priest, Abiathar, escaped the slaughter. He fled to David and reported to him what had happened. David had suspected that Doeg would tell Saul what had transpired at Nob. He felt personally responsible for the death of the priests. He invited Abiathar to join him and promised to give the priest protection from Saul.

17
MAJOR ATTACKS
ON DAVID
1 Samuel 23-27

Chapter Chronology

	1011
Four Years of Saul's Reign	
1015	

FIRST MAJOR ATTACK
1 Samuel 23:1-29

Date: ca. 1014 BC

David and Keilah
1 Samuel 23:1-14

A. David Rescues Keilah (23:1-5)

In the Forest of Hereth David heard how the Philistines were plundering the threshing floors of Keilah. Through the prophet Gad he inquired of Yahweh as to whether or not he should go to the rescue of this city. The oracle was positive. Since his men objected to doing battle with the Philistines, David made a second inquiry with similar results. So David's small band went to Keilah and engaged the Philistines. Not only did he deliver the town of Keilah from being plundered, he was able to capture the Philistine livestock which his men desperately needed.

B. Saul's Plan (1 Samuel 23:6-8)

David's location at Keilah soon became known throughout the land. Abiathar (cf. 22:20-23) found him there. Saul also heard the reports. The king was confident that David could now be captured since he apparently had made the strategic mistake of occupying a walled city. Saul interpreted David's mistake as an indication that God had now rejected David. He still failed to grasp that he was the one who had been rejected. Nevertheless, Saul mobilized his army and marched toward Keilah

C. David Flees Keilah (1 Samuel 23:9-14)

Sympathizers soon sent the report of Saul's plans to David. He immediately inquired of the priestly oracle whether or not the reports about Saul were true, and whether or not the men of Keilah, if threatened with annihilation, would surrender David to his enemy. On both counts the priestly oracle was positive. David and his men—now numbering some six hundred—quickly returned to their wilderness haunts. When he heard that David had escaped Keilah, Saul canceled his campaign against that city and chased David into the Wilderness of Ziph

David in the Wilderness of Ziph
1 Samuel 23:15-29

A. Visit from Jonathan (1 Samuel 23:15-18)

While David was at Horesh ("thicket") in the wilderness of Ziph Jonathan came to *encourage him in God.* The Saulides knew that someday David would be king, and Jonathan would be his lieutenant. The two made another covenant to this effect. Then Jonathan departed for his home.

B. Betrayal by Ziphites (1 Samuel 23:19-25)

The Ziphites reported David's general location to Saul. They promised to deliver David into the hands of the king. Saul sent the Ziphites back as scouts before his army to get an exact fix on David. They found that David had moved to the Wilderness of Maon to the south of Jeshimon, a wasteland along the western shore of the Dead Sea. When he heard that Saul was again in hot pursuit, David retreated to *the rock* in the wilderness of Maon.

C. David's Narrow Escape (1 Samuel 23:26-29)

With the aid of intelligence supplied by the Ziphites, Saul marched straight toward the mountain where David was camped. Saul was in the process of positioning his men to surround David when a messenger arrived who reported that the Philistines had invaded the land. Saul withdrew his troops to deal with the new threat. Because of David's narrow escape the rock in the wilderness of Maon became known as the Rock of Escape. David then relocated to the strongholds of Engedi, a mountain oasis midway along the western side of the Dead Sea.

SECOND MAJOR ATTACK
1 Samuel 24:1-22

Date: 1012 BC

David Spares Saul's Life
1 Samuel 24:1-7

Once the Philistine threat was over, Saul again turned his attention to tracking down his rival. In response to reports that David was hiding in the area of Engedi, Saul took three thousand men and marched in that direction. En route Saul entered one of the caves that was part of a sheepfold to *cover his feet* (KJV), i.e., relieve himself. David and some of his men were hiding in the inner recesses of that very cave.[24] One of his men reminded David that Yahweh had promised one day to deliver his enemies into his hand. David crept forward in the dark and cut off the edge of Saul's robe. He returned to his men guilt stricken because he even had dared to cut the robe of God's anointed. David's attitude persuaded his men not to touch Saul.

David Defends Himself
1 Samuel 24:8-15

After Saul had gone a safe distance, David went out of the cave and called after him. He bowed to the ground and addressed Saul respectfully as *my lord the king*. With great emotion he tried to make his father-in-law see that he was being manipulated by certain men who stood to profit by removing David from the scene. He pointed out that he could have slain Saul in the cave had he been so minded. The missing edge of Saul's robe was proof of that. Perhaps Yahweh would avenge the wrong that Saul had done to him, but David would not. Saul was wasting his time seeking him, for David was no more a threat than a single flea on a dead dog. David concluded his speech by appealing to Yahweh to deliver him from the hand of Saul.

---

[24]Coming into the dark cave from the bright sunlight meant that Saul's eyes were not as accustomed to the darkness as were the eyes of David. Evidently the king left his outer garment near the entrance of the cave while he went into a side chamber to relieve himself. The noise of men and animals outside the cave drowned out any noise David might have made in getting to the robe.

Saul's Response to David's Speech
1 Samuel 24:16-22

Saul was moved to tears by the words of David. He acknowledged that David had been more righteous than he. He recognized for the moment that David must not have considered him as an enemy else he would have slain him in the cave. Saul prayed Yahweh's blessing on David because he had refrained from slaying the king. Saul acknowledged that David one day would be king. He concluded by requesting an oath from David that he would not wipe out the family of Saul, an action frequently taken when a new dynasty came to power (24:16-21).

The request for an oath must have been a face-saving action by Saul. If David refused to kill the king, he would have no reason to kill the descendants of the king. Nonetheless, David quickly gave Saul the oath he wanted. Saul then returned home. David went up to *the stronghold,* in this case, the most rugged part of the Wilderness of Judea.

NABAL INCIDENT
1 Samuel 25:1-43

Date: ca. 1012 BC

Setting for the Incident
1 Samuel 25:1-3

During the days of wilderness hiding, Samuel died. All Israel mourned for the prophet. They buried him at his house in Ramah. Meanwhile, David kept on the move. He relocated temporarily about a hundred miles to south in the Wilderness of Paran on the border between Canaan and the Sinai peninsula (25:1).

In the vicinity where David was hiding, a wealthy businessman was shearing his sheep. Nabal was a descendant of Caleb, but he certainly did not possess the disposition of his ancestor. Nabal was harsh and evil in his dealings. His wife Abigail, however, was both beautiful and intelligent (25:2-3).

David's Request for Assistance
1 Samuel 25:4-13

A. Grounds of the Request (1 Samuel 25:4-8)

When he heard that Naboth was shearing sheep in Carmel (eight miles SE of Hebron) David sent ten of his men to request a donation of provisions. Sheep shearing was a festival time in which the spirit of generosity prevailed. All the time he had been in that area, David's men had never taken any of Nabal's livestock. In fact the presence of the small army of men probably kept thieves and raiding parties at bay. In any case, David felt he had a solid basis upon which to make his request.

B. Nabal's Reaction (1 Samuel 25:9-11)

The ten messengers were rudely rebuffed by Nabal. He regarded David as nothing more than an ordinary rebel. Nabal had no intentions of sharing what belonged to him with the likes of a David.

C. David's Wrath (1 Samuel 25:12-13, 21f)

When the ten messengers reported back to camp, David was furious. He ordered his four hundred men to strap on their swords. David prepared to lead the attack personally. He felt that Nabal had returned to him evil for good. In a fit of rage David swore that by morning no male associated with Nabal would be alive.

Abigail's Intervention
1 Samuel 25:14-31

A. Preparation (1 Samuel 25:14-17)

One of the servants told Abigail what had happened. He confirmed what the messengers of David had asserted, viz., that David's men had provided protection for those who tended sheep for Nabal in the field. The servant rightly judged that David would not ignore the insults of Nabal. The entire household was facing danger. Yet no one could approach the know-it-all Nabal because he was such a *worthless man.*

B. Mission (1 Samuel 25:18-31)

1. Abigail's encounter (25:18-22): Abigail gathered a sizable amount of provisions from all the good things that had been prepared for the festival. She loaded this food on donkeys and secretly departed for David's camp, led by one of her servants. As it happened, David

249

and his men were coming down from their mountain stronghold even as Abigail approached.

3. Abigail's appeal (25:23-25): When she saw David, Abigail dismounted, and bowed herself to the ground. She accepted the total blame for the lack of hospitality shown the ten messengers. She urged David to pay no attention to *this worthless man* Nabal, for he lived up to the meaning of his name. The name Nabal means "fool" and this man acted the part.

4. Abigail's argument (25:26-27): Abigail used sweet but persuasive logic to urge David to accept the gift that she had brought on the donkeys and to forgive *your maidservant.* She argued that 1) through her actions God had kept David from the guilt associated with shedding blood and avenging himself; 2) God was the true avenger of folly like that of Nabal; and 3) David should accept her gift for the sake of his men.

5. Abigail's plea (25:28-31): Abigail then made a direct plea for forgiveness. Since David was one who will be greatly blessed, he could afford to be gracious. David's blessing included 1) an enduring house, i.e., a long-lasting dynasty; 2) divine protection of his life; and 3) the casting out of his enemies as a stone is hurled from a sling. Should David take vengeance on Nabal his conscience would bother him for having avenged himself rather than allowing the Lord to take vengeance for him.

C. David's Response (1 Samuel 25:32-35)

In David's reply he 1) praised God for having sent Abigail; 2) thanked Abigail for keeping him from bloodshed; 3) graciously thanked the woman for the gifts; and 4) dismissed her in peace.

D. Nabal's Death (1 Samuel 25:36-44)

1. Circumstances (25:36-38): Abigail returned to find Nabal already feasting. Since he was very drunk, she did not attempt to tell him at that time what she had done. The next morning when he was sober Nabal learned of his wife's mission. When he heard, *his heart died within him so that he became like a stone.* The text appears to be describing a paralyzing stroke triggered by rage. Nabal lingered ten days. Then Yahweh struck him, i.e., he had another seizure, and he died.

2. Marriage proposal (25:39-42): The news of Nabal's death caused David to bless Yahweh. The Lord had restrained David from the evil of personal vengeance, but at the same time Nabal had been repaid for the reproach that he had heaped upon God's anointed. David then sent servants to invite Abigail to become his wife. She greeted the offer with humility. Nonetheless, she arose quickly, and with her five maidservants, followed the emissaries to David's camp.

3. David's wives (25:43-44): Abigail was the third wife of David. During his absence from court, Michal, his first wife, had been given to a certain Palti. At some point prior to marrying Abigail, David had taken Ahinoam of Jezreel as a wife. Polygamy stands condemned in Scripture both by the original marriage pattern of the Garden and by the Law of Moses (cf. Leviticus 18:18).

THIRD MAJOR ATTACK
1 Samuel 26:1-25

Date: ca. 1012 BC

Saul's Pursuit
1 Samuel 26:1-3

The Ziphites again reported to Saul that David was hiding in the hill of Hachilah which was before the Jeshimon. Saul led his three thousand troops to the vicinity of that hill. David took evasive action when he ascertained that Saul was on his trail again. From a distance David noted that Saul was spending the night ringed by his troops.

David's Plan
1 Samuel 26:6-11

David determined to enter the camp of Saul that night. Abishai, brother of Joab, volunteered to go with David on this dangerous mission. The two invaders found the entire camp of Saul asleep. No one was guarding the king. Abishai sought permission to take the spear that was stuck in the ground near the king and run his enemy through. David, however, had qualms about striking Yahweh's anointed. Saul may die a natural death, or be smitten by Yahweh, or die in battle; but David will not touch him. Instead, David told Abishai to take the king's spear and jug of water.

David's Taunt

1 Samuel 26:12-21

A. Accusation against Abner (1 Samuel 26:12-16)

David and Abishai were able to escape from Saul's camp undetected. Yahweh had caused all the troops of Saul to sleep with a sound sleep. The two men crossed the road and climbed the mountain on the other side. From that distance David shouted to awaken Saul's camp. He first addressed Abner. He accused Abner and his troops of being guilty of dereliction of duty worthy of death for failing to guard the life of the king. He then displayed the spear and jug that proved the security in Saul's camp had been breached.

B. Appeal to Saul (1 Samuel 26:17-20)

David then addressed Saul. He asked why his father-in-law was pursuing him. Was it Yahweh who had stirred Saul up against David? Perhaps a sacrifice by the two of them would suffice to placate the Lord. Was it his advisers who had stirred up Saul against David? Let them be cursed before Yahweh. These advisers were attempting to drive David from *the inheritance of Yahweh,* i.e., from Israel. They could care less if David rendered devotion to the gods of one of the surrounding nations. David did not wish to die on foreign soil. He pled with Saul not to hound him into foreign exile.

C. Saul's Response (1 Samuel 26:21-25)

1. Saul's remorse (26:21): Once again David's words struck a responsive chord in Saul. He confessed his sin. Saul summarized his life with serious self-condemnation: *I have played the fool and have committed a serious error.* He invited David to return. Saul promised not to harm him because David had spared his life that day.

2. David's confidence (26:22-24): David then invited one of Saul's servants to come and fetch the royal spear. He further expressed his confidence that Yahweh will reward his righteousness and faithfulness in not taking the life of the king that day. Yahweh will regard David's life as precious just as he had regarded Saul's life. David concluded his speech by expressing his desire for Yahweh to deliver him from distress.

3. Saul's blessing (26:24-25): Saul responded by pronouncing a blessing on David. In it he expressed confidence that David will both accomplish much and surely prevail one day in receiving the crown.

After these words, the two men went their separate ways never to see one another again.

David at Ziklag
1 Samuel 27:7-12

A. Attack on Enemies (1 Samuel 27:7-9)

1. Identification of the enemies (27:7-8): David spent sixteen months in the land of the Philistines. Out of his headquarters at Ziklag, he attacked the old pagan inhabitants of the land: Geshurites, Girzites and Amalekites. The first two peoples are otherwise unknown in the Bible. Saul virtually had wiped out the Amalekites (1 Samuel 15:8-9), but a new wave of these desert marauders was attempting to press into Canaan out of the desert.

2. Nature of the attacks (27:9): David apparently launched retaliatory attacks against the desert peoples whenever they attempted to invade the south of Judah. He exterminated these enemies of Israel and took all their plunder. These raids accomplished two things. First, David was able to supply the needs of his followers. Second, his victories over the enemies of his people helped him build a base of support in Judah.

B. Reports to Achish (1 Samuel 27:10-12)

When Achish inquired about the raids, David gave deliberately misleading reports. They were worded in such a way that Achish assumed the raids were against Israelite territory. He became confident of David's loyalty. Achish was prepared to integrate David's six hundred soldiers into the Philistine army.

The conduct of David during the sixteen months in Ziklag cannot be condoned. These were dark days in the life of the future king. He was spiritually depressed. During this period there is no record of any communication with the Lord.

History of Israel

18
END OF SAUL
1 Samuel 28-2 Samuel 1

Chapter Chronology

1010		1010
	1 Year	

During his reign Saul had been fairly successful in preventing the Philistines from making significant inroads into Israel. From the viewpoint of these enemies, however, the time was now ripe for a major thrust into Israel. Samuel, the spiritual leader of the nation, was dead. The most capable soldier in Israel's army had defected to the Philistines. Saul was losing his political grip and perhaps even his sanity. These factors convinced the lords of the Philistines to band together under the leadership of Achish to attempt an invasion of Israel.

SAUL AND THE WITCH
1 Samuel 28:1-25

Date: 1010-1009 BC

Philistine Invasion
1 Samuel 28:1-14

The Philistine invasion came about 1010 BC. The plan was to march north along the coastal plain to the Valley of Jezreel, then knife eastward across that valley. In this region Saul's defenses were thin, and the flat terrain gave the Philistines military superiority because of their chariotry.

A. David's Awkward Position (1 Samuel 28:1-2)
The Philistine attack put David, who was now a trusted ally of King Achish, in an awkward position. The king insisted that David go to war with him against Israel. David was in no position to refuse since he had placed himself at the disposal of the Philistine king.

Achish trusted David so much that he appointed his men to be the royal bodyguard during the battle.

B. Saul's Desperate Plight (1 Samuel 28:3-14)

1. No divine revelation (28:3-6): The plight of Saul is indicated in three statements in the text. First, the author reminds the reader that Samuel was dead. In this national crisis Saul could count on no counsel from the great prophet. Second, Saul had removed from the land those who were mediums and spiritists. This statement indicates that Saul had attempted to fulfill his responsibilities as king to remove from the land all practitioners of the occult. This action meant, however, that in this crisis he could not easily consult with these prognosticators. Third, the Philistines camped in Shunem seven miles east of Megiddo in the Valley of Jezreel. The Israelites were camped just across a narrow valley on the slopes of Mount Gilboa. When he saw the Philistine camp, Saul trembled with fear. Finally, when he tried to inquire of the Lord, the king received no answer by any of the unusual means of revelation: dreams, Urim (the priestly oracle), or prophets.

2. Inquiry about a medium (28:7): In his desperation Saul decided to resort to necromancy (consulting the dead). He ordered his servants to seek out a woman who was a medium. Though outlawed, witches still secretly practiced their Satanic religion. The servants knew of a woman in Endor who was a medium. In Jewish tradition this woman is identified as the mother of Abner, Saul's general.

3. Visit to the witch (28:8-11): Saul disguised himself by changing his clothes in order to conceal his identity from Philistine patrols and from the medium. He and two men made the perilous journey through the night around the Philistine lines to Endor. The witch was cautious when the unidentified visitor requested to contact a dead spirit. She suspected the request might be an effort at entrapment. Saul swore an oath in Yahweh's name that no punishment would come to the woman. The woman inquired about whom she should call up.

4. Appearance of Samuel (28:12-14): As soon as Saul mentioned the name Samuel, the prophet appeared. The witch, who had performed none of her usual séance antics, *saw* him. She cried out in fear. If she had any suspicions as to the identity of her tall visitor they now were confirmed. She chided Saul for having deceived her. The king calmed her fears and begged her to describe

256

what she saw. The witch said she saw a *divine being* (NASB), i.e., supernatural being, coming out of the earth. Saul then inquired as to the form of what she saw. The witch described the form as 1) an old man who was 2) wrapped in a robe. At this point it seems that Saul himself saw the spirit. He *knew* that this was the spirit of Samuel. Out of respect for the old prophet, Saul bowed himself to the ground.

Samuel's Ominous Prophecy
1 Samuel 28:15-25

A. Reproof by the Prophet (1 Samuel 28:15-16)

A conversation took place between Samuel and Saul apparently without the mediation of the witch. First, Samuel asked Saul why he had disturbed him by bringing him up, i.e., causing him to return from Sheol, the abode of the dead. The language suggests that Sheol for the saint was peaceful. Second, Saul responded by describing his plight. In the face of the Philistine invasion he needed divine counsel, but Yahweh had departed from him. Third, Samuel raised a second question. If Yahweh had become his enemy, why then did he now seek the counsel of Yahweh's prophet?

B. Prediction by the Prophet (1 Samuel 28:17-19)

Samuel then spoke ominous prophetic words to the king. He announced 1) political judgment. By the violence of the coming battle God will tear the kingdom from Saul's hand and give it to David. The disobedience regarding Amalek (1 Samuel 15) will be avenged even as Samuel had predicted years before. Then Samuel spoke of 2) military judgment. On the morrow Yahweh will deliver the army of Israel into the hands of the Philistines. In this battle Saul will also experience 3) personal judgment. He and his sons will join Samuel in Sheol on the morrow, i.e., they will die in battle.

C. Provision by the Witch (1 Samuel 28:20-25)

Faint with hunger and overwhelmed with fear, Saul fell prostrate on the ground. Seeing the terror in the eyes of her king, the woman tried to be a source of comfort to him. Since she had done as Saul had asked, she now requested him to listen to her. He should eat some food before attempting to return to the camp. With the assistance of his servants, the woman finally persuaded Saul to eat. The king arose from the ground and sat on the bed while the kindly witch quickly prepared meat and bread for him. After they had eaten the royal entourage departed.

CAPTURE OF ZIKLAG
1 Samuel 29:1-30:31

Date: 1010 BC

The Philistine invasion of 1010 BC created problems for David as well as Saul. David faced problems with Achish, at Ziklag and with his own troops.

Problems with Achish
1 Samuel 29:1-11

A. Concern of the Captains (1 Samuel 29:1-5)

The Philistines gathered their forces to Aphek. There they organized their army for the thrust into Israel. As royal bodyguard, David's unit was to the rear of the attacking forces. The Philistine commanders were very uncomfortable with a sizable "Hebrew" unit to their rear. Achish, however, defended David. In all the time he had been in the land of the Philistines, never had Achish ever had occasion to find fault with David. Yet the commanders angrily insisted that David be sent back to Ziklag. They were afraid that in the heat of battle David might attack the Philistines in order to win his way back into the good graces of Saul.

B. Dismissal of David (1 Samuel 29:6-11)

Achish summoned David and dismissed him, but not without first praising him for his fidelity during his years of service. The text seems to suggest that the king could not overrule the collective will of the Philistine lords. David protested his dismissal, but it is hard to believe that in his heart he did not breathe a silent sigh of relief. Achish reiterated his own satisfaction with David who had been as pleasing as *an angel of God.* Nevertheless, because the commanders had insisted, he ordered David to leave at first light. In the morning David and his men went south toward the land of the Philistines while the armies of Achish marched east toward Jezreel to confront Saul.

Problems at Ziklag
1 Samuel 30:1-6

The trip from Aphek to Ziklag—about seventy-five miles—took three days. The troops arrived only to find the city in ruins. In the absence of the fighting men, those pesky Amalekites had made a raid on the city. They had taken captive all those who remained in the city. Then they had burned the place. David and his men burst forth in agonizing lamentation at the realization that their wives, sons and daughters were in the hands of Amalekites. Ahinoam and Abigail, David's wives, were among those who had been kidnapped. The agony over this loss was compounded by the murmuring of the troops. Blaming him for leaving the city without adequate defenses, they spoke of stoning David. *But David strengthened himself in Yahweh, his God,* i.e., his faith in God enabled him to deal with this crisis effectively.

Problems with his Troops
1 Samuel 30:7-25

A. Pursuit of the Amalekites (1 Samuel 30:7-20)
1. Priestly oracle (30:7-10): David sought the counsel of God through the priestly oracle administered by Abiathar. By this means he ascertained that a pursuit of the Amalekites into the desert would be successful. Forgetting their fatigue, the six hundred desperate men set out in pursuit of the enemy. Exhausted by their three-day trip from Aphek two hundred of David's men collapsed at the Brook Besor, about ten miles from Ziklag. David left them there to guard the baggage while he and four hundred stalwarts proceeded with the chase.

2. Egyptian informer (30:11-15): The search for the Amalekites discovered an Egyptian lying in the sand. Because he had had neither food nor water, the man was all but dead. He was taken to David where he received food and drink. When questioned, the Egyptian reported that he had been a servant of the Amalekites. When he had fallen sick three days earlier, the Amalekites left him to die in the desert. He agreed to lead David to their camp if David would swear not to kill him or hand him over to the Amalekites.

3. Attack on Amalekites (30:16-17): At what they considered a safe distance from the scene of their attack, the Amalekites were celebrating when David came upon them. They were eating, drinking and dancing because of the great spoil that they had taken both from the Philistines and from the people of Judah. David launched a night attack against the sprawling camp. Until evening the next day his men chased and cut down fleeing Amalekites. Only four hundred young men who rode camels were able to escape.

4. *Success of the mission (30:18-20):* So David was able to rescue his two wives. He recovered all that the Amalekites had taken. The other livestock in the Amalekite camp were regarded as David's personal spoils of victory.

B. Aftermath of Battle (1 Samuel 30:21-31)

1. *Dispute among the troops (30:21-25):* On the return trip to Ziklag, David had to settle a dispute among his men. Some of the worthless men among David's four hundred thought that the spoils of war should go only to those who actually went into battle. Those who had guarded the baggage should receive only their family members *that they may lead them away and depart.* Apparently they wanted these baggage handlers excommunicated from the community. David, however, would have none of that. Credit for the victory belonged to Yahweh, not the four hundred. Therefore, David issued a ruling that became part of Israelite military law: those who guard the baggage in war receive equal share of the spoils with those who actually fight.

2. *Gifts to Judah (30:26-31):* Upon his return to Ziklag, David sent part of the spoils from the victory to the elders of various towns throughout Judah. By this diplomatic move David was positioning himself to be elevated to kingship by his native tribe immediately after the death of Saul.

DEATH OF SAUL
1 Samuel 31-2 Samuel 1

Date: 1010 BC

Battle of Mount Gilboa
1 Samuel 31:1-13

While David was defeating the Amalekites in the desert, Saul was facing the judgment of God at Mount Gilboa.

A. Death of Saul (1 Samuel 31:1-6)

The Philistines initiated the attack against Israel. Saul's troops fled. The slopes of Mount Gilboa were covered with the corpses of

260

his fallen men. Three of Saul's sons fell that day. Then the battle pressed in on the king himself. He was wounded by Philistine archers. Fearing that he might fall into enemy hands to be abused and finally slain, Saul ordered his armorbearer to thrust him through. The armorbearer, however, feared to take the life of the king. So Saul took his sword and fell on it. His loyal armorbearer followed the example of the king. Thus was fulfilled the prophecy made by Samuel in his post-mortem appearance.

After describing how the Philistines had forced Saul to suicide, the Chronicler affirms that Yahweh slew him. He cites two reasons for the downfall of Saul: 1) his trespass that he committed against Yahweh *because of the word of Yahweh that he did not keep;* and 2) he did not inquire of Yahweh, but rather sought counsel of a witch. For these reasons Yahweh turned the kingdom over to David (1 Chronicles 10:13-14).

B. Valor of Gileadites (1 Samuel 31:7-13)

1. Philistine desecration (31:7-10): In the aftermath of the Philistine victory at Gilboa, the Israelites withdrew from the Valley of Jezreel and even certain vulnerable areas east of Jordan. For a time the Philistines occupied those cities. When the Philistines returned to Gilboa to strip the slain of valuables, they discovered the bodies of Saul and his sons. They decapitated Saul's corpse and stripped his weapons. These trophies of victory triggered joyous celebration throughout the land of the Philistines. Saul's weapons were eventually deposited in the temple of Ashtaroth, the goddess of sex and war. The Philistines nailed Saul's body and those of his sons to the wall of the town of Beth-Shan near the Jordan River.

2. Gileadite daring (31:11-13): Across the Jordan in Jabesh-gilead courageous men decided to end the desecration of Saul's body. They marched all night to Beth-Shan. They took the bodies of the royal family from the wall and returned to Jabesh. There they cremated the bodies in order to prevent any further desecration of them. Then they buried the remains beneath a tree near their city. To show respect for the dead the Gileadites fasted for seven days.

A Battle Report
2 Samuel 1:1-26

A. Report of an Amalekite (2 Samuel 1:1-10)

History of Israel

1. *Verbal report (1:1-4):* Three days after returning to the burned out site of Ziklag, David received news from the battle at Mount Gilboa. An Amalekite, who had been in the camp of Saul, came to Ziklag to report to David the outcome of the battle. The man was tattered and torn. He had dust on his head to symbolize lamentation. This man related the sad news that Israel had been put to flight before the Philistines. Saul and Jonathan were dead. To this point the report was accurate. The remainder of the report was fabricated by the Amalekite for self-serving purposes.

2. *Physical evidence (1:5-10):* David wished more verification that the king and prince were dead. The Amalekite then reported coming upon Saul leaning on his spear on Mount Gilboa. With Philistine chariots pressing in on him Saul supposedly asked this Amalekite to end the agony of his wound by slaying him. The Amalekite reported that he did as Saul had asked. He produced Saul's crown and bracelet as evidence of the truth of his account. The Amalekite apparently thought that he could curry favor with David by claiming that he had been the one to kill the king. The truth is that he must have been lurking nearby when Saul committed suicide.

B. A Just Execution (2 Samuel 1:11-16)

The reaction in Ziklag to the news of Saul's death must have shocked the Amalekite. David's men followed their beloved leader in the ritual mourning until evening. Then David summoned the Amalekite and rebuked him for having stretched out his hand against Yahweh's anointed. He then ordered one of his men to slay this servant who claimed to have slain his king. The Amalekite had condemned himself to death by his own testimony.

C. A Bitter Lamentation (2 Samuel 1:17-27)

1. *Saul and Jonathan in death (1:17-22):* David then composed a poetic lament over the deaths of Saul and Jonathan. The composition was called *the song of the bow*. It appeared in the extra biblical Book of Jashar as well as here in 2 Samuel. The poem began with a reference to the royal figures as *the beauty* and *mighty* of Israel. David could not bear the thought that the *uncircumcised* Philistines might be rejoicing over the death of the royal family. He called for Mount Gilboa to remain barren to mark the tragedy. There the royal shields were defiled in spite of the fact that both Saul and Jonathan had been valiant in battle.

2. Saul and Jonathan in life (1:23-24): David's lament continued by describing the loving relationship between Saul and Jonathan in life. They were not separated in their death. David described their physical prowess as *swifter than eagles* and *stronger than lions.* He called on the daughters of Israel to weep over Saul who had brought them prosperity.

3. Special word about Jonathan (1:25-27): The lament concluded with a special word about Jonathan. David was especially distressed over the death of this man that he considered a *brother.* His relationship with Jonathan brought David more satisfaction and joy than his relationship with any woman in his life.

Chart 9 LIFE OF DAVID *Proposed Chronology*		
EVENT	**DATE** BC	**AGE**
Birth	1040	
Anointed by Samuel	1028	12
In Saul's Court	1027	13
Fought Goliath	1021	19
In Saul's Army	1019	21
Flight from Saul	1015	25
In Achish's Army	1011	29
Anointed by Judah	1010	30
Anointed by Israel	1002	38
Sin with Bathsheba	981	59
Rebellion by Absalom	976	64
Death	970	70

19
DAVID'S EARLY REIGN
2 Samuel 2-5

CHAPTER CHRONOLOGY

		1000
	David's Reign over Judah	David Begins Reign
	7.5 Years	in Jerusalem
1009		1002

DAVID'S
REIGN OVER JUDAH
2 Samuel 2:1-3:5

Date: 1009-1002 BC
David's Anointing over Judah
2 Samuel 2:1-7

A. Move to Hebron (2 Samuel 2:1-4a)

Following the period of lamentation over Saul and Jonathan,
David inquired of Yahweh regarding his next step. By this means he
ascertained that he should move immediately from Ziklag to Hebron,
the political and geographical center of the region. All of his men and
their families relocated in the villages around Hebron. The tribal
leaders then came to Hebron and anointed David king over the house
of Judah.

B. Proper Recognition (2 Samuel 2:4b-7)

When he learned of the heroic actions of the men of Jabesh,
David immediately sent a congratulatory message to that city. He
wished Yahweh's lovingkindness upon them. He promised to show
goodness to them because they had shown kindness to Saul. David's
message closed with mention of the fact that the house of Judah had
anointed him king. The congratulatory message was an oblique
appeal to the elders of this distant city of Israel to recognize him as
king.

David's Reign Challenged
2 Samuel 2:8-3:5

Saul had many loyal followers throughout the land who were determined to prevent David from becoming king of Israel. Their problem was that the most qualified successor of Saul had died with his father at Gilboa. Abner, Saul's uncle and general, sought to rally support for Ish-bosheth the sole surviving son of the late king.

A. Plot of Abner (2 Samuel 2:8-11)
Mahanaim in Transjordan was Abner's base of operations. The presence of the Philistines west of Jordan made it impossible to maintain a capital in that region. Gradually Abner was able to secure for Ish-bosheth the support of various regions of the country. After about five years it could be said that Ish-bosheth ruled over *all Israel,* i.e., all of the tribes besides Judah. He ruled all Israel for two years. Meanwhile, David ruled in Hebron over Judah for seven and a half years.

B. Clash at Gibeon (2 Samuel 2:12-32)
1. Military entertainment (2:12-17): When he had gathered sufficient support, Abner decided to challenge David's rule of Judah. To thwart this offensive David's men advanced to Gibeon in the territory of Benjamin. At the pool there the two forces met. Joab the nephew of David was commanding the forces of Judah. Abner proposed that before the battle, champions from the opposing sides *make sport,* i.e., fight a mini battle for the entertainment of the soldiers in both armies. Joab agreed. Twelve men from each side competed. The twenty-four soldiers were so skilled in hand to hand combat that all of them eventually fell wounded. The place thereafter was named Helkath-hazzurim, "the field of sword-edges." If this contest was meant to settle the dispute between the two armies, it did not. A general battle of severe intensity followed. Abner and his men were thoroughly defeated.
2. Death of Asahel (2:18-23): An incident occurred in the battle at Gibeon that was to have serious repercussions. Asahel was killed. He was the third son of Zeruiah and younger brother of Joab and Abishai. This youth was *swift of foot.* During the course of the battle he set his sights on Abner. He determined to chase down the old general and kill him. As he scampered up and down the rough hills of

266

Benjamin, Abner spotted the young soldier bearing down on him. Twice Abner warned Asahel to turn aside lest he be killed. Abner knew that if he killed this young warrior Joab would never forgive him. Asahel, however, refused to be deterred. As he closed in on Abner, the wily old general abruptly stopped and thrust backward with the butt of his spear. Asahel was struck with such force that the butt of the spear ripped through his belly and exited his back. Asahel died on the spot. Those who came on that spot the rest of the day paused in silent tribute to the valor of this young soldier.

3. Conclusion of the battle (2:24-29): Joab and Abishai continued to press the attack on Abner out into the wilderness. Abner was eventually able to rally his fleeing soldiers in a strategic position on the top of a certain hill. Abner called to Joab and suggested that it was time to end hostilities. After all, both the pursuers and those being pursued were *brothers*. Observing that an all-out assault on the position of Abner would be extremely costly, Joab signaled his men to halt the attack. Under cover of darkness, Abner and his men marched through the Arabah (Jordan Valley), crossed the river and returned to the safety of Mahanaim.

4. Battle results (2:30-31): In the battle at Gibeon twenty of David's men were lost while Abner's losses were 360. Asahel was buried with honors in the family tomb at Bethlehem. Then by an all-night march Joab and his troops returned to Hebron.

C. Summary Statement (2 Samuel 3:1-5)

Apparently the clash at Gibeon was the first of many encounters between those who supported the son of Saul, and those who followed David. Gradually the house of Saul grew weaker. During the seven plus years at Hebron David continued to prosper. He took three additional wives, one of whom was the daughter of the king of Geshur. Each of his wives bore him one son during this period.

COLLAPSE OF SAUL'S HOUSE
2 Samuel 3:6-4:12

Date: 1003 BC

David's bid to succeed Saul as king of a united Israel was strengthened considerably by a strange turn of events among the supporters of the opposition.

Accusation against Abner
2 Samuel 3:6-11

A. Abner's Ambitions (2 Samuel 3:6-7)

Early on Abner was intensely loyal to the house of Saul. At the same time he viewed David as a threat to the nation. In Abner's view, David's associations with King Achish of Gath disqualified him from any consideration of kingship. The text hints at some point Abner began to have some personal ambition. With the weak Ish-bosheth totally dependent on him, Abner *was making himself strong in the house of Saul* (NASB). Ish-bosheth accused Abner of a sexual relationship with Rizpah, one of Saul's concubines. To take the wives of a king was a method of positioning oneself for a bid for the crown. Whether or not Abner was guilty as charged is difficult to ascertain from the text.

B. Abner's Anger (3:8-11)

Abner exploded with anger at the accusation of Ish-bosheth. He could not believe that after all the kindness he had shown to the house of Saul that anyone could think him guilty of such treachery. At any time Abner could have delivered Ish-bosheth over to David. Now because he had been (falsely?) accused, Abner swore that he would use his influence to see David acknowledged as ruler of Israel from Dan to Beersheba. Ish-bosheth was so intimidated by this outburst that he could not say a word to his general.

Negotiations with Abner
2 Samuel 3:12-21

A. Condition for Reconciliation (3:12-16)

1. David wants Michal back (3:12-14): Abner immediately sent messengers to Hebron. He wanted David to enter into a covenant with him. If that came about, Abner promised to bring all Israel over to him. Before David was willing to consider a covenant, however, he insisted that his first wife Michal, daughter of Saul, be returned to him. To re-establish his marriage with the daughter of the former king was meant to strengthen David's claim to the throne in the eyes of many supporters of Saul.

2. Michal's sad return (3:15-16): With his chief military officer negotiating with his rival Ish-bosheth was in no position to deny

David's request. He took Michal from her current husband Paltiel (Palti) and had her escorted to Hebron. Her husband sorrowfully followed, helpless to reclaim his wife. When Paltiel reached Bahurim, Abner ordered him to return. The text gives no indication of Michal's attitude about being returned to her rightful husband.

B. Summit at Hebron (2 Samuel 3:17-21)

1. Abner's efforts for David (3:17-19): True to his word, Abner began to consult with the elders of Israel about supporting David. He pointed out to them that in time past they had preferred David to Saul. Now Abner urged them to recognize David. He told them that Yahweh had designated David as the savior from the Philistines. After he had secured the support of the other tribes, Abner approached the tribe of Benjamin. This tribe was the base of Saul's support. Abner agreed to carry the concerns of the northern elders to David.

2. Abner's trip to Hebron (3:20-21): Abner with a twenty-man honor guard came to David at Hebron. They were welcomed with open arms. Details of the negotiations are not related. At the end of the feast, however, Abner was prepared to gather all Israel that they might make a covenant with David. Abner was dismissed with David's blessing.

Murder of Abner
2 Samuel 3:22-39

A. Duplicity of Joab (2 Samuel 3:22-27)

At this point Joab returned with the troops from a raid. When he was informed that Abner had just left with the king's blessing, Joab rebuked David. He was suspicious that Abner was feigning support in order to spy out the strength of Judah. Without notifying David, Joab sent messengers to bring Abner back to Hebron. When he returned, Joab took him aside into the middle of the gate on the pretext of speaking to him privately. There he slew Abner *on account of the blood of Asahel his brother.*

B. Reaction of David (2 Samuel 3:28-39)

1. David's shock and anger (3:28-30): David was shocked when he heard what his general had done. He publicly proclaimed his innocence in the matter. He pronounced a malediction on Joab and his

269

descendants. He wished sickness, poverty, weakness and hunger on Joab's family perpetually.

2. *Formal lamentation (3:31-34):* The king ordered his supporters, including Joab, publicly to lament the death of Abner. David himself followed the bier to the grave. There he and all his followers wept. The king chanted a lamentation that he had composed in honor of Abner. The man had experienced a death unworthy of him. He had not died in battle, nor had he been executed as a common criminal. Abner had been treacherously murdered.

3. *Dealing with the murderer (3:35-39):* After the burial, the people tried to get David to eat. He vowed he would not taste food until sundown. The people were pleased with this demonstration of grief over the murder of his former enemy. They rightly concluded that David had nothing to do with the cold-blooded murder of Abner. The king regarded Abner as *a prince and a great man* in Israel. His sense of justice called for punishment against Joab. Yet, even though he was king, he regarded the two sons of Zeruiah as *too difficult* to handle. All he could do was to call upon Yahweh to punish the evil that Joab had done.

Death of Ish-bosheth
2 Samuel 4:1-12

A. Plotters (2 Samuel 4:1-4)

The death of Abner sent shock waves throughout Israel. Ish-bosheth lost his courage (lit., "his hands went limp") and all his subjects were *disturbed.* Two Benjamite brothers, who were commanders in Ish-bosheth's army, decided to take advantage of the situation. They decided to assassinate the king so as to gain some recognition from David. The author then notes parenthetically that no other viable candidate for the throne could be found within the royal family. The son of Jonathan was now only twelve. He had been crippled from childhood. He was unwilling or unable to press any claims to the throne.

B. Execution of the Plot (2 Samuel 4:5-7)

On a hot day when Ish-bosheth was taking a siesta in his house, Baanah and Rechab made their move. Under the pretext of entering the house to get some wheat (probably rations for their troops), they entered the royal chamber and assassinated their king. They then decapitated Ish-bosheth. After making good their escape from Mahanaim, the two traveled all night through the Arabah (Jordan Valley) to make their way to Hebron.

C. Execution of the Assassins (2 Samuel 4:8-12)

The assassins presented the head of Ish-bosheth to David. They thought they would be rewarded for having eliminated David's enemy. They suggested that through their action Yahweh had taken vengeance on the house of Saul. David, however, was of a different mind. If he had ordered the execution of a man who thought he had brought good news of Saul's death, how much more would he execute those guilty of murdering an innocent man in his own bed. At that sentence David's men fell on Rechab and Baanah and slew them. The hands and feet were removed from the corpses, and their bodies were hung up beside the pool in Hebron. The mutilation of the dead bodies was a sign that these men had raised their hands against royalty. Then David took the head of Ish-bosheth and buried it in the grave of Abner in Hebron.

DAVID RECOGNIZED
BY ALL ISRAEL
2 Samuel 5:1-25

Date: 1002 BC

During the long years after his anointing at Bethlehem, David made no effort to seize the throne by force. He patiently waited for the prophecy of Samuel to be fulfilled. He trusted God to work his will. In 2 Samuel 5 the text chronicles the steps by which David finally was established on the throne of united Israel.

Coronation at Hebron
2 Samuel 5:1-5

A. Anointing by Elders (2 Samuel 5:1-3)

In response to the efforts of Abner the elders of the tribes came to Hebron after the death of Ish-bosheth. They acknowledged that 1) they were David's *bone and flesh.* 2) Even when Saul was king it was David who had been their military leader. 3) Yahweh had promised David that he would be *shepherd,* i.e., ruler, of Israel. David then made a covenant with these elders. What concessions he may have made to secure the recognition of these elders is not stated. The elders responded by anointing David to be king of Israel.

B. Celebration by Tribes (1 Chronicles 12:23-40)

The Chronicler relates more details about the glorious three-day celebration in Hebron at the anointing of David. Each tribe sent a sizable contingent of armed men. These all came *with perfect heart* to make David king. The celebration lasted three days. The locals provided most of the provisions; but tribes as far as Issachar, Zebulun and Naphtali brought great quantities of food on all means of conveyance. *There was joy indeed in Israel.*

David was thirty when he became king (of all Israel?). In round figures, he reigned forty years. Seven and a half years he ruled over Judah from Hebron. His rule over all Israel was thirty-three years (2 Samuel 5:4-5).

Capture of Jerusalem
2 Samuel 5:6-10

A. Jebusite Challenge (2 Samuel 5:6-7)

Perhaps as a result of the covenant with the elders of the northern tribes, David's first order of business was to establish a new capital for the united nation. Jebus (Jerusalem), which was strategically situated on the border of Judah and Benjamin, was selected. The fortress of this city was still occupied by Jebusites. They were so confident of the impregnability of their city that they boasted that even blind and lame men could defend the place against David.

B. David's Challenge (2 Samuel 5:8)

By three statements David challenged his men to capture Zion. 1) He indicated that those Jebusites who had sarcastically referred to themselves as *blind and lame* were *hated* by David, i.e., they were his enemies. 2) The way into the fortress was through the water tunnel. 3) Whoever struck down a Jebusite first would be commander of the entire army.

C. Joab's Actions (2 Samuel 5:9-10)

Joab was the first to scale the vertical water tunnel and enter Jebus. He therefore became commander of the army. Once the city was secure David took up residence in that stronghold. Since the place had been conquered by David's men and since David resided there, the place was called *the city of David.* Jerusalem's fortifications were repaired and extended. Once established in his new capital David became greater and greater because Yahweh of hosts was with him.

Growth in the Family
2 Samuel 5:13-16

Unfortunately David followed the example of foreign kings in building up a large harem. He had six sons by six wives while living in Hebron (cf. 2 Samuel 3:2-5). Thirteen sons are named as having been fathered by David in Jerusalem. David also fathered several unnamed sons by concubines. Tamar, one of his many daughters, is named because of the prominence that she will have in later narrative (1 Chronicles 3:9).

Victories over the Philistines
2 Samuel 5:17-25

During the seven years in which David ruled in Hebron the Philistines appear to have been dormant. Perhaps they looked on David as a friend. The text says nothing about what became of the Philistines who occupied the villages of the Valley of Jezreel in 1010 BC (1 Samuel 31:7). Presumably Abner had driven them out of the land at some point. Now that the tribes were united, however, the Philistines became concerned. They were determined to cut David off from his northern subjects by driving a military wedge through the center of the Israel.

A. First Philistine Invasion (2 Samuel 5:17-21)
The first Philistine invasion was intended to capture David. Most likely it should be dated prior to David's move from Hebron to Jerusalem. When David heard these old enemies were marching eastward in search of him, he went down to the *stronghold,* probably the old cave of Adullam. The Philistines spread out their forces in the Valley of Rephaim, the western approach to Jerusalem. His actions sanctioned by the priestly oracle, David attacked the Philistines and broke through their ranks. He named that spot Baal-Perazim ("the master of breaking through"). In their flight the Philistines abandoned

273

their idols. David and his men carried them away and burned them (cf. 1 Chronicles 14:12).

B. Second Philistine Invasion (2 Samuel 5:22-25)

Sometime later the Philistines returned to the valley of Rephaim. Again David inquired of Yahweh about a possible attack. He was told to circle behind the enemy. When he heard *the sound of marching,* i.e., rustling, in the tops of the balsam trees, then he should attack. God promised to go before him into battle. David followed these instructions and secured the victory. His men struck down the army of the Philistines from Gibeon (six miles northwest of Jerusalem) and Geba even as far as Gezer, some fifteen miles further to the northwest. As a result of this victory the fame and fear of David spread to surrounding lands (cf. 1 Chronicles 14:13-17).

Chart 10
PREACH THE WORD
The Youth Who Pursued Death

Text: 2 Samuel 2:18-23
Basic Idea: Asahel a picture of every sinner who chases after the things of the world until he is destroyed.

    A. The Danger that Confronted him.
    B. The Deception that Emboldened him (trusting youth & speed)
    C. The Determination that Gripped him
    D. The Disaster that Met Him

Appeal: Turn aside from your wild pursuit of death.

20
EARLY
PROBLEMS FOR DAVID
2 Samuel 6, 9, 21

Chapter Chronology

1000	2 Years	998

DAVID AND
MEPHIBOSHETH
2 Samuel 9:1-13

Summons
2 Samuel 9:1-5

The benevolence of David toward the son of Jonathan indicates the soft side of his personality. Normally oriental kings made the total elimination of the former royal house the first order of business in a new regime. David, however, was of a different spirit. From Ziba, a former servant in Saul's house, David learned that a crippled son of Jonathan was still living. David sent to Lo-debar in Transjordan for this son.

Arrangements
2 Samuel 9:6-8

Mephibosheth must have feared the worst as he prostrated himself before the king. David assured him, however, that he had nothing to fear. For the sake of Jonathan he promised to restore all the lands of Saul to this young man. In addition, David decreed that Mephibosheth eat at the royal table regularly, i.e., he was to be part of David's court. At this good news, Mephibosheth again prostrated himself and confessed his unworthiness to receive such honor.

David then summoned Ziba and appointed him to manage the lands of Mephibosheth. With fifteen sons and twenty servants of his own, Ziba was certainly in a position to assume such responsibility. This he agreed to do.

Explanation

So Mephibosheth lived in Jerusalem. He ate at the king's table where he was treated like one of David's sons. In trying to ascertain the chronology of this incident, these facts need to be considered: 1) Mephibosheth was five when he was dropped by a nurse and became a cripple (2 Samuel 4:4). David ruled seven and a half years at Hebron before becoming king of Israel (2 Samuel 5:5). That makes Mephibosheth almost thirteen at the time David was recognized as king by all the tribes. Since Mephibosheth had *a young son* at the time he received his court position, one must place the recognition of Mephibosheth at least five years (and possibly more) into David's reign over all the tribes.

Why has the author of Samuel included the account of David's kindness to Mephibosheth here? At least three reasons have been suggested. 1) God had kept his word to David; so David now kept his word to Jonathan. 2) The account introduces two characters (Ziba and Mephibosheth) who figure prominently in the struggles of David later. 3) The account demonstrates that David was secure in the throne. He could afford to be magnanimous to a representative of the former royal family.

DEALING WITH A FAMINE
2 Samuel 21:1-14

Date: ca. 1000 BC

Reason for the Famine
2 Samuel 21:1-2

At some point in the reign of David Israel experienced three years of famine. When the famine persisted, David concluded that this was no ordinary quirk of nature. The king *sought the presence of Yahweh,* i.e., he consulted the priestly oracle, in order to verify his hunch.

The oracle indicated that Israel was being punished for Saul's criminal acts against the Gibeonites. The lives of the Gibeonites were protected by an ancient covenant that Joshua had made with these people (Joshua 9). In his zeal for Israel, Saul attempted to rid the land of these Amorites. Perhaps he wished to confiscate their property to reward the Benjamites who were loyal to him (cf. 1 Samuel 22:7). In any case, Saul's actions were a national crime since a national covenant had been broken. The people were guilty in that they permitted their king to act in this lawless manner. Murder left unpunished polluted the land (Numbers 35:33). The famine was the punishment for that pollution.

**Consultation
With the Gibeonites**
2 Samuel 21:3-6

A. David's Commitment (2 Samuel 21:3-4)

David asked the Gibeonite leaders what he should do to make atonement for Israel's transgression of a solemn covenant. He desired for the aggrieved people to turn their curses into blessings for *the inheritance of Yahweh,* i.e., the land that Yahweh had given to his people for their inheritance. The Gibeonites indicated that no amount of monetary payment could make things right. They further stated that it was not their place to execute any Israelite. To do so might only bring on them the wrath of the more powerful Israelites around them. The hint here was that execution—the shedding of blood—was the only way atonement could be made for the many Gibeonites who had died at the hands of Saul. David then committed himself to do for these Gibeonites whatever they stipulated as being just.

B. Gibeonite Requirement (2 Samuel 21:5-6)

Saul had tried to exterminate the Gibeonites. Only the execution of seven of his sons (descendants) could atone for the violation of the covenant with Gibeon. The Gibeonites wished to *hang them before Yahweh in Gibeah,* i.e., impale them on sharp stakes in their native village. Perhaps some stipulation to this effect was actually written in the treaty that Israel had with Gibeon. In any case, David agreed to hand over the seven Saulides.

Guilty Punished
2 Samuel 21:7-9

A. Execution of Saulides (2 Samuel 21:7-9)

277

David took two sons of Saul by the concubine Rizpah, Armoni and Mephibosheth (not to be confused with the son of Jonathan who was spared). Merab's five sons—grandsons of Saul—were also taken. These men all *fell together,* i.e., they were executed, at the same time in the first days of the barley harvest. They were then handed over to the Gibeonites for impalement.

B. Explanation

If these seven men were innocent of any involvement in the crimes of Saul, then David violated God's law. No innocent family member was to be executed for the crimes of another member of the family. Since David is not here condemned for any violation of the law, one must assume that these seven had been personally involved in the ethnic cleansing attributed to Saul.

C. Chronological Issues

Does the chronology, however, allow for personal involvement of the seven men? Certainly Saul's two sons could have been involved; but what about his grandsons? Would they have been old enough? That depends on when this episode is dated.

Most likely, the famine occurred early in David's reign over all Israel. That was the earliest David would have controlled the tribal territory of Benjamin and consequently be responsible for the actions of those living there. Merab had been married even before David was forced to leave Saul's court. The chronological clues sprinkled through the account of David indicate that at least twenty years elapsed between Merab's marriage and David's coronation as king of all the tribes. Thus Merab's sons were teenagers at the time David became ruler of all Israel. They certainly would have been old enough to have joined other Saulides in the ethnic crimes against the Gibeonites.

Devotion Rewarded
2 Samuel 21:10-14

A. Rizpah's Guardianship (2 Samuel 21:10)

Rizpah, the mother of two of the executed men, could not give the corpses of her sons proper burial without violating the royal edict. She did the next best thing. She spread out sackcloth on a rock and sat down near the decaying bodies of the seven men. She made sure neither the birds by day nor the beasts by night had access to the bodies. This dedicated, living scarecrow kept her faithful watch until the famine ended and the rains fell. By that time only the skeletons remained.

B. David's Recognition (2 Samuel 21:11-14)

David was deeply moved by the dedication of Rizpah. Therefore he issued two commands. First, he ordered the bones of Saul and Jonathan brought from Jabesh-gilead and reburied in the tomb of Kish, the father of Saul. This action demonstrated that David had no personal animosity toward the house of Saul. Second, he ordered the bones of the seven recently executed descendants of Saul buried in the same tomb. Only after these men had been given a proper burial was God moved by the entreaty for the land.

MOVING THE ARK
TO JERUSALEM
2 Samuel 6

Date: ca. 998 BC

Establishing Jerusalem as a center of worship for the entire nation was the priority of the early years of David's reign. The obvious first step in bringing this about was to transport the ark, the ancient symbol of the covenant, to Jerusalem. This was accomplished in two stages.

Learning Reverence
2 Samuel 6:1-10

A. Honor Guard (2 Samuel 6:1)

After consulting with his military commanders, David proposed to the assembly of Israel that the ark be transported to Jerusalem, the new capital. The assembly concurred. The king then assembled an honor guard of thirty thousand men from all of Israel to escort the ark of God to Jerusalem. This representative force traveled the ten miles from Jerusalem to Baale-judah (Baalah; Kiriath-Jearim) where the ark had resided for some seven decades.

B. Ark Transportation (2 Samuel 6:2-5)

Unfortunately David did not take time to research the proper manner of transporting the ark. He placed the sacred chest on an ox

279

cart. Two brothers, Uzzah and Ahio, who been custodians of the ark, were accompanying the cart. Ahio was out in front; Uzzah was walking beside the cart. David and all his men were celebrating with religious fervor using musical instruments of various kinds.

C. Death of Uzzah (2 Samuel 6:6-7)
When the procession had reached the threshing floor of Nacon a tragedy took place. The oxen stumbled. The ark nearly toppled to the ground. Uzzah reached out his hand to steady the ark. Uzzah's good intentions notwithstanding, Yahweh's anger burned against him. Because of his irreverence, Uzzah died there beside the ark. As a Levite and one who had watched over the ark during its stay at Kiriath-Jearim, Uzzah should have known the proper manner in which the ark was to be transported. (See Numbers 4:5, 15, 19-20). Touching the ark was the proverbial straw that broke the camel's back. It was but the culmination of a cavalier attitude that gave little consideration to sacredness of the ark.

D. Ark at Rest (2 Samuel 6:8-10)
David was angry over the incident. He probably blamed himself for not being more careful in his plans for moving the ark. Because he now feared the Lord, David wondered if the movement of the ark to Jerusalem would ever be possible. The king ordered the ark to be taken aside off the road to the nearby house of the Levite Obed-Edom the Gittite, i.e., a man from Gath Rimmon.

Celebrating Success
2 Samuel 6:11-19

A. Reason for Second Attempt (2 Samuel 6:11-12)
The ark remained at the house of Obed-Edom for three months. During that period Yahweh blessed this man with a blessing that must have been noticeable to others. David decided to try again to move the ark to Jerusalem for two reasons. 1) Yahweh was blessing Obed-Edom; and 2) David had learned the reason for the initial failure.

B. Involvement of Priests (1 Chronicles 15:3-15)
Again David assembled *all Israel,* i.e., representatives of all Israel, at Jerusalem. The assembly included the elders and the captains over thousands (cf. 1 Chronicles 15:25). The second

movement of the ark, however, was attended primarily by 862 priests
and Levites rather than military units. By royal order these religious
leaders first consecrated themselves. After this had been done, the
Levites reverently attached poles to the ark and hoisted the sacred
chest to their shoulders *as Moses had commanded according to the
word of Yahweh.*

C. Interim Celebration (2 Samuel 6:13-15)

After they cautiously had moved the ark but six paces, the
procession stopped and David offered an ox and a fatling to God.
Apparently at various intervals along the way the procession paused
to offer similar sacrifices *because God was helping the Levites who
were carrying the ark* (cf. 1 Chronicles 15:26).

David was jubilant that all was going well. He enthusiastically led
the procession with vigorous dancing. For this he had removed his
royal robes and was wearing only an ephod, a short, sleeveless,
garment. The people were shouting praise. Stringed instruments,
horns and cymbals accompanied the loud praise. Chenaniah, chief of
the Levites, directed the singing *because he was skillful.*

D. Ark Positioned (2 Samuel 6:17-19)

The ark was placed inside a special tent that David had erected
for it. Again the king offered sacrifice before the Lord. This was
followed by a fellowship meal for which David provided the food.
The king then blessed the people in the name of Yahweh.

Defending Zeal
2 Samuel 6:16, 20-23

A. Michal's Scorn (2 Samuel 6:16, 20-22)

As the procession enter Jerusalem Michal observed the religious
zeal of her husband from a window in the royal residence. In her heart
she despised David (6:16). Why Michal found David's actions so
disgusting is not stated. Returning to his home in a joyous mood,
David was greeted by a sullen, sarcastic wife. She verbally chastised
her husband for acting like a fool by uncovering himself in the eyes of
the maids of Israel. Though the actions of the king may have been
undignified, they were not immodest. David defended himself by
saying that he had been celebrating before Yahweh. He was happy to
abase himself before God and honor the Lord before the people. He

281

reminded Saul's daughter that Yahweh had selected him over her father. He assured her that although he might in the future be even more lightly esteemed by people with the mindset of Michal, he would in fact be distinguished in the eyes of those maids to which his wife had referred.

B. Michal's Punishment (2 Samuel 6:23)

Michal had no child to the day of her death. The placement of the verse at this point suggests that Michal's barrenness may have been a punishment for the attitude that she manifested toward the religious zeal of her husband. Others think the verse points to the permanent estrangement between David and Michal.

Ordering Worship
1 Chronicles 16:4-42

A. Musical Appointments (1 Chronicles 16:1-36)

When the ark was installed in Jerusalem, David appointed priests and Levites to ministerial posts. Asaph was the chief of those appointed to lead the praise before the ark. A lengthy psalm, apparently composed for the occasion, is recorded in Chronicles. It is not clear who authored this beautiful composition.

B. Other Appointments (1 Chronicles 16:37-42)

In addition to the Levites and priests who led the musical celebration at the tent in Jerusalem, David appointed Obed-Edom and sixty-eight of his relatives as gatekeepers. Zadok was the priest in charge at the tabernacle which was now located at Gibeon. The prescribed morning and evening sacrifices were reinstituted. Levitical musicians were also assigned to the tabernacle. Heman and Jeduthun led the praise service there with trumpets and cymbals.

ORGANIZING
THE KINGDOM

The growth of the kingdom necessitated the creation of new administrative positions.

Top Positions

2 Samuel 8:15-18

The greatness of David's kingdom is indicated by the growth in the royal court. Joab had won appointment as military commander by his heroics in the capture of the stronghold of Zion. Jehoshaphat was the recorder, charged with the responsibility of keeping the royal records. Zadok, the priest under Saul, shared the priesthood with Ahimelech the son of Abiathar, David's priest. Seraiah was secretary who penned the royal proclamations. Benaiah commanded a unit made up of mercenary Cherethites and Pelethites—peoples closely related to the Philistines—that served as the royal bodyguard. David's sons served as *chief ministers,* (lit., "priests"). Thus Saul's simple court now had evolved into a complex royal bureaucracy.

Other Officers
1 Chronicles 26:20-27:34

A. Treasury Officers (1 Chronicles 26:20-28)
Apparently often various national leaders dedicated valuable objects to the Lord. These were stored in the temple under the watchful eye of royal officials.

B. "Outward Business" (1 Chronicles 26:29-32)
David had officers who were in charge of the affairs of the kingdom in respect to the work of the Lord and the service of the king. The king had 1,700 *capable* men west of Jordan, and 2,700 east of the river. The exact duties of these officers are not known.

C. Military Officers (1 Chronicles 27:1-15)
David organized his army into divisions numbering 24,000, each with its own commander. These divisions served on active duty one month each year. Some of the commanders are familiar to the student of Israel's history, e.g., Benaiah and Asahel.

D. Tribal Officers (1 Chronicles 27:16-24)
Each of the tribes had its own *prince.* In Judah David's brother Elihu held this position. Here the author includes a note about David's census. David did not count those under twenty years of age. To do so would have called in question the promise of Yahweh to

multiply Israel as the stars of heaven. Joab had started to count them, but did not finish. Because he started, however, wrath came upon Israel. The incomplete census numbers were not included in the account of the chronicles of King David.

E. Overseers of Property (1 Chronicles 27:25-31)

Crown officers supervised storehouses, agricultural workers, vineyards, wine cellars, oil stores, vineyards, and livestock of various kinds.

F. Counselors (1 Chronicles 27:32-34)

Jonathan, David's *uncle* or near relative was a counselor and scribe. The reference is probably to the Jonathan mentioned in 1 Chronicles 20:7 who was a nephew of David. Jehiel *was with the king's sons,* i.e., he was their tutor. The counselor Ahithophel was the Judas of the Old Testament. He deserted David during the Absalom rebellion. Hushai was *the king's friend* or close advisor. During the Absalom rebellion he remained loyal to David and frustrated the counsel of Ahithophel (cf. 2 Samuel 15:32ff, 17:5ff).

Jehoiada the son of Benaiah replaced Ahithophel after the latter committed suicide. Abiathar was chief priest along with Zadok. He advised David in ritual matters. Joab was over the host. He advised David in military matters.

21
ACCOMPLISHMENTS IN
DAVID'S REIGN
2 Samuel 5, 8, 10, 12, 23

Chapter Chronology

	988
7 Years	
995	

MILITARY
ACCOMPLISHMENTS

Date: ca. 995-988 BC

David expanded the territory controlled by Israel significantly in all directions. His conquests resulted in foreign tribute flowing into the coffers of his kingdom. Distant kings swore vassal allegiance to David.

Against Old Enemies
2 Samuel 8:1-2

A. Against Philistines (2 Samuel 8:1)

Early in his reign David decisively had turned back two major Philistine invasions of Israel. When he was sufficiently strong he went on the attack against these old enemies. He subdued them and took control of their chief city, probably Gath.

A number of heroes in David's army distinguished themselves in various campaigns against the Philistines early in David's reign. The episodes have in common that in each case one of the sons of *the giant* was defeated. These giants employed by the Philistines were the last surviving members of the Rephaim, a tall race that once inhabited parts of Canaan in large numbers. With each new giant they could put forward, the Philistines took new courage in their ongoing battles with the Israelites. In each engagement, however, the giant was slain and the Philistines were trounced.

1.   *First Philistine campaign (2 Samuel 21:16-17):* In one battle David became weary. A Philistine giant named Ishbi-benob pressed down upon him. This powerful man wielded a spear that had a point weighing three hundred shekels of bronze (8 lbs). Had not Abishai aided the king he surely would have been killed. This near escape caused the troops to insist that David no longer go into battle with them lest *the lamp of Israel,* i.e., the king himself, be extinguished.

2.   *Two more Philistine campaigns (2 Samuel 21:18-19):* Two battles with the Philistines were fought at Gob near Gezer (cf. 1 Chronicles 20:4), about twenty miles southeast of modern Tel Aviv. In the first Sibbecai smote Saph, another of the Philistine giants. Sibbecai was a member of the Thirty, a military order attained through gallantry in battle (1 Chronicles 11:29). At some point he was made commander of the eighth division of David's army (1 Chronicles 27:11). In the second battle at Gob, Elhanan killed Lahmi the brother of Goliath the Gittite (cf. 1 Chronicles 20:5).

3.   *Fourth Philistine campaign (2 Samuel 21:20-22):* A fourth Philistine giant had six fingers on each hand and six toes on each foot. He defied Israel before the battle much like Goliath had done (cf. 1 Samuel 17:8-10). David's nephew Jonathan struck down this formidable adversary.

B. Against Moabites (2 Samuel 8:2)

After defeating the Moabites, David was especially harsh with the captives. They were forced to lie on the ground and then were measured with a line. Two lines were executed, and one was spared. These men had committed such notorious atrocities that David deemed the death penalty appropriate. The sparing of one third of the captives was viewed in the ancient world as a benevolent act. These remaining Moabites became servants of David, sending him annual tribute.

Against the Arameans
2 Samuel 8:3-12

A. Defeat of Hadadezer (2 Samuel 8:3-4)

David won a major victory when he defeated Hadadezer of the kingdom of Zobah near the Euphrates River. The captives numbered 7,000 cavalrymen, 1,000 chariots, and 20,000 foot soldiers. Since the Israelite army at this time had neither cavalry nor chariotry, David ordered all but a hundred of the chariot horses hamstrung (lamed). This action rendered the horses useless for military purposes.

B. Second Victory over Arameans (2 Samuel 8:5-6)
When the Arameans of Damascus attempted to come to the aid of Hadadezer, David won a second impressive victory in the north. Some 22,000 of the enemy were killed. Israelite occupation forces were stationed among the Arameans of Damascus. The Aramean people sent tribute to David throughout his reign.

C. Spoils from the North (2 Samuel 8:7-12)
1. War booty (8:7-8): From his campaigns in the north David returned to Jerusalem with valuable spoils. For example, from the servants of Hadadezer he had captured a number of golden shields. These eventually were housed in the treasury of the temple. Some of the cities in Hadadezer's kingdom yielded to David a large amount of bronze. Solomon later made use of this bronze to construct the brazen "sea," the huge pillars, and bronze utensils of the temple.
2. Gift from Toi (8:9-12): Toi (or Tou), king of Hamath, was grateful to David for defeating Hadadezer. He expressed his appreciation by dispatching his son with valuable gifts of gold, silver and bronze. Toi apparently was seeking either an alliance, or protection from David. These items, as well as all similar tribute, were dedicated to Yahweh.

Against the Edomites
2 Samuel 8:13-14

David's reputation as a military genius was enhanced when he won a decisive battle over the Edomites[25] in the Valley of Salt. Some 18,000 Edomites fell. The field commander in this operation was Abishai (1 Chronicles 18:12). David was able to put garrisons throughout Edom. The Edomites became his vassals.

---

[25]The Masoretic Text reads *Arameans*. That this is a likely scribal error for *Edomites* is indicated by the following considerations: 1) It is improbable that the Arameans would have such a large force in the Valley of Salt near the southern end of the Dead Sea. 2) In Hebrew the words *Arameans* and *Edomites* look almost alike. 3) The parallel passage in 1 Chronicles 18:12, the Septuagint, and 2 Samuel 8:14 all indicate that the war was against Edom.

Campaign against Ammon
2 Samuel 10:1-19; 12:26-31

The results of the war against Ammon were summarized in 2 Samuel 8:3-8. That campaign here receives expanded treatment because 1) it was an extremely fierce struggle, one in which Israel met with near disaster; 2) it explains how distant Aramean city states became involved in hostilities with the kingdom of David; and 3) during this campaign David committed his greatest sin.

A. Diplomacy Rejected (2 Samuel 10:1-5)

The Ammonite King Nahash, who once had attacked Jabesh-gilead, had shown kindness to David. When he died his son Hanun ascended the throne. David sent high-ranking diplomats to convey his condolences over the father's death. Hanun's advisors, however, poisoned his mind against David. They suggested that these diplomats had come to spy out Rabbah—modern Amman, about twenty miles east of the Jordan—the Ammonite capital. The new king decided to humiliate David's representatives. He 1) shaved off half of their beards; and 2) cut off their robes at the hips thus shamefully exposing them. He then sent them away. The humiliated ambassadors were directed by David to tarry in Jericho until their beards had grown back before returning to Jerusalem.

B. First Ammon Campaign (2 Samuel 10:6-14)

1. Hiring mercenaries (10:6-7): The Ammonites realized that their disrespect for the Israelite ambassadors would lead to war. Consequently Hanun hired 33,000 mercenaries from the Aramean states to the north. When he received news of this large troop movement, David dispatched Joab and the army to attack Rabbah.

2. Ammonite deployment (10:8): The Ammonites formed their battle ranks at the entrance of their capital. The Aramean mercenaries were strategically positioned nearby in the open field, probably out of sight. Their assignment was to attack Joab from the rear once the Israelite army launched a frontal attack on the Ammonites.

3. Coping with ambush (10:9-12): The Israelites apparently marched into a trap at Rabbah. Joab was forced to divide his army. He quickly selected some of the better units to lead personally against the Arameans. The remainder of the army was placed under the command of his brother Abishai to fight the Ammonites. Joab urged all the troops to fight courageously.

4. *Ammonites defeated (10:13-14):* While Abishai held the Ammonites in check Joab took the battle to the Arameans. After a fierce struggle the enemy broke ranks and fled. When the Ammonites saw that their allies had fled, they retreated behind the walls of their capital. At that point Joab terminated the campaign either because the casualties had been too heavy, or because he did not have the resources to lay siege to the city.

Another Aramean Campaign
2 Samuel 10:15-19

A. Aramean Threat (2 Samuel 10:15-16)

The Arameans were determined to avenge the earlier defeat at the hands of Israel. Hadadezer assembled troops from several Aramean city states. A strong force assembled at Helam on the northeast border of Israel. The unified command was given to Shobach, the commander of Hadadezer's army.

B. Israelite Victory (2 Samuel 10:17-19)

In response, David mobilized his army and crossed the Jordan. He may have surprised the enemy with this rapid mobilization and deployment of troops. In the battle of Helam again the Arameans fled before Israel. David's forces killed 700 charioteers and 40,000 horsemen. General Shobach also lost his life in the battle. All of Hadadezer's vassals then made peace with David. No more did they come to the aid of the Ammonites.

OTHER ACCOMPLISHMENTS

Musical Accomplishments

Five Davidic poems are found in the historical books:

- Song of the Bow (2 Samuel 1): Death of Saul & Jonathan.
- Lament over Abner (2 Samuel 3): Death of Abner.
- Song of Rest (2 Samuel 22): Deliverance from Saul.

- Song of the Ark (1 Chronicles 16): Ark brought to Jerusalem.
- David's Last Words (2 Samuel 23): Just before his death.

In addition to these poems found in the historical books, David made a hefty contribution to the Book of Psalms. In the Psalm headings seventy-three psalms are attributed to David; five additional psalms are attributed to him in the New Testament. David may have written most of the anonymous psalms as well. He may have been responsible for gathering the first collection of psalms (Psalms 1-41).

Building Accomplishments

David was responsible for building a wall of defense against the Philistines which has been discovered by archaeologists. He built a royal palace as well.

In the technological realm, the mastery of manufacturing iron implements in Israel took place during David's reign. See 1 Chronicles 22:3.

Diplomatic Accomplishments
2 Samuel 5:11-12

One of David's diplomatic triumphs was a trade agreement with Hiram king of Tyre that resulted in an economic boom. The mention of King Hiram's recognition of David as early as 2 Samuel 5 gives the impression that he was among the first to enter into a covenant with David. Actually, archaeologists provide information that makes it clear Hiram did not begin to reign until 979 BC. At that time David was in his last years of life. Thus it is clear that the author of 2 Samuel was not narrating events in a strictly chronological sequence. The only other possibility is that Hiram was active in the government of his father prior to becoming king in 979 BC.

Certainly the author regarded the covenant between Hiram and David as a most significant development. The Tyrian king sent cedar wood and skilled craftsmen to Jerusalem to build a palace for David. This gesture of recognition caused David to realize that 1) Yahweh truly had established him as king of Israel; and 2) Yahweh had exalted his kingdom for the sake of his people Israel.

290

HEROES OF
DAVID'S ARMY

The second list of military heroes contains the names of those who helped David win the throne and conquer Zion. The names in 2 Samuel are arranged in three groups which are military orders of honor. Twelve from these groups were appointed commanders of divisions of David's army (1 Chronicles 27). Chronicles adds the names of others that David deemed worthy of special honor for their commitment to him in the period before he received the crown.

Supreme Honor
2 Samuel 23:8-12

A. Josheb-basshebeth (2 Samuel 23:8)
Three warriors received the supreme recognition from King David. The group was simply known as "the Three." The commander of this group was Josheb-basshebeth, also known as Adino the Eznite. He had slain eight hundred men with his spear in one encounter.

B. Eleazar the Ahohite (2 Samuel 23:9-10)
The second member of the Three was Eleazar the Ahohite. In one battle against the Philistines he had refused to withdraw. He struck the enemy until his hand was weary and *clung to the sword.* Because of his valor that battle was won. The other Israelites reappeared when the danger was past to strip the enemy corpses.

C. Shammah the Hararite (2 Samuel 23:11-12)
Supreme honor also was bestowed on Shammah the Hararite. In a battle with the Philistines he took his stand in a bean patch and refused to retreat though his unit fled from the field of battle.

Superior Honor
2 Samuel 23:13-23

Within a military order known as the Thirty were certain men who stood out. Though their exploits were not deemed as valiant as those of the Three, yet they enjoyed superior honor within the group known as the Thirty. These three may be called "the overshadowed,"

291

for while their deeds were valiant, they were made to appear less important by the courageous acts of others.

A. As a Group (2 Samuel 23:13-17)

Three officers qualified for this honor. They first distinguished themselves during a Philistine invasion. David had taken refuge temporarily in the cave of Adullam. He was overheard expressing a desire to taste again the water from a well in Bethlehem which he had known in childhood. For these loyal men David's wish was their command. They broke through the camp of the Philistine garrison which currently occupied Bethlehem to fetch the water for their king. David, when he learned of the circumstances, poured the water out on the ground. He would not drink of water which was secured at the risk of the lives of his men. Their well-being was more important to him then his personal comfort.

B. Individually (2 Samuel 23:18-23)

The individual deeds of valor of two of the three men who received superior honor are recorded. First, Abishai the brother of Joab was chief of the Thirty. He had slain three hundred with his spear in one battle. Second, Benaiah had distinguished himself with several deeds of valor. 1) He struck down *two of Moab's best men* (NIV). 2) He also had faced a lion in the middle of a pit on a snowy day. 3) Using only a club, he disarmed an impressive Egyptian warrior and slew him with his own spear. This valor earned Benaiah the position of captain of David's bodyguard.

Presumably the third unmentioned member of this second group of three was Joab. Perhaps the record of his deeds was erased when he lost command because of the Absalom incident.

Secondary Honor
2 Samuel 23:24-39

Nothing is known of the exploits of the rest of David's heroes. Their names are merely listed in honor roll fashion. Certain things, however, stand out about the list. First, the group known as the Thirty was not actually limited to thirty men. The group may have started out as literally thirty men. Others, however, were added to the roster when their deeds were equivalent to those of the original members. Perhaps other soldiers were elevated to the honor to fill vacancies created by death or retirement from military service. In any case the text explicitly states that there were thirty-seven members of the order at the time the list which appears in 2 Samuel 23 was composed.

A study of the names here recorded indicates that these heroes came from throughout the land. Several were even foreigners who were fighting in David's army. The last name on the list in 2 Samuel is Uriah the Hittite. One wonders if the brave deed that earned him this honor was the battle in which he lost his life because David had ordered him to be abandoned on the battlefield. The Chronicles version of the list includes sixteen names following Uriah. These were men added to the order after the list in 2 Samuel was compiled.

Special Honor
1 Chronicles 12:1-22

The Chronicler has named certain individuals and groups for special honor, not so much for specific acts of heroism, as for their general courage.

A. Benjamite Marksmen (1 Chronicles 12:1-7)

When Saul was still king and David was living in Ziklag (1 Samuel 27), a unit of twenty-three expert marksmen from the tribe of Benjamin cast their lot with David. These men could sling stones or shoot arrows with either hand. They risked loss of property, and even their lives, by taking their stand with David at a time when the kingship issue had not yet been settled. Their marksman eye was equaled by their keen insight into David's future role in Israel.

B. Skilled Gadites (1 Chronicles 12:8-15)

During the earliest days of David's flight from Saul he was joined by a group of highly skilled soldiers from the tribe of Gad in Transjordan. They joined David when he was hiding out in the stronghold in the wilderness. These valiant men were particularly expert in the use of spear and shield. Because of their shaggy beards, they are said to have the faces of lions. Quickness of foot was also an attribute of this unit. These Gadites all became captains in David's army. In battle the least of these officers was equal to a hundred men, the greatest to a thousand. These men had made a reputation for themselves on one occasion by a surprise attack across the Jordan

293

when it was in flood. They drove the enemy—probably the Philistines—from the valleys that opened onto the plain of Jordan.

C. A Spirit-directed Band (1 Chronicles 12:16-18)

During those wilderness days David was joined by several from Benjamin and Judah. At first David was suspicious that this group might be intending to betray him to Saul. He committed judgment as to the intentions of this group to God. Then the Spirit came upon Amasai and caused him to deliver to David a message of commitment and encouragement. What an unlikely mouthpiece for the message of God! These men were also made captains in David's army.

D. Defectors from Manasseh (1 Chronicles 12:19-21)

The last group to cast their lot with David before the days of his glory was from Manasseh. David had been dismissed by King Achish before the battle of Mount Gilboa (cf. 1 Samuel 29:4-5). As he was returning to Ziklag, seven high ranking officers from Saul's army defected to him. They aided David in dealing with the desert raiders who had destroyed Ziklag and kidnapped its population. David was not remiss in honoring these men who, though tardy in their commitment, nonetheless risked everything by casting their lot with him while the issue of kingship was still in doubt.

22
DAVID'S TROUBLES
2 Samuel 7, 11-14

Chapter Chronology

	976
10 Years	
985	

After discussing the triumphs of David, the author of the Samuel text narrates the troubles that David experienced as a result of his great sin with Bathsheba. The king's problems started during a protracted second campaign against the Ammonites. The Ammonites retreated behind the walls of Rabbah where they hoped they could outlast the siege efforts of Joab.

DAVID'S GREAT SIN
2 Samuel 11:2-12:25

Date: ca. 981-980 BC

While the army was fighting successfully on foreign soil, David was losing the battle of temptation at home. His adultery marks the spiritual low point of the king's life, and a turning point in his reign.

Sin of Adultery
2 Samuel 11:2-13

A. Circumstances (2 Samuel 11:3-5)

After an afternoon nap, David was walking on the flat roof of his palace. From that height he spied a beautiful woman bathing, probably on the roof of a house at lower elevation. David inquired about the woman and learned that she was the wife of one of his finest officers, Uriah the Hittite. Undeterred by her marital status, David sent messengers to fetch this woman. When she came to him—apparently voluntarily—he lay with her. Bathsheba *purified herself of her uncleanness* and then returned to her house. Apparently the two only spent the one night together. That night of sinful sex was to have repercussions that nearly destroyed the reign of David. A short time later the woman discovered she was pregnant. She promptly notified David of this fact so that he might protect both himself and her.

B. Failed Cover-up (2 Samuel 11:6-13)

1. Uriah recalled (11:6-9): In an attempt to cover up the infidelity of Bathsheba, David ordered Uriah, a naturalized foreigner (Hittite), home from the battlefield. The king interviewed this officer concerning the conduct of the war. Then he urged the man to go to his house and refresh himself. As Uriah departed from the palace, David ordered a present (a guilt offering?) to be sent after him. Uriah, however, spent that night with the royal bodyguard at the door to the king's house. Whether Uriah suspected anything was amiss is difficult to determine. He may have heard reports from guards at the palace that Bathsheba had spent a night with the king. He also may have become suspicious because of the king's insistence that he visit his house.

2. Uriah intoxicated (11:10-13): When David was told that Uriah had not gone down to his house, he questioned the man. Uriah explained that as a professional military man he could not in good conscience enjoy the comforts of home as long as his troops were experiencing the deprivations of a long military campaign. For two more days Uriah remained in Jerusalem. At a royal banquet, David got Uriah drunk thinking that under the influence of the wine his inhibitions would erode. Still Uriah spent his nights with the king's servants outside the palace door.

Sin of Murder
2 Samuel 11:14-25

A. Orders to Joab (2 Samuel 11:14-17)

David was driven by Uriah's obstinate refusal to visit his wife to a desperate scheme. He drafted orders to be carried to the battlefront by Uriah. Joab was to assign Uriah to the frontline where the battle was fiercest. Then he was to order the supporting troops to withdraw, leaving Uriah to be struck down and killed by the Ammonites. General Joab faithfully executed the orders of his king. In one of the Ammonite sallies against the Israelite forces Uriah was killed.

B. Report to David (2 Samuel 11:18-24)

1. Messenger prepped (11:18-21): Joab anticipated that David would be angry when he heard the report of heavy losses at Rabbah. He directed the messenger to respond to any royal outburst by reporting as a postscript the death of Uriah.

2. Messenger's report (11:22-24): The messenger reported to David the details of the battle. The Ammonites had pushed the Israelites away from the city. Joab, however, had been able to rally his forces and push the Ammonites back to the gates of their capital. There the Ammonite archers were able to pick off many Israelites including Uriah.

C. Message to Joab (2 Samuel 11:25)

Hearing the news of Uriah's death, David realized that his royal orders led to the irresponsible conduct of Joab in ordering the men so close to the walls. He sent word back to his general urging that he not be distraught over the losses or of his complicity in the death of Uriah. In a rather calloused comment the king said *the sword devours one as well as another.* He ordered Joab to continue the attack against Rabbah.

Consequences of the Sin
2 Samuel 11:26-12:25

A. Marriage to Bathsheba (2 Samuel 11:26-27)

Bathsheba went through the motions of mourning for her dead husband. Whether this mourning was sincere or just part of the cover-up plot is not clear. In any case, following this time of mourning (usually seven days), David married Bathsheba. Some weeks later she brought forth the child that had been conceived in adulterous union. How many, if any, suspected what had taken place is not indicated. David's actions, however, were evil in the sight of Yahweh.

B. Prophetic Rebuke (2 Samuel 12:1-12)

1. Nathan's parable (12:1-4): Yahweh left David in his guilty state for almost a year. He then dispatched the prophet Nathan to administer a rebuke to the sinful king. He chose to use a parable in order to elicit from David a pronouncement of self-condemnation. The parable was simple. A poor man and rich man lived beside one another. While the rich man had many flocks and herds, the poor man had only a little lamb that was a family pet. When a traveler came to the rich man he was unwilling to feed him from his own flock or herd. Rather he took the poor man's pet lamb and made a meal of it for his guest.

2. David's anger (12:5-6): David's anger boiled as he heard the story which he took to be a real occurrence. David swore an oath in the name of Yahweh that the rich thief deserved to die. He ordered that this man make a four-fold restitution for the stolen lamb.

3. Nathan's application (12:7-9): Nathan then made the devastating application. *You, David, are the man!* You have pronounced judgment upon yourself. God had anointed David as king and had delivered him from the hand of Saul. He had given Saul's house including his wives into the care of David along with both Judah and Israel. The Lord would have given him many similar blessings. David, however, had despised the word of Yahweh by committing a horrendous evil. David was as guilty of murder as if he had struck Uriah with his own sword. He then had taken to himself the wife of the man whose death he had orchestrated. David had despised the Lord by taking Bathsheba for he denied by his conduct the omniscience of his God.

4. Penalty for the sin (12:10-12): The penalty for David's sin was threefold. First, the sword was never to depart from the house of David. Second, God would raise up evil against David from within his own house. Third, one of David's associates would take his wives from him and lie with them in full public view.

C. David's Confession (2 Samuel 12:13-14)

David was moved deeply by the words of the prophet. He made no excuses for his conduct. He acknowledged forthrightly his sin. Nathan accepted the confession. He announced that God was not going to take David's life on account of the sin. However, because his conduct had given occasion to the enemies of Yahweh to blaspheme, God was going to punish David by taking the child that recently had been born.

D. Punishment of David (2 Samuel 12:15-23)

1. His son smitten (12:15-18): Yahweh struck the child of Bathsheba with serious illness. David inquired of God for the child, i.e., he prayed for him. He humbled himself by fasting and lying all night prostrate on the ground. His advisers encouraged him to eat with them, but he refused. After seven days of illness, the child died.

The courtiers were afraid to tell their king of the infant's death. Observing how the child's illness had affected David, they feared that he might take his own life when he learned of the death.

2. After his son's death (12:19-20): From the whispering of the courtiers David sensed that the fortunes of the child had changed for the worse. When he ascertained that the child had died, David arose from the ground, washed, anointed himself, changed his clothes and went to the house of God to worship. Then he returned to his own house and requested food.

3. David's perspective on death (12:21-23): The royal servants were completely dumbfounded by the king's behavior. David explained that he had fasted and wept while the child was alive, hoping that Yahweh would be gracious and spare the life of his son. After the death, however, fasting was of no avail. No amount of mourning could bring back the dead. Then David's faith soared when he stated: *I shall go to him, but he will not return to me.* The statement suggests a belief in infant salvation and immortality.

E. Birth of Solomon (2 Samuel 12:24-25)

David comforted Bathsheba over the loss of their son. Eventually she become pregnant a second time by David. The son who was born was named Solomon. Yahweh loved this child. He sent the prophet Nathan to bestow on the infant a special name: *Jedidiah,* "beloved of Yahweh."

F. Fall of Rabbah (2 Samuel 12:26-31)

1. Joab sends for David (12:26-28): Although he sustained heavy losses, Joab was eventually able to overcome the lower city, *the city of waters,* i.e., the area where the water supply was located. With the end of the siege in sight he sent for David to bring the remaining forces in order to administer the final blow. The loyal general wanted his king to receive the credit for capturing this important capital.

2. David's recognition (12:29-31): David did as Joab had suggested. He led the final assault against the citadel and thus was credited with having conquered Rabbah. The massive crown—it weighed 75 lbs.—displayed on the statue of the Ammonite god Milcom (*their king*) was captured. A jewel from this crown was put in David's crown. An enormous quantity of spoil was brought out of the city. Those who survived the siege were put to forced labor.

GOD'S COVENANT
WITH DAVID
2 Samuel 7:1-29

David's Obsession
2 Samuel 7:1-3

The placement of chapter 7 in 2 Samuel may again mislead one regarding the chronology of the event. Most likely the chapter relates an event which occurred fairly late in David's reign. Once David was firmly established on the throne, he became obsessed with the desire to build a house for the ark of God. His conscience bothered him that he dwelled in house of cedar, i.e., a luxurious palace, while the ark of God resided in a tent. The prophet Nathan, David's counselor, thought this was a splendid idea. He encouraged the king to proceed with all that was in his heart.

God's Promise
2 Samuel 7:5-17

A. Divine Revelation (2 Samuel 7:4-5)
Nathan's encouragement for David's building plans was premature. The prophet learned that very night that it was not God's will for David to build a temple to house the ark. Nathan was dispatched to bear that news to David.

B. Reminders to David (2 Samuel 7:6-9a)
The prophetic oracle began with two reminders. First, God had never requested a house. Since the days of the exodus Yahweh had been content to dwell in a tent. Second, God had selected David to be ruler over his people. He had given him victory over all his enemies.

C. Grand Promises to David (2 Samuel 7:9b-17)
1. To David personally (7:9b-11): Next, several specific promises were made to David. 1) God will make David's name great. 2) David and God people will enjoy a rest from their enemies such as they had not experienced since the days of the Judges. 3) God will build a house, i.e., a dynasty for David.

2. To David's descendants (7:12-17): Finally, Nathan's oracle outlined promises for David's posterity. 1) God will establish the kingdom for one of David's direct descendants. 2) This future ruler will build a house for God's name. 3) The throne of his kingdom will endure forever. 4) This ruler will occupy the position of a son in relationship to God. 5) As such he will be corrected with the disciplinary rod of divine judgment. 6) Yet the covenant faithfulness of God will not depart from him. 7) The house, kingdom and throne of David will endure forever.

The "foreverness" of these promises points beyond David's son Solomon. Jesus the Messiah is a son of David. He is God's son par excellence. He is currently building a spiritual temple. On the cross Jesus experienced the disciplinary rod of God, not for his own sins, but the sins of others. He sits even now upon the throne of God in the heavenly places.

David's Prayer
2 Samuel 7:18-29

A. David's Praise (2 Samuel 7:18-24)

Moved by the breadth and depth of these promises, David *went in and sat before Yahweh,* i.e., he entered the tent where the ark was housed. He opened his prayer by expressing amazement that God had brought him this far. Yet now through Nathan's oracle the Lord was making commitments to David concerning the distant future. The king then began to praise God 1) for this most recent revelation of his plans for David. 2) Such revelation set Yahweh apart from all other so-called deities. 3) With mighty acts God had redeemed Israel from nations and their gods. In so doing he had made a name for himself. 4) Yahweh had established a relationship with Israel as his people forever.

B. David's Petition (2 Samuel 7:25-29)

David then called upon God to confirm forever the word that he had just spoken through his servant. The fulfillment of these promises will cause the name of Yahweh to be magnified forever. The prayer concluded with a petition that God will indeed do what he had just promised to do.

PROBLEMS IN THE FAMILY

2 Samuel 13:14-33

Date: ca. 981-976 BC

The prophesied trouble within David's household was not long in making its appearance. By their lawless conduct, two of David's sons brought incalculable pain to the heart of their father.

Amnon's Incestuous Rape
2 Samuel 13:1-22

A. Amnon's Plot (2 Samuel 13:1-10)

1. Ammon's lust (13:1-2): Amnon, the eldest son of David, lusted after his stepsister. From a distance he watched in the courtyard where the unmarried women were kept in seclusion. The frustration of not being able to devise a way by which he might be alone with Tamar made Amnon physically ill.

2. Ammon's advisor (13:3-7): Unfortunately Amnon had a *friend* and cousin named Jonadab. He is described as *a very shrewd man* (NASB). Jonadab had the solution to Amnon's problem. He suggested that Amnon feign illness. When David came to see him he should request that Tamar come and prepare some fancy cakes for him. David suspected nothing. He sent word for Tamar to go to her brother's house and prepare food for him.

3. Tamar's naiveté (13:8-10): If David was naive about Amnon's request, Tamar was even more so. When she entered his house Amnon was lying on his bed. Tamar took dough, kneaded it, made cakes in the sight of Amnon and baked them. She then set the cakes on a table in view of her half brother, but he refused to eat. Instead Amnon ordered everyone out from his presence. Then he asked Tamar to bring the cakes into the bedroom and feed him. Suspecting nothing improper, Tamar took the food to the bedroom.

B. Tamar's Rape (2 Samuel 13:11-19)

1. Tamar's protest (13:11-14): Amnon seized his half sister and demanded that she lie with him. Tamar resisted as best she could. First, she pled with Amnon not to do such a horrible deed. Second, she argued that such disgraceful things were simply not done in Israel! Third, she pointed out that both of them would be ruined by such an act. Amnon would be considered a fool, i.e., a godless man, for having raped his own half sister. Finally, Tamar urged Amnon to

302

ask the king for her in marriage if he could not control his lust. The king—so Tamar affirmed in the desperation of the moment—will not refuse such a request. At least marriage to his half sister, though forbidden in the law (Leviticus 18:9, 11; 20:17), was more honorable than rape! Amnon was in no mood to reason. He overpowered his sister and violated her.

2. *Ammon's hatred (13:15-17):* Perhaps because Tamar refused to cooperate, the sexual experience was not what Amnon had fantasized. Immediately Amnon's feelings went to the opposite extreme. He hated Tamar more than he ever had *loved* her. Because of his guilt and fear of exposure he ordered Tamar out of his presence. Tamar again tried to reason with Amnon. Sending her away after violating her was even worse than the violation itself. Sending her away would make it appear that Tamar had initiated the seduction. Amnon again refused to listen. He ordered his attendant to throw Tamar out of the house and lock the door.

3. *Tamar's humiliation (13:18-19):* Humiliated by her experience, Tamar went into public mourning. She put ashes on her head. She tore the long-sleeved garment that virgin daughters of the king wore as distinctive garb. She placed her hand on her head to replace the veil that had been ripped off in Amnon's chamber. She cried aloud as she ran toward her brother's house.

C. Immediate Consequences (2 Samuel 13:20-22)

Absalom comforted his sister by inviting her to come and live in his house. There Tamar remained *desolate,* i.e., childless and despondent. David heard about the incident, and he was very angry. The Scripture, however, does not indicate that he took any disciplinary action against his lawless firstborn. Perhaps he found it difficult to punish in his son the same sin that had marred his own life. On his part, Absalom refused to speak to Amnon. He hated his half brother for what he had done to Tamar.

Absalom's Revenge
2 Samuel 13:20-29

A. Absalom's Plot (2 Samuel 13:23-27)

After two years of seething anger, Absalom was ready to take his revenge on Amnon. He requested that the king and his sons attend a sheep shearing celebration at Baal-Hazor about ten miles from the

History of Israel

capital. David declined because he did not wish to burden Absalom with the expense of providing for the entourage that accompanied the king on all his outings. Absalom then requested that Amnon, the eldest son, be permitted to attend the festivities as a stand-in for the king. If David had any suspicions they are not indicated here. Permission was granted. Amnon and all the king's sons went with Absalom to Baal-Hazor near Ephraim.

B. Ammon's Assassination (2 Samuel 13:28-29)

When Amnon became drunk, Absalom ordered his servants to slay him. When this happened all the other sons of David mounted their mules and fled.

Aftermath of the Murder
2 Samuel 13:30-39

A. David's Agony (2 Samuel 13:30-36)

The initial report that reached David was that all his sons had been massacred by Absalom. David immediately went into mourning. Jonadab, however, came in to assure the king that only Amnon had died, the victim of a plot that had been in motion since the day Tamar had been raped. Shortly thereafter the king's sons were spotted returning on the Jerusalem road. They entered the palace to join David and his servants in mourning over the death of Amnon.

B. Absolom's Flight (2 Samuel 13:37-39)

Absalom fled to the land of Geshur northeast of the Sea of Galilee where his maternal grandfather was the ruler. He remained there for three years. Meanwhile, David mourned for *his son,* probably the absentee Absalom. He longed to send for him to invite him to return. The king probably thought that to do so was equivalent to endorsing the murder of his oldest son.

Neglect of Absalom
2 Samuel 14:1-33

A. Joab's Plan (2 Samuel 14:1-19)

1. A wise woman (14:1-3): Joab sensed that David was agonizing over the exile of Absalom. He also may have assumed that Absalom as the eldest son of David would succeed to the throne.

304

Therefore Joab contacted a wise woman from Tekoa six miles south of Bethlehem. Joab urged the woman to feign mourning. He told her exactly what she was to say to the king. She was to tell a story similar to that of the king's situation.

2. *The woman's feigned plight (14:4-7):* The woman in the guise of a mourner fell prostrate before David beseeching his help. She told David that she was a widow with two sons. The two young men, however, had gotten into a fight while working in the field. One of her sons had been killed in the struggle. Now other family members were demanding that the murderer be handed over for execution. If this should happen, however, her husband would have no one to perpetuate his name.

3. *David's response to the woman (14:8-11):* David responded to the woman's problem in three stages as the woman continued to press for decisive action. First, the king attempted to brush aside the woman by saying that he would issue orders concerning the situation. Apparently David felt that if he defended the son, he would become involved in his guilt. The woman then offered to take upon herself any associated guilt. Second, David promised that if the woman would bring her tormentors to him he would order them not to harass her about the matter any longer. Finally, David swore an oath that not one hair of the surviving son would fall to the ground, i.e., he would not be harmed in any way.

4. *Application of the woman's story (14:12-14):* The wise woman then made an application of her drama. While the king was willing to guarantee the safety of this "widow's son," yet David would not guarantee the safe return of Absalom, favorite prince of the people. Life is like water spilled on the ground. It cannot be gathered up again. Therefore David should waste no time restoring his son. In so doing David will be acting in a God-like way, for the Lord is constantly looking for ways to restore the wayward. The woman completed her appeal by complimenting David on his keen sense of right and wrong. In this respect the king was like *the angel of God.*

5. *David suspects Joab (14:15-19):* To continue to throw off David, the woman then returned to her fictitious story. She wanted the king to think that was her only reason for coming to him. David, however, now saw through the deception. He suspected that Joab was behind the ruse of the woman from Tekoa. Perhaps Joab had attempted on various occasions to get David to take action regarding

Absalom. Under questioning, the woman admitted that Joab had told her exactly what she should say.

B. Absalom's Return (2 Samuel 14:20-27)

1. David's orders (14:20-24): The king then summoned Joab and ordered him to bring Absalom back home. The general prostrated himself before David and thanked him for granting this request. Joab went to Geshur immediately and brought Absalom back to Jerusalem. David, however, did not forgive Absalom completely. The crown prince was not restored to the royal court. Absalom was forced to take up residence in his own house.

2. Absalom's status (14:25-27): Absalom was a favorite of the people. No one was as handsome as the crown prince. There was no defect in his physical appearance. Once each year he had his hair cut. The shorn hair weighed two hundred shekels (about 5 lbs.). Absalom had three sons and one daughter. His beautiful daughter was named Tamar after his disgraced sister.

C. Absalom's Restoration (2 Samuel 14:28-33)

1. Audience with Joab (14:28-32): Two years passed and still there was no reconciliation between David and his oldest surviving son. Twice Absalom attempted to get Joab to come and discuss his status. The general refused to come. Finally Absalom ordered his servants to burn Joab's barley field that was right next door. That got Joab's attention immediately. Absalom demanded that he be restored to the court or executed as a murderer.

2. Absalom returns to court (14:33): Joab made the king realize that by allowing Absalom to return he had recognized that the murder of Amnon was justifiable homicide. Therefore there were no legal grounds to deny the prince his rightful place in the royal court. David then sent for Absalom. The prince did obeisance before his father. David kissed his son. Reconciliation had been effected, or so it seemed.

23
POLITICAL DISRUPTION
2 Samuel 15-19

Chapter Chronology

976	4 Years	972

Nathan predicted that the sword would never depart from the house of David as a result of his adultery with Bathsheba (2 Samuel 12:10). The rape of Tamar and the subsequent murder of Amnon were but the first installments of this judgment. In his last years David faced two political rebellions led by his sons as well as one revolt led by a Benjamite.

REVOLT OF ABSALOM
2 Samuel 15-18

Date: 976 BC

Preparation for Revolt
2 Samuel 15:1-12

From the moment Absalom set foot on Israelite soil he plotted the overthrow of his father. The handsome devil, as some have called him, used several tactics not unfamiliar to the Christian. Satan often uses the same tactics in an effort to get people to join his rebellion against heaven's King.

A. Stealing the Hearts (2 Samuel 15:1-6)
1. Big show (15:1): First, Absalom put on a big show to impress his countrymen. He secured a chariot and horses. This is the first recorded use of horses by a member of the royal family. Compared to the mule that David used for transportation, these horses must indeed have been impressive. Furthermore, fifty runners preceded Absalom as he rode into the city. These advance PR men stirred up the crowds to give the crown prince a royal welcome.

2. *Hard work (15:2a):* Second, Absalom worked hard. He rose early and stood beside the way of the gate to greet the people much as a modern politician might "pump the flesh" at a factory entrance at the start of the morning shift. No palace hours for this prince!

3. *Flattery (15:15:2b-3a, 5):* Third, he showed a personal interest in all who came to the gate with court cases. He inquired about the litigant's city and the nature of his case. Fourth, Absalom used flattery to good advantage. He always agreed that the legal claim of each petitioner was right. Fifth, he treated the litigants as more or less equals. If any came near to do obeisance Absalom took hold of the man and greeted him with a kiss upon the cheek. This crown prince developed the reputation of being down to earth, just one of the common folks.

4. *Undermining the king (15:3b-4):* Sixth, Absalom sought to discredit the king in the eyes of his subjects. He pointed out to each petitioner that no one was present to hear cases on behalf of the king. The implication was that King David was derelict in duty. Absalom openly expressed the desire that he might be appointed judge so that he might render justice to all who sought it.

By these six stratagems Absalom was able to steal away the hearts of the men of Israel. After four[26] years of preparation Absalom was ready to launch his rebellion (15:6).

B. Selecting the Launch Pad (2 Samuel 15:7-12)

1. *Using religion as a cloak (15:7-9):* Absalom went to his father and requested permission to go to Hebron to honor a vow that he had made while still living in Geshur. While in exile, he had sworn that if he was restored to Jerusalem he would *serve Yahweh.* Since David was a man of piety, he was anxious to encourage any spiritual inclination on the part of a son, especially this son. Suspecting nothing, David put his blessing on Absalom's trip. Absalom chose Hebron as the site to launch his rebellion because 1) it was in the heart of Judah, his base of support; 2) it was a royal city antedating Jerusalem; 3) it was the town where Absalom had been born (2 Samuel 3:3); and 4) it was a safe distance from Jerusalem and the watchful eyes of David's men.

---

[26]Following the Septuagint and the Syriac versions. Josephus (*Ant.* 7.9.1) also reads *four years.* The Masoretic Text reads *forty years* in 15:7. Some think that this revolt came when Absalom was forty years old, or in the fortieth year of David's reign. Most likely, however, the *forty years* of the Masoretic Text is a scribal error.

2. Spreading the word (15:10): Absalom dispatched secret agents throughout the tribes of Israel to alert his supporters that the moment was near. A trumpet signal relayed across the land will indicate that Absalom had been declared king.

3. Duping national leaders (15:11-12): Two hundred of the leading citizens of Jerusalem were invited to accompany the crown prince to Hebron. They had no idea that they were being used by a rebel. Absalom wanted it to appear in Jerusalem that his rebellion had massive support among the national leaders. He sent for the influential Ahithophel, David's counselor, who previously had assured Absalom of his support. Why Ahithophel was willing to back a revolt against David is not stated in the text. His support, however, gave the entire effort credibility. The sacred historian indicates that the conspiracy was strong. Absalom's following kept on increasing.

David's Flight
2 Samuel 15:13-16:13

A. Evacuation Order (2 Samuel 15:13-18)

1. His motivation (15:13-15): A messenger arrived at David's palace with the news that the hearts of the men of Israel were with Absalom. David seems to have panicked. He ordered an immediate evacuation of Jerusalem. He probably wished to spare the capital the agony of a protracted siege. The king stressed the urgency of quickly departing from the city lest the forces loyal to Absalom overtake and slaughter them. The servants pledged themselves to do whatever the king ordered. Their support for David's plan to flee indicates that militarily evacuation was the best option.

2. His anticipation (15:16): David probably anticipated that his absence from Jerusalem would be of short duration. He therefore left ten of his concubines to tend the palace. He never anticipated that these women were to become pawns in Absalom's bid for power.

3. Review of fugitives (15:17-18): The royal entourage stopped at the last house within the city limits. David sadly watched his servants and his six hundred foreign personal bodyguards march out before him.

Portraits of the Fugitives
2 Samuel 15:19-16:14

David's humiliating flight from Jerusalem provoked two very different responses. Some heroically pledged themselves to serve David unto the death. Others took advantage of the situation to further their own interests or vent their anger toward the king.

A. The Committed (2 Samuel 15:19-37)

At various points along the exit route David was met by friends who in different ways expressed their support for their humiliated king.

1. Ittai the Gittite (15:19-23): David questioned Ittai the Gittite, the commander of the king's guards, as to why he was leaving. The royal bodyguard should remain with the new king. Ittai only recently had cast his lot with David. He did not need to feel obligated to follow David into an uncertain future. Ittai, however, vowed to serve David wherever he went and even to death. After hearing this resolute commitment, David permitted Ittai and his men and their families to leave Jerusalem with him. The sad procession marched down Mount Zion, across the Kidron, up the ascent of Olivet in the direction of the wilderness. All the country was weeping with a loud voice.

2. Zadok and Abiathar (15:24-29): The chief priests Zadok and Abiathar and the Levites who where in Jerusalem stood beside the ark of God as David and his supporters exited the city. David ordered the ark returned to the city. He reasoned that if God showed him favor he would eventually return to Jerusalem to the ark and Yahweh's habitation. Yet if the Lord no longer took delight in David, this man of faith was prepared to accept whatever future God might have planned for him. Zadok and his sons could do David a great service by keeping him informed of developments in Jerusalem. David planned to wait at the fords of the Jordan until he received directions from Zadok. Since this priest was also a seer (prophet), David trusted his insight into the actions he should take in response to Absalom's threat.

3. Hushai the Archite (15:30-37): The royal fugitives slowly made their way up the ascent of the Mount of Olives. David was barefoot, his head was covered, and he was weeping. His agony was even greater when he learned that his close adviser Ahithophel was among the conspirators. David prayed that the counsel of Ahithophel might be turned to foolishness. As if in answer to his prayer, Hushai, another royal counselor, met David near the summit of Olivet. His clothing was torn and he had dust on his head in mourning over the

310

turn of events. David suggested that Hushai would be of more help to return to Jerusalem and offer his services to Absalom. David wanted Hushai to 1) frustrate the counsel of Ahithophel; and 2) report Absalom's plans to Zadok and Abiathar. Zadok's two sons in turn were to relay that information to David.

B. The Opportunist (2 Samuel 16:1-4)

Ziba, the servant of Mephibosheth (son of Jonathan), met David a little beyond the summit. This opportunist was confident that Absalom's rebellion would fail. He was trying to position himself for a greater influence and power in the post-rebellion kingdom.

Ziba brought with him two donkeys loaded with foodstuffs for the royal family and the king's servants. With these timely gifts Ziba won over the heart of the king. When David inquired about the whereabouts of Mephibosheth, Ziba slandered his master. He said that Mephibosheth had remained in Jerusalem anticipating that in all the political confusion the kingdom of his father Saul would be returned to him. This accusation was certainly plausible. Without making any further inquiry into the truth of this serious accusation, David on the spot decreed that all of Mephibosheth's possessions now belonged to Ziba.

C. The Antagonist (2 Samuel 16:5-14)

1. Shimei's outrageous conduct (16:5-8): At Bahurim, a village east of the Mount of Olives, David was met by Shimei, a man who was related to King Saul. The deep animosity of the Saulides towards David is indicated in this episode. Shimei walked along a ridge above the road David was traveling. He continuously cursed David, called him foul names and pelted his entourage with stones. He called David a man of blood and a son of Belial (worthless man). In Shimei's opinion David's misfortune had befallen him because of what he had done to the household of Saul.

2. Abishai's request (16:9-14): Abishai wanted to chase down Shimei (*this dead dog*) and decapitate him. The sons of Zeruiah (Joab and Abishai) were addicted to the use of the sword to solve all problems. David, however, immediately disassociated himself from such a vengeful spirit. He accepted this treatment by Shimei as part of God's judgment against him. If his own son Absalom was trying to kill him, how can this Benjamite be condemned for what he was doing? David had determined to place himself at the mercy of God.

Perhaps the Lord would turn this cursing to good. So the procession continued on its way even as Shimei continued his harassment.

Absalom in Jerusalem
2 Samuel 16:15-17:23

A. Hushai Feigns Loyalty (2 Samuel 16:15-19)

Absalom entered Jerusalem unopposed. His chief counselor Ahithophel was at his side. Hushai, David's friend, approached and rendered homage to the new king. Absalom questioned Hushai about why he had not departed with *his friend.* Hushai declared that his allegiance was to whatever king Yahweh, the people and the army selected. He was prepared to serve Absalom just as he had served David.

B. Ahithophel's Advice (2 Samuel 16:20-17:4)

1. Regarding David's concubines (16:20-23): Absalom asked Ahithophel what his next step should be. This Old Testament Judas advised the young man publicly to go into the concubines of his father. Such an act would 1) serve as a public claim to the throne; 2) signal that the rebellion was irreversible; and 3) therefore strengthen the will of all who had committed themselves to his cause. Absalom immediately followed Ahithophel's advice. In those days this counselor's advice was regarded as equivalent to an oracle of God. A tent was pitched on the roof of the palace. There Absalom sexually humbled the concubines of his father.

2. Regarding pursuit of David (17:1-4): Ahithophel next urged Absalom to let him take 12,000 men and immediately pursue David. The wise man reasoned that David was weary and exhausted from his flight. A swift attack will discourage his supporters. They will flee, and Absalom could then smite the king himself. Ahithophel felt he was the one who could secure for Absalom the support of all of those who had supported David. This plan was designed to secure peace in the land quickly rather than a protracted conflict. Ahithophel's plan pleased both Absalom and the elders of Israel.

C. Hushai's Advice (2 Samuel 17:5-14)

1. A contrived warning (17:5-10): Absalom submitted Ahithophel's plan to Hushai to see what he thought of it. David's friend, stalling for time, proclaimed the plan to be bad advice. David was a mighty warrior. His men were skilled soldiers. No doubt he was already hiding out in a cave in the wilderness ready to pounce on any force that might try to pursue him. Should David score a quick victory over Absalom's forces, those committed to the rebellion would lose heart and desert the cause.

2. *Hushai's counter plan (17:11-14):* Hushai then advanced his own plan to Absalom, one that was advantageous to his friend David. He recommended that Absalom muster a huge army and then personally lead that army against his father. This army will search out David and totally crush him leaving not one of his supporters alive. If David attempted to take refuge in a city, that city would be totally dismantled. Hushai painted a picture that stirred the macho mentality of Absalom and his soldiers. They declared the counsel of Hushai to be superior to that of Ahithophel. The narrator explains that Yahweh had appointed that the wise advice of Ahithophel be frustrated so that calamity might befall Absalom.

D. Warning to David (2 Samuel 17:15-23)

1. *Message committed to runners (17:15-16):* Hushai immediately went to the temple to convey the news to Zadok and Abiathar about what Absalom was contemplating. David must be advised to cross over the Jordan. He would be in grave danger at the fords of the Jordan should Absalom revert to the plan of Ahithophel.

2. *Danger to the runners (17:17-20):* The sons of Zadok, Jonathan and Ahimaaz, were hiding at En-rogel in the Kidron Valley southeast of Jerusalem. The plan was for a maidservant to relay information to them. They in turn were to carry the news to David. This plan was nearly upset when a lad spotted the two loyal supporters of David and reported their whereabouts to Absalom. The two young soldiers fled to Bahurim to the house of a man who had a well in his courtyard. They climbed down into the well, and a woman spread a covering over the opening of the well. On the covering she spread grain. Just at that moment the agents of Absalom arrived. They questioned the woman about Jonathan and Ahimaaz. She misdirected them across the brook of water. Not finding David's two friends in the area, Absalom's men returned to Jerusalem.

3. *David's response to the warning (17:21-23):* Jonathan and Ahimaaz conveyed their warning to David at the fords of the Jordan. David ordered a nighttime crossing of the river. Thus by frustrating the counsel of Ahithophel, Hushai saved David's life. When

313

Ahithophel saw that his advice was not followed, he was so depressed that he went to his home and committed suicide.

War with Absalom
2 Samuel 17:24-18:33

A. David in Mahanaim (2 Samuel 17:24, 27-29)

David made Mahanaim, the old capital of Ish-bosheth, his Transjordan headquarters. The people of this region were solid supporters of David. Three of the local leaders brought supplies for David and his men. Shobi was an Ammonite, the son of Nahash. Machir from Lo-debar had been a friend of Mephibosheth (cf. 2 Samuel 9:4). Barzillai was a very aged and loyal supporter of David. These friends brought food, bedding and utensils of various kinds to David's troops.

B. Preparation for Battle (2 Samuel 17:25-26; 18:1-5)

1. Invasion by Absalom (17:25-26): Absalom soon led his army across Jordan into Gilead for the inevitable confrontation. His army was led by Amasa, Joab's illegitimate cousin.

2. David organizes his forces (18:1-5): At Mahanaim David numbered and organized his forces. He appointed three commanders, each in charge of one third of the force: Joab, his brother Abishai, and Ittai. David intended to lead the army, but his troops vetoed this idea. His presence on the battlefield might become the focal point of the enemy attack. It would be better if David remained in the safety of the city with whatever reserve forces there may have been. The king reluctantly agreed. So David stood by the gate and reviewed his troops before the battle. In the hearing of the entire army David charged his three commanders for his sake to deal gently with his son Absalom. In spite of all that had happened, David still loved that rebellious son.

C. Battle in the Forest of Ephraim (2 Samuel 18:6-8)

The two armies clashed in the forest of Ephraim. David's troops gained the advantage almost immediately. In the wide-ranging battle the forest proved a formidable obstacle for Absalom's less skilled partisans. In all, Absalom lost twenty thousand troops that day, a good portion to the pits and perils of the forest.

314

D. Absalom's Death (2 Samuel 18:9-18)

1. Joab's violation of orders (18:9-15): As Absalom tried to escape the battle his head became lodged in a low hanging tree. He was jerked from the back of his mule and left dangling in mid air. His predicament was reported to Joab. The old general rebuked his troops for not slaying the rebel. They could have earned ten pieces of silver for their effort. The troops, however, respected the wishes of their king so much that a hundred times that amount could not have induced them to slay Absalom. The soldiers knew their general. Had they disobeyed the orders of the king Joab would not have stood up for them. Joab then took matters in his own hands. He took three spears and thrust them into the heart of Absalom while he was yet alive in the midst of the oak. Taking their cue from their commander, ten of the general's armor bearers gathered around Absalom and completed the execution.

2. Burial of Absalom (18:16-18): Once Absalom was dead there was no need to continue the carnage. Joab blew the trumpet signaling an end to hostilities. His men unceremoniously threw the body of Absalom in a deep pit in the forest and piled stones over it. Absalom's supporters fled *each to his tent,* i.e., home. The prince himself had no male heir. Once earlier he had erected a monument and placed it in the King's Valley to perpetuate his name. The point of mentioning that monument here is to underscore what a tragic end came to this talented and charismatic young prince.

E. Battle Report (2 Samuel 18:19-33)

1. Ahimaaz's run (18:19-23): David's close friend Ahimaaz wished to carry the news of the battle to David. For some reason unexplained in the text Joab denied the request of Ahimaaz.[27] He dispatched instead a Cushite (Ethiopian) runner. Still Ahimaaz pressed Joab for permission to carry the news to David. Perhaps he felt that the Cushite would not present the news of Absalom's death in a sympathetic manner. Joab finally consented to dispatch Ahimaaz. Taking a longer but quicker route, Ahimaaz outran the Cushite.

---

[27]Commentators have reached exactly opposite conclusions as to why Joab did not at first dispatch Ahimaaz: 1) because he did not wish to have the news of Absalom's death softened; or 2) because he wished to soften the blow by sending a more detached messenger. Another possibility is that Joab wished to spare Ahimaaz the unpleasantness or even animosity of David's reaction to the news.

2. *David's anxious wait (18:24-27):* David waited anxiously *between the two gates* of Mahanaim for news from the battle. At last a watchman saw a man running alone. David reasoned that the news must be good else the watchman would have seen many men fleeing in all directions from the battlefront back to the safety of the city. Then the watchman spotted the second runner. Again David consoled himself with the assessment that the news must be good. As the runners drew nearer, the watchman thought he recognized the unique running style of Ahimaaz. David was convinced now. Ahimaaz was a good man. He would surely be brining good news.

3. *Messengers arrive (18:28-33):* Ahimaaz approached his king and breathlessly blurted out the message: *All is well.* He then prostrated himself and praised Yahweh who delivered up all those who had lifted their hands against the king. David anxiously inquired about the well being of Absalom. Ahimaaz avoided giving a direct answer. *I saw great tumult,* he said. The king ordered Ahimaaz to stand aside. At that moment the Cushite arrived with a similar message of good news. Again David asked about Absalom. The Cushite gave a forthright but discreet indication of his death. He wished that all the enemies of David might be as that young man. He needed to say no more. The king went to the chamber over the gate and sobbed uncontrollably. He sincerely wished that he had died that day in place of his son Absalom!

RESTORATION OF DAVID
2 Samuel 19

Date: 972 BC

Reaction to Absalom's Death
2 Samuel 19:1-8

A. David's Agonizing (2 Samuel 19:1-4)

As the troops returned from the battle their joyous spirit was quickly turned to gloom by the news that David was grieving over his dead son. His troops sulked back into the city as though they had lost the battle. The king continued to agonize over his son with such a loud voice that the men in the city could hear his wailing.

B. Joab's Rebuke (2 Samuel 19:5-8)

Sensing a major morale problem, Joab came and spoke bluntly to David. The king's agony had caused the men who had saved the lives of the royal family to feel as though they had done something wrong. David appeared to love those who hated him, and to hate those who loved him. Had the result of the battle been reversed, said the general, David would have been more pleased. If David did not immediately go out and express appreciation to his troops all of them would desert him that very night. Joab may have been threatening to lead the troops away from David. In any case, David was jarred into action. He went out and sat in the city gate. All his supporters gathered around him.

**Participants
in David's Restoration**
2 Samuel 19:9-43

Following the victory over Absalom David waited in Mahanaim until a ground swell for his return developed on the other side of the Jordan. Several different reactions to the restoration of the king are indicated in chapter 19.

A. The Bickering (2 Samuel 19:9-10)
The people of Israel were in a dilemma. The king they had chosen for themselves was now dead. David was in exile in Transjordan. In the past David had delivered them from the hands of their enemies, especially the Philistines. The implication here is that without a strong king they again would be at the mercy of these enemies. Some action needed to be taken formally to reinstate David on his throne. David wisely waited until popular support for his return to power developed.

B. The Reluctant (2 Samuel 19:11-15)
Though the northern tribes were debating about how best to reinstate David, Judah had made no moves in that direction. David contacted his avid supporters Zadok and Abiathar in Jerusalem. They were to speak to the elders of Judah regarding their lack of initiative in this matter. After all, David was their flesh and bone. David's agents were to inform Amasa, who had been Absalom's commander, that he will replace Joab as general of the army. This popular and diplomatic move united the men of Judah behind David. They sent word for David and his servants to return to Jerusalem. David made

his way to the Jordan. The men of Judah assembled at Gilgal in order to assist the king in crossing the river.

C. The Desperate (2 Samuel 19:16-23)

1. Assistance in river crossing (19:16-18a): Two of the first men to greet David at the Jordan were Shimei and Ziba, both of the tribe of Benjamin. The former brought with him a thousand men; the latter brought his fifteen sons and twenty servants. Both men feared that David, once he was restored to power, would direct his wrath toward them, Shimei for cursing the king, Ziba for twisting the truth for personal advantage. These Benjamites kept crossing the river to assist the king's household in transit.

2. Shimei's plea (19:18b-20): As the king was about to cross the Jordan, Shimei fell down before him. He begged David to forget what he had done as he was climbing the ascent of Olivet. He confessed his curses on the king to be sin. He asked David to take into account that he was among the first to greet him on his return to Jerusalem.

3. David's oath (19:21-23): Abishai raised the legal question of whether Shimei had committed a capital crime by cursing Yahweh's anointed. Technically Abishai was right. David, however, disassociated himself from this attitude of vindictiveness. This was a day for celebration, not revenge. Furthermore, as chief judicial officer in the land it was David's prerogative to decide if clemency would be extended. David swore an oath to Shimei that he would not die for the crime he had committed.

D. The Aggrieved (2 Samuel 19:24-30)

1. Mephibosheth professes loyalty (19:24-28): Mephibosheth the grandson of Saul met David when he crossed Jordan. His appearance indicated that he had been in mourning for a long time. He had given himself no personal care since the day that David had departed from Jerusalem. David questioned him, however, about why he had not gone with him into exile. Mephibosheth explained that he had been deceived by Ziba. He intended to saddle a donkey and depart with David, but his lameness had prevented him from doing this. Moreover, he charged, Ziba had slandered him. Yet Mephibosheth regarded David as *an angel of God* in respect to discerning between truth and falsehood. Mephibosheth knew that the house of Saul was as good as dead until David befriended him and allowed him to eat at the royal table. Therefore, whatever David might decide, Mephibosheth would utter no word of complaint.

2. *David's decision (19:29-30):* David was not sure whether Ziba or Mephibosheth had told him the truth. He therefore decided that they will split the land which once had belonged to Saul. Mephibosheth said he was willing for Ziba to have it all. The only thing that mattered to him was that David had returned safely. Whether or not these words were spoken sincerely is difficult to ascertain from the text.

E. The Benefactor (2 Samuel 19:31-39).

1. *David's invitation (19:31-33):* Barzillai the Gileadite had come down to the Jordan to escort David across the river. This wealthy octogenarian had supplied the king with his necessities while he was in Mahanaim. David invited Barzillai to go to Jerusalem with him so that he might return the hospitality.

2. *Barzillai's response (19:34-39):* Barzillai politely declined. He had few years yet to live. At his age he would not appreciate the finery of court life. In his declining years he did not want to be a burden to the king. He begged leave to return to die in his own land near the grave of his parents. Yet Barzillai was not reluctant to request that David take his son Chimham with him. So David announced that he will take the son of his friend with him to Jerusalem. The king will do for the son whatever the father thought appropriate. The king then kissed the old man, blessed him, and sent him on his way. Then David followed his supporters across the Jordan.

F. The Childish (2 Samuel 19:40-43)

David was escorted to Gilgal by Chimham, the people of Judah, and half of the people of Israel. At Gilgal brouhaha developed. Some of the northern tribes complained they had been left out of the privilege of bringing the royal family across the Jordan. The men of Judah defended their right to take the lead in escorting the king by pointing out that the king was a member of the tribe of Judah. They further pointed out that they had received no royal compensation for what they had done. The men of Israel responded that they were ten tribes and therefore had ten times more claim to David than did Judah. Furthermore, they were the first to propose bringing back the king. Why then should the men of Judah treat them with contempt?

Yet the words of the tribe of Judah were harsher than the words of the men of Israel.

24
DAVID AFTER
ABSALOM'S REBELLION
2 Samuel 20, 23-24

Chapter Chronology

	971
2 Years	
972	

SHEBA REBELLION
2 Samuel 20

Date: ca. 972 BC

Beginning of the Rebellion
2 Samuel 20:1-2

The tribal argument at Gilgal abruptly concluded when a Benjamite named Sheba blew a trumpet and announced that the northern tribes had disowned David as their king. The men of Israel then withdrew from following David and went after Sheba. The men of Judah, however, remained with their king from the Jordan to Jerusalem.

Royal Business in Jerusalem
2 Samuel 20:3-7

A. David's Concubines (2 Samuel 20:3)
The first order of business upon returning to Jerusalem was to deal with the ten concubines who had been humiliated by Absalom. David decided that they should be treated as widows, since Absalom, who had claimed them as his wives, was now dead. The king provided for these unfortunate ladies security and sustenance.

B. Dealing with the Rebellion (2 Samuel 20:4-7)
1. Commission of Amasa (20:4-5): The next order of royal business was to dispatch Amasa to deal with the rebellion among the

321

northern tribes. He was to recruit an army from the men of Judah within three days. Apparently the men of Judah had no taste for more war at this time. At the end of the three days Amasa still had not been successful in recruiting his force.

2. *Commission of Abishai (20:6-7):* Time was of the essence as far as David was concerned. The rebellion in the north needed to be crushed immediately lest it become worse than that of Absalom. Abishai was commissioned to take the royal guard and pursue Sheba before he could find some fortified city to hole up in. So Joab's men, now under the command of Joab's brother Abishai, along with the palace bodyguard of foreign mercenaries, pursued Sheba. David left himself completely unprotected in the palace. This indicates how urgent he felt the situation was in the north.

Murder of Amasa
2 Samuel 20:8-10

Amasa met the northward bound force at the large stone in Gibeon. Joab feigned friendship with Amasa. He rushed forward to greet him. Joab arranged for his sword to drop from its sheath as he rushed forward. He then picked it up with his left hand. He took Amasa's beard by the right hand as he pretended to want to give his rival a kiss of greeting. Amasa was completely off guard. Joab then smote him with such a blow that the viscera of the man began to ooze out the wound.

End of the Sheba Rebellion
2 Samuel 20:11-22

A. Pursuit of Sheba (2 Samuel 20:11-13)

Joab and Abishai left to pursue Sheba. One of Joab's soldiers then challenged those loyal to David to follow Joab. The troops, however, were paralyzed by the dastardly deed they had just witnessed. They did not wish to walk past the writhing body of Amasa lying in the middle of the road. Joab's servant removed the body to a field beside the road and threw a robe over it. The soldiers then hastened after Joab who had now assumed command of the forces.

B. Siege of the City of Abel (2 Samuel 20:14-19)

1. Progress in the siege (20:14-17): Joab pursued Sheba through the tribes of Israel to the city of Abel Beth-maacah, about four miles west of Dan. The men of Judah laid siege to the city. They built a siege ramp up to the level of the walls. From the height of that ramp they were wreaking destruction on the walls of the city. When it appeared that the city was about to fall, a wise woman from within the city summoned Joab to a conference.

2. Appeal of a wise woman (20:18-19): The woman pled for a cessation of hostilities. She argued that 1) the city of Abel was a part of Israel's heritage with a reputation as a place of wisdom; 2) the city was among the most peaceful and loyal in Israel; 3) the city was *a mother in Israel,* i.e., a city that had produced much offspring for the nation; and 4) the city was part of the inheritance that Yahweh had given his people.

C. Beheading of Sheba (2 Samuel 20:20-22)

Joab assured the unnamed woman that he had no desire to destroy the place. Yet a rebel had taken refuge in that city. If the city surrendered this rebel, Joab would withdraw from the area. The woman promised to throw the head of Sheba over the wall to Joab. The woman then returned to her people to persuade them to execute Sheba. When the head of the rebel came over the wall, Joab signaled an end to the conflict. His troops returned to their homes.

Footnote to the Account
2 Samuel 20:23-26

In view of all the turmoil he has narrated, the author of Samuel felt it was necessary to record the officers of David's government once again (cf. 8:16-18). For the most part the two lists are the same. Joab was reinstated as commander of the army. Benaiah commanded the mercenary royal bodyguard. Adoram (NASB) or Adoniram (NIV) was over the forced labor battalion. Jehoshaphat was the recorder. Sheva replaced Seriah as scribe. Zadok and Abiathar continued as priests. Ira the Jairite replaced the sons of the king in the office of *priest,* i.e., personal adviser.

DAVID'S 'LAST WORDS'
2 Samuel 23:1–7

The second song in the appendix to 2 Samuel is designated as *the last words of David*. These are certainly not the last words that David ever spoke (cf. 1 Kings 2:1-9). This poem must be the last prophetic or inspired utterance of the king (23:1a).

David's Self Description
2 Samuel 23:1b-3a

The poem begins with a description of David himself. He was of lowly origin, *the son of Jesse*. Yet God had exalted him. This shepherd became *the anointed of the God of Jacob*. As such David was a type of Christ, the anointed one par excellence. He was *the sweet psalmist of Israel*. Some seventy-three psalms in the Book of Psalms are attributed to him. Yet he was no ordinary song writer. The Spirit of Yahweh spoke through David. Inspiration is not a quality attributed to writings centuries after they were written. The biblical writers were aware that they were being used as the instrument of the Holy Spirit. David claims that what he was about to write in this particular song was an oracle of God. The Rock of Israel had given him these words.

Messianic Implications
2 Samuel 23:3b-7

A. David's Growing House (2 Samuel 23:3b-5)

The language of this song is difficult. The words seem to have messianic implications. David anticipates the rise of a king who will rule over mankind in righteousness, i.e., justice. He will rule in the fear of God, i.e., reverence for God. His appearance will signal a new day for the world. Just as the warmth of the morning brings refreshment and stimulates growth, so the reign of this king will result in spiritual growth. This ruler will come from the house (descendants) of David. That was the thrust of the everlasting covenant which God had made with David. Because of that covenant David was confident that God will provide salvation, i.e., deliverance from physical threat, for David personally. He will also make his house grow in stature.

B. Removal of Thorns (2 Samuel 23:6-7)

In contrast to the glorious future of David's house, the ungodly are compared to thorns that men dig up and burn in order to clear the land. They must be well armed (protected) for the task. So the future king—Messiah—will root out of his kingdom all such *thorns*. These will be cast into the furnace of God's judgment fire.

DAVID AND HIS CENSUS
2 Samuel 24

Date: ca 971 BC

Sin of the Census
2 Samuel 24:1–10

A. Temptation for the Census (2 Samuel 24:1-4)

After the Absalom rebellion the anger of Yahweh burned against Israel. God permitted Satan (1 Chronicles 21:1) to incite David to take a census in Israel. The king ordered Joab to register the people from Dan to Beersheba *so that I may know the number of the people*. Joab, worldly man that he was, sensed that this census was very wrong. His objections, however, were probably more on political and social grounds than theological ones. In spite of Joab's remonstration, the king could not be dissuaded. So Joab and his commanders went out from the presence of the king to register the people.

B. Execution of the Census (2 Samuel 24:5-9)

Joab began the census in the southern part of Transjordan. He then proceeded in a wide arc through Gilead to Dan, then to Tyre and Sidon, then south through Cis-jordan to Beersheba in southern Judah. After almost ten months Joab returned to the capital and presented the king with the census figures. He had found 800,000 valiant swordsmen in Israel, and 500,000 in Judah.[28]

C. David's Troubled Heart (2 Samuel 24:10)

---

[28]The census figures in 1 Chronicles 21:5 are 1,100,000 for Israel and 470,000 for Judah. Undoubtedly the original report to David had the numbers broken down into various categories, e.g., standing army, aliens, age categories, as well as tribal and village numbers. The authors of Samuel and Chronicles have simply added together the categories they thought most important. Figures would be very different, for example, if Samuel omits the king's personal bodyguard from the count, or if Chronicles included but Samuel excluded the 288,000 men of the regular army in Israel (1 Chronicles 27:1-15). Another suggestion is that Chronicles included the resident aliens in the count for Israel.

David's heart troubled him after the census. He confessed to the Lord that he had sinned greatly and acted foolishly. He begged God's forgiveness. Since merely taking a census was not sinful—Moses took two of them—the sin here must have been connected with David's attitude. This was a military census. David must have been anticipating a military campaign on some grand scale. The cities of the Hivites and Canaanites were included. Perhaps David planned to draft these peoples into his army.

Punishment of Israel
2 Samuel 24:11-17

A. David's Options (2 Samuel 24:11-14)
In the morning Yahweh dispatched Gad, David's seer, with a message for the king. The Lord in his grace will allow David to choose what punishment he should experience because of his sin. The alternatives were 1) seven years of famine, 2) three months of flight from before his enemies, or 3) three days of pestilence. These alternatives brought David great distress. Nonetheless, he elected to *fall into the hand of Yahweh* in the pestilence. He concluded that since the mercies of the Lord are great, that punishment might be the less disruptive both for him personally and for his people.

B. Deadly Pestilence (2 Samuel 24:15-17)
Yahweh then sent a pestilence upon the land. It lasted from morning to *the appointed time,* i.e., the time of afternoon sacrifice. Seventy thousand men from Dan to Beersheba died within a matter of hours. As the angel of death approached the major population center of Jerusalem, Yahweh stayed his hand. This cessation came in response to David's intercessory prayer. The king could "see" the angel who was striking down the people, i.e., the angel was visible. David was prepared to accept the wrath of God for what he had done, but why *these sheep,* i.e., innocent people? God heard that prayer, and the angel of pestilence stopped his deadly work by the threshing floor of Araunah the Jebusite.

The sentiment of David's prayer was right, but his facts were not accurate. Israel had in fact sinned. By supporting the rebellion of Absalom in such large numbers they had repudiated for a time God's anointed. Thus God accomplished a twofold judgment in this pestilence. Israel was punished for tolerating the Absalom and Sheba rebellions. David was punished by seeing his potential military force devastated.

Purchase of a Threshing Floor
2 Samuel 24:18–25

The seer Gad returned to David, instructing him to build an altar on the threshing floor of Araunah the Jebusite. First, however, the king had to purchase that ground. The Jebusite, suspecting that sacrifice at this spot might put an end to the pestilence, offered to give David the land and even the sacrificial animals. The king, however, insisted on purchase. His words on this occasion have challenged believers through the centuries: *I will not offer burnt offerings to Yahweh my God which cost me nothing.*

So the purchase was made. David paid fifty shekels of silver for the threshing floor and the oxen.

End of the Pestilence
1 Chronicles 21:26-30

As David was offering burnt offerings and peace offerings on the new altar *he called to the Lord.* Yahweh answered him with fire from heaven on the altar of burnt offering. This was a visual demonstration that David's prayers for the land had been answered. The Lord commanded his death angel to put his sword back into his sheath, i.e., the pestilence was restrained.

When David saw that the Lord had answered his prayer for relief from the pestilence, he offered additional sacrifices on his new altar. At that time the tabernacle of the Lord with its massive bronze altar was a Gibeon a few miles north of Jerusalem. During the time that the sword of the Lord's angel was poised over Jerusalem David was terrified to leave the city. This is why he continued to offer sacrifices on the threshing floor of the Jebusite.

DAVID AND HIS DREAM
1 Chronicles 22

David's magnificent obsession was to build a temple for Yahweh. That he was forbidden to do. Nonetheless, he did everything he could to make that task easier for his son Solomon.

Temple Preparations
1 Chronicles 22:1-4, 14

A. Temple Site (1 Chronicles 22:1)

The selection of the site for the temple was linked to the episode of the plague that was stayed at the threshing floor of Araunah (Ornan). David had offered sacrifices at that spot in celebration of the cessation of the plague. During that time David was shown (2 Chronicles 3:1) that his personal altar on the threshing floor of Araunah was to become a national altar. On that site the house of God was to be located.

B. Temple Materials (1 Chronicles 22:2–5, 14)

David knew that when he died a young and inexperienced Solomon would succeed him. The task of building a world famous temple would be a challenge for any ruler. David determined to gather as much material as he could for the project before his death. Resident aliens were organized to hew out stones. David prepared a large quantity of iron for making nails and clamps. More bronze was collected than could be weighed. David also secured a large quantity of timber from Tyre. Thus did David make *ample preparation* for the construction of the temple before his death.

Charge to Solomon
1 Chronicles 22:6–16

A. Explanations (1 Chronicles 22:6-10)

David charged his son Solomon to build a house to the name of Yahweh. He explained first why he himself had not undertaken the project. The word of Yahweh (through the prophet Nathan?) indicated that because he had shed so much blood in his many wars, he was forbidden to build the temple. Through the prophetic word the Lord promised to give the land rest in the days of Solomon. This man of rest had been chosen to build the house of God. The Lord also indicated that David's son will be the son of God in a special sense. God promised to establish the throne of David's son forever.

B. Prayers (1 Chronicles 22:11-13)

328

David expressed his prayer that Yahweh might be with Solomon, that he might be successful in building the house of Yahweh. He then prayed that Yahweh would give Solomon discretion and understanding in his governance of Israel. If the young man would be careful to observe the Mosaic Law, he would prosper. Then David urged his sons, in the same words that Moses charged Joshua, *Be strong and courageous.* If one knows he is in step with God he has no reason to fear whatever the future might hold.

C. Enumeration (1 Chronicles 22:14-16)
David then enumerated all the materials that he had gathered for his son to use in temple construction: 100,000 talents of gold (3,750 tons NIV), a million talents of silver (37,500 tons NIV), bronze and iron beyond weight, timber and stone. Many skilled in masonry, carpentry and stone cutting had been identified and organized. All was ready for Solomon to begin the task.

The amount of gold and silver gathered by David has been dismissed by some commentators as a gross exaggeration.[29] The fact is that it is impossible to estimate with any degree of certainty what the "talent" was worth in the days of David. Both a Babylonian and a Phoenician system of weights were current in Canaan, and the value of the talent of the former was twice that of the latter. Each of these systems also had a heavier and a lighter scale, the former again being double the latter. In view of the fact that the system of weights employed by the author of Chronicles—perhaps neither of the systems mentioned above—is unknown, it is presumptuous to speak of the figures here being preposterous.

Charge to the Princes
1 Chronicles 22:17–19

David next addressed the leaders of the nation. He commanded them to assist Solomon in building the temple. He pointed out to them that Yahweh had subdued the land before David and his people. The land now enjoyed rest on every side. With these military challenges behind them, the leaders should now set their heart to seek Yahweh.

---

[29]Pliny (*Nat. Hist.*, 32.15) gives some standard by which to compare the figures given in 1 Chronicles 22:14. Pliny reports that Cyrus in a single campaign in Asia captured half as many talents of silver as are here mentioned, and 34,000 lbs. of gold.

They should build the temple for the Lord. Then they should move the Ark of the Covenant and the *holy vessels* (other furnishings of the tabernacle) to that sacred house.

25
SOLOMON
COMES TO POWER
1 Kings 1-3

Chapter Chronology

		967
David/Solomon Co-regency	Solomon Deals with Opponents	
971	969	

It is difficult to determine is the precise relationship between the events recorded in 1 Kings 1 and the final days of David as depicted in 1 Chronicles 23-29. Various reconstructions are possible. The most reasonable scenario is that Solomon's initial formal nomination and elevation to the throne is recorded in 1 Kings 1. The national convention of 1 Chronicles 23-29 must have occurred shortly after the first anointing of Solomon. At that convention Solomon was made king *a second time* (1 Chronicles 29:22).

INITIAL ANOINTING
OF SOLOMON
1 Kings 1:5–53

Date: ca 971 BC

David's final years were full of turmoil and tribulation. As he lay critically ill he was yet to experience another heartbreak. David's disgruntled eldest son, Adonijah, tried to take advantage of his father's condition to usurp the throne.

David's Decrepitude
1 Kings 1:1-4

When David was advanced in age he became for a time decrepit. He could no longer maintain his body temperature. The royal counselors (physicians?) advised that he secure a young virgin to *stand before the king,* i.e., become his servant. She was to become his *nurse* (NASB) or companion. The text implies, but does not clearly

331

state, that this virgin became a concubine of the king. With David's consent the search was conducted. In the town of Shunem in the tribal area of Issachar a suitable maiden was found. Abishag was very beautiful (lit., fair to exceeding degree). She was apparently willing to become the intimate companion of the decrepit king. Yet David *did not know her*. This remark helps to underscore the wane of David's physical faculties.

Adonijah's Attempted *Coup*
1 Kings 1:5–10

Adonijah, the son of Haggith, was the fourth, and now apparently the eldest surviving son of David (2 Samuel 3:4). He considered himself to be entitled to the throne. Yet Yahweh had bestowed a name of affection on Solomon at his birth (2 Samuel 12:25). David discerned in this that God had designated Solomon to be his successor. Long before any public announcement was made, the palace personnel knew that Solomon, not Adonijah, was David's choice to succeed him on the throne.

A. Adonijah's Tactics (1 Kings 1:5)

While David's physical condition deteriorated, Adonijah was exalting himself. He boasted to his confederates that one day he would be king. He made no effort to conceal his conspiracy. Borrowing a tactic from Absalom, Adonijah prepared for himself a chariot, horses, and fifty men to run before him to herald his movements.

B. Explanation (1 Kings 1:6-8)

Adonijah's calloused disregard for his father's wishes and physical condition is explained in four ways. First, he was a spoiled brat who had never been disciplined. Though David was a great man in many respects, he was a failure in parenting. Second, because of his natural gifts, especially physical attractiveness, Adonijah had an ego that simply would not allow him to acquiesce in being bypassed in the succession to the throne. Third, he felt he was entitled to the throne because he was the eldest surviving son. Fourth, Adonijah was encouraged in his claim to the throne by two powerful national leaders: Joab, David's general, and Abiathar the priest. Both of these men had unwavering fidelity to David. Why they encouraged

Adonijah in his plot can only be a matter of conjecture. In any case, other equally influential leaders—Zadok the priest, Benaiah the general, and Nathan the prophet—supported Solomon.[30] Solomon also had the backing of "the mighty men who belonged to David," i.e., the palace guard, who refused to be swayed by the charisma of Adonijah.

C. Adonijah's Feast (1 Kings 1:9-10)
Adonijah planned to proclaim himself king at a great feast held at En-rogel in the valley southeast of Jerusalem. All the king's sons, except Solomon, were invited. The courtiers from the tribe of Judah, those who did not openly support Solomon, were in attendance. The fact that Solomon was excluded proves that Adonijah knew him to be David's choice as successor.

Counter *Coup*
1 Kings 1:11–37

A. Nathan's Plan (1 Kings 1:11-14)
1. Bathsheba's help (1:11-12): When Nathan heard of Adonijah's coronation festivities, he took prompt action to thwart the conspiracy. First, he enlisted Bathsheba, Solomon's mother, in his effort. The prophet stressed the urgency of the situation by suggesting that unless the plot could be countered, the life of both Bathsheba and her son would be in jeopardy.

2. Bathsheba's role (1:13-14): The plan called for Bathsheba to approach the king first. She was to present the danger from her perspective as wife and mother of the designated successor. Lest David think that his wife had exaggerated the intentions of Adonijah, Nathan promised to come in on her heels to confirm what she had told the king.

B. Plan Executed (1 Kings 1:15-27)

---

[30]The other two prominent supporters of Solomon named in 1 Kings 1:8 are not easily identified. Rei is completely unknown except from this passage. Shimei may have been David's brother whose name appears as Shammah in 1 Samuel 16:9, and Shimeah in 2 Samuel 13:3 and 21:21. Others think he is the son of Elah named in 1 Kings 4:18. A third view is that he is the Shimei who once had cursed David (2 Samuel 16:5), but who now was *with Solomon.*

1. Bathsheba alerts the king (1:15-21): Bathsheba went immediately to the king's private chamber, which was probably a breach of etiquette since the old king was there with his young companion Abishag. First, Bathsheba reminded David of a solemn oath regarding the succession that he had made to her privately. Then she informed David about Adonijah's feast with its suspicious guest list. Third, Bathsheba impressed upon the king that the entire nation was looking to him for a clear declaration regarding his successor. Finally, she warned her husband that should he die without installing Solomon on the throne, both Bathsheba and her son would be viewed by the new king as *offenders,* i.e., criminals.

2. Nathan confirms the report (1:22-27): As Bathsheba was finishing her emotional appeal to her husband, Nathan's presence was announced to the king. After paying proper respects, Nathan spoke his piece in a masterful manner. He innocently assumed that David must have authorized Adonijah's feast. He pointed out that David's closest friends—Nathan, Zadok and Benaiah—had not been invited to En-rogel. Neither had Solomon been invited. If David was responsible for what was happening at En-rogel he must have changed his plans regarding his successor without consulting with his closest advisers. Nathan's words were framed in such a way as to elicit from David a strong denial that he had authorized Adonijah's coronation.

Anointing of Solomon
1 Kings 1:38–40

A. David's Actions (1 Kings 1:28-35)

1. Assurance to Bathsheba (1:28-31): The impassioned plea of Bathsheba and then timely confirmation of Nathan served to impress the ailing king with the urgency of royal action in favor of Solomon. First, he summoned Bathsheba again into the bed chamber. He assured her that he intended to honor his oath. He gave the order for Solomon to be enthroned that very day.

2. Instructions regarding Solomon (1:32-35a): Second, David ordered Zadok, Nathan, and Benaiah to take Solomon to the spring Gihon and anoint him as king immediately.[31] They were to blow the

---

[31]In Old Testament times the spring Gihon was on the slope of the City of David. Why David selected this spot is not clear. Perhaps it had something to do with the

trumpet and render to Solomon the traditional coronation greeting. They were then to bring the young man back into the city and have him sit on David's throne.

3. Position of Solomon (1:35b): Third, David declared that he had appointed Solomon to be *prince (nagid)* over Israel and Judah. Apparently David could nominate Solomon as *nagid,* but it remained for the tribal leaders to declare him king *(melek).*

B. Benaiah's Prayer (1 Kings 1:36-37)

Benaiah as captain of the king's personal guard could constrain himself no longer. He responded to the king's order with an expression of hearty agreement ("Amen!") and a prayer for God's blessing upon the future reign of Solomon. With most of the military leaders supporting Adonijah, the support of the palace guard was essential if Solomon were to secure the throne. Benaiah prayed that the throne of Solomon might exceed in greatness the throne of David. History records that God answered that prayer in a marvelous way.

C. Solomon's Anointing (1 Kings 1:38-40)

In short order Zadok, Nathan and Benaiah organized the coronation processional. The Cherethites and Pelethites—the royal palace guard—provided armed escort for the brief march to and from the Gihon. Zadok anointed Solomon with a horn of holy oil (cf. Exodus 30:23-25) taken from the sacred tent on Mount Zion (cf. 2 Samuel 6:17). A trumpet sounded and the crowds roared, "Long live King Solomon." The procession then moved back to the palace on Mount Zion. The ground seemed to tremble with the tumultuous sounds of the joyous crowds.

Adonijah's Capitulation
1 Kings 1:41–53

A. Feast Interrupted (1 Kings 1:41-48)

The sounds of the tumult at Gihon reached Adonijah's company at En-rogel just around the bend in the valley. The conspirators—even Joab—were filled with apprehension. The guests, however, did their

---

symbolism that as Gihon was vital to the life of Jerusalem, so also was the king. That the king in his frail condition thought of such symbolism, however, is difficult to imagine.

host the courtesy of finishing their meal. Then a breathless messenger arrived with the news the conspirators dreaded most: David had made Solomon king! Jonathan the messenger then went on to report the details of what had happened that day at Gihon and at the palace.

B. Conspirators Scatter (1 Kings 1:49-53)
Jonathan's report sent the conspirators scurrying in all directions. Adonijah fled immediately to an altar where he thought he could find sanctuary by grasping the *horns*. He refused to leave that place of sanctuary until *King* Solomon swore that he would not execute him. Solomon responded to Adonijah with a simple promise—not an oath—that he would be safe as long as he proved to be a loyal subject. If, however, he committed any fresh crime against the crown, he would be executed. With that assurance, Adonijah *came down* from the elevated altar. He was then escorted into the presence of King Solomon where he rendered homage to his younger half-brother.

FORMAL ANOINTING
OF SOLOMON
1 Chronicles 23–29

Date: ca 970 BC
Convention Summoned
1 Chronicles 23:1–2

Chronicles begins the description of David's last days by stating that in his old age he *made his son Solomon king over Israel.* The author of Chronicles makes no mention of the *coup* in which Adonijah almost succeeded. Energized by that episode, David regained sufficient strength to call for a national convention. At that time he organized the various groups of leaders for more effective service under Solomon.

Kingdom Re-organization
1 Chronicles 23:3–27:34

A. Religious Personnel (1 Chronicles 23:3-26:32)
1. Levites (23:3-32): The Levites over thirty years of age numbered 38,000. The majority of these Levites were charged with oversight of the house of God. Others served as officers and judges,
336

gatekeepers, and musicians. The tribe of Levi consisted of three clans: the Gershonites, Kohathites, and Merarites. David organized these Levites into twenty-four "houses."

In the days of Moses the primary work of the Levites was the transportation of the tabernacle. David ordered the Levites over twenty counted. Since the duties of Levites will be increased when the temple was erected, a larger number of attendants was required. Hence David lowered the age of service from thirty to twenty (23:24).

Chart 11 Levites in David's Day 1 Chronicles 23	
WORK	COUNT
Oversee Temple Work	24,000
Officers and Judges	6,000
Gatekeepers	4,000
Musicians	4,000
TOTAL	38,000

The Levites were assigned to assist the sons of Aaron with the service of the house of God by 1) purifying all holy things; 2) offering praise morning and evening; and 3) offering burnt offerings to the Lord on special occasions. The duties of Levites appear to have been expanded during the monarchy, possibly due to the inadequate number of those in priestly families.

2. *Priests (24:1-19):* Two sons of Aaron (Eleazar and Ithamar) survived long enough to establish households in Israel. The representatives of these two great priestly families in the days of David were Zadok and Ahimelech. These two priests assisted David in organizing the descendants of Aaron for priestly service. Sixteen of the courses of priests came from the descendants of Eleazar, the other eight from the descendants of Ithamar. In a formal service before the king, the princes and chief priests cast the lot to determine the order of the courses. The results were recorded by a Levitical scribe. The twenty-four courses of priests rotated in serving two week shifts of ministry in the temple.

3. Singers (25:1-31): David and his military commanders organized musicians for use in the praise service of the temple. These were all Levites, but with a specialized ministry. The musicians came from three main families: Asaph, Heman and Jeduthun. These men were all able *to prophesy* (i.e., praise God) with various musical instruments. The singers were under the direction of David. The total of those trained in singing was 288. These, like the priests and Levites, were organized by lot into twenty-four courses.

4. Gatekeepers (26:1-19): Another group of Levites had the duty of guarding the temple precincts. Several of these men are called *mighty men of valor* or *valiant men.* They guarded the gates leading to the temple, the storerooms, and temple treasuries. One name in this list—Obed-Edom—stands out. David deposited the ark at his house where it remained for three months (1 Chronicles 13:13f). The list here contains ninety-three names (cf. verses 8, 9, 11), all of whom were chiefs (v. 12). The total number of gatekeepers was 4,000 (cf. 1 Chronicles 23:5).

B. Other Officers (1 Chronicles 26:20-27:34)

1. Treasury officers (26:20-28): Apparently often various national leaders dedicated valuable objects to the Lord. These were stored in the temple.

2. "Outward business" (26:29-32): David had officers who had charge of the affairs of the kingdom in respect to the work of the Lord and the service of the king. The king had 1,700 *capable* men west of Jordan, and 2,700 east of the river. The exact duties of these officers are not known.

3. Military officers (27:1-15): David organized his army into divisions numbering 24,000, each with its own commander. These divisions served on active duty one month each year. Some of the commanders are familiar to the student of Israel's history, e.g., Benaiah and Asahel.

4. Tribal officers (27:16-24): Each of the tribes had its own *prince.* In Judah David's brother Elihu held this position. Here the author includes a note about David's census. David did not count those less than twenty years of age. To do so would have called in question the promise of Yahweh that he would multiply Israel as the stars of heaven. Joab had started to count them, but did not finish. Because he started, however, wrath came upon Israel. The incomplete census numbers were not included in the account of the chronicles of King David.

5. Overseers of crown property (27:25-31): Crown officers supervised storehouses, agricultural workers, vineyards, wine cellars, oil stores, vineyards, and livestock of various kinds.

6. Counselors (27:32-34): Jonathan, David's *uncle* (*dod*) or near relative was a counselor and scribe. The reference is probably to the Jonathan mentioned in 1 Chronicles 20:7 who was a nephew of David. Jehiel *was with the king's sons,* i.e., he was their tutor. The counselor Ahithophel was the Judas of the Old Testament. He deserted David during the Absalom rebellion. Hushai was *the king's friend* or close advisor. During the Absalom rebellion he remained loyal to David and frustrated the counsel of Ahithophel (cf. 2 Samuel 15:32ff, 17:5ff). Jehoiada the son of Benaiah replaced Ahithophel after the latter committed suicide. Abiathar was chief priest along with Zadok. He advised David in ritual matters. Joab was over the host. He advised David in military matters.

David's Last Address
1 Chronicles 28:1–8

A. David's Obsession (1 Chronicles 28:2-3)

Because of the size of the group, David *rose to his feet* to speak. He explained to the assembly that he had intended to build a permanent home for the ark of God that was *the footstool of our God.* To this end he had made preparation. The Lord, however, overruled his good intention. Because he was a man of war and had shed blood in battle, God had said that David must not be the builder of the temple.

B. God's Revelation to David (1 Chronicles 28:4-7)

1. Nathan's oracle (28:4): David then shared with the assembly—perhaps for the first time publicly—the substance of the Nathan oracle (cf. 2 Samuel 7). Although he was not permitted to build a house for God, the Lord had promised to build an enduring *house,* i.e., dynasty, for David.

2. God's choice of Solomon (28:5-7): Through prophetic revelation—David was a prophet as well as a king—God had made known his choice of Solomon. Since Israel was the kingdom of Yahweh, God alone had the right to establish throne succession. The

339

revelation had indicated also that Solomon would 1) be the temple builder, 2) be the *son* of God in a special sense, and 3) have a permanent kingdom if he faithfully followed the law of God as did David.

C. David's Exhortation (1 Chronicles 28:8)
David concluded his address to the assembly by exhorting them to observe all the commandments of Yahweh. Only thus could they ensure that they will be able to bequeath the good land of Canaan to their sons.

Instructions to Solomon
1 Chronicles 28:9–21

A. First Charge to Solomon (1 Chronicles 28:9-10)
Before the entire assembly David charged Solomon to *know,* i.e., have a personal walk, with God. He urged him to serve Yahweh, not just outwardly, but with his whole heart and mind. Mere outward observance of the law was not sufficient because Yahweh *searches all hearts, and understands every intent of the thoughts* (NASB). If Solomon sought Yahweh, he would allow himself to be found. On the other hand, if Solomon should forsake the Lord, he in turn would be forever rejected. Solomon then should *consider,* i.e., take seriously, the fact that Yahweh had chosen him for a purpose. His duty was to build the sanctuary of the Lord. The young prince needed to *be courageous and act.*

B. Revelation of the Plans (1 Chronicles 28:11-19)
Next in the public ceremony David delivered to Solomon the divinely revealed plans regarding the temple. David had felt the hand of God upon him as he drew those plans. They included the design of the temple proper, its courtyards and accompanying structures, the organization of the priests and Levites and all the other temple personnel. Even the amount of gold or silver that was required for each major piece of furniture and its accompanying utensils had been computed. Though this structure is frequently called "Solomon's temple," this text indicates that David had a great deal to do with the design. What is more important, the temple constructed by Solomon was built according to a pattern revealed by God himself.

C. Final Charge to Solomon (1 Chronicles 28:20-21)

David realized that the construction of the temple was a formidable task in spite of all the preparations that he had made. He therefore encouraged his son to *be strong and courageous and act.* Solomon should not be intimidated by the magnitude of the project because, his father assured him, *my God is with you.* The Lord promised to stay with Solomon until the task was completed. At the same time the young king had at his disposal the divisions of priests and Levites as well as the non-clerical officials. These men will faithfully carry out any commands the king might issue.

Contributions for the Temple
1 Chronicles 29:1–9

A. David's Example in Giving (1 Chronicles 29:1-5)

David reminded the assembly of the tremendous task that the youthful Solomon faced in building the temple. David pointed out that he already had provided precious metals and stones in abundance for the work. Now he announced yet another 3,000 talents of the most precious gold (*gold of Ophir*) and 7,000 talents of silver. He then challenged the assembled rulers to be equally generous.

B. Response of the Leaders (1 Chronicles 29:6-9)

The princes, officials and commanders responded generously to the challenge of their beloved king: Gold (5,000 talents + 10,000 darics), silver (10,000 talents), brass (18,000 talents) and iron (100,000 talents). Whoever possessed precious stones gave them to the treasury of the house of Yahweh. All present rejoiced *because they had given willingly.*

Thanksgiving and Prayer
1 Chronicles 29:10–19

A. Praise (1 Chronicles 29:10-15)

The generous contribution to the work of the Lord prompted David to lead in a prayer of praise and thanksgiving. The opening words of this prayer remind one of the model prayer in the Sermon on the Mount. David addressed God as *our father.* He spoke of the greatness, power, majesty, victory and dominion of the Lord. Then David acknowledged that riches and honor come from God. He alone deserves the praise for the "miracle" offering since he is the one who had provided the wealth that had now been contributed.

B. Petition (1 Chronicles 29:16-19)

God knows the hearts of all men. He therefore knew that the gifts presented both by David and his officers had been given cheerfully. David prayed that God preserve forever in the hearts of his people this focus on things divine. He asked that the Lord give Solomon a *perfect* (NASB) heart to keep the divine commandments and to build the temple for which he had made such abundant provision.

Close of the Convention
1 Chronicles 29:20–22

Following his prayer, David called on the assembly to *bless* Yahweh. All present bowed low and did homage to the Lord and his earthly representative King David. The next day the group offered sacrifices to the Lord: a thousand each of bulls, rams and lambs. These peace offerings were accompanied by feasting *before Yahweh* with great gladness.

Chart 12 *Two Coronations of Solomon*	
First Coronation	**Second Coronation**
1 Kings 1:1-2:11	1 Chronicles 28:1-29:30
At Gihon	At the Palace
Necessitated by	Planned by David's Authority
Adonijah's Actions	Made King by the Assembly
Made King by David	Anointed by the Assembly
Anointed by Zadok	

DEATH OF DAVID
1 Kings 2:1–11

Participation in the great national convention drained the last bit of strength from the old king. Feeling death's grip tightening upon him, David summoned Solomon to his side to impart to him his final private instruction.

Private Words to Solomon
1 Kings 2:1–9

A. General Encouragement (1 Kings 2:1-4).

First, David urged Solomon to *be strong and be a man.* Second, he urged his son to *keep the trust of Yahweh.* He could prosper only by faithful adherence to the Law of Moses. Third, the young man should walk before Yahweh in truth with all his heart. Thereby Solomon will experience the fulfillment of God's promise of everlasting possession of the throne.

B. Special Instructions (1 Kings 2:5-11).

1. Regarding Joab (2:5-6): Certain obligations that David had neglected to fulfill, or had promised to fulfill, now devolved upon his son and successor. First, Solomon must deal with Joab who literally had gotten by with murder during the reign of David. The fact that Joab had *shed the blood of war in peace* (cf. 2 Samuel 3:22-27; 20:4-10) cried out for justice. Solomon should not allow Joab *to go down to Sheol* (the abode of the dead) *in peace,* i.e., he must not be allowed to die a natural death. Solomon must *act in wisdom* in this matter. He must find a plausible pretext for bringing Joab's just deserts upon him. Otherwise a rebellion in the ranks of the army might occur.

2. Regarding sons of Barzillai (2:7): The situation was completely different with the sons of Barzillai. David owed this family a debt of gratitude dating back to the days when he fled into Transjordan to escape Absalom. Barzillai the Gileadite had brought David much needed supplies in those dark days (cf. 2 Samuel 17:27-30). David encouraged Solomon to allow Barzillai's family to be included among those who ate at his table, i.e., provide them with a perpetual royal food allowance.

3. Regarding Shimei (2:8-9): Shimei the Benjamite had cursed David in the hour of his humiliation by Absalom (cf. 2 Samuel 16:5-8). Cursing the king was a capital crime (cf. Exodus 22:28). Yet when David was restored to his throne, he pledged not to execute Shimei. Solomon, however, was not bound by the oath of his father. He should be wise enough to realize that a man like Shimei could not be trusted. Though Shimei was *with Solomon,* i.e., had supported his

343

claim to the throne, the new king must *bring down his gray hair in blood to Sheol,* i.e., execute the man.

4. *Moral issue:* The morality of David's instruction concerning Shimei and Joab has been called into question. These points, however, must be observed. First, no hint of malice or vindictiveness is evident in the passage. Second, verses 2-4 set the tone for these special instructions. What was uppermost in David's mind was strict observance of the law of God. That included the execution of the murderer and the blasphemer. Third, David is tacitly admitting to failure on his own part in enforcing the law. To know that these errors will be corrected in the reign of his son gave David great comfort in his last hours.

Chart 13 *Reign of David* *1010-970 BC*			
Hebron Years	**War Years**	**Rest Years**	**Trouble Years**
King of Judah	King of all Israel		
Civil War	Defensive Wars Offensive Wars David's Sin Ark Moved	Nathan Oracle Family Problems	Absalom Revolt Sheba Revolt Adonijah Plot
7.5 Years	21 Years	5 Years	7 Years
Age 30-38	Age 38-59	Age 59-64	Age 64-70
2 Samuel 1-4	2 Samuel 5, 8, 10-12	2 Samuel 6-7, 9	2 Samuel 13-20 1 Kings 1-2
1010-1002 BC	1002-981 BC	981-976 BC	976-970 BC

Concluding Summary
1 Kings 2:10–12

Shortly after David's final instructions to Solomon, the old man *lay down with his fathers,* i.e., he died. The language seems to suggest an awareness of reunion with his relatives in Sheol, the abode of the dead. David was buried in the City of David—that part of Jerusalem that his personal troops had conquered from the Jebusites. His sepulcher on Mount Zion still existed in the time of Christ (Acts 2:29). The total length of David's reign was forty years. He had reigned seven years in Hebron, and thirty-three years in Jerusalem.

SOLOMON AND HIS CHALLENGERS
1 Kings 2:13–46

At the national convention in David's last days Solomon was made king *a second time.*[32] He was anointed again by Zadok the priest. The military leaders and all the other sons of David pledged their allegiance to the young king. God highly exalted Solomon in the sight of all Israel. He bestowed on Solomon royal majesty which neither Saul nor David had possessed (1 Chronicles 29:22b-25). The actions of the national convention firmly established Solomon on the throne (1 Kings 2:12). Those who were his enemies, however, had not relinquished all hope of seizing the throne.

Date: ca 969

Second Plot of Adonijah
1 Kings 2:13–25

After the collapse of his attempted coup, Adonijah had pledged his allegiance to Solomon (1 Kings 1:53). Not long after the death of David, however, Adonijah attempted to lay the groundwork for another coup.

A. A Subtle Plan (1 Kings 2:13-18)

---

[32]Rabbinic tradition has Solomon ascending the throne at age twelve. Josephus (*Ant.* 8.7.8) says he was fourteen. Modern scholars estimate that he was seventeen or eighteen. Solomon already had one child at the time of his accession as is indicated by the fact that he reigned forty years and his son Rehoboam was forty-one at the time of his father's death (1 Kings 14:21).

345

1. Adonijah's request for Abishag (2:13-14): By means of Abishag, the former concubine of King David,[33] Adonijah hoped to accomplish what his chariots, horsemen and banquets had not accomplished earlier. He won the sympathies of the most powerful woman in the land, Bathsheba the queen mother. She was suspicious at first when Adonijah came calling. His tactics, however, disarmed her and turned her into an ally.

2. Adonijah's request to Bathsheba (2:15-17): First, Adonijah resorted to self pity as a means of appealing to the sympathies of Bathsheba. The kingdom belonged to him, and *all Israel*—an obvious exaggeration—was prepared to make him king. Things turned around, however, and the kingdom became Solomon's. Second, he used hypocritical piety. He feigned resignation to the will of Yahweh in respect to the throne. Third, he pled with Bathsheba to help him: *Do not deny me this one last request.* Fourth, he flattered Bathsheba by asserting that the king will never refuse a request from his mother. Fifth, he pretended to be in love. All he wanted as compensation for losing the throne to Solomon was the hand of Abishag the Shunammite.

3. Adonijah's motives (2:18): Apparently Bathsheba did not question Adonijah about his motives for wanting to marry the Shunammite. That love (or lust) partially may have motivated the request cannot be denied. Higher aspirations, however, were certainly involved as Solomon instantly recognized. Be that as it may, Bathsheba was taken in by Adonijah's tactics. She agreed to speak to the king on his behalf.

B. Bathsheba's Petition (1 Kings 2:19-22)

1. Formal request (2:19-20): Bathsheba went immediately to the throne room of Solomon. After the exchange of courtesies, she got right to the point. She referred to her petition as a *small favor,* and so it seemed to her. Solomon expressed his willingness to fulfill whatever request his mother might make, never dreaming that she

---

[33]Abishag is never actually called David's concubine or wife in the text. Some think that had she actually been married to David, Adonijah would have been committing incest by marrying her under the laws of Leviticus 18:8 and 20:11. It may have been on the legal technicality that David had never been able to consummate the marriage with Abishag (assuming that he had married her) that Adonijah thought he stood a chance to gain her hand. What is clear is that in the eyes of the people Abishag would have been considered the wife of David regardless of her legal status.

would ask for anything that he could not grant. Thus reassured, Bathsheba stated her request on behalf of Adonijah.

2. *Solomon's reaction (2:22):* Solomon exploded in rage when he heard his mother's request. He could not believe that his own mother did not realize the implications of her request. She might as well have asked the kingdom to be given to Adonijah, for that would be the upshot of a marriage to the concubine of the former king. Why so? Taking possession of a wife or harem of a deceased king was equivalent to a claim to the throne (cf. 2 Samuel 12:8; 16:22). The mention of Joab and Abiathar in connection with Adonijah's request makes it appear that Solomon had received from his intelligence officers some prior information indicating that another plot was brewing. Be that as it may, Solomon viewed the petition of Adonijah as conclusive proof that Adonijah was involved in another conspiracy.

C. Adonijah's Execution (1 Kings 2:23-25)

1. *Ordered by the king (2:23-25):* Having been lenient with his elder brother once, Solomon was in no mood to ignore further the threat that Adonijah posed to his rule. In the presence of all those in the throne room he swore a solemn oath that Adonijah will die that very day. He then dispatched Benaiah, captain of the palace guard, to execute his half brother. The order was immediately carried out. This was the first in a bloody trilogy of executions.

2. *Explanation:* Those who might be tempted to look on the execution of Adonijah as a ruthless misuse of royal power should ponder the following points. 1) Had Adonijah's first rebellion succeeded both Solomon and his mother would have been killed (cf. 1 Kings 1:12). 2) By fleeing to the altar following the collapse of his conspiracy, Adonijah was admitting that he deserved the death of a traitor. 3) Solomon displayed the greatest magnanimity toward Adonijah when, instead of executing him, he placed him on probation. 4) Adonijah had been warned that if wickedness were found in him, he would be killed (1 Kings 1:52). 5) For Solomon to ignore this second offense might suggest that the king was weak, and such weakness would be an encouragement to sedition throughout the land.

Solomon Deals
with other Opponents

1 Kings 2:26–34

A. Abiathar (1 Kings 2:26–27)

1. Removed from office (2:26): That Abiathar was again involved in the conspiracy to give the throne to Adonijah is suggested by the actions that Solomon took against him. This priest, who on the occasion of the earlier conspiracy escaped even censure, was summoned to the palace. The king curtly ordered him to retire from the priestly office and return to his hometown of Anathoth. As far as Solomon was concerned, Abiathar was worthy of death (lit., a man of death) for his treasonous conduct. On account of his past associations with David, however, the king sentenced the old man to banishment rather than death.

2. Fulfillment of prophecy (2:27): Abiathar was the last descendant of the Ithamar branch of the priestly family. When he was banished, the high priesthood reverted to the descendants of Eleazar who was represented in Solomon's day by Zadok. Thus was fulfilled a prophecy made by an anonymous prophet (cf. 1 Samuel 2:31-36) concerning the house of Eli (Ithamar branch) more than a century earlier.

B. Joab (1 Kings 2:28–34)

1. Flight to the altar (2:28): When Joab heard of the execution of Adonijah and the expulsion of Abiathar, he knew that he was next. Though Joab had not supported Absalom in his rebellion against David, he had lent his support to the ill-fated conspiracy of Adonijah. Realizing that his treason was a capital crime, Joab fled to the tent of Yahweh on Mount Zion and clasped the horns of the altar. There he sought sanctuary as Adonijah done before him (cf. 1 Kings 1:50). His flight to the altar indicates that he had been involved in the Abishag incident.

2. Execution orders (2:29-30): Solomon regarded Joab's flight to the altar as proof of his continuing treasonous intentions. He ordered Benaiah to go and slay the old general. When Joab refused the command to step away from the altar, Benaiah was in a quandary. He finally returned to Solomon for further orders.

3. Major justification (2:31): Good reasons existed for denying sanctuary to Joab. Solomon spelled out those reasons to Benaiah. The altar provided no sanctuary to murderers (Exodus 21:14). Therefore the king ordered Benaiah to slay Joab at the altar. Only by the

348

shedding of the blood of this guilty man could the innocent blood of Abner and Amasa be washed away from the house of David (cf. Numbers 35:33). As chief magistrate of the land, Solomon considered it his obligation to avenge the death of murder victims.

4. Supporting justification (2:32-33): As if the execution of Joab needed any further justification, Solomon added that the victims of Joab's sword were better men than their assassin. Though many people, no doubt, suspected David of criminal complicity in these murders, the deeds were actually done without his knowledge. By avenging the death of the innocent, the stain of blood (obligation to punish) could be removed from the house of David. As a consequence, the descendants of David will prosper. On the other hand, the children of Joab will always have to live with the stigma that their father had been executed as a murderer.

5. Execution carried out (2:34-35): Having received royal authorization to slay Joab in the tabernacle, Benaiah hastened back to the altar to perform the deed. Joab was buried in the courtyard of his own house which was located near Bethlehem in the wilderness of Judah. To be so buried was considered an honor (cf. 1 Samuel 25:1). This honor was accorded Joab in recognition of his years of faithful service to his country. Solomon filled the vacant posts of army commander and high priest with his friends Benaiah and Zadok.

Shimei's Challenge
1 Kings 2:36-46

A. Shimei's Probation (1 Kings 2:36-38)

Even though Shimei had recently been *with Solomon* (cf. 1 Kings 1:8), his earlier bitter outburst against David made Solomon suspicious of him. He was summoned to the palace and ordered to build a new home in Jerusalem. Shimei was told never to leave the capital. Solomon wanted to keep Shimei under surveillance; he also wished to neutralize his considerable influence in his tribe of Benjamin.

Solomon warned Shimei that should he ever leave the city for any reason, he would be executed for his past crime against the crown. Specifically the king mentioned crossing the brook Kidron east of Jerusalem, for that would be the direction that Shimei might be expected to go in an effort to return to his home at Bahurim just over the Mount of Olives. Having been clearly warned, Shimei would be responsible for his own death should he venture out of the city. Shimei swore an oath to comply with the terms of the probation. The sentence was better than Shimei deserved and probably better than he had expected especially in view of the fact that Solomon was not bound by the oath of David to refrain from slaying him.

B. Shimei's Execution (1 Kings 2:39-46a)

After three years of probation in Jerusalem, two of Shimei's slaves ran away. They took refuge with Achish, king of Gath. Learning of their whereabouts, Shimei immediately set out for Gath to retrieve them. Upon his return he was summoned to the palace. Solomon lodged a threefold charge against him. First, he had profaned the name of God by violating a solemn oath taken in the name of the deity. Second, he had violated the terms of his probation, thus disregarding the commands of the king. Third, Shimei had cursed and blasphemed the Lord's anointed, David. For these transgressions Shimei received divine recompense at the hands of Solomon. By executing Shimei, Solomon was acting in the service of God. He fully expected God to be pleased with his action and to bless him accordingly. Thus with no further hesitation, Solomon ordered Benaiah to execute Shimei.

Pharaoh's Concession
1 Kings 3:1

By swiftly eliminating four potential antagonists—Adonijah, Abiathar, Joab and Shimei—Solomon firmly established himself as king (1 Kings 2:46b). He further strengthened his position by arranging a marriage to Pharaoh's daughter. This marriage was strictly political. Treaties between nations were customarily sealed by intermarriage of the two royal houses. This alliance, however, must have been shocking to the average Israelite since Egypt was the ancestral foe of Israel.

Solomon brought his new wife to the city of David. There she lived in the palace formerly occupied by David (2 Chronicles 8:11) until Solomon was able to complete his building projects. The text does not state that Pharaoh's daughter gave up her idols when she became Solomon's wife. Certain factors, however, lead to the conclusion that such was the case.[34]

350

ENDOWMENT OF SOLOMON
1 Kings 3:4–15

Date: ca 969 BC

Public Sacrifices at Gibeon
1 Kings 3:2-4

A. High Place Worship (1 Kings 3:2-3)

Because they had no temple, the children of Israel were sacrificing to Yahweh in the *high places.* The only blemish on Solomon's commitment to the Lord in these early days was his participation in the high place worship. He loved Yahweh and walked in *the statutes of David,* i.e., the laws of God which David had kept and which he commanded Solomon to keep (cf. 1 Kings 2:4). The author of Kings does not say that worship in the high places was sinful at this time. He only is suggesting that it was less than ideal. God winked at this imperfection in the period before the temple was built.

B. Solomon at Gibeon (1 Kings 3:4)

The Bible explains Solomon's famous wisdom as a supernatural endowment that he received while worshiping at *the great high place* in Gibeon. At this spot, six miles northwest of Jerusalem the tabernacle with its huge bronze altar was now located (2 Chronicles 1:3). Upon that altar a thousand whole burnt offerings were offered (i.e., provided by) Solomon with the intention of seeking God's blessing upon his reign.

Solomon's Dream
1 Kings 3:5–15

A. Yahweh's Appearance (1 Kings 3:5)

---

[34]That Pharaoh's daughter may have surrendered her idols is suggested by three factors: 1) Solomon at this period of his life was an enthusiastic observer of the law of Yahweh; 2) the king is never condemned for this particular marriage; and 3) no trace of Egyptian idolatry or religious rites can be found in Israel at this time.

While he was at Gibeon, the Lord appeared to Solomon in a dream. The young king was instructed to name whatever he might desire from God.

B. Solomon's Request (1 Kings 3:6–9)

Solomon's reply was marked by both perception and piety. He began by acknowledging the great favor that Yahweh had bestowed on David to permit his son to follow him on the throne. He then humbly confessed his inability to handle the task that had been thrust upon his shoulders. He referred to himself as a *little child.* He did not know how *to go out or come in,* i.e., conduct himself in the office of king. Furthermore the nation had become so vast that the governance of it would be a major challenge even to the most mature man. In view of these circumstances, Solomon asked God to give him a discerning heart (lit., a hearing heart) that would qualify him to judge (i.e., rule) the people to God, to know the difference between what was true and false.

C. God's Response (1 Kings 3:10–14)

Solomon's response pleased Yahweh. Solomon might have asked for long life, or wealth, or victory over enemies. Since, however, he had asked for a gift that would enable him to better meet the needs of his people, God granted his petition. Solomon's wisdom will surpass all who had gone before him, and all who followed him. In addition God gave the young king what he had not requested, viz., riches and honor. The blessing of long life, however, had a condition attached. Only if Solomon continued to walk in the way of Yahweh would his days be lengthened.

D. Solomon's Worship (1 Kings 3:15)

Solomon awoke to discover that he had been dreaming. This, however, was no ordinary dream; it was a dream in which a divine revelation had been given to him. Solomon proceeded immediately to the other major sanctuary of that period, the tent that housed the Ark of the Covenant. There he offered new sacrifices to Yahweh. In addition to the burnt offerings made at Gibeon, he added peace offerings in gratitude for the endowment he had just received.

Solomon's Wisdom
1 Kings 3:16-28; 4:29-34

A. Character of his Wisdom (1 Kings 4:29-34)

1. Magnitude of his wisdom (4:29-31): God gave to Solomon practical wisdom, understanding (ability to solve difficult problems), and *largeness of heart,* i.e., comprehensive knowledge. The magnitude of his wisdom is indicated by four comparisons. His wisdom was like 1) *the sand of the seashore,* i.e., measureless. 2) It exceeded the wisdom of the *children of the east,* i.e., the various Arab tribes dwelling east of Canaan including the Edomites who were famous for their wisdom. 3) His wisdom exceeded that of Egypt which was famous for the knowledge of geometry, arithmetic, astronomy and medicine. 4) His wisdom exceeded that of the wisest men of his own nation: Ethan, Heman, Calcol and Darda.[35] Solomon's reputation as a polymath spread throughout all the surrounding nations.

2. Fruit of his wisdom (4:32-34): Only a small portion of the literary fruits of Solomon's wisdom has been incorporated into the Bible. During his reign this king spoke three thousand proverbs of which less than one third are preserved in the Book of Proverbs. Of his 1,005 songs, only three have survived: the beautiful Song of Songs, and two of the psalms (72 and 127). In addition, Solomon made observations based on his botanical and zoological studies. Solomon's great wisdom attracted the attention of the kings throughout the Near East.

B. Example of his Wisdom (1 Kings 3:16-28)

1. Conflicting claims (3:16-22): The classic case of two harlots, both claiming to be the mother of a baby, demonstrated the judicial wisdom that had been given to Solomon. The women had given birth to children out of wedlock within three days of one another. No third party was present at the births, hence independent collaboration was impossible. The plaintiff charged that her friend had smothered her child one night. She then allegedly switched her dead baby for the living one that was sleeping at the side of his mother. In the morning light the plaintiff discovered that the dead baby was not her own. The

---

[35]Ethan, Heman, Calcol and Darda were the sons of Zerah (1 Chronicles 2:6). Heman and Ethan authored Psalms 88-89, two of the wisdom psalms.

defendant naturally disputed all these contentions. She tenaciously maintained that the living child was really hers. Back and forth the women made their claims and counter claims.

2. *Discernment strategy (3:23-26):* Finally Solomon was ready to make a decision. He first summarized the problem as it had been presented to him. Then he ordered a sword to be brought. The child will be divided and half given to each woman. The real mother, the plaintiff as it turned out, was emotionally stirred by the decision that in effect mandated the death of her son. In desperation she cried out to the king to spare the child and give it to her rival. She preferred to lose her case and see her rival rewarded than to have the child killed. The defendant, on the other hand, was perfectly content to allow the execution to take place. She did not really love the child. Her only objective was to deprive her rival of the fruit of her womb.

3. *Result (3:27-28):* Through this stratagem Solomon learned the identity of the real mother. He ordered the plaintiff to be given custody of the disputed child. The people of Israel were impressed and even awed by this demonstration of royal sagacity. They rightly concluded that the wisdom of God was in this young king.

Chart 14		
Solomon's Work Force		
Cabinet	Adoniram 1 Kings 4:6; 5:14	
Superior Officers	250 Israelites 2 Chronicles 8:10	300 Canaanites (Each Over Four Crews)
Foremen	Hiram Men (Served as Crew Foremen)	3,300 Canaanites (Each Over a Crew of About 45 men; 2 Chronicles 2:18; 1 Kings 5:16)
Laborers	30,000 Israelites (Cut Timber)	70,000 Canaanites (Burden Bearer) 80,000 Canaanites (Stonecutters) 1 Kings 5:15; 2 Chronicles 2:18
Total	30,250 Israelites	153,600 Canaanites

26
SOLOMON'S
WISDOM & WORK
1 Kings 4-8

969	10 Years	960

KINGDOM OF SOLOMON
1 Kings 4:1–28

Administration of the Kingdom
1 Kings 4:1–19

Solomon's wisdom was also demonstrated in the area of kingdom administration. To select faithful servants is one of the most difficult tasks of rulers. The welfare of the whole state depends on the choices. That the list of appointees reflects Solomon's wisdom is indicated by the following considerations: 1) Priority in this list is given to officers of peace. 2) In several positions Solomon retained the experienced servants of his father. 3) Positions of trust were filled by persons of piety—sons of priests or prophets.

A. Kingdom Officers (1 Kings 4:1-6)

- Azariah was prime minister.[36]
- The scribes, Elihoreph and Ahijah, wrote letters and proclamations, drew up edicts and apparently had certain fiscal duties (2 Kings 12:10).

---

[36]Azariah is designated in Hebrew as *ha-kohen, the priest*. The term *kohen* must have had a secular as well as a sacred meaning. In 2 Samuel 8:18 David's sons are called *priests* whereas the parallel passage in 1 Chronicles 18:17 refers to them as *first men*. Just as the sacred *kohen* represented the people before God, so the secular *kohen* represented the people before the king and vice versa.

- Jehoshaphat, a carryover from David's court (cf. 2 Samuel 8:16), was the recorder. He scheduled palace activities and introduced people to royal audiences.
- Benaiah commanded the host.
- Zadok and Abiathar were the high priests.
- Azariah son of Nathan (the prophet?) was over the twelve district governors.
- Zabud, another son of Nathan, was chief minister (lit., priest) and *friend of the king* or confidential adviser.
- Ahishar was the steward and manager of the palace.
- Another carryover from David's administration was Adoniram (Adoram). He was in charge of the forced labor force.

B. Tax System (1 Kings 4:7-19)

Solomon is credited with originating the first scientific system of taxation. He divided his entire realm into twelve tax districts, nine west of Jordan and three east of the river. The boundaries of the districts corresponded roughly to the old tribal boundaries. Over each district he set a governor who was responsible one month of the year to supply the produce and meat necessary to sustain the king's household. Judah is not included in the list of districts, probably because that area had been organized on a different basis by David.

The governors are listed in the order in which they were responsible for the royal provisions during the year. Two of them were married to daughters of Solomon (verses 11, 15). Five are known only by the names of their fathers. No satisfactory explanation of this curious circumstance has yet been proposed.

Extent of the Kingdom
1 Kings 4:21, 24

Solomon's empire was vast, stretching from *the river,* i.e., the Euphrates in the north, to the land of the Philistines in the west and Egypt in the south. The northernmost point in his empire was Tiphsah, a town on the west bank of Euphrates River at its most important crossing place. The southernmost point was Azzah (Gaza), the last town in Palestine on the frontier of Egypt. All the kings in this region rendered tribute to Solomon. In spite of the large extent of his kingdom, peace prevailed.

Felicity of the Kingdom
1 Kings 4:20, 25

The wisdom of the tax district system is indicated in 1 Kings 4:20. The population was so numerous that it was easier for the governors to collect the royal tribute. Solomon's subjects were *eating, drinking and rejoicing.* Apparently the king's exactions did not deprive the people of necessary food; they had plenty to eat and drink.

Judah and Israel prospered under Solomon. From Dan, at the headwaters of the Jordan, to Beersheba, on the edge of the southern wilderness, every person sat *under his vine and under his fig tree.* This proverbial expression denotes rest and the undisturbed enjoyment of the fruits of the earth.

Expenses of his Kingdom
1 Kings 4:22–23 + 26–28

The court provisions were commensurate with the size of Solomon's kingdom. Each day the royal household consumed approximately 340 bushels of fine flour and 155 bushels of meal. Thirty head of beef, a hundred sheep, as well as wild game, were required for the palace table. Such a quantity of bread and meat could feed at least fourteen thousand people.

The peace was maintained by means of a huge cavalry and chariot force. The addition of these two units revolutionized the Israelite army which heretofore had been entirely infantry. Solomon had four thousand[37] stalls for his chariot horses. In

---

[37]That the figure 40,000 in the Masoretic Text of 1 Kings 4:26 is a scribal error is indicated by two facts: 1) the parallel passage in 2 Chronicles 9:25 reads 4,000; and

addition the king kept twelve thousand cavalry horses. This great number of horses threw an extra burden on each of the twelve district governors (cf. 4:7-19). Yet these officers faithfully brought barley and straw to the various depots throughout the land where the animals were kept. Multiplication of horses by the king was a violation of God's law (cf. Deuteronomy 17:16).

PREPARATION FOR
BUILDING THE TEMPLE
1 Kings 5:1-18

Treaty with Hiram of Tyre
1 Kings 5:1-12

A. Solomon's Appeal (1 Kings 5:1-6)
When Hiram (Huram) king of Tyre heard that Solomon had succeeded his father, he dispatched ambassadors to congratulate the youthful king. In a letter of response Solomon indicated that he now intended to pursue the dream of his father to build a house for the name of Yahweh. He made two requests of Hiram. First, he asked that Hiram continue to make available to him the valuable timber from the Lebanon Mountains. Second, he requested that a skilled craftsman be sent to Jerusalem (2 Chronicles 2:7). In exchange for these provisions, Solomon agreed to supply manpower to assist in the logging operation and to pay the wages of the Sidonian laborers. In a closing complimentary remark, Solomon alluded to the skill of the Sidonians in woodsmanship.

B. Hiram's Response (1 Kings 5:7-9)
1. Praise (5:7): Hiram rejoiced at the prospect of continued friendly relations with Israel. He praised Yahweh the God of Israel for having given David so wise a son as his

---

2) the lower figure is more in line with the number of chariots (1400) possessed by Solomon (I Kings 10:26). Normally two horses were yoked to each chariot. A third horse was usually provided for each chariot in case of an accident.

successor. The wisdom of the youthful king was evident to Hiram because 1) Solomon had chosen the path of peaceful coexistence; 2) he earnestly desired to fulfill the purposes of his father; and 3) he had made the worship of God the foremost concern of his reign.

2. *Proposal (5:8-9):* In his letter of reply, Hiram agreed to furnish the timber that Solomon had requested. The plan called for Hiram's servants to bring the logs down the rugged mountain road from Lebanon to the sea. There the timber was lashed into rafts and floated down the Mediterranean seacoast to Joppa (2 Chronicles 2:16). At that point the logs were separated and delivered to the Israelites. Solomon's men were responsible for moving those logs the forty steep miles to Jerusalem. In exchange for these services Hiram asked that "bread," i.e., grain, might be supplied to his palace in Tyre.

C. Treaty Obligations (1 Kings 5:10-12)

The formal treaty negotiated with Hiram is regarded by the author of Kings as another manifestation of the wisdom of Solomon. Hiram sent the timber southward toward Jerusalem. Solomon paid Hiram annually, in addition to the wages of the laborers, 20,000 kors of wheat (103,200 bushels), twenty kors (1,100 gallons) of *beaten* oil, i.e., oil that was obtained   by pounding the olives before they ripened.

Solomon's Levy of Workers
1 Kings 5:13-16

A. Lebanon Force (1 Kings 5:13-14)

Solomon made further preparation for the construction work by drafting out of Israel a labor force numbering some thirty thousand. These men were divided into three shifts of ten thousand. Each shift was compelled to labor in Lebanon four months of the year. Apparently these Israelites worked alongside of Hiram's servants and under their direction.

B. Canaanite Force (1 Kings 5:15-16)

In addition to the thirty thousand Israelite draftees, Solomon compelled the remnants of the Canaanites to become tribute slaves (cf. 1 Kings 9:20, 21). The census by the king found 153,600 Canaanite men remaining within the borders of Israel (2 Chronicles 2:17). Of these 70,000 became burden bearers, 80,000 became hewers of stone *in the mountains,* i.e., in the hill country of Canaan. The remaining 3,600 were Canaanite supervisors (2 Chronicles 2:18). Over these supervisors were 550 superior officers (cf. 1 Kings 9:23).

Materials Prepared
1 Kings 5:17-18

Having secured and organized the laborers, Solomon issued the order for the foundation stones to be cut out and brought to the temple site. Although the foundation stones would not be seen, equal care was given to their preparation. Ordinarily plain stones were used in foundations. The king, however, ordered for the temple great, costly, hewn stones. Some of these very stones can be viewed at the excavations on Mount Moriah today. Solomon's laborers worked alongside the Phoenician construction crews preparing both the stone and the wood. Among the latter were the Gabalites. Gebal (Byblos) was a Phoenician city about twenty miles north of modern Beirut. The men of this town had a reputation as skilled builders (cf. Ezekiel 27:9).

CONSTRUCTION WORK
1 Kings 6:1-7:51

Date: ca 967-960 BC
Without question the greatest achievement of Solomon's glorious reign was the construction of the Jerusalem temple. Using plans designed by David, and the expertise of Phoenician craftsmen, Solomon brought into being what surely must have been one of the wonders of ancient architecture.

The material presented in Scripture is sufficient to allow one to get a general idea of what the temple was like. The omission of

360

crucial architectural details, however, renders impossible absolute certainty about many points. The careful and detailed dimensions are proofs of the tender veneration with which the people of God regarded the temple. They are also indications of the belief that this house was for the Lord and not for man.

Construction of the Temple
1 Kings 6:1-35

A. Chronological Note (1 Kings 6:1)

1 Kings 6:1 furnishes the key to biblical chronology prior to the monarchy period. Temple construction began in Ziv, the second month (April), in the fourth year of Solomon's reign (967 BC). This was 480 years after the Israelites had come out of Egypt. This text seems to necessitate a date for the exodus of about 1447 BC.

B. Exterior of the House (1 Kings 6:2-10)

1. Size (6:2): The temple proper was a rather small building. Exclusive of the porch and side chambers, the building measured about 90 feet long, 30 feet wide, and 45 feet high. The temple was never meant for the congregation of worshipers, but only for the presence of God and the priests who ministered before that presence. The congregation never met *within* this building; rather they offered their worship *towards* it. Worshipers congregated in the great courtyard that surrounded the temple.

2. Porch and side chambers (6:3-6, 8): In front of the main building was a porch or vestibule fifteen feet deep that extended across the entire front (east end) of the temple. An unspecified number of immovable lattices were the windows of the house. Around the outside wall of the entire building (exclusive of the porch) were three stories of staggered width that were divided by partitions into distinct compartments. There were about thirty of these chambers. The upper chambers were reached by means of a door through the external wall of the side chambers that led to a spiral stairway. The chambers were fastened to the house by means of cedar beams resting on abatements in the walls of the house. The chambers served 1) as storage areas for temple treasures and gifts, 2) lodging for priests who were serving in the temple, and 3) possibly as a buttress to support the walls of the house.

History of Israel

3. *Building materials (6:7, 9):* The stones used in the temple
were *perfect,* i.e., they were so hewn and prepared at the quarry that
no sound of any iron tool was heard at the temple site when the stones
were brought together. The roof of the house, which was most likely
flat, was made of beams and boards of cedar wood.

C. Promise to Solomon (1 Kings 6:11-14)
During the course of the building of the temple, the divine word
came to the king, probably through a prophetic intermediary
(Nathan?). That God spoke directly is ruled out by 9:2 which alludes
to the *second* direct revelation to Solomon. In effect the divine word
contained an implied commendation of Solomon for having begun
such a noble work. If Solomon continued to follow the direction of
Yahweh 1) God would confirm the promise spoken to David in 2
Samuel 7:12ff; and 2) God would dwell in the midst of his people.
Thus encouraged by the gracious promise of Yahweh, Solomon
proceeded with the construction of the interior of the temple.

D. Interior of the House (1 Kings 6:15-35)
The sacred historian next describes some of the outstanding
features of the interior of the temple.
1. *Holy place (6:15-18, 29-30).* The interior stone walls of the
house were lined with wood that was engraved with gourds and
flower blossoms. The wood was in turn overlaid with small gold
plates that were attached to the wood with nails. The walls were also
ornamented with precious stones (2 Chronicles 3:6, 9). The floor was
covered with cypress wood. Thirty feet from the west end of the
house a floor-to-ceiling partition separated the most holy place (the
debir) from the rest of the house.
2. *Debir (6:19-22):* The holy of holies (the *debir*) at the rear of
the structure housed the Ark of the Covenant. This part of the
building was a cube (symbolizing perfection) of thirty feet. The *debir*
was overlaid with pure gold (2 Chronicles 3:8) which weighed 600
talents (23 tons). Immediately in front of the *debir* was a stone altar
covered with cedar which was overlaid with gold. Gold chains hung
in front of the *debir*. The purpose of these chains is not stated. Above
the *debir* were the *upper chambers* (2 Chronicles 3:9) which were
also overlaid with gold. The relics of the old tabernacle may have
been stored here.

362

3. *Cherubim (6:23-28):* Two huge cherubim (15 feet high) made of precious olive wood overlaid with gold dominated the interior of the *debir.* They faced east (2 Chronicles 3:13). Their outstretched wings reached across the entire width of the *debir* (30 feet). Between their bodies was a space of several feet where the Ark of the Covenant rested. Cherubim were angelic creatures that are usually depicted guarding something sacred. Their appearance is a matter of speculation.

4. *Doors (6:31-35):* The doors leading to the *debir* were made of olive wood. They contained relief carvings similar to those on the walls. They were overlaid with gold. A curtain hung inside the *debir* that prevented any priest from gazing within when the doors were opened once each year on the day of atonement (2 Chronicles 3:14). The outer doors of the house were made of fir decorated with figures of cherubim, palm trees and flowers overlaid with gold. These doors were made of two panels, but it is impossible to determine whether they were divided lengthwise into two narrow leaves (Hammond) or width-wise about halfway up (Keil).

5. *Other construction details (6:36-38).* The inner court of the temple was enclosed by a low wall formed by three rows of hewn stones and a row of cedar beams. The size of this court is not stated. If it was twice the size of that of the tabernacle, the court would have measured 300 feet by 150 feet. The temple project was completed in the eleventh year of Solomon's reign, in the month of Bul (October). This means that the temple was 7.5 years in the building, rounded off by the sacred historian to seven years.

Hiram's Work
1 Kings 7:13-51

A. Identity of Hiram

To construct the metallic furnishings of the temple, Hiram the king sent to Solomon, at his request (2 Chronicles 2:6), a workman who also bore the name Hiram, or according to Chronicles Huram-Abi (2 Chronicles 2:13).[38] His mother was a Danite by birth (2 Chronicles 2:14) who had married into the tribe of Naphtali. His father was a man of Tyre. Like his father before him, Hiram was a

---

[38]Some think *Abi* ("my father") was a title equivalent to the English word "master." Others think it was part of his name, rather than a title.

skilled worker in bronze as well as wood, cloth and other metals (2 Chronicles 2:14).

B. Works of Hiram (1 Kings 7:15-51)

1. Bronze pillars (7:15-22): Perhaps the greatest achievement of Hiram was the casting of two enormous, hollow bronze pillars. The circumference of the pillars was eighteen feet. The pillars stood 27.5 feet.[39] A bronze, ornate capital roughly resembling a full-blown lily-cup added an additional 7.5 feet to each pillar. The pillars appear to have stood within the porch, not in front of it as some have suggested. These two pillars in front of the sanctuary symbolized the power and eternity of God. They were named *Jachin* ("he shall establish") and *Boaz* ("in him is strength").

2. Bronze sea (7:23-26): Hiram made for the temple courtyard a great bronze water basin that was called *the sea* on account of its unprecedented capacity. The sea was circular and measured fifteen feet in diameter, forty-five feet in circumference. The sea rested on twelve bronze oxen, three of which faced each direction. The capacity when filled to ordinary height was 2,000 baths (11,500 gallons). The weight of this giant laver must have been about thirty tons. Rabbinic tradition indicates that the sea was provided with taps or faucets. The text gives no indication how the sea was filled.

3. Stands and basins (7:27-39): Hiram constructed ten identical movable lavers for the temple court. These were made of bronze. They were decorated with cherubim, lions, palms and wreaths. Each laver could contain forty baths (230 gallons). Five of these lavers were positioned along the north side and five along the south side of the court. At these lavers the flesh and fat that were used in sacrifice were first washed. They were also used for the purification of worshipers (2 Chronicles 4:6), and for cleansing of the altar and court after bloody sacrifices. When filled with water these lavers weighed over a ton.

4. Recap and other bronze objects (7:40-46): In addition Hiram was also responsible for a number of the smaller implements used in

---

[39]2 Chronicles 3:15 gives the length as 35 cubits (52.5 feet). Chronicles may be giving the total length of both pillars minus the pedestals to which they were anchored; Kings may be giving the height of each pillar individually, including the height of the pedestal. Another possibility is that the actual height of each pillar was 17.5 cubits which Kings has rounded off to 18. The 17.5 cubits of each pillar combined equals the 35 cubits of 2 Chronicles 3:15.

the temple. The text explains that Hiram did the casting in Gilead between Succoth and Zarethan. No doubt this spot was chosen because of the abundance of water and good clay with which to form the molds (1 Kings 7:40-47). No attempt was made to discover the exact weight of the metal used on account of the vast quantities of bronze required. No mention is made here of the huge bronze altar. Someone other than Hiram must have constructed it.

5. Interior temple vessels (7:48-51): All the vessels used inside the temple were made of gold. Apparently Hiram had nothing to do with the making of these objects. The furniture within the holy place included 1) the altar of incense, 2) the golden table—actually ten of them (2 Chronicles 4:8)—upon which the twelve loaves of unleavened bread were displayed; and 3) the ten lampstands, each with seven oil lamps. They were arranged five on each side of the *debir*.[40] The instruments used with the furnishings of the holy place included 1) tongs, 2) cups, 3) snuffers, 4) bowls, 5) spoons, and 6) fire pans. Even the door hinges of the temple were of gold!

Even after the construction of all the temple vessels and furniture there was a surplus of precious metal and bronze. This excess was stored in the temple treasuries.

DEDICATION
OF THE TEMPLE
1 Kings 8:1-66

Date: 960 BC

The temple was dedicated in the seventh month, but of what year is not stated. Either the year was the eleventh year of Solomon (960 BC), in which case the ceremony was conducted month before the construction work was complete,[41] or the twelfth year, in which case

---

[40]Some hold that the lampstands were arranged in a single row, in front of and parallel to the *debir*. Others picture the lampstands being arranged in two rows perpendicular to the partition of the *debir*. In the latter arrangement the lamps furnished the light throughout the Holy Place. In the former arrangement the lamps served as a barrier before the *debir*. The idea that the ten lampstands rested on the ten tables mentioned in Chronicles is not supported in the text.

[41]The date for the completion of the temple in 6:38 may have been reckoned from the completion of the dedication that lasted for fourteen days, and therefore continued into the eighth month. This explanation eliminates the difficulty of having the dedication a month before the temple was completed.

he wanted almost a year after construction so as to make the dedication coincide with the sacred seventh month.

Because of its importance in the history of redemption, the sacred historian devotes considerable space to the dedication of Solomon's temple. Thousands of people flocked to Jerusalem to share in the paramount event. Without question the dedication of Solomon's temple was the grandest ceremony ever performed under the Mosaic dispensation. The solemn dedicatory transaction consisted of six acts.

Procession
1 Kings 8:1-13

A. Royal Summons (1 Kings 8:1-2)

1. Leaders (8:1): Solomon summoned all the leaders of the nation to Jerusalem to share in the dedication ceremonies. After years of waiting, a national sanctuary was to be dedicated that superseded the tabernacle of Moses at which their forefathers had worshiped for five centuries. The first order of business was the transfer of the Ark of the Covenant from Mount Zion, the city of David, to its permanent resting place in the *debir* of the temple on Mount Moriah. Because it housed the sacred ark, the newly-built temple enjoyed the sanctity and national prestige of the sanctuary in Shiloh which had been destroyed by the Philistines about 145 years earlier.

2. All Israel (8:2): In addition to the princes summoned by Solomon, *all the men of Israel* also came to Jerusalem to participate in the feast. Since the gathering took place in the month of Ethanim, the seventh month, the particular feast must have been the feast of tabernacles. No doubt the dedication was scheduled for this time of year because this feast was the greatest and most joyous gathering of the year.

B. Ark Moved (1 Kings 8:3-9)

1. Manner (8:3-5): As on former occasions of extraordinary solemnity, the priests rather than Levites carried the Ark of the Covenant (cf. Joshua 3:6ff; 6:6). The Levites transported the tabernacle and its holy furniture. Innumerable sacrifices were offered before the ark to express the grateful joy of the populace.

2. Positioning (8:6-8): The priests deposited the ark in its assigned place in the *debir*—the holy of holies—between the two giant cherubim. The wings of the cherubim completely covered the ark so that it was enveloped in darkness. The priests drew the staves forward toward the front end of the ark. These staves could be seen by one who might be standing in the holy place immediately in front of the *debir*.[42]

3. Contents (8:9): At the time the ark was placed in the temple it contained only the two tables of stone that had been put there by Moses at Horeb. The golden pot of manna and Aaron's rod (Hebrews 9:4) probably had been removed by the Philistines when they had temporary possession of the ark (cf. 1 Samuel 6:19).

C. Divine Glory (1 Kings 8:10-13)

1. Timing of it (8:10-11): As the priests withdrew from the *debir,* the singers and trumpeters standing at the east end of the altar began their service of praise (2 Chronicles 5:13). At that exact moment the cloud that was indicative of the divine presence filled the house of the Lord (cf. Exodus 40:34f). Because of the cloud the priests for a time could not continue their ministrations.

2. Reaction to it (8:12-13): As Solomon witnessed this divine manifestation, he was stirred to the depths of his being. That glorious cloud proved that his work of piety had been accepted. The almighty God had entered that earthly shrine to dwell in the darkness of the *debir*. Solomon could only turn his eyes heavenward and utter a prayer of declaration in which he reaffirmed his purpose in building the temple. The structure was intended to be *a house* for God in contrast to the portable shrine of the tabernacle.

Declaration
1 Kings 8:14-21

Turning his gaze from the house where the cloud appeared, Solomon faced the congregation assembled there and perhaps gestured to them that they might stand up. The king then *blessed,* i.e., greeted the people, and addressed them. First, Solomon praised God for bringing to pass what he had spoken through Nathan the prophet. Then the king enumerated the circumstances that led to the building of the temple. 1) God had selected David to rule Israel. 2) David

---

[42]The meaning may be that the staves could be seen occasionally when the curtain was pulled aside to allow the high priest to enter the *debir* on the day of atonement. The traditional Jewish view is that the staves pressed against the veil that was hung before the *debir*.

desired to build a temple, and God approved of that desire. 3) Nevertheless, God had decreed that David's son have the honor of being the temple builder. 4) The Lord had raised up Solomon and had aided him in building the temple that was a resting place for the ark.

Adoration
1 Kings 8:22-24

The dedicatory prayer of Solomon is one of the most beautiful passages in the Bible. In it the temple is depicted as a house of prayer rather than a place of sacrifice.

Solomon began his prayer standing upon a bronze platform in the courtyard of the temple (2 Chronicles 6:13). His hands were spread toward heaven in a gesture of supplication. Solomon declared that no god in heaven or earth compared to Yahweh. This expression does not suggest that other gods really exist, but in effect means that Yahweh is the only God. What distinguished Yahweh from the non-entities worshiped by other peoples is that he kept his covenantal word and extended mercy to those who sincerely tried to live by the terms of that covenant. As a particular example of God's faithfulness, Solomon cited the promises made to David. In the light of his succession and the completion of the temple, Solomon regarded those promises as fulfilled.

Supplication
1 Kings 8:25-50

In the second part of the prayer, Solomon presented his supplications before the Lord.

A. General Petitions (1 Kings 8:25-30)
God had also promised that David's descendants will continue to reign over God's people as long as these rulers were faithful to Yahweh. Solomon first asked that the Lord to keep that promise. The Israelites knew that God could not be contained in man-made buildings. Yet the king prayed for the Lord to take notice of the earnest prayer offered to him at the temple. This petition was not presumptuous because God had designated the temple as the place where his name, i.e., his revelation of himself, will dwell. Solomon

prayed for the Lord to respond to penitent prayers by forgiving whatever trespass had been committed.

B. Specific Petitions (1 Kings 8:31-50)

Solomon next details seven specific situations that might arise in the future. Each situation is cast in the "if ... then" framework. Frequently Solomon alludes to *God in heaven.* Four times he mentions praying toward the temple.

The seven petitions may be briefly summarized as follows: 1) may God hear every oath taken before the temple altar and then intervene to punish the guilty and justify the innocent. 2) After military defeat may God restore to Israel those who might have been taken captive. 3) May God hear the penitent prayers of his people when they have been chastised by drought. 4) In the midst of plagues may God listen to the cry of his people. 5) May God hear the prayers of any foreigners who might come to the temple to pray. 6) May God hear those who were fighting wars far removed from Jerusalem who might address their petitions toward the temple. 7) In his last petition Solomon contemplated the captivity of Israel. He prayed that God might intervene on behalf of his people when they came to their senses and repented.

C. Final Appeal (1 Kings 8:51-53)

Solomon brought his prayer to a conclusion by citing several reasons why God should hearken to the present prayer and all future prayers that might be offered before him. First, Israel was God's people. Second, God had brought this people out of the furnace of Egyptian bondage. Third, Yahweh had separated Israel from all peoples of the earth for his very own inheritance. The prayer closed with an appeal to the Lord to cause salvation and grace to go forth from the temple over his people (2 Chronicles 6:40-42).

Benediction
1 Kings 8:54-61

A. Praise (1 Kings 8:54-56)

At the conclusion of his prayer, Solomon rose up from his knees—he must have fallen to his knees at some point during the prayer—and, with hands spread toward heaven, blessed the congregation. The benediction began with praise to the Lord for the

369

fulfillment of his promises, especially the promise of *rest* given through Moses.

B. Petition (1 Kings 8:57-60)

The king then summed up his wishes for the good of his kingdom. First, he prayed that God might choose to teach Israel his commandments by positive guidance rather than through divine discipline. Second, he prayed that God might incline their hearts toward the Lord so that they might obey his commandments. Third, he prayed that the words of his dedicatory prayer might ever be before the Lord that he might execute justice on behalf of both the king and the people. Finally, he prayed that Israel will be so blessed of God that all people of the earth will recognize that he alone is God.

C. Exhortation (1 Kings 8:61)

Solomon concluded his prayer with a brief exhortation that the people continue to demonstrate the piety and loyalty to Yahweh that they had demonstrated in building the temple. According to 2 Chronicles 7:1 at that moment fire came down from heaven and consumed the sacrifices; and the glory of the Lord filled the house.

Celebration
1 Kings 8:62-66

A. Sacrifice (1 Kings 8:62-63)

The king and his people celebrated the dedication of the temple with an enormous sacrifice. Some 22,000 oxen and some 100,000 sheep were slaughtered. In the peace offering only the fat was burned on the altar. The rest of the animal was eaten by the worshipers. The enormous number of animals was required to feed the vast multitudes that gathered for the dedication.

B. Accommodation (1 Kings 8:64)

Even though the bronze altar in the temple courtyard had a top surface of 900 square feet, it was not large enough to accommodate the offerings at the dedication. In addition to the enormous number of peace offerings just mentioned, burnt offerings and meal offerings appropriate to such an occasion were also offered. Therefore Solomon *sanctified the middle court,* i.e., the entire area of the court of priests that was before the house. This probably was done with holy anointing oil (cf. Exodus 40:1-15). The whole space may have been regarded as one huge altar (Rawlinson), or temporary altars may have been erected all over the courtyard (Keil).

C. Conclusion (2 Chronicles 7:9-10)

A great congregation had assembled from as far as the entrance of Hamath on the Orontes river in the north to the Wadi of Egypt in the south, i.e., from one end of the land to the other. These worshipers joined Solomon in a seven-day feast of dedication that was in turn followed by the seven-day feast of tabernacles. On the eighth day of the second feast (the twenty-second day of the seventh month) Solomon dismissed the multitude. The crowd reciprocated by blessing, i.e., saluting, their king. The next morning they departed for their tents, i.e., dwellings, full of joy because of what the Lord had done for his servant David and his people Israel.

27
SOLOMON IN
ALL HIS GLORY
1 Kings 7, 9-11

Chapter Chronology

		930
960	30 Years	

CONSTRUCTION OF
THE PALACE COMPLEX
1 Kings 7:1-12

General Information
1 Kings 7:1, 9-11

The palace complex dominated the outer court that surrounded the temple mount. This complex was thirteen years in construction. This longer period spent on the palace does not argue for selfishness on the part of Solomon. On the contrary, his piety caused him to build the temple first. The temple construction was much faster because 1) David had gathered enormous quantities of materials in advance; 2) Solomon employed a special force of laborers on the temple; and 3) the temple was small in comparison to the palace complex. The palace complex consisted of five major buildings.

All the stones used in the palace complex were of the finest quality, smoothed on all sides. The *great court* that enclosed both the temple and the palace complex was formed by a wall consisting of three rows of hewn stones and a coping of cedar. It thus resembled the wall surrounding the temple courtyard.

Individual Structures
1 Kings 7:2-8

A. Forest of Lebanon House (1 Kings 7:2-5)

This building received its name because it contained a virtual forest of cedar pillars. This huge building (150 by 75 feet) seems to have served as a treasury and armory. Possibly it also served as the residence of the royal bodyguard (cf. 1 Kings 10:17; Isaiah 22:8).

B. Porch of Pillars (1 Kings 7:6)

The porch of pillars was no doubt a covered colonnade, i.e., it had a roof but no sides. It connected the house of the forest of Lebanon and the hall of justice. Litigants probably waited here until called to present their case before the king.

C. Hall of Justice (1 Kings 7:7)

This building was open in the front, and shut in by solid walls on the other three sides. It was covered with cedar. Here the king held court and granted audiences.

D. Palace (1 Kings 7:8a)

The hall of justice served as the principal entrance into the king's personal residence. Little is known of this structure except that it was within a courtyard, and it was built on the same order as the hall of justice.

E. House of Pharaoh's Daughter (1 Kings 7:8b)

The queen's private residence seems to have been directly behind the palace.

Post-Construction Revelation
1 Kings 9:1-9

A. General Significance (1 Kings 9:1-2)

After Solomon had completed his building projects in 957 BC, Yahweh appeared to him a second time as he had appeared in the dream at Gibeon. This communication is clearly God's response to the dedicatory prayer of Solomon. At least thirteen years had elapsed since that great prayer. Solomon was now at the height of his prosperity. With his building projects completed the king's heart was puffed up with pride. His love for the Lord was waning. He had begun that spiritual decline which eventually led to idolatry. This divine word served to remind Solomon of that wonderful prayer and youthful devotion that he was in danger of losing.

B. Assurances (1 Kings 9:3-5)

The Lord made the following points in this revelation: First, the Lord pledged himself to answer the prayers of his penitent people. *I will hear from heaven, will forgive their sin, and will heal their land.* Second, Yahweh assured Solomon that he had chosen and consecrated the temple *that my name may be there forever.* Third, he reminded Solomon of the conditional promise made to David. If his descendants were obedient to the Lord, then David's sons would continue to occupy the throne in Jerusalem (2 Chronicles 7:12-18).

C. Warnings (1 Kings 9:6-9)

1. Rejection of land and temple (9:6-7): The warnings against unfaithfulness are stern and uncompromising. If Solomon or any of his children turned from following Yahweh, God would deprive the nation of the land he had given them. Furthermore, the Lord would utterly reject the temple that he had so recently acknowledged. The condition of the nation would become so deplorable that people would allude to Israel when they wished to use an apt illustration of folly and unfaithfulness.

2. Response of onlookers (9:8-9): In case of unfaithfulness, the house of God will be a conspicuous example of the fate which befalls an unfaithful people. Those who observed the ruins on the temple mount will hiss or whistle in astonishment. They will ask one another why Yahweh treated the land of the temple in this manner. The answer will come back from those close at hand that Israel had forsaken the God who had brought them out of Egypt.

Additional Payment to Hiram
1 Kings 9:10-14

A. Solomon's Debt to Hiram

Solomon spent twenty years on his major building projects—seven years on the temple and thirteen years on the palace complex. That Solomon was able to build such magnificent buildings was due largely to his alliance with Hiram king of Tyre, from whom he had received enormous amounts of timber. At some point during the twenty years of construction, Solomon had run short of gold. He again turned to Hiram to supply his need. Probably the 120 talents (4.5 tons) of gold were a loan rather than a gift advanced on the

375

strength of anticipated profits from Solomon's share in the joint naval expedition to Ophir described in 1 Kings 9:26-28.

B. Solomon's Payment to Hiram (1 Kings 9:10-11)

At the end of the twenty years of construction, Solomon ceded to Hiram the sovereignty over twenty cities in the land of Galilee, i.e., the northern part of the tribal territory of Naphtali.[43] Elsewhere this region is called *Galilee of the Gentiles* (Isaiah 9:1) because of the large number of Phoenicians who lived there. The villages given to Hiram were undoubtedly Canaanite communities that had not been taken over and developed into Israelite cities. Exactly why Solomon gave the twenty cities to Hiram is unclear.

C. Hiram's Response (1 Kings 9:12-13)

When Hiram went out to inspect his newly acquired territory, he was greatly disappointed. He had hoped to be awarded a rich grain-producing area, but had received instead a barren mountainous tract. Immediately he fired off a letter to Jerusalem to express his disappointment. Hiram addressed Solomon as *my brother,* the diplomatic language employed by friendly nations of that day. The letter referred to the recently acquired territory as *Cabul.* Though the exact meaning of this word is not known, it is almost certainly an expression of disparagement intended to mock Solomon's stinginess. The Chronicler intimates that Solomon regained possession of the cities (2 Chronicles 8:1-2). Perhaps Hiram simply refused to take jurisdiction of the area.

Compulsory Labor
1 Kings 9:15-23

The second means by which Solomon was able to construct so many buildings was the compulsory labor force (Heb. *hammas*). The object of the forced labor was the building of public works, the temple, palace, fortifications and strategic points in the provinces.

---

[43]Three views can be found in the commentaries: 1) the cities were a gift in appreciation for the help Hiram had rendered throughout the twenty years of building; 2) Solomon was forced to cede these towns to Hiram because he could not keep up with his annual financial obligations; and 3) the towns were put up as security for the loan of 120 talents of gold.

A. Jerusalem Projects (1 Kings 9:15a)

In addition to the temple and palace complex, two projects constructed by compulsory labor are identified. The first, the Millo, is mentioned six times in Scripture, each time with the definite article. The Millo seems to have been a bastion that filled some weak point in the walls of the city. Second, Solomon's labor force extended the wall of Jerusalem, probably to enclose the temple mount.

B. Fortress Cities (1 Kings 9:15b-18)

Outside of Jerusalem Solomon constructed six fortresses located at points strategic for controlling the movement of caravans.

- Hazor, situated in northern Galilee, controlled the routes from the north.
- Megiddo the great fortress commanded one of the major passes through the mountains that intersected the coastal plains. The main highway from Egypt to Damascus passed through Megiddo.
- Gezer was Solomon's fortress guarding the southern frontier of Israel.
- Lower Beth-horon guarded a main route leading from the coastal plains up to the highlands were Jerusalem was located.
- Baalath was located in the tribal territory of Dan southwest of Beth-horon.
- Tamar appears to have protected the route to the important Red Sea port of Ezion-geber. To the list of outer fortresses the Chronicler adds Upper Beth-horon and Tadmor, which was 150 miles northwest of Damascus (2 Chronicles 8:4f).

C. Other Cities (1 Kings 9:19)

In some cities public storage facilities were constructed. Such provisions were used for the troops and royal household, and possibly as insurance against seasons of scarcity. These may have been the cities where Solomon's twelve district administrators lived (cf. 1 Kings 4:7). Other cities served as bases for Solomon's chariot forces and cavalry units.

D. Organization of the Levy (1 Kings 9:20-23)

Solomon's levy of bond slaves was taken from among the foreign peoples that the Israelites had not destroyed. No Israelites were forced to become permanent bond slaves (cf. Leviticus 25:39), although some Israelites were compelled to render temporary government service (cf. 1 Kings 5:13). For the most part Solomon used Israelites for the more exalted service in the army or in the royal court. At the top administrative level over Solomon's levy of bond men were 550 officers. As previously explained (cf. comments on 1 Kings 5:16), 300 of these superior officers were Canaanites.

Pharaoh's Daughter
1 Kings 9:24

After completing the palace complex, Solomon had Pharaoh's daughter brought up from the city of David to the loftier summit where her palace was situated. The Chronicler explains Solomon's motives for moving his Egyptian wife out of the city of David (cf. 1 Kings 3:1). The ark of God had once been housed on that hill. The presence of this foreign princess in a place sanctified by the ark was not considered appropriate (cf. 2 Chronicles 8:11).

Solomon's Worship
1 Kings 9:25

After the temple was built, Solomon ceased to sacrifice upon the altars of the high places (cf. 3:2). *Solomon sacrificed burnt offerings and peace offerings to Yahweh* on the bronze altar in the temple court. *He also burned incense upon the altar that was before Yahweh* (1 Kings 9:25). The meaning is that Solomon as the builder of the temple provided the resources that were necessary to conduct the temple ritual properly (cf. 2 Chronicles 8:12f).

After the completion of the temple, Solomon implemented the arrangements that David had made for the priests, Levites, and gatekeepers. Nothing that David had ordered was left undone (2 Chronicles 8:14-15).

SOLOMON'S FAME
AND FORTUNE
1 Kings 9:26-10:13

Jesus once referred to *Solomon in all of his glory* (Matthew 6:29). The author of Kings underscores the wisdom of Solomon's rule and the material blessing that resulted from it. Solomon's kingdom was surely the most glorious the world had yet seen, not because it was the largest or even the most prosperous, but because of the wisdom of its king and the perfection of its government.

Solomon's Navy
1 Kings 9:26-28

Another source of Solomon's wealth was his commercial fleet. The king built ships at Ezion-geber in the land of Edom (cf. 2 Samuel 8:14). Solomon himself made a trip to Ezion-geber (2 Chronicles 8:17), possibly to launch the fleet. In this maritime venture the Israelites and Phoenicians were partners. Phoenicians were renowned in the ancient world for their seamanship. The Chronicler adds that Hiram even provided the ships (2 Chronicles 8:18). This probably means that the ships were transported overland in sections, and then reassembled at Ezion-geber. Hiram's interest in this venture was opening up the Red Sea trades routes to which he otherwise had no access.

The location of Ophir is uncertain. Modern scholarship has attempted to narrow the location to either India or East Africa. Wherever its location, Ophir supplied Solomon with enormous quantities of gold—420 talents (16 tons). Whether all this gold was brought back on one voyage, or whether this figure represents the profits from several voyages to Ophir cannot be determined.

The "Hiram fleet" also brought large quantities of almug trees and precious stones. From this precious wood Solomon constructed *pillars,* stairs (2 Chronicles 9:11) and various types of stringed musical instruments. The precise identification of the almug tree depends on the view one has of the location of Ophir. Only during Solomon's reign was this wood imported into Israel (1 Kings 10:11-12).

Solomon's Wealth
1 Kings 10:14-29

In Deuteronomy 17:14-20 God stipulated three things that the future kings of Israel were not to do. They were not to multiply 1) horses unto themselves, or 2) wives, or 3) wealth. As the years went by Solomon violated all three of these stipulations.

A. Extent of his Wealth (1 Kings 10:14-15)

1. Gold revenues (10:14): In one year—probably the year of the Sheba's visit—the gold revenues of Solomon weighed 666 talents (25 tons). According to the Berkeley Version, this gold was worth $20,000,000. No doubt this amount includes the receipts from all sources—taxes, tribute, and voyages. This enormous income marked a turning point in the king's relationship to God. From this point on the story of Solomon is one of steady decline.

2. Revenues in kind (10:15): Solomon also received vast annual revenues from caravans who passed through his territory, the sheiks of the nomad tribes in Arabia, and *the governors of the land,* i.e., the twelve officers mentioned in 1 Kings 4. These contributions probably were in kind, i.e., produce or animals or goods. This explains why the author distinguished them from the gold revenues of the previous verse.

3. Horses (10:26): In contravention of Deuteronomy 17:16 Solomon multiplied to himself horses. His force of 1,400 chariots was maintained largely for the sake of pomp and display. The chariot is of little tactical value in the hilly terrain of Palestine and, furthermore, Solomon's reign was peaceful. Hence, he did not actually need such a large chariot force. The maintenance of 12,000 cavalry troops is further indication of Solomon's materialistic disposition. The various chariot and cavalry units were stationed in Jerusalem and throughout the land (cf. 9:19).

4. Silver and wood (10:27): In an obvious hyperbole the author declares that during the reign of Solomon, silver became as common as ordinary stones which cover the environs of Jerusalem. The highly valued cedar wood, imported from Phoenicia, became as common as the much less prestigious sycamore wood that heretofore had been used for building purposes.

B. Use of his Wealth (1 Kings 10:16-21)

1. Gold shields (10:16-17): From his enormous gold treasures Solomon made two hundred bucklers, i.e., body-length shields. Six hundred *bekas* (NIV) of gold (7.5 lbs.) went into each shield. In addition, Solomon made three hundred smaller shields, each containing three minas or 300 *bekas* (2 Chronicles 9:16), i.e., 3.75

380

lbs., of gold. These golden shields were carried by the royal bodyguard on special occasions. When not in use during royal ceremonies, the shields were suspended from the walls of the house of the forest of Lebanon.

2. *Throne (10:18-20):* Solomon's throne, located in the porch of judgment, was another indication of the glory of his kingdom. It was made of ivory that was overlaid with pure gold. Six steps led to the elevated throne. Perhaps the seven levels symbolized the perfection in the decisions rendered by the king when he was sitting in judgment. The top of the throne was rounded or arched in form. On either side of the arm rests were two wooden lions overlaid with gold. Twelve other lions were situated two on each step leading to the throne. The lion was a symbol of royalty in the ancient Near East. This animal also had special significance for the tribe of Judah (cf. Genesis 49:9; Numbers 23:24). The twelve lions may represent the twelve tribes as the guardians of the throne of Israel. No throne in any kingdom of the time equaled that of Solomon.

3. *Drinking vessels (10:21):* All of Solomon's drinking vessels were of gold, as were also the vessels used in the house of the forest of Lebanon. None were made of silver, since silver had become so plentiful that it had lost its value.

C. Sources of his Wealth (1 Kings 10:22-25)

The author of Kings already has referred to one major source of Solomon's wealth, viz., the Red Sea fleet (cf. 9:26ff). Now he mentions two other sources of his wealth.

1. *Tarshish fleet (10:22):* Solomon also had a Tarshish fleet, i.e., a fleet that sailed to Tarshish on the southern coast of Spain.[44] This fleet operated on a three-year schedule. It brought back exotic products from distant lands. The gold and silver were secured in Tarshish; the apes, baboons (NIV) and ivory were available through the trading colonies along the coast of Africa. The Tarshish fleet was probably based at some Mediterranean port.

---

[44]Most commentators insist that the fleet mentioned in 10:22 is the same as the fleet mentioned in 9:26-28. The term *Tarshish fleet* is then taken to be a general name for all large, ocean-going ships or merchant vessels. That the term *can* have this meaning is clear from 1 Kings 22:48, *Jehoshaphat made ships of Tarshish to go to Ophir.* 2 Chronicles 9:21, however, proves that Tarshish in reference to Solomon's fleet is a geographical designation.

2. *Gifts (10:23-25):* Dignitaries from distant lands came to Jerusalem to hear the wisdom of the man so richly endowed of God. These visitors bestowed upon Solomon luxurious presents including gold and silver vessels, garments, arms, spices and riding animals. The visit of the queen of Sheba is an example of what must have been occurring regularly.

3. *Horse/chariot trade (10:28-29):* The source of Solomon's enormous silver reserves was his control of chariot and horse trading. He secured horses from Egypt and Kue, i.e., Cilicia in Asia Minor. During this period the Egyptians imported wood from Syria in order to manufacture chariots. Since Solomon controlled all the important trade routes from Cilicia and Egypt to Syria, he seems to have held a virtual monopoly on the horse and chariot trade in this region of the world. Thus, the neo-Hittite and Aramean kings to the north depended upon Solomon for Egyptian chariots, while the Egyptians depended on him for Cilician horses. As the middleman in this lucrative trade, Solomon no doubt made a handsome profit for himself. The established rate of exchange was 150 shekels (3.75 lbs.; $100 BV) for one Cilician horse, and for one Egyptian chariot 600 shekels (15 lbs.; $400 BV).

VISIT OF SHEBA
1 Kings 10:1-13

Date: ca. 935?

The wide-ranging voyages of the fleet spread the fame of Solomon to distant lands. An incredulous queen from Arabia came to inspect firsthand the marvels of Solomon's city and court.

Purpose of her Visit
1 Kings 10:1

The precise identity of the queen of Sheba has not yet been ascertained. She was one of several prominent queens ruling trading colonies in southern Arabia during this period. The visit of the queen of Sheba was probably a trade mission rendered necessary by the Israelite control of the major land routes to the north and the economic threat to south Arabian trade with East Africa posed by Solomon's naval enterprise.

The queen was informed that Solomon's greatness was due to his relationship with the God of Israel. Part of her reason for going to Jerusalem was to test the king by means of enigmatic riddles in order to see for if he had supernatural wisdom. Such tests of practical sagacity were part of the diplomatic encounters of that time. A king's wit and poetic skill were evidence of the extent to which he was conversant with affairs and culture in the world of his day.

The journey to Jerusalem from Sheba—a trip of some fifteen hundred miles—was no small undertaking in that day. The queen brought with her a very heavy force which included an armed escort and court attendants. She brought camels bearing spices, gold and precious stones to be bestowed upon her host.

Impressions of the Queen
1 Kings 10:2-8

A. What the Queen Saw (1 Kings 10:2-5)

When she reached Jerusalem, the queen spoke unto Solomon *all that was in her heart.* The king was able to answer appropriately all the questions that were put to him. The queen was quite impressed with the wisdom of Solomon, and with the palace he had built as well. She was amazed as she watched Solomon's hundreds of servants gathered about the bountiful tables that the king spread for them. The rich and costly apparel of Solomon's personal attendants and his cupbearers (cf. 2 Chronicles 9:4) particularly caught her eye. The queen also took special note of the ascent[45] or private entrance by which the king entered the temple. The reaction of the queen to all the grandeur of Solomon's court is expressed in the words *and there was no more spirit in her,* i.e., she was beside herself with amazement.

B. What the Queen Said (1 Kings 10:6-8)

The queen was not reluctant to express her feelings and reactions to Solomon. All that she had heard concerning his words and wisdom had proved to be true. While she had been incredulous prior to making her journey to Jerusalem, she now was of the opinion that the

---

[45]Some think the *ascent* was an arched bridge or viaduct over the Tyropoeon Valley between Mount Zion and the western wall of the temple area. Such a bridge would have been at least 350 feet high. Others, however, think the reference is not to some architectural achievement, but rather to the splendid retinue which accompanied Solomon on his visits to the temple.

wisdom and prosperity of Solomon far exceeded any report that had come to her ears.

Conclusion of the Visit
1 Kings 10:9-10

A. Praise to Yahweh (1 Kings 10:9)
The queen rightly discerned that Solomon's prosperity and sagacity came from the God of Israel. For this reason, she directed her praise heavenward. Yahweh delighted in Solomon and set him upon the throne of Israel. The Lord loved Israel and desired a king to rule over his people who executed justice and righteousness. Such sentiments were consistent with the polytheistic religion of this queen. Nothing in the text indicates that she became a worshiper of Yahweh after visiting Solomon's court.

B. Exchange of Gifts (1 Kings 10:10)
The state visit concluded with an exchange of gifts. For her part, the queen gave Solomon 120 talents (4.5 tons) of gold, a vast amount of spices, and precious stones. Solomon made appropriate gifts to the queen in return for her generosity, and in addition gave her whatever she asked. This might well have included a satisfactory trade agreement.

SOLOMON'S
FALL AND END
1 Kings 11:1-43

Solomon's Wives
1 Kings 11:1-13

Solomon violated the law regarding kings by multiplying wives. Besides his marriage to Pharaoh's daughter, the uniqueness of which has already been indicated, Solomon married many other *strange* or foreign women. If chapters 9-10 describe the fame of Solomon, chapter 11 sets forth his shame.

A. Extent of the Marriages (1 Kings 11:1-2)
1. Wives of cousin nations (11:1a): Among his wives were women of Moab and Ammon. Ammonites and Moabites were not to

be received into the congregation of the Lord until the tenth generation (cf. Deuteronomy 23:3). While marriage to a woman of these nations was not, strictly speaking, forbidden, such marriages must have been regarded as especially repugnant. The Edomites were viewed with more favor, being allowed to enter the congregation of the Lord in the third generation (cf. Deuteronomy 23:7).

2. *Phoenician and Hittite wives (11:1b):* The mention of Sidonians among the wives of Solomon gave rise to the tradition that Solomon married a daughter of Hiram. The *Hittite* women were from those northern kingdoms that had once been subject to the Hittite empire prior to its collapse about 1200 BC. With the exception of Jehoram who married Athaliah, the semi-Phoenician daughter of Ahab, none of Solomon's successors on the throne of Judah married foreign princesses so far as the record goes.

3. *Sinful marriages?* The law expressly forbade intermarriage with daughters of any of the seven nations of Canaan (Exodus 34:11-16; Deuteronomy 7:1-4). Strictly speaking, only Solomon's Hittite, and possibly his Sidonian, wives violated this prohibition. The Sidonians were considered Canaanites. The rationale for the prohibition of marriage to the seven nations of Canaan, however, applied equally to all other idolaters, viz., *they will turn away your sons from following after me* (Deuteronomy 7:4). Thus by marrying any of these foreign women Solomon was certainly violating the spirit of the law.

4. *Disastrous marriages (11:2):* Solomon clung unto these women in love. By placing the object of the preposition before the verb, the Hebrew suggests an emphasis that may be missed in the English: *even them Solomon clung to.* Instead of clinging to God as commanded in the law (Deuteronomy 4:4; 10:20; 30:20), Solomon chose to cling to his women!

B. Reason for the Marriages (1 Kings 11:3)

1. *Incredible numbers?* Seven hundred of Solomon's wives were princesses, i.e., members of the royal houses of neighboring nations. His concubines—wives of secondary rank—numbered three hundred. These numbers, when compared with the practice of other monarchs of the Near East, are not found at all to be incredible.

2. *Pride not passion:* The vast number of the harem suggests that Solomon was not motivated by sensuality in gathering these women. The mention that 700 of these women were *princesses*

385

suggests that his object was to enhance his renown. As he exceeded other kings in glory, wisdom, chariots and horses, so he must also supersede them in the number of his wives. Pride rather than passion drove this king to violate God's command against the multiplication of wives.

C. Influence of the Marriages (1 Kings 11:4-8)

1. Pagan temples (11:4, 7): Solomon paid the price for his pride. When he was old, i.e., toward the end of his reign, those women turned his heart away from God. This need not be taken to mean that Solomon himself took part in idolatrous practices, but only that he sanctioned such practices in the vicinity of Jerusalem. In his early reign he had been uneasy at the mere presence of Pharaoh's daughter in the city of David; but now he crowned the hills overlooking the temple precincts with monuments to idolatry.

2. Pagan deities (11:5-7): Three of the deities to whom Solomon showed favor are named in the text. First, Solomon *went after* Ashtoreth *the goddess of the Sidonians.* Ashtoreth is the Hebrew name of Astarte, one of the principal Phoenician goddesses. She was viewed by her adherents as a fertility goddess. As such she was worshiped by means of sexual intercourse in her temples. Small clay figurines of her with her breasts and pudenda accentuated have been found in Palestinian excavations in great abundance.

Second, Solomon went after Milcom or Molech *the abomination of the Ammonites.* The worship of this deity involved the sacrifice of little children. Whether or not Solomon permitted the child sacrifice rituals to be performed in Jerusalem cannot be determined.

Third, Solomon built a high place for Chemosh, *the abomination of the Moabites.* Chemosh seems to be the Moabite name for the god called by the Ammonites Molech.

3. Solomon's involvement (11:7-8): The extent to which *Solomon went after* pagan gods is spelled out in the text. First, his heart was not wholly devoted to Yahweh as the heart of David had been. Second, Solomon did not follow Yahweh fully as David had done. Third, he did evil in the eyes of Yahweh by building shrines for the foreign gods. Two high places were located on the Mount of Olives east of Jerusalem, a site elsewhere called *the mount of corruption* (2 Kings 23:13). The women made use of these sanctuaries by offering incense and animal sacrifices to their

386

respective deities. The text never asserts that Solomon personally worshiped in the temples.

D. Yahweh's Anger (1 Kings 11:9-13)

1. Reason (11:9-10): Yahweh was extremely angry with Solomon because his allegiance to his God had grown cold. Exceptional favors had been granted to this king. Twice he had been permitted to receive direct revelations from God (cf. 1 Kings 3:5; 9:2). Solomon had been solemnly warned about pursuing other gods, but he had disregarded this command of the Lord.

2. Announcement of judgment (11:11): In his anger the Lord pronounced a solemn judgment upon Solomon. No doubt the pronouncement came through the mouth of one of God's prophets, for it hardly seems likely that God would condescend to grant this apostate prince yet another direct revelation. The message is dreadful. Because Solomon had failed to live up to his obligations before God, the Lord determined to rend the kingdom from him. A mere servant will become heir to all of Solomon's glory and treasure.

3. Divine mercy (11:12-13): God tempered the judgment with two gracious and merciful limitations. 1) The blow will not fall until after the death of Solomon; and 2) the disruption will only be partial. One tribe, Judah, will remain under the Davidic dynasty. Two reasons are given for these merciful limitations. Judgment will be mitigated 1) for David's sake, i.e., because of the promises made to David (cf. 2 Samuel 7:13); and 2) for Jerusalem's sake. God had chosen Jerusalem as the site of his temple and as the appropriate capital of his earthly kingdom.

Solomon's Adversaries
1 Kings 11:9-28

At the close of the account of Solomon the author of Kings has gathered all the significant information concerning the adversaries of this king. These accounts have been placed here because 1) it is the habit of the author to collect into one passage material related to a particular facet of Solomon's reign; 2) it was only in his later life that these adversaries materially affected his position; and 3) because these troubles are regarded as a chastisement for Solomon's sin that has just been described. One should not conclude that these adversaries appeared only in the last days of the king.

A. Rebellion of Hadad (1 Kings 11:14-22)

1. Slaughter in Edom (11:14-16): The first adversary raised up by Yahweh was Hadad, a member of the royal family of Edom. The Edomites had initiated hostilities with Israel by a fierce attack in the days of David. After Joab had buried the dead Israelites, he led the armies of David into Edom in retaliation. The campaign there lasted six months. Every male who could be captured was executed.

2. Sanctuary in Egypt (11:17-20): To escape the slaughter, Hadad and some of the royal servants took refuge in the trackless desert of Midian south of Edom. Eventually he and his company pressed on toward Egypt, stopping in Paran to secure guides who led them across the Sinaitic peninsula to the kingdom of the Pharaohs.

In Egypt Hadad and his party were graciously received. The Pharaoh gave to the young Edomite prince a house, land and provisions for his table. Pharaoh also gave Hadad the hand of his sister-in-law, the sister of Tahpenes the queen consort. This action reflects the political hopes that the Egyptians pinned on the Edomite heir. Hadad's wife gave birth to a son, Genubath, who was reared in Pharaoh's palace with all the privileges of an Egyptian prince.

3. Rebellion in Edom (11:21-22): When Hadad heard about the deaths of David and Joab, he requested that Pharaoh allow him to return to his own land. Pharaoh was reluctant to see Hadad, who now had lived in Egypt for at least twenty-five years, leave his court. Nonetheless, Hadad insisted that he be allowed to return to Edom. When he returned Hadad fomented rebellion against Solomon in Edom. Whether he succeeded in wresting any territory from Solomon's control or merely acted as a constant gadfly to the Israelite merchant caravans is unclear.

B. Rezon of Damascus (1 Kings 11:23-25)

The second adversary raised up by God as an antagonist to Solomon was Rezon, an Aramean who established himself in Damascus. Damascus, as part of the kingdom of Zobah, fell to David when Hadadezer of Zobah was defeated (cf. 2 Samuel 8:3-12; 10:6-19). At that time Rezon deserted his master Hadadezer. He became the leader of an outlaw gang that preyed on Israelite interests in the north "all the days of Solomon." At some point—probably late in Solomon's reign—Rezon led a group of warriors against Damascus. He captured the city, settled in it, and finally established himself as the ruling power there. Eventually the entire region of Aram recognized Rezon as their king. Thus Solomon was faced with opposition simultaneously on the northern and southern frontiers of his empire.

D. Jeroboam the Ephraimite (1 Kings 11:26-28)

1. Humble origins (11:26): The third adversary of Solomon was an Israelite, Jeroboam the son of Nebat. He was an Ephrathite, i.e., an Ephraimite (cf. Judges 12:5; 1 Samuel 1:1) from the insignificant village of Zeredah. His mother's name, *Zeruah*, means *leper*. She was a widow. Perhaps these facts are recorded to emphasize Jeroboam's humble origins.

2. His rebellion (11:27-28): Because of his industry, Jeroboam had been appointed superintendent over the workers of the house of Joseph (Ephraimites) who had been drafted for service in the corvée. For the proud Ephraimites to be forced to labor on fortifications around Jerusalem must have been particularly galling. Jeroboam sensed the unrest among the workmen. He *lifted up his hand against the king*. No account of this rebellion has survived. It apparently took place at the time Solomon was building the Millo (cf. 1 Kings 9:25), about the twenty-fifth year of his reign.

Ahijah's Prediction
1 Kings 11:29-41

A. Commitment to Jeroboam (1 Kings 11:29-31)

Ahijah the Shilonite (i.e., one from the town of Shiloh) sought out Jeroboam and privately conferred with him in a field near Jerusalem. The prophet was clad in a new outer garment that he took in his hands and tore into twelve pieces. Israel is always reckoned as made up of twelve tribes. Since the tribe of Joseph had been divided into two, Ephraim and Manasseh, the total should have risen to thirteen. Levi, however, was omitted from the count because that tribe was scattered throughout all Israel. Ahijah instructed the young Ephraimite to take ten of the pieces of cloth, symbolizing the ten tribes that God intended to rend from the hand of Solomon.

B. Faithfulness to David's House (1 Kings 11:32-36)

1. One tribe left to Davidic kings (11:32): One tribe, Benjamin, was left to the rulers of Judah (cf. 1 Kings 12:21; 2 Chronicles 11:3,

389

23). God's graciousness to the house of David is based on two principles: 1) God's love for and promises to David himself; and 2) God's love for and choice of Jerusalem as his holy dwelling place. Judah and Benjamin shared possession of Jerusalem.

2. Division deferred (11:33-35): The disruption of the kingdom came about because of the idolatrous leanings of Solomon. The king certainly tolerated and perhaps subsidized the worship of Ashtoreth, Chemosh, Milcom and other deities. He had rejected the Davidic path of absolute commitment to God. Nevertheless, the divine judgment against the house of David was tempered in two ways. 1) The entire kingdom will not be taken from the Davidites; and 2) the judgment will be deferred until after the death of Solomon.

3. Davidic lamp theme (11:36): God's graciousness to Solomon was based on his faithfulness to David. Solomon may have broken his covenant with God, but God will not break his covenant with David. A major theme is reiterated here. David will always *have a lamp* before God. The lighted lamp is frequently used in the Old Testament as a symbol of life, happiness, and prosperity. The figure may have been derived from the custom of keeping a lamp burning in the tent or home. The extinction of the lamp symbolized the breaking up of the home.

C. Conditional Promise (1 Kings 11:37-39)

In Ahijah's closing words Jeroboam was assured that he will indeed become king. As king his every desire will be gratified. If he faithfully followed the Davidic path of steadfast obedience to God, Yahweh would 1) be with Jeroboam, and 2) give him a sure house, i.e., family or dynasty. Jeroboam was advised, however, that it was not God's intention to take away the kingdom from the house of David forever. Ahijah here intimates what later prophets specifically would predict, viz., that in the future, the kingdom will be restored to the house of David.

D. Danger to Jeroboam (1 Kings 11:40)

1. Solomon attempts to slay Jeroboam (11:40a): As a consequence of Jeroboam's rebellion, Solomon sought to slay his Ephraimite overseer. Perhaps the rebellion was triggered by Ahijah's private prophecy. Still in no way did this justify any treasonous act on the part of Jeroboam. The fact that God had revealed his purposes to the young man was no reason for him to attempt to bring these things

390

to pass. The rebellion was all the more inexcusable in view of the fact that Ahijah specifically had declared that Solomon was to retain the kingdom during his lifetime.

2. *Refuge in Egypt (11:40b):* Jeroboam fled for his life to Shishak in Egypt. The fact that this pharaoh granted asylum to the fugitive proves that he was no friend of Solomon. The official attitude of Egypt towards Israel drastically had changed since the days when one of Shishak's predecessors had given Solomon the hand of his daughter in marriage.

Conclusion of Solomon's Reign
1 Kings 11:41-43

Scripture writers list four sources that they used, guided by the Holy Spirit, in reconstructing the events of Solomon's reign: 1) the book of the acts of Solomon (1 Kings 11:41); 2) the book of Nathan the prophet; 3) the prophecy of Ahijah the Shilonite; and 4) the visions of Iddo the seer concerning Jeroboam the son of Nebat. Neither the royal nor prophetic records of Solomon's reign are extant.

Like David, Solomon ruled for forty years. Scholars have computed that he could not have been more than sixty at the time of his death. Solomon was buried in the city of David—that portion of Jerusalem that David had conquered from the Jebusites. Solomon was succeeded by Rehoboam, his only son to be mentioned in Scripture.

END OF THE SINGLE KINGDOM PERIOD
We have now covered 476 years of Israel's history

SISTER KINGDOMS
Quarrelling Sisters

Biblical Location: 1 Kings 12-2 Kings 17 + Chronicles chapters.

Beginning Point: Kingdom Split (931 BC)

Ending Point: Samaria Destroyed (723 BC)

Duration: 208 Years

Key Players: Jeroboam, Ahab, Jehu, Elijah, Elisha, Asa, Jehoshaphat, Joash, Jezebel, Athaliah

Key Events: Religion Founded; Pharaoh Invades, Carmel Meeting, Jehu Revolt, Revivals, Attack on House of David

Scripture Theme:
When all Israel saw that the king refused to listen to them, they answered the king: "What share do we have in David, what part in Jesse's son? To your tents, O Israel! Look after your own house, O David!" So the Israelites went home (1 Kings 12:16 NIV)

Christian Application:
James used events of the Sister Kingdom Period to encourage prayer. *Therefore confess your sins to each other and pray for each other so that you may be healed. The prayer of a righteous man is powerful and effective. Elijah was a man just like us. He prayed earnestly that it would not rain, and it did not rain on the land for three and a half years. Again he prayed, and the heavens gave rain, and the earth produced its crops* (James 5:17-19 NIV).

Jesus mentioned Sister Kingdom Period events to expose Jewish prejudice. *"I tell you the truth," he continued, "no prophet is accepted in his hometown. I assure you that there were many widows in Israel in Elijah's time, when the sky was shut for three and a half years and there was a severe famine throughout the land. Yet Elijah was not sent to any of them, but to a widow in Zarephath in the region of Sidon. And there were many in Israel with leprosy in the time of Elisha the prophet, yet not one of them was cleansed--only Naaman the Syrian"* (Luke 4:24-27 NIV).

NOTE

Chronological notes about the reigns of kings are based on a series of articles by Rodger Young published in *Journal of the Evangelical Theological Society*: 48/2 (June 2005): 225-48; 46/4 (Dec 2003): 589-603; 47/4 (Dec 2004): 577-95.

28
KINGDOM DIVISION
1 Kings 12-14

Chapter Chronology

			910
	JEROBOAM		
931			
	REHOBOAM	**Abijah**	
932		**915**	

SECESSION OF
THE TEN TRIBES
1 Kings 12:1-19

Date: ca 931 BC

When Solomon died about 932 BC the kingdom appeared to be in good shape outwardly. Yet because of the idolatry introduced in his last days, the seeds of kingdom disintegration already had been sown. Even so, the speed with which that glorious kingdom shattered, and the devastating spiritual, political and economic consequences of that event are somewhat shocking and certainly sad.

Assembly at Shechem
1 Kings 12:1-20

A. Reason for the Assembly (1 Kings 12:1)

Rehoboam was forty-one at the time his father Solomon died (1 Kings 14:21; 2 Chronicles 12:13). His succession to the throne does not seem to have been questioned in Judah. The northern tribes, however, insisted on their right to ratify the coronation of the new king. All Israel (the northern tribes) assembled at Shechem, the most important city in Ephraim, *to make him king*. They had no concrete plans for rebellion at this time. Nonetheless, these tribes were disgruntled because of Solomon's high-handed tactics and rigorous taxation policies. Their insistence that Rehoboam meet with them on their own territory should have been a clear indication that they would brook no negative response to their demands.

B. Israel's Request (1 Kings 12:2-5)

1. Israel's spokesman (12:2-3): Jeroboam son of Nebat served as the spokesman for the dissident tribes at Shechem. Since the time of his abortive rebellion against Solomon, Jeroboam had resided in Egypt. When Solomon died, the elders of Israel immediately sent to Egypt to invite Jeroboam to speak on their behalf to Solomon's would-be successor. Putting forth Jeroboam as their spokesman was a second clear indication that the elders of the north did not mean to be ignored.

2. Israel's complaint (12:4): The dissidents complained that Solomon had placed a heavy yoke upon them. They requested that Rehoboam grant them a measure of relief. If this relief was forthcoming, the elders promised to serve Rehoboam. There is, of course, an implied threat in this conditional pledge of allegiance. The grievance of the northern tribes was real. While it is true that the reign of Solomon had brought prosperity to Israel, national glory had been achieved only by means of a galling conscription and heavy taxation.

3. Rehoboam's dilemma (12:5): Rehoboam wisely postponed his decision regarding the northern ultimatum for three days. The new king did not suffer from impetuosity. He evidently sensed how much depended upon his reply. If he complied with the request, he was accepting the crown conditionally. On the other hand, if he denied their request, he faced the danger of revolt. Viewing Rehoboam's proposed three day delay as a reasonable interval, the dissidents peacefully departed.

B. Counselors' Recommendations (1 Kings 12:6-11)

1. Advice of senior counselors (12:6-7): Rehoboam turned for advice first to the older men who were experienced in statecraft from their service in the court of Solomon. They advised him to *be a servant* to the people for this day, i.e., accede to their demands. A little humility at this point will gain for the new king many servants forever.

2. Consultation with junior counselors (12:8-9): Rehoboam was not in a mood to compromise. Spurning the advice of his father's counselors, Rehoboam turned to young men who served as his personal courtiers and counselors. These were men who had grown up with Rehoboam in Solomon's harem. Of these friends Rehoboam asked the same question that he had asked the elders with three slight changes: 1) He emphasized the pronoun *you* in the Hebrew as though he anticipated a very different answer from what he had heard from the elders. 2) In the words *that we may respond* he identified these young men with himself. 3) He repeated the request of the dissidents, no doubt expressing his contempt for their audacity by the tone of his voice.

3. *Advice of junior counselors (12:10-11):* The young men viewed the request of the dissidents as presumptuous. They urged the king to follow a "get tough" policy. They suggested that he use what must have been a proverbial expression: *My little finger is thicker than the loins of my father.* The idea here is that Rehoboam's weakness was stronger than his father's strength. The advice of the young counselors was based on the premise that appeasement will not work. Any attempt to placate the people by kindly words, they feared, might be interpreted as weakness.

C. Rehoboam's Reply (1 Kings 12:12-15)

1. *Rehoboam's arrogance (12:12-14):* On the third day Jeroboam and the representatives of the northern tribes appeared again before Rehoboam. The new king spoke harshly to the petitioners, repeating verbatim the declaration of his young advisers. Whereas Solomon had chastised them with whips, Rehoboam promised to use *scorpions.* This term may be a reference to a particular kind of whip, one with barbed points like the point of a scorpion's sting. On the other hand, the term may be purely figurative for an even greater pain to be administered by Rehoboam.

2. *Assessment (12:15):* Rehoboam's pride is inexcusable and reprehensible. Nevertheless, Yahweh used his incident to accomplish his purpose of bringing about a division within the kingdom. God may even use the sinful acts of men to accomplish his will. What happened at Shechem led to the fulfillment of the predictions made by the prophet Ahijah to Jeroboam some two decades earlier.

D. Israel's Rebellion (1 Kings 12:16-20)

1. *Walk-out (12:16):* After briefly consulting among themselves, the representatives of the northern tribes defiantly replied to the king: *What portion have we in David?* i.e., we are receiving no consideration from David's seed, so why should we yield homage to him?[46] The dissidents further declared: *Neither have we inheritance in*

the son of Jesse, i.e., his tribe is not ours; his interests are not ours. *To your tents, O Israel,* they shouted. As they angrily stomped out of the audience chamber they shouted one last warning: *Now see to your own house, David,* i.e., let the seed of David henceforth reign only over the tribe of Judah. With these ominous words the northern representatives departed for their tents, i.e., dwellings.

2. *Fall-out (12:17):* Those members of the ten tribes who happened to be settled within the territory of Judah (e.g., the Simeonites) rendered homage to Rehoboam. So also did the tribe of Benjamin (cf. verse 21). Probably the fact that Benjamin shared the magnificent city of Jerusalem with Judah induced that tribe to adhere to the house of David. In any case, from this point on, the term *Israel* is used by the author of Kings in its restricted sense as referring to the northern kingdom.

3. *Strong-arm tactics (12:18):* Rehoboam was determined to demonstrate to the rebels that he was not intimidated. He therefore sought immediately to force the northern tribes to pay tribute and thereby recognize his sovereignty. The king ordered Adoram, the superintendent of forced labor, to collect the tribute. The rebels stoned Adoram to death. Rehoboam realized the gravity of the situation. He therefore hastened south to the safety of Jerusalem.

4. *Crowning of Jeroboam (12:19-21):* The representatives of the northern tribes returned to their respective communities and reported what had transpired at Shechem. When the people heard that Jeroboam had returned from Egypt, they were anxious to crown him king. The text gives no indication where the ceremony took place. Most likely the event took place at Shechem. With the coronation of Jeroboam the secession of the northern tribes was complete.

PERIOD OF ADJUSTMENT
1 Kings 12:21-33

Rehoboam in Judah
[932-915 BC]

---

[46]Sheba used these same words (cf. 2 Samuel 20:1) to lead a rebellion against David, but the circumstances were quite different from those that launched this rebellion. Sheba believed in the dynastic principle. He believed that the scepter should remain in the house of Saul. In this case the northern representatives rejected the dynastic principle. They believed that the right to bestow sovereignty rested with the people.

1 Kings 12:21-24

Rehoboam was determined to crush the northern uprising by military means. He gathered a force of some 180,000 men from Judah and Benjamin. Rehoboam's actions, however, did not meet with the approval of God. Shemaiah *the man of God,* i.e., prophet, ordered a halt to plans for an invasion of the north. Two reasons are given for the prohibition. First, the northern tribes were still *brethren* of those who lived in the south. Second, the national disruption was God-ordained. Thus a prophet of Judah (Shemaiah) confirmed what a prophet of Israel (Ahijah) had predicted. Because of the prophetic prohibition, the men of Judah called off the planned attack on the north and returned to their homes.

Jeroboam in Israel
[931-910 BC]
1 Kings 12:25-31

A. Selection of a Capital (1 Kings 12:25)
Jeroboam's first concern as king of Israel was to find a suitable capital. First he *built,* i.e., fortified, Shechem, the most prominent city in the north. Then he was forced temporarily to move the seat of government across the Jordan to Penuel in the area of Gilead. This action may have been necessitated by the invasion of Pharaoh Shishak about which the text will speak later.

B. Creation of a Cult (1 Kings 12:26-33)
1. His need for change (12:26-27): Another urgent concern of Jeroboam was the creation of a cult in the north that rivaled the divinely revealed religion practiced in Jerusalem. Jeroboam feared that if people continued to travel to the temple three times each year for the major festivals, the sentiment for the house of David would reassert itself in the north.
2. Golden calves (12:28-30): After taking counsel of his closest advisers, Jeroboam determined that the new religion should center about the images of two golden calves. He erected shrines for these calves at two convenient locations, Dan and Bethel. Propaganda poured forth from the palace in an attempt to persuade the people to change their religious affiliation. The king argued that it was inconvenient for his people to travel to Jerusalem for worship.

Furthermore, he presented the golden calves as symbols of the deity who had led Israel out of Egypt. Jeroboam intended to link his calves to the calf erected by Aaron at Mount Sinai (cf. Exodus 32:4-8), i.e., he passed off his innovations as a restoration of something old. The people of the north zealously embraced their new religion.

Chart 15	
Two Kingdoms Contrasted	
ISRAEL	**JUDAH**
Northern Kingdom	Southern Kingdom
Ten Tribes	Two Tribes
First King: Jeroboam	First King: Rehoboam
Capitals: Shechem, Samaria	Capital: Jerusalem
Temples: Dan, Bethel, Samaria	Temple: Jerusalem
Dynasties: 9	Dynasty: 1
Kings: 19	Kings: 19 + a Queen
All Bad Kings	Good and Bad Kings
Duration: 209 Years	Duration: 344 Years
Destruction: 722 BC	Destruction: 586 BC
Land of Exile: Assyria	Land of Exile: Babylon
Longest Reign: Jeroboam II	Longest Reign: Manasseh
41 Years	55 Years
Shortest Reign: Zimri	Shortest Reign: Jehoahaz
7 Days	3 Months
Last King: Hoshea	Last King: Zedekiah

3. *Significance:* Jeroboam's effort could hardly have succeeded if the calves erected at Bethel and Dan had been presented as images of the invisible Yahweh. The Semitic peoples never represented their gods as animals. The calves must have represented the animal upon which Yahweh was understood to ride.[47] Eventually, however, theological distinctions faded. The calves became identified with Yahweh himself in popular religious understanding. For this reason Hosea regarded the calves as idols (Hosea 13:2).

4. *Worship system (12:31-33):* Jeroboam built shrines on high places for his new faith. He made priests of *all classes of the people,*

---

[47]The biblical cherubim, which were so prominent in the decorations of the temple, are often described as winged bulls. If that is the case, Solomon's cherubim would look very much like Jeroboam's calves. Cf. 1 Kings 6:23.

thus rejecting the priestly prerogatives of the tribe of Levi. He ordered a great festival to be held on the fifteenth day of the eighth month, one month after the appointed time for the feast of tabernacles. Jeroboam himself officiated as high priest, offering sacrifices and incense on special occasions before the calves that he had made. Every aspect of the religion in the north was devised in Jeroboam's own heart.

CONDEMNATION OF THE NORTHERN KINGDOM
1 Kings 13:1-14:18

Date: ca. 930 BC and 920 BC

Because Jeroboam had initiated his apostate religion in Israel, he lost the support of the prophetic order. He was denounced by a prophet from Judah as well as the prophet Ahijah within his own kingdom.

A Man of God from Judah
1 Kings 13:1-23

A. An Urgent Mission (1 Kings 13:1-10)

1. A long-range prediction (13:1-2): God did not permit the inauguration of Jeroboam's first great feast at Bethel to proceed without prophetic protest. An unidentified prophet from Judah was dispatched to deliver the divine word of warning to the king. With a precision rare, but not unique, in Bible prophecy, Josiah, a man who would not be born for some three hundred years, was named as the instrument to bring God's wrath upon Bethel and its altar. For the fulfillment of this prediction see 2 Kings 23:20.

2. An immediate sign (13:3-5): To give credibility to his long-range prediction, the prophet offered an immediate sign of confirmation. The altar will be rent and the ashes (lit., fatness, i.e., the fat of the sacrificial victim) poured out. These words brought the proceedings to an immediate halt. In violent rage Jeroboam put forth his hand against the prophet, at the same time ordering him to be seized. The arm of the king, however, was stricken with paralysis so that he could no longer control it. At that very instant the altar was smitten by God as the prophet had announced. In one dramatic act God 1) demonstrated that the sacrifice being offered was

401

unacceptable; 2) symbolized the ultimate overthrow of that altar; and 3) humbled a proud king.

3. Request of the king (13:6-7): Alarmed by the judgment he had experienced in his own body, Jeroboam begged the prophet to entreat God on his behalf. Sensing that he was no longer in danger, the man of God prayed. The king's arm was made whole again. In grateful appreciation (and perhaps with some ulterior motive) Jeroboam invited the prophet to the palace for refreshment.

4. Refusal of the man of God (13:8-10): The man of God refused to accept the hospitality of the apostate king. No matter what inducements might be offered, he was under orders to return immediately to Judah by a different route. Sharing in a meal was a sign of close fellowship. This prophet was to leave no doubt that the God he served had repudiated the northern calf cult. The prophet probably returned by a different route in order to make it more difficult for his movements to be traced.

B. A Brazen Deception (1 Kings 13:11-19)

1. An old Bethel prophet (13:11-13): While devout worshipers of Yahweh had moved to Judah (cf. 2 Chronicles 11:13-16), at least one old prophet remained in Bethel. This man's commitment level was obviously quite low; but he could not personally participate in the apostate worship in Bethel. His sons, however, had witnessed the events in the temple. The account of the fearless pronouncement of the man of God stirred the old prophet's heart. After ascertaining the route taken by the young prophet, the Bethel prophet rode off after him. The text gives no clue as to the motivation here. Did he merely crave prophetic fellowship? Or was it his intention to persuade the man of God to reverse the pronouncement he had made against the Bethel cult?

2. Old prophet's lie (13:14-19): The old prophet caught up with the man of God taking a brief respite under an oak along the road to Judah. When he invited the man to his home in Bethel, the old prophet was rebuffed with the same words used in response to Jeroboam's invitation. The old prophet then fabricated a story about an angelic visitation in which he was told to bring the man of God back to Bethel.[48] The motives of the old prophet are not clear. Putting

---

[48]Some argue that a communication through a celestial messenger was regarded as a higher form of revelation than a subjective communication to the mind of the

his actions in the best possible light, his lie was born out of an ardent desire for fellowship with the man of God. On the other hand, he may have been acting on behalf of his king.[49]

C. An Ominous Prediction (1 Kings 13:20-26)

1. Pronouncement by the old prophet (13:20-22): The man of God believed the lie. He returned to Bethel to share the hospitality of the old prophet. During the meal the old prophet received a genuine revelation from God. The Holy Spirit compelled him to cry out against the man of God. He who denounced disobedience in Jeroboam is now himself denounced. The rebuke was followed by a devastating announcement: *Your body shall not come to the grave of your fathers.* Part of the punishment of the old prophet was that he was forced 1) to admit that he had told a lie; and 2) to pronounce the doom of a godly man.

2. Death of the man of God (13:23-26): The gloomy meal at an end, the Bethel prophet saddled his donkey for the man of God who seems to have been traveling on foot. As he was making his way south toward Judah, a lion pounced upon the man of God and slew him. That this death was no accident is indicated by the peculiar behavior of the donkey and the lion, both of which simply stood near the corpse of the fallen prophet. Those who traveled that highway reported in Bethel the corpse and the strange behavior of the two animals. The old prophet knew instantly the identity of the corpse and the reason for the tragedy.

D. A Bitter Lamentation (1 Kings 13:27-32)

Immediately the old prophet went to the spot where the man of God had fallen. He found the scene just as the travelers had reported it. Both the lion and the donkey were still there. With great sorrow the old prophet brought the corpse back to Bethel. There he bestowed profound respect upon that corpse by burying it in his own grave. He

---

prophet. Others suggest that the angel was mentioned in order to avoid telling a deliberate lie in the name of God, an action that might have called down immediate wrath.

[49]Two more sinister interpretations have been put on the actions of the old prophet. 1) If the man of God could be lured back to Bethel to break bread, that action would in effect cancel the implied curse that he had placed on the city by refusing to eat with the king. 2) If the young prophet survived an act of direct disobedience to a command of God, the threats that he recently had made would not need to be taken seriously.

mourned for the young man with the customary lamentation formula: *Alas, my brother!* He instructed his sons to bury him beside the man of God. The old prophet was now convinced that the predictions regarding the Bethel altar and other sanctuaries in the north would come to pass.

E. A Defiant Reaction (1 Kings 13:33-34)

The dramatic demonstration at the Bethel temple and the subsequent death of the man of God for disobeying the word of God failed to make any lasting impression on the apostate Jeroboam. Shortly after these events the king returned to his policy of appointing priests from the population in general rather than restricting that high privilege, as the law required, to the sons of Aaron. Because of his contemptuous defiance of the law of God, Jeroboam forfeited his claims to all promises made to him by Ahijah the prophet (cf. 1 Kings 11:37f). From the moment he introduced the religious schism into Israel, his dynasty was doomed to destruction.

By Ahijah the Prophet
1 Kings 14:1-18

Nearly the entire reign of Jeroboam is passed over in silence. At some point he moved his capital from Penuel (1 Kings 12:25) to Tirzah west of the Jordan. Toward the end of his reign a crisis arose in the royal family that brought Ahijah the prophet back into the picture. The same prophet who foretold Jeroboam's reign over Israel now issued a decree of judgment against his dynasty.

A. Jeroboam's Sick Son (1 Kings 14:1-6)

1. Queen's mission (14:1-2): About the year 920 BC the crown prince Abijah fell desperately sick. Suspecting that the illness of his son was punitive, Jeroboam determined to secure from Ahijah some word as to the prognosis for the lad. The king's decision to seek help from Ahijah was based on the prophet's support of him in the past. He realized, however, that his own religious activities were calculated to bring only censure and perhaps an unfavorable prediction. Therefore he determined to send his wife to seek the oracle. Even she had to disguise herself so that neither the prophet nor the populace was able to recognize her.

404

2. King's plan (14:3): The queen took with her gifts to bestow on the prophet—ten loaves, some cakes, a leather bottle of honey. The present was purposely a poor one for the sake of maintaining the deception. Probably Jeroboam hoped for more than just information; he may have hoped to trick the old prophet into a declaration that the son will recover. In godless superstition he apparently believed that whatever the prophet said would come to pass even if he were tricked into saying it.

3. Prophet's condition (14:4-5): The queen hastened toward Shiloh, some thirty difficult miles from Tirzah. Ahijah spent his days there in darkness because his eyes *had set,* his pupils did not adjust to the light. Probably because of his advanced age Ahijah had not followed other godly Israelites in moving to Judah. In any case, the attempted deception was frustrated by a direct revelation from the Lord to the blind prophet. Ahijah was told who was coming to his house and for what purpose she was coming.

4. Shocking announcement (14:6): When the queen stood at the door, the prophet ripped away the deception. He identified the queen, and asked why she had attempted to perpetrate the masquerade. No favorable oracle will fall from the lips of the prophet, for he had been instructed by God to bring to her heavy tidings.

B. Jeroboam's Egregious Sin (1 Kings 14:7-9)

Before pronouncing sentence, the prophet briefly stated the divine case against Jeroboam. God had raised the lowly Jeroboam to the throne. The king was but God's vice-regent ruling over God's people. God had torn away a large part of the kingdom from the house of David and had given it to Jeroboam. Yet the northern king had not walked the paths of spiritual fidelity that David had trod. In fact, Jeroboam had committed a more grievous sin than any of his predecessors whether kings or judges. In defiance of the Decalogue (Exodus 20:4), Jeroboam had made *other gods* that were merely *molten images,* i.e., the calves of Bethel and Dan. God did not accept whatever theological explanation Jeroboam used to justify his golden calves. The king had pushed Yahweh behind his back, i.e., had contemptuously disregarded divine revelation. He thus had aroused the anger of God.

C. Jeroboam's Doomed House (1 Kings 14:10-14)

1. *Thoroughness of judgment (14:10-11):* The judgment that Ahijah pronounced against the house of Jeroboam was to be swift and thorough. Every male of his house will be cut off. The expression *as one takes away dung* indicates the contempt with which the members of the royal house will be treated in that day of judgment. The corpses of those pathetic princes will be left unburied. Those who fell in the city will be eaten by roving packs of savage dogs, those who fell in the open field, by birds of prey. To the eastern mind, to be left unburied was the ultimate disgrace. Yet this is exactly what will take place because *Yahweh has spoken.*

2. *Sign of judgment (14:12-13):* As a sign that the long-range prediction concerning the dynasty of Jeroboam was certain, Ahijah gave a prediction that could be verified within a matter of hours. At the precise moment that the queen arrived back at the palace, her son will die. The entire nation will mourn for the crown prince and they will bury him. He will be the one exception to the previous prediction that the sons of Jeroboam will be left unburied. Of all the members of the royal household, this young prince alone had lived a life deserving divine recognition. These words almost suggest that Abijah dissented from his father's religious policies.

3. *Means of judgment (14:14):* To accomplish his divine purposes against the house of Jeroboam, Yahweh will raise up a king that later history reveals to be Baasha (cf. 1 Kings 15:29). Judgment against Jeroboam will begin with the death of Abijah.

D. Jeroboam's Corrupt Kingdom (1 Kings 14:15-16)

The people of Israel as well as their king will taste of divine judgment. They had joined in the calf worship. Thus God will smite Israel and sweep it away as easily and swiftly as a reed is swept down a turbulent stream. Israel will be removed from the Promised Land and carried into captivity beyond the Euphrates. This terrible fate will befall the nation because they had provoked Yahweh by making their Asherahs, i.e., wooden poles representing the female deity Asherah. The old Canaanite cult flourished alongside Jeroboam's recently established calf worship in the northern kingdom. So because of all the sins inaugurated and tolerated during the reign of Jeroboam, God was forced to give Israel over to her enemies.

E. Judgment Administered (1 Kings 14:17-18; 15:25-31)

With sad heart the queen made the long trek back to Tirzah. When the distraught lady entered the threshold of the palace, her son died. The prince was buried and mourned just as Ahijah had prophesied.

Adjustments in Judah
2 Chronicles 11:5-23

A. Advantages of Judah

At the time of the schism of 931 BC Judah had several advantages over her sister kingdom to the north. Rehoboam had the privilege and advantage of ruling in Jerusalem, the city that God had chosen for his temple. The population of Judah was more heterogeneous. Furthermore, an influx of pious priests and Levites from the northern kingdom strengthened Judah in its earliest years (2 Chronicles 11:13-17).

B. Military Preparation (2 Chronicles 11:5-12)

Rehoboam faced some major adjustments as king of Judah. In the schism he had lost well over half the territory that his father had ruled. No longer was the Jerusalem government able to control the trade routes. The loss in revenues were enormous. A hostile sister kingdom forced Judah to undertake emergency military construction. Rehoboam built fifteen fortified cities to protect his tiny country from any attempted invasion by Jeroboam. He stored food and weapons in each of these cities and stationed officers over them. Only in this way was he able to hold Judah and Benjamin in the face of the superior forces of his northern rival.

C. Facade of Glory (2 Chronicles 11:18-21)

Though his kingdom was in the throes of poverty, Rehoboam still attempted to live in the grand style of his father Solomon. He followed his father down the path of polygamy. He had eighteen wives and sixty concubines. By these women he fathered twenty-eight sons and sixty daughters. Three of his wives (Mahalath, Abihail and Maacah) are named.

D. Royal Family (2 Chronicles 11:22-23)

Rehoboam is said to have dealt wisely with his sons. He scattered them throughout the land so as to weaken them by division. Yet he kept them all content by giving to them responsibilities, abundant food, and many wives. Rehoboam designated Abijah (Abijam) as crown prince.

Rehoboam was forty-one when he began to reign. He ruled Judah seventeen years (932-915 BC).

CONDEMNATION OF THE SOUTHERN KINGDOM
2 Chronicles 11-12

For three years (932-929 BC) Judah walked in the way of David and Solomon (1 Kings 14:21). Then the southern kingdom also became involved in a great apostasy in the early years of Rehoboam. In large measure this may be attributed to the influence of Naamah, the Ammonite mother of Rehoboam.

Apostasy Described
1 Kings 14:22-24

When the kingdom of Rehoboam was secure, Judah forsook the law of Yahweh (cf. 1 Chronicles 12:1). The people built high places where they could worship the astral deities. They erected the pillars that symbolized Baal and the poles that were symbols of Asherah. These abominations were found throughout the land *on every high hill and under every green tree.* Such shady spots were ideal for the immoral rites associated with the Baal cult. Most shocking of all, male cult prostitutes sprang up around the land. Whether these were homosexual or heterosexual prostitutes is uncertain. The people whom the Lord had called to holiness had adopted all of the corrupt practices of the Canaanites that God had driven out before them. They provoked the Lord to jealousy with their attachment to idols. Israel was the bride of God. Whenever the nation engaged in the worship of other gods, Scripture speaks anthropomorphically of God's jealousy.

Invasion by Shishak
1 Kings 14:25-28

A. Pharaoh's Campaign (1 Kings 14:25)
Judah's apostasy was punished swiftly. In the fifth year of Rehoboam (928 BC), Pharaoh Shishak invaded the land. With Israel

408

divided into two quarreling kingdoms, the ambitions of the Egyptians to control Palestine could be realized. A record of this invasion is inscribed on one of the pylons of the great Amon temple at Karnak (Thebes) in Lower Egypt. This inscription contains the names of between fifty and sixty localities in Israel and about a hundred in Judah that were captured on this expedition.

B. Repentance in Judah (1 Kings 14:26)

At the approach of Shishak, Rehoboam and his people repented of their transgressions. They begged for God's mercy. God heard that prayer and spared Jerusalem from destruction at the hands of Shishak (2 Chronicles 12:5-8). Nevertheless, to teach his people a lesson, God permitted them to be brought under tributary obligation to Shishak. The Pharaoh took away all the treasures of the house of God and the king's palace, including the beautiful shields of gold that Solomon had hung in the house of the forest of Lebanon.

C. Rehoboam's Pretense (1 Kings 14:27-28)

Rehoboam could do no better than to replace the golden shields with shields of bronze. These were carried by royal bodyguards whenever the king made an official visit to the temple. After the parade the shields were immediately returned to guard chambers so as to conceal from the people the humiliating fact that bronze had been substituted for gold. What a contrast! Solomon's golden shields were put on public display; but the shields of bronze were of so little value that they were stored in a guard chamber. Those bronze shields bear eloquent testimony that Rehoboam was but a pale imitation of his father.

SISTER KINGDOMS QUARRELING
1 Kings 15:1-16:12

Chapter Chronology

Jeroboam	Nadab		Baasha	Elah	Zimri
	910	909		886	885
Abijah			ASA		
915	912				

A state of war existed between the sister kingdoms throughout the seventeen years in which Rehoboam and Jeroboam simultaneously reigned. Border clashes must have occurred regularly. No massive invasions, however, are reported. Rehoboam died a peaceful death. He was buried with his fathers in the city of David. He was succeeded by his son Abijah, or Abijam as it is spelled in Chronicles.

JUDAH UNDER ABIJAH
[ca. 915-912 BC]

Although Abijah was a worshiper of Yahweh, he continued the policy of toleration of idolatry during his three years of rule. Abijah's heart *was not perfect with Yahweh his God.* Nevertheless, God gave him a *lamp,* i.e., progeny, and a successor on the throne of Judah for the sake of David. For four hundred years the descendants of David continued to sit on the throne of Judah. Thus did God demonstrate his faithfulness to David, the man after God's own heart, who had observed the commandments of God except in the matter of Uriah the Hittite (1 Kings 15:1-5).

ABIJAH'S INVASION OF ISRAEL
2 Chronicles 13:2-20

Date: 914 BC

Abijah's Strength

411

2 Chronicles 13:3

The state of hostilities between Israel and Judah erupted into open warfare during the days of Abijah. He invaded the northern kingdom with 400,000 men. The Hebrew term *'lph*, usually translated *thousand*, when used in military contexts can refer to military chieftains and/or the military unit they commanded. A unit commanded by an *'lph* may have contained as few as ten soldiers. If we read the text *mathematically* we have two enormous armies; if we read the text *militarily* we have two considerably smaller armies the exact sizes of which are unknown. See *Expositor's Bible Commentary*. The important point is that Abijah was outnumbered two to one.

Abijah's Sermon
2 Chronicles 13:4-12

The king of Judah stood on Mount Zemaraim and preached a sermon to Jeroboam and his troops. Abijah defended the right of the house of David to rule over all Israel. He belittled Jeroboam and the *scoundrels* who had helped him intimidate *the young and timid* Rehoboam. He pointed out that Mosaic worship was being faithfully conducted in Judah, while the northern tribes were following the calf cult created by Jeroboam. He warned the northern troops that they were fighting against Yahweh. They could not possibly succeed.

Abijah's Success
2 Chronicles 13:13-20

While Abijah continued to ramble on with his hypocritical discourse, Jeroboam's troops were encircling the army of Judah. When the army of Judah realized it had been surrounded, the soldiers cried to Yahweh. The priests blew the sacred trumpets. Abijah's army fought with such valor that the sons of Israel fled before Judah. *God gave them into their hand.* Israel's army suffered 500,000 casualties. *The sons of Judah conquered because they trusted in Yahweh.* Several northern towns, including Bethel, were (temporarily) captured by Abijah. Jeroboam was not able to recover strength during the rest of the reign of Abijah.

TRANSITIONS

South: Abijah's Death
2 Chronicles 13:21-22

The military victory at Mount Zemaraim is the distinctive accomplishment of Abijah's reign. The only other information related about this lackluster monarch is that he married fourteen wives and begat thirty-eight sons and daughters. Abijah was succeeded by his son Asa.

North: Judgment on Jeroboam
1 Kings 14:19-20

Jeroboam ruled Israel for twenty-two years (932-910 BC). His son Nadab succeeded him on the throne (1 Kings 14:20). Nadab was only able to hold the throne for parts of two years. He continued the schismatic religious policies of his father. An upstart from the tribe of Issachar conspired against him. When the plot unfolded, Nadab was leading a campaign to recover Gibbethon, a Levitical city on the frontier of Dan, from Philistine control (1 Kings 15:25-27).

Upon assuming the throne, Baasha launched a bloody purge that utterly wiped out the house of Jeroboam. By thus eliminating all potential rivals, Baasha was unconsciously fulfilling the prophecies of Ahijah the Shilonite. The massacre of Jeroboam's descendants is regarded by the author of Kings as being divine retribution for the sins of the first king of Israel (1 Kings 15:28-31).

JUDAH UNDER ASA
[912-871 BC]

First Great Reformation
1 Kings 15:9-24

After some two decades of apostasy in Judah, a dedicated worshiper of Yahweh took the throne. King Asa led the first of five great reformations in Judah. Unfortunately, toward the end of his reign this good king experienced a failure of faith.

In spite of the fact that he grew up in a palace dominated by an idolatrous grandmother and a hypocritical father, Asa did what was right in the eyes of Yahweh. He removed the cult prostitutes and wooden idols from the land (1 Kings 15:9-13).

God blessed Judah with ten years of peace and prosperity which Asa attributed to the reformation. During these years Asa built fortified cities and strengthened his army. Spearmen from Judah numbered 300,000 while bowmen from Benjamin numbered 280,000 (2 Chronicles 14:1-8).

ASA'S VICTORY OF FAITH
2 Chronicles 14:9-15

Date: ca. 902 BC

Prayer before Battle
2 Chronicles 14:9-11

About 902 BC Judah was invaded by a vast host led by Zerah the Ethiopian. Asa met the invaders in the valley of Zephathah at Mareshah. Prior to battle the king prayed one of the greatest prayers of Scripture. He confessed total dependence on Yahweh. He asked for help because *we trust in you, and in your name we have come against this multitude.* The prayer concluded with the appeal *let not man prevail against you.*

Defeat of the Invaders
2 Chronicles 14:12-15

Yahweh routed the Ethiopians before Asa. The armies of Judah pursued them as far as Gerar, five miles south of Gaza. Much plunder was carried away. Several cities in the vicinity of Gerar were sacked as well.

Prophetic Warning
2 Chronicles 15:1-7

The Spirit of God directed Azariah to go out and meet Asa as he returned from the victory over Zerah. This prophet reminded the victorious host that *Yahweh is with you when you are with him.* Azariah rehearsed what happened during the period of the Judges

414

when the people forsook Yahweh. Those priestless, kingless and lawless days were full of internal strife and external oppression. *God troubled them with every kind of distress.* For Asa, however, Azariah had a word of encouragement. If he was strong and courageous, there would be reward for his work.

Renewed Revival
2 Chronicles 15:8-15

A. Zeal of Asa's Effort (2 Chronicles 15:8-9)
The words of Azariah encouraged Asa in his reformation. He extended to the newly captured territories his efforts to remove the paraphernalia of idolatry. He restored the altar of Yahweh at the temple. Many of the pious citizens of the northern kingdom defected to Asa when they saw that he was making a sincere effort to restore the true faith.

B. Covenant Renewal (2 Chronicles 15:10-15)
In his fifteenth year Asa orchestrated a covenant renewal ceremony in Jerusalem. Some 700 oxen and 7,000 sheep were sacrificed to Yahweh. The people entered into a covenant to seek the Lord with all their heart. They agreed that whoever did not seek Yahweh will be executed. All present rejoiced at the renewal of the ancient covenant. They sought the Lord earnestly, *and he let them find him.* The result was that God gave them rest on every side (2 Chronicles 15:10-15).

C. Removal of his Grandmother (2 Chronicles 15:16)
Asa continued his reform efforts. He removed his grandmother from her powerful position as principal lady because she had made an idol (lit., a horrible thing) to Asherah. He burned that idol at the brook Kidron.

D. High Place Issue (2 Chronicles 15:17-18)
A problem arises in reference to what Asa did to the high places, the unauthorized shrines scattered throughout the land. Did he remove those high places (2 Chronicles 14:3), or did he not (1 Kings 15:14; 2 Chronicles 15:17)? The answer is that Asa removed the pagan high places, but did not remove the high places that were devoted to Yahweh. In spite of this defect in the devotion of Asa, his heart was

blameless with the Lord. All of the valuables captured in wars fought by his father and by himself, Asa dedicated to Yahweh and placed in the house of God.

Threat from Baasha
1 Kings 15:16-24

A. Reason for Baasha's Actions (1 Kings 15:16-17)

1. State of hostilities (15:16, 32): The second dynasty in the northern kingdom was founded by Baasha ben Ahijah. He killed the son of Jeroboam about 909 BC and exterminated all other relatives of that first dynasty. This change of dynasty in the north, however, did not induce Asa of Judah to change his attitude toward the sister kingdom. Twice the author of Kings states that a state of hostilities existed between the two kingdoms throughout the twenty-four years in which Baasha and Asa simultaneously ruled.

2. Ramah fortress (15:17): In the thirty-sixth year of the kingdom of Judah (894 BC) the northern king committed an overt act of aggression that could not be ignored by Asa. Baasha attacked Judah in an effort to re-conquer the territories lost to Abijah and Asa. At Ramah, only five miles north of Jerusalem, he began to build a fortress by which he intended to seal off the northern approaches of Judah.

B. Lapse of Faith (1 Kings 15:18-22)

Asa was alarmed by this turn of events, yet for some unexplained reason he did not undertake an attack against Baasha. He resorted to political strategy. He sent an enormous gift to Ben-Hadad of Damascus with a request that he attack Israel from the north. Ben-Hadad gladly complied with Asa's request. He attacked several northern cities of Israel. The invasion forced Baasha to withdraw to his capital at Tirzah. Asa then dismantled the fortifications that Baasha had started. The confiscated materials were used to build two prominent Judean fortresses, one at Geba and one at Mizpah.

C. Prophetic Warning (2 Chronicles 16:7-12)

1. Condemnation by Hanani (16:7-9): Hanani the seer (prophet) condemned Asa for his failure of faith in this crisis. He asserted that Asa could have defeated Baasha just as he had earlier defeated the Ethiopians when he had relied upon Yahweh. *For the eyes of Yahweh move to and fro throughout the earth that he may strongly support those whose heart is completely his.* In choosing to bribe Ben-Hadad, Asa had acted foolishly. From this point on he would experience war.

2. *Asa's reaction (16:10-12):* Asa was enraged at the seer for this forthright condemnation. Hanani was thrown into prison. Asa oppressed some of the people—presumably pious souls like Hanani—at the same time. In his final years Asa was diseased in his feet. Yet in his disease he did not seek Yahweh, but only the physicians. This man who had begun as such a dynamo of faith had forgotten the God who had made him strong.

ANARCHY IN ISRAEL
[886-885 BC]

Following Ben-Hadad's invasion of the northern kingdom in 895 BC the reign of Baasha of Israel rapidly deteriorated. The text briefly narrates the sad account of the turbulence surrounding Baasha's last years and those of his immediate successors.

Doom of Baasha Predicted
1 Kings 16:1-7

A. Prophet Jehu (1 Kings 16:1)

Most likely the prophets had encouraged Baasha to take the initiative against the house of Jeroboam in 908 BC. When it became apparent, however, that Baasha intended to follow in the same spiritual path as his two predecessors (Jeroboam and Nadab) he lost prophetic support. Yahweh eventually dispatched a prophet from Judah, Jehu, the son of the prophet Hanani, to publicly proclaim in Israel the doom of Baasha.

B. Judgment on Baasha's House (1 Kings 16:2-4)

Yahweh had used Baasha as a tool to punish the Jeroboam dynasty. For this purpose he had been elevated from the lowliest ranks to the highest position in the land. Yet Baasha had not proved faithful to Yahweh. In words almost identical to those used by Ahijah against Jeroboam (cf. 1 Kings 14:6-16), Jehu pronounced the doom of Baasha's dynasty. The relatives of Baasha will fall in the city and in the field. Their corpses will be left unburied to be eaten by beast and bird.

417

End of the Baasha Dynasty
1 Kings 16:5-14

A. Assessment of Baasha (1 Kings 16:5-6)

The sacred historian speaks of Baasha's *might* (ESV). That he was able to fortify Ramah just five miles from Jerusalem, and that Asa dared not directly challenge him are two indications of that "might." Baasha died a natural death. He was buried at Tirzah.

B. Prediction against Baasha's House (1 Kings 16:7)

Baasha's son Elah tried to succeed him. The hand of divine destruction, however, fell swiftly on the family of Baasha just as the prophet Jehu had predicted. The judgment fell on Elah for two reasons. First, he continued to *provoke Yahweh with the deeds of his hands,* i.e., he participated in the calf worship. Second, Baasha was guilty of murdering his predecessor. Had Baasha been a righteous man, his destruction of the house of Jeroboam would have been regarded as a divine mission; but since he was just as evil as the man he had killed, his act was only motivated by personal ambition. For this reason he stood condemned for the murder.

C. Fulfillment of the Prediction (1 Kings 16:8-14)

1. Conspiracy against Elah (16:8-9): Jehu's prophecy was fulfilled in this manner. When Elah had reigned two years, one of his military officers, Zimri, the commander of half of the Israelite chariot force, conspired against him. Elah seems to have been a dissolute and drunken incompetent. As king, he should have been with the army, which was engaged in a campaign at Gibbethon. Instead the king was in the house of one of his attendants participating in a drunken orgy. Perhaps Elah remained in Tirzah because he remembered the fate of Nadab, who had been assassinated at Gibbethon (cf. 1 Kings 15:27). In any case for a king to accept the hospitality of one of his subjects was a serious breach of monarchical etiquette. Arza, the steward or attendant, may have been a part of the conspiracy, in which case Elah is made to look all the more naive. In any case, it was during this drinking party that Zimri assassinated his king.

2. Execution of Baasha supporters (16:10-14): As soon as Zimri had been enthroned in 885 BC, he ordered all male relatives of Baasha to be executed. Thus he followed the precedent established in the first

418

dynastic upheaval. This action eliminated all potential rivals to the throne as well as all those who might feel obligated to avenge the blood of their relative. Zimri went a step beyond what Baasha had done back in 908 BC. He also executed the friends of the royal house, any who might be sympathetic to Elah. The bloodshed fulfilled the predictions made against the Baasha dynasty by the prophet Jehu. This dynasty had incurred the wrath of God because of its commitment to *vanities,* i.e., the golden calves.

Zimri's Seven-day Reign
[885 BC]
1 Kings 16:15-20

A. Zimri's Lack of Army Support (1 Kings 16:15-16)
Zimri was only able to hold the throne of Israel for one week. Upon hearing that Zimri had assassinated the king, the army in the field immediately declared their general, Omri, to be king. That the troops refused to recognize Zimri is not surprising. First, he was an inferior officer who was not even present on the great campaign at Gibbethon. Second, by murdering Elah's friends, Zimri doubtless made many enemies throughout the army.

B. Siege of Zimri's Palace (1 Kings 16:17-18)
Omri was not hesitant about accepting the office thrust upon him by his troops. He immediately broke off the siege of Gibbethon and led the army back up through the mountain passes to Tirzah. In a show of force he deployed his troops about the capital. Omri no doubt ordered Zimri to surrender. Seeing that his position was hopeless, Zimri went into the fortress of the palace—one of the innermost rooms—and committed suicide by setting the place on fire.

C. Divine Retribution (1 Kings 16:19-20)
Even though Zimri died by his own hand, the Bible regards his death as being the result of divine retribution *because of the sins that he had committed.* He is said to have walked *in the way of Jeroboam,* i.e., he continued to condone the calf worship in the north. Perhaps even before his seven-day rule Zimri had demonstrated his zeal for the counterfeit religion introduced by Jeroboam. On the other hand, the author may simply mean Zimri's revolt was not religiously

419

motivated. In any case, the text is certainly making the point that the anarchy in the north was the bitter fruit of Jeroboam's apostasy.

A Civil War
1 Kings 16:21-22

The entire nation did not rally to the standard of Omri. For some unexplained reason, a rival emerged to challenge Omri's claim to the throne. Perhaps this counter-movement was the protest of the religious community against the power of the army. In any case, Tibni was probably the favorite of the part of the army that was not involved in the encampment at Gibbethon.

Once the hereditary principle was overthrown, the crown in the north became a prize to be possessed by the strongest. Tibni determined not to let Omri have the throne uncontested. A fierce civil war erupted between the two factions. The text suggests that this struggle lasted about four or five years (885-880 BC). Finally Omri was able to subdue the forces of Tibni and slay the rival.

Conclusion

The political and spiritual conditions in the northern kingdom continued to worsen. In Judah, however, a valiant effort was made to bring the nation back to the Lord. A radical change in the relationship between the two kingdoms occurred sometime during the reign of Omri or Ahab. After nearly fifty years of conflict, Israel and Judah entered into a covenant of peace. Hostility gave way to harmony between the two sisters.

30
BATTLE AGAINST BAAL
1 Kings 16:13-18:46

Chapter Chronology

Omri	Ahab	
874		855
	Jehoshaphat	
873		

By 880 BC Omri's claim to the northern throne was no longer contested. The official records, however, list Omri as coming to power in the thirty-first year of Asa of Judah (885 BC), The Omri dynasty—the fourth in Israel—became one of the most important because of a new religious policy and a new foreign policy.

REIGN OF OMRI
[885-874 BC]
1 Kings 16:23-28

A New Capital
1 Kings 16:23-24

For the first six years of his reign Omri resided in Tirzah. During that time he was building a new capital. He chose a strategic location, a large oblong mound that dominated two main highways. Samaria, as the new city was named, was forty-two miles north of Jerusalem and twenty-five miles inland. The name was derived from that of its former owner, Shemer. Omri paid Shemer two talents of silver (about $4,250 BV) for the ground. Subsequent history proves the wisdom of Omri's choice of Samaria. The city remained the capital of Israel until the fall of the northern kingdom in 722 BC.

Religious Developments
1 Kings 16:25

The religious situation continued to deteriorate under Omri. Micah 6:16 refers derogatorily to the *statutes of Omri* which may suggest some new development in the calf worship. Perhaps the calf worship was organized into a formal system at this time. Another possibility is that Omri took additional measures to prevent those living in the north from attending the temple in Jerusalem. In any case, the practices of this king angered Yahweh even more than those of his five predecessors.

Accomplishments

In sources outside the Bible Omri appears as one of the most prominent kings of Israel. Two other significant accomplishments of Omri can be deduced from subsequent narrative. First, he reestablished David's policy of friendly relations with Phoenicia. Second, he (or his son) brought to an end the era of confrontation with Judah. The old general appears to have been a very capable diplomat! The biblical writer, interested as he was in the religious history of the kingdoms, saw little that was significant in his reign.

TWO FRIENDLY KINGS

Ahab in the North
[874-853 BC]
1 Kings 16:29-34

A. Political Policy
From the political and commercial point of view the alliance between Israel and Sidon was wise and necessary. The rising power of Aram made such an alliance desirable from the military standpoint. The Phoenicians needed the agricultural products of Israel, and land-locked Israel needed the markets available to the wide-ranging fleets of the Phoenicians. Thus, to the secular historian the marriage of Ahab and Jezebel was a brilliant diplomatic coup. From a religious point of view, however, the marriage was disastrous.

B. Religious Policy (1 Kings 16:29-34)
1. General assessment (16:29-30): Ahab succeeded his father Omri on the throne of Israel in 874 BC. He did evil in the eyes of Yahweh *more than all who were before him.* The worship of Yahweh under the image of the calf continued to be the official state religion. Under Ahab, however, Canaanite idolatry was tolerated, even

encouraged, due to the influence of the Phoenician princess Jezebel, Ahab's wife.

2. Influence of Jezebel: Jezebel was the daughter of Ethbaal, the ruler of Sidon. Tradition identifies him as the priest of Astarte who assassinated the king and usurped the throne. This tradition may account for Jezebel's fierce character and her fanatical devotion to the gods of her country. This woman was a pagan missionary. She came to Israel with the avowed purpose of making her god Baal Melqart the supreme god in the land.

3. Baal temple erected (16:31-33): King Ahab was led into the corruption of Canaanite idolatry. He apparently served and worshiped Baal as well as Yahweh. For Jezebel's god Ahab erected a temple, an altar and a pillar or image in Samaria. In addition the king made an Asherah, i.e., a wooden pillar symbolizing the goddess Asherah. In Canaanite theology Asherah was the consort of Baal. Ahab was following the dictates of international courtesy that required a foreign queen to have a sanctuary of her own religion in her adopted land. No less a king than Solomon could be cited as a precedent for such a policy among the Israelites.

4. Example of religious deterioration (16:34): A concrete example of the effects of counterfeit calf worship and Phoenician idolatry is cited at the end of 1 Kings 16. Hiel, a Bethelite, undertook what no one had dared to do for five centuries, viz., rebuild the walls of Jericho. These efforts at Jericho were probably part of Ahab's program to provide better protection on his southern border. Hiel may have been superintendent for a royal project.

Joshua's curse rested on anyone who dared undertake rebuilding Jericho. The impiety of Hiel was punished swiftly and severely. His eldest son died when the foundations of Jericho were laid. By the time he rebuilt the gates, the last of his sons died. The swift and exact fulfillment of the prophetic threats made through Joshua was a forceful witness to the fact that the law of God could not be violated with impunity.

5. Prelude to Elijah: The concluding chapters of 1 Kings and the opening chapters of 2 Kings focus, not upon the king, but rather upon the king's prophetic opponents—Elijah, Micaiah and Elisha. In these chapters the sacred historian traces the efforts of Israel's spiritual leaders to help their people in the spiritual crisis precipitated by governmental policy.

Jehoshaphat in the South
[873-849 BC]
2 Chronicles 17-19

Jehoshaphat began his sole reign in 869 BC. Like his father Asa, Jehoshaphat followed Yahweh. Unlike his father, his commitment did not wane in his later years. Four chapters in Chronicles shed light on why Ahab of Israel cultivated an alliance with Jehoshaphat.

A. Strength of Jehoshaphat (2 Chronicles 17:1-19)

1. Manifestation (17:1-2; 10-19): The strength of Jehoshaphat was manifested in two ways. First, the king of Judah was militarily strong. He stationed troops in fortified cities throughout Judah. He had garrisons in the towns of Ephraim which his father Asa had captured. He had a huge army of experienced soldiers numbering in the hundreds of thousands. Second, Jehoshaphat was enormously wealthy. He had *great wealth and honor*. The fear of Yahweh fell on the surrounding kingdoms so that they, for the most part, did not make war with Judah. The Philistines rendered tribute in silver to him, the Arabs in thousands of rams and goats.

2. Explanation (17:3-9): The source of Jehoshaphat's strength was Yahweh. The Lord was with this king because he followed the example of David. He did not seek after the Baals as did his counterparts in the northern kingdom. So Yahweh *established the kingdom in his control.* Jehoshaphat took great pride in the ways of Yahweh. He continued the efforts of his father to remove the high places and the Asherahs from Judah. He even dispatched government officials and Levites throughout the land to instruct his people in the book of the law.

B. Reforms of Jehoshaphat (2 Chronicles 19:5-11)

Jehoshaphat appointed judges in the land in each city. An appellate system brought difficult cases to one of two supreme courts in Jerusalem. One court, presided over by the high priest, considered religious questions. A government official was supreme judge over the civil court.

C. Criticism of Jehoshaphat (1 Kings 22:41-44)

The prophets had two main criticisms of Jehoshaphat. First, he did not remove the high places outside Jerusalem. These were shrines where Yahweh was worshiped illegally (1 Kings 22:43). Second, he made peace with Ahab of Israel (2 Chronicles 19:2-3). To seal this alliance, Jehoshaphat arranged a marriage between his son Jehoram, and Athaliah the daughter of Jezebel (2 Chronicles 18:1). Probably the mutual fear of the rising power of Damascus forced the rival kingdoms to seek reconciliation.

JUDGMENT FAMINE IN ISRAEL
1 Kings 17:1-7

If there ever was a time when God needed to intervene in a mighty way in the stream of human history it was in the time of Ahab. In that dark hour a determined effort was being made to stamp out faith in Yahweh. Only mighty miracles such as were performed by Elijah and Elisha were sufficient to counteract the influence of Jezebel and her 850 priests and prophets. The greatest prophet is reserved for the worst age. Israel had never had such an impious king as Ahab, or such a miraculous prophet as Elijah.

Elijah at the Court
1 Kings 17:1

Since the founding of the kingdom of Israel in 930 BC the prophets and the kings had been at odds with one another. The king had as his primary goals military security, economic expansion and a higher standard of living for his people. The prophets, on the other hand, were concerned first and foremost about fidelity to Yahweh. They viewed with suspicion the foreign treaties negotiated by the government. The antagonism between the government and prophets reached its climax in the Ahab-Elijah clash.

A. Abrupt Appearance (1 Kings 17:1a)

Elijah ("my God is Yahweh") came from the town of Tishbe, about eight miles north of the Jabbok River in the rugged region of Gilead. Because his manner matched the terrain from which he came, Elijah was frequently called simply *the Tishbite*. The abrupt way in which Elijah appears on the scene without a word of introduction or explanation is certainly remarkable. Elijah's sudden appearances and disappearances gave birth to the belief of his contemporaries that he was borne hither and yon by the Spirit of God.

B. Bold Announcement (1 Kings 17:1b)

1. In Yahweh's name: The ministry of Elijah began with an announcement of judgment upon Israel. This pronouncement is introduced with an oath formula that was appropriate for the situation: *As Yahweh God of Israel lives.* By these words Elijah was asserting that Yahweh, not Baal, was the God of Israel. Furthermore, Yahweh was a living God, not a figment of vain imagination as was Baal. Slaves normally stood to wait upon their masters. Therefore the words *before whom I stand* serve to identify Elijah as the ambassador or spokesman for Yahweh.

2. Nature of the judgment: The judgment announced by Elijah is one that was threatened by Moses if the covenant people were to fall into idolatry (cf. Deuteronomy 11:16; 17:18-20). Neither dew nor rain would fall in Israel. The normal rainy season in Palestine is from December to March. The rest of the year the earth receives moisture from the dew which at times could be as heavy as a drizzle.

3. Duration: The duration of the drought depended upon Elijah's word, and the prophet's word depended on some evidence of repentance from the people. The prophets of Baal were not able to remove the curse though they claimed that their god controlled the elements of nature. Thus the drought served a polemical as well as a judicial function.

Elijah at Cherith
1 Kings 17:2-7

A. Protection (1 Kings 17:2-3)

Shortly after Elijah announced the drought in Israel, he was directed by Yahweh to proceed eastward to the brook Cherith in some secluded area of Gilead. There he was to hide himself both to escape royal punishment and to avoid the importunity of his countrymen who might cry out to him because of the drought.

B. Provision (1 Kings 17:4-7)

At the Brook Cherith God provided for Elijah in a miraculous manner. The Lord of nature commanded the ravens to bring the prophet's food to him. With unfailing regularity the birds brought bread and meat to the prophet until the brook dried up.[50]

MIRACLES IN PHOENICIA
1 Kings 17:8-24

When the water supply at Cherith failed, God instructed Elijah to leave the land of Israel and journey to the Sidonian village of Zarephath. This was the very heart of the dominions of Ethbaal, the fanatical father of Jezebel. There God had commanded a widow to feed Elijah (17:8-9). Two great miraculous occurrences are connected with the prophet's sojourn there.

Multiplication of Food
1 Kings 17:10-16

A. Requests of a Poor Widow (1 Kings 17:10-12)

1. Request for water (17:10): Always obedient to the voice of God, Elijah hastened to Zarephath, probably taking the indirect route east of Jordan to avoid any contacts with agents of the king. At the gate of the city Elijah providentially met the very woman for whom he was looking, though he did not at first realize it. The woman was gathering sticks—a sign of her poverty—when the weary prophet approached her and requested that she secure for him a cup of water. Because Phoenicia is watered by the fresh streams from the Lebanon Mountains, the drought does not seem to have affected that area as much as Israel. Supplying water to the thirsty in that region is considered a duty almost sacred. So the woman scurried off in the direction of the well or water pot.

2. Request for bread (17:11-12): As the woman was going to fetch the water the prophet also mentioned that he would like *a morsel of bread.* The woman burst forth in an oath in the name of Yahweh. She apparently recognized Elijah, either by his features or dress, as an Israelite. Hence she referred to Yahweh as *your God.*

---

[50]Some have argued that the vowels of the word traditionally rendered *ravens* can be altered to produce the word *Arabs.* According to this view Elijah was cared for by some Bedouins who lived in the region of Cherith. Since the vowel points were not part of the inspired consonantal Hebrew, this suggestion cannot be ruled out. All ancient versions, however, attest the reading *ravens.*

With this oath she indicated that she did not have so much as one small cake of bread. All she had was a handful of meal in a jar and a little oil. Even as Elijah approached she was gathering sticks to make a fire to prepare a final meal for herself and her son. Since the Phoenicians were in large measure dependent upon Israel for foodstuffs, the drought to the south must have created great scarcity of grain in Phoenicia. The poor no doubt were the hardest hit. This widow was evidently reduced to the greatest extremity.

B. Faith of the Widow (1 Kings 17:13-14)

Now the faith of the Phoenician woman was put to the test. Elijah challenged the woman to feed him first, afterward she and her son could eat. To this outlandish request the prophet added a precious promise. If the woman put God's servant first, her jar of meal and flask of cooking oil would be miraculously preserved until the rains returned to the land.

C. Reward of the Widow (1 Kings 17:15-16)

Perhaps it was the authoritative manner of the man, or his prophetic garb, or the fact that he had spoken an oracle in the name of Yahweh that caused this heathen woman to believe and obey. In any case, her faith was rewarded. For many days she, her son, Elijah and *her house,* i.e., poor relatives, ate of that meal. All attempts to rule out the miraculous in this passage fail. God was doing more for that widow than merely sustaining her providentially by natural means. God was supernaturally multiplying the woman's food supplies. This widow received a prophet in the name of a prophet, and she received a prophet's reward (cf. Matthew 10:41).

Resurrection from the Dead
1 Kings 17:17-24

A. Death of the Widow's Son (1 Kings 17:17-18)

While Elijah was in residence at the widow's home, her son fell ill and died. The woman immediately jumped to the conclusion that the prophet's presence had drawn the attention of God to the sinfulness of her house. She interpreted the death of the child as retribution for sins that never would have been noticed had Elijah left her alone.

428

B. Elijah's Mighty Prayer (1 Kings 17:19-24)

With calm confidence Elijah asked the desperate woman to give him the limp corpse of her son. He took the child into his chamber where he laid him on his own bed. In mighty intercessory prayer the prophet cried out to God with a question. Had God repaid the kindness of this widow with such a blow? Then in an "action prayer" the prophet stretched himself upon the child in order to keep the body warm for the expected return of life. Three times Elijah repeated this "action prayer." Each time he accompanied it with earnest entreaty that God permit the child's life to be restored. Yahweh heard that prayer of faith. The lad revived.

CARMEL CONFRONTATION
1 Kings 18:1-46

Elijah's Return to Israel
1 Kings 18:1-15

In the third year, Yahweh ordered his prophet back to Israel. He was to show himself to Ahab, and then Yahweh promised again to send the rains (18:1). Undoubtedly the Lord also gave the prophet instructions to challenge the Phoenician prophets to a showdown on Mount Carmel.

A. Elijah and Obadiah (1 Kings 18:2-16)

1. What Obadiah had done (18:2-4): Obadiah ("the servant of Yahweh") was the governor of Ahab's palace in Samaria, a position of no little importance. He was a god-fearing man. He risked the wrath of Jezebel by hiding a hundred prophets in caves by fifties. The division of the prophets into two companies was partly for the sake of security and partly for the sake of convenience. The large number to be fed increased the chance of detection. Throughout the period of Jezebel's ruthless persecution, Obadiah took care of these men of God by supplying them with food and water. In view of the severity of the famine, this was truly an amazing feat.

2. What Obadiah was doing (18:5-6): While Obadiah was on an errand for his king, he encountered Elijah. Ahab had sent his steward throughout the land in search of water near which grass might still be growing. The king was facing the unpleasant prospects of having to slaughter a portion of his livestock if fodder was not soon located.

429

The king and Obadiah divided the land between them to facilitate the search. This personal inspection by the king and one of his chief officers indicates the extreme straits to which the Israelites were now reduced. Whether or not the two men were accompanied by a retinue is uncertain.

3. *Obadiah's surprise (18:7-8):* Obadiah's humble obeisance and the terms in which he addressed the prophet reveal the profound reverence with which Obadiah regarded Elijah. The question, *Is this you?* expressed the surprise of Obadiah at seeing Elijah, not any uncertainty about his identity. Elijah acknowledged that he was the long-missing prophet. He ordered Obadiah to go and inform the king that he was back.

4. *What Obadiah feared (18:9-14):* Obadiah was horrified at the thought of announcing to Ahab that Elijah had returned, because he knew the disposition of his master. Ahab had communicated with all neighboring kingdoms in search of Elijah. He even had made foreign kings swear that they were not harboring the prophet. Obadiah was afraid that when he went to inform the king of Elijah's whereabouts, the prophet would disappear. If such should happen, then Ahab would feel that his steward had lied to him or trifled with him. In either case, the king surely would have ordered his steward executed. Obadiah pled that Elijah take note of his lifetime commitment to Yahweh and his compassion for the prophets. He begged the prophet not to give him such a dangerous assignment.

5. *Obadiah's obedience (18:15-16):* Elijah set the mind of Obadiah at ease when he swore an oath in the name of *Yahweh of hosts* in which he promised to appear to Ahab that very day. Obadiah then went to find his king. Ahab in turn hastened to confront the prophet.

B. Elijah and Ahab (1 Kings 18:17-20)

1. *Ahab's arrogance and sarcasm (18:17):* Ahab did not meet the prophet with a humble and contrite heart, but with sarcasm and belligerence. By means of a rhetorical question the king expressed his amazement that Elijah had ventured back into his presence. He addressed the prophet as the *troubler of Israel.* This noun is derived from a verb that is used to denote alienation from society or from God which results from some heinous crime or act. Ahab thus charged Elijah with being the one who by his actions had alienated the deity (Baal?) so that the rains had been withheld.

2. *Elijah's defiance (18:18):* In words seething with defiance, the Tishbite hurled the epithet back into the teeth of the king. *It is you and your father's house that have brought the trouble on Israel!* Elijah accused the Israelites of having *forsaken the commandments of Yahweh;* he accused Ahab of having *walked after the Baals.*

3. *Elijah's challenge (18:19):* The text does not indicate how Ahab reacted to the defiant response of Elijah. The unexpected calmness and boldness of the prophet may have completely unnerved the king so that he could make no reply. In any case, Elijah hurled a challenge at the king. Let all Israel, i.e., the representatives of the nation, gather to Mount Carmel along with the 450 prophets of Baal and 400 prophets of Asherah. These Asherah *prophets* were Jezebel's ministers, probably imported from Sidon. They were fed from the bounty of the queen.

4. *Location for the showdown:* Mount Carmel was the site for the prophetic showdown. Carmel is a ridge some twelve miles in length. Near the summit is a plateau where the contest might well have taken place. A spring of water is close at hand which is said to flow even in the driest seasons. The selection of Carmel as the site of the confrontation was also dictated by the fact 1) that it was a central and convenient location; 2) that it was near the sea, from whence the rain clouds normally came; and 3) that an altar of Yahweh had once been located here.

Carmel Showdown
1 Kings 18:20-40

Ahab immediately complied with the demands of Elijah. He summoned the nation and the prophets of Baal to Mount Carmel. The king *sent unto the people,* i.e., invited the people to attend the contest. He *gathered* the prophets of Baal, perhaps implying that they were unwilling to come and were forced to do so by the king. The prophets of Asherah probably did not attend the convocation because they were under the personal control of the queen. She did not allow their participation (18:20).

A. Contest Preliminaries (1 Kings 18:21-24)

1. *Challenge to the witnesses (18:21):* No indication is given of the size of the crowd that assembled on Mount Carmel. No doubt the dramatic confrontation attracted hundreds, if not thousands. Elijah

431

hoped to reach these masses. To them he directed his rhetorical question: *How long are you going to hobble upon two crutches,* i.e., seek the support of both Yahweh and Baal simultaneously. Elijah was calling for a clear-cut decision. Let the people choose Baal or Yahweh, then let them commit themselves wholeheartedly to that deity who was truly God. Awed by the presence of the king and the prophets, the people answered not a word. Perhaps also they were convicted in their own consciences and were consequently speechless.

2. Elijah's confidence (18:22): To set the stage for the contest Elijah called the attention of the people to the fact that he stood alone that day as sole representative of Yahweh. On the other hand, Baal's prophets numbered 450. Thus did Elijah underscore the fact of his absolute confidence even though he was outnumbered. Certainly he was trying to stress the fact that truth is not determined by numbers.

3. Preparation of sacrificial animals (18:23): Since his opponents were so numerous, and since they were supported by the crown, Elijah proposed that they supply the two sacrificial bullocks. One was to be selected and prepared by the Baal prophets, the other by God's prophet. Elijah offered his rivals their choice of the oxen. He did not want them to use the excuse that their animal was less fit for sacrifice. The bullocks were to be placed on the altar wood, but no fire was to be set to the wood.

4. Prayer to the deities (18:24): Once the sacrificial animal was in place, the people were told to call on the name of their god Baal. The failure of the people to take a clear-cut stand for Yahweh was tantamount to their choosing Baal as their god. Elijah, on the other hand, would call on the name of Yahweh. The deity who responded to the prayers of his worshipers and consumed the sacrificial bullock with fire from heaven was be recognized as the true God.

6. Challenge accepted: The Baal sympathizers agreed to Elijah's challenge. As they saw it, the advantage was with Baal. He was the god of storm and lightning. Furthermore, the Baal prophets were allowed to select the sacrificial animal of their choice, go first, and use as much time as they needed for their incantations.

B. Efforts of the Baal Prophets (1 Kings 18:25-29)
1. Baal prophets go first (18:25): Having gained the assent of the people, Elijah repeated the proposal to the splendiferously clad prophets of Baal. They had been put in a position in which they could hardly refuse the test and still retain the respect of their constituents.

Because the prophets of Baal were so numerous, Elijah suggested that they go first in the contest. He was anxious that the impotence of Baal be fully manifested before Yahweh demonstrated his power.

2. *Sacrificial bull prepared (18:26):* The prophets of Baal declined the opportunity to select the bullock. They took the one that was given them by representatives of the people or by Elijah himself. They then prepared the animal in the prescribed manner, and began to call on the name of Baal. From morning until noon they continued to cry out that Baal might hearken to their prayers. They then began to limp, i.e., dance about the altar, in an attempt to attract the attention of their mute master.

3. *Elijah's taunting (18:27):* At noon Elijah began to ridicule his opponents. He urged them to cry louder. In condescending tones Elijah offered some possible explanations for Baal's lack of response. Perhaps he was meditating or talking; or maybe he was on a trip; or then again, maybe he was just a late sleeper and needed to be awakened!

4. *Fanatical prophesying (18:28-29):* Elijah's barbs stirred the Baal prophets to renewed vigor as if to testify to their undying faith in their god. Grabbing the swords and spears of soldiers standing nearby they engaged in acts of self-mutilation to attract the attention of their god. This fanatical *prophesying* continued for some six hours—from early morning to the time of the offering of the evening sacrifice about three in the afternoon. Without question, these men were absolutely sincere in their faith.

C. Efforts of Elijah (1 Kings 18:30-38)

1. *He repaired an altar (18:30):* When the Baal prophets retired from the field exhausted, Elijah called the people to him. He wanted them to have a good view of all he was about to do in order to remove suspicion of hoax or magic. The prophet began his demonstration by rebuilding the altar of Yahweh. This altar may have been one of the high places where Israelites worshiped prior to the establishment of the temple in Jerusalem. On the other hand, this altar may have been built by some of the faithful Yahweh worshipers in the north who refused to bow the knee to Baal or to the golden calf. Scarcely any doubt can exist that this was one of the altars that the government had ordered torn down (cf. 19:10). By repairing the altar, Elijah was casting himself in the role of the restorer of the law and true faith.

2. *He drenched his sacrifice (18:31-35):* Twelve stones were used to restore the altar, symbolizing the twelve tribes of Israel. By this action Elijah was silently protesting the schism in the north. With the twelve stones from the old altar, Elijah built a new one *in the name of Yahweh,* i.e., by his authority and for his glory. A trench was dug about the altar as deep as the grain measure containing two seahs (about thirteen quarts) of seed. The sacrificial bullock was cut in pieces and laid on the altar wood. The prophet then ordered four pitchers of water to be poured on the sacrificial animal and on the wood beneath. Then he ordered for this drenching to be repeated two more times. So much water was poured over the altar that it ran down and filled the trench around the altar. Apparently these actions were taken to exclude all suspicion of fraud.

3. *He prayed (18:36):* At about three o'clock in the afternoon (cf. verse 29) Elijah drew near his water-drenched altar. He lifted his eyes heavenward and began to pray. He addressed Yahweh as the God of Abraham, Isaac and Israel. He prayed for God to vindicate himself and his prophet there on that mount. The prophet asked for fire from heaven to prove that everything Elijah had said with regard to the famine three years earlier, and all that he had done with regard to organizing the confrontation with the Baal prophets, had been done through the word of Yahweh.

4. *Answer by fire (18:37-38):* Earnestly Elijah called upon Yahweh to hearken to his prayer so the people might be convinced that he alone was God, and being thus persuaded, might turn back to the God of their fathers. This dramatic prayer had no sooner fallen from the lips of Elijah when *fire from heaven* (lightning) fell upon the altar. The tongues of fire not only consumed (lit., ate up) the sacrificial animal and wood, they also disintegrated the stones, scorched the dust about the altar, and even licked up the water in the trench.

D. Execution of the Baal Prophets (1 Kings 18:39-46)

1. *Proclamation of the people (18:39):* The people reacted to the divine demonstration instantly and decisively. Recognizing in the fire the token of the divine presence, they fell on their faces and continued to shout in unison, *Yahweh is God, Yahweh is God!* Seizing the initiative of that emotion-packed moment, Elijah ordered the Baal prophets to be apprehended. He then led the throng down to the base of the hill where he slew, i.e., ordered to be slain, the pagan prophets.

Apparently this was done beside the River Kishon so that the corpses could be flushed out of the land into the sea.

2. Explanation of the slaughter: The slaughter of the Baal prophets has been called an act of gross fanaticism and cruelty by some; others have seen in it a wild and terrible *vendetta* for Jezebel's persecutions of Yahweh's prophets. The following considerations may help to put this incident in proper perspective.

- The law required the execution of those who worshiped false gods, and especially those who taught others in Israel to so worship (Exodus 22:20; Deuteronomy 13; 17:2-7).
- Whereas it was normally the duty of the theocratic ruler to carry out such executions, in Elijah's day the king was corrupt, powerless, and an idol worshiper.
- Elijah had just proved that Yahweh was God; now he must likewise prove the law of God was not dead.
- These prophets had been instrumental in corrupting the people of God. They thus had threatened the very existence of true religion.
- The action was allowed and approved by God who otherwise would hardly have answered the prayer that Elijah offered following the massacre.
- Idolatry and irreligion are not today to be avenged by sword or fire, not because these sins are any less grievous, but because the duty of punishing these crimes has been reserved for God himself.
- Whereas the law specified stoning as the punishment for idolatry (Deuteronomy 13:10; 17:5), the sword was used in this instance because of the numbers involved and the lateness of the afternoon hour.

End of the Famine
1 Kings 18:41-46

A. Instructions to Ahab (1 Kings 18:41)

King Ahab was wise enough to realize that he could not intervene to rescue the condemned prophets from the angry throng. Apparently he accompanied the crowd to the Kishon. In the excitement of the day the king had eaten nothing. Elijah therefore instructed Ahab to go up and have a meal. The king's attendants must have spread a tent for

435

him upon the higher plateau. They had brought food for their master, but until now he had not cared to eat. By encouraging the king to eat, Elijah was suggesting that there was no longer any cause for anxiety or alarm on his part. Since the people had repented, and the wicked had been cut off from the land, the drought could now be removed. In Elijah's prophetic mind he could already hear the sound of a great rain.

B. Intercession by Elijah (1 Kings 18:42-44)
  1. Intensity of it (18:42): Elijah then made his way to one of the prominent knolls of Carmel where he could enter into earnest intercession. The prayer posture of the prophet was somewhat peculiar. He seems to have been squatting with his head between his knees. The purpose here was to induce concentration. After some moments of petition, Elijah dispatched his servant to a higher elevation from which the Mediterranean Sea could be clearly viewed. His concentration in prayer was so intense that Elijah could not stop to scan the sky to see if his prayer had been answered.
  2. Persistency of it (18:43-44): Seven times the servant was instructed to return to his observation post. God had promised rain (cf. verse 1), and Elijah was confident that God would keep that promise. Without murmur the devoted servant executed the prophet's orders. On his seventh trip to the summit, he spotted a small cloud no bigger than the palm of a man's hand. Such small clouds were harbingers of rain in Palestine (cf. Luke 12:54). Elijah then dispatched his servant to the plateau where Ahab was dining to announce to the king that he should make haste to go to Jezreel lest he be caught in the downpour and be unable to cross the flood-swollen Kishon.

C. Return to Jezreel (1 Kings 18:45-46)
  Shortly the sky blackened, a wind arose, and a great rain swept across the Plain of Esdraelon. Ahab made his way toward Jezreel as fast as he could. The hand of Yahweh came upon Elijah giving him supernatural strength. Girding up his loins, i.e., gathering about his waist his long flowing robe, Elijah set out running toward Jezreel. He actually arrived at the gate of the city prior to Ahab and his chariot. Over this distance it would not be impossible for a man to outstrip a horse and chariot, especially since the man would run cross-country while the chariot would have to stick to the now muddy roadbed.

Elijah believed he had struck the death blow to the pagan practices promoted by the royal court. He wished to be in Jezreel to further any reformation efforts that the hapless Ahab might inaugurate. He knew Ahab would need all the help he could get to bolster his courage as he came face to face with his domineering wife.

History of Israel

31
LAST DAYS OF AHAB
1 Kings 19-21

Chapter Chronology

		853
AHAB		
874		
	JEHOSHAPHAT	

Elijah expected the triumph on Carmel to be followed by a great religious reformation in Israel. Such was not the case. Elijah had won a battle, but the outcome of the war against Baal was still in question.

RETREAT TO HOREB
1 Kings 19:1-18

Date: ca 867 BC

Crisis in the Desert
1 Kings 19:1-8

A. Elijah's Flight (1 Kings 19:1-4)

1. Jezebel's threat (19:1-2): Upon learning of the defeat of her god and the death of her prophets, Jezebel publicly vowed that she would see Elijah dead. A messenger was dispatched to the city gate to find the prophet and to convey to him the queen's solemn vow in the name of the gods she revered that she would have his life within twenty-four hours. If, however, she meant to slay Elijah, why did Jezebel forewarn him by means of this messenger? Perhaps she felt that she would find no one that night with the courage to carry out the execution order against a man whose supernatural powers had been so widely heralded. The dispatching of the messenger was more an act of rage than of rationality. In her exasperation she had to give vent to her impotent wrath. Her husband may have been convinced and even converted by what he had seen, but *she* was unconquered and unrelenting.

439

2. *Elijah's discouragement (19:3a):* This unexpected turn of events caused the prophet great discouragement. In a moment of spiritual weakness he resigned as it were from his prophetic ministry, and fled the country. Profound depression mingled with fear in the heart of this man of God. He had expected the contest on Carmel to settle the Baal issue once and for all. His dream of Israel in the fold of fidelity was smashed by the defiant declaration of the queen.

3. *Dismissing his servant (19:3b):* At Beersheba, ninety-five miles south of Jezreel on the southern boundary of Judah, the prophet dismissed his faithful servant. The journey to that point must have occupied at least three days. The lad was probably too exhausted to go any farther. There was no reason why this faithful servant should be subjected to the uncertainties and privations of desert travel. Besides, Elijah wanted to be alone in his depression.

4. *Under the juniper tree (19:4):* When Elijah came upon a juniper (broom) tree, he sat down to rest beneath its bushy branches. There he sat alone, exhausted physically and depressed psychologically. He requested that he might die.[51] In agonizing lament he cried, *I am no better than my fathers.* He had thought himself to be a special messenger of God, raised up mightily to bring the people of God to repentance. So long as he had a ray of hope that he might influence the moral and religious life in Israel, nothing was too difficult for him. Under that juniper tree, however, Elijah came to feel that his life was fruitless, that he had failed in his mission. He had accomplished no more than those prophets who had preceded him in the task of preaching.

B. An Angel's Assistance (1 Kings 19:5-8)

1. *Food (19:5):* The pathetic prophet closed his eyes and prayed that he would never open them again. God, however, had other plans for this man. An angel awakened him and directed him to arise and eat. Elijah probably had eaten little or nothing during his journey from Jezreel. His profound depression may have been due partly to physical weakness. Therefore before God could deal with his spiritual problem he had to take care of the man's physical needs.

---

[51]Literally, *he requested his life to die.* In this expression is reflected the conception that life proceeds directly from God and consequently belongs to him. A person might wish to die, but he was not at liberty to commit suicide.

440

2. More food and rest (19:6-7): Opening his eyes, Elijah found near his head a cake of bread and a jug of water. After partaking, the prophet again dozed off. Once again the angel awakened him and bade him partake of the food because he yet had a long journey before him.

Theophany at Horeb
1 Kings 19:8-12

A. Journey to Horeb (1 Kings 19:8)
From that meal Elijah gained enough strength to sustain himself for several days. Like Moses before him and Jesus after him, Elijah fasted for forty days. These three great fasters were reunited gloriously on the Mount of Transfiguration. The journey from Beersheba to Mount Horeb is about one hundred miles. Obviously Elijah did not spend the entire forty days traveling. Rather his total time in the wilderness was forty days.

A. Yahweh's Censure (1 Kings 19:9-10)
1. Yahweh's question (19:9): At Horeb Elijah took up residence in a cave.[52] There the word of Yahweh came to him in the form of a question designed at once to reprove Elijah and to make him analyze his situation. At every other point in the ministry of this prophet, the Lord had been sending him to his destinations; Elijah, however, had left Jezreel without on his own. He had left in fear and distrust of God. So God asked the probing question, *What are you doing here?* The implication is that Elijah had deserted his post.
2. Elijah's self-justification (19:10): Elijah did not accept censure without some self-justification. In the face of the terrible apostasy in Israel, Elijah had been very zealous for Yahweh. On the other hand, the children of Israel broke the covenant with God, threw down his altars, and slew his prophets. Yet Elijah stood firm and, so it seemed to his despondent mind, stood alone. Now Elijah's own life was in jeopardy even though he had won a mighty victory on Carmel.
3. Implied criticism: In these words there is tacit reproof of God. Why had the Lord looked upon the deterioration in the northern

---

[52]The Hebrew reads *the cave.* This could be taken to be a generic article meaning the cave region. Others think the article points to a particular cave, possibly that from which Moses saw the back of Yahweh (Exodus 33:21ff).

kingdom for so long without intervening? Elijah resented the growing corruption of the age and the frustration of his efforts to reverse it. Here is the old cry found throughout the Old Testament, the complaint that God is silent and indifferent, that the righteous are persecuted while the wicked prosper.

C. Elijah's Instruction (1 Kings 19:11-12)

1. What Elijah experienced (19:11-12): If Elijah thought his depression and his desertion of the field of battle were justified, he was mistaken. He was about to experience a theophany, a manifestation of the power and presence of God, through which he was to learn a very important lesson. The Lord directed the prophet to stand at the entrance of the cave. As soon as he stepped from the cave, Elijah was confronted with a veritable tempest that ripped rocks loose from the mountain and sent them crashing to the valley below. Yahweh, however, was not in the wind. Shortly after the wind subsided, the earth began to shake. Once again the Lord was not present in the earthquake. Next came fire—perhaps a thunderstorm with bolts of lightning the likes of which the prophet never had seen before. Yahweh, however, was not in the fire. Then came the still small voice (lit., a sound of gentle silence). Elijah then knew that he was standing in the presence of God.

2. What Yahweh taught Elijah: Through the Horeb signs God taught Elijah an important lesson. The spectacular and dramatic have their place in God's order of things. Most often, however, the divine program is carried forward through the still small voice that speaks to the hearts of people. While Yahweh is a God of judgment, he is also the God of mercy and grace. Elijah needed to be reminded of that fact. He needed to see that the time of fire, sword and slaughter had passed. Now the time had come to proclaim the word of Yahweh in gentle silence. The still small voice of protest was to become in the course of time a powerful force; it must not be allowed to die! A successor must be chosen to carry on the work.

Commission of Elijah
1 Kings 19:13-18

A. Another Rebuke (1 Kings 19:13-14)

Wrapping his sheepskin mantle about his face lest he look upon God, Elijah stepped forth from his cave into which apparently he retreated during the manifestations of divine power. Again Elijah heard the voice of God raising the same embarrassing question that was asked previously: *What are you doing here, Elijah?* Elijah repeated verbatim the answer he had given God earlier. The tone of his voice, however, must surely have changed. Formerly defiant, loud, belligerent, he now spoke with the still small voice, the voice of self-abasement. The facts had not changed. He knew of no other way to respond to the divine query. Now, however, he had reservations about his course of conduct. Elijah thought he knew best how God's work should be done. The theophany taught him that he had a faulty understanding of God's goals and methods. That Elijah had indeed repented is indicated by the fact that he was given a new commission by the Lord.

B. Three Anointings (1 Kings 19:15-17)

Elijah was commissioned to *anoint,* i.e., appoint or call, Hazael, Jehu and Elisha. Elijah was to see to it that these three individuals were made aware of their divinely appointed destiny. Hazael was to become king of Damascus, Jehu was to become king of Israel, and Elisha was to become Elijah's successor. The three were to be God's agents of judgment upon apostate Israel. Jehu was commissioned to slay those who escaped the sword of Hazael; Elisha, by the sword of the spirit, was to *slay* those who escaped the physical judgment of Jehu. The two kings were destined to create in Israel tumultuous upheavals just like the wind, earthquake and fire did at Horeb. The word of God spoken by Elisha, however, was what God will use to constrain men to humble themselves before the Lord. Rightly understood, the commission to Elijah is a concrete application of the great spiritual lesson that he learned through the theophany at Horeb.

The Horeb commission answered Elijah's implicit criticism that God was not doing enough to thwart the sinners in Israel. God was suggesting that bold action was about to be taken against the ruling dynasty and the religion that it fostered. A ruthless foreign invader and a dynastic upheaval were going to be necessary to root out Baalism in Israel.

C. Final Note (1 Kings 19:18)

In a final note, Yahweh refuted Elijah's twice-stated allegation that he alone had remained faithful to the Lord in Israel. God revealed that seven thousand still had not bowed the knee to Baal. The figure is

443

not only a round number it is a symbolic one as well. The still small voice had been at work in Israel; a faithful remnant was still to be found there (cf. Romans 11:5) that had not *kissed* (embraced) Baal.

CALL OF ELISHA
1 Kings 19:19-21

A. Elijah's Symbolic Action (1 Kings 19:19)

Upon returning to Israel, Elijah set about to carry out the duty God had assigned him at Horeb. He came upon Elisha plowing in a field. Elisha must have come from an affluent family for twelve yoke of oxen were working the field. Elijah passed by Elisha and cast his mantle upon the young man. This rough hairy garment had become the trademark of Elijah and the symbol of his prophetic office. To cast the cloak to or upon Elisha was therefore an appropriate way of calling Elisha to be his successor.

B. Elisha's Acceptance (1 Kings 19:20)

1. His request (19:20a): After casting his mantle upon Elisha, Elijah strode on. He left it for the young man to take or reject this call as he saw fit. Elisha made up his mind at once. He ran after his new master. His request to be allowed to give his mother and father a parting embrace is altogether fitting, even touching. Had he asked permission to stay and *bury* his parents he would have merited rebuke (cf. Luke 9:59-61). Consequently Elijah granted the reasonable request. The call to be his servant did not require a repudiation of his own flesh and blood.

2. Farewell feast (19:20b): Elisha bade farewell to his parents and friends at a hastily prepared meal. He slew a yoke of oxen and boiled the meat thereof over a fire he had built with the wood of his plow. He may have meant this to be symbolic of his repudiation of his secular calling. The farewell feast completed, Elisha arose and went after Elijah. The young man became Elijah's attendant.

The reign of Ahab (874-853 BC) was crucial in the religious history of Israel. Through several prophets Yahweh continued to demonstrate his superiority to the gods of surrounding nations.

YAHWEH AND

THE ARAMEAN THREAT
1 Kings 20:1-43

The focus now shifts from the internal threat of Baalism to the external threat of the neighboring Aramean kingdom of Damascus. The policy of harassment had characterized Ben-Hadad's dealings with Israel in the days of Baasha (cf. 1 Kings 15:18). Now "the" Aramean king determined that he would subdue Israel totally.

Siege of Samaria
1 Kings 20:1-22

About 860 BC Ben-Hadad of Damascus went up and besieged Samaria with thirty-two "kings," i.e., heads of tiny allied principalities. This invasion may have been prompted by Omri's conquest of Moab and consequent control of the Transjordan trade route, the famous King's Highway (20:1).

A. Initial Demands (1 Kings 20:2-4)

1. Ben-Hadad's demands (20:2-3): Aramean messengers were sent to Ahab with the demands of Ben-Hadad. The demands were excessive; they were designed to provoke all-out war. Ben-Hadad wanted silver and gold; but also he wanted Ahab's harem and the best of his children as hostages. Surrender of the harem would be tantamount to surrendering the throne itself (cf. 2 Samuel 16:21), not to mention all manhood and self-respect.

2. Ahab's response (20:4): Faced with an overwhelming Aramean host, Ahab deemed it advisable to make every concession, to cast himself, as it were, on the mercy of Ben-Hadad. He may have hoped that a soft answer would turn away the wrath of his adversary. He may have assumed that a verbal acknowledgment of the claims of Ben-Hadad would be sufficient to placate the foe thus eliminating the necessity of having actually to hand over his family as hostages.

B. Additional Demands (1 Kings 20:5-9)

1. Demand to enter Samaria (20:5-6): Since Ahab had yielded so easily to his initial demands Ben-Hadad demanded more. The initial proposal was vague and allowed Ahab to select what to deliver over to the Aramean; the second proposal was definite and immediate. It provided for Ben-Hadad's servants to pass through the palaces of Samaria seizing whatever appeared to be valuable.

2. *Ahab's response (20:7-9):* Realizing that his previous conciliatory submission had only stirred the Aramean braggart to make greater demands, Ahab called the elders of the land together to seek advice. They urged the king to resist these latest demands. Total capitulation was unthinkable. Ahab sent word back to Ben-Hadad that whereas he had been willing to comply with the initial demands, he could not permit enemy soldiers to pillage his palaces.

C. An Empty Boast (1 Kings 20:10-12)

1. *Ben-Hadad's bluster (20:9-10):* Infuriated by this response, Ben-Hadad fired back a blustering reply. He vowed to make Samaria a heap of dust. He boasted that his troops were so numerous that this dust would be insufficient to fill the hands of each of his soldiers.

2. *Ahab's proverb (20:11-12):* Ahab's third response to the king was a pithy and incisive proverb that consists of only four words in the Hebrew: *It is not the one who girds on his harness who should boast, but he who survives to remove it.* When this curt reply was reported to Ben-Hadad, the king and his vassals were drinking in their campaign huts. In furious rage the king issued the command—one word in the Hebrew—to commence the siege.

D. A Prophetic Word (1 Kings 20:13-14)

1. *Assurance of divine help (20:13):* God dispatched an unnamed prophet to offer encouragement to Ahab in this national crisis. The prophet promised to deliver Ben-Hadad and his host into the hand of Ahab that very day. Whatever other reasons God may have had for intervention on behalf of Israel, the supreme purpose of this divine help was that Ahab might know assuredly that Yahweh was God. On Carmel Yahweh had appeared as a God of fire, wrath and judgment; now he was about to reveal himself as God of deliverance. On Carmel he had shown himself to be superior to the idols of Phoenicia; now he planned to demonstrate his power over the gods of Aram.

2. *Strategy (20:14):* Ahab welcomed this word from Yahweh, but he was puzzled by it. So the king inquired further of the prophet. Who will secure the victory? Which side is to commence the hostilities? In the name of Yahweh the prophet related the strategy. The *young men* or servants of the district governors will gain the

victory. Just who these young men were is not clear. Probably God selected a group that was weak and feeble in order that the victory might be attributed to him. This band of young men, whoever they were, was to commence the attack against the Arameans.

E. Deliverance (1 Kings 20:15-21)

1. Ahab's young men (20:15-18): Ahab found only 232 of the *young men*[53] in the capital. The rest of his army numbered only seven thousand. At noon, when normally people of the Near East take a lengthy respite from all activity, the tiny force of Ahab marched forth from Samaria. Ben-Hadad and his vassals were carousing and giving little thought to their military endeavors. The camp sentries immediately reported the troop movements out of the gate of Samaria. Ben-Hadad gave the orders that the Israelites were to be taken alive, no doubt so that he might torture them and mock them before they were executed.

2. Success of the strategy (20:19-21): The 232 *young men* may have been used as a decoy to lull the Aramean troops into a false sense of security. When the Arameans came forward to take them into custody, the seven thousand troops poured forth from the city to engage the enemy. When several Arameans fell in battle, panic seized the rest. They fled for their lives with Israel in hot pursuit. Ben-Hadad fled by horse along with some of his cavalry. Thus did Israel defeat the Aramean host with a great slaughter.

F. Warning (1 Kings 20:22)

Shortly after the victory over the Arameans, the unnamed prophet came to Ahab again, this time with a warning. The danger was not over. At the turn of the year, i.e., in the spring of the following year, when military campaigns were normally launched, Ben-Hadad was going to return. Therefore Ahab should take every military precaution by strengthening both his army and the fortification of his capital.

Confrontation at Aphek
1 Kings 20:23-43

---

[53]The traditional view is that the young men were the sons of vassal princes left as hostages as an assurance that they did not rebel. Modern commentators prefer the view that the *princes* were governors of various districts of Israel. The *young men* were cadets who were recruited by these princes and sent to the capital for special training. Others depict the young men as "shock troops" or "commandos."

A. Aramean Preparation (1 Kings 20:23-25)

Ben-Hadad's advisers were not long coming up with an explanation for the humiliating defeat at Samaria. They suggested that the Israelites had been successful because their gods were gods of the hills, whereas the Aramean gods were gods of the plains. If the armies of Israel could be lured out of the hilly terrain of Samaria and into the plains, the Arameans were convinced that they would prove to have the stronger army. In addition to suggesting that the king pick his battlefield more carefully, the advisers also suggested that the thirty-two kings, with their diverse interests and lack of military expertise, be replaced with professional officers over the host. Finally, they suggested that Ben-Hadad, if he would be assured of victory, would need to have an army at least as large as the one he had lost at Samaria. The king listened to this advice and implemented it at the appropriate time.

B. Battle (1 Kings 20:26-29)

1. Faceoff at Aphek (20:26-27): In the spring of the year Ben-Hadad mustered his troops and went up against the Israelite fortress of Aphek. Emboldened by their previous victory, the Israelites went out to challenge the invaders. They found the whole plain swarming with Aramean legions. In comparison the Israelites appeared like two bands of stragglers separated from the main body of the flock.

2. Encouraging prophecy (20:28): Under these circumstances Ahab was more than cheered by the appearance of a man of God—perhaps the same prophet who had brought news of victory a year earlier. Once again the message from the Lord was positive. Because the Arameans had relegated the Creator God to the level of a tribal deity, because they had said Yahweh was only a god of the hills, therefore Yahweh promised to intervene again on behalf of his people. Neighboring nations will learn of the power of the living God through this deliverance, and wavering Israel will be provided with yet another incontrovertible proof of Yahweh's divinity.

3. Seven-day standoff (20:29): For seven days the two armies camped opposite one another. The Arameans waited for the Israelites to descend from the mountains; but Israel was reluctant to attack such a great host. On the seventh day the army of Israel charged down the hillsides and into the plains. The reason for the delay of seven days is not stated, but it is entirely possible that the sacred number seven had

448

come to be regarded superstitiously as the most advantageous time for attack. In any case, the historian reports that the men of Israel smote a hundred thousand Aramean infantry in that one day of battle. The term *smote* may include wounded as well as slain.

C. Treaty with Aram (1 Kings 20:30-34)

1. Collapsing wall (20:30a): Those who survived the slaughter took refuge in the fortress at Aphek, which at the time would appear to have been in the control of the Arameans. There a second tragedy befell the invading host. A city wall collapsed killing 27,000 men. Probably these soldiers were manning the defenses of the city when an earthquake threw down the walls.

2. Advice for Ben-Hadad (20:30b-31): Following the defeat in the plains of Aphek, Ben-Hadad had fled into an inner chamber of the fortress (lit., chamber within a chamber). There his counselors advised that he surrender to Ahab because, they argued, the kings of Israel had a reputation for showing mercy to their enemies. If the king and his staff were to put on sackcloth as a token of humility and ropes on their heads, i.e., around their necks, to demonstrate complete submission, there was a good chance that Ahab would allow them all to live.

3. Ben-Hadad's surrender (20:32-33): Ben-Hadad had no alternative but to acquiesce in this suggestion. The counselors were dispatched so garbed to plead for the life of their master. Ahab seemed surprised to hear that Ben-Hadad was alive. Upon receiving the news he immediately declared his willingness to enter into a peace treaty with the Aramean by declaring, *He is my brother.* Seizing upon this favorable word, the messengers replied, *Ben-Hadad is your brother,* by which they declared their willingness to accept the generous offer of a covenant. Then Ahab ordered that Ben-Hadad be brought to him. When the Aramean king came forth from his place of hiding, Ahab invited him to come up with him into the royal chariot. This signaled great favor and reconciliation.

4. Terms of the treaty (20:34): All of the details of the covenant worked out between Ahab and Ben-Hadad are not recorded. The Aramean agreed to return to Israelite control the territories his father had taken from Ahab's *father,* i.e., predecessor, Baasha (cf. 15:20). Furthermore, Ben-Hadad conceded to Ahab the right to establish Israelite bazaars or quarters in Damascus where Israelites might live and trade. Ahab was pleased with these concessions. After formalizing the agreement, the Israelite king dismissed his enemy.

5. Explanation of the treaty: Ahab had good reason for being lenient with Ben-Hadad. A new power was rising in the east. Assyrian texts state that both Ahab and Ben-Hadad contributed troops to a coalition army that successfully withstood the Assyrian advances in the famous battle of Qarqar in 853 BC. In the face of the rising power of Assyria, Ahab probably thought it was better to have a friend and ally to the north than a belligerent. Others, however, think Ahab was motivated by purely commercial considerations.

D. Ahab Condemned (1 Kings 20:35-43)

1. A disobedient prophet (20:35-36): The prophets were not happy with the actions of Ahab. A certain member of the *sons of the prophets* went about to bring rebuke to the king. He directed his companion, i.e., one of his fellow prophets, to smite him, i.e., bruise and wound him. When the companion refused to comply, the prophet pronounced a severe judgment against him. As soon as the two parted, a lion slew the companion. This now is the second account of a prophet who violated an explicit commandment of God and paid for it with his life, in both cases by being slain by a lion (cf. 1 Kings 13:24).

2. A lesson in obedience: The unnamed prophet intended to illustrate to the king the principle of unquestioning obedience to the commandments of Yahweh. Ahab had just transgressed the law of God by allowing one to escape whom God had appointed to destruction. He had to be taught that he had no right to be generous at the expense of others, that God's will must be done even when it goes against the grain and seems to contradict impulses of kindness. A prophet ordered to smite a brother, and that for no apparent reason, no doubt refused because he found such an order repugnant. That prophet who followed his benevolent impulses instead of the command of God forfeited his own life. The duty of unquestioning obedience was thus emphatically taught.

3. A wounded prophet (20:38): When the prophet gave the command to wound him to another man, the second man instantly complied. He probably had seen or heard what had happened to the first man who rejected that command. The prophet next put bandages over his head wound to conceal his identity. Then he went to wait for the return of the king.

450

4. A prophet's parable (20:39-40): As the king passed by, the prophet, playing the role of a wounded soldier, cried out to Ahab to render a royal judgment. He pretended to be the victim of an unjust penalty assessed against him by a superior officer. He told the king that during the battle he had been ordered to guard a prisoner. If that prisoner escaped, he forfeited his life or else must pay a talent of silver (about 75 lbs.). Since common soldiers never carried so much money, the penalty for allowing escape of the prisoner was death. The prisoner did in fact escape *while I was busy with other duties.* Upon hearing these circumstances, Ahab declared the death penalty to be fair and just. A soldier who allowed a prisoner to escape should be executed.

5. Ahab condemned (20:41-42): The prophet then ripped away his bandage disguise. Ahab recognized him immediately as one of the prophets. Slowly the prophet pronounced the doom of the king. God had appointed Ben-Hadad to utter destruction; he was a condemned man. Yet the king to whom God had granted the victory had dismissed Ben-Hadad instead of executing him. Therefore Ahab will forfeit his life for that of Ben-Hadad. By means of his parable the prophet had succeeded in getting Ahab to pronounce his own judgment.

6. Assessment of Ahab's conduct: In spite of the clear condemnation of Ahab's conduct, some commentators seek to commend him on his merciful dealings with Ben-Hadad. An assessment of his conduct must be made in the light of three facts. 1) Ahab was not free to do as he pleased with Ben-Hadad. This was God's war and God's victory. Yahweh should have been consulted through priestly or prophetic oracle before disposing of the prisoners. 2) Ahab's previous dealings with Ben-Hadad (cf. 20:6) should have indicated to him the character of this king. In the interest of future peace and security, Ahab should have executed the Aramean. 3) Surely the fate of Agag, Oreb and Zeeb as well as other aggressors against Israel should have signaled Ahab as to how to deal with Ben-Hadad.

7. Ahab's apprehension (20:43): Under the divine threat and rebuke, Ahab returned to his campaign quarters sullen and angry. He realized that the prophet's prediction regarding the outcome of the battle had been fulfilled; he was therefore filled with apprehension that this new prediction will also prove true. With all the joy of victory removed, Ahab returned to the capital in Samaria.

451

YAHWEH AND
A SOCIAL THREAT
1 Kings 21:1-15

Shortly after the battle of Aphek, another incident transpired that brought further prophetic condemnation to Ahab. This time the bearer of bad news was Ahab's bitter enemy Elijah.

Covetousness of the King
1 Kings 21:1-7

A. Ahab's Pouting (1 Kings 21:1-4)

Near Ahab's second palace in Jezreel was a vineyard possessed by a man named Naboth. This plot of ground Ahab dearly coveted. The vineyard was not required for the public welfare, but to satisfy a purely selfish personal whim. Ahab tried to induce Naboth to sell the vineyard, or to exchange it for one the king already owned. He, however, refused to sell his property to one outside his family. Rebuffed by Naboth, Ahab returned to the palace to give vent to childish grief. Sullen and angry he pouted in his private chambers, refusing to partake of food.

B. Jezebel's Plotting (1 Kings 21:5-7)

Jezebel went to Ahab's room to inquire as to the reason for the king's loss of appetite. The queen was shocked when she heard what triggered her husband's depression. She did not even bother to ask why Naboth had refused to sell his property. This queen came from a royal family that was accustomed to get whatever it wanted. She urged Ahab to arise and eat. She promised to see to it that he got his vineyard.

Conspiracy against Naboth
1 Kings 21:8-16

A. Instructions to Thugs (1 Kings 21:8-10)

In short order Jezebel set in motion a plot to eliminate Naboth. Letters, written in the name of the king and sealed with the royal seal, were sent to the elders and judges of Jezreel. Jezebel's plan was simple. A fast was to be proclaimed in Jezreel, as though the city had

452

come under a curse because of some undisclosed sin. Naboth was to be accorded his usual seat of honor. During the assembly two *sons of Belial,* i.e., worthless men, publicly were to accuse Naboth of having cursed both God and the king. Such cursing, according to the law, was a capital crime (cf. Exodus 22:28; Deuteronomy 13:11). Naboth then was to be stoned. Because the alleged crime was treason, all of Naboth's property would be forfeited to the crown.

B. Plot Executed (1 Kings 21:11-14)

1. Naboth executed (21:11-14): The elders of Jezreel must have been as wicked as their queen. Their ready compliance with the directive of Jezebel shows not only the moral degradation of the day, but also the terror that the name of Jezebel inspired. The crowd believed the testimony of the two witnesses over the protests of Naboth. Convinced that this man had brought down the curse of God on their city, the crowd shoved Naboth outside the city walls where they stoned him to death. The elders returned their word to Jezebel in Samaria that the dastardly deed had been done.

2. Ahab jubilant (21:15-16): Jezebel immediately informed Ahab that the way was now clear for him to claim the property of Naboth. The queen's words were full of irony. Naboth had refused to sell his property; now he had lost his life and his property. The moody Ahab was jubilant when he heard that Naboth was dead. He arose immediately to go down to Jezreel to take possession of the vineyard.

Condemnation by Elijah
1 Kings 21:17-26

A. Confrontation (1 Kings 21:17-20)

1. Elijah's pronouncement (21:17-19): God did not allow the ruthless murder of Naboth to go unrebuked. Elijah was dispatched to meet Ahab in the vineyard that he had confiscated. The prophet opened the conversation with a penetrating rhetorical question: *Have you murdered and also taken possession?* This indictment was followed by a pronouncement of doom on Ahab. In the place where the dogs licked Naboth's blood, dogs will lick the blood of Ahab!

2. Ahab's reaction (21:20): Ahab was shocked at the sudden appearance of Elijah whom he had not seen since the Carmel contest. The conscience-stricken king could only mutter: *Have you found me out, O my enemy?* Ahab considered Elijah his enemy because it

453

seemed that this prophet always opposed him. Yet it was not because of personal animosity that Elijah sought out Ahab, but because the king had *sold himself,* i.e., completely surrendered himself, to do what was evil in the eyes of Yahweh.

3. *Explanation:* Ahab, the supreme magistrate of the land, may have been ignorant of the tactics by which Jezebel had procured the vineyard for him; but he had acquiesced in her infamous crime after its accomplishment, and he was anxious to reap the benefits of it. Thus instead of punishing his guilty wife and those who had carried out her instructions, the king, by his actions, had sanctioned the crime. Therefore, the prophetic pronouncement was directed against Ahab.

B. Elaboration (1 Kings 21:21-24)

After he explained the reason for the sentence, Elijah elaborated upon it. The judgment involved every male descendant of Ahab. Just as the royal houses of Jeroboam and Baasha had been exterminated, so now the house of Ahab will be wiped out. By his actions Ahab had provoked God to anger. He had also encouraged Israel to sin; therefore he must be punished. Furthermore, the queen must also taste the wrath of God. The dogs will eat Jezebel beside the wall of Jezreel, the scene of her latest crime. Dogs and birds will devour the unburied corpses of Ahab's family.

C. Significance (1 Kings 21:25-26)

The Naboth incident clearly reveals the social breakdown of Ahab's kingdom and the extent to which Jezebel's Phoenicianization had succeeded. Years of flirtation with pagan practices were taking their toll. The rights of individuals guaranteed in the Sinai covenant were being ignored. The king was no longer under the law, but was superior to it. No predecessor had so completely abandoned the ways of Yahweh. Through Jezebel, Canaanite Baal worship had been reintroduced in the northern kingdom.

Contrition of Ahab
1 Kings 21:27-29

Ahab was deeply affected by the dire predictions of Elijah. By several outward signs he manifested his inward repentance for the crimes he had condoned. He rent his garments, put on sackcloth, fasted and even slept in his sackcloth. He also *went about softly,* i.e., humbly, contritely. Taking note of this royal repentance, Yahweh sent an important word to Elijah that in effect deferred the threatened judgment until the days of his son. This is no example of the innocent suffering for the guilty. God knew in advance that the son was going to be worse than his father. Furthermore, the son would also have the option of repentance by which still further reprieve could be granted. Judgment was deferred to give the house of Ahab another chance. How marvelous is the divine patience!

32
JEHOSHAPHAT
THE COMPROMISER
1 Kings 22-2 Kings 1, 3

Chapter Chronology

		852	
AHAB		Ahaziah	Joram
		853 852	
			849
JEHOSHAPHAT			
873			

Following the second defeat of Ben-Hadad, the Arameans and Israelites remained at peace for over two years. At that time Ahab received a state visit from King Jehoshaphat of Judah, a king with considerable military strength (2 Chronicles 17:10-19). The northern king needed the help of his southern ally to help recover territory which Ben-Hadad had failed to return to Israel in compliance with the treaty of Aphek (cf. 1 Kings 20:34).

JEHOSHAPHAT'S
ALLIANCE WITH AHAB
1 Kings 22:1-40

Exactly at what point Jehoshaphat and Ahab formalized an alliance the text does not say. The alliance, however, was sealed by Jehoshaphat taking the daughter of Ahab and Jezebel as a wife for his son Jehoram. Shortly thereafter Jehoshaphat made a state visit to the sister kingdom. At that time Ahab pressed Jehoshaphat for a joint military action.

Proposal
1 Kings 22:1-5

A. Focal Point (1 Kings 22:1-3)

The focal point of Ahab's concern was the fortress of Ramoth-Gilead that was located east of the Sea of Galilee on the frontier with

457

Aram. During the course of Jehoshaphat's visit, Ahab broached the question of a possible joint campaign to recapture the city. The alliance between Israel and Judah was new. Ahab probably wondered how the pious prince of Judah would respond to this proposal.

B. Response (1 Kings 22:4-5)
Jehoshaphat should have forthrightly refused aid to Ahab (cf. 2 Chronicles 19:2). Instead, however, he expressed his enthusiastic interest in engaging in this war. Probably Jehoshaphat feared the growing power of Damascus and considered that it was in his own best interest to dislodge Ben-Hadad from his stronghold in Gilead. Being the godly man that he was, Jehoshaphat insisted that the will of Yahweh be sought regarding the proposed campaign.

Court Prophets
1 Kings 22:6-12

A. Their Unified Prediction (1 Kings 22:6)
Having primed his court prophets, Ahab was not unwilling to comply with the request of Jehoshaphat. When the king put the question of the campaign to the four hundred prophets, they dutifully and unanimously urged Ahab to go up to Ramoth-Gilead. They promised that the Lord (*adonay*) will give the city into the hands of the king. These four hundred were not the prophets of Baal or Asherah. They were renegade prophets of Yahweh who were part of the apostate official calf worship of the northern kingdom. They were king-appointed rather than God-called prophets.

B. Jehoshaphat's Suspicion (1 Kings 22:7-9)
Jehoshaphat was suspicious of the four hundred. He asked if there might yet be another prophet of Yahweh whose advice could be solicited. Indeed Micaiah the son of Imlah could be consulted. Ahab, however, admitted that he hated this man of God because he consistently had prophesied evil concerning the royal family. Jehoshaphat then administered a mild rebuke to Ahab for insinuating that a prophet of God could be motivated by personal dislike for the king. Under the circumstances Ahab could hardly refuse to permit his guest to hear what Micaiah might have to say. So he dispatched an officer to fetch the man of God.

C. Antics of the Prophets (1 Kings 22:10-12)

The four hundred continued their prophesying even while Micaiah was being summoned. In order to convince the dubious Jehoshaphat that the campaign was safe, Zedekiah, the leader of the four hundred, constructed *horns of iron.* These symbols of power may have been nothing more than two iron spikes held on the forehead. *With these you shall thrust through Aram until you have consumed them.* This dramatic prediction was made in the form of a *thus says Yahweh.* The rest of the four hundred continued to repeat their initial promises of success except that they followed the lead of Zedekiah in using the name Yahweh in this utterance.

Micaiah's Prophecy
1 Kings 22:13-28

A. Micaiah's Summons (1 Kings 22:13-14)

The messenger sent to fetch Micaiah knew that Ahab needed to secure an endorsement of the proposed campaign from all the prophets. Any negative note might cause the pious Jehoshaphat to withdraw from the venture. So the messenger pled with the man of God to join the four hundred in approving the campaign. The messenger, however, misunderstood this man of God as much as did his king. Micaiah could not be intimidated or bribed. He was not afraid to stand alone. He would speak only what Yahweh revealed to him.

B. Micaiah's Sarcastic Assurance (1 Kings 22:15-16)

Ahab put to Micaiah the same question that he had put to the four hundred. The prophet responded with the identical answer that the court prophets had given. Ahab's hollow tone had revealed the insincerity of his question. He really did not want to know the will of God; he wanted to be deceived. No doubt Micaiah's mocking tone showed that his words were sarcastic. In an effort to impress Jehoshaphat, Ahab pretended to be greatly distressed over the prophet's manifest insincerity. Before he realized what he was saying, Ahab blurted out that what he wanted to hear was the word of Yahweh. This was a tacit admission that what he had heard from the four hundred was not the word of the Lord.

C. Micaiah's First Vision (1 Kings 22:17-18)

At this juncture the tone and demeanor of Micaiah suddenly changed. The man of God became deadly serious. He had seen a vision of Israel scattered upon the hills with no shepherd; he heard the voice of God directing those scattered ones to return to their homes in peace. No one in the royal assembly failed to see that Micaiah was foretelling the dispersion of the Israelite army as a result of the death of their king. Ahab certainly understood the thrust of these words. He had demanded the word of Yahweh and had received it. Lest Jehoshaphat be unduly influenced by this dire prediction Ahab quickly suggested that these words were but further evidence of the prophet's prejudice toward the king.

D. Micaiah's Second Vision (1 Kings 22:19-23)

The insinuation that Micaiah spoke out of malice brought forth a vigorous rebuttal from the man of God. At sometime in the past Micaiah had seen another vision relating to Ahab. He had seen Yahweh on his heavenly throne surrounded by all the hosts of heaven, i.e., angels. Yahweh asked for suggestions as to how Ahab might be enticed to go up to Ramoth-Gilead that he might be slain there. Various schemes were suggested. Finally *the spirit,* i.e., the evil spirit, affirmed that he could entice Ahab. The plan was for this spirit to take control of the mouths of Ahab's prophets that they in turn might persuade the king to go up against Ramoth-Gilead. Yahweh then granted to this spirit permission to so entice Ahab. Thus, declared Micaiah, Yahweh had put a lying spirit in the mouths of all Ahab's prophets; they had spoken falsehood. Furthermore, the prediction of calamity against Ahab had not just come from Micaiah, but from Yahweh who spoke through him.

E. Important Issues

Several important questions remain to be answered concerning Micaiah's vision.

1.   How can it be that Yahweh found it necessary to take counsel from the angelic hosts? Prophetic visions are anthropomorphic. They do not always correspond to reality. Such visions are the vehicle used to convey a cardinal truth to the mind of the prophet. In this case the truth is that Ahab's death in battle had been foreordained in the counsels of God, and that divine wisdom had devised a means for accomplishing this goal.

460

2. Who was the spirit who volunteered to entice Ahab? Keil and others see the spirit as a personification of the spirit of prophecy which takes hold of a man and makes him a prophet. Other commentators, however, are probably correct when they identify the spirit as Satan. That Satan has or at least did have access to the heavenly council chambers is attested by the opening chapters of the Book of Job.

3. How can the all Holy One give his sanction to deceit and lying for the purpose of tempting Ahab to his death? Here one must distinguish between the permissive and the positive will of God. Yahweh permitted the evil spirit to do his evil work. The same thought is expressed in Ezekiel 14:9: *If the prophet be deceived ... I, Yahweh, have deceived that prophet.* Ahab *wished* to be guided by false prophets. The justice of God permitted him to be so guided.

F. Micaiah and Zedekiah (1 Kings 22:24-25)

1. Assault on Micaiah (22:24): Zedekiah, one of the four hundred, bristled at the charge that he and his cohorts had been possessed by a spirit of lies. Without warning he stepped forward and smote Micaiah on the cheek. At the same time Zedekiah shouted: *Where did the spirit of Yahweh pass over from me to speak to you?* Zedekiah was conscious of some force beyond himself that compelled him to speak his prophetic word. How could the Spirit of Yahweh speak one message through Zedekiah, and something quite different through Micaiah? This scoffing question was intended to counter the story Micaiah had related so dramatically. Ridicule is one of the most effective ways of countering the arguments of an opponent.

2. Micaiah's response (22:25): Micaiah was not intimidated by the bombastic Zedekiah. He did not answer directly the insolent question. Rather he confidently affirmed that one day Zedekiah will *see,* i.e., perceive the truth. Only then will Zedekiah have the prophetic vision correctly to assess the political situation. In that day when Micaiah's predictions concerning the defeat of the armies of Israel were fulfilled, Zedekiah will hasten into hiding out of shame and perhaps fear of reprisals at the hand of the queen.

G. Conclusion (1 Kings 22:26-28)

1. Micaiah imprisoned (22:26-27): The two kings looked on the assault of Micaiah without protest. When the brief prophetic confrontation was over, Ahab ordered Micaiah returned to his prison cell. There he was to remain under the watchful eye of Amon the governor of the city and Joash, one of Ahab's own sons. Instructions were given that Micaiah was to receive only bread and water until the king returned from Ramoth-Gilead in peace.

2. *Micaiah's defiant shout (22:28):* Probably owing to the presence of Jehoshaphat, Micaiah escaped with no more severe punishment. Still the man of God was undaunted. He was willing to stake his prophetic reputation on the fulfillment of this one prediction. If Ahab returned in peace, then Yahweh truly had not spoken to him. He was willing to face the capital punishment to which he was liable in that case. Before being dragged from the place, Micaiah shouted forth a call for all peoples to take note of the predictions that he just had made.

Death of Ahab
1 Kings 22:29-40

A. Ramoth-Gilead Campaign

The two kings were not deterred by the ominous predictions of Micaiah. They proceeded immediately to Ramoth-Gilead. Ahab's action is in character; that of Jehoshaphat is more difficult to explain. Why did the godly king of Judah reject the advice of God's prophet? Some (or all) of the following considerations may help to explain his actions.

- Jehoshaphat already had committed himself to the war effort (cf. verse 4).
- The hospitality extended by his host may have obligated Jehoshaphat to acquiesce.
- He may have feared being labeled a coward.
- Those present in the assembly were treating Micaiah's prophecy with disdain.
- Ahab may have convinced Jehoshaphat to dismiss the threats of Micaiah in view of the long-standing animosity that existed between the king and this prophet.
- Jehoshaphat's own interests were threatened by the rising Aramean power.

B. Worthless Precautions (1 Kings 22:29-30)

On the eve of battle Ahab came up with what he thought was an ingenious plan to frustrate the dire predictions that had been made against him. Micaiah had seen *Israel* scattered as sheep having no master. To thwart this prediction, Ahab decided in effect to relinquish his role of leader of the host. He decided not to lead the army, as kings were accustomed to do, in his royal robes. Rather he disguised himself as a lesser officer. Since Jehoshaphat's life had not been threatened by the prophet, it was unnecessary for him to take similar precautions.

B. Jehoshaphat's Danger (1 Kings 22:31-33)

Ben-Hadad directed his thirty-two chariot officers to concentrate their attack on the king of Israel. The Aramean rightly reasoned that the death of the king will terminate the war. Seeing the royal robes of Jehoshaphat, the chariot captains pressed in that direction. When the king of Judah realized he had been singled out for concentrated attack, he cried out in desperation to God. Yahweh intervened on his behalf (2 Chronicles 18:31). The charioteers recognized that it was not Ahab that they were pursuing. So they turned away from Jehoshaphat.

C. Ahab's Wound (1 Kings 22:34-36)

1. Attempt to disguise it (22:34): Ahab's disguise could not avert the judgment of God. During the course of the battle, an Aramean soldier launched an arrow that was destined to find its mark in the breast of the king. Ahab knew he had been mortally wounded. He ordered his chariot driver to wheel about and carry him away from the battle. Ahab did not want the army to discover what had happened lest they become discouraged and abandon the field. The fury of the battle, however, did not allow the chariot driver to comply with his king's order. To maintain a facade of normality, Ahab's servants propped him up in the chariot. Unable to attend to his wound, the king slowly bled to death.

2. Death of Ahab (22:35-36): At evening Ahab died. His blood poured out into the floor of the chariot. When the army saw that their king had fallen, a shout went up among the troops. They urged one another to terminate the battle and make their way to their homes.

D. End of the Campaign (1 Kings 22:37-38)

463

What a sad sight that must have been as the battle-weary, leaderless troops made their way back to Samaria. There they buried their fallen king. At the city pool, where harlots customarily bathed, they washed the chariot of the king. Packs of scavenger dogs licked up the blood that had been flushed from the chariot. This fulfilled the word that Yahweh had spoken concerning Ahab through Micaiah and, in essence, through Elijah as well.

E. Ahab's Accomplishments (1 Kings 22:39-40)

As the account of Ahab's long reign concludes, two other brief notices about his accomplishments are given. He, like his father, was a city builder. Ahab built several towns. He was perhaps most famous for his ivory palace, i.e., a house with ivory inlays. His son Ahaziah ("whom Yahweh upholds") succeeded him as king. This name perhaps suggests that, notwithstanding his flirtations with Baal worship, Ahab remained a believer in Yahweh.

Alliance Condemned
2 Chronicles 19:1-3

When Jehoshaphat returned to Jerusalem after his narrow escape at Ramoth-Gilead, Jehu the prophet went to see him. Jehu was the son of Hanani the seer who had condemned Asa for his alliance with Ben-Hadad (cf. 2 Chronicles 16:7). Jehu rebuked the king for entering an alliance with those *who hate Yahweh*. Jehu warned that compromise with the enemies of the Lord could bring the wrath of God against the king. Because of his reform efforts and his personal efforts to seek God, however, Yahweh promised to be lenient with Jehoshaphat.

JEHOSHAPHAT'S ALLIANCE WITH AHAB'S SON
1 Kings 22:48-53

Transition in the North
1 Kings 22:51-53

When Ahab fell at Ramoth-Gilead in 853 BC, he was succeeded on the throne of Israel by his son Ahaziah. This king, like his father, did evil in the eyes of Yahweh. He tolerated the calf worship that Jeroboam had instituted. In addition he served Baal. The sacred

464

historian points the finger at Jezebel as being one of the reasons for the evil direction of this eighth king of Israel.

Maritime Alliance
2 Chronicles 20:35-37

A. Planned Venture (2 Chronicles 20:35-36)
Ahaziah joined Jehoshaphat of Judah in attempting to revive the maritime enterprise of Solomon. The two kings had *Tarshish ships,* i.e., large sea-going vessels. They intended to sail these ships to Ophir and Tarshish (cf. 2 Chronicles 20:36). These ships were launched from the Red Sea port of Ezion-geber.

B. Prophetic Warning (2 Chronicles 20:37)
The prophet Eliezer appeared on the scene to *prophesy* against Jehoshaphat. He denounced Jehoshaphat for his alliance with Ahaziah. He announced that *Yahweh will destroy what you have made.* A tremendous storm dashed the ships to pieces before they got out of the harbor (cf. 1 Kings 22:48).

C. Second Venture Proposed (1 Kings 22:49)
The northern king attributed the smashing of the ships to the inexperience of Jehoshaphat's sailors. He proposed a second joint venture with the seamen from Judah. Because of their close association with the Phoenicians, some subjects of the northern kingdom may have been highly skilled sailors. Jehoshaphat, however, accepted the explanation of the prophet. He refused any further commercial alliance with Ahaziah.

ELIJAH'S CONFRONTATION
WITH AHAZIAH
2 Kings 1:1-17

Date: ca. 852 BC

Background
2 Kings 1:2

In his second year of rule, Ahaziah accidentally fell through the lattice that enclosed his upper chamber. As a result of this fall, the king was so injured that he lingered upon his bed hovering between life and death. In this desperate condition, Ahaziah dispatched messengers to Baal-Zebub, the god of the Philistine city of Ekron, to inquire as to his prognosis. The king, of course, wanted more than just information; a favorable oracle from a deity meant that the god will intervene on his behalf.

That a son of Jezebel preferred to consult Baal rather than Yahweh is not surprising. Why he chose this particular Baal god, however, is not clear. Perhaps Baal-Zebub had a reputation for granting favorable oracular verdicts. On the other hand, perhaps Ekron was the nearest of the ancient Baal shrines. The name Baal-Zebub means "lord of flies." Apparently this particular Baal was thought to prevent plagues of flies, or else was thought to send such plagues against his enemies.

Elijah's Announcement
2 Kings 1:3-8

A. Divine Commission (2 Kings 1:3-4)

For the second time (cf. 1 Kings 19:5, 7) an angel of God visited Elijah the prophet, instructing him to intercept the delegation that had been dispatched to Ekron. The actions of Ahaziah were a complete denial of the lordship of Yahweh. To consult a foreign oracle was tantamount to saying that the voice of God was wholly silent. The God of Israel did have a word for Ahaziah, albeit an unsolicited one. Because he had so grievously apostatized, God sentenced this king to die from the effects of his fall.

B. Ahaziah's Consternation (2 Kings 1:5-8)

Ahaziah inquired as to the reason for the hasty return of his messengers. They reported the message that the prophet had delivered. They described the man of God as being a hairy man (lit., a lord of hair) who was wearing a leather girdle. Normally the girdle was of soft material. From this description Ahaziah knew immediately that the message of doom had come from the same man who had predicted the death of his father. Some take the description of Elijah to mean that he was rough and unkempt with his hair and beard long. Others think the reference is to a shaggy garment that Elijah wore. In any case, Ahaziah realized that the dreaded adversary of his father and mother suddenly had reappeared.

Attempted Arrest
2 Kings 1:9-15

A. Soldiers Dispatched (2 Kings 1:9)

No doubt Ahaziah had been instructed by his wicked mother to take strong action against Elijah should this religious radical reappear. Though lying on his bed of affliction under the divine sentence of death, this king was so hardened, unrepentant and defiant that he ordered a unit of fifty soldiers to arrest Elijah. The size of the arrest force suggests that Ahaziah was challenging directly the power of the prophet and his God. Meanwhile, Elijah had positioned himself on a hill where he calmly awaited the showdown with the king.

B. Elijah Protected (2 Kings 1:10-12)

The captain of fifty approached the prophet, addressed him by his customary title, and ordered him to surrender. Elijah then prayed for God to vindicate his prophetic authority by destroying this band of soldiers. God heard that prayer. Fire (lightning?) came down from heaven to consume the captain and his fifty. Ahaziah sent another fifty to demand that Elijah come down *quickly*. The king apparently had grown impatient. Again the prophet prayed. Again fire from heaven consumed his adversaries.

C. Elijah's Surrender (2 Kings 1:13-15)

A third captain dispatched by the king escaped with his life because he humbled himself before God's prophet. He ascended the hill on which Elijah was still seated. He bowed himself before the prophet to beseech his compassion. Having heard of the fate of the previous units, he acknowledged that this man of God held his life and the lives of his men in his hand. He begged that Elijah might spare these men. The battle was now won. The honor of Elijah and the God he represented had been vindicated. An angel of God intervened at this point, directing the prophet to go with this captain.

Ahaziah's Death
2 Kings 1:16

Elijah did not change his message once he came face to face with this bitter antagonist. Boldly in the name of his God Elijah repeated the message that he originally had sent to the king by his messengers. Because of his gross apostasy, Ahaziah will die from his injuries. Shortly thereafter the king expired. Ahaziah's official reign is said to have been two years, but in actual time he reigned about a year overlapping 853-852 BC (1 Kings 22:51).

Because he had no son, Ahaziah's brother Jehoram (short spelling Joram) ruled in his stead. Thus a Jehoram ruled in Israel simultaneously with a Jehoram in Judah who in fact was his brother-in-law (2 Kings 1:17).[54] While Jehoram of Israel was evil, he was not as bad as his father and brother. Perhaps he had taken warning from the fates of his two predecessors. In any case, he *put away* the image of Baal that Ahab had erected in Samaria. This may indicate that he abolished the official status of Baalism in the northern kingdom. Jehoram's wickedness was that he continued the apostate calf worship introduced by Jeroboam back in 930 BC (2 Kings 3:2-3).

JEHOSHAPHAT
AND AHAB'S SECOND SON
2 Kings 3:1-17

Date: ca. 851 BC

For over three decades (874-841 BC) Jezebel was the most powerful figure in the northern kingdom. She dominated her husband Ahab, and her two sons Ahaziah and Jehoram. To a certain extent her influence reached Judah. In that southern kingdom Jezebel's son-in-law and grandson ruled as legitimate monarchs. In the year Jezebel died her daughter Athaliah seized the throne of Judah and ruled for seven years.

Moab Campaign
2 Kings 3:4-15a

A. Background (2 Kings 3:4-5)

---

[54]That Jehoshaphat and Ahab both named their sons Jehoram may have been intended as a symbol of the friendship between the two kingdoms. 2 Kings 1:17 states that the northern Jehoram came to the throne in the second year of the reign of the southern Jehoram. On the other hand, 2 Kings 3:1 states that the northern Jehoram came to the throne in the eighteenth year of Jehoshaphat. Experts in biblical chronology conclude that Jehoshaphat and his son Jehoram had a co regency that began in 853 BC.

For some years the Moabites were put under oppressive tribute by the Omri dynasty. They were forced to send to Samaria the wool of a hundred thousand sheep and goats. This extraordinarily heavy tribute drove the Moabites to rebellion at the first opportunity which, as it turned out, was the death of the powerful Ahab.

Jehoram mobilized his forces for an invasion of Moab. In this effort Jehoshaphat of Judah was again an ally. The good king does not seem to have learned anything from his disastrous military alliance with Ahab (1 Kings 22) and his equally disastrous commercial alliance with Ahaziah (2 Chronicles 20:35f).

B. Invasion Plan (2 Kings 3:6-10)

1. Reason for the plan (3:6-8): The plan suggested by Jehoshaphat called for the combined forces to take the circuitous route around the southern tip of the Dead Sea to attack Moab from the south. Two reasons dictated this decision. First, the king of Edom, currently a vassal of Judah, could contribute a contingent of troops if the expedition took the southern route. Second, Moab was probably less fortified on the southern frontier.

2. Near disaster (3:9-10): The torturous trip of a hundred miles through the barren wilderness of Judah took the allies seven days. What was thought to be a perennial stream in that region had failed due to a lengthy drought. The allies found themselves facing a desperate situation. The impious Jehoram was ready to blame their plight upon Yahweh. Yet no prophet of God had sanctioned this campaign. The allies had come together on their own accord, guided strictly by political interests. In despair born of unbelief, Jehoram assumed that Yahweh meant to deliver this host into the hands of the king of Moab.

C. Prophetic Presence (2 Kings 3:11-12)

1. Hopeful news (3:11): Being a man of faith, Jehoshaphat was not ready to throw up his hands in despair. In this desperate hour he wanted to confer with a prophet of God. How relieved he must have been to learn that Elisha had accompanied the expedition, apparently without the knowledge of Jehoram. In time past Elisha had been known as the one who *poured water on the hands of Elijah,* i.e., had been his servant. Now God demonstrated his power through this man for the first time before the kings of both Israel and Judah.

2. *Search for Elisha (3:12):* Jehoshaphat was delighted to learn that Elisha was present. He was convinced that *the word of Yahweh is with him.* Just how Jehoshaphat had come to have such regard for Elisha is uncertain. Perhaps it was the fact of Elisha's close association with Elijah that led Jehoshaphat to endorse Elisha as an authorized exponent of God's will. In any case, the allied kings were so desperate that *they* sought out Elisha rather than merely summoning him to their pavilion.

3. *Elisha's initial reaction (3:13):* When the three supplicants approached, Elisha unleashed a sarcastic verbal barrage against Jehoram. The halfhearted repentance of this monarch had not ingratiated him to this uncompromising man of God. Jehoram had no ground of appeal to the prophet. If this son of Jezebel wanted prophetic counsel, he should seek out the prophets of his father or mother.

4. *Plea of Jehoram (3:14-15a):* Jehoram responded to the prophetic sarcasm with meek deportment. In effect he begged the prophet that his initial response not be his final response. After all, it was not just the king of Israel who was in desperate straits. *Three* kings were in danger of falling to the king of Moab. To this Elisha responded with solemn adjuration that it was only because of the presence of the godly Jehoshaphat that he condescended to help the expedition. The prophet then called for a musician to play some soothing song so that he could bring himself into the proper frame of mind to receive the divine revelation.

Prophecy of Elisha
2 Kings 3:15b-25

A. Prediction (2 Kings 3:15b-18)

While the musician played, the *hand of Yahweh,* the power of the Spirit of God, came upon Elisha. He was able to reveal to the royal petitioners that Yahweh will deliver them from their plight. The kings were to have pits dug in the valley by means of which the precious water that they needed might be retained. A great storm was to arise many miles from the camp of the allies. The parched valley will shortly be filled with the runoff of that storm. Not only will Yahweh deliver the allies from their present danger, he will also deliver Moab into their hands.

B. Fulfillment (2 Kings 3:19-23)

True to the word of the prophet, the next morning about sunrise (*when the meal offering was offered*) a mighty stream of water filled the pits dug the day before. The Moabite army saw the reddish early morning sun reflecting off the water. Since there had been no rain during the night, the Moabites never suspected that the wadi near the allied camp was full of water. The confused movement of men and beasts about the trenches seen from a distance suggested hostilities. The Moabite officers concluded that the three invading armies had turned against one another in a bloody slaughter. Nothing remained to do but to gather the spoil from the camp of the allies. For this purpose the hosts of Moab surged forward in a disorderly rush.

C. Allied Victory (2 Kings 3:24-25)

The allies had anticipated the onrush of Moabites. They kept the main body of their men concealed within the camp as an ambush. When the first wave of greedy Moabites reached the camp, the allies rose up to smite and completely rout them. True to the prediction of Elisha, the allies destroyed the cities of Moab, spread stones over the fields, stopped up the wells, and felled the fruit trees. This devastation continued until finally only the stronghold of Kir-hareseth remained untouched. Allied slingers began to hurl their missiles over the wall of Kir-hareseth, thus grievously harassing the defenders.

Siege of Kir-hareseth
2 Kings 3:26-27

A. Attempted Breakout (2 Kings 3:26)

The fortunes of Moab continued to decline. The king then decided on a desperate gamble. Gathering seven hundred expert swordsmen, he attempted to break through the allied lines to reach the king of Edom.[55] Perhaps he regarded the king of Edom as the weakest member of the coalition, the least likely to offer effective resistance. This attempt failed. The Moabites were again forced back into their beleaguered fortress.

---

[55]By a very slight emendation in the text another reconstruction is possible. In Hebrew the words *Edom* and *Aram* are quite similar. It is possible that originally the text read *break through to the king of Aram,* in which case the text is pointing to a desperate effort on the part of the king of Moab to break through the allied lines to safety in the territories of Aram.

B. A Desperate Act (2 Kings 3:27)

The Moabite king then tried to appeal to his deity Chemosh for a miraculous deliverance. He took the crown prince and offered him up as a burnt offering upon the city wall in full view of both the defenders and the attackers. The sight of their king sacrificing his own firstborn son so stirred up the fury of the Moabites against Israel that they fought with almost superhuman strength. In the face of this determined opposition the allies began to weaken. Finally, the campaign was called off. Each of the confederates returned to his own land.

RETALIATORY
INVASION OF JUDAH
2 Chronicles 20:1-30

Date: ca. 850 BC

In retaliation for assisting Jehoram in his effort to re-subjugate Moab, Judah itself experienced an invasion. The Moabites, Ammonites and the Meunites came to make war against Jehoshaphat (2 Chronicles 20:1).

Judah's Plight
2 Chronicles 20:2-4

The invasion of the army from beyond the Dead Sea caught Jehoshaphat by surprise. By the time he got the word the enemy was at Engedi on the western bank of the Dead Sea well within the territory of Judah. The king was afraid. He *turned his attention to seek Yahweh*. He proclaimed a fast. Citizens from throughout Judah gathered to seek the Lord.

Jehoshaphat's Prayer
2 Chronicles 20:5-13

The king stood before the assembly of his people in the court of the temple and led in a wonderful prayer. He acknowledged the great and irresistible power of Yahweh. He expressed confidence that the Lord heard the cries of distress that came to him from before his temple. In narrative prayer the king described how Judah had been

472

invaded by a force determined to drive God's people out of their inheritance. Jehoshaphat closed the prayer by admitting powerlessness and ignorance in the face of this invasion. In this situation Judah was totally dependent upon Yahweh.

Jahaziel's Prophecy
2 Chronicles 20:14-19

A. Prediction of Assistance (2 Chronicles 20:14-17)

In the midst of that assembly the Spirit of Yahweh came upon a Levitical singer named Jahaziel. He urged the nation not to fear before the invaders. *The battle is not yours, but God's.* Tomorrow they should march against the enemy, but they will not need to fight. They will *stand and see the salvation of Yahweh.*

B. Response (2 Chronicles 20:18-19)

In response to this encouraging word, Jehoshaphat bowed his face to the ground. All his subjects joined their king in worshiping Yahweh. The Levitical singers stood up to praise the Lord *with a very loud voice.*

Confident Praise
2 Chronicles 20:20-23

A. Marching to Confrontation (2 Chronicles 20:20-21)

In the morning Jehoshaphat addressed his troops as they prepared to march against the enemy. He urged them to put their trust in Yahweh and his prophets. He ordered the Levitical choir, dressed in their holy attire, to lead the military procession.

B. Divine Intervention (2 Chronicles 20:22-23)

Even as the army of Judah marched toward the confrontation singing praises, God *set ambushes* among the invaders. The Ammonites and Moabites destroyed those from Mount Seir (Edom). Then they turned on one another. So the entire invading force was routed before the army of Judah even arrived at the scene.

Abundant Plunder
2 Chronicles 20:24-30

A. Praise on the Spot (2 Chronicles 20:24-26)

Gathering the spoils from the camp of the invaders took three days. On the fourth day the jubilant army of Jehoshaphat assembled publicly to bless the Lord. They named the spot the Valley of Beracah, i.e., "blessing."

B. Praise at the Temple (2 Chronicles 20:27-30)

The army returned to Jerusalem triumphantly to the sound of various musical instruments. A joyous throng filled the courts of the temple where only days before they had stood trembling. News of the miraculous deliverance put the dread of Judah's God in surrounding nations. From that day forward *the kingdom of Jehoshaphat was at peace, for his God gave him rest on every side.*

33
JEZEBEL BATTLES
CONTINUE
2 Kings 2, 4-8

Chapter Chronology

			841
	Joram		
852			
		841	
Jeho-shaphat	Jehoram		Ahaziah
	848		

JEZEBELIAN
INFLUENCE IN JUDAH
2 Chronicles 21-22

Jezebel's Son-In-Law
2 Kings 8:16-24

A. Apostasy

Jezebel's son-in-law Jehoram reigned as a coregent with Jehoshaphat from 853 BC until the death of his father in 849 BC. The independent reign of Jehoram lasted eight years (848-841 BC). Influenced by his evil wife Athaliah—Jezebel's daughter—Jehoram departed from the righteous course of his father. Shortly after taking the throne he put to death his six brothers in order to solidify his position. At the same time he executed many princes, no doubt for the same reason. Soon afterwards he *made high places in the mountains of Judah, and caused the inhabitants of Jerusalem to commit fornication,* i.e., become idolaters (2 Chronicles 21:11).

B. Grace (2 Kings 8:18-19)

The apostasy of Jehoram of Judah merited national destruction. God, however, had made promises to David and to his seed after him. These promises would not be fulfilled if Judah's lamp of national existence were now removed. The long-suffering of God with respect to David's dynasty was demonstrated in that he bore with Judah for about three centuries longer until at last their cup of iniquity was full. Though he could not yet destroy Judah, the Lord did bring certain chastisements upon Jehoram.

C. Warning (2 Chronicles 21:12-15)
    1. Condemnation (21:12-13): Jehoram received a letter from Elijah who, as of 848 BC had not yet been translated to heaven. The prophet condemned the king of Judah for 1) rejecting the ways of his father Jehoshaphat and his grandfather Asa; 2) walking in the ways of the kings of Israel; 3) leading his people to engage in idolatrous worship; and 4) slaying his brothers who were better than he.
    2. Punishment (21:14-15): Because of Jehoram's wickedness, Yahweh will strike Judah, the royal family and the king himself with a heavy blow. Jehoram would experience a slow and painful disease of his bowels.

D. Political Chastisements (2 Kings 8:20-22)
    Judah experienced two major political setbacks during the reign of Jehoram.
    1. Edomite revolt (2 Kings 8:20-21): The Edomites revolted and appointed for their nation an independent king. Jehoram tried to crush this rebellion, but his efforts were almost disastrous. Edomites surrounded his position at Zair near the southern tip of the Dead Sea. Only by a daring night dash was Jehoram able to break through the enemy lines and thus prevent annihilation. His army was so unnerved by this experience that they dispersed to their homes. Jehoram was never in a position to make any further invasion of Edom.
    2. Philistine invasion (2 Chronicles 21:16): Second, the Philistines invaded Judah in the days of Jehoram. Probably in connection with this invasion Libnah, located in the lowlands of Judah on the edge of Philistia, also revolted (2 Kings 8:22).

E. Illness and Death (2 Kings 8:23-24)
    For two years Jehoram suffered with an incurable disease of his bowels. The king was buried in that portion of Jerusalem built by David, but not in the royal tombs there (2 Chronicles 21:20). He was followed on the throne by his son Ahaziah, who is also called Jehoahaz (2 Chronicles 21:17) and Azariah (2 Chronicles 22:6).

TRANSLATION OF ELIJAH
2 Kings 2:1-25

Date: ca. 849 BC

Elijah continued as the leader of the prophetic opposition to the house of Ahab until about 848 BC. When he was translated into heaven, his assistant Elisha became the leader of the prophets.

Final Visits
2 Kings 2:1-5

After his call at Abel-meholah (cf. 1 Kings 19:21), Elisha had become the constant companion and faithful attendant of Elijah. The latter had no fixed residence, but wandered from place to place as the Spirit of God led him (2 Kings 2:1).

A. Gilgal Visit (2 Kings 2:2)

In the course of their travels the two prophets arrived at Gilgal. Three times Elijah asked his attendant to remain behind. He knew his days on earth were numbered, and he wished to spend these final days in solitude. Under ordinary circumstances Elisha would have complied with the request of his master. The younger prophet had a premonition if not a revelation that Elijah shortly was going to be departing from the earth. Elisha refused to allow himself to be deprived of those final hours of fellowship and instruction. Three times in this narrative Elisha took a double oath not to leave the side of Elijah.

B. Bethel Visit (2 Kings 2:3-4)

1. Concern of the students (2:3): From Gilgal the two men of God went to Bethel, the religious capital of the northern kingdom. Elijah may have had instructions for the prophets there. The student prophets called Elisha aside and warned him that he was about to lose his master and teacher. Elisha answered the students curtly. He knew what was about to transpire without being forewarned by this band of students. *Keep still,* he instructed them. Such a solemn event should not be the subject of idle chatter.

2. Elisha's commitment (2:4): At Bethel Elijah again instructed Elisha to tarry at that place. The old prophet had yet another journey to take, down the rugged descent from the mountains of Ephraim to

477

Jericho in the Jordan valley. Again Elisha refused to turn aside. Elisha repeated the same oath he had earlier taken. Once again his master yielded. So the two men of God came to Jericho twenty miles distant. Once again the sons of the prophets called Elisha aside and shared with him their prophetic premonition. Once again Elisha administered a gentle rebuke to the students.

C. Jericho Visit (2 Kings 2:5-6)

At Jericho, Elijah made his third and final attempt to separate himself from his faithful attendant. Yahweh had directed the grand old prophet to go to the Jordan. Perhaps Elisha should remain at Jericho where there was food and fellowship and shelter. Elisha, however, was staunch in his insistence that he spend these last hours with his master regardless of where the Lord might lead.

Final Words
2 Kings 2:7-10

A. River Crossing (2 Kings 2:7-8)

Fifty prophetic students followed Elijah and Elisha from Jericho. Out of respect for Elijah's desire for solitude at this moment, these students hung back and finally stopped altogether on a little hill where they had a commanding view of the Jordan Valley. They watched with eager curiosity as the two prophets reached the bank of Jordan. There Elijah took his mantle, rolled it up so that it resembled a rod, and smote the waters with it. Instantly the waters parted so that the two men walked across on dry land.

B. Conversation (2 Kings 2:9-10)

1. Elisha's request (2:9): With his time on earth very short, Elijah wished to leave his faithful follower some parting gift as a sign of his love. Whatever Elisha desired, if it were within his power, the older prophet would grant. Elisha requested a double portion of Elijah's spirit. The *double portion* was the right of the eldest son who also had authority over members of the family once the father was gone. Asking for the *double portion* was equivalent to asking that he be regarded as Elijah's successor.

2. Elijah's response (2:10): Granting such a request was not directly within the power of Elijah. Only God could designate a man as spiritual leader of the nation. Elijah could do no more than leave the matter in the hands of God. If God should grant to Elisha the privilege of actually witnessing Elijah's departure into heaven, this would be the sign that his request had been granted. From this it appears that the chariot and horses that Elijah saw were not ordinarily visible to the physical eye.

Final Moments
2 Kings 2:11-12

A. Chariot of Fire (2 Kings 2:11)
The conversation of the two men of God was interrupted by the appearance of a chariot of fire pulled by horses of fire. The *fire* is probably an earthly description of celestial glory. The atmosphere was in turbulence at the moment the chariot whisked Elijah away up into the heavens. Elisha saw this stupendous sight. He knew that his request for a double portion of Elijah's spirit had been granted.

B. Elisha's Response (2 Kings 2:12)
At first sight of that heavenly chariot, Elisha cried out in dazed wonder: *My father, my father! The chariot of Israel and its horses!* The term *father* suggests that Elisha regarded Elijah as his teacher. Perhaps he even felt like Elijah's adopted son. Elijah himself was the chariot of Israel and its horsemen. He was the great protector of the nation. Later this same figurative form of address is used of Elisha (cf. 2 Kings 13:14).

Recognition of Elisha
2 Kings 2:13-25

When his friend and spiritual father disappeared into the clouds, Elisha tore his clothes in grief. Sadly Elisha picked up the mantle that had fallen from the shoulders of Elijah and walked back to the edge of Jordan (2:12).

A. Miracle at the Jordan (2 Kings 2:13-15)
1. Divine confirmation (2:13-14): In imitation of the actions of his master, Elisha smote the waters of the river with the mantle. At the same time he cried: *Where is Yahweh God of Elijah?* Elisha wondered if the all-powerful God who had so blessed the ministry his master was still with his people now that Elijah had departed. When

479

the waters instantly parted, Elisha knew the answer to that question. By enabling him to repeat Elijah's last miracle, Yahweh gave assurance to Elisha that the divine power was going to be available to him throughout his prophetic ministry.

2. *Recognition by the students (2:15):* When the sons of the prophets saw Elisha returning from the Jordan alone they concluded that the spirit of Elijah rested upon him. On what basis they reached this conclusion is not clear. Perhaps they had witnessed the miracle that Elisha had performed at the river; or they may have inferred that the leadership had passed to Elisha because he was now wearing the mantle of his master. In any case, they came forth and bowed before him. Thus the student prophets accorded to Elisha the recognition they previously had given to Elijah.

B. Request of the Students (2 Kings 2:16-18)

1. *Concern about Elijah (2:16):* The sons of the prophets, having been informed of the ascension of Elijah, were quite concerned about the well-being of their former master. They assumed that the Spirit of God had whisked him away only to cast him down in some remote place. So they requested that Elisha give permission for fifty of the more robust men among them to make a thorough search of the rocky ridges and ravines of the Transjordan territory. They could not bear the thought of leaving the old prophet in such a barren spot. Elisha knew that the effort would be futile. So he rejected the first petition made of him as leader of the prophetic band.

2. *Search for Elijah (2:17-18):* The sons of the prophets continued to urge Elisha to permit them to undertake the search until he was ashamed to refuse them any longer. He reluctantly gave them the permission that they sought. Fifty men searched for three days. They found nothing. Elisha waited patiently at Jericho for the zealous young men to return from their futile mission. Because his veracity and wisdom to some extent had been questioned, Elisha reminded these young men of his previous advice to them.

C. Healing Noxious Waters (2 Kings 2:19-22)

1. *Request of the local officials (2:19):* Having heard of the recent miracle performed by Elisha at the Jordan, the civic authorities of Jericho came to the prophet to seek his aid in removing the one unfortunate drawback to their otherwise pleasant community. A bitter spring of water gushed forth near Jericho that sent its waters in

rivulets across the plain to the Jordan. Nothing could grow near this water; cattle drinking this water aborted.

2. *Elisha's response (2:20-22):* Elisha called for a new vase filled with salt. As he poured the salt into the spring, he uttered a pronouncement in the name of Yahweh to the effect that never again will that spring produce death and miscarrying among people and stock. The waters were instantly and permanently made whole. The so-called Spring of the Sultan near the ancient ruins of Jericho may be the very spring referred to in this passage. The salt and the *new* vase were intended to teach that impurity can only be cleansed by what is wholly pure.

D. Cursing the Bethel Youth (2 Kings 2:23-24)

1. *Mockery by the youth (2:23):* After a brief stay at Jericho, Elisha visited Bethel, probably to inform the sons of the prophets there about what had transpired in Transjordan. On the outskirts of the city the prophet was confronted by a gang of ruffians who viciously mocked him. They jeered: *Go up, O baldhead!* This may be an allusion to the recent rumor that Elijah had ascended to heaven. These unbelieving urchins were urging the prematurely bald Elisha to imitate his master.

2. *Elisha's curse (2:24a):* The juvenile delinquents continued to follow behind, hooting and jeering at this man of God who now was the official representative of God on earth. Having endured this mockery and potential personal danger as long as he could, Elisha turned and calmly *cursed* these hoodlums in the name of Yahweh. This cursing consisted of pronouncing a negative prophecy against them. He may have said something like this: May evil and calamity fall upon you. Under the Law of Moses, God's ministers were required to "curse" the disobedient (Deuteronomy 27:14-26).

3. *Two bears (2:24b):* In order to teach these young men a lesson and at the same time vindicate his prophet in Bethel, God stirred up two she-bears to come out of a nearby woods and attack the offenders. These angry bears *tore* forty-two of these fellows. The text does not indicate to what extent these young men were injured. This frightening example of God's wrath was no doubt intended to serve as an unforgettable lesson to a new generation that was growing up in contempt of God and true religion.

E. Further Travels (2 Kings 2:25)

481

From Bethel, Elisha went up to Mount Carmel where presumably another group of the sons of the prophets was located. The purpose of his trip was doubtlessly the same as for his trip to Bethel, viz., to share with these men of God his firsthand knowledge of the exodus of Elijah. This trip also might have been to commemorate the great victory over Baal that had been won at that place. Having completed this mission, Elisha returned to the capital at Samaria. This prophet did not choose to imitate the semi-ascetic lifestyle of his master. He stayed for the most part in the capital working with and through the various kings.

Elisha became leader of the prophetic schools in Israel about the year 848 BC. He lived into the reign of Jehoash who came to the throne of Israel in 798 BC. Thus for half a century Elisha led the sons of the prophets. During those years Baalism finally was defeated in the northern kingdom.

ELISHA'S
MIRACULOUS MINISTRY
2 Kings 4-8

Date: 848[56]-798 BC

Elisha's ministry was undergirded by a large number and wide variety of miracles. This man's ministry stretches over half a century and spans the reigns of four northern kings: Jehoram, Jehu, Jehoahaz and Jehoash. The author of the Book of Kings seems to have grouped his miracles topically rather than relating them chronologically.

Elisha's Private Miracles
2 Kings 4:1-6:7

Six of Elisha's miracles were performed for individuals, four of them for two faithful female disciples. Two other miracles were performed on behalf of a community of student prophets.

A. Widow's Oil (2 Kings 4:1-7)

---

[56]Beginning of the period when Elisha was recognized leader of the prophetic ministry in Israel. His public ministry actually began two or three years earlier ca. 851 BC before the departure of Elijah (2 Kings 3).

1. A widow's need (4:1): A destitute widow did not hesitate to ask Elisha for assistance because 1) her husband had been a member of the prophetic order over which Elisha presided; and 2) because her husband was a God-fearing man. When her husband died, some creditor demanded immediate payment of a family debt. Since the widow could not pay off the loan, the creditor had taken her two sons into slavery as payment for the loan.

2. Elisha's directive (4:2-7): Elisha instructed the woman to secure from all her neighbors empty vessels of every size and description. This not only served to test her faith, but to undergird the eternal principle that God helps him who helps himself. She was told to take those empty vessels into the privacy of her home and pour into them the small amount of oil that she possessed. As each vessel became full it was set aside and replaced by another empty vessel in order that the pouring might be continuous. When every last vessel in the house was filled, the oil ceased flowing. God did not permit waste. The miracle was performed inconspicuously lest the prophet be overwhelmed with requests for similar aid to others. Elisha directed the woman then to sell the oil and pay off the debt. After satisfying the claims of her creditor with part of the money, she was able to support herself and her sons on the remainder.

B. Birth Prediction (2 Kings 4:8-17)

1. A gracious hostess (4:8-10): On his travels about the country, Elisha was accustomed to take his meals with *a great woman,* i.e., a woman of means, when in the town of Shunem. With the passage of time, the wealthy Shunammite became convinced that Elisha was truly worthy of the title he bore, *man of God.* She and her husband built a special room for the prophet to use both as a sleeping chamber and as a study.

2. A shocking announcement (4:11-17): Elisha wished to repay his Shunammite hosts in some way. At the suggestion of his servant Gehazi—here mentioned for the first time—Elisha announced to the childless woman that within a year she will embrace a son. Like Sarah before her, the Shunammite was incredulous in the face of this shocking announcement. Nevertheless, at that very season a year later the woman gave birth to a son, just as the prophet had predicted.

C. Resurrection (2 Kings 4:18-37)

483

1. *Child's death (4:18-21):* Some years later the Shunammite's son died as a result of sunstroke. The woman put the lifeless corpse on the bed in the prophet's chamber. She then set out for Mount Carmel some fifteen miles distant where Elisha was ministering. She believed that the prophet was able to duplicate the resurrection performed by Elijah in Zarephath some years earlier.

2. *Interim action (4:22-31):* Elisha responded to the emergency in two ways. First, he dispatched Gehazi immediately to the Shunammite's house. Gehazi was to lay Elisha's staff upon the lad's face. This action was designed to comfort the mother and to raise in her a firm expectation of a resurrection. Second, as soon as he was able Elisha set out for Shunem along with his friend. En route they were met by Gehazi returning from carrying out his master's directions. He reported that the lad was showing no signs of life in spite of the prophet's staff.

3. *Elisha's action prayer (4:32-34):* Elisha entered the chamber where the dead child lay. He closed the door in order that he might not be disturbed during his efforts to revive the body. Falling to his knees, the inarticulate prayer that had been upon his heart from the moment he left Carmel was verbalized. Following the example of his master Elijah (cf. 1 Kings 17:21), Elisha stretched himself upon the lad and brought his flesh as close as he could to that of the lad. The idea in this seems to be to prepare the body for re-inhabitation of the soul or spirit by restoring warmth to it. Aside from this practical purpose, the act also demonstrated the faith of the prophet that God will permit this great miracle to take place. Elisha's efforts accomplished their purpose; the child's body was actually warmed.

4. *Child restored (4:35-37):* Still no signs of life appeared. The prophet, somewhat perplexed, got up from his prone position and paced in the room, doubtlessly analyzing the situation, praying as he did so. Then he again stretched himself upon the child. Shortly the child sneezed seven times—showing the recovery of his suspended respiration—and opened his eyes. The Shunammite was summoned, no doubt from the lower story of the house. She was instructed to take up her restored child. As anxious as the woman was to once again embrace her son, she first bowed before the prophet in humble gratitude; then she took up her son and went out to spend those precious first moments alone with the lad.

D. Healing Noxious Pottage (2 Kings 4:38-41)

1. Dangerous accident (4:38-39): During a famine Elisha visited the prophetic school at Gilgal. He ordered that the large communal pot be put on the fire, and pottage or vegetable stew be prepared. Then students fanned out in the neighborhood to look for wild fruits or vegetables that might be put into the stew. Perhaps because of the famine the men could not be as selective as they normally were. One young fellow brought back as many *gourds* as he could carry.[57] He sliced them up into the stew. None of the more experienced students were paying attention to what he was doing.

2. Alarm (4:40): As the students were eating the vegetable stew, they realized, either by the bitter taste or nauseous effects, that they were eating unwholesome food. They cried out to Elisha, *O man of God, there is death in the pot!* No one was able to continue eating the stew.

3. Elisha's response (4:41): Elisha took prompt action. He called for some meal and cast it into the pot. Meal, of course, has no power in itself to neutralize poison any more than salt has to purify bitter waters (cf. 2 Kings 2:19-21). While it is possible that this action might have modified some of the bitterness of the brew, the primary purpose of the meal was to symbolize purification. In any case, the pottage was served anew, and those who had faith in Elisha and continued to eat of it were in no way harmed.

E. Food Multiplication (2 Kings 4:42-44)

1. A gift for the students (4:42): A man came from Baal Shalishah near Gilgal to bring Elisha twenty cakes of bread made from the firstfruits of his harvest. Each loaf was the equivalent of what one person ate at one meal. Along with these cakes, the man brought a few ripe stalks of grain that were a token of his gratitude (cf. Leviticus 23:10) for God's harvest mercies.

2. Enough for all (4:43-44): Elisha ordered that the loaves be placed before the sons of the prophets who resided at Gilgal. Elisha's servant—presumably Gehazi—was incredulous. The amount of food was scarcely sufficient to suffice for a fifth of the hundred men living at Gilgal! In the face of the objection, the prophet repeated his

---

[57]Gustaf Dalman attempts to identify the particular plant here involved. He points to a vine that grows in the vicinity of Jericho that produces yellow fruit like melons. These melons have powerful laxative properties. If eaten in great quantity they indeed can be fatal. See *Sacred Sites and Ways,* Trans. P. Levertoff (New York: Macmillan, 1935) p. 81ff.

instructions, and added an explanation in the form of a prophetic oracle. God had revealed to him that the quantity of food was ample for the hundred men, and that they will show that they had eaten enough by leaving some of it. The result was as the prophet predicted.

F. Recovering a Lost Ax (2 Kings 6:1-7)

1. Expanding ministry (6:1-3): The school of the prophets at Jericho had outgrown its facilities. When Elisha next visited Jericho, the students proposed to him that a new dwelling be constructed a few miles from Jericho near the Jordan where trees for such a purpose were readily available. To this proposal Elisha gave his encouragement. Upon their insistence, he agreed also to supervise the work.

2. Valuable loss (6:4-5): As the men were working an ax head flew from one man's shaft into the murky waters of the river. The man was distraught. He cried out to Elisha, *Alas, my master, for it was a borrowed one!* The man made no direct request for assistance, but the tone of his exclamation constituted an oblique call for help.

3. Elisha's response (6:6-7): Elisha, being always interested in the personal problems of his disciples, asked to be shown the spot where the ax head entered the stream. The prophet then cut off a branch and cast it upon the water at that spot. The ax head miraculously was caused to rise to the surface of the water.[58] In order to test the faith of the student, Elisha then ordered him to take up the ax head. He must show that he really believed that the ax head was floating on the surface, and that he was not merely experiencing an optical illusion.

HEALING OF NAAMAN
2 Kings 5:1-27

Date: ca. 845 BC

Elisha performed two great miracles that resulted in greater respect for Yahweh among Israel's neighbors. The first of these miracles involved the healing of an Aramean officer.

Background

---

[58]Naturalistic explanations of this miracle—that Elisha used the stick to pry the ax head from the bottom of the stream—do violence to the account.

2 Kings 5:1-7

A. Naaman hears of a Prophet (2 Kings 5:1-4)

1. Witness of an Israelite maid (5:1-3): As captain of the Aramean host, Naaman had achieved honor and wealth. He was *a mighty man of valor,* i.e., a good soldier; but he was a leper. A maid, captured on a raid into Israel, became distressed over the grievous affliction of Naaman. One day she expressed her sentiment that he might be brought into contact with the powerful prophet in Samaria. She was confident that Elisha could cure him of his leprosy.

2. Directive of a king (5:4): Convinced by his wife's persistence to pursue the matter, Naaman reported the suggestion of the Israelite maid to the king. Much to his surprise, the king took the whole matter seriously. He agreed to send a letter by Naaman's hand to the king of Israel urging that he do what he could for the captain.

B. Preparation for the Journey (2 Kings 5:5)

When Naaman departed, he took with him an enormous treasure with which he thought he could pay for his cleansing. Ten talents of silver is roughly equivalent to $20,000. The unit of measure is omitted for the gold, but it is likely that the amount was six thousand shekels' weight, roughly equivalent to $60,000. Finally, in addition to the silver and gold, Naaman took ten changes of garments to bestow upon his benefactor. Naaman's first mistake is that he thought he could purchase his cleansing.

C. Letter to an Israelite King (2 Kings 5:6-7)

Naaman went straight to the palace of the king of Israel. He presented the letter from Ben-Hadad which, when stripped of diplomatic niceties, demanded that his general be healed. Naturally the king of Israel was upset by the letter. He tore his clothes and cried: *Am I God, to kill and make alive?* i.e., am I omnipotent? He did not think of Elisha, probably because he gave no credence to the reports circulating about him. The only conclusion the king could reach was that Ben-Hadad was making these extravagant demands as a pretext for more hostility. Here was Naaman's second mistake: he went to the wrong place in search of his cleansing.

Naaman's Cleansing
2 Kings 5:8-14

A. Elisha's Actions (2 Kings 5:8-10)

1. His invitation (5:8): News of the king's distress reached Elisha. He sent word to the palace inviting the king to send the foreign dignitary to his house. The Aramean will then be convinced that Yahweh had a prophet in the land.

2. His rebuke (5:9): Soon Naaman and his entourage arrived at the humble abode of Elisha in the city of Samaria. A man of his station was not about to enter such humble quarters, and so he simply waited impatiently at the door of the house. Regarding the pride of his visitor as worthy of rebuke, Elisha remained within the house and sent his servant out to communicate with the dignitary.

3. His instructions (5:10): If the actions of the prophet insulted the inflated ego of Naaman, his instruction did even more: *Go wash in the Jordan seven times.* The nearest point of the Jordan River from Samaria was some twenty miles distant. If Naaman had the faith to go to the river, and there persisted in the formal act of dipping in the river seven times, the scaly leprous skin would disappear.

B. Naaman's Anger (2 Kings 5:11-12)

Naaman was angered by the treatment he received from the unseen prophet. He expected to receive every possible attention; but the prophet had not even greeted him at the door. The captain expected an instantaneous cure. Instead he was told that *he* must do something—dip in the muddy Jordan. The rivers of Damascus (Abanah and Pharpar) were fresh, clear and beautiful. If the leprous taint was to be *washed* away, would not the crystal clear waters of his native land have more cleansing power than the clay-colored waters of Jordan? Disgusted and perturbed, Naaman wheeled his chariot around and departed in a cloud of dust. Here were Naaman's third and fourth mistakes: he had a preconceived notion of how cleansing should be effected; and he got angry with the prophet who told him how to achieve cleansing.

C. A Servant's Wisdom (2 Kings 5:13-14)

Fortunately for Naaman, his servants did not share in his wild indignation. When their master had cooled somewhat, one of his servants reasoned with Naaman. He suggested that if Elisha had directed Naaman to do some difficult thing, the captain would have attempted to do it. How much more should he be willing to do the simple, if somewhat silly, thing that the man of God prescribed. The irresistible logic persuaded Naaman. At the first opportunity, he turned his chariot eastward and began to make his way through the rapidly descending valleys toward the Jordan. When he exactly complied with the prophet's instructions, the miracle occurred. Not only was the leprosy removed, Naaman's flesh became as soft as that of a little baby.

Naaman's Conversion
2 Kings 5:15-19

A. Evidence of Conversion (2 Kings 5:15-18)

A number of facts indicate that at the Jordan Naaman's heart was transformed as well as his flesh.

- Naaman was determined to express his appreciation to the man of God even though the return trip to Samaria took him at least forty miles out of his way and delayed his return to Damascus by at least one day.
- The once pompous Aramean was now contrite. He descended from his chariot, went into the prophet's abode, and stood before him.
- Naaman confessed faith in the supremacy of Yahweh.
- Naaman was anxious that Elisha should accept a *blessing,* i.e., a present, in appreciation for what he had done. Elisha thought it best, however, to decline the gift. Naaman needed to learn that Yahweh was his true healer, Elisha but his representative.
- Naaman took two mule loads of soil back to Aram with him. Commentators conjecture that he intended to use the soil to consecrate a plot of ground and make it a suitable place upon which to worship Yahweh. In the mind of this newly converted heathen, the ground of Israel was more holy, more appropriate for the worship of the God of Israel.
- Naaman declared his intention to cease offering sacrifice to any god other than Yahweh.
- Naaman indicated that as captain of the host he was required to attend the temple of Rimmon with his king. There he was compelled to bow before the image of that

god. He therefore expressed the hope that Yahweh will pardon him of this wrong.

B. Elisha's Blessing (2 Kings 5:19)

Elisha did not declare that God will overlook this departure from strict monotheism. Naaman had not asked a question but had only expressed a wish. Elisha's *Go in peace* should be taken simply as wishing the peace of God to be on the departing Aramean.

Aftermath
2 Kings 5:20-27

A. Gehazi's Deception (2 Kings 5:20-26)

1. His covetousness (5:20): Gehazi could not bear the thought of the Aramean going home with all his treasure. He convinced himself that this foreigner deserved to be spoiled because he was an enemy of Israel. He swore an oath using the name of God to run after the captain and take *something* of him. *As Yahweh lives* are strange words in the mouth of one who has set his mind on a course of lying and stealing.

2. His lie (5:21-23): Naaman's entourage, traveling at a leisurely pace so as not to exhaust those servants who might have been on foot, was easily overtaken by the fleet-footed Gehazi. He told Naaman that Elisha had changed his mind regarding the gifts that had been offered. Two needy sons of the prophets from Mount Ephraim had happened along, and Elisha requested Naaman to donate to them a talent of silver ($2,000) and two changes of garments. Naaman believed the story of Gehazi and wanted to do even more than the servant had requested. He suggested that two talents ($4,000) be taken, probably because the strangers who had arrived were two. Following the conventions of the Near East, Gehazi pretended to decline the more generous offer.

3. His precaution (5:24): Naaman took the two talents and, along with the changes of garments, put them upon the shoulders of two of his servants. At a hill just outside Samaria, Gehazi took the money from Naaman's slaves, and dismissed them. He could not run the risk of having these foreigners seen entering Samaria again. Gehazi took the bags of money and hid them in the house of his master, probably in the courtyard thereof.

4. His condemnation (5:25-26): The sins of Gehazi escalated when he lied to his master regarding his whereabouts. Elisha then claimed that he had been with Gehazi in prophetic spirit. The prophet then reflected back to Gehazi his inner thoughts about what he planned to do with the newly acquired wealth, viz., purchase olive groves and vineyards, as well as sheep and oxen. Those desperate days were no time to think of acquiring property and luxury for oneself! Such actions could bring the prophetic office into contempt with unbelievers and undermine the credibility of Elisha's ministry.

B. Gehazi's Punishment (2 Kings 5:27)

Elisha pronounced sentence against his servant. Since Gehazi had taken of Naaman's goods, he will also partake of his leprosy. Should this servant decide to marry and father children, they too would be lepers. In that instant the plague fell on Gehazi. His skin turned white as snow. Gehazi departed from the presence of Elisha to spend his remaining days with the outcast lepers.

ELISHA'S PREDICTIVE MIRACLES
2 Kings 6:24-8:15

Aramean Troop Movements Revealed
2 Kings 6:8-23

The Arameans again began to assert their power against Israel in the days of Jehoram the son of Ahab. Two miracles of Elisha demonstrated God's compassion for Israel and his superiority over the gods of Aram.

A. Aramean Plans Revealed (2 Kings 6:8-12)

1. Elisha's ability (6:8-10): Through his supernatural insight, Elisha was able to reveal to the king of Israel the secret military plans of the Arameans. The prophet had a strong personal dislike for King Jehoram, but he did not allow these personal feelings to interfere with his patriotism. The king of Israel learned to avoid those spots where Elisha indicated he would encounter an Aramean ambush.

2. Elisha identified (6:11-12): The king of Aram became greatly concerned at the repeated failure of his best laid plans. One officer—perhaps Naaman—suggested that the plans were being revealed by the Israelite prophet. Perhaps the Aramean had learned this through intelligence agencies in Israel. On the other hand, perhaps this official was merely surmising that a man who could heal the dreaded leprosy would have no difficulty reading the secret thoughts of a man.

B. Aramean Troops Captured (2 Kings 6:13-23)

1. Arresting force (6:13-14): Aramean spies ascertained that Elisha was currently residing in Dothan, a village about twelve miles north of Samaria. A strong force was dispatched with orders to kidnap the prophet. In order to take Elisha by surprise, the Arameans marched by night and encompassed the city.

2. Fearful servant (6:15): Elisha's new servant arose early in the morning to discover the city surrounded by a force that included infantry, cavalry, and even a chariot force. Faced with the prospect of capture and consequent slavery, the young servant rushed to his master to report his alarming discovery. *How shall we do?* he cried, i.e., is there any way we can save ourselves?

3. Revelation of divine protection (6:16-17): Elisha was quite calm in the face of this serious threat. He knew that God protected him, and it mattered not how many might be arrayed against him outside the walls of Dothan. The servant, however, needed reassurance. So Elisha prayed that the servant's eyes might be permitted to see that great angelic host that hovers just beyond the realm of sight and sound. The prophet's prayer was answered. The eyes of the servant were opened, and he beheld round about the hill of Dothan a heavenly force—chariots and horses *of fire,* i.e., glowing with an unearthly brightness.

4. Delusion of the soldiers (6:18-19): Rather than waiting for the Arameans to come up the slopes of Dothan to arrest him, Elisha and his servant went down to the attacking host. As they approached the enemy, Elisha prayed for God to smite the Arameans with blindness, i.e., a state of confusion in which they willingly follow the directions of the prophet. As a result of that prayer, the soldiers allowed Elisha to convince them that they had attacked the wrong city. Under this miraculous delusion, the soldiers allowed Elisha to lead them into Samaria. The behavior of these soldiers is absolutely inexplicable apart from direct working of God in their mental processes.

492

5. *Intention of the king (6:20-21):* Once inside Samaria, Elisha prayed for God to *open their eyes,* i.e., remove the bewilderment that had seized them at Dothan. The soldiers awoke from their delusion to realize that they were surrounded by a great throng of Israelite soldiers. King Jehoram, though not on the most cordial terms with Elisha (cf. 2 Kings 3:11-14), addressed the prophet by the honorable title *father.* The king was eager to slay the helpless invaders, but he felt compelled to seek the permission of the one who had delivered them into his hand.

6. *Elisha's instructions (6:22-23):* Elisha declined permission to slay these men. They were not prisoners of war in the usual sense. The ultimate purpose of the miracle at Dothan was to teach these foreigners and their king to fear the God of Israel, and to respect his people and prophet in particular. Therefore, instead of slaying the Arameans, the prophet directed that they be treated hospitably and then be sent back to their own land. As a result of this episode, the Aramean raiders, who had heretofore harassed the Israelite countryside, suspended their activities for a time, and Israel had a respite.

Prediction of
Deliverance of Samaria
2 Kings 6:24-7:20

The kind treatment of the Aramean troop was soon forgotten. Ben-Hadad gathered his entire force and invaded Israel. Realizing that he was no match for the invaders in the field, King Jehoram withdrew to his capital at Samaria and prepared for a long siege.

A. Samaria's Plight (2 Kings 6:24-29)

1. *Inflated prices (6:24-25):* Ben-Hadad blockaded the city and attempted to starve its inhabitants into submission. The situation in the city deteriorated to such a degree that an donkey head, the worst part of an unclean animal, which would normally never be eaten, sold for eighty pieces of silver ($50), and a *cab* (pint) of dove's dung (ESV) for five pieces of silver ($3). *Dove's dung* may have been the popular name for some food such as roasted chickpeas. If actual dove's dung is intended, it was probably sold as fuel.

2. *Cannibalism (6:26-29):* King Jehoram made regular inspections of the fortifications and guard posts on the broad walls of

493

Samaria. On one such tour a woman cried out to the king for a judicial decision. She and a neighbor had entered a pact to eat their two sons on two successive days. Her boy was boiled and eaten the appointed day. The following day the neighbor reneged on the agreement and hid her son to avoid the ordeal of seeing him killed and eaten.

B. Elisha's Prediction (2 Kings 6:30-33)

1. Elisha blamed (6:30-31): The king was horrified to learn how deplorable the conditions had become within the city. He tore open his clothes in anguish. Beneath his robes he was wearing sackcloth. In his distress the king swore an oath to have Elisha decapitated that very day. Why the king blamed Elisha for the horrors of the famine is not clear. Perhaps he felt that the prophet should work some mighty miracle to relieve the city of its suffering.

2. Elisha under death warrant (6:32): Elisha was sitting in his home in Samaria with the elders of the land sitting before him at the time the king dispatched the prophet's executioner. Their conversation was interrupted when Elisha received a supernatural revelation of what was about to take place. The prophet called upon those present with him to resist the royal messenger and bar the door to him, because the king himself was en route to the prophet's house. He would either confirm or countermand the original order.

3. Elisha confronted by the king (6:33): The messenger of the king arrived at that very moment. The elders barred the door as Elisha suggested. Then the king himself appeared on the scene. He was immediately admitted into the presence of the prophet. Jehoram seems to have repented of his hasty order to slay the prophet. He had hurried after his own messenger in order to give the prophet a final opportunity to live. The question of the king—*Why should I wait for Yahweh any longer?*—implies that Elisha previously had urged Jehoram to wait for divine interposition. The king interpreted the calamity as being from Yahweh. Why should he try to hold out any longer? Why should he not break with God, slay his lying prophet, and surrender the city to the Arameans?

C. Elisha's Prediction (2 Kings 7:1-2)

1. Prediction announced (7:1): Elisha responded to the king in the most solemn manner. Within a short period of time the whole nation will know whether or not Elisha was a true spokesman for the living God. Within twenty-four hours such a quantity of grain will be available to the inhabitants of Samaria that barley and fine flour will again be bought and sold at the pre-siege prices.

2. Prediction challenged (7:2): The king's personal attendant was vocally incredulous. With scoffing sarcasm he insisted that the prediction was utterly impossible of fulfillment. Even if the Lord were to make windows in the heavens, and pour down through them grain instead of rain, this prediction could not come to pass. Since the disdain of the officer was directed not only at Elisha but at the power of God, the prophet answered him sternly. *You shall see with your eyes, but you shall not eat!* By these words the officer, if he were wise enough to discern it, was forewarned of his imminent death.

D. Joyous Discovery (2 Kings 7:3-11)

1. Desperate lepers (7:3-7): Four lepers were on the verge of perishing at the gate of Samaria. Friends within the city no longer had food to share with them. The only hope of survival was to desert to the Arameans. At twilight they approached the enemy camp only to find it totally deserted. Yahweh had caused the Arameans to hear what they thought was the sound of an enormous army sweeping down upon them. They jumped to the illogical conclusion that Jehoram had hired Hittite and Egyptian mercenaries to attack them from opposite directions. The Arameans fled for their lives.

2. Guilty lepers (7:8-11): The lepers first satisfied their hunger. Then they began hiding the valuables left by the enemy. The lepers wanted to make sure they got their share of the spoils of war. During the process of plundering, however, their consciences began to bother them. Many were perishing within Samaria while they were enjoying their good fortune. To withhold such good tidings from their desperate countrymen must surely be a criminal act for which God will punish them. So, belatedly the lepers determined to carry the news to the *king's house,* i.e., his officers and court.

E. Precise Fulfillment (2 Kings 7:12-20)

1. Verification (7:12-15): Aroused from his sleep, the king greeted the news of the Aramean retreat with incredulity. He suspected some kind of trick. Two chariots were dispatched to check out the report. This patrol followed the main road to the Jordan. All along the way they saw the garments, weapons, and baggage

495

discarded by the fleeing troops. Convinced that the Arameans had fled, the patrol reported back to the king.

2. Celebration (7:16-20): News of the good fortune spread through Samaria that morning like wildfire. The whole population *en masse* descended on the Aramean camp to feast and take spoil. The officer who the previous day had scoffed at the predictions of Elisha was trampled by the mob in the gate of the city.

Famine Prediction
2 Kings 8:1-6

A. Warning to the Shunammite (2 Kings 8:1-2)

A great famine occurred during the reign of Jehoram (cf. 2 Kings 4:38). Prior to the approach of that famine Elisha had warned his wealthy Shunammite friend to leave her home and take up residence wherever she might choose. God had determined to bring a famine upon the land that was to last for seven years. The faithful woman regarded the prophet as a spokesman for God. She accepted his advice as equivalent to a divine command. The Shunammite and her household migrated to the fertile Philistine plain which, though not totally exempt from famine, did not suffer from such natural calamities nearly as much as did Samaria or Judah. For seven years the Shunammite resided in that foreign land.

B. Plight of the Shunammite (2 Kings 8:3-4)

When the famine abated, the Shunammite returned to her native land to discover that some neighbor had seized her unoccupied house and land. The woman had no recourse but to appeal to the king that her properties be restored. The king happened to be talking to Gehazi (clearly these miraculous accounts are not in chronological order) when the woman came into his presence to plead her case. Apparently Jehoram had sent for Gehazi to satisfy his curiosity with regard to the miraculous deeds of Elisha. This king and the prophet were not on friendly terms, hence the best source for accurate information about the deeds of this man of God was his servant.

C. Relief for the Shunammite (2 Kings 8:5-6)

As Gehazi was relating the most stupendous of all of Elisha's miracles—the resurrection of the Shunammite's son—this woman began to cry for the attention of the king. Gehazi was pleased to point

496

out his old friend and her son, who by this time must have been a lad of ten years or more. The king made inquiry of the woman, not only about the miracle that had been done in her house, but also about her property claims. Convinced that her cause was just, the king appointed an officer of the court to expedite the return of the woman's property. In addition, he awarded her all the profits that the land had produced during the seven years of her absence.

Assassination Prediction
2 Kings 8:7-15

A. Elisha Visits Damascus (2 Kings 8:7)

For reasons not stated Elisha at some point in his ministry made a trip to Damascus. Some have tried to link this visit to the commission given many years earlier to Elijah that he (or his surrogate) was to anoint Hazael. Others speculate that Jezebel was stirring up trouble for the prophet, forcing him to leave the country temporarily. Still another possibility is that Elisha was spending part of the time of the national famine outside the land even as his predecessor had done. Whatever his reason for going to Damascus, the move was most bold. Not too long previous to this visit, the king of Damascus had made a determined effort to arrest Elisha and punish him for revealing Aramean military plans to Jehoram (cf. 2 Kings 6:13-19). Probably Yahweh directed Elisha to make this trip, and the prophet, putting his trust in the Lord, carried out the command.

B. Consultation with the Prophet (2 Kings 8:8-9)

The aged Ben-Hadad was quite ill at the time Elisha visited the city. Ben-Hadad, knowing of the reputation of this man of God, immediately dispatched his trusted servant Hazael with presents for the prophet. He was instructed to make inquiry of Yahweh through the prophet concerning the prognosis for the king. The miracles of Elisha had convinced even these idolaters that Yahweh was a powerful God. The Aramean king paid great respect to the prophet by referring to himself in the message as *your son*.

C. Message to Ben-Hadad (2 Kings 8:10)

Elisha instructed Hazael to tell his master that he will recover from his current illness. However, God had revealed to Elisha that the king will die, not of his illness, but of another cause. After giving this

497

answer to Hazael, the prophet fixed a hard stare upon his visitor until Hazael became uncomfortable. Hazael already had formed a plan to eliminate his master. The stare of the prophet made him realize that his plans were known.

D. Prediction about Hazael (2 Kings 8:11-13)

As Elisha mentally observed what lay in store for his people at the hand of Hazael, he began to weep. Hazael inquired as to the reason for this unexpected outburst. Elisha explained his actions by describing the brutal warfare that Hazael was going to launch against Israel—the burning of cities, slaughter of youth, dashing to pieces of little children, and ripping open of pregnant women. Hazael shrugged off the implications of this prediction by asking how he, a lowly servant—*a contemptible dog*—would ever be able to launch war against Israel and do the terrible things Elisha predicted of him. Elisha responded that Hazael was not to continue in his lowly position, for Yahweh had revealed that one day he will be king of Aram.

E. Assassination of Ben-Hadad (2 Kings 8:14-15)

Hazael returned to Ben-Hadad and reported only the first half of Elisha's answer to the king. He suppressed the part of the answer that announced that Ben-Hadad will die, but not of the illness. On the very next day Hazael made his move against the king. He took a thick piece of cloth, dipped it in water, and held it over the ailing king's face until Ben-Hadad died of suffocation. Hazael then claimed the throne.

34
END OF
THE JEZEBEL ERA
2 Kings 9-12

Chapter Chronology

					814
Joram			**JEHU**		
852		841			
	Ahaz-iah	**Athaliah**		**Joash**	
			836		

JEZEBEL'S GRANDSON
2 Kings 8:24-28

In Judah Ahaziah began to reign in the twelfth year of Joram of Israel (841 BC). He was twenty-two when his father died of bowel disease. His mother was Athaliah, the Jezebel of Judah. She influenced him to follow the religious policy of the house of Ahab (2 Kings 8:25-27).

Battlefield Setback
2 Kings 8:28

Following the example of his grandfather Jehoshaphat, Ahaziah joined in a military alliance with his uncle, Jehoram of Israel. The objective of the alliance was to go to the relief of Ramoth-Gilead which was under attack by Hazael, the new Aramean king. During the course of the defense of the city, Jehoram was severely, but not fatally, wounded. Leaving a strong garrison under General Jehu to defend the city, the two kings retired to their capitals.

Visit to Jezreel
2 Kings 8:29

King Joram stopped off at the royal retreat in Jezreel in the plains to recuperate rather than make the more arduous ascent back to

499

Samaria. After some time passed, Ahaziah of Judah made a trip to
Jezreel to visit his convalescing relative. As things turned out,
Ahaziah never returned from that fateful visit.

JEHU REVOLUTION
2 Kings 9:1-10:31

Date: 841 BC
At Mount Horeb God had told Elijah that the day of retribution
for the Baal worshipers in the northern kingdom was surely coming.
The judgment was to be administered by three men: Hazael, Jehu and
Elisha. *The one who escapes the sword of Hazael, Jehu shall put to
death, and the one who escapes the sword of Jehu, Elisha shall put to
death* (1 Kings 19:17). That program of divine retribution began to
unfold in the closing years of the reign of Ahab's son Jehoram.

Anointing of Jehu
2 Kings 9:1-13

A. Details of Anointing (2 Kings 9:1-10)
When the time was right, Elisha carried out the divine
commission to anoint Jehu to execute the divine wrath against the
Omri dynasty. The prophet dispatched one of the prophetical students
to Ramoth-Gilead where Jehu was the commander. The young man
took Jehu behind closed doors and anointed him to be king of Israel.
Along with the anointing came a commission. Jehu was to smite the
house of Ahab in order that God might avenge the deaths of the
prophets at the hands of Jezebel. Jehu was to make the house of Ahab
like the houses of Jeroboam and Baasha. The corpse of Jezebel
herself was to be left for the dogs to devour. Having completed his
mission, the young prophet hastily departed. Secrecy was of the
utmost importance.

B. Recognition (2 Kings 9:11-13)
1. Jehu pressed for information (9:11-12): When Jehu emerged
from the house, his colleagues quizzed him about the crazy-acting
messenger who had disappeared almost as suddenly as he had
appeared. Jehu suspected that the whole scene had been arranged
beforehand by his junior officers in an effort to get him to make a
move against the unpopular Jehoram. The officers firmly disavowed
500

any knowledge of what the young man might have said. They pressed their commander to relate it to them. Jehu then reported to the junior officers all that the prophet had said.

2. Jehu proclaimed king (9:13): The officers at Ramoth-Gilead received the news enthusiastically. They immediately began to render to Jehu royal homage by spreading their garments upon the dust for him to walk upon. They improvised an enthronement ceremony by having Jehu ascend the outside stairs that led to the upper story of the house. When he took his position on the top-most step, they blew the trumpets and proclaimed Jehu to be king.

Death of King Jehoram
2 Kings 9:14-26

The revolution of 841 BC may well have been the most important political development in the history of the separate monarchies since the schism of 930 BC. Both kingdoms were affected immediately by what transpired. Besides the obvious political changes brought on by the revolution, the effects of this *coup* were felt in the religious, economic and social realms as well.

A. Signs of Trouble (2 Kings 9:14-20)

1. Jehoram's initial evaluation (9:14-17): Jehu and his supporters made their way immediately for Jezreel where King Jehoram was convalescing. A watchman spied the chariot forces approaching. Jehoram at first thought that the small group of chariots was bringing news from the war front. The king dispatched a messenger to find out if the news was good or bad.

2. Two messengers defect (9:18-20): Jehu ordered the king's messenger to join his ranks. The royal watchmen noted this suspicious behavior and reported it at once to Jehoram. The king dispatched a second messenger with the same results. Jehoram now realized that the commander of that chariot force was acting in defiance of the crown. From the reckless pace at which the chariots were approaching Jezreel the watchman concluded that Jehu was leading the force.

B. Confrontation with Jehu (2 Kings 9:21)

Since Jehu was known for his loyalty to the crown, Jehoram's apprehension disappeared. Jehoram decided to ride out with his nephew Ahaziah of Judah to meet his commander. The two kings met Jehu and his company in the portion of ground that Ahab had taken from Naboth so ruthlessly. The king greeted Jehu with the question: *Is all well?* Jehu answered in the negative. No peace could exist between Jehu and Jehoram so long as the *witchcrafts,* i.e., idolatrous influence, of the queen mother Jezebel were allowed to continue in Israel.

C. Jehoram Killed (2 Kings 9:22-26)

Jehoram now grasped the seriousness of the situation. He shouted a warning to his young nephew, wheeled about and attempted to flee the scene. Jehu immediately shot an arrow through the back of the king. Jehoram slumped into his chariot dead. Jehu ordered the corpse to be cast into the portion of ground that once had belonged to Naboth. Thus was the house of Ahab recompensed for the murder of Naboth at the very spot announced by Elijah some fifteen years earlier.

Death of Ahaziah
2 Kings 9:27-29

King Ahaziah of Judah escaped the scene at Jezreel unscathed. He fled southward toward the land of Judah by the way of Beth Haggan, a village due south of Jezreel. Jehu ordered his men to pursue and slay Ahaziah because he was the grandson of Ahab. As Ahaziah's chariot slowed down at the steep ascent of Gur near the southern edge of the Plain of Esdraelon, Jehu's archers were able to inflict a wound upon him. Ahaziah then changed directions and headed west toward Megiddo, partly because he was now in no condition to make the rugged climb back to Jerusalem, and partly because he wished to throw off his pursuers. King Ahaziah died in Megiddo either of the wounds he had received at the ascent of Gur, or as a result of some new violence on the part of Jehu (cf. 2 Chronicles 22:8-9).

Death of Jezebel
2 Kings 9:30-37

A. Jezebel's Gamble (2 Kings 9:30-31)

After pursuing Ahaziah as far as Ibleam, Jehu returned to Jezreel. About three hours had elapsed since the death of King Jehoram. Jezebel was resignedly waiting for her confrontation with Jehu. When she heard he was coming, she put on eye make-up, adorned her head, and took up her position near a window. Even though she was a grandmother and at least fifty years old, Jezebel still hoped to be able to capture the affections of Jehu with her beauty. She attempted to flatter him by calling him *Zimri*. This name recalled the fact that another Israelite general had revolted and slain his master and reigned as king.

B. Jezebel's Death (2 Kings 9:32-33)

Jehu was not deterred by the wiles of Jezebel. He challenged two palace eunuchs to throw her from the window. The eunuchs grabbed the screaming queen and flung her to the courtyard below. Her falling body bounced off certain wall projections at once smearing her blood on the walls and showering it on Jehu's chariot horses as well. The captain then had his driver race over her crumpled corpse.

C. Jezebel's Burial (2 Kings 9:34-35)

Jehu was completely unaffected by the bloodshed in which he had been involved. He entered the palace and ordered a meal for himself. Not until after Jehu had satisfied his appetite did he give any thought to the corpse of the late queen ignominiously lying untended on the ground. He then ordered this *cursed woman* to be given a decent burial. When the servants went to carry out these orders, all they could find of Jezebel was the skull, the feet and the palms of her hands. Scavenger dogs had eaten the rest.

D. Fulfillment of Prophecy (2 Kings 9:36-37)

When the servants reported back to Jehu, the general remembered a prophecy delivered many years earlier by Elijah (cf. 1 Kings 21:23). As Jehu remembered it, Elijah had said four things about the fate of Jezebel: 1) that dogs will devour her; 2) that this will take place in the *portion* of Jezreel, i.e., the cultivated space or portion of land outside the wall of the city; 3) that the carcass of Jezebel will be as dung upon the face of the ground; and 4) that the fragments of the body will be so scattered that all her remains will not be buried in one tomb.

Aftermath of the

Revolution in Israel
2 Kings 10:1-27

The deaths of Jehoram and Jezebel were only the start of a bloody campaign to free Israel of the influence of this ungodly family. Jehu moved quickly to eliminate all potential rivals.

A. Massacre of Ahab's Family (2 Kings 10:1-11)

1. Intimidation of the elders (10:1-3): Jehu sent letters to the elders of the nation, those who had tutored Ahab's sons. Jehu taunted these potential adversaries. He urged them to select the boldest son of Jehoram, make him king, and come out against him with the weaponry that was stored in Samaria. Jehu was quite certain the garrison at Samaria was not going to venture forth against the army of Ramoth-Gilead that was backing Jehu.

2. Capitulation of the elders (10:4-5): The elders of Samaria were intimidated by the scornful tone of Jehu's letters. They knew that they could not muster any military support for an unpopular regime against a popular general. The elders sent back to Jehu a letter of capitulation. They placed themselves unreservedly on Jehu's side.

3. Execution order (10:6-7): Jehu immediately fired back a letter that demanded a demonstration of the professed loyalty of Samaria's leaders. He ordered them to decapitate Ahab's seventy *sons,* i.e., descendants, and bring their heads the twenty miles to Jezreel within twenty-four hours. Having committed themselves in their letter to obedience, the leaders of Samaria had little choice but to allow themselves to become the tools of Jehu. Without hesitation they slew the seventy princes, put their heads in baskets, and sent them to Jezreel by messenger.

4. Jehu's defense of his actions (10:8-10): Jehu ordered the royal heads to be put on public display in two heaps at the city gate. The next morning Jehu addressed the spectators there. He openly admitted that he had slain his master; but he pretended to have nothing to do with the deaths of the seventy relatives of Ahab. By this time everyone knew how those men had met their deaths. Did this not prove that the leaders of the nation were weary of the Ahabites? Did this not clear Jehu of any private or selfish motive in what he had done? Furthermore, Jehu argued, what had transpired had been predicted by Elijah the prophet.

5. Additional executions (10:11): Next, Jehu slew *all that remained of the house of Ahab in Jezreel.* This probably included the princesses as well as princes. In addition he executed *his great men,* and the Baal priests who were on the royal payroll. Thus did Jehu destroy the entire Ahabite faction from the land.

B. Massacre of Judean Princes (2 Kings 10:12-14)

Having eliminated all potential opposition both in Jezreel and throughout the land, Jehu set out for Samaria. En route he happened upon a group of forty-two relatives of the deceased King Ahaziah of Judah. They were on their way to visit their northern cousins and also the queen mother Jezebel. At least that was what they claimed. Jehu realized that it was hardly possible that these men could be ignorant of recent events in the north. They must surely be coming north to give aid and assistance to their relatives of the house of Ahab. The forty-two princes of Judah who were also descendants of Ahab were taken captive and later slain.

C. Alliance with Jehonadab (2 Kings 10:15-17)

1. Public show of support (10:15): Near Samaria Jehu happened upon Jehonadab, the founder of a remarkable sect of conservative Yahwists. He was somewhat of an ascetic who required his sons to live in tents, to possess neither house, nor field, nor vineyard, and to abstain wholly from the use of wine (cf. Jeremiah 35:8-10). Jehu was anxious for the endorsement of this noted leader. Without a moment's hesitation Jehonadab cast his lot with Jehu. The venerable old man rode about in the new king's chariot thus giving the impression that he was in accord with the bloody anti-Ahab policy of Jehu.

2. Hints of further executions (10:16-17): Jehu hinted to his new ally that further severe measures were about to be taken. When the two entered Samaria Jehu demonstrated his *zeal for Yahweh* by slaying all that remained of Ahab's house, the wives and perhaps children of the seventy sons already slain. This action fulfilled the word that God had spoken against the house of Ahab by the mouth of Elijah.

D. Massacre of Baal Worshipers (2 Kings 10:18-27)

1. Jehu's duplicity (10:18-19): Up to this point, the revolution of 841 BC had appeared to be nothing more than a dynastic change such as had been forced upon the nation by Baasha (1 Kings 15:27-

505

29), Zimri (1 Kings 16:9-12), and Omri (1 Kings 16:17-19). No one, except a few trusted associates, as yet suspected that deep religious motives were at the root of this revolution. Publicly Jehu announced his intention to serve Baal even more zealously than had his predecessors. Consequently the prophets, priests, and worshipers of Baal were summoned to a great inaugural sacrifice. All of this Jehu did deceitfully, for his intention was utterly to destroy the Baal worshipers.

2. *Ethical issues:* Idolaters were liable to death under the Law of Moses. Jehu had a perfect right to eradicate Baal worship throughout the land. The end, however, does not justify the means. To draw several hundred of his subjects by false pretenses into a trap and then slay them for doing what he himself invited them to do is an act wholly unjustifiable.

3. *Exclusion of Yahweh worshipers (10:20-23):* When the Baal worshipers assembled, Jehu followed the custom of supplying them all with proper garb. Keeping up the pretense that he was a devotee of Baal, Jehu himself entered the temple along with Jehonadab whom he wished to have as a witness to his *zeal for Yahweh.* He urged the Baal worshipers to make sure no Yahwists were present in the building. They might have attended this festival out of curiosity, or to curry favor with the new king. Restricting sacred temple rites to true devotees was routine.

4. *Elimination of the Baal cult (10:24-28):* Once the Baal worshipers were within the sacred precincts, Jehu stationed eighty of his men at the entrance. When the officiating priest had finished offering the sacrifices, Jehu ordered his men to enter the temple and slay the worshipers. All the wooden images representing deities subordinate to Baal were brought out and destroyed. The stone pillar representing Baal himself was broken in pieces. The temple of Baal was torn down. The ruins became a dump for city waste. Thus did Jehu eliminate the worship of the Tyrian Baal from Israel.

E. A Prophetic Word (2 Kings 10:28-31)

1. *Jehu's partial reform (10:28-29):* While Jehu was zealous for Yahweh as over against Baal, he was not of a mind to lead a reformation of Yahweh worship. The calf worship of the north had been under the curse of God from its inception (cf. 1 Kings 13:2). Jehu never intended to reform this aspect of worship in his kingdom.

His partial reformation brought no permanent blessing upon the nation.

2. Jehu's partial reward (10:30-31): Through some prophet (probably Elisha) Yahweh spoke to Jehu commending him for executing the divine wrath against the house of Ahab and the Baal worshipers. Nothing is said here about the motives of Jehu. They were largely selfish. For his external obedience, God rewarded Jehu with an external earthly honor. His sons to the fourth generation will follow him on the throne of Israel. The Jehu dynasty ruled for nearly a century, twice as long as any other dynasty in the north.

Aftermath of the
Revolution in Judah
2 Kings 11:1-21

The revolution of 841 BC was crucial in the history of Judah as well as Israel. The execution of the forty-two princes by Jehu (cf. 2 Kings 10:12-14) set the stage for a usurper to take over the throne of David in Jerusalem.

A. Queen Athaliah (2 Kings 11:1-3)

1. Her murderous rampage (11:1): Athaliah was the daughter of Ahab and Jezebel and the wife of Jehoram of Judah. Through her influence King Jehoram had introduced the Tyrian Baal into Judah (2 Kings 8:18; 2 Chronicles 21:5, 11). When Ahaziah was slain by Jehu in the early hours of the revolution, the powerful position of Athaliah as queen mother was jeopardized. The regular line of succession required the enthronement of one of her grandsons, the eldest son of Ahaziah. Were this enthronement to happen, the position of queen mother would pass on to the widow of Ahaziah. For this reason Athaliah ordered all the members of the house of David put to death. This included Athaliah's own grandsons, and probably other descendants of David belonging to branches of the house other than that of Rehoboam.

2. Rescue of an infant (11:2): Athaliah's plot to wipe out completely the house of David was frustrated by the determined efforts of Jehosheba, the sister of Ahaziah. She hid the royal infant Joash in the *chamber of mattresses,* i.e., a storage room of the palace. After a few days she transferred him to one of the chambers of the temple. There the child remained until he was six. Jehosheba was

507

married to Jehoiada the high priest (2 Chronicles 22:11). Hence she had ready access to the temple precincts.

3. Conditions under Athaliah (11:3): For seven years (841-835 BC) Athaliah ruled Judah. During that period Baalism was temporarily triumphant. The temple of Yahweh was allowed to fall into decay. A temple of Baal was erected in Jerusalem to rival it (cf. 2 Kings 11:18). The usurper was held in check to some extent by the Yahwist party. She apparently was afraid openly to challenge the position of Jehoiada, so he was left in charge of the temple with its treasures and armories (cf. 2 Kings 11:10). Athaliah allowed the temple services to continue (2 Chronicles 23:4-7), and permitted the priests and Levites to serve in their regular courses (2 Chronicles 23:8). Nonetheless, the zealous Yahwists chafed under the arrogant rule of the Jezebel of Judah.

B. Coronation of Joash (2 Kings 11:4-12)

1. Commitment of the royal guard (11:4): When Joash was seven years of age Jehoiada determined that the time had come to make the effort to restore the throne to the line of David. He summoned to the temple the five captains of the Carites, the royal guard, for a secret meeting. These men had entered the service of Athaliah under the notion that the house of David was extinct. By long standing tradition, however, the Carites were strongly attached to David and his seed. These men took an oath of support for the young king.

2. Commitment of other leaders (2 Chronicles 23:4-7): The captains visited the cities of Judah and gathered a strong force of Levites, priests, and other representative men. This larger group came to the temple and also swore an oath to Joash.

3. Positioning of the forces (11:5-11): On the fateful day three of the five companies of royal bodyguards were deployed about the palace. The other two companies, supplemented by the forces recruited from the cities of Judah, were assigned to guard the young king in the temple. To those guards Jehoiada issued shields and spears that had been captured years earlier by David in battle. Armed with these weapons the guards took up their positions in ranks stretching from one side of the temple court to the other, both before and behind the king.

4. Anointing of the king (11:12): When all was ready, Jehoiada brought forth the young king and placed the crown upon his head. He then laid on the head of Joash a copy of the Law of Moses to symbolize that the king must rule in accordance with the law. The priests then anointed the young prince with oil and declared him to be king (2 Chronicles 23:11). The crowds expressed their appreciation by clapping their hands and shouting: *May the king live!*

C. Death of Athaliah (2 Kings 11:13-16)

1. Her reaction to the coronation (11:13-14): When Athaliah heard the noise accompanying the coronation she was naturally suspicious. Though it was not her custom to enter the temple of Yahweh, she hurried next door to investigate the commotion. Entering the courtyard she was astonished to see young Joash standing upon the special platform that the king normally occupied when he attended temple services. In utter dismay Athaliah ripped her robes and shouted: *Treason!*

2. Her execution (11:15-16): Jehoiada ordered the soldiers to close ranks about the queen and conduct her out of the courtyard. Anyone who attempted to rescue the queen was to be slain. The queen, however, was not to be slain in the temple. Once outside the temple precincts, Athaliah was executed.

RESTORATION OF THE
DAVIDIC DYNASTY
2 Kings 11:17-12:20

Date: ca. 835 BC

Minority of Joash
2 Kings 11:17-12:3)

A. Covenant made by Jehoiada (2 Kings 11:17-18)

1. Terms of the covenants (11:17): Two solemn covenants were made—one between the king and the people, and the other between the people and God. The first bound the king to govern according to the law, and the people to render allegiance to the new king. The second covenant bound the nation to maintain the worship of Yahweh.

2. Reaction to the covenants (11:18): The Baal temple in Jerusalem was destroyed. The altars and images of Baal were smashed. The priest of Baal was executed. Officers were appointed over the temple. This included priests, Levites, singers and gatekeepers. The regular daily sacrificial ritual was re-established.

B. Enthronement of Joash (2 Kings 11:19-20)

Joash was escorted in triumphant procession from the temple to the royal palace. Once the rightful heir was seated on the throne of his ancestors the land was content. No opposition showed itself. The removal of Athaliah ended at long last the evil reign of the children of Jezebel.

C. Temple Repair Project (2 Kings 12:1-16)

1. Initial fund raising failure (12:1-6): For over half of his reign of forty years (835-796 BC) the priest Jehoiada was the counselor of King Joash. During those years Joash did right in the eyes of Yahweh. When his minority came to an end, Joash's first act was to order a restoration of the temple. All the monies collected by the priests were to be directed toward this project. The priests, however, showed no urgency about collecting these funds.

2. Second fund raising effort (12:7-16): Together with Jehoiada, Joash worked out a new fund raising program. A public chest was set up conspicuously in the temple court near the great altar. Worshipers were encouraged to offer free will offerings for the renovation project. Periodically Jehoiada and a royal secretary emptied the chest and weighed its contents. These monies were then given to superintendents who employed the skilled laborers. Everyone had complete confidence in those overseers for they *dealt faithfully,* i.e., honestly. After the repair work was completed, the surplus monies were used to replace the temple vessels that had been spoiled by successive kings to bribe foreign invaders.

35
SAD DAY, HEYDAY
& PAYDAY
2 Kings 13-17

Chapter Chronology

Jehoahaz 814	Jeho-ash 798	Jeroboam II 793	Menahem 752	Pekah 742	Hoshea 732	723
Joash	Amaziah 797	Uzziah 768	Jotham 751	Ahaz 736	Hezekiah 715	

SAD DAY IN
BOTH KINGDOMS

Later Reign of Joash
2 Chronicles 24:15-22

A. Death of Jehoiada (2 Chronicles 24:15-19)

Jehoiada died at the age of 130. After his death Joash followed the advice of counselors who were sympathetic to paganism. The house of Yahweh was abandoned and the nation served the Asherahs and other idols. Because of this new apostasy, the wrath of Yahweh came on Judah and Jerusalem. Prophets arose to call the people back to the Lord, but the people refused to listen.

B. Zechariah son of Jehoiada (2 Chronicles 24:20-22)

The Spirit of God came upon Zechariah the son of Jehoiada the priest. He *stood above the people* in the court of the temple and rebuked them for having transgressed the commandments of Yahweh. At the command of King Joash the people conspired against Zechariah and stoned him to death in the temple court. What an ingrate Joash turned out to be. As the prophet died he cried out: *May Yahweh see and take vengeance!*

Sword of Hazael
2 Kings 10:28-36

A. Jehu of Israel Punished (2 Kings 10:28-36)

To punish Israel for continuing in calf worship, Yahweh unleashed the sword of Hazael. He began to *cut Israel short* by means of the king of Aram. Hazael wrested the entire Transjordan territory (Bashan and Gilead) from the control of Israel. Jehu's only consolation was that he was able to keep Hazael from crossing the Jordan. The Aramean oppression got even worse during the reign of Jehu's son Jehoahaz.

B. Jehoahaz of Israel Punished (2 Kings 13:1-9).

1. Failings of Jehoahaz (13:2, 6): Jehoahaz succeeded his father Jehu on the throne of Israel. He ruled seventeen years (814-798 BC). Like all previous kings of Israel, he sinned by continuing to condone the calf worship at Dan and Bethel. The record also indicates that Jehoahaz did not remove the Asherah—the wooden image of the consort of Baal—from Samaria. This Asherah had been set up by Ahab at the instigation of Jezebel (cf. 1 Kings 16:33). That Jehu had not removed this last vestige of the Ahab-Jezebel era during his long reign is surprising.

2. Humiliation by Hazael (13:7): Jehoahaz was punished for his sin even more severely than Jehu. God delivered Israel into the hand of the ruthless Aramean kings Hazael and his son Ben-Hadad II *all the days,* i.e., all the days that God appointed for the calamity. The Arameans inflicted heavy casualties upon the Israelite army. Hazael *made them like the dust by threshing.* This may be a way of figuratively describing the utter destruction that Hazael inflicted on the armies of Israel. On the other hand this language may be an allusion to the execution of prisoners by driving threshing implements over them—a barbaric practice known to have been practiced by the Arameans (cf. Amos 1:3). Hazael was able to limit the standing army of Israel to fifty horsemen, ten chariots, and ten thousand infantry, virtually nothing more than a police force. Jehoahaz, it would appear, was a vassal of Hazael.

C. Joash of Judah Punished (2 Kings 12:17-21)

1. Successes of Hazael (12:17): After taking the Transjordan area from Israel, Hazael cast his eye upon the coastal plains of Palestine. The city of Gath, which may have been under control of Judah (cf. 2 Chronicles 11:8), fell easily to him. Encouraged by this victory, the Aramean king took his small army into the mountain region where he defeated the army of Joash and took much spoil (2 Chronicles 24:23f). Then he commenced the siege of Jerusalem. The date of this attack was about 805 BC.

2. Joash resorts to bribery (12:18): Like Rehoboam and Asa before him, Joash bought off the invader with temple treasures. Valuables from the palace were also given to Hazael. The Aramean was sufficiently satisfied with the tribute rendered to him and withdrew from Judah.

3. Assassination of Joash (12:20-21): Shortly after the attack by Hazael, Joash was assassinated by two of his servants. Perhaps sensing his unpopularity, the king had taken refuge in *the house of Millo,* a fortress built by David and Solomon. Both of the assassins had foreign mothers. No indication is given in the text as to their motive. Perhaps the humiliating capitulation to Hazael caused the people to lose all confidence in their king. Joash was forty-seven when he died.

D. Continued Aramean Oppression (2 Kings 13:3)

The oppression continued under Hazael's son Ben-Hadad II who succeeded Hazael in 801 BC. For a time Ben-Hadad was able to intensify the Aramean oppression against Israel by capturing certain unidentified cities from Jehoahaz (2 Kings 14:25).

E. Unnamed Deliverer (2 Kings 13:4-5)

1. Jehoahaz's repentance (13:4): In the midst of this Aramean oppression, Jehoahaz repented and cried out to God for deliverance. Jehoahaz did not abandon the practice of the calf worship, perhaps because he did not suspect that this was the sin that had provoked the anger of Yahweh. He did repent, however, and God accepted that repentance as imperfect as it was. God delivered his people from the destruction that they otherwise might have experienced at the hands of the Aramean kings.

2. Identity of the deliverer (13:5): God raised up one to deliver his people from their oppressors. This *deliverer* may have been Jehoash, the son of Jehoahaz who began to extricate Israel from the grip of the Arameans. More likely, however, the reference is to Jeroboam II who was able to restore all the borders of Israel. Under his reign peace again returned to the northern kingdom.

Chart 16 *Jehu Dynasty* *841-753 BC*		
Kings	**Dates** BC	**Summary**
Jehu	841-814	Revolution
Jehoahaz	814-798	Retribution
Jehoash	798-782	Recovery
Jeroboam II	782-753	Restoration
Zechariah	753	Ruin
God's promise to Jehu: "Your sons to the fourth generation shall sit on the throne of Israel" (2 Kings 10:30)		

3. Unexpected help: Help came to Israel in the midst of the Aramean oppression from an unexpected quarter. About 800 BC the Assyrian king Adad-nirari III attacked Damascus. He inflicted serious casualties on Ben-Hadad II. From that point on, Israel gradually began to recover her lost territories and to emerge from the half century of humiliating submission to Damascus.

Recovery from Aramean
Oppression in Israel
2 Kings 13:10-14:22

In Israel the recovery began under Jehoash (short spelling Joash) who reigned sixteen years (798-782 BC). He followed in the footsteps of his father Jehoahaz by continuing to condone and participate in the calf worship inaugurated by Jeroboam (2 Kings 13:10-13).

A. Final Predictions of Elisha (2 Kings 13:14-25)
1. A death-bed visit (13:14): The prophetic ministry of Elisha which had spanned over fifty years came to a close in the early years of Jehoash of Israel. The venerable old prophet must have been at least eighty years old. As he lay dying, the king came to the prophet's bedside. As he wept, Jehoash bestowed upon Elisha the familiar titles that were addressed to Elijah when he departed from this world. The term *father* recognized Elisha as the spiritual leader and teacher of Israel. The term *chariot* depicted him as national defender. When Elijah left this earth he left behind a capable successor; but when

514

Elisha died, there was no one to assume spiritual leadership. King Jehoash realized that a great era of God's dealings with Israel was coming to an end.

2. *First symbolic act (13:15-17):* Moved by the compassion of the king, Elisha mustered his strength to give Jehoash assurance that God was standing by his people. The old prophet instructed the king to take a bow and arrows from one of the soldiers who accompanied him on this visit. The prophet then instructed the king to place his hands on the bow as one would normally do when about to shoot that weapon. When the king assumed this position *Elisha put his hands upon the king's hands* i.e., he arose from his bed and also took the position of an archer covering the king's two hands with his own. The shooting of the arrow was to be a joint act of the prophet and the king. The window shutter was then opened, and the arrow was released in the direction of Transjordan where the Arameans had won such impressive victories over the Israelites. Elisha explained that the arrow symbolized deliverance from Aramean oppression. Israel will inflict a crushing defeat upon the Arameans at Aphek in Gilead.

3. *Second symbolic act (13:18-19):* Next the king was told to take in hand the arrows remaining in the quiver and to smite them upon the ground. Jehoash smote the arrows against the floor three times. He did not enter into the spirit of the symbolic act, which represented the smiting of enemies. Elisha was angry at this evident lack of enthusiasm. If the king had been earnestly desirous of victory he would have kept striking until instructed to stop, or at least until he had smitten the floor five or six times. From his prophetic perspective Elisha could see the great opportunity that was forfeited because of Jehoash's lethargic response. The Israelites will now defeat their enemies but thrice.

B. Bones of Elisha (2 Kings 13:20-21)

Because of the weakness of the northern kingdom at this time marauding bands of Moabites invaded Israel at the beginning of each year, i.e., in the spring of the year. Sometime after the death of Elisha, some Israelite men were carrying the corpse of a comrade for burial when the funeral party spotted one of these bands of raiders. With no time for ceremony, the burial party hastily and perhaps somewhat roughly cast the corpse into the nearest sepulcher which just happened to contain the bones of Elisha. When that corpse touched the bones of Elisha, the dead man revived and rose to his feet inside

515

the sepulcher. God was teaching Israel respect for his prophet even after death.

C. Victories over the Arameans (2 Kings 13:22-25)

1. Compassion of Yahweh (13:22-23): During the Aramean oppression God had compassion upon his people. *He turned unto them for the sake of the covenant with Abraham, Isaac and Jacob.* The time was coming for God to cast off these people; but that time had not yet come.

2. Successes of Jehoash (13:24-25): Though he was not able to completely extricate the nation from the Aramean grip, Jehoash was able to inflict three smashing defeats upon Ben-Hadad just as Elisha had predicted. This enabled him to recover the cities that Ben-Hadad had taken from his father. Much of the Transjordan territories, however, remained firmly under the control of Ben-Hadad until the reign of Jeroboam II.

**Recovery from Aramean
Oppression in Judah**
2 Kings 14:1-22

When Joash was assassinated, he was succeeded by his twenty-five year old son Amaziah. The new king ruled for twenty-nine years (797-768 BC). Amaziah, the *thistle king,* is another example of a good start and a tragic end.

A. Hopeful Beginning (2 Kings 14:1-7)

1. Similarities with his father (14:1-3): The authors of both Kings and Chronicles number Amaziah of Judah among the good kings. Yet in his reign there was much amiss. In several respects Amaziah's reign resembles that of his father Joash. Both were zealous for Yahweh at first, but turned to idolatry at last. Both opposed prophets and treated their critics with scorn. Both roused conspiracy against their rule by their misconduct. Both were assassinated by malcontents. Further, both were unsuccessful in war. Both had to withstand a siege on their capital. Both bought off their enemy by the surrender of the greater part of their wealth, including the treasures of the temple.

2. Commendable justice (14:4-6): Only on one score does Amaziah receive the reproof of the author of Kings. He failed to remove the high places. Not until the reign of Hezekiah was any attempt made to abolish the use of these local shrines and to enforce the law that insisted on a central sanctuary for national worship. On the other hand, the sacred historian points to one very commendable action of this king. Once he had the kingdom firmly under his control, Amaziah ordered those who had assassinated his father to be executed (cf. 2 Kings 12:20). He refused, however, to follow what was standard policy among rulers of his time and have the sons of the assassins slain as well. Here Amaziah was submitting to the Law of Moses that stipulated sons were not to be executed for the sins of their fathers (Deuteronomy 24:16).

B. Campaign against Edom (2 Chronicles 25:5-16)

1. Issue of Israelite mercenaries (25:5-10): Subjugation of Edom was vital to the prosperity of Judah. Amaziah resolved to launch a massive effort once again to conquer that land. He mustered an army of 400,000 men, which included 100,000 mercenaries from the northern kingdom. Rebuked by a prophet for lack of faith in enlisting the services of the Israelites, Amaziah dismissed the mercenaries.

2. Success in Edom (25:11-16): Amaziah's Edom campaign met with great success. Ten thousand of the enemy fell in battle, and an equal number were captured and ruthlessly executed by being thrown from a high cliff. The climax of this campaign was the capture of the almost impregnable Edomite capital of Sela, later known as Petra. Following the lead of many great conquerors, Amaziah gave the city a new name—Joktheel, i.e., "subdued by God" (2 Kings 14:7).

C. War with Israel (2 Kings 14:8-14)

1. An ill-advised challenge (14:8): Upon returning to Judah, Amaziah discovered that the Israelite mercenaries whom he had dismissed had vented their anger by rampaging through cities of Judah killing some 3,000 men and taking much spoil (2 Chronicles 25:13). His confidence bolstered by his successes in Edom, Amaziah determined to avenge the actions of those Israelite soldiers by challenging the northern king, Jehoash, to a military showdown.

2. A mocking fable (14:9): Jehoash responded to the challenge of Amaziah by means of a fable. The thistle, the lowest and most despised plant of the forest, sent to the stately cedar to request the hand of his daughter in marriage. In antiquity such a request was

517

tantamount to a claim to equality. A mere beast of the field happened by and trampled the thistle into the dust of the earth.

3. Explanation of the fable (14:10): The application of Jehoash's parable is obvious. Amaziah had enjoyed a measure of success against Edom. Now, like the thistle, he thought he was equal to the cedar, the mightiest of kingdoms. Amaziah had best stay at home and glory in his past triumphs. If he ventured forth against Israel he would find himself as easily crushed as the thistle beneath the feet of a wild animal. Jehoash was as confident of success as was Amaziah. His three recent triumphs over the powerful Arameans were just as impressive as Amaziah's victory over the Edomites.

4. A sneak attack (14:11): The message from Jehoash did not deter Amaziah. Jehoash anticipated that confrontation was inevitable. He decided that the best defense was an offense. Jehoash crossed the border and launched a sneak attack through the Philistine plain. The two forces met at Beth-shemesh, which lies almost due west of Jerusalem on the western frontier of Judah.

5. Amaziah's defeat (14:12-14): In this test of strength between the two kingdoms—the first since the days of Abijam over a hundred years earlier—the armies of Judah were utterly crushed with each soldier fleeing to his *tent,* i.e., home. Amaziah himself was captured and brought to Jerusalem. There under threat of death he was forced to order the gates of Jerusalem opened to Jehoash. The king of Israel broke down some six hundred feet of the northern wall of Jerusalem. The spoils of war fell to the conqueror—the objects of value that had accumulated in the temple since Joash of Judah had bribed Hazael with its treasure. The treasures of the royal palace, including all the spoils Amaziah had captured in Edom, were also taken. To discourage a retaliatory attack by Judah at a later time, hostages were taken by Jehoash.

D. Death of Amaziah (2 Kings 14:15-22)

1. Assassination (14:15-20): Amaziah maintained himself on the throne of Judah for several years after his humiliating defeat by Jehoash of Israel. Like his father before him, Amaziah died in a conspiracy. He had aroused much dissatisfaction by his importation of foreign idols (2 Chronicles 25:27) and by fifteen years of inaction after his defeat by Jehoash. When he heard rumors of the conspiracy against him, Amaziah fled to Lachish on the southwestern frontier of Judah. His enemies, however, were too numerous and powerful.

518

Amaziah was assassinated in Lachish. Though he had died in disgrace at the hands of his own servants, the conspirators were minded to treat the royal corpse with respect. The body was brought back to Jerusalem *upon horses,* i.e., a horse-drawn chariot, where it was buried.

2. *Uzziah, the people's choice (14:21-22):* For the first time in the history of Judah *the people* took the initiative in determining who ruled. Azariah (also called Uzziah) was elevated to the throne. One passage suggests that this took place after the death of Amaziah (2 Kings 14:21). Chronological considerations, however, indicate that Uzziah had been made king in place of his father some twenty-four years earlier (c. 792 BC), perhaps not long after Amaziah's ignominious defeat at the hands of Jehoash of Israel. Uzziah was sixteen years old at the time. He was thirty-nine when he became sole ruler. Only after the death of his father did Uzziah achieve greatness.

HEYDAY PERIOD
2 Kings 14:23-15:7

Israel and Judah achieved their greatest glory under the reigns of Jeroboam II in the north and Uzziah in the south. This somewhat unexpected turn of events resulted from two factors. About 800 BC, after crushing the Arameans, the Assyrians withdrew to their own territory. Then for over half a century, until 745 BC, the Assyrians remained politically dormant. This gave the states that had been oppressed by the Arameans an opportunity to recover.

Jeroboam in Israel
[793-753 BC]
2 Kings 14:23-29

A. General Assessment (2 Kings 14:23-24)

Jeroboam II was the greatest king of the northern kingdom, and yet his reign of forty-one years (793-753 BC)[59] is passed over with

---

[59]A study of all the data from both kingdoms indicates that Jeroboam II served as coregent with his father Jehoash for twelve years. Thus the total of Jeroboam's reign was forty-one years (793-753 BC). He became sole ruler in 782 BC. See Edwin R. Thiele, *A Chronology of the Hebrew Kings* (Grand Rapids: Zondervan, 1977), pp. 25, 75.

great brevity in the Bible. Like all the kings of the Jehu dynasty, Jeroboam II continued to follow the apostate calf worship. For this reason Jeroboam II is said to have done evil in the eyes of Yahweh.

B. Kingdom Expansion (2 Kings 14:25-27)

1. Geography of expansion (14:25a): The military successes of Jeroboam II were considerable. He was able to restore the borders of Israel as they had been in the earlier days of the northern kingdom. His kingdom stretched from the *entrance of Hamath*—the high slopes in the valley between the two ranges of the Lebanon Mountains—to *the sea of the plain,* i.e., the Dead Sea. The recovered territory included all of Transjordan as far south as the river Arnon, the border of Moab. Some think that Moab itself may be included in this general description of the territorial conquests of Jeroboam II.

2. Contribution of Jonah (14:25b-26): The success of Jeroboam II is attributed to the guidance of Jonah the prophet. This is the same prophet famous for what happened to him as he tried to flee the responsibility to preach in Nineveh. The author of Kings explains the divine aid to Jeroboam II as being due to unfathomable divine compassion. God saw the extreme suffering of his people under the Arameans and thus raised up his prophet to give inspired advice to the king in his efforts to free Israel from this oppression.

3. God's patience and provision (14:27): Although the nation was deserving of judgment, Yahweh decided not to blot out the name of Israel at this time. He gave the nation a grace period, an opportunity to repent, an Indian summer before the winter of retributive judgment. He gave to Israel the deliverance promised by Elisha (cf. 2 Kings 13:17) and later by Jonah. This deliverance which began under Jehoash was brought to a successful completion by Jeroboam II. Thus one Jeroboam founded the northern kingdom; another restored it to its ancient glory.

C. A Puzzling Reference (2 Kings 14:28)

One note concerning Jeroboam II has puzzled commentators for years. He is said to have recovered Hamath and Damascus *which belonged to Judah.* These two cities north of Israel had belonged to Israel during the days of David and Solomon. How these two cities could be said to have belonged to Judah in this period has not been explained successfully. The question of the relationship between

Judah and the kingdoms of Hamath and Damascus in the north must be left open.

Uzziah in Judah
[791-740 BC]
2 Kings 15:1-7

A. General Assessment (2 Kings 15:1-4)

Uzziah (also called Azariah) began his independent reign over Judah in 767 BC when his father and coregent of twenty-four years was assassinated. Altogether Uzziah reigned fifty-two years. The author of Kings rates him as a good king with one exception, viz., he failed to confine the worship to the place that Yahweh had designated. The Chronicler mentions the positive influence of a prophet named Zechariah upon his life. *As long as he sought Yahweh, God prospered him* (2 Chronicles 26:5).

B. Military Accomplishments (2 Chronicles 26:2-8)

Judah experienced its heyday under Uzziah's reign. This king was a conqueror. He was able to recover Elath from the Edomites in the south. He captured and dismantled certain Philistine fortresses, then built his own cities in the area. He defeated the Arabians and the Maonites. Uzziah forced the Ammonites to pay him tribute. Because of his large standing army (307,500) which was both well-trained and well-armed, the power of Uzziah was feared far and wide.

C. Other Accomplishments (2 Chronicles 26:9-15)

Uzziah was a builder. He refortified Jerusalem and installed catapults and other *engines of war invented by skillful men.* He also built towers in outlying areas to protect his vast herds of cattle. He built cisterns to provide water for his vineyards and fields. He *loved the soil.*

D. Pride and Punishment (2 Chronicles 26:16-28)

The marvelous prosperity that Uzziah enjoyed caused him to be filled with pride. He attempted to usurp the position and prerogatives of the priesthood, something that was forbidden to anyone who was not descended from Aaron. Uzziah took a censer, entered the temple over the protests of the priests, and burned incense on the golden altar. At that moment God struck him with leprosy. The king was

521

forced to spend the final years of his reign in a *house of separation* isolated and alone. His son Jotham then assumed the royal functions.[60] Uzziah's sin and the beginning of Jotham's co regency took place about 750 BC (2 Kings 15:5).

PAYDAY PERIOD
2 Kings 15:8-16:20

The history of Israel and Judah was radically affected by the rise of Tiglath-pileser III of Assyria. Heretofore the Assyrian military thrusts into Syria-Palestine had been merely tribute-gathering raids. A new policy, however, was inaugurated by Tiglath-pileser. This monarch was determined to build an empire. He designed the policy of massive population deportation that was so effective in holding captive peoples in check. By removing the upper classes of a conquered nation and resettling them in some remote portion of his empire, Tiglath-pileser was able to reduce the threat of local rebellions throughout his domain.

Israel Submits to Assyria
2 Kings 15:8-26

The heyday period for Israel ended abruptly with the death of Jeroboam II in 753 BC. In the next thirty years Israel had six kings representing five dynasties.

A. Reign of Zechariah (2 Kings 15:8-12)
Zechariah was the last representative of the Jehu dynasty. He reigned but six months in 753 BC. The fact that he succeeded to the throne at all was a fulfillment of promises made to the founder of his dynasty (cf. 2 Kings 10:30). God promised Jehu his sons were going to hold the throne to the fourth generation.

B. Reign of Shallum (2 Kings 15:13-15)

---

[60]Jotham assumed control of the government when his father was banished to a *separate house* in 750 BC. Uzziah died in 740 BC. Jotham handed the government over to his son Ahaz in 735 BC, but he continued to serve as king emeritus for another four years (cf. 2 Kings 15:30). See Edwin R. Thiele, *A Chronology of the Hebrew Kings* (Grand Rapids: Zondervan, 1977), p. 78.

522

Shallum, the assassin of Zechariah, was able to hold the throne for only thirty days. Hearing of his conspiracy, Menahem, an army general, marched from Tirzah to Samaria, got Shallum into his power, and put him to death.

C. Reign of Menahem (2 Kings 15:16-22)

1. Attack on Tiphsah (15:16-18): Zechariah had plans to continue the expansionist policies of his father Jeroboam. At the very time he was assassinated, the armies under Menahem were garrisoned at Tirzah awaiting orders to march northward to attack Tiphsah on the Euphrates River. After rather easily disposing of Shallum, Menahem launched the expedition that previously had been planned. When the city of Tiphsah refused to surrender, Menahem treated it in a most cruel way. Even pregnant women were ripped open and their unborn children bandied about on the swords of his soldiers. All the territory from Tirzah in Israel to Tiphsah fell temporarily under the control of Menahem. Assyria was weak and unable to resist these incursions.

2. Tribute to Assyria (15:19-20): Menahem's conquests in the north were short-lived. In 745 BC the mighty Tiglath-pileser, known in Babylonia as King Pul, came to the throne of Assyria. In one of his early campaigns Tiglath-pileser invaded Israel and forced Menahem to pay an enormous tribute of a thousand talents of silver ($2,000,000 BV). This payment in effect made Menahem a vassal of Tiglath-pileser and placed his throne under the protection of the Assyrian monarch. To secure this tribute money, Menahem taxed the wealthy landowners fifty shekels ($2,000 BV) each. Content for the moment with his take, Tiglath-pileser returned to Assyria. Menahem reigned ten years over the northern kingdom (752-742 BC).

D. Reign of Pekahiah (2 Kings 15:23-26)

Menahem was succeeded by his son Pekahiah who reigned two years (742-740 BC). Nothing of significance happened during his reign. One of his captains, Pekah the son of Remaliah, conspired against him and slew him in the tower (i.e., lofty part) of the royal palace. Joining Pekah in this conspiracy were fifty Gileadites who may have been part of the royal bodyguard.

Anti-Assyrian Coalition
2 Kings 15:27-31

Throughout the reigns of Menahem and his son Pekahiah, Pekah had maintained a rival dynasty, perhaps in Transjordan. This reconstruction is based on the statement that Pekah ruled for twenty years. The independent rule of Pekah began in 740 BC and ended in 732 BC.

Pekah was radically anti-Assyrian in his foreign policy. He joined with Rezin of Damascus in forming a coalition of western states that hoped to be able to withstand further Assyrian incursions into the area. This alliance is an extraordinary and somewhat unexpected political development. Not since the early days of Ben-Hadad I had either Israel or Judah been allied with the Aramean state. For a century and a half the kings of Damascus had been bitter enemies of the people of God. The military resurgence of Assyria under the dynamic leadership of Tiglath-pileser (745-727 BC) forced the states of Syria-Palestine into a political realignment.

Turmoil in Judah
2 Kings 15:33-16:9

A. Reign of Jotham in Judah (2 Kings 15:32-38)

The period of independent prosperity continued in Judah for about fifteen years longer than in Israel. The southern kingdom remained strong during the sixteen year reign (751-736 BC) of Jotham, son of Uzziah.

1. Building accomplishments (15:34-35): Jotham is evaluated as a good king. He is said to have done according to all that his father did except that he did not repeat the tragic mistake of attempting to enter the temple (2 Chronicles 27:2). Yet he made no effort to destroy the high places that were so offensive to the Lord. He did, however, build the *high gate* of the temple, which appears to have been on the north side of that structure. This gate probably was intended to serve as further fortification against possible attack from the north. The Chronicler relates that Jotham also restored other fortifications (2 Chronicles 27:3).

2. Conquest of Ammon (2 Chronicles 27:5): One of the significant accomplishments of Jotham was the subjugation of Ammon. For three years the Ammonites paid enormous annual tribute to Judah—a hundred talents of silver and 10,000 measures of both wheat and barley.

B. Ahaz Seizes the Throne (2 Kings 15:32-16:4)

Perhaps fearing that his father could not deal with the impending crisis created by the anti-Assyrian coalition, Ahaz seized the throne in 735 BC. He rejected the overtures of the anti-Assyrian coalition. He either did not feel threatened by Assyria, or else he feared Tiglath-pileser so much that he did not wish to offend the Great King in any way.

C. Invasion of Judah (2 Kings 16:5-9)

1. Extent of the invasion (16:5-6): In 734 BC Pekah and Rezin invaded Judah with the purpose of deposing Ahaz and putting someone more sympathetic to the anti-Assyrian cause on the throne. Jerusalem was besieged, but did not fall. The fortifications of Uzziah (2 Chronicles 26:9) and Jotham (2 Chronicles 27:3) had, no doubt, greatly strengthened the city since the time it was captured so easily by Jehoash (cf. 2 Kings 14:13). Frustrated at Jerusalem, the coalition roamed farther south and captured Elath driving out the garrison that had been stationed there since the days of Uzziah (cf. 2 Kings 14:22). From that time on the Arameans (or perhaps Edomites) occupied this important seaport city.[61]

2. Judean losses (2 Chronicles 28:5-15): Ahaz suffered severe casualties at the hands of the coalition. Rezin carried off a great number of captives to Damascus. Pekah is said to have inflicted 120,000 casualties in one day *because they had forsaken Yahweh.* Several prominent members of Ahaz's administration, including one of his sons, lost their lives in this war. Some 200,000 *women, sons and daughters* were taken captive to Samaria. These captives were quickly released at the insistence of the prophet Oded.

3. Other losses (2 Chronicles 28:16-19): At the same time Ahaz was trying to deal with the Syro-Ephraimitic invasion, the Philistines took from Judah a number of prominent villages in the lowlands and Negev. Through this combination of calamities Yahweh humbled

---

[61]The difference in the Hebrew spelling of *Edomites* and *Arameans* is so slight that it is conceivable that a scribal error occurred here. It is difficult to imagine Arameans from Damascus remaining in far distant Elath for any length of time. It is far more reasonable to regard the capture of Elath as a blow against Judah. Once the city fell, it was returned to the native people.

Judah *because of Ahaz king of Israel, for he had brought about a lack of restraint in Judah and was very unfaithful to Yahweh.* Perhaps the Philistines were also members of the anti-Assyrian coalition.

Judah Submits to Assyria
2 Kings 16:7-20

The Syro-Ephraimitic invasion of Judah forced Ahaz to make a crucial political decision that had religious consequences for decades to come.

A. Appeal to Assyria (2 Kings 16:7-9)

In his extreme desperation, Ahaz turned to Tiglath-pileser of Assyria for relief from the invaders. He asked the mighty king to deliver him from the Syro-Ephraimite threat. Sacred and royal treasuries were drained in order to send to Nineveh the appropriate gift intended to seal the alliance between the two countries. In 732 BC the Assyrian attacked and captured the city of Damascus. King Rezin himself was slain when the city fell. The immediate threat to Judah from Syria and Ephraim (Israel) ceased. Ahaz, however, had sold his soul for temporary security.

B. Corruption in Judah (2 Kings 16:10-18)

1. Ahaz fancies a pagan altar (16:10): Following the conquest of Damascus, Tiglath-pileser summoned Ahaz and other vassal kings to confirm officially their submission to him through a formal treaty. While in the city, Ahaz saw an altar that struck his fancy. To curry favor with his new master, Ahaz sent back to Jerusalem to Urijah the high priest detailed instructions for making this altar. By this action he was acknowledging the superiority of the gods of Assyria.

2. Ahaz worships at the altar (16:11-18): Being a man with no backbone, Urijah did not resist the royal orders. When he returned from Damascus, Ahaz personally made use of the new altar for his private sacrifices. Eventually the old Solomonic altar was removed from its place of prominence, and all temple sacrifices were offered on the Assyrian altar. In the course of time temple courtyard objects were stripped of decorative accessories probably to meet Judah's tribute obligations to Tiglath-pileser.

3. Increasing corruption (16:1-4): Ahaz's sixteen year reign (732-716 BC) was one of the most decadent on record. Of the kings of

Judah, only Manasseh and Amon receive greater condemnation. Eventually Ahaz shut up the temple and suspended the sacrificial offerings and burning of incense. To replace temple worship he erected altars *in every corner of Jerusalem* (2 Chronicles 28:24; 29:7). Ahaz tolerated and participated in the corrupt worship in the high places and groves. He reintroduced and personally participated in the worship of Canaanite deities, even to the extent of immolating his son (cf. 2 Chronicles 28:3).

FALL OF THE
NORTHERN KINGDOM
2 Kings 17:1-41

The nationalist King Pekah of Israel who headed the anti-Assyrian coalition was assassinated in 732 BC. The last king of the northern kingdom, Hoshea, sought to preserve the kingdom of Israel by pledging fidelity to Tiglath-pileser.

Reign of Hoshea
[732-723 BC]
2 Kings 17:1-4

A. Corruption (2 Kings 17:1-2)

Hoshea ruled for nine years in Israel (732-723 BC). Like his predecessors in the north, Hoshea did evil in the eyes of Yahweh. He continued the apostate calf worship, leaned upon the arm of flesh, and turned a deaf ear to the voice of God's prophets. His guilt, however, did not equal that of the kings who immediately preceded him.

B. Conspiracy (2 Kings 17:3-4)

1. Attempt to regain independence (17:3): When Tiglath-pileser died in 727 BC, Hoshea tried to regain his independence by withholding the annual tribute money. The new Assyrian king, Shalmaneser, came up against him and forced him to resume his position as a vassal.

2. Alliance with King So (17:4): Hoshea searched for some other means by which he might extricate himself from the grip of Assyria. Grasping at straws, he was persuaded to enter alliance with a certain King So of Egypt. This So is probably to be identified with Sib'e, a commander of one of the small monarchies of the Egyptian

527

delta.[62] With this backing, the Israelite monarch tried once again to withhold tribute from Shalmaneser. This act of rebellion brought down the wrath of the Assyrian upon Samaria. The text as it stands gives the impression that Hoshea may have gone out to meet Shalmaneser to sue for peace and pardon. He was then arrested and imprisoned.

Fall of Samaria
2 Kings 17:5-6

The Assyrian army began to besiege the kingless capital of Israel. According to the Hebrew mode of reckoning parts of years as full years, the siege lasted three years. Actually the siege need not have lasted longer than one full year and parts of two other ones, i.e., a little over one year. Samaria held out as long as it could, anticipating the promised aid from Egypt. Finally in 723 BC Samaria fell[63] to *the king of Assyria,* either Shalmaneser, or to Sargon who claimed the throne that same year. The Assyrian records relate that 27,290 persons were carried captive from Samaria, and doubtless many others from smaller villages round about.[64] These captives were taken and distributed in the distant eastern provinces of the Assyrian empire.

Explanation of Israel's Fall
2 Kings 17:7-23

---

[62]J.A. Wilson, "So," *Interpreters' Dictionary of the Bible,* vol. R-Z, p. 394. Others think "So" is not a person, but a place—the Egyptian capital of this period, Sais. The Hebrew text as it stands suggests that a person is intended.

[63]The commonly accepted date of 722 BC for the fall of Samaria is based on the claims of Sargon to have captured the city in his accession year. Assyriologists today generally regard these claims as inaccurate. Royal scribes were involved in revisionist history in an attempt to camouflage the difficulties that Sargon had in consolidating his claims to the throne. Sargon did at a later time re-capture Samaria. A reasonable reconstruction is that Samaria was captured by Shalmaneser in 723, but rebelled shortly thereafter when Shalmaneser died. Sargon recaptured the city and deported (more?) of its inhabitants.

[64]In his annals Sargon mentions deporting people from Mesopotamia to the "Hatti land" (Syria-Palestine) in the first year of his reign (721 BC). A similar repopulation of Samaria took place in Sargon's seventh year (715 BC). In the days of Esarhaddon (681-669 BC) Samaria received another infusion of foreign colonists (Ezra 4:2).

Prophets interpreted history as well as outlined future events. The prophetic author of Kings now offers an explanation of the calamity that befell the northern kingdom. He also hints that the same fate will fall on Judah.

A. Initial Apostasy in Israel (2 Kings 17:7-12)

1. Calf cult (17:7-8, 16): After God had delivered his people from the oppression in Egypt they had taken up the worship of other gods. They followed the *statutes of the heathen,* i.e., their customs and religious observances, even though these were the very "statutes" that caused God to order the Canaanites expelled from the land. The kings of the northern kingdom compounded the apostasy when they introduced into the nation the calf cult as a substitute for the pure worship ordained by Yahweh. The author of Kings regarded those calves as *molten images.*

2. Other religious offenses (17:9-12): In private the Israelites participated in all kinds of rites that were not pleasing to Yahweh. High places were built throughout the land in open violation of the divine command that there be one temple and one altar. In the most insignificant locations as well as in the population centers stone pillars and the wooden Asherahs were set up. The worship in the high places followed the pattern of Canaanite worship with the offering of incense. By these actions Israel indicated allegiance to the idols.

B. Aggravated Apostasy (2 Kings 17:13-17)

1. Rejecting God's word (17:13-15): In spite of the blatant apostasy in Israel, God graciously continued to plead with his people and warn them through *prophets* and *seers.* God's people responded to the prophetic efforts by continuing to *harden their necks,* i.e., to be obstinate, just as their *stiff necked* fathers who had failed God so often in the wilderness period. Rejecting the *statutes* of Yahweh, the people of Israel rejected the covenant with God into which they had entered at Mount Sinai (cf. Exodus 19:5-8). Yahweh's *testimonies*—those commandments that witness of him and reveal his nature—they also rejected. The people chose to follow *vanity,* the empty, futile, impotent pagan gods. As a result they themselves became vain, i.e., impotent. Whereas God commanded his people to be separate and distinct from all nations, they chose instead to follow the way of the heathen.

529

2.   *Adopting foreign deities (17:16-17a):* In the days of Ahab, Phoenician deities were introduced alongside the apostate calf worship. For a time both Baal and his consort Asherah had companies of prophets in Samaria. At some stage, astral deities were introduced into Israel, the worship of the various planets. Such worship must have been imported from Mesopotamia.

3.   *Pagan practices (17:17b):* With the pagan deities came pagan practices such as child immolation (cf. 2 Kings 16:3), and various magical practices (cf. 2 Kings 9:22). The people of Israel had sold themselves to do evil with the deliberate intention of provoking Yahweh to wrath.

C. Rejection of National Israel (2 Kings 17:18-23)

1.   *Northern Israel cast off (17:18):* When their cup of iniquity was full, God's wrath, long restrained, descended upon Israel. God removed them out of his sight. They were cast off, removed from their land. They were disowned and disinherited as the people of God (cf. Hosea 1:9). Judah alone was left to carry the torch as God's peculiar people.

2.   *Judah's waywardness (17:19):* By God's grace the southern kingdom was preserved for a few years after the destruction of the northern kingdom. Judah, however, also rejected the commandments of Yahweh and embraced the *statutes of Israel,* i.e., the Baal worship and all the vile practices connected with it. The only sin of Israel not attested in Judah is that of the calf worship.

3.   *All Israel rejected (17:20):* Since God is no respecter of persons, he rejected *all the seed of Israel,* i.e., Judah as well as Israel. He afflicted them by the hand of foreign oppressors—the Arameans, the Assyrians and the Babylonians. In addition to these powers, God gave his people into the hand of *spoilers,* i.e., neighboring nations that took advantage of the weakness of Israel and Judah to attack and plunder them. This divine program of harassment and humiliation lasted until Judah as well as Israel had been removed from God's land and God's favor.

4.   *Stages of rejection (17:21-23):* The rejection of *all the seed of Israel* took place in three great stages. First, God tore the ten northern tribes away from the house of David. By the introduction of the calf worship, Jeroboam *drove Israel from following Yahweh.* Throughout the history of the northern kingdom, the people never turned from this great sin introduced by Jeroboam. Second, God removed Israel from

his sight, i.e., from the land that was under the guardianship of Yahweh. In fulfillment of prophetic warnings dating back to Moses, Israel was carried away captive to Assyria. The third stage of the rejection of *all the seed of Israel* unfolds in the remaining chapters of the book of Kings.

5. *Lost tribes of Israel:* A great deal of speculation has arisen about the fate of the northern tribes. At the time the Book of Kings was written, they were still scattered throughout the Assyrian empire (2 Kings 17:23). Some of the former citizens of the northern kingdom returned to Palestine with Zerubbabel in 538 BC, and others with Ezra in 458 BC. Those who remained in the lands of the captivity either united with the Jewish colonies that were established there, or else simply adopted fully the practices of the heathen, intermarried with them, and disappeared as a distinct people. Theories of migrations of these tribes into Europe and/or the New World are spun out of fertile imaginations.

Repopulation of Samaria
2 Kings 17:24-41

A. Assyrian Policy (2 Kings 17:24)

Following the precedent of Tiglath-pileser, King Sargon replaced those Israelites taken into captivity with subjects from Mesopotamia and Syria. By separating people from their native lands and from their leadership, the Assyrians hoped to be able to prevent rebellions from subject peoples.

B. Plague on Colonists (2 Kings 17:25-28)

1. *Burgeoning lion population (17:25):* The foreign colonists were ignorant of Yahweh. They therefore failed to pay the Lord proper respect. To teach them a lesson, Yahweh sent against them a plague of lions. Since rural areas of Israel were depopulated, conditions were favorable for the rapid increase of the lion population. Several of the colonists lost their lives. The situation became a matter of grave concern.

2. *Request for a Yahweh priest (17:26):* Word spread to the Assyrian king along with the suggestion that the colonists needed to learn the proper ritual to perform in order to please the God of Israel. The king then ordered one of the priests of Yahweh to return to Samaria to teach the colonists. While a remnant of the former

531

citizenry of Israel remained in the land (2 Chronicles 34:9), they were familiar with the details of the religious ritual practiced in the temples. Apparently all the priests had been deported by Sargon.

3. *Work of the Yahweh priest (17:27-28):* The priest and his entourage returned to dwell in Bethel, the religious capital of the old Kingdom of Israel. He taught the new settlers to *fear Yahweh,* i.e., the perverted form of worship once practiced in Bethel. No positive evidence exists, however, that this priest set up a new calf image to replace the one which had been carried off to Assyria (Hosea 10:5).

C. Religion of the Samaritans (2 Kings 17:29-41)

1. *Blended religion (17:29-31):* Those who settled in the region of Samaria were polytheists. In spite of the teaching of the priest of Yahweh, they continued to worship their native deities.[65] They set up their idols in the high places that had been constructed by the Samaritans throughout their cities. The Sepharvites were even offering up their children as sacrifices to their gods.

2. *Their practices (17:32-33):* Polytheism by its very nature is syncretistic. Thus it is not strange to find that the foreign colonists in the territory of Samaria *feared Yahweh and served their own gods.* The Samaritans followed the apostate practice of recruiting priests from all ranks of society (cf. 1 Kings 12:31). These priests were willing to officiate in the illegitimate high places that were maintained contrary to the Law of Moses.

3. *Ignored God's word (17:34-40):* Had the Samaritans really wanted to serve Yahweh they would have attended to the *statutes and ordinances* that were binding upon all who would truly worship the Lord. The Sinai covenant required that God's people worship no other God. All religious devotion belonged exclusively to Yahweh who had brought these people out of the land of their bondage. God's promise of deliverance and protection for Israel was conditioned upon their

---

[65]The Babylonians worshiped Succoth-benoth, which is generally regarded as a corruption of the name of the goddess who was the wife of Marduk, viz., Sarpanitu. The men of Cuth or Cuthah continued to honor Nergal the god of war, which was the titular deity of their native city. The colonists from Hamath worshiped Ashima, a deliberate misvocalization of Asherah, the Canaanite mother goddess. Nibhaz and Tartak were purely local deities of the Avites. Adram-melech may be a special title of Shamash the sun god. Anammelech may be an intentional Hebrew corruption of the name of the goddess Anunit, the consort of Shamash (17:29-31).

faithfulness to him. All warnings about recognizing other gods were ignored by the colonists in Samaria.

4. New Testament Samaritans: The syncretistic worship of the Samaritans continued right down to the time of the author of Kings (17:41). By the time of Christ, however, the Samaritans had become devoted followers of Yahweh and devout followers of the Law of Moses in most respects. To this day a small community of these Samaritans still can be found in Nabulus, Israel.

END OF THE SISTER KINGDOM PERIOD

We have now covered 683 years of Israel's history

ASSYRIAN PERIOD

Brink of Destruction

Biblical Location: 1 Kings 18-23 + Chronicles chapters

Beginning Point: Samaria Fell (723 BC)

Ending Point: Carchemish Battle (605 BC)

Duration: 118 Years

Key Players: Hezekiah, Isaiah, Manasseh, Josiah, Jeremiah, Sennacherib

Key Events: Hezekiah Revival; Assyrian Invasion; Manasseh Apostasy; Jeremiah Call; Josiah Revival; Nineveh Fall

Scriptural Theme:
The LORD will bring on you and on your people and on the house of your father a time unlike any since Ephraim broke away from Judah--he will bring the king of Assyria (Isaiah 7:17).

Christian Application:
For this reason they could not believe, because, as Isaiah says elsewhere: "He has blinded their eyes and deadened their hearts, so they can neither see with their eyes, nor understand with their hearts, nor turn--and I would heal them." Isaiah said this because he saw Jesus' glory and spoke about him (John 12:39-41 NIV).

36
KING WHO
COULD NOT DIE
2 Kings 18-20

Chapter Chronology

Hezekiah		687
Co-regent	HEZEKIAH	
728	715	

After the fall of Israel, the kingdom of Judah continued to survive for another 136 years. Hezekiah was ruling in the southern kingdom when the Assyrians captured Samaria and deported the northern tribes. Seven others followed him on the throne of David. The Assyrian Period was characterized by two thoroughgoing revivals followed by periods of apostasy.

HEZEKIAH'S REFORM
2 Chronicles 29:3-31:21

Stirrings of Revolt

Hezekiah was twenty-five when he came to the throne as a co-regent with his father in 728 BC. His father Ahaz died in 715 BC. After his father died, Hezekiah reigned twenty-nine years, until 687 BC. This king receives unqualified praise from the author of Kings (2 Kings 18:3). No other king before or after manifested such complete confidence in the Almighty. Throughout his life he faithfully observed the Law of Moses. Because of his obedience, *Yahweh was with him.* Of no other king except David is this statement made (cf. 2 Samuel 5:10).

Clergy Commissioned
2 Chronicles 29:3-11

A. State of Worship (2 Chronicles 29:3-7)

Immediately after the death of his wicked father, Hezekiah ordered the priests and Levites to cleanse the temple of all the *filthiness* that Ahaz had allowed to accumulate there. During those dark days the temple doors had been locked, the lamps extinguished. No incense had been burned, no burnt offerings had been presented.

B. State of the Nation (2 Chronicles 29:8-11)
As Hezekiah assessed the situation, the deplorable political position of the nation was due to the neglect of the things of God. *The wrath of Yahweh* had been turned against Judah. The nation had experienced humiliating military defeats during the reign of Ahaz. Women and children had been carried into captivity. The kingdom was an object of ridicule. Only by entering into a new covenant would the burning wrath of Yahweh be turned away from the nation.

Temple Cleansed
2 Chronicles 29:12-19

Fourteen Levites representing the major branches of the tribe assumed leadership in the reformation. The cleansing of the temple precincts took eight days. For an additional eight days the priests consecrated the house itself. Every unclean thing was removed from it to the Kidron Valley. On the sixteenth day of the first month the clergy reported to King Hezekiah that the cleansing of the temple was complete. Even the utensils that Ahaz discarded had been consecrated and returned to their place beside the altar of burnt offering.

Worship Restored
2 Chronicles 29:20-36

A. Atonement Offerings (2 Chronicles 29:20-28)
Early the next morning the king and princes of the city went to the temple to worship. Sacrifices were offered to purge the altar and to *atone* (lit., cover over) the sin of *all Israel.* Hezekiah apparently intended to include those who once belonged to the northern kingdom in the benefits of his sacrifice. The sacrifices were to the accompaniment of the Levitical musical arrangements of David, Gad and Nathan.

B. Voluntary Offerings (2 Chronicles 29:29-36)

538

At the completion of the burnt offerings provided by the king, the assembly began to bring voluntary burnt offerings. All the while the Levites were singing praises to Yahweh *with the words of David and Asaph the seer.* The number of priests who consecrated themselves was too small to handle the ritual slaughtering of the thousands of animals. Levites were pressed into service to assist them. On this occasion the Levites had been more conscientious to consecrate themselves than the priests. The sudden re-establishment of the divine order of worship brought joy to the heart of the king and his people.

Royal Proclamation
2 Chronicles 30:1-12

A. Invitation to the Feast (2 Chronicles 30:1-9)

Temple cleansing was not completed in time for the regular observance of Passover on the fifteenth day of the first month. Consequently, Hezekiah, his princes and the assembly decided to celebrate the feast in the second month. Couriers carried the royal proclamation throughout all the land, and even into the region of Ephraim and Manasseh. Hezekiah particularly pled with those who had escaped the hand of the king of Assyria to come again to that sanctuary that Yahweh had consecrated forever. He urged them to serve Yahweh so that his burning wrath might be turned away from them. Hezekiah assured the former citizens of the northern kingdom that they will find compassion from God.

B. Response to the Invitation (2 Chronicles 30:10-12)

For the most part the hardened sinners of the north were unreceptive to the gracious invitation of Hezekiah. Nevertheless, some from Asher, Manasseh and Zebulun humbled themselves and came to Jerusalem for the Passover celebration. *The hand of God* was on Judah. The citizens there were united to do what the king and princes commanded *by the word of Yahweh.*

Passover Celebration
2 Chronicles 30:13-27

A. Passover Observance (2 Chronicles 30:13-20)

A large throng assembled in Jerusalem for the Passover. Their zeal for Yahweh was demonstrated when they removed the illegitimate altars from Jerusalem and cast them into the Brook Kidron. Many in the assembly—especially those who came from the north—were not ritually consecrated. The Levites slaughtered the Passover lamb for them. Though technically in violation of the Law of Moses, these people went ahead and ate the Passover. Hezekiah prayed that the good Lord pardon those who sincerely desired to partake even though they were ritually impure. Yahweh heard that prayer and *healed* the people.

B. Passover Extension (2 Chronicles 30:21-27)

Passover was followed by the weeklong celebration of the Feast of Unleavened Bread. Each day during the offering of the peace offerings the Levites and priests praised Yahweh with loud instruments. Hezekiah continued to encourage the Levites in these ministries. The assembly determined to extend the glorious celebration for another seven days. They had more than enough to eat. The king and his princes contributed 2,000 bulls and 17,000 sheep. Great joy filled Jerusalem because both as to attendance and unanimity of spirit, this celebration exceeded any since the days of Solomon. The proceedings concluded with a blessing by the Levitical priests. *Their voice was heard, and their prayer came to his holy dwelling place, even heaven.* God intended to bless his people once again.

Other Reforms
2 Chronicles 31:1-21

A. Cleansing (2 Chronicles 31:1)

Those who had been present at the great Passover celebration in Jerusalem returned to their cities determined to serve Yahweh alone. They removed every vestige of idolatry throughout the cities of Judah, and even in the territories of the former northern kingdom. Meanwhile the king also pressed forward in his reform efforts. Even the bronze serpent that Moses had erected in the wilderness was destroyed by Hezekiah because it had become an object of worship. The people affectionately referred to it as Nehushtan, "the little bronze thing" (2 Kings 18:4).

B. Contributions (2 Chronicles 31:2-19)

1. Priestly portions (31:2-10): Hezekiah reorganized the twenty-four courses of priests and Levites. He restored the royal subsidy so that the daily set offerings could be presented as well as the special offerings for special days. He ordered the people to give the portion due the priests and Levites so that they could devote themselves full time to the law of Yahweh. The people responded to the king's order enthusiastically. In less than four months Azariah, the high priest, reported that the priests had an overabundance of food. Hezekiah blessed Yahweh and his people.

2. Excess contributions (31:11-19): Under royal directive, the storage rooms in the temple were prepared to house the surplus contributions and consecrated things. Levitical officers were appointed to oversee collection, storage and distribution of these gifts.

C. Blessing (2 Chronicles 31:20-21)

Hezekiah did what was *good, right, and true* before Yahweh his God. Every work he undertook he did with *all his heart.* Consequently he prospered in his reign.

HEZEKIAH'S PERSONAL CRISIS
2 Kings 20:1-21

Date: 702 BC

Two clues aid in the chronological placement of 2 Kings 20. First, fifteen years were added to the life of King Hezekiah. Since that king died in 687 BC, his miraculous healing reported in 2 Kings 20 must have taken place in 702 BC. Second, in 2 Kings 20 Hezekiah still had possession of his treasure (cf. verses 13-17). Thus the illness and recovery must have taken place prior to the Assyrian invasion when the king was forced to drain his treasury to pay tribute to Sennacherib (cf. 2 Kings 18:13-16).

Hezekiah's Illness
2 Kings 20:1-4

A. Prophetic Announcement (2 Kings 20:1-2)

In those crucial days just prior to the great Assyrian invasion, Hezekiah was smitten with a life-threatening malady. To the royal chambers Isaiah the prophet was dispatched with a message of warning. *Set your house in order for you shall die and not live!* In the face of this shocking announcement the good king turned on his bed away from his numerous attendants and faced the wall so that he might pray to his God with more concentration.

B. Hezekiah's Prayer (2 Kings 20:3-4)

1. He claimed God's promises (20:3a): The king's prayer is a model for those who are afflicted with serious illness. He first called upon Yahweh to remember how he had tried his very best to walk throughout life so as to meet with divine approval. This was not presumptuous self-righteousness. Hezekiah knew that he honestly had endeavored to serve God and do his will. Under the old covenant, length of days was promised to the righteous (cf. Proverbs 3:2; 9:11; 10:27). Hezekiah could not comprehend why he should be cut off in middle age—he would have been thirty-nine—when kings far less righteous had lived two and more decades longer. The king's opening statement is thus a form of expostulation and laying hold on divine promises.

2. He petitioned for God's mercy (20:3b): The earnestness of the king was manifested in the tears that accompanied his prayer. Besides the natural fear of death, there were other good reasons for Hezekiah's earnest petition. For one thing, at this point in his life Hezekiah had no male offspring (cf. 2 Kings 21:1). Furthermore, Hezekiah knew his early reformation efforts would surely bring upon Judah the wrath of the mighty Sennacherib. He wished to live to see his country through this crisis.

3. Prayer heard (20:4): Before Isaiah had reached the second of the three courtyards that surrounded the royal palace, God stopped him. The prophet was ordered to retrace his steps, enter the king's bedchamber, and reverse the thrust of the oracle he had delivered only moments before.

<h2 style="text-align:center">Hezekiah's Recovery</h2>
2 Kings 20:5-11

A. Announcement (2 Kings 20:5-6)

Hezekiah's fervent prayer was effectual. God promised the king that within three days he will be able to worship the Lord in the temple. God, however, did more than the king had asked. He granted Hezekiah fifteen additional years of life which, in effect, would more than double the length of his reign (cf. 2 Kings 18:2). Furthermore, God promised to deliver Hezekiah and Jerusalem from the hand of the king of Assyria. For the sake of his reputation both in Judah and among the heathen, and for the sake of his commitment to David, the Lord pledged himself to be Jerusalem's defender.

B. Symbolic Action (2 Kings 20:7)

Isaiah directed those present to place a lump of figs on the malignant boil. Figs were used as a remedy for such boils. The prophetic order, however, seems to have been more in the nature of a symbolic act. The fig poultice underscored that from that moment forward God intended gradually to heal the king of his terminal malady.

C. Sign (2 Kings 20:8-11)

1. Request for a sign (20:8): Even the prophet's symbolic act did not fully set the mind of Hezekiah at ease. Under the old covenant God frequently offered miraculous signs to substantiate promises that he made to people in desperate straits. That Isaiah had offered a sign to wicked Ahaz during the Syro-Ephraimitic crisis was well known (cf. Isaiah 7:11). Hezekiah assumed that such a sign was available to him as well. He therefore asked his friend Isaiah what the sign was going to be. Neither God nor the prophet was angry with this request. For Christians today to demand signs is faithless; but in an age of miracles, when prophets were empowered to give signs, faithful people might request them without incurring God's displeasure.

2. Nature of the sign (20:9-11): The sign involved the sundial, perhaps clearly visible from the window of the bedchamber. The king could indicate whether he wanted the shadow to go forward or backward on the steps. Hezekiah requested that the shadow change its direction and ascend the steps. Isaiah then prayed. God responded by bringing the shadow ten steps backward. This miracle did not necessarily involve the temporary reversal in the rotation of the earth. That the miracle was local is made clear in the parallel passage (2 Chronicles 32:31). Probably a very abnormal refraction of the rays of the sun caused the retreat of the shadow on the sundial.

D. Hezekiah's Poem (Isaiah 38:9-20)

After he recovered from his dreadful disease, Hezekiah composed a poem. In it Hezekiah reflected upon his thoughts during his illness.

543

For this reason the poem is a lament rather than a thanksgiving psalm. It emphasizes the mortality of the flesh rather than the miraculous healing.

Hezekiah's Pride
2 Kings 20:12-19

A. Embassy from Babylon (2 Kings 20:12)
Following his recovery, Hezekiah was visited by an embassy from Berodach-baladan. For some twenty years this Babylonian king had been a thorn in the flesh of the Assyrian rulers. Scholars generally have concluded that the object of the embassy was to persuade Hezekiah to enter into an anti-Assyrian alliance with Babylon.

B. Hezekiah's Response (2 Kings 20:13)
Hezekiah was dazzled by the attention bestowed upon him by these visitors from Babylon. He *hearkened unto them,* i.e., listened to their suggestions of an alliance between Judah and Babylon. Hezekiah showed the Babylonian emissaries all of his treasure and armaments both in Jerusalem and in fortresses throughout Judah. He may have been trying to convince these guests that he had the potential to be a valuable ally.

Hezekiah's Rebuke
2 Kings 20:14-19

A. Penetrating Question (2 Kings 20:14-15)
When the Babylonian embassy left, Isaiah appeared before Hezekiah with a message of rebuke. In order to elicit a confession about what had taken place, the prophet interrogated the king about his visitors. The prophet's question (*What have they seen in your house?*) got to the heart of the matter. Isaiah was asking whether Hezekiah treated his guests as ordinary ambassadors, or whether instead he courted an alliance with their master. To the credit of the king, he answered forthrightly and made no effort to conceal what had taken place. He readily acknowledged that he had shown these particular guests everything.

B. Divine Revelation (2 Kings 20:16-18)

The divine word of rebuke for Hezekiah was a revelation of what the future held in store for Judah. Hezekiah had gotten involved with the nation that ultimately will destroy Judah. All the treasures he boastfully had displayed to the ambassadors one day will be carried off as plunder to far-off Babylon. Hezekiah's *sons,* i.e., descendants, will one day become eunuchs in the court of the king of Babylon. Mere human foresight is incapable of suspecting that within a century, insignificant Babylon will completely turned the tables on mighty Assyria.

C. Disappointing Response (2 Kings 20:19)

Hezekiah accepted the prophetic rebuke. He thereby acknowledged that he had been in the wrong. As far as Hezekiah was concerned, the pronouncement was *good* because he himself was not personally involved. The king felt that God might have justly brought down on him personally some affliction or calamity in punishment for his political indiscretion. It was a relief to hear that the blow will not fall during his lifetime. The self-centeredness of this evaluation of the prophecy caused the attendants standing nearby to raise their eyebrows. Noticing their chagrin, Hezekiah turned to his courtiers to ask the rhetorical question: *Is it not good, if peace and steadfastness be in my days?*

ASSYRIAN
INVASION OF JUDAH
2 Kings 18:13-19:37

Date: 701 BC

For the king to appear so unconcerned about the future of his land was not very statesmanlike. The irony, however, is that Isaiah had said nothing about *peace and steadfastness* in the days of Hezekiah. Shortly Hezekiah's faith was tested by a confrontation with Sennacherib.

Siege Preparation
2 Chronicles 32:1-8

A. Physical Preparations (2 Chronicles 32:1-5)

Anticipating an invasion by Sennacherib, Hezekiah took actions to make a siege of Jerusalem more difficult. Water was *cut off* from the springs around the city. The meaning may be that they shut off the flow of the water in one direction, and guided it into another. A tunnel constructed in this period carried the water of the Gihon spring back into the city to the pool called Siloam. Other preparations included 1) strengthening the wall of the city; 2) building another outside wall; 3) making weapons and shields in great number; and 4) appointing military officers.

B. Psychological Preparations (2 Chronicles 32:6-8)

The king encouraged his people to be *strong and courageous* in the face of the impending Assyrian attack. He reminded them that *the one who is with us is greater than the one with him.* The Assyrian relied upon the arm of flesh. With the Jews, however, was Yahweh. He will fight for his people. The Jews *relied* on the words of Hezekiah.

Initial Stage of Invasion
2 Kings 18:13-16

A. Sennacherib's Success (2 Kings 18:13)

In the fourteenth year of Hezekiah's (independent) reign (701 BC), Sennacherib attacked Judah. On the famous Taylor Prism the Assyrian scribes recounted the details of this campaign. The Great King first smashed Tyre, one of the allies of Hezekiah. Most of the other anti-Assyrian confederates then capitulated, but Ashkelon, Ekron and Judah refused to submit. Sennacherib subdued the Philistine cities of the plains as well as an Egyptian relief column that attempted to come to their aid. He then launched an attack against Lachish which at this time was actually larger than Jerusalem.

B. Hezekiah's Payment (2 Kings 18:14-16)

1. Assyrian demands (18:14): With his outlying fortified cities under Assyrian control, Hezekiah decided that it was pointless to continue the rebellion. He acknowledged his transgression in rebelling against his overlord, and entreated Sennacherib to withdraw his forces. Whatever penalty the Great King chose to impose upon him, Hezekiah was willing to bear. Sennacherib pretended to be willing to accept Hezekiah's offer of surrender, and imposed upon his rebellious vassal the enormous tribute of three hundred talents of silver ($600,000 BV) and thirty talents of gold ($900,000 BV).[66]

According to the Assyrian records, Hezekiah was also compelled to 1) make certain territorial concessions; 2) surrender an Assyrian vassal king who was being detained in Jerusalem; and 3) send two or more of his daughters to Nineveh to become part of Sennacherib's harem.

2. *Hezekiah's tribute (18:15-18):* In order to meet the tribute demands of Sennacherib, Hezekiah emptied the treasuries of both the temple and the palace. Only some thirty years before (cf. 2 Kings 16:8) Ahaz had emptied these same treasuries in order to hire the services of Tiglath-pileser. Apparently Hezekiah had little or no gold readily available. He was forced to strip the gold from the pillars and doors that he himself had overlaid with the precious metal. Sennacherib relates that in addition to the two large sums of gold and silver, Hezekiah sent to him at this time "woven cloth, scarlet, embroidered; precious stones of large size; skins and horns of buffaloes; and two kinds of woods."

Surrender Demands
2 Kings 18:17-37

A. Confrontation at Jerusalem (2 Kings 18:17-18)

Sennacherib was not satisfied with the tribute paid by Hezekiah. He wanted nothing less than the total surrender of Jerusalem. While he himself was engaged in military operations in the lowland region of Palestine, he sent an embassy to Jerusalem to demand capitulation. At the head of the contingent were three officers bearing the titles Tartan, Rab-saris, and Rabshakeh. All three titles are known from Assyrian records. Hezekiah sent out to the wall three of his highest officials to hear what the Assyrians had to say. Because he could speak fluent Hebrew, Rabshakeh acted as spokesmen for the Assyrians.

B. Assyrian Intimidation (2 Kings 18:19-25

Rabshakeh came right to the point. Hezekiah obviously had been making military preparations for a siege of Jerusalem. How had he

---

[66]Sennacherib states that he imposed on Hezekiah a tribute of thirty talents of gold and eight hundred talents of silver. Perhaps the three hundred talents mentioned in the Bible was the amount available in stamped ingots, and the extra talents mentioned in the Assyrian inscription were obtained from other sources, such as the despoliation of the temple.

dared to take these steps? What was the basis for his confidence? One by one Rabshakeh attempted to eliminate the possible grounds upon which Hezekiah based his rebellion (2 Kings 18:19).

1. Empty boasting (18:20): Rabshakeh imagined Hezekiah boasting of his counsel and strength for war, i.e., of the wisdom of his advisers and his military capabilities. Such boasts were *merely words.*

2. False expectations (28:21): Expectations of aid from Egypt were doomed to frustration. Egypt was nothing but a *bruised reed* that will snap the moment any weight was applied to it.

3. Religious miscalculation (18:22): Hezekiah could expect no help from Yahweh since he had been desecrating his high places. Perhaps the Assyrians had also learned that Hezekiah's reform efforts actually angered some segments of the population. Rabshakeh may have been trying to exploit the religious unrest within Judah.

4. Military weakness (18:23-24): Rabshakeh resorted to ridicule. He mocked the fact that the Judean army lacked cavalry. Hezekiah did not have enough fighting men to turn back even one unit of the Assyrian army.

5. Fighting against Providence (18:25): Finally, Rabshakeh argued that Yahweh himself had dispatched Sennacherib against Jerusalem. Perhaps the Assyrian had heard of the prophecies of Isaiah (Isaiah 7:17-24; 10:5-12) that foretold the Assyrian invasion of Judah.

C. Request of Judeans (2 Kings 18:26-27)

The propaganda of Rabshakeh was having its intended effect on the Jewish soldiers manning the walls. Hezekiah's officers interrupted the Assyrian at this point. They request that he speak to them in Aramaic, the diplomatic language of the day. Rabshakeh, of course, refused to comply with this request. His very purpose in coming to Jerusalem was to intimidate the soldiers and weaken the resolve of the citizens to resist. He wanted Jerusalem's defenders to realize that soon they will be brought to the last extremity of hunger and thirst. They will be forced even to consume their own excrement and drink their own urine.

D. More Propaganda (2 Kings 18:28-37)

1. Don't trust Hezekiah (18:28-29): The urgent request of the Judean diplomats only stirred Rabshakah to greater efforts. He rose and addressed himself directly to the citizens on the walls. He urged the defenders not to allow Hezekiah to deceive them, particularly with his assurances of supernatural deliverance.

2. Exile is not so bad (18:30-32a): From threat Rabshakeh turned to grandiose promises. If Jerusalem will but surrender, each one in the city will be allowed to return to his own land where he might live a peaceful life. Then after a time, Sennacherib will come and transplant them to a new land. Such national deportations were so common in the Assyrian Empire that Rabshakeh knew he must mention this possibility if his remarks were to enjoy any measure of credibility. So he attempted to place this practice in the best possible light. He tried to persuade the Judeans that being transported hundreds of miles from their homes really was not so bad—that they were to be envied rather than pitied for being about to experience it. The gracious Sennacherib will even try to settle them in a beautiful land just like Judah! In any case, if they followed Rabshakeh's advice they would live; if Hezekiah's, they would die.

3. No god has resisted Assyria (18:32b-35): Rabshakeh continued by ridiculing Hezekiah's faith as fanatical and unrealistic. No local deity thus far had been able to deliver his people from the mighty Assyrian army. To make his point more emphatically, Rabshakeh ticked off the recent victories of the Assyrian war machine, including Samaria. Since the Jews could produce no example of a national god that had been able to withstand Assyria's might, they should abandon their hope of supernatural deliverance from Sennacherib.

4. Response of the defenders (18:36-37): Rabshakeh's efforts to foment some insurrection within Jerusalem failed. The Judeans on the walls strictly followed their king's orders to maintain silence. Horrified at the blasphemies of the Assyrian, Hezekiah's three ministers ripped their robes and returned to the royal palace to report all that had been said.

Isaiah's Initial Prophecy
2 Kings 19:1-7

A. Isaiah Consulted (2 Kings 19:1-5)

1. Messengers dispatched (19:1-2): Hezekiah tore his garments and donned sackcloth when he heard the report of his ministers. He then went to the temple to seek divine counsel. At the same time the king dispatched a delegation to Isaiah the prophet. The messengers wore sackcloth to emphasize the horror that Rabshakeh's threatening boasts had engendered.

2. *Messengers' request (19:3-5):* Hezekiah's messengers described the crisis to Isaiah. The nation had no strength to face up to the impending attack. Perhaps Yahweh will take note of the contemptuous words that Rabshakeh had spoken against the living God, and then reprove those words with some mighty act of judgment. Perhaps he will intervene on behalf of the remnant of his people.[67]

B. Isaiah's Response (2 Kings 19:6-7)

Isaiah seems to have already formulated a reply to the king even before the delegation arrived at his home. Hezekiah did not need to be afraid of the blasphemous words of the Assyrian. God will send a destructive blast against Sennacherib. The Assyrian will be forced to retreat to his own land. There Sennacherib will be assassinated.

Sennacherib's Letter
2 Kings 19:8-13

A. Reason for the Letter (2 Kings 19:8-9)

Failing in his mission to secure the surrender of Jerusalem, Rabshakeh returned to his master. By that time Sennacherib had taken Lachish and was warring against nearby Libnah. When the Assyrian king heard that the Ethiopian general Tirhakah was marching against him, he knew that he might be forced to make a strategic retreat from Palestine. For this reason he made one last effort to secure the surrender of Hezekiah. Messengers were dispatched to Jerusalem with a letter from the Great King.

B. Content of the Letter (2 Kings 19:10-13)

The letter suggested that Hezekiah had been deceived by the prophets who were promising that Jerusalem was going to be delivered from the Assyrians. Thus far any nation that had tried to match might with Assyria had been crushed. Sennacherib documented

---

[67]Sennacherib claims to have carried away 200,150 persons in this expedition. He already had captured all the outlying fortresses of Judah. Hence those residing in Jerusalem were truly a remnant.

this assertion by enumerating a number of cities that already had fallen to Assyria.

Hezekiah's Prayer
2 Kings 19:14-19

Hezekiah took the letter to the temple and spread it out before the Judge of all the earth. In mighty prayer the king called upon his God to recognize this challenge by Sennacherib. He admitted that the Assyrian monarchs could boast of an impressive list of conquests. The gods of these cities had been carried off as trophies of war or burned as worthless. That, however, only proved that the gods of the nations were but the creation of man's hands. Yahweh was the living God who could not be lumped together with gods of wood and stone. Hezekiah called upon God to remember his covenant with Israel, to deliver Jerusalem from this blasphemous invader in such a way as to vindicate his name among the nations of the earth.

Isaiah's Oracle
2 Kings 19:20-34

A. Condemnation of Sennacherib (2 Kings 19:20-26)

Hezekiah received an answer to his prayer through Isaiah. The prophet's oracle first rhetorically addressed the Assyrian invader. By the boisterous and blasphemous conduct of Rabshakeh, Sennacherib had reviled the Holy One of Israel. Furthermore the Assyrian had offended Yahweh with his boundless self-confidence that no natural barrier could impede his conquest. Did this foreigner not realize that Yahweh determined the rise and fall of kingdoms? Yahweh had enabled Sennacherib to lay waste fortified cities. He had placed within the hearts of the nations a fear that made them wither before the armies of Assyria.

B. Restraint of Sennacherib (2 Kings 19:27-28)

The omniscient God of Israel knew every movement of Sennacherib and every thought of his heart. He knew of the *rage* of the Great King against Hezekiah and against the God in whom Hezekiah trusted. Yahweh, therefore, will take action against Sennacherib. He will treat him as Assyrian kings customarily treated their captives. Yahweh will force a hook through Sennacherib's nose

551

and a bridle through his lips. This wild animal will be turned back from the walls of Jerusalem. He will return home hastily along the same route by which he had entered Palestine.

C. A Future for Judah (2 Kings 19:29-31)

1. A sign for Hezekiah (19:29): Isaiah's oracle included a sign for Hezekiah. In this case the prediction of a near event became the pledge that God will keep his word with regard to a more distant prediction. Since the Assyrians had come in the spring of the year, the Jews had not been able to plant their crops that year. They had to eat what grew of itself. The next year—probably a sabbatical year—they will have to do the same. In the third year, however, things will return to normal. This *sign* had reference to the promise that Jerusalem will be free from any further attack on the part of Sennacherib.

2. Hope for Judean remnant (19:30-31): The *remnant* that had escaped deportation at the hands of Sennacherib will again be firmly established in their land. That remnant will once again *bear fruit,* i.e., exhibit all the outward signs of prosperity. From the human perspective such a prospect seemed dim indeed at the time Isaiah uttered this oracle. The *zeal of Yahweh,* his zealous love for his people, will bring about this restoration to prosperity and glory.

D. Failure of Sennacherib (2 Kings 19:32-34)

Isaiah's oracle concludes with a forceful declaration regarding the present emergency. Sennacherib will not come to besiege Jerusalem. Rather he will be forced to leave off operations in Palestine and retrace his steps to Assyria. Yahweh will defend Jerusalem because his own honor was at stake and because of the great love that he had toward David.

Judah's Deliverance
2 Kings 19:35-37

A. Assyrian Army Slaughtered (2 Kings 19:35)

On the very night following Isaiah's dramatic prediction, the divine stroke fell against the armies of Sennacherib. The angel of Yahweh passed over the Assyrian camp and smote 185,000 of the enemy. When the survivors awoke in the morning they found their comrades absolutely dead, not sick or dying. Such a massive overnight catastrophe must be attributed to direct intervention by Yahweh himself.

B. Sennacherib Assassinated (2 Kings 19:36-37)

His army decimated, Sennacherib could do nothing other than beat a hasty retreat to Nineveh. Some twenty years later as he was worshiping in the temple of Nisroch he was assassinated by his own sons. Thus was fulfilled the prediction of Isaiah (cf. 2 Kings 19:7) that Sennacherib was going to *die by the sword in his own land.*

History of Israel

37
END OF
ASSYRIAN DOMINATION
2 Kings 21-23

Chapter Chronology

						609
Manasseh		Amon		Josiah		
697		643	641			
Sen-nach-erib	Esar-haddon		Ashurbanipal		627	
	681	669				

VASSAL REIGNS OF
MANASSEH AND AMON
2 Kings 21:1-24

Good King Hezekiah was followed on the throne by the wickedest king to ever rule in Judah. All the religious gains brought about by Hezekiah were soon lost. The nation plunged anew into idolatry and all its attendant evils. Political independence, so bravely engineered by the father, was willingly surrendered by the son. Judah again fell into the orbit of Assyrian vassal kingdoms.

Sin of Manasseh
[697-643 BC]
2 Kings 21:1-18

A. Wicked Deeds (2 Kings 21:1-9, 16)
1. What he permitted (21:1-5): Considering the length of his reign—fifty-five years—very little is known about the reign of Manasseh. He came to the throne at the age of twelve. Wicked princes were soon able to sway the boy king to their more liberal point of view. As a result Manasseh followed all the abominations of the heathen. High places dedicated to Canaanite deities reappeared. The worship of the Tyrian Baal, first introduced by Athaliah in Judah (cf. 2 Kings 11:18), again made its appearance. A wooden image symbolic of the goddess Asherah was erected by the king. Worship of

555

the heavenly bodies which had been so popular in the days of Ahaz again was tolerated. Altars to other gods were erected in both the outer and inner courts of God's temple.

2. *What he practiced (21:6-9):* Manasseh dedicated his sons to Molech. The crown prince he offered up as a burnt offering. Manasseh superstitiously kept track of his lucky days. He resorted to enchantments, i.e., spells and the like. Necromancers (those who call up the dead) and wizards (psychics) were placed in official positions. The defilement of the temple by an Asherah image annulled God's promises to abide permanently in that sacred place.

3. *Persecution (21:16):* The national decadence culminated in a bloody persecution of the faithful. Jerusalem was filled with blood from one end to the other. A widespread ancient tradition named Isaiah as one of the victims of this persecution.

B. Prophetic Condemnation (2 Kings 21:10-15)

God did not leave himself without a vigorous voice of protest during the corrosive reign of Manasseh. The great prophets of that period remain anonymous; but their message was plain. Because Manasseh had done more evil than the peoples who inhabited the land before Israel, God will judge Jerusalem as he earlier had judged Samaria. The plummet that God had placed alongside the house of Ahab in the north will now be placed alongside the house of David. Jerusalem will be emptied of its inhabitants as one empties garbage from a pan. Judah will be conquered and spoiled by her enemies.

C. Assyrian Vassal

The Assyrian annals add one detail about the reign of Manasseh. He is mentioned as a faithful vassal of Esarhaddon (681-669 BC). Manasseh even contributed troops for the Great King's invasion of Egypt in 669 BC.

Manasseh's Repentance
2 Chronicles 33:11-17

Toward the very end of his reign, Manasseh offended his master Ashurbanipal (669-627 BC). The Assyrians took him captive to Babylon. While in his *affliction* there, Manasseh repented of his sins against God and man. When the Assyrians restored him to his throne, Manasseh made a valiant effort to put away the idolatrous practices that he himself had introduced into the land. He repaired the altar of Yahweh, and re-established so far as he could the worship of the Lord.

Reign of Amon
[643-641 BC]
2 Kings 21:19-26

The short two-year reign of Amon receives scant attention in Kings. Like his father in the early part of his reign, Amon *forsook Yahweh the God of his fathers* and embraced all the gods of neighboring nations. Amon's allegiance to Assyria aroused the indignation of many patriots who desired freedom. Some of the attendants of the king fell on him in his own house and slew him. The assassins apparently did not have the support of the powerful *people of the land,* the landed gentry, for those who had murdered the king were swiftly executed. If the conspirators had intended to bring about a change of dynasty, their plot failed. The people of the land sought out the rightful heir, though he was but a lad of eight, and made him king.

REIGN OF JOSIAH
[641-610 BC]
2 Kings 22:1-23:30

The death knell sounded for Judah during the reign of Manasseh (Jeremiah 15:4). Because of the national reformation led by his grandson Josiah, however, God granted to Judah a temporary reprieve. This king, who came to the throne at the tender age of eight, determined to steer his nation out of the Assyrian orbit in which worship of pagan gods was mandatory. He led the last great reformation of the monarchy period.

Freedom from Assyria
2 Kings 22:1-23:27

Josiah reigned for thirty-one years. As in the case of Hezekiah the author of Kings states that Josiah did *what was right in the sight of Yahweh and walked in all the ways of David his father.* This good king never deviated from the right path.

A. Initial Reforms (2 Chronicles 34:1-7)

1. Two steps in the right direction (34:1-7): Josiah began his reform movement in his eighth year when he was but sixteen years old. In that year he began *to seek the God of his father David.* The reformation gained momentum in Josiah's twelfth year (628 BC) when he began *to purge Judah and Jerusalem from the high places, the Asherahs, carved Images, and molten images.* The reformation may have proceeded in stages so as to test the reaction of Assyria which doubtlessly would have regarded such reform as tantamount to rebellion.

2. Call of a teenage prophet (Jeremiah 1:2): In the thirteenth year of Josiah, a young teenager named Jeremiah was called to preach. The ministry of this great prophet must have given powerful impetus to the king's reform efforts.

Temple Repair Project
2 Kings 22:1-7

The reformation reached its climax in the king's eighteenth year (622 BC). Josiah appointed a three-man committee led by Shaphan the scribe. This committee counted the monies that had been collected to pay for much needed repairs in and around the temple. The monies probably had been accumulating since the twelfth year of the king when the reformation intensified. The high priest Hilkiah distributed the monies among the Levitical superintendents who were in charge of the renovation project. These were men of impeccable honesty in whom full confidence was placed to properly administer the funds.

SCROLL DISCOVERED
2 Kings 22:8-13

Date: 622 BC

Impact of the Scroll
2 Kings 22:8-11

A. Identity of the Scroll (2 Kings 22:8)

When they were bringing out the money that had been stored in the temple, Hilkiah made a striking discovery. In one of the numerous temple storage areas he found an ancient scroll. Opinions differ as to exactly what this book was. Some think that it was only the Book of Deuteronomy or some portion thereof. Others think the entire Pentateuch was discovered. Hilkiah handed the scroll over to Shaphan. He read enough of it to determine that the book was exceedingly valuable. Shaphan brought the scroll to the attention of the king.

B. Concern about the Scroll (2 Kings 22:9-11)

When Josiah heard the tone and contents of the scroll, he was quite upset. He tore his garments to demonstrate his sorrow. He recognized the language of the scroll as that of the law of God. Even though that book had for many years been lost, much of its contents had been preserved and handed down orally by the pious within the nation.

Verification of the Message
2 Kings 22:12-13

A. Committee Appointed (2 Kings 22:12-13)

1. Reason (22:12): The king appointed a five-man committee to make further investigation regarding the scroll. Apparently Hilkiah the high priest was the chairman of this committee. Prior to the time of David such inquiry was made through the high priest as he utilized the Urim and Thummim. Since David's day, however, this type of revelation was sought from a prophet of God.

2. Issue (22:13): The issue was not whether or not the scroll was authentic. Of this there was no doubt. Rather the king wished to ascertain whether or not the threats that the scroll contained were to have an immediate fulfillment. Josiah recognized that the nation had been doing, and to some extent continued to do, those very things that were forthrightly condemned in the law. In view of the grave threats that Moses had made against apostasy, the king perceived that the wrath of Yahweh was about to be poured out upon his nation.

Word of Huldah
2 Kings 22:14-20

A. Identity of Huldah (2 Kings 22:14)

The royal committee consulted Huldah, a prophetess who was readily available *in the second city,* i.e., lower district of Jerusalem.

559

History of Israel

Her immediate availability seems to be the reason she was selected over Jeremiah or Zephaniah, the more prominent prophets of the period. Huldah is the only prophetess in Israel who seems to have ranked on an equal footing with the prophets.

B. Oracle of Huldah (2 Kings 22:15-20)

1. *God's wrath on Judah (22:15-17):* After examining the contents of the scroll, Huldah sent a prophetic oracle back to the king. Josiah's worst fears were justified. All the threats in the scroll will shortly befall Jerusalem. Such drastic punishment was justified in view of the fact that Judah had turned completely from God. The Judeans had burned incense to other gods. They had constructed abominable images with what appeared to be a determined effort to provoke the wrath of Yahweh. The unquenchable wrath of God had been kindled by this apostasy. That wrath was about to be poured out on Jerusalem.

2. *Encouraging word for Josiah (22:18-20):* Yahweh had taken note of the piety of Josiah and the determined reformation effort that he had launched. Because the king had humbled himself when he heard the message of the scroll, he received prophetic assurance that the threatened destruction of Judah was not going to occur during his reign. Josiah will *die in peace,* i.e., he will not personally see the judgment envisioned in the scroll.

Covenant Renewal
2 Kings 23:1-7

A. National Assembly (2 Kings 23:1-3)

1. *Reading the scroll (23:1-2):* After hearing the verdict of Huldah, the king's first action was to call for a national assembly. Josiah read (or caused to be read) in the courts of the temple *all the words of the book of the covenant* that had been discovered. The entire Pentateuch could scarcely be read through in less than ten hours. For this reason many scholars feel that the book which is referred to here is Deuteronomy. The reading of the legal portions of the entire Pentateuch, however, cannot be ruled out entirely.

2. *Renewing the covenant (23:3):* The king renewed the old covenant with God that had been broken during the grossly wicked reigns of Manasseh and Amon. He pledged to obey from the heart the totality of the Law of Moses. To this commitment the representatives

of the people gave their assent. Thus they also became parties to the covenant.

B. Jerusalem Cleansed (2 Kings 23:4-7)

1. Pagan paraphernalia burned (23:4): Josiah ordered the priests and Levites to remove from the house of God all vessels that had been made for and dedicated to any pagan deity. This included the two altars that had been set up in the inner and outer courts. In compliance with the law, Josiah burned this pagan paraphernalia (cf. Deuteronomy 7:25; 12:3) in *the fields of the Kidron valley,* i.e., the upper part of the valley to the northeast of Jerusalem. Josiah did not want even the smoke from this fire to pollute the capital. He then carried the ashes of this material to Bethel so as to remove them completely from the vicinity of the Holy City. How appropriate that the ashes of these pagan objects be returned to the city in which, to large measure, the idolatrous impurities that had corrupted both Israel and Judah had originated.

2. Pagan priests removed (23:5): Josiah also removed the pagan priests who had been imported during the reigns of Manasseh and Amon. These priests offered incense to Baal, the sun, the moon and other heavenly bodies at high places throughout the land.

3. Asherah destroyed (23:6): Josiah also destroyed the Asherah, wooden symbol of the Canaanite goddess, from the temple. Manasseh originally set up this idol (2 Kings 21:3). After his repentance he had removed the Asherah (2 Chronicles 33:15). Later Amon replaced it (2 Chronicles 33:22). Following the example of Asa, Josiah took this abominable image to the brook Kidron. He burned the wooden parts to ashes and crushed the metal parts to a fine powder. This powder was then sprinkled on the graves of the common people. Burial places were regarded as unclean and thus fit receptacles for any kind of impurity.

4. Sacred prostitutes removed (23:7): Josiah tore down the houses of the male temple prostitutes (lit., consecrated ones). These men were an essential element in the worship of Astarte. The houses of these prostitutes were in close proximity to Yahweh's temple. God's house had been defiled by the foul lust of these "consecrated ones." The *women who wove hangings for Asherah* were doubtless the priestesses of Asherah who were themselves prostitutes. The curtains that were used in the shrines where the impure fertility rites were performed were of dainty fabrics of many colors (cf. Ezekiel 16:16).

Josiah's Reformation
2 Kings 23:8-20

A. Reform in Judah (2 Kings 23:8-14)

1. Centralized priesthood (23:8): In order to prevent further illicit worship at the outlying high places, Josiah summoned to Jerusalem the Levitical priests who had served at these shrines. He forced them to remain in the capital. Throughout Judah, from Geba (near Bethel) to Beersheba in the south, Josiah *defiled* or desecrated the high places where these Levites had served. This action he hoped would render these shrines permanently unsuitable for religious services. The high place type worship had even invaded the city of Jerusalem. Altars and other religious paraphernalia had been set up in the large open buildings that were part of the gates of the city.

2. Restrictions on apostate priests (23:9): Josiah did not permit the apostate Levitical priests who had been summoned to Jerusalem to approach the altar of Yahweh or to have any part in the temple ritual. Nevertheless, they were permitted to partake of the priestly revenues. They were allowed to eat of the unleavened bread that only the priests could touch, and probably the portion of the sacrificial animals that were designated for priests. In other words, Josiah did not deprive these Levites of their livelihood.

3. Defiled Topheth (23:10): Topheth was the name given to the place in the valley of Hinnom where sacrifices were offered to Molech. The exact meaning of the word Topheth is unknown. The valley of Hinnom is that depression that sweeps around the more western of the two hills where on Jerusalem was built. This spot, sacred to Molech, was defiled by Josiah so that the abominations practiced there could not continue.

4. Blow against astral worship (23:11-12): One of the idolatries introduced during the Manasseh-Amon era was the worship of the sun. Sacred chariots and horses were stationed near one of the entrances of the temple to be ready for use in pagan processions. The sacred horses were *removed,* and the wooden chariots were burned. Rooftop altars, generally associated with the host of heaven, Josiah crushed into dust and then cast that dust in the Brook Kidron.

5. *High places defiled (23:13-14):* Josiah also destroyed the high places that Solomon had erected in the vicinity of Jerusalem for the benefit of his pagan wives. The entire ridge of hills on the east of the city came to be known as the "mount of corruption" because of the evil rites practiced there. These ancient shrines Josiah defiled by breaking their sacred pillars in pieces, cutting down the Asherahs, and by filling these areas with human bones. Form the earliest times bones were considered unclean.

6. *Occult practices banned (23:24-25):* Occult practices had flourished during the long reign of Manasseh. Josiah was determined to banish these devilish deeds from the land. Those with familiar spirits, i.e., mediums, and wizards who pretended to possess supernatural knowledge, were removed. The *teraphim* or household gods were destroyed whenever possible. *Idols* (lit., shapeless, formless things) probably again refers to objects used in private, perhaps figures used as amulets. Private superstitious practices (*abominations*) were uncovered and banished. Josiah conscientiously tried to fulfill all the precepts of the Law of Moses with regard to these matters. In his exact obedience to the law, Josiah was without equal among the kings of Judah.

7. *Response by the Lord (23:26-27):* In spite of Josiah's valiant efforts to reform the nation, the anger of Yahweh was not turned aside from Judah. At best, the reformation only gained a temporary reprieve for Judah. The sinister shadow of Manasseh still hovered over the hearts of the men of Judah in spite of all that Josiah had attempted to do. Therefore God determined to remove Judah *from his sight* just as he had removed Israel. Jerusalem, the city chosen by God as site of his temple, will be abandoned.

B. Reform in the North (2 Kings 23:15-20)

1. *Bones burned on Bethel altar (23:15-16):* When Jeroboam set up his altar at Bethel in 930 BC, he in effect made that city a high place. The buildings connected with this high place were torn down by Josiah. Whether the Bethel temple was still standing at this time is hard to determine. Probably the mixed race imported to the area by the Assyrians continued to worship at the site. The Asherah that was there Josiah crushed to powder and burned. From Israelite sepulchers Josiah ordered human bones to be brought out and burned on the Bethel altar. By this action he was unconsciously fulfilling the

prophecy made by the unnamed man of God some three hundred years earlier (cf. 1 Kings 13:2).

2. *Prophet's tomb spared (23:17-18):* The king inquired of the local inhabitants about the significance of a pillar in the area of the tombs. He was told that this pillar marked the sepulcher of the man of God from Judah who had predicted the very things that Josiah had done to the altar. Josiah then ordered his soldiers to leave undisturbed that particular sepulcher and the bones of the two prophets buried therein.

3. *High places defiled (23:19-20):* Josiah's army roamed at will throughout the former territory of the northern kingdom destroying and defiling the high places. This was the period of Assyrian decline, and the kings in Nineveh were no longer able to defend their outlying provinces. Taking advantage of this weakness, Josiah seems to have established his hegemony over the Assyrian provinces north of Judah. He reunited under his authority all the scattered portions of the old Israelite kingdom, except, perhaps, the Transjordan area. He levied taxes in Samaria as freely as in Judah (2 Chronicles 33:9). Throughout these territories Josiah slew the pagan priests and defiled the altars of the heathen shrines by burning human bones upon them just as he had done at Bethel.

C. Reform Celebrated (2 Chronicles 35:1-19)

1. *Levites replace ark (2 Chronicles 35:1-3):* The Passover feast became a focal point of Josiah's reform. The king set the priests in their offices. He *encouraged* them in the service of the house of God. The Levites were directed to put the ark in the temple. No longer was it to be a burden upon their shoulders. This suggests that the ark had been removed from the temple and hidden by the Levites during the days of wicked Manasseh. Another suggestion is that the ark had been removed during the time of temple renovation.

2. *Levites reorganized (2 Chronicles 35:4-6):* The Levites were to organize themselves by the ancient divisions that dated back to David and Solomon. They then were to position themselves in the holy place for the slaughter of the Passover animals. All was to be done *according to the word of Yahweh unto Moses.* The parallel passage in Kings alludes to *the book of this covenant,* an obvious reference to the scroll recently found in the temple.

3. *Unselfish spirit (35:7-15):* The king and royal officials contributed thousands of lambs to the lay people for Passover and the

feast of Unleavened Bread, which followed Passover. Priests and Levites worked together in preparing the Passover animals. After taking care of the Passover needs of the lay people, the Levites prepared the appropriate sacrifices for themselves and the priests. The singers and gatekeepers did not have to leave their posts because the Levites took care of the preparation for them.

4. *Assessment (35:16-19):* Thus did Josiah orchestrate the observance of the Passover and the Feast of Unleavened bread which followed. Not since the days of Samuel had a Passover been so numerously attended and so meticulously observed. The festival was attended not only by the citizens of Judah, but by many Israelites from among the ten tribes who still remained intermixed with the Assyrian colonists in the area of Samaria.

EGYPTIAN INTERLUDE
2 Kings 23:29-37

Confrontation at Megiddo
2 Chronicles 35:20-22

A. Egyptian Troop Movements (2 Kings 23:29)

With the fall of Nineveh to the Medo-Babylonian coalition in 612 BC, a refugee Assyrian government was established at Haran. In 610 BC that city also fell to the Chaldean king Nabopolassar. Fearing that the international balance of power was about to be upset, Pharaoh Neco (609-593 BC) decided to intervene on behalf of the tottering Assyrian kingdom. Neco's trip to the Euphrates River took him along the coastal plain of Palestine and through the pass at Megiddo.

B. Death of Josiah (2 Chronicles 35:20-25)

1. *Josiah warned (35:20-22):* Why Josiah took his tiny army to Megiddo in an attempt to stop the advance of Neco is not entirely clear. The Pharaoh tried to dissuade Josiah from this foolish confrontation. Neco assured Josiah that he had no quarrel with Judah. The Egyptian even insisted that God had directed him to undertake this mission. To resist him was to oppose God. The Chronicler seems to concur that the action of Josiah was contrary to the will of God for he declares that Josiah *hearkened not unto the words of Neco from the mouth of God.*

2. *Josiah wounded (35:23-25):* The battle was joined and Josiah was mortally wounded (2 Kings 23:29). Josiah's servant put the wounded king in his *second chariot*—a chariot of much lighter construction and drawn by fleeter horses—and hastened toward Jerusalem. The Chronicler implies that Josiah succumbed to his wound en route to the capital. Jeremiah seems to have led the nation in lamenting the death of this good king. The last year of Josiah's reign began in the fall of 610 BC. He was killed in July of 609 BC.

Removal of Jehoahaz
[July-October 609 BC]
2 Kings 23:31-35

After the death of Josiah, *the people of the land*, i.e., the landed gentry, placed his son Shallum on the throne. On what grounds the people preferred this son to his elder brother Eliakim is not known. Upon assuming the throne, Shallum adopted the name Jehoahaz. He reigned but three months. Jehoahaz was summoned by Neco to the Egyptian military headquarters at Riblah about two hundred miles north of Jerusalem. Why Jehoahaz left the safety of Jerusalem is not clear. In any case, for him the trip was ill-fated. He was deposed and deported to Egypt. The land of Judah was put under a tribute of a hundred talents of silver ($200,000 BV) and a talent of gold ($30,000 BV) annually.

Jehoiakim's Enthronement
[609-598 BC]
2 Kings 23:34-24:7

A. **Pharaoh's Vassal** (2 Kings 23:34-35)

Neco installed his own man, Eliakim, the older son of Josiah, on the throne. Pharaoh required his vassal to take a new name as a symbol of subjection, but Eliakim himself seems to have had the right to select the new name. He chose Jehoiakim ("Yahweh will set up"). Jehoiakim was unable to meet his tribute obligations to Neco from the depleted national treasuries. He was forced to impose a real estate tax upon the land owners for this purpose.

B. **Jehoiakim's Character** (2 Kings 23:36-37)

During Jehoiakim's eleven years on the throne all the idolatrous practices of the Manasseh era were reintroduced. In spite of the national poverty, this petty little king spent huge sums of money on himself. In one of Jeremiah's blistering sermons he condemned Jehoiakim for building for himself a fancy new palace (Jeremiah 22:13-14). Jehoiakim was the villain of the closing years of Judah's history. He was everything that is despicable in a national leader. He was a spendthrift, a bigot, an arrogant and irreverent tyrant who brooked no criticism, not even when that criticism came from a man of God. A prophet named Uriah was too bold in his denunciation of the king, and paid for his boldness with his life (Jeremiah 26:21). Jeremiah was in danger on more than one occasion during those eleven years.

C. Battle of Carchemish (2 Kings 24:1-7)

Jehoiakim carefully watched the political developments on the Euphrates River. From July 609 to June 605 BC the armies of the Babylonians and the Assyro-Egyptian coalition sparred. For the most part during those years the Babylonians were on the defensive. Finally, the Babylonian army under the brilliant young crown prince Nebuchadnezzar was able to launch a mighty offensive against the Egyptian stronghold at Carchemish. The Babylonians won a crushing victory. The tattered Egyptian armies fled southward from Carchemish in disarray. Nebuchadnezzar was able to roam at will through Syria-Palestine, the Hatti-land as he calls it in his annals.[68]

END OF THE ASSYRIAN PERIOD

We have now completed 795 years of biblical history

---

[68] See *Documents from Old Testament Times*, p. 79.

BABYLONIAN PERIOD
Deportation and Desolation

Biblical Location: 2 Kings 24 + Daniel, Jeremiah,
Ezekiel chapters

Beginning Point: Carchemish Battle (605 BC)

Ending Point: Babylon Fall (539 BC)

Duration: 67 Years

Key Players: Daniel, Ezekiel, Nebuchadnezzar, Belshazzar

Key Events: Jews Deported; Ezekiel Called; Jeremiah Persecuted;
Jerusalem Destroyed; Nebuchadnezzar Humbled

Scriptural Theme:
This is what the LORD Almighty, the God of Israel, says to all those I carried into exile from Jerusalem to Babylon: "Build houses and settle down; plant gardens and eat what they produce. ...When seventy years are completed for Babylon, I will come to you and fulfill my gracious promise to bring you back to this place (Jeremiah 29:4, 5, 10 NIV).

Christian Application:
So when you see standing in the holy place 'the abomination that causes desolation,' spoken of through the prophet Daniel [Daniel 9:27; 11:31; 12:11]--*let the reader understand--then let those who are in Judea flee to the mountains* (Matthew 24:15-16).

38
FALL AND EXILE
OF JUDAH
2 Kings 24-25

Chapter Chronology

Jehoi-akim	586 Zede-kiah 597	JUDEANS IN BABYLON		
Nebuchadnezzar 605		Amel-Marduk 562	Neriglissar 560	Nabonidus 556 ... 539

POST-CARCHEMISH
REPURCUSSIONS
2 Kings 24:1-17

In Judah
2 Kings 24:1

The battle of Carchemish changed the dynamics of the politics of the Near East. The Babylonians were now the masters of the world. Tiny Judah soon was forced to capitulate to the Babylonian juggernaut.

The battle of Carchemish occurred in the fourth year of the reign of Jehoiakim (Jeremiah 46:2). In that year Nebuchadnezzar came against Jerusalem. Jehoiakim was bound with bronze chains to be carried away to Babylon (2 Chronicles 36:6). Apparently Nebuchadnezzar changed his mind. He was content to take some hostages (e.g., Daniel) and some of the vessels of the temple (Daniel 1:1-2; 2 Chronicles 36:6). Jehoiakim became a servant, i.e., a vassal, to Nebuchadnezzar for three years.

In Babylon
Daniel 1-3

A. Hebrews Elevated (Daniel 1)

Four teenage Judeans were selected to receive training to serve in the royal administration in Babylon. The four were offered access to the finest food and drink. They sought permission, however, to eat a simple died that conformed to the regulations of the Law of Moses. At the end of the training period the four proved to be physically and mentally superior to all the other young men in the program.

B. Daniel: Dream Interpreter (Daniel 2)

In the second year of his reign Nebuchadnezzar had a dream that he perceived was communicating divine revelation. He insisted that his dream interpreters first tell him the dream he had experienced then interpret it for him. When they could not, the king ordered them executed. Daniel assured the king that he could interpret the dream if given time to pray about it. God revealed to Daniel that the dream concerned the entire sweep of history from Nebuchadnezzar to the end of time. Daniel and his companions were promoted in the royal service after this spectacular revelation.

C. Rescued from a Fiery Furnace (Daniel 3)

Nebuchadnezzar erected a huge image on the Plain of Dura and ordered all his subjects to worship it. Three Judean young men refused to bow. They were thrown into a fiery furnace. The king looked into the furnace and saw four persons walking about, and the fourth was like a celestial being. When the Judeans were brought out of the furnace they were unharmed. Even their clothing did not smell like smoke.

JEHOIAKIM'S REBELLION
AGAINST NEBUCHADNEZZAR
2 Kings 24:1-7

Occasion
2 Kings 24:1

In 601 BC Nebuchadnezzar brought his army down the coastal plain of Palestine. He apparently intended to invade Egypt and destroy Neco once and for all. On the borders of Egypt, however, Nebuchadnezzar met with a stinging defeat. This unexpected turn of events encouraged Jehoiakim to rebel against Nebuchadnezzar.

Judah's Peril
2 Kings 24:2-4

A. From Local Contingents (2 Kings 24:2)

Unable to attend to Jehoiakim personally, Nebuchadnezzar ordered bands of Edomites, Moabites and Ammonites to join local contingents of the Chaldean army in harassing Judah. Though these small units were probably unable to do much damage to the fortified cities of Judah, they did force the rural people to seek refuge in Jerusalem (Jeremiah 35:11). In ordering these attacks on Judah, Nebuchadnezzar was really the unconscious agent of Yahweh. The prophetic threats against Judah now started to be fulfilled.

B. From the Lord (2 Kings 24:3-4)

The final destruction of Judah had been decreed by the mouth of Yahweh. Judah had to be removed from his sight—carried off into a foreign land—because of the sins of Manasseh that survived into the reign of Jehoiakim.

Jehoiakim's Death
2 Kings 24:5-7

A. Issues about his Death (2 Kings 24:5-6a)

Jehoiakim died December 9, 598 BC. The circumstances of his death are not entirely clear. Jeremiah had predicted that he would be *buried with the burial of a donkey.* His death, said the prophet, will be unlamented (Jeremiah 22:18f). These words suggest that Jehoiakim was assassinated, or at least that his body was dishonored after death by his own countrymen. Another possibility is that when the Chaldeans arrived in force at Jerusalem to punish the rebellious city, they disinterred the corpse and heaped indignities upon it.

B. Jehoiakim's Son (2 Kings 24:6b-7)

Whether by violence or natural death, Jehoiakim was dead when the Chaldeans arrived. His young son Jehoiachin was left to face the wrath of the mighty Nebuchadnezzar. No further aid from Egypt was forthcoming. Even though Neco had successfully defended his land from the Babylonian threat of 601 BC, the Egyptians were in no position to challenge Nebuchadnezzar's hegemony over Syria-Palestine.

573

Jehoiachin's Deportation
2 Kings 24:8-17

A. General Assessment (2 Kings 24:8-9)

Jehoiachin was eighteen years old when he began to reign. His reign was but three months and ten days (2 Chronicles 36:9)—from December 10, 598 BC to March 16, 597 BC. During his brief reign he allowed the idolatries and superstitions that had prevailed under his father to continue. Jeremiah called this king *a despised, broken jar* and *a vessel wherein is no pleasure* (Jeremiah 22:28).

B. Jehoiachin's Peril (2 Kings 24:10-11)

Nebuchadnezzar's army was encamped around the walls of Jerusalem during most of the reign of Jehoiachin. The Great King himself was detained in a siege at Tyre. He sent his servants to deal with Jerusalem. During the course of the siege Nebuchadnezzar himself appeared on the scene, probably bringing with him additional forces.

C. Jehoiachin's Surrender (2 Kings 24:12-16)

1. Explanation: Jerusalem was well fortified. The city could have withstood several months of siege. Jehoiachin, however, realized that further resistance would only bring upon his people incalculable hardship. Perhaps he hoped that if he surrendered Nebuchadnezzar might allow him to retain his throne as a vassal king. Whatever his motives, Jehoiachin and the leading citizens of Jerusalem walked through the gates of the city and surrendered on March 16, 597 BC.[69]

2. Extent of deportation (24:12-16): In addition to the royal captives, Nebuchadnezzar carried away from Jerusalem additional treasure from the temple. Solid gold objects were taken; gold plated furniture was stripped. Some ten thousand of the leading citizens of the nation were also deported to Babylon.

---

[69]The date of the surrenders of Jehoiachin "is undoubtedly the most precise (date) in Israelite history during the biblical period and constitutes one of the cornerstones of biblical chronology." See Gershon Galil, "The Babylonian Calendar and the Chronology of the Last Kings of Judah" *Biblica* 72 (1991) 367. The biblical record of Jehoiachin's surrender is substantiated and supplemented by the Babylonian Chronicle. See James B. Pritchard, ed. *Ancient Near Eastern Texts Relating to the Old Testament* (third ed.; Princeton: University Press, 1969), p. 564.

574

ZEDEKIAH'S FIRST REBELLION
AGAINST NEBUCHADNEZZAR
2 Kings 24:17-20

Zedekiah's Vassal Reign
[597-587 BC]
2 Kings 24:17

Nebuchadnezzar appointed Mattaniah, another son of Josiah, to reign on the throne of David. Mattaniah took the throne name of Zedekiah ("righteousness of Yahweh"). This last king of Judah certainly made no attempt to live up to his new name. He allowed the people to continue their pollutions and abominations (2 Chronicles 36:14).

Inclination toward Rebellion
2 Kings 24:18-20

A. Plotting in the Western Empire

Zedekiah was inclined toward rebellion from the moment Nebuchadnezzar put him on the throne. Jeremiah the prophet thundered forth against the folly of resistance against Babylon, but still the political leaders clung to their suicidal course. When a new Pharaoh, Psamtik II, came to power in 594 BC Judah and neighboring countries began to make plans for a concerted effort against Babylon. Ambassadors from Edom, Moab, Ammon, Tyre and Sidon met in Jerusalem to plan the rebellion (Jeremiah 27:3ff). The plan must have been uncovered. That very year Zedekiah was summoned to Babylon to reaffirm his allegiance to Nebuchadnezzar (Jeremiah 51:59ff). Zedekiah's first major effort to break with Babylon was nipped in the bud.

B. Call of Ezekiel in Babylon (Ezekiel 1-3)

In 592 BC God called a man from a priestly family to be his prophet in Babylon. Ezekiel's ministry prior to the fall of Jerusalem back in the homeland was one of demolishing delusions that somehow Judah could survive as a nation through political strategy. Ezekiel's ministry was characterized by visions, allegories and action parables bordering on the bizarre.

575

C. Final Rebellion against Babylon (2 Kings 24:20)

A still more aggressive Pharaoh took the throne of Egypt in 588 BC. Pharaoh Apries—Hophra, as he is called in the Bible—actively encouraged a western coalition against Babylon. Zedekiah sent ambassadors to Egypt (Ezekiel 17:15) and entered wholeheartedly into the rebellion.

SIEGE OF JERUSALEM
2 Kings 25:1-7

A. First Nine Months (2 Kings 25:1)

1. Fall of outlying fortresses: The Babylonian army arrived at Jerusalem on January 4, 587 BC. They blockaded the city and began systematically to eliminate the out-lying strong points. The fortified towns of Lachish and Azekah were among the last to fall (Jeremiah 34:7).[70]

2. Intensified siege of Jerusalem: The siege of Jerusalem now began in earnest. Siege towers were constructed. These movable towers enabled the attackers to approach the walls on the same level as the defenders. Sometimes the siege towers contained battering rams. Jeremiah was viewed by his contemporaries as a collaborator with the enemy; he was in custody during the first phase of the siege (Jeremiah 34:1-7; chap. 32).

B. Break in the Siege (2 Kings 25:2-3)

In the summer of 587 BC an Egyptian army marched northward with the intention of relieving the pressure on Zedekiah. Nebuchadnezzar was forced temporarily to lift the siege in order to deal with this threat (Jeremiah 37:5; Ezekiel 17:17). Apparently with little effort the Babylonians were able to send the Egyptians scurrying back home. During the siege Jeremiah was arrested and thrown into a dungeon where he nearly died (Jeremiah 37:16).

C. Last Nine Months

---

[70]In 1935 eighteen ostraca that date to the time of the siege of Jerusalem were found in the ruins of Lachish. These ostraca are military communiqués between a field commander and his superior in Lachish. See Victor Matthews and Don Benjamin, eds. *Old Testament Parallels* (New York: Paulist, 1991), pp. 134-136.

Nebuchadnezzar then resumed the siege of Jerusalem. King Zedekiah sought counsel from Jeremiah (Jeremiah 34:17-21). The prophet was placed back in the court of the guard (Jeremiah 38:1-3). He subsequently was thrown into a cistern (Jeremiah 38:4-13). The defenders began to suffer from famine (Jeremiah 21:7, 9; Lamentations 2:12, 20). All the bread of the city was soon consumed. Famine was followed by pestilence (Jeremiah 21:6-7). After a time the city was reduced to the last extremity, viz., cannibalism (Lamentations 4:10).

D. Zedekiah's Flight (2 Kings 25:4-5)

On August 15, 586 BC, after a siege of eighteen months, the Babylonians were able to make a breach in the walls of Jerusalem. Zedekiah and his soldiers fled the city. Under cover of darkness the desperate king slipped past the enemy outposts and made his way toward the plains of the Jordan. He was intercepted, however, by the Babylonians. When his bodyguard deserted him, Zedekiah was helpless to defend himself.

E. Zedekiah's Capture (2 Kings 25:6-7)

Zedekiah was taken captive to Riblah where Nebuchadnezzar had made his headquarters. There the rebel stood trial before the officers of the Great King. Zedekiah was forced to witness the execution of his young sons. Then the Babylonians blinded the eyes of Zedekiah, probably by means of a red-hot rod. He was then placed in fetters and carried away to Babylon. There he remained in prison until the day of his death (Jeremiah 52:11).

Destruction of Jerusalem
2 Kings 25:8-17

Following the capitulation of Jerusalem, the Babylonian soldiers awaited further instructions regarding the fate of the city. A month after the successful breaching of the walls, Nebuzaradan, the captain of the guard, arrived from Riblah with orders to raze Jerusalem and prepare its inhabitants for deportation (2 Kings 25:8-10).

A. Captives Prepared (2 Kings 25:11-12)

Nebuzaradan ordered all Judean hostages—those taken in the siege together with deserters—prepared for deportation. Only the very poorest of the citizens were allowed to remain in the land. The Babylonians did not wish the area to uninhabited, since it could then have paid no tribute.

	**Chart 17** ***Deportations to Babylon***
Date	References	Numbers	Notes
605 BC	Daniel 1:1 2 Chr 36:6-7		Daniel and his friends taken
597 BC	2 Kgs 24:13-16 Jer 52:28 Ezek 1:2 2 Chr 36:10	10,000 3,023	Ezekiel and King Jehoiachin taken
586 BC	2 Kgs 25:3-7 Jer 52:29	832	King Zedekiah blinded, taken captive
582 BC	Jer 52:30	745	

B. Temple Plundered (2 Kings 25:13-17)

Before setting fire to the temple, the Babylonians plundered that edifice of all its treasures once again. The giant pillars of bronze—Jachin and Boaz—were broken up to facilitate transportation to Babylon. The same applies to the ornate bases of the portable lavers and the mammoth laver called *the sea*. All the smaller items of bronze were also carried off, along with what few vessels of gold and silver remaining from the previous despoliations of the temple in 605 and 597 BC. So much bronze was carried away by the conquerors that the scribes thought it to be an impossible task to weigh it all.

Jerusalem was totally burned and destroyed August 3, 586 BC.

Aftermath of Jerusalem's Fall
2 Kings 25:18-30

The Book of Kings closes with an appendix discussing three events which transpired after the destruction of Jerusalem.

A. Execution of Leaders (2 Kings 25:18-21)

Nebuzaradan selected the leaders most responsible for the prolonged resistance of Jerusalem to send to Riblah for execution. The high priest Sereiah and *the second priest* Zephaniah headed the list. Three Levitical supervisors, nine state officials, and sixty *people of the land who were found in the midst of the city* were also slain there (cf. Jeremiah 52:25).

B. Governorship of Gedaliah (2 Kings 25:22-26)

1. Gedaliah's appointment (25:22-23): After the fall of Jerusalem, Judah became a province of the Babylonian Empire. Gedaliah was appointed by Nebuchadnezzar to be governor over the poor of the land who had been left behind. He set up his headquarters at Mizpah. Gedaliah immediately launched a campaign to rebuild Judah. His first goal was to unite the various factions into which the remnant of the people was divided. Once the Babylonian army had withdrawn from the area, various guerrilla bands began to come out of hiding. They joined Gedaliah at Mizpah.

2. Gedaliah's program (25:24): Gedaliah urged the captains to use their influence to secure peace throughout the land. First, he assured them, they had no reason to fear serving the Chaldeans. This suggests that Gedaliah had used his influence with Nebuchadnezzar to secure amnesty for those who had participated in the war against Babylon. Second, he called upon these leaders to dwell peacefully in the land and render service to the king of Babylon. If they continued to do this, he promised them a life of peace.

3. Gedaliah's assassination (Jeremiah 41:1-16): The tranquility of the tiny remnant of the Jews was soon shattered. Ishmael, a member of the royal family, began plotting behind the scenes to assassinate Gedaliah. In the seventh month, Ishmael and ten cutthroats proceeded to Mizpah. Suspecting nothing, Gedaliah entertained these men hospitably (Jeremiah 41:1). During the course of the banquet, Ishmael and his men rose up and slew the governor, the Jewish officials who served with him, and his Babylonian bodyguard.

4. Flight to Egypt (25:26): Fearful of Babylonian retaliations, the remnant departed immediately for Egypt. At their first camping spot near Bethlehem, Jeremiah pleaded with them to trust the Lord and remain in the land (Jeremiah 41:17-42:22). The worldly captains, however, accused Jeremiah of attempting to deceive them. They pushed on to Egypt. Thus two Jewish communities survived during the exile, one in Babylon, and the other in Egypt.

JEWS IN EXILE AFTER THE

DESTRUCTION OF JERUSALEM

A. In Egypt (Jeremiah 43:8-44:30)

On Egyptian soil the Judean remnant again embraced pagan worship in the form of the Queen of Heaven. Jeremiah tried to reason with them, but they were committed to their goddess. The prophet warned that Nebuchadnezzar would overtake them in Egypt and deport yet more of them to Babylon. He offered them a sign of the impending invasion of Egypt. Pharaoh Hophra will fall into the hands of his enemies. In 568 BC Jeremiah's predictions regarding the Pharaoh and the Babylonian invasion of Egypt came true.

B. In Babylon (Daniel 4-5)

For the most part the thousands of Jews living in Babylon followed the advice of Jeremiah and settled down to live as normal a life as possible until the day of their deliverance (Jeremiah 29). Daniel continued to impress Nebuchadnezzar with his dream interpretation. He interpreted a dream about a great tree being cut down to mean that Nebuchadnezzar himself was going to lose his throne for a time. For seven years the king would live like an animal (Daniel 4). Daniel's prediction came to pass a year later.

No doubt the words written by Isaiah in anticipation of the exile to Babylon encouraged Jews in that area, especially as they saw Cyrus rising to power east of Babylon (Isaiah 44:28-45:13).

C. Release of Jehoiachin (2 Kings 25:27-30)

1. Explanation (25:27-28): King Jehoiachin was taken captive to Babylon in 597 BC. Until the end of the reign of Nebuchadnezzar, the king of Judah was kept in prison. When the Great King died in 562 BC, his son Evil-Merodach (Amel-Marduk) *lifted up the head of Jehoiachin,* i.e., restored him to royal favor. This encouraging development occurred in the last month of the thirty-seventh year of Jehoiachin's captivity. Perhaps due to the influence of Daniel, Jehoiachin's throne was placed above the thrones of the other captive kings in Babylon. The presence of these kings each on a throne of honor was thought to enhance the dignity of Evil-Merodach ("stupid one of Marduk").

2. Confirmation (25:29-30): The Babylonian king supplied suitable garments to the released monarch and invited him to dine daily at his royal table. Jehoiachin enjoyed this dignity until the day

580

of his death. In addition, Jehoiachin received a daily allowance of all that he needed for himself and his family, besides the food that he enjoyed at the royal table. Documents have been found in the Babylonian archives listing the royal provisions for Jehoiachin and his family.[71]

3. Significance: The release and subsequent elevation of Jehoiachin no doubt bolstered the morale of the Jewish captives and made them ever more confident that one day God would fulfill his promise to put an end to their banishment and restore them to their native land.

Following Nebuchadnezzar Babylon was ruled by a series of lackluster kings: Amel-Marduk (562-560 BC), Neriglissar (560-556 BC), Labashi-Marduk (556 BC) and finally Nabonidus (556-539 BC) who shared the throne with his more famous son Belshazzar.

END OF THE BABYLONIAN PERIOD

We have now completed 867 years of biblical history

---

[71]See *Documents from Old Testament Times*, pp. 84-86.

PERSIAN PERIOD
Restoration and Reconstruction

Biblical Location: Ezra, Nehemiah, Esther

Beginning Point: Babylon Fall (539 BC)

Ending Point: Malachi Death (ca. 400 BC)

Duration: 139 Years

Key Players: Zerubbabel, Joshua, Esther, Ezra, Nehemiah

Key Events: First Return; Temple Rebuilt; Genocide Thwarted; Reforms Enforced; Walls Rebuilt

Scriptural Theme:
Now these are the people of the province who came up from the captivity of the exiles, whom Nebuchadnezzar king of Babylon had taken captive to Babylon (they returned to Jerusalem and Judah, each to his own town) (Ezra 2:1 NIV).

Christian Application:
At that time his voice shook the earth, but now he has promised, "Once more I will shake not only the earth but also the heavens." The words "once more" indicate the removing of what can be shaken--that is, created things--so that what cannot be shaken may remain. Therefore, since we are receiving a kingdom that cannot be shaken (Hebrews 12:26-28 NIV).

Chart 18		
Structure of the Book of Ezra		
538	516	458
Return Under Zerubbabel Chapters 1-6 22 Yrs.	**Gap of 58 Years in Ezra**	Reform Under Ezra Chapters 7-10 1 Yr.
Kings: Cyrus Darius	**Events in the Book of Esther**	*King:* Artaxerxes

39
RETURN TO
THE HOMELAND
Ezra 1-6

Chapter Chronology

Zerubbabel Return		Temple Rebuilt	516
537		520	
530			486
Cyrus	Cambyses	Darius I	
539	522		

JEWS UNDER CYRUS
[539-530 BC]

Problem of Darius the Mede
Daniel 6

After the fall of Babylon in 539 BC Darius the Mede received the kingdom (Daniel 5:31). He was made king (Daniel 9:1). No person of this name is attested in the Babylonian records of the period. Did Cyrus the Persian wear a special title as ruler of the Median people that he had conquered? Or is Darius the Mede the Jewish name for Gubaru who served as governor of Babylon under Cyrus? Conservative scholars are divided over the issue. In any case, this Darius was manipulated by jealous subordinates into issuing an edict regarding prayer that got Daniel arrested and thrown into a den of lions (Daniel 6).

Edict of Liberation
Ezra 1:1-11

Date: ca. 538-537 BC

The focus of Ezra 1 is on an edict of emancipation by which the Judeans were permitted to return to their homeland. After briefly indicating the background of that decree, the author presents a synopsis of the edict itself. He then describes the response of the Judeans to that edict.

A. Background of the Edict (Ezra 1:1)

The first verse of the Book of Ezra states succinctly the facts concerning the emancipation proclamation that freed the Judeans from captivity.

1. Author of it: The edict was issued by Cyrus king of Persia. What a surprise! The ruler of the world became the agent by which exiled Judeans were allowed to go home. The Cyrus Cylinder, discovered by Rassam in the nineteenth century, indicates that Cyrus permitted all peoples who had been deported by the previous empires to return to their native lands.

2. Time of it: The edict was issued in *the first year of Cyrus,* i.e., the first year of his rule over Mesopotamia which began on New Year's Day (March 24) of 538 BC. Cyrus had become master of the world when he conquered Babylon on October 12, 539 BC.

3. Result of it: The edict of Cyrus had the effect of fulfilling the word of Yahweh spoken through the mouth of Jeremiah seven decades earlier. The word of God cannot fail. Even before the captivity Jeremiah had predicted that Babylon's world rule was going to last but seventy years (cf. Jeremiah 25:11; 29:10). Still earlier Isaiah the prophet had predicted that Cyrus, the conqueror of Babylon, was going to allow God's people to return to rebuild their land (Isaiah 44:28-45:7).

4. Reason for it: The edict of emancipation was issued because *Yahweh stirred up the spirit of Cyrus.* The means by which the Lord did this is not stated. To the author of Ezra God worked in mysterious ways. Josephus *(Antiquities* 11.1.2) preserves the tradition that the Jews showed Cyrus the specific prophecies of Isaiah 44-45 in which the Persian king was named as the deliverer of God's people 150 years before he was even born! This suggests that God used Scripture to stir up the spirit of Cyrus. The important truth is that God can influence the hearts of even those who are not among his people. He is sovereign over Gentiles as well as Jews.

5. Publication of it: Heralds were dispatched to various Jewish communities throughout the empire to make known the decision of the king. The official written document was then given to the communities to substantiate the oral proclamation.

586

B. Paraphrase of the Edict (Ezra 1:2-4)

The Judean scribe has given a Hebrew paraphrase of the official decree of Cyrus much as a news reporter might give a synopsis of a statute passed by a state legislature.[72] First, Cyrus acknowledged that Yahweh had placed under his authority all the kingdoms of the earth. Second, the Persian realized, perhaps from prophecies of Isaiah, that Yahweh had appointed him to build his house in Jerusalem. Third, Cyrus authorized Yahweh's people to go up to Jerusalem and rebuild the house of the Lord. Fourth, those who chose not to return to Judah were encouraged to support the émigrés and to make freewill offerings for the reconstruction of the temple.

C. Issues regarding the Edict

1. Cyrus as agent of Yahweh: Some see a contradiction between the religious sentiments of Cyrus represented in the edict, and those that appear in some of the contemporary documents of his reign. Here Cyrus regards himself as the agent of Yahweh. In the Cyrus Cylinder, however, Cyrus views himself as a righteous ruler chosen by the god Marduk to restore the ancient worship in Babylon. Further, Cyrus speaks of his worship of Marduk. He also calls on other gods to intercede on his behalf before the superior gods Bel and Nebo.

2. Possible explanations: Actually little is known about the personal religious faith of Cyrus. If he were a polytheist, it would not be inconsistent for him to recognize Yahweh as one of many gods who assisted him in becoming world monarch. Some assume that Cyrus was a monotheistic worshiper of Ahura Mazda. In that case Cyrus might have regarded both Yahweh and Marduk as local representations of the deity that he himself worshiped. On the other hand, Cyrus may have left it up to the scribes of each ethnic group to represent his edicts in the most appropriate religious terms.

3. Yahweh God of heaven: The title *God of heaven* occurs twenty-one times in the Hebrew Bible, twelve times in Ezra-Nehemiah. The title appears frequently in the context of Persian-Jewish communication. This was a title that communicated with the

---

[72]The Hebrew proclamation (Ezra 1) and the Aramaic memorandum (Ezra 6) represent two independent records. The former was for heralds to announce to the exiles; the latter contained the specifics and was destined for the archives. A memorandum drafted by Persian authorities was sent to a Jewish community in Elephantine Egypt authorizing them to rebuild their temple. See James Pritchard, ed., *Ancient Near Eastern Texts,* 3rd ed. (Princeton: University Press, 1969), p. 492.

pagan mind. The title stresses that Yahweh is superior to all the astral deities worshiped in Mesopotamia.

D. Response to the Edict (Ezra 1:5-11)

1. Stirring by God (1:5): Those who responded to the edict of Cyrus are said to be from the tribes of Judah, Benjamin and Levi. These tribes had been carried into captivity first by the Assyrians in 701 BC, and then by the Babylonians between 605 and 582 BC. In later Old Testament history the tribes of Judah and Benjamin were closely associated. Just as Yahweh stirred up the heart of Cyrus, so he also stirred up the hearts of the family heads of these tribes. These families were all motivated by spiritual concerns. Above all else, they wanted to see the house of God rebuilt.

2. Encouragements to return (1:6-7): Those who made the commitment to return to Judea were encouraged by two developments. First, the Judean community in Babylon collected a freewill offering for the temple project and for the pilgrims. Second, Cyrus restored to the Judeans the temple vessels that Nebuchadnezzar had carried away almost seventy years before.

3. Temple vessels returned (1:8-11): Mithredath[73] the royal treasurer counted out the vessels to Sheshbazzar *the prince* or ruler of the Judeans.[74] He transported 5,400 vessels of gold and silver from Babylon to Jerusalem.

Register of Returnees
Ezra 2:1-70

God honors those who pioneer in his program. Ezra 2 is an honor roll of those who accepted the challenge to rebuild a desolate land. These people did not harden their hearts to the stirring of God's Spirit. They understood that the restoration of Judea and the reconstruction of the temple were essential to the eternal purpose of God. However unappealing Ezra 2 might be to a modern reader, this

---

[73]Mithredath is a well-known Persian name meaning "given to (the god) Mithra." The term *treasurer* (Heb. *haggizbar*) is a hapax legomena in the Old Testament. It is also of Persian origin.
[74]The Hebrew term translated *prince* carries no necessary implication of royal descent. Sheshbazzar is a Babylonian name for which two interpretations have been offered: 1) "Shamash [the sun-god] protects the son;" and 2) "Sin [the moon god] protects the father."

chapter is a monument to God's care. Here are people being given by a gracious God a second chance to live up to a holy calling.

A. Leaders (Ezra 2:1-2a).

1. Twelve leaders: The choice of twelve senior leaders[75] to head the group of returnees appears to have been deliberate. The community they led was the reconstituted people of Israel. To this group of pilgrims now belonged all the promises given to the people of Israel in Patriarchal times.

2. Zerubbabel the governor: At the head of the list is Zerubbabel, a grandson of King Jehoiachin, next to the last king of Judah. Various interpretations have been offered regarding the relationship between Zerubbabel and Sheshbazzar. Most likely Jewish tradition is correct that the leader of the returnees had both a Jewish and a Babylonian name.

3. Jeshua the high priest: Second on the list of leaders is Jeshua, elsewhere called Joshua (in Greek "Jesus"). He was the high priest (Zechariah 3:1). His name is frequently linked with that of Zerubbabel.

4. Other leaders: Among the other leaders only two names are familiar to Bible students: Nehemiah and Mordecai. Neither, however, was the famous personage of the same name. The famous Nehemiah did not return to Judea until some nine decades later. Mordecai was an old Jew living in Susa when he was made prime minister of the Persian Empire about sixty-five years after the events of Ezra 2.

B. Pilgrims (Ezra 2:2b-35)

The sacred writer did not attempt to list every individual who returned in 538 BC. He does, however, the next best thing. He provides two groupings of the returnees. The first is by families, the second by cities. Apparently an Israelite could establish his "roots" and hence his legal right to be part of the national assembly by producing a family genealogy or village roster.

---

[75]A copy of this list in Nehemiah 7 adds one additional name, Nahamani, which evidently had dropped out of the text of Ezra in the course of copying. No evidence supports the contention that each of these men was a prince of one of the twelve tribes of Israel.

1. *By family (2:2b-20):* Family solidarity was very important in Israel. Eighteen prominent families supplied some 15,604 of those who made the dangerous journey home.

2. *By town (2:21-35):* The author next lists the returnees by their native towns. Twenty-one villages are named from which 8,540 pilgrims came.

C. Religious Personnel (Ezra 2:36-58)

Six groups of religious personnel are named and numbered as having participated in the return from exile.

1. *Priests (2:36-39):* The 4,288 priests who returned represented four different families.[76] The priests formed about a tenth of the total of returnees. Only four of the twenty-four courses of priests organized by David were represented among the returnees.

2. *Levites (2:40):* Only seventy-four Levites were among the pilgrims. The Levites were to assist the priests in their ministry. The lowliness of this service perhaps explains why so few Levites chose to join the pilgrimage back to Judea.

3. *Singers (2:41):* The descendants of Asaph were temple singers. They numbered 128. Sometimes the signers are identified with Levites (cf. Nehemiah 11-12), and sometimes, as here in Ezra, they are listed separately.

4. *Gatekeepers (2:42):* Representatives of six families of gatekeepers numbering 139 were among those who returned. The gatekeepers had the duty to lock and unlock the doors of the temple and to guard the treasury (cf. 1 Chronicles 9:17-29).

5. *Nethinim (2:43-54):* The Nethinim ("those given") or temple servants were the lowest class of religious personnel. Thirty-five families of Nethinim were represented among the pilgrims. Some have traced this class back to the Gibeonites who were to be *hewers of wood and drawers of water* for the house of God (Joshua 9:23). This group may have been supplemented from time to time by the addition of war captives who were made to serve in the sanctuary (cf. Numbers 31:25-47).

6. *Servants of Solomon (2:55-58): The descendants of Solomon's servants* were a separate group within the Nethinim. Ten

---

[76]The Tosephta indicates that the Jews eventually reconstructed twenty-four priestly courses out of these four families. These twenty-four courses, which existed in the time of Jesus, where designated by the names of the original twenty-four of David's day.

different families of these servants are named. The origin of this group is uncertain. Perhaps their ancestors were among certain servants given to Solomon by one of the many countries with which he had treaty relations. These servants may have been a special scribal guild. In any case, the combined total of the Nethinim and Solomon's servants was 392.

D. Unconfirmed Claims (Ezra 2:59-63)

A number of those who wished to migrate to Judea could not verify their Israelite descent. This is not surprising. The devastation of the kingdom of Judah, the destruction of Jerusalem and the temple archives probably destroyed many of the public genealogical records. The text distinguishes two groups of those with unconfirmed ancestry.

1. Laymen (2:59-60): Family records were important for two reasons: 1) to establish ownership of property; and 2) to insure that the citizens of the restored community had an unbroken descent from the original Israel.

2. Priests (2:61-63): Only descendants of Aaron could serve as priests in Israel (Numbers 16:40). Some of the pilgrims claimed priestly descent but offered no documentation of that claim. The case finally was appealed to the governor. His final ruling was that these undocumented priests should have no part of priestly ministry until a high priest arose who could receive divine revelation. The implication of the governor's ruling is that 1) the Urim and Thummim were not available to the postexilic high priest; or 2) that the ability to use them had been withdrawn.

E. Statistics (Ezra 2:64-70)

1. Totals (2:64): The entire company of pilgrims who made the journey back to Judea numbered 42,360. The actual total of all the separate numbers given in Ezra 2, however, is only 29,818. Comparison with the parallel list in Nehemiah indicates that several families appearing in one list are not included in the other and vice versa. The surplus families in both lists are exactly the same figure: 1,765. Adding this 1,765 to the 29,818 yields the figure 31,583. This figure still falls short 10,777 of the grand total stated in Ezra 2:64. Obviously not all those who returned are enumerated in Ezra 2. The list contains those from Judah and Benjamin who settled in the vicinity of Jerusalem. The other 10,777 must have been from the

591

other tribes. Though they settled outside Judea, they were still considered part of the *assembly,* i.e., the religious community.

2. Other statistics (2:65-67): Other statistics of interest include the number of servants (7,337), singers (200), horses (736), mules (245), camels (435), and donkeys (6,720). The ratio of slaves to freemen (1 to 6) indicates that those who returned were people of wealth. The singing men and women mentioned here may have been the non-Levitical singers who joined the great choirs on the major festivals.

3. Contributions (2:68-69): Upon arriving at the old site of the temple the heads of the various family groups made a substantial contribution for the work of reconstruction. In so doing they were consciously imitating their forefathers of the Exodus period who donated various precious objects to build the tabernacle (cf. Exodus 25:4-7; 35:2-9). Their offering consisted of 61,000 gold drachmas (1,100 lbs.), 5,000 silver minas (3 tons), and a hundred priestly garments.

4. Application: A chapter like Ezra 2 is regarded as boring by all but the most pedantic scholars. The believer, however, can discover even in this desert several oases of devotional stimulation. First, any effort made for God's kingdom is precious in God's sight. Though these names have long since disappeared from the face of the earth, they are known to God. Second, all people need to feel a sense of belonging, if not to family, at least to a place. Family relationships are extremely important in God's eyes. Third, every community of faith must give attention to preserving its core values or it may lose its character, even its life. For the Jews of the Restoration genealogy was a means of protecting the community from those who might be disruptive. One became a member of the covenant community by birth.

Reconstruction Efforts
Ezra 3:1-13

A. Altar (Ezra 3:1-3a)

1. How they built (3:1-2): After settling in their respective villages, the children of Israel gathered *as one man,* i.e., with common purpose, to Jerusalem. It was now the sacred seventh month (Tishri = Sept/Oct), presumably of the second year of the return (537 BC). The people, no doubt by prearrangement, were now ready to devote themselves to the restoration of proper worship. On the site of the old temple they watched Jeshua the high priest and Zerubbabel the governor lead their respective families in the reconstruction of the altar of burnt offering. The new altar was set on the foundation of the old altar of Solomon's temple. These men were not religious innovators. Thus they built according to the specifications set forth in the Law of Moses (Exodus 27:1-8).

2. *Why they built (3:3a):* Because of their fear of the *peoples of the lands* the repatriated Jews had made the reconstruction of the altar a priority. Apparently they believed that only the faithful observance of the sacred sacrificial rituals could fortify them against the attacks of their enemies.

3. *Sacrificial system restored (3:3b-6):* The open-air altar became the center of the religious life of the returnees. The priests reinstituted the morning and evening regimen of burnt offerings (cf. Exodus 29:38-42). The week-long Feast of Tabernacles was observed with appropriate sacrifices each day of the festival (cf. Numbers 29:12-38). The foundation of the temple, however, had not yet been laid.

B. Temple (Ezra 3:7-13)

1. *Preparations (3:7):* Once the altar had been restored, attention turned to the major project of rebuilding the temple of God. At that first great worship gathering in the seventh month a collection was taken. Masons and carpenters were hired. Negotiations with the Sidonians and Tyrians were completed. Like Solomon before them, the Judeans exchanged agricultural products for cedar from Lebanon. The logs were transported from the mountains to the Mediterranean Sea, lashed together, and floated to the seaport at Joppa. Then those logs were hauled by animal power up to the heights of Jerusalem. This transaction between two separate provinces of the Persian Empire would not have been possible without the permission of King Cyrus.

2. *Commencement (3:8-9):* In the second month of the second year of their return (537 BC), seven months after the rebuilding of the altar, the work on the temple was ready to begin. Again Zerubbabel (representing the Davidic line) and Jeshua (representing the priestly lineage) were in the forefront. The enthusiasm of the group is indicated by the fact *all that came from the captivity* offered their services. The Levites as a group supervised the work of the laymen.

Three families of Levites—Jeshua, Kadmiel, Henadad—were appointed to supervise the Levite foremen. All of this Levitical involvement was to make sure everything was ritually correct.

3. *Celebration (3:10-11):* When the foundations of the temple were in place the work stopped for a celebration. The priests wore their special garb. The Levites led in a praise service following directions that went back to David. The singing was accompanied by the clashing of cymbals and resounding trumpets. They praised Yahweh for his goodness and covenant faithfulness. All the worshipers shouted their agreement with the praises of the Levities.

4. *Mixed reaction (3:12-13):* For the younger worshipers the laying of the temple foundations was an occasion of great joy. The old men, however, wept with a loud voice. They had seen the glorious temple of Solomon that had been destroyed some fifty years earlier. The foundation before them gave little promise of duplicating the glories of the first temple.[77] Those who listened from afar could not distinguish between the joyous shouting and the loud wailing. While young people tend to be overly exuberant, old people often miss the excitement of the present by dwelling on the past.

Resistance to the Work
Ezra 4:1-24

No work done for God's glory will go unchallenged. The author now documents the major attempts of the enemies of the Jews to thwart the efforts of the postexilic community.

A. Offer of Assistance (Ezra 4:1-2)

The enemies of Judah and Benjamin approached Zerubbabel and the other leaders of the postexilic community to request permission to assist in the building project. They claimed to worship the same God. As proof they cited the fact that they had been sacrificing to Yahweh since the days when the Assyrian king Esarhaddon (688-669 BC) had settled them in the area. God's verdict of the commitment of these people to him makes a lie of their claim (2 Kings 17:33f). These

---

[77]Solomon's temple was 60 x 20 x 30 cubits (1 Kings 6:2). Ezra 6:3 authorizes a temple sixty cubits high and sixty cubits wide. The length dimension has probably fallen from the text, or perhaps could not be read by Darius in the original memorandum. In any case, Cyrus was giving the maximum possible dimensions of the temple to ensure the building costs stayed within limits.

people were polytheists. They worshiped Yahweh only because they believed him to be the God who controlled the new land where they had settled. In no way does their worship of Yahweh indicate that they regarded him as the only God.

B. Rejection of Assistance (Ezra 4:3)
The Jewish leaders were firm in refusing the proffered aid from the surrounding peoples. They responded that ethnically, religiously, and legally these surrounding peoples had no claim in the temple that was under construction. This temple was for Yahweh who had entered into a special covenant with Abraham and his seed. He was uniquely the *God of Israel.* Only the Judean community had royal authorization to build this temple. Working together, they will be able to accomplish that task without outside help.

C. Legal Red Tape (Ezra 4:4-5, 24)
The true spirit of those who offered to *help* with the temple now became manifest. The people of the land discouraged (lit., weakened the hands of) the people of Judah and *frightened* them from building. This intimidation took the form of hiring (bribing?) royal counselors (probably Persian governors) to throw up bureaucratic road blocks to the construction effort. Among other things, they probably cut off the supplies of lumber from Phoenicia. These hostile efforts continued through the reigns of Cyrus and his son Cambyses, a period of about sixteen years. As time went on the Jews became discouraged. They lost their vision. The temple project was abandoned. Not until the reign of Darius (522-486 BC) was the climate favorable for a resumption of the work.

REBUILDING THE TEMPLE
Ezra 5-6

Scriptures are silent about the remnant in Judea during the reign of Cyrus' son Cambyses (530-522 BC). When Cambyses died under mysterious circumstances on a campaign to Egypt, his general Darius assumed the throne. For two years Darius faced wide-spread rebellion throughout his empire. He documents his successful restoration of order in the famous trilingual Behistun Inscription.

Resumption of Temple Work
Ezra 5:1-17

In the second year of King Darius (522-486 BC) the work of rebuilding the temple resumed after a hiatus of sixteen years. Again the work was challenged, this time with different results.

A. Divine Assistance (Ezra 5:1-2)

1. A divine stirring (5:1): God raised up two prophets to speak to the shameful indifference that had stymied the temple project. Haggai stepped forward first. On August 29, 520 BC, he preached a powerful message in which he urged the temple work to resume (Haggai 1:1-11). Temple construction began on September 21, 520 BC (Haggai 1:15). In October of that same year Zechariah delivered his first message. Stirred by the powerful preaching of these two great prophets the temple work continued apace. Every spiritual advance from Genesis to Revelation began with a word from the Lord.

2. A divine supervising (5:2): Two other reminders of divine help are found in these verses. First, God was *over them* (NASB), i.e., it was his work that was being done. They were accountable to the Lord, and he was responsible to provide the leadership to see the job completed. Second, the two prophets of God were *with them supporting them.* The prophetic word did more than launch the new initiative. God sustains his people in their work as much as he stirs them to begin the task.

B. Official Challenge (Ezra 5:3-17)

A new Persian official in the region considered it his duty to investigate what was going on in Jerusalem. Most likely this government investigation was triggered by the reports of the local enemies of the Jews. This governor, Tattenai, did his duty both in making the on-site investigation, and reporting what he found to the king.

1. Site inspection (5:3-5): Tattenai and his lieutenant came to Jerusalem to see what authorization the Jews had for rebuilding their temple. He secured a list of the builders, in case any legal action had to be taken against them. The governor, however, elected not to stop the construction until he had time to seek direction from King Darius. The author of Ezra sees this restraint as due to the providence of God who was watching over the leaders of the Jews.

2. *Report on Tattenai had done (5:6-10):* Tattenai's letter to Darius factually reported what was taking place in Jerusalem. First, he reported that he personally had observed the construction proceeding on the temple of *the great God.* Huge stones and great beams were being put in place *with great care.* The huge stones (lit., stones that had to be rolled) were of particular concern to the governor. They seemed larger than necessary for a worship center. Tattenai might have suspected some military fortress was being constructed. Second, Tattenai indicated that he had questioned the authorization of the project. Third, he had secured a list of the leaders of the construction effort.

3. *Report on what the Judeans had said (5:11-16):* Tattenai reported how the Judeans defended their actions. First, the Judeans argued that they were rebuilding a temple that had been erected by a great king of Israel many years before. This construction effort was motivated by religious zeal. The builders were *servants of the God of heaven and earth.* Second, the temple had been destroyed by Nebuchadnezzar the Chaldean because their forefathers had *provoked* the God of heaven. The people of Judah had then been deported to Babylon. Third, in his first year King Cyrus had issued a decree that the temple was to be rebuilt. Fourth, Cyrus had returned various temple vessels that had been confiscated by Nebuchadnezzar. He had given those valuable vessels to Sheshbazzar his governor. These were to be deposited in the rebuilt temple. Fifth, the governor Sheshbazzar had initiated the project. The present construction was but an effort to finish his work. Thus the work was proceeding under a building permit issued sixteen years earlier.

4. *Request (5:17):* Tattenai concluded his letter by asking that a search be made of the *king's treasure house* in Babylon to see if the decree of Cyrus could be verified. In any case, Darius should send his governor directions as to how to deal with the construction effort in Jerusalem.

Completion of the Task
Ezra 6:1-22

The official inquiry of Tattenai set in motion a series of actions which gave legal authorization to the construction work which was continuing apace in Jerusalem.

A. Cyrus Memorandum (Ezra 6:1-5)

1. Located (6:1-2): Darius decreed that the royal archives be searched. That search began in Babylon and extended eventually to Ecbatana, a fortress in the province of Media. There a royal memorandum containing the seal of King Cyrus was found.

2. Question of authenticity: A Hebrew summary of Cyrus's decree appeared in Ezra 1. An excerpt from the more detailed official Aramaic version is recorded here. Because of the Jewish phraseology contained here, an older generation of scholars questioned the authenticity of one or the other or both of these proclamations. Documents from the Persian period, however, have provided convincing evidence of the authenticity of both versions.

3. Provisions (6:3-5): The portion of the memorandum cited here contains four points. First, Cyrus limited the size of the project. The Jerusalem temple should be rebuilt on the foundations of the first temple. The building should be sixty cubits high and sixty cubits wide. Second, Cyrus prescribed the manner in which the temple should be built. The building should consist of three layers of huge stones and one layer of timber.[78] Thus the huge stones that had aroused the suspicion of Tattenai were specifically authorized in the original building permit. Third, the cost of the construction should be paid out of the royal treasury from taxes collected in the Trans-Euphrates province. Fourth, the gold and silver vessels confiscated by Nebuchadnezzar should be returned to their place in the temple.

B. Edict of Darius (Ezra 6:6-13)

1. Gracious provisions (6:6-10): On the basis of this old decree by Cyrus, Darius issued his own decree. Governor Tattenai and his associates were to refrain from interfering with the work in Jerusalem. Tattenai's subordinate, the Jewish governor (Zerubbabel), was to be permitted to build the temple on its ancient foundation. Tattenai was ordered speedily to back the project financially using revenues of the Trans-Jordan province. Furthermore, whatever the priests might need to carry on the sacrificial ritual should be supplied to them. Darius desired that acceptable sacrifices be offered in that temple on behalf of the royal family. The accurate list of materials for worship suggests

---

[78]Solomon's temple was also built with one layer of timber for every three layers of stones (cf. 1 Kings 6:36). This construction method can be documented elsewhere in the ancient Near East. The layers of timber may have minimized the damage by earthquakes.

that Darius received advice from Judean scholars before drafting his decree.

2. Frightening warning (6:11): Darius' decree concluded with an order and a wish. First, for the person who dared violate this decree, Darius ordered that he be impaled on a beam pulled from his own house.[79] Then the house of that man should be made a refuse heap. The ancients appreciated poetic justice in punishments. Hence it was deemed appropriate that one who hindered the building of God's house witness his own house demolished before dying on one of its beams.

3. Encouraging wish (6:12): Second, the king wished that *the God who has caused his name to dwell there,* i.e., in Jerusalem, should overthrow any king or people who attempted to change his edict or destroy the temple. The concept that God's name, i.e., a revelation of himself, rather than his physical presence dwelled in Jerusalem also indicates Judean influence on the contents of this decree.

C. Work Completed (Ezra 6:13-15)

Tattenai the governor of the Trans-Euphrates province, and his associates, carried out the decree of Darius *with all diligence.* Through the encouragement of the prophets Haggai and Zechariah the temple work was brought to a successful conclusion in the last month (Adar = Feb-Mar) of the sixth year of Darius (March 12, 515 BC). This was four-and-a-half years after Haggai's initial call for action (Haggai 1:1). In so doing the Judeans were obeying the command of the God of Israel and the decrees of Cyrus, Darius, and Artaxerxes. The mention of Artaxerxes in 6:14 suggests that it was the author's purpose to lump together here the three great Persian patrons of God's people. The particular benefits bestowed by Artaxerxes will be taken up in the Book of Nehemiah.

D. Temple Dedicated (Ezra 6:16-18)

The dedication of the second temple was celebrated with great joy. Some seven hundred special sacrifices were offered to mark the

---

[79]In impalement, the sharp end of a post was thrust through the belly, esophagus and lungs. The victim was then left to die. Herodotus (3.159) attests that Darius impaled three thousand Babylonians when he captured the rebellious city. According to the Behistun inscription Darius impaled numerous rebels, oftentimes after mutilating them.

599

occasion, small in comparison to the tremendous numbers offered at the dedication of Solomon's temple. Most significant was the offering of twelve goats as a sin offering for the twelve tribes of Israel. This action indicated two things: First, the sins of Israel had accumulated during the absence of the temple (586-515 BC) when no sin offering for the nation could be made. Second, this action indicates that the postexilic community considered itself as the surviving remnant of the entire covenant nation. Thus the twelve sin offerings were a confession of both failure and faith. Forgiveness was still possible. The covenant with the whole people of God was still intact. In accordance with the Law of Moses, priests and Levites were organized for continuing service in the new temple.

E. Victory Celebrated (Ezra 6:19-22)

1. Joy grounded in Yahweh (6:19-22): On the fourteenth day of the first month (515 BC) the feast of Passover was observed by the postexilic community in their new temple. The priests and Levites purified themselves in accordance with the Law of Moses. They slaughtered the Passover lamb for themselves. They were joined in the celebration by those who had returned from exile and those who had separated themselves from the impurity of the nations of the land, i.e., proselytes or converts. In so doing, the postexilic community collectively was seeking Yahweh the God of Israel. The seven days of the Feast of Unleavened Bread that followed were celebrated with joy. They celebrated the friendly disposition of *the king of Assyria* that had encouraged them in rebuilding the temple. Their joy was grounded in Yahweh to whom they attributed the unexpected edict of Darius.

2. Footnote: The reference to King Darius as *king of Assyria* is most appropriate. First, Darius now ruled the old Assyrian Empire. Second, the author is attempting to make a striking point. The Lord had used the Assyrian kings to chastise his people. The long process of deportation to foreign lands had begun under the Assyrian Tiglath-pileser in 745 BC. Now the Lord had used the Assyrian king (Darius) to grant favor to his people. With the rebuilding of the temple the restoration was complete.

Conclusion

Thus ends the account of the first phase of the restoration of God's people. This generation witnessed anew the stirring of God's Spirit. At the beginning Yahweh stirred up the spirit of Cyrus (Ezra 1:1); at the end he stirred up a complacent leadership and people (Haggai 1:14). The curtain falls on Act One of the Restoration to the joyous shouts of God's people celebrating their Feast of Freedom (Passover). For almost six decades the record is silent regarding conditions in Judea, except for one hint of continued harassment by local enemies (Ezra 4:6). The spotlight now shifts to a foreign capital and a Judean queen who saved her people from extermination.

History of Israel

40
PRESERVATION
THE NATION
Esther 1-10

Chapter Chronology

	Vashti Removed 483	Esther Queen 479	Haman Plot 474-473	
485	Greece Invasion 481-479	Xerxes		465

The Book of Esther has as its chronological setting *the days of Ahasuerus* who was known in secular history as Xerxes (485-465 BC). [80] This king ruled over 127 provinces that stretched from India to Ethiopia.[81] Even scholars who do not advocate the historicity of Esther admit that the portrayal of Xerxes in this book corresponds to what the classical writers had to say about this monarch. The geographical setting of the book is Susa (Heb., Shushan), one of the Persian capitals.

JEWS UNDER XERXES
[485-465 BC]

Assembly of Xerxes
Esther 1:1-9

God sees the needs of his people long before those needs become a reality. He providentially places those he can use in strategic places so that they will be available when the crisis unfolds. In the third year

---

[80]The Septuagint translators thought that Ahasuerus was Xerxes' son Artaxerxes. Josephus followed the LXX in this identification. Modern scholars identify Ahasuerus as Xerxes.

[81]The Hebrew term *medina* refers to smaller governmental (or racial) units of the empire such as Judea (cf. Nehemiah 1:3). Herodotus (3.89-94) documents that for tax purposes the empire was broken down into twenty larger areas that consolidated a number of the smaller provinces.

of his reign (483 BC) King Xerxes made important decisions that were to have enormous implications for God's people. The fast moving action of this crucial year began with a banquet and concluded with the demotion of the king's leading lady.

A. Banquet for the Nobles (Esther 1:3-4)

Xerxes gave a banquet for his princes, military leaders, and provincial officials. This banquet introduced a lengthy period of open court. For 180 days the king put all of his great wealth on display. The exact purpose of this assembly is not stated in the Bible. The gathering in Esther 1, however, seems to be the same one described by Herodotus (7.8). In order to avenge a defeat suffered by his father Darius I at Marathon, Greece in 490 BC, Xerxes was making plans for one of the greatest invasions of all time.

B. Banquet for the Citizens (Esther 1:5-8)

At the end of the planning period the king gave a seven day banquet (lit., "drinking feast") for all the citizens of Susa. The banquet of Xerxes was held in *the court of the garden of the king's palace,* i.e., on the grounds surrounding the palace. The author, who describes in detail the magnificent setting, gives every impression of having been an eyewitness. Drinks were served in golden vessels of various kinds.[82] The royal wine was plentiful. The drinking was done *according to the law.* Ordinarily, guests would drink together at the direction of the toastmaster. For this occasion, however, Xerxes had ordered the household servants to give to each guest whatever he desired. Such rousing Persian drinking parties are confirmed by the ancient historians.

C. Women's Banquet (Esther 1:9)

Simultaneously Queen Vashti was hosting the women at a separate banquet within the palace. Vashti is probably the same person called by Herodotus (9.108-13) Amestris.

---

[82]Magnificent Persian drinking goblets such as are mentioned in Esther 1:7 have been found by archaeologists. A golden cup in the form of a winged lion dating to the fifth century BC is part of the collection of the Metropolitan Museum of New York. A picture of such a vessel is found in C.A. Moore, "Archaeology and the Book of Esther," reprinted from *The Biblical Archaeologist* in *Studies in the Book of Esther* (New York: Ktav, 1982), p. 376.

Problem for Xerxes
Esther 1:10-22

A. Defiance of the Queen (Esther 1:10-12)

On the last day of the feast, the drunken Xerxes dispatched his seven harem eunuchs to summon Queen Vashti to the banquet chamber. She was to appear with the royal crown. Traditional Jewish interpretation understands this to mean that Vashti was to appear wearing nothing but the crown. The king wished to put on public display the exceptional beauty of his wife. The queen refused the summons.[83] Though she knew her modesty would cost her crown, Vashti would not compromise her moral standards.

B. Consultation with Advisers (Esther 1:13-20)

1. Identity of advisers (1:13-14): Xerxes was enraged when Vashti refused his summons. He immediately consulted with his seven advisors. Four things are said about these men. 1) They were experts in Persian laws and customs. 2) They where men *who knew the times.* This either means that they were astrologers or, more likely, that they were familiar with historical precedents that had the force of law. 3) They saw the face of the king. Ordinarily the Persian king was inaccessible to his subjects. These advisors, however, could personally converse with the king at any time except when he was in the presence of one of his wives. 4) They sat in first place in the kingdom, i.e., they were officials of the highest order.

2. Offense of the queen (1:15-18): The king could not allow the disobedience of Vashti to go unpunished. One of the counselors, Memucan, made an observation and a suggestion. Vashti's actions were an offense, not only to her own husband, but to all the princes of the realm. Those women present at Vashti's banquet knew of the queen's defiance. They might be encouraged to treat their own husbands with contempt. Soon after the women of nobility (who apparently were not at the banquet of 1:9) would hear what the queen had done. This would result in *plenty of contempt and anger* (NASB).

---

[83]Contemporary evidence does not support Josephus' explanation that Vashti's refusal was the result of a Persian law that wives should not show their faces to strangers. Vashti may have been fortified in her refusal by her own excessive use of wine. Others have suggested that Vashti/Amestris was pregnant with her child Artaxerxes at the time of this drinking feast in 483 BC.

Thus actions taken against Vashti should not be considered personal revenge, but public policy benefiting the entire kingdom.

3. Specific recommendations (1:19-20): The council recommended that an edict be issued that would 1) banish Vashti forever from the presence of the king; and 2) give her royal position to another. These two stipulations may in reality be one. Vashti was no longer to see the face of Xerxes in the sense that she would no longer appear by his side in her official capacity. This punishment, so the council reasoned, will cause all women throughout the empire to respect their husbands. The edict should be written in the laws of Persia and Media *which cannot pass away*.

C. Edict of Xerxes (Esther 1:21-22)

1. Dispatch of the edict (1:21-22a): Memucan's suggestion pleased both the king and the council of seven. Letters were drafted in the language of each province, and then dispatched by swift messengers. The Persians had a communication system that was the marvel of the ancient world. It resembled the pony express system of the American West.

2. Gist of the edict (1:22b): The thrust of the Xerxes' edict was twofold. 1) Each man was to be the master in his own house. 2) The language of the husband should be the language of the household. Just how Xerxes intended to enforce his edict is not indicated.

Silent Years

A. Failed Invasion of Greece

The Book of Esther passes over four years—from the third to the seventh regnal years—of Xerxes. Herodotus, the Greek historian, fills in the gap. With an army of 200,000 men and a navy of hundreds of ships, Xerxes launched a massive invasion of Greece in 481 BC. At Salamis (480 BC) the Persian navy suffered a devastating defeat. A few months later the land force was defeated at Plataea, northwest of Athens (479 BC).

B. Vashti Surfaces Again

While Xerxes was in Sardis after the invasion of Greece he fell in love with his niece. Vashti (Amestris) waited until the king's birthday to make a request of her husband which, according to palace custom, he could not refuse. Vashti was granted the right to mutilate the mother of the king's young lover. Nothing further is known of Vashti (Amestris) until she surfaced in the reign of her son Artaxerxes as a powerful figure.

Selection of Esther
Esther 2:1-23

A. Proposal by Advisers (Esther 2:1-4)

After the war with Greece, Xerxes began to long for the company of his queen. The king's attendants suggested that he select a new queen from among the most beautiful virgins of the entire realm. This was a bold departure from the usual procedure of taking the queen from the families of the seven senior counselors (Herodotus 3.84). Provincial overseers were to gather eligible candidates to Susa. The virgin who pleased the king was to be made queen to replace Vashti. The king recognized the suggestion as sound personal and political advice. He therefore ordered its implementation.

B. Opportunities for Esther (Esther 2:5-12)

1. *Taken into Xerxes' harem (2:5-8):* Living in Susa was a Jew named Mordecai. He was a Benjamite, the great-grandson of one of those who had been taken captive in 597 BC. He was raising his orphaned cousin Hadassah ("myrtle") whose Persian name was Esther ("star"). This young Jewish girl was among those taken by royal officials into the harem of Xerxes. No indication is given as to the number of virgins taken by the king. Josephus suggests that there were four hundred. The text gives no concrete indication of Esther's attitude toward the prospect of becoming a concubine of the king and potentially a queen.

2. *Favor in the harem (2:9):* Esther found favor in the eyes of Hegai, the harem overseer. His favor was demonstrated by 1) immediately providing her with cosmetics and *portions,* i.e., food. Esther did not refuse to eat the food of the heathen as did Daniel. This may say something about the spiritual maturity of this Jewish maiden. 2) He assigned her seven choice maids from the king's palace. 3) He transferred her to the best place in the harem.

3. *Mordecai's interest (2:10-11):* Following the advice of Mordecai, Esther did not reveal her ethnic origins. Mordecai must have feared for Esther's safety. Perhaps he had sensed the rise of an anti-Semitic faction within the empire. Every day Mordecai walked

607

back and forth in front of the court of the harem. In some manner, information regarding Esther's well-being was smuggled out to him.

4. Beauty treatment (2:12): The virgin candidates went through an extensive beauty treatment. Six months they were treated with oil and myrrh and six months with spices and other feminine cosmetics. Archaeology has illuminated the particular beauty treatment involved here. Certain cosmetic "incense" burners have been found. Women of the Persian period saturated their hair and skin pores with pleasant odors from these burners.

C. Xerxes' Choice (2:13-19)

1. Esther's appointment (2:13-14): At the end of the twelve months each candidate went into the king. She took anything she desired—ornaments, apparel, jewels—from the harem to the palace. Having spent the night with the king, the candidate was now considered a concubine. She was assigned to *the second harem*. She never again entered the king's presence unless she was summoned by name.

2. Esther's wisdom (2:15): When Esther's night arrived, she requested nothing except what Hegai, the king's eunuch, advised. Her natural beauty needed little enhancement from excessive ornamentation.

3. Esther's honor (2:16-19): Esther found favor with the king more than all the virgins. With Esther, Xerxes' search for a queen ended. The king elevated her to the position once occupied by Vashti. A banquet was ordered in Esther's honor and a holiday was proclaimed throughout the provinces. Esther was made queen in December 479 BC.

Report of Mordecai
Esther 2:19-23

A. Mordecai's Position

At this time Mordecai was *sitting at the king's gate*. This phrase, which appears five times in the book, has an official connotation. Mordecai had received appointment as a royal officer, perhaps a judgeship. This appointment might have been made because of the influence of Esther. In the ancient Near East the gate was a complex of buildings comparable to a modern day county courthouse. One of the strongest arguments for the historicity of the Book of Esther is the mention in a cuneiform tablet of a certain Marduka. He was a high official at the court of Susa during the early years of Xerxes. That this Marduka is the biblical Mordecai is all but certain.

B. Assassination Plot Exposed (Esther 2:19-23)
1. Occasion (2:19-20): Apparently Xerxes ordered a second gathering of virgins. This may have been a final procession honoring the unsuccessful candidates. By displaying the beauty of the runners-up the beauty of Esther was set off in more striking relief.
2. Reported (2:21-23): At that time two disgruntled royal guards were plotting the assassination of Xerxes. Possibly they were seeking revenge for the treatment of Vashti. In some manner this plot became known to Mordecai. He got the word to the queen. She in turn informed the king in Mordecai's name. The plot was investigated. Those found guilty were impaled on a tree, i.e., a sharpened post. Royal scribes carefully noted this incident in the official annals of the king. Fourteen years later Xerxes became the victim of a similar palace conspiracy.

PRESERVATION
OF THE JEWS
Esther 3:1-10:3

Plot of Haman
Esther 3:1-4:17

Some four years after Esther became queen, King Xerxes promoted Haman to the position of prime minister of the realm. He is called *the Agagite,* i.e., from the province called Agag[84] (3:1). This Haman plotted to destroy the Jewish people.

A. Reason for the Plot (Esther 3:1-6)
1. Mordecai offends Haman (3:2-6): Among the king's servants only Mordecai refused to render homage to Haman. Other royal

---

[84]J. Oppert published an inscription from the time of Sargon of Assyria (c. 725 BC) that mentions Agag as a place in Media (which later was incorporated into the Persian Empire). Gleason Archer, *A Survey of Old Testament Introduction,* rev. ed. (Chicago: Moody, 1974), p. 421. Jewish tradition considered Haman a descendant of that Amalekite king slain by Samuel some five hundred years earlier (cf. 1 Samuel 15:8).

609

officials questioned Mordecai about his non-compliance with the royal edict to render homage to the prime minister. The old man replied only that he was a Jew. His refusal to bow to Haman was Mordecai's way of expressing Jewish national spirit and pride. These officials called Haman's attention to Mordecai's disrespect. When the prime minister saw for himself the insolence of Mordecai he was filled with rage. Yet Haman did not take vengeance on Mordecai personally. Rather he determined to rid the entire kingdom of the Jewish race.

2. *Charges against the Jews:* An accusatory letter from the enemies of the Jews in Palestine was written to the Persian court early in the reign of Xerxes (Ezra 4:6). This letter may have been one of the factors that made it easy for the prime minister to initiate his pogrom against the Jews.

B. Authority for the Plot (Esther 3:7-11)

1. *Casting the pur (3:7):* On New Year's Day in the year 474 BC Haman had his personal astrologers cast the *pur* (lot) *from day to day and from month to month*. The purpose here was to determine the most propitious day for the extermination of the Jewish race. New Year's Day was an appropriate day for Haman's divination because in Babylonian religion that was the day when the gods came together to fix the fate of men. The method employed is not clear. The lot itself may have resembled the object found by excavators in the ruins of Susa. This was a quadrangular prism that had the numbers one, two, five and six engraved on its sides. The lot indicated that the thirteenth day of the twelfth month (March 7, 473 BC) was the most auspicious time to implement the attack against the Jews. The providence of God, however, overruled chance (cf. Proverbs 16:33). The Jews were to have nearly a year to take countermeasures against Haman's program of ethnic cleansing.

2. *Purchasing the right (3:8-11):* Haman persuaded Xerxes that an unnamed people were dangerous to the unity of the Persian kingdom because they observed their own laws and not the laws of the realm. Haman cleverly omitted the name of the group he wished to attack for fear that the king would recall previous occasions when his predecessors had rendered favorable edicts on behalf of the Jews. He offered to reimburse the royal treasury with ten thousand talents of silver—equivalent to two-thirds of the annual income of the entire empire—to pay for implementation of a decree to exterminate the

Jews. Haman must have been enormously wealthy. Xerxes feigned lack of interest in the monetary offer. The text, however, clearly implies that the money went into the royal treasury (cf. 4:7; 7:4). The king so trusted Haman that he did not even inquire as to what people were to be affected. He handed Haman his signet ring so that the prime minister might authorize the extermination.

C. Implementation of the Plot (Esther 3:12-15)

On thirteenth day of the first month (April 17, 474 BC) the scribes penned the royal orders at the dictation of Haman. These orders, sealed with the king's seal, where dispatched to officials of various rank throughout the empire. On the thirteenth day of the twelfth month (March 7, 473 BC)[85] all Jews regardless of age or sex were to be slaughtered. Their possessions were to be seized as plunder. No doubt Haman planned to take a portion of that plunder. The Jewish population of Susa and their many friends were thrown into confusion by the edict. Meanwhile, Haman and the king callously celebrated the edict over drinks.

D. Reaction to the Plot (Esther 4:1-8)

1. Mordecai's mourning (4:1-3): When Mordecai heard of the decree, he donned the garb of a mourner and went out into the city weeping loudly. He probably felt personally responsible for what had happened. By revealing his national identity he had brought this fate on his people. Mordecai stopped short of entering the king's gate because no one could enter the royal structures wearing sackcloth. Mordecai's mourning was duplicated by Jews throughout the empire when they heard the edict of the king.

2. Mordecai informs Esther (4:4-8): When Esther heard of the anguish of Mordecai, she sent a change of garments to him. When he refused the gift, Esther dispatched one of her attendants to ascertain the reason for this bitter public mourning. The attendant found Mordecai in the city square in front of the king's gate. The Jew sent back to Esther 1) an account of all that had happened to him because of his refusal to honor Haman; 2) the information regarding the amount that Haman had pledged for the destruction of the Jews; 3)

---

[85]Others suggest a rational explanation for the long delay in the implementation of the edict. Haman anticipated that many Jews would leave their possessions and flee beyond the borders of the empire to preserve their lives. He then would be rid of the Jews and could confiscate their possessions with little difficulty.

the text of the royal edict; and 4) an request for Esther to go to the king to plead for the deliverance of the Jewish people.

E. Counterplot (Esther 4:9-17)

1. Esther's hesitancy (4:9-12): Esther sent her attendant to remind Mordecai that it was a capital offense to approach the king in his private residence without a summons. Only if the king raised the royal scepter would the death sentence be canceled. In the past thirty days Esther had not been summoned by Xerxes.

2. Mordecai's insistence (4:13-14): Mordecai sent the attendant back with an ominous message. He reminded Esther that she would not escape the general order to exterminate Jews just because she lived in the palace. He assured his adopted daughter that if she remained silent at this time, deliverance would arise for the Jews from another source. Here the faith of the old Jew in the covenantal position of the Jewish people shines through. Esther, however, should realize that Providence had placed her in her royal position for just such an emergency as this.

3. Esther's courage (4:15-17): Esther was moved to action by Mordecai's words. She sent word back to him to request that all the Jews living in the capital assemble and fast—an act always accompanied by prayer—for three days on her behalf. During that same period the queen and her maidens also planned to fast. Fortified by this intercession, she promised to break the law and approach the king. Esther had now conquered her natural fears. She was now ready to lay her life on the line for her people. Rashness acts without fear; bravery, in spite of it.

Plan of Esther
Esther 5:1-14

A. Esther's Banquet (Esther 5:1-10)

1. She entered the throne room (5:1-3): After the three days of fasting Esther put on her royal robes. She dared not approach the king in sackcloth. Esther stood in the inner court of the king's palace. From his throne room the king could see Esther standing in the court. He extended the royal scepter to her thus allowing her to approach. Esther drew near and touched the top of the scepter. The king inquired as to what was troubling his queen. Whatever she needed, he promised, he would give her, even to the half of his kingdom.

2. *She presented her request (5:4-8):* Esther wished for the king and prime minister to come to a banquet that she had prepared. The king summoned Haman and immediately departed for the quarters of the queen. During the course of the banquet again the king repeated his willingness to grant any request that Esther might make. Esther, sensing that the time was not right to make her appeal, simply invited the king and Haman back the next day to another banquet. At that time she promised to make her request.

3. *Haman deflated (5:9-10):* Haman left the banquet elated that the queen had included him in her invitation. At the king's gate, however, he encountered Mordecai. Haman was enraged when the old Jew did not pay homage to him. He maintained his composure, however, and returned to his house. There he sent for some friends and his wife Zeresh.

B. Haman's Depression (Esther 5:11-14)

1. *He explained his depression (5:11-13):* Haman was bewildered by his own depression. He recited to his friends all the reasons why he should be very happy. Besides ten sons, wealth, and position, he alone had been invited by Esther to attend a banquet with the king. Yet every time he happened upon Mordecai in the king's gate he became dissatisfied again. Mordecai was making his life miserable!

2. *He planned to execute Mordecai (5:14):* Zeresh and his friends urged Haman to eliminate Mordecai, to make an example of him. With the king's permission the next morning he should have Mordecai impaled on a *tree* fifty cubits (75 feet) high. Then he could attend Esther's banquet with a joyful heart. This advice pleased Haman. He ordered the impalement *tree* to be erected during the night. The enormous height is probably due to the fact that the *tree* was erected on a high hill or on a previously existing structure. The drama of the account should not be missed. Esther had not yet presented her petition to the king; the king did not know that Mordecai had once saved his life; and now an impalement *tree* had been set up for Mordecai.

Pronouncement of the King
Esther 6:1-8:2

The king's insomnia that very night was to lead to a pronouncement that suddenly and dramatically changed the direction of the Book of Esther.

A. Xerxes' Negligence (Esther 6:1-3)

Providentially that very night the king could not sleep. God accomplishes some of his greatest work during sleepless nights. Xerxes ordered a scribe to read to him from the royal records. In the course of this reading the king was made aware of how Mordecai had reported the assassination plot of the two doorkeepers. The records indicated that no honor had yet been bestowed on Mordecai for his loyalty to the crown. The king desired to remedy this oversight immediately.

B. Haman's Suggestion (Esther 6:4-9)

Morning dawned. The king asked which of his counselors might be standing in the court. Haman had arrived first that morning. He was anxious to speak to the king about impaling Mordecai. As Haman entered the throne room the king posed this question: What should be done with a man whom the king desires to honor? Haman immediately assumed that the king was about to bestow another honor on him. Imagining himself as the beneficiary, Haman proposed a fourfold honor. The man whom the king wished to honor should 1) wear a robe once worn by the king; 2) ride on one of the king's own horses on whose head was a crown; 3) be led by one of the king's most noble princes through the city square; and 4) the prince should proclaim before the honoree that he was being honored by the king.

C. Mordecai's Honor (Esther 6:10-14)

1. King's order (6:10): The king then ordered Haman to implement his suggestions with regard to Mordecai the Jew. The king thus knew from the royal records that Mordecai was a Jew. He did not make the connection between that fact and the ethnic cleansing that his prime minister authorized in the king's name.

2. Haman's humiliation (6:11): What the prime minister intended for his personal honor became the greatest humiliation of his life. Haman left the court in utter shock. One can only imagine how he must have felt when he bestowed these honors on the man he had hoped to execute that very day.

614

3. Zaresh's reminder (6:12-14): After he led Mordecai on horseback through the city square, Haman returned to his home utterly humiliated. In great personal agony he related to his wife and friends what had taken place. The gloom of the moment lifted, however, when his wife and friends pointed out that Mordecai was a Jew. According to the irrevocable law of the king, all Jews were to die on the thirteenth day of the twelfth month. Haman's gloom turned immediately to malicious glee. At that very moment royal servants arrived to escort the prime minister to Esther's banquet.

D. Esther's Second Banquet (Esther 7:1-8:2)

1. Esther's revelation (7:1-4): At the banquet again Xerxes inquired about Esther's petition. The queen then asked for her own life and the life of her people for her request. She quickly explained that the Jewish people had *been sold* to be destroyed. The reference is to the price Haman had offered the king for the privilege of exterminating the Jews.

2. King's outrage (7:5-7a): Xerxes demanded to know who intended to do such a thing. Esther forcefully pointed to Haman as the *foe and enemy*. At this unexpected accusation Haman trembled. The king was outraged. He stormed out into the garden to let his anger cool and to collect his thoughts. His absence permitted the incident that finally sealed Haman's fate.

3. Haman's plea (7:7b): Haman remained in the room alone with Esther. He realized that only through Esther's intercession would his life be spared. So Haman approached the couch where Esther was reclining in true Persian fashion as she ate. There he pled for his life. Apparently in a gesture of contrition he either seized Esther's feet or perhaps even kissed them. In so doing he threw caution to the wind. No one was to come so near the wife of a Persian king!

4. King's orders (7:8-10): The king returned to catch Haman in what could be interpreted as a compromising position. In shock the king asked if Haman were brazen enough to assault the queen with the king in the house. At that moment they *covered Haman's face,* i.e., put Haman under arrest. One of the king's servants pointed out that Haman had erected an impalement *tree* fifty cubits high where he had intended to execute Mordecai, one of the benefactors of the king. The king ordered the immediate execution of Haman. Thus did they hang Haman on the tree that he had prepared for Mordecai.

615

5. Other fallout (8:1-2): Xerxes gave the house of Haman to Esther. She in turn appointed Mordecai to manage that property. The old Jew was permitted to come before the king. He received the royal signet ring that had once been worn by Haman.

Protection of the Jews
Esther 8:3-9:19

A. Need for Protection (Esther 8:3-8)

1. Esther's request (8:3-6): Though Haman was dead, his plot was still alive. Esther fell at the feet of the king, imploring him to reverse the evil scheme of Haman. Again Xerxes raised the scepter to signal the attending bodyguards that the queen had the right to touch him. Encouraged by this gesture Esther stood, regained her composure, and presented her petition rationally to the king. She wanted a letter to be written to revoke the earlier letters devised by Haman. Esther pled that she personally would not be able to endure should her people be destroyed.

2. King's authorization (8:7-8): Xerxes first reminded Esther and Mordecai what he already had done to demonstrate sympathy for their plight. He had ordered Haman to be hung and had given his house to Esther. Now he authorized another step. Esther and Mordecai were to compose letters to be sent, under the king's seal, to the Jews throughout the realm. Technically the previous edict could not be revoked. A new decree, however, might have the desired effect. He left the matter up to Esther and Mordecai.

B. Mordecai's Letters (Esther 8:9-14)

1. Jewish defense authorized (8:9-14): In the third month (Sivan), on the twenty-third day (June 25, 474 BC), Mordecai dispatched letters in the various languages to the officials and Jews throughout the realm. Some two months and ten days had elapsed since the earlier letters were sent out by Haman. Under royal seal, these letters granted the Jews of the realm the right to assemble to defend their lives on the fateful thirteenth day of the twelfth month. The Jews could destroy any who came against them, and seize their spoil. They were thus given eight months to plan for their collective defense.

2. Further explanation: The wording in 8:11 has generally been misunderstood. Most take this verse to be an authorization by

Mordecai and Esther for the Jews to go on the offensive against their enemies, killing them along with their wives and children. Another interpretation, however, is possible. The Jews were authorized to kill the entire army that might attack *them, their children and wives, and to plunder their spoil.* These words are a citation of Haman's original edict. The exact wording of the original decree had to be cited so as to remove any ambiguity from the second edict. The Jews had a right to defend themselves against any attack against their men, women, children or possessions.

C. Mordecai's Promotion (Esther 8:15-17)

Mordecai went out from the presence of the king dressed in royal robes. A large crown (i.e., headdress or turban) symbolized his office. The promotion of Mordecai was an occasion for great joy in the Jewish community. Sensing that the Jews were a people favored by the crown, many Gentiles *became Jews.*

D. Deliverance Day (Esther 9:1-19)

1. General description (9:1-4): When the thirteenth day of the twelfth month arrived the Jews were able to gain the mastery over their enemies. They assembled in their cities throughout all the provinces to lay hands on those who sought their harm. This show of strength put fear in the hearts of non-Jews. Even the government officials assisted the Jews because they feared Mordecai who had become very powerful within the kingdom.

2. In Susa (9:5-10): In the acropolis of Susa *(the capital* NASB)—a section separated from the rest of the city—five hundred enemies were killed including the ten sons of Haman. One may assume that most of these were the cronies of the former prime minister. The Jews, however, did not lay their hands on the plunder.

3. Esther's further requests (9:11-15): The king was shocked at the numbers who were killed in Susa. Yet he did not back down on his commitment to grant Esther any request she might have regarding this crisis. Esther had two more requests. First, she requested permission for Jewish war against their enemies to be extended by one day. This request should not be viewed as vindictiveness on Esther's part but as precaution against rumored attacks upon the Jews the following day. Second, she asked that the corpses of Haman's ten sons be impaled. The exposure of the bodies of these men was intended to be a warning to all who aimed to exterminate the Jews. The king ordered these actions to be taken. As a result, on the fourteenth day of the twelfth month the Jews defended themselves against attacks in the rest of Susa. Three hundred additional enemies were slain. Still the Jews did not plunder their enemies as they were entitled to do under the Mordecai edict.

4. *Report from the provinces (9:16-19):* Out in the provinces the casualties among those who attacked the Jews was 75,000. Again no plunder was taken. The fourteenth day of the month became a holiday devoted to feasting. In Susa, however, the celebration took place on the fifteenth day. Among the Jews both days were subsequently observed as holidays.

A Footnote
Esther 9:20-10:3

The Book of Esther closes with material that may have been added several years after that initial celebration of Purim.

A. Letter of Mordecai (Esther 9:20-28)

At some point Mordecai determined that there should no longer be two separate holidays, the fourteenth in the provinces and the fifteenth in the capital. He authorized the annual observance of both days. The days were to be celebrated by feasting, exchanging gifts and charity to the poor. These two holidays were called Purim because Haman had decided by the *pur* or lot the month and day in which he planned to destroy the Jews. In this manner the feast of Purim became a universal custom among the Jews.

B. Letter of Esther (Esther 9:29-32)

Queen Esther herself wrote letters to all the provinces concerning Purim. These letters, different from those mentioned in 9:20, were cosigned by Mordecai. Apparently some in the provinces were resisting the idea of observing both the fourteenth and fifteenth days of Adar. Esther's letter confirmed the time for the observance of Purim. It also authorized a time of fasting on the day previous to the two days of merry making. Even today some Jews still keep "Esther's fast" on the day before the celebration of Purim. The command of Esther was written in *the book,* i.e., the record that Mordecai was

618

keeping of all these events (cf. 9:20). Eventually that "book" became the nucleus of the present Book of Esther.

C. Career of Mordecai (Esther 10:1-3)

1. Mordecai's reputation (10:1, 3): Because of his association with Mordecai, King Xerxes learned that taxation was a better way to finance his administration than using plunder. The text suggests that the king prospered during the days of Mordecai. The old Jew was second only to the king himself in the kingdom. He was held in high regard among his own people. Mordecai was known as one who sought the good of his people and one who spoke for the welfare of the whole nation.

2. Verification (10:2): In the concluding verses of the book the author challenges his critics to check for themselves the facts he has narrated. Verification of Mordecai's advancement to prime minister could be found in the Book of the Chronicles of the kings of Media and Persia. Unfortunately this document is no longer extant. The author's words, however, leave no doubt that he intended his work to be taken as sober history.

Conclusion

During the reign of Cyrus (539-530 BC) the Jews returned to Judea, rebuilt their altar, and laid the foundation of the temple. Under Darius (522-486 BC) they completed the temple (515 BC). During the reign of Xerxes (486-465 BC) Samaritan opposition to the postexilic community continued (Ezra 4:6). Even more significantly, the Jews survived a plan to exterminate them as a people (Book of Esther). The last chapters of the story of restoration were written during the reign of the Persian King Artaxerxes (465-423 BC) which are the focus of the following chapter.

41
INSTRUCTION
OF THE NATION
Ezra 7-10

Chapter Chronology

			423
ARTAXERXES			
464			
		445	
	EZRA		
	458		

The second phase of the restoration began in the seventh year of King Artaxerxes (458 BC). In that year Ezra was able in some unexplained way to secure an appointment from the king to return to Jerusalem as a religious reformer. About fifty-eight years had elapsed since the completion of the temple. The godly Zerubbabel and Jeshua had died. The people in Judea were in a backslidden and despondent condition.

EZRA'S CREDENTIALS
Ezra 7:1-28

Ezra's Qualifications
Ezra 7:1-10

A. A Priestly Scholar (Ezra 7:1-6a):

Ezra was a priest. Like all priests, he could trace his ancestry back to Aaron the first high priest. Though he was born and raised in Babylon, he was also a *ready* (lit., quick) or skilled scribe or scholar with special expertise in the Law of Moses. The language suggests that he was one of those brilliant minds who could grasp with ease the complex materials found in the Mosaic Law. That Ezra was so well educated is one indication that the Jews in Babylon prospered under Persian rule.

B. Complaints from Judea (4:7)

The situation in Judea, however, was a different story. Opposition from the Samaritans was a continuing problem. During the reign of Artaxerxes another effort was made to hinder the work of the postexilic community. Those behind this effort were Bishlam, Mithredath and Tabeel. Nothing further is known about the contents of their letter to the king, the circumstances that produced it, or the results of it.

C. Favor with the King (Ezra 7:6b)

The text does not make clear how Ezra came into the favor of King Artaxerxes. What is clear is that this godly scholar requested permission to travel from the land of captivity to Judea. He also requested the authority to enforce the law of God among the Jews of that area. Because God's hand (i.e., favor) was upon him, all the efforts of this man were blessed. So it was that the king granted to Ezra all that he requested. Perhaps the commissioning of Ezra was Artaxerxes' way of responding to the formal complaint that he had received from Bishlam and the others.

D. Secret of his Preparation (Ezra 7:10)

Ezra's preparation for service in God's kingdom began with his heart. *He prepared his heart,* i.e., he was determined, to do three things: 1) study the law of Yahweh, 2) to practice that law, and 3) to teach that law to Israel.

Ezra's Commission
Ezra 7:11-26

By means of a diplomatic note King Artaxerxes granted to Ezra wide-ranging authority. In modern terminology, he might be called Secretary of State for Jewish Affairs. After a formal introduction, the king specified four areas of authority. This letter, like the others in the Book of Ezra, is cited in Aramaic, the language of official correspondence in the Persian Empire.

A. Stipulations regarding Ezra (Ezra 7:11-26)

- Permission was granted for any of the people of Israel living in the Persian Empire to go with Ezra to Jerusalem (7:13).

- Ezra was commissioned to *inquire concerning Judah and Jerusalem according to the law of your God.* He was to assess the situation as to what degree the pilgrims in Judea were following God's law (7:14).
- Ezra was to carry to Jerusalem an offering for the temple. He was to supplement a gift from the royal treasury with monies secured from provincial officers and freewill offerings from Jewish exiles. The money was to be used primarily to underwrite sacrifices to be offered on the altar (7:15-18).
- The king sent by the hand of Ezra certain utensils that were for use in the service of the house of God. These were to be delivered to the temple authorities (7:19).
- Ezra was authorized to tap the royal treasuries for any additional resources he might need for his work (7:20).
- He was mandated to do zealously whatever *the God of heaven* might require at his temple. Artaxerxes believed that to ignore any requirement regarding temple ritual might subject the king and his sons to divine wrath (7:23).
- Ezra was to appoint magistrates and judges for the Jews who lived throughout the Trans-Euphrates province (7:25a).
- He was to teach any Jews who were ignorant of the laws of God (7:25b).
- The king authorized Ezra to enforce both the law of God and the law of the king among the Jewish people. He had the authority to administer various punishments,[86] including the execution of law breakers (7:26).

B. Stipulations regarding Officials

A second decree (or perhaps a section within the one decree) was directed to the various royal treasurers in the Trans-Euphrates province. These officials were ordered to supply Ezra whatever he needed up to a hundred talents of silver (about 3.75 tons), a hundred kors of wheat (650 bushels), a hundred baths of wine (607 gallons), and a hundred baths of oil and salt as needed. Furthermore these treasurers were ordered not to impose any form of taxation of the temple personnel (Ezra 7:21, 22, 24).

---

[86]The punishments were not derived from the law of God, although some of them are mentioned in the Pentateuch. These laws are state penalties. *Banishment* (NASB) is better understood as corporal or physical punishment.

623

C. Praise Interlude (Ezra 7:27-28)

Ezra burst forth in praise as he contemplated the way God was working for the benefit of his people. He recognized that God had put the desire in the heart of King Artaxerxes to adorn the house of Yahweh in Jerusalem. To the Lord belonged the credit for the favorable treatment that Ezra had received from the king and his associates. The realization that God was opening doors strengthened Ezra. He realized that *the hand of Yahweh,* i.e., empowerment by God, was upon him. He therefore organized a group of Jewish leaders to make the trip to Jerusalem.

EZRA'S RETURN
Ezra 8:1-36

Ezra's journey to Jerusalem began on New Year's Day in the seventh year of Artaxerxes (April 8, 458 BC). The trip took four months (Ezra 7:8-9).

Roster of Travelers
Ezra 8:1-14

A group of 1,514 *leading men from Israel* and their families left Babylon with Ezra. With women and children, the group could have numbered six or seven thousand, about one sixth the size of the group that returned in 538 BC.

The émigrés were honored by having their names recorded. Most of the families mentioned here were also involved in the earlier return under Zerubbabel. In this list of names the heads of two priestly families are mentioned first. They are followed by the head of the descendants of King David. The number of the men who accompanied the heads of these first three families has not been included in the text. Then follow the leaders of twelve family groups with the numbers of émigrés in each group. Some think that the twelve families are representative of the twelve tribes and are another clue that the author regarded the return from Babylon as a second exodus.

Rest at the Ahava Canal
Ezra 8:15-31

A. A Discovery (Ezra 8:15)

After traveling about nine days, Ezra and his group camped at the river of Ahava, probably one of the many canals of the Euphrates River. During the three day encampment Ezra discovered that no Levites had joined the group. That these men should be reluctant to make the trip back to Jerusalem is understandable. They faced a double difficulty. First, like all pilgrims, they would have to uproot their families. Second, they faced the drastic change from ordinary pursuits to the strict routines of the temple.

B. Recruitment of Levites (Ezra 8:16-17)

Ezra dispatched a delegation to nearby Casiphia (location unknown) to recruit Levites. Nine men were chosen because of their standing in the community (*leading men*); two for their diplomatic skills (*teachers*). Ezra carefully coached his emissaries about those to whom they were to appeal and what they were to say. They were to address their appeal to Iddo, the leader of the Levites, to *bring ministers to us for the house of our God.*

C. Response (Ezra 8:18-20)

Again God's hand of blessing was upon the group. Two Levitical families totaling thirty-eight heads of households volunteered to return to Jerusalem. In addition 220 Nethinim or temple servants joined the travelers.

D. Prayer and Fasting (Ezra 8:21-23)

Before undertaking the trip, Ezra ordered a solemn fast. The group entreated the Lord for a safe journey. Ezra had been ashamed to request a military escort to protect the group from bandits along the way. He had assured King Artaxerxes that *the hand of God*, i.e., his power and blessing, was upon those who seek him, but his wrath is directed against those who forsake him. Having publicly stated his conviction regarding the protective providence of God, Ezra thought it was inconsistent to request an armed guard. So the group resorted to prayer, and the Lord heard that entreaty.

E. Finance Committee (Ezra 8:24-30)

Ezra appointed a committee of twelve leading priests and twelve leading Levites to be responsible for the transportation of the gifts for the temple. The law required priests to handle the sacred objects and the Levites to carry them (cf. Numbers 3:8, 31; 4:5ff).

Ezra carefully weighed out the gold, silver and other valuables that had been contributed to the work of the temple. These offerings amounted to 650 talents of silver (24.5 tons) plus silver utensils worth an additional hundred talents (3.75 tons). The gold weighed one hundred talents (3.75 tons). The contributions also included twenty bowls of gold weighing a thousand darics (19 lbs.) and two fine articles of polished bronze *as precious as gold*.

Safe Arrival
Ezra 8:31-36

A. Protection in the Journey (Ezra 8:31)

After twelve days of organizing at the River Ahava, the group departed for Jerusalem. The journey of a thousand miles around the Fertile Crescent was uneventful, a circumstance attributed to the fact that *the hand of our God was over us.* Just as God protected his people from their enemies at the exodus from Egypt, so now he guarded these who made their exodus from Babylon. The Lord delivered them from the hand of potential enemies while en route.

B. Valuables Delivered (Ezra 8:32-34)

After arriving in Jerusalem the group rested for three days. On the fourth day, the committee of twenty-four publicly weighed out the gifts from Babylon and then delivered them over to the custody of the appropriate temple officials. *Everything was numbered and weighed, and all the weight was recorded at that time* (NASB). Both those who carried the valuables and those who received them acted in business-like manner.

C. Sacrifices (Ezra 8:35)

The exiles that had come from captivity went to the temple to offer sacrifices. Twelve bulls and ninety-six rams (a multiple of twelve) and seventy-seven lambs were offered as burnt offerings *for all Israel.* Likewise, twelve male goats were offered as a sin offering. The inhabitants of postexilic Judea considered themselves the survivors and representatives of all the tribes of Israel. They were the covenant people.

D. Royal Edicts Delivered (Ezra 8:36)

After religious duties had been fulfilled, Ezra's people delivered the edicts of Artaxerxes to the government officials in the Trans-Euphrates province. These officials *supported the people and the house of God* (NASB) as required by the royal decree.

EZRA'S WORK
Ezra 9:1-10:44

Within five months (cf. 7:9 with 10:9) Ezra's efforts to teach the law of God in Judea began to bear fruit. He had pricked the conscience of the nation by his emphasis on Israel as *the holy seed.* With no prompting from their teacher, a group of leaders approached Ezra with some bad news. The postexilic community had been unfaithful to its calling by tolerating illegal marriages with pagan women. These reports of unfaithfulness among the leaders of the Jews challenged Ezra's wisdom and courage.

Israel's Problem
Ezra 9:1-6

A. Report (Ezra 9:1-2)

Some *princes* (civil authorities) reported to Ezra that the people of Israel, including some Levites and priests, had not separated themselves from the peoples of the surrounding lands. *Abominations* (i.e., pagan worship objects) were being tolerated and even condoned. The ecumenical spirit threatened to destroy the distinctiveness of God's people! Some had even married foreign women so that *the holy race has intermingled with the peoples of the lands* (NASB). What was worse, this *unfaithfulness* was most in evidence among the princes and rulers of the people. Religiously and ethnically Israel was in danger of disappearing as a distinct people.

B. Reaction (Ezra 9:3-5)

Ezra was devastated by this news. He went beyond the usual signs of mourning (tearing his garments) and plucked out some of his beard. This was a sign of indignation as well as grief. He then *sat appalled,* i.e., speechless with astonishment. He was astounded to think that after all the troubles of Israel and their subsequent restoration by God they should once again start down the same path

627

of disobedience. Others who *trembled* over the implications of this deliberate violation of the word of God joined Ezra in his demonstration. Ezra's *humiliation* ended at the time of the evening sacrifice (about 3:00 pm). He then fell on his knees, stretched out his hands to God in a gesture of entreaty, and prayed.

Ezra's Prayer
Ezra 9:6-15

A. A Sinful Record (9:6-7)

Great revivals begin when great souls go to a great God with great fervor. Ezra's prayer is a model for revival prayer. First, he acknowledged the sinful record of his people. Ezra was ashamed to lift up his face to God. His people were drowning in a sea of guilt. That however, was nothing new. Since the days of the fathers—as long as anyone could remember—the nation had been guilty before God. On account of national iniquities, Israel had been given by God into the hand of powerful kings. The people had experienced the sword (war), captivity, plunder, and open shame (lit., shame of faces). The shame continued to that very moment since Judea was but a tiny province within the vast Persian Empire.

B. God's Grace Acknowledged (Ezra 9:8-9)

Second, Ezra acknowledged the grace of God. A remnant had escaped exile to return to the Promised Land. That remnant was like a peg upon which hung all hope for the fulfillment of the glorious promises made to Israel by her prophets. Through that remnant God intended to *enlighten* the eyes, i.e., revive the nation, in the midst of her bondage. Like Ezekiel (37:1-14), Ezra regarded the people as dead during the exile. God, however, had not forsaken them in their captivity. He had caused a trio of Persian kings—Cyrus, Darius, Artaxerxes—to show favor toward the Jews. The newly built temple bore testimony that the revival of Israel had begun. God's people had *a wall* (lit., a fence)[87] in Judah and Jerusalem, i.e., a secure place.

C. Present Transgression Confessed (Ezra 9:10-14)

---

[87]The term *wall* (*gader*) is not used for a city wall, but for an enclosure of a vineyard. The phrase *in Judah and Jerusalem* also is a clue that no literal wall is intended. It would be impossible to build a wall around Judah. Thus the *wall* mentioned in Ezra 9:9 does not refer to the wall of the city of Jerusalem that had not yet been built.

Third, Ezra confessed the magnitude of the present transgression. This prayer was intended for the ears of the spectators. It was a kind of sermon prayer. The confession is couched in first person (*we*). Great intercessors include themselves among the sinners for whom they pray. Several reasons are given as to why the intermingling with heathen peoples was such a horrendous sin.

- Separation from the peoples of the land was commanded by God (9:10). The violation of any divine commandment is a serious matter.

- The commandment in question was ancient (cf. Deuteronomy 7:3). It had been given before Israel ever entered Canaan (9:11).

- The commandment had been repeated by various prophets through the ages. Thus no one could plead ignorance (9:11).

- The commandment had been explained. God is not required to explain his commands (9:11). When he does, however, no one could plead that his directives were arbitrary or inappropriate. The words *unclean, uncleanness, abominations* and *impurity* describe pagan worship and those associated with it.

- The commandment was specific (9:12a). Israelites were not to give their daughters to pagan men, nor take pagan wives for their sons. They were not to seek the peace and prosperity of the heathen in the land, i.e., they were not to have any sort of business agreement with them.

- The commandment was accompanied by a promise and an implied threat (9:12b). By remaining separate from the heathen, Israel will be strong. God's people will continue to enjoy the land their God had given them. They will be able to leave that land to their offspring. The implication here (clearly stated in other passages) is that if they intermingled with the heathen they will lose the land. That, of course, is exactly what had happened in 586 BC.

- The commandment had been broken in spite of the fact that this people already had been punished once for this same transgression (9:13a).

- The commandment had been broken in spite of all the grace that God had recently shown them (9:13b). God had requited his people less than their past iniquities deserved. He had given his people *an escaped remnant* (NASB).

- The violation of the commandment placed the remnant in jeopardy of total extinction (9:14).

D. God's Righteousness Acknowledged (Ezra 9:15)

Fourth, Ezra concluded the prayer with an acknowledgment of the righteousness of God. The remnant stood guilty before him. The righteous judgment of God will result in the total destruction of the remnant. Ezra did not ask for forgiveness. He knew that repentance that manifests itself in the removal of the sin is required before divine forgiveness can be requested.

Initial Steps
Ezra 10:1-8

A. A Plan Offered (10:1-2)

Ezra's actions and prayer before the house of God attracted a large crowd of men, women and children. His tears were contagious. Soon the crowd was weeping along with their leader. Finally, Sechaniah could stand it no longer. He publicly admitted the fact that sin had been committed through the marriages to foreign wives. Yet, in spite of this, he voiced his opinion that there was still hope. He had a plan by which he believed that the sin could be removed from the land thus making possible divine forgiveness.

B. Details of the Plan (Ezra 10:3)

Shecaniah's plan was bold. All of those present should make a covenant to put away their foreign wives and the children born of them. This should be carried out according to the counsel of Ezra (*my lord*) and *those who tremble at the command of our God,* i.e., those who were truly concerned over the issue. The wives should be put away legally (cf. Deuteronomy 24:1). If sending away the children seems unduly harsh, these facts must be kept in mind.

- First, the major problem being addressed was the religious influence of the mothers on their children.
- Second, sending away the children with their mothers was less cruel than forcibly separating the mothers from their children.

- Third, keeping the religion of the Lord pure was the one and only aim of Ezra.
- Fourth, only by insulating themselves from the sea of pagan influence around them could the religious identity of God's people be maintained (10:3).

C. **Promise of Support** (Ezra 10:4)

Shecaniah urged the emotionally distraught Ezra to take the lead for this was his responsibility. Shecaniah, however, promised that those present were committed to back him. In addition he encouraged Ezra in this difficult assignment with the words *be courageous and act*.

D. **Pertinent Considerations:**

To place the actions in Ezra 10 in proper perspective, several factors must be understood.

- First, the marriages here dissolved were illegal in the first place. Sending away the foreign wives signaled willingness to cease perpetuating an illegal act.
- Second, divorce was permitted in Israel, though not without some serious cause (Deuteronomy 24:1).
- Third, Moses permitted divorce and remarriage because of *the hardness of heart* of the men of Israel (Mark 10:5).
- Fourth, a number of Jewish wives had been divorced for no good reason in order that these heathen women might be married (Malachi 2:10-16).
- Fifth, God hates divorce (Malachi 2:16) because of what it does to individuals, families, and his cause in this world.
- Sixth, the situation described in Ezra 10 was one in which the lesser of two evils (divorce) was chosen.
- Seventh, If a serious reason for divorce ever existed, this had a better claim than most to come within that category.
- Eighth, the problem of intermarriage with unbelievers is handled differently under the New Covenant than it was under the Old (cf. 1 Corinthians 7:12-14, 16).

E. **An Oath Secured** (Ezra 10:5-8)

631

For a leader of the local community to speak up was all that Ezra needed. He immediately secured an oath from the leading priests, Levites and laymen that they would carry out the proposal of Shecaniah. Ezra then retired to one of the temple chambers to continue his prayer and fasting over the unfaithfulness of the exiles. Those who took the oath sent out a proclamation throughout Judea that all of the exiles should assemble at Jerusalem within three days. Anyone who failed to appear forfeited his possessions and his position as a member of the assembly of exiles.

Actions of the Assembly
Ezra 10:9-15

A. Uncomfortable Gathering (Ezra 10:9)

The proclamation got results. In the ninth month (December) the family heads in the regions of Judah and Benjamin appeared in Jerusalem within three days. They all sat in the open square before the house of God (i.e., in the great court). As they waited for Ezra to address them, they were trembling because of 1) this matter, i.e., the potential consequences of their intermarriages; and 2) the heavy winter rain.

B. Ezra's Sermon (Ezra 10:10-11)

Finally the scribe stood up. The inclement weather prohibited a long speech. In a few carefully crafted sentences Ezra exposed the guilt of those people. He accused the assembly of being unfaithful to God because they had married foreign wives. While it is true only a fraction of those present had actually committed this trespass, the others were guilty for having tolerated it. Ezra urged the assembly to *make confession* to the Lord, then to separate themselves from the peoples of the land including their foreign wives.

C. A Problem (Ezra 10:12-13)

A loud chorus of voices from the assembly agreed with Ezra on the action that needed to be taken. They pointed out, however, that the problem was more widespread than Ezra realized. More than a couple of days were needed to deal with the problem. The assembly was too large to move indoors, and the wintry rain made standing in the open square unbearable.

D. Plan of Action (Ezra 10:14-15)

A motion was made that the sensitive issue of the foreign wives be handled by a committee of leaders. By appointment those from a given village were to be required to appear before this tribunal. The testimony of the accused and the elders and judges of his village could then be heard and evaluated. The tribunal will continue to function until all alleged violations of the law had been investigated and resolved. Then the anger of God could be turned away from the postexilic community. This motion won overwhelming support of the assembly with only two negative votes. Two Levites, apparently not voting members of the assembly, supported the two men who were in opposition.

Marriage Tribunal
Ezra 10:16-19

A. Work of the Tribunal (Ezra 10:16-17)

Ezra appointed a blue ribbon committee consisting of the heads of households. The group began to meet on the first day of the tenth month a bit over a week after the assembly had authorized this approach. Seventy-five days were required to make the fair investigation of all cases where men had married foreign wives. The point at issue in each case was whether or not the wife genuinely had converted to the worship of the Lord. If the wife had converted, the marriage was valid; if not, the marriage had to be dissolved. Less than one case per day resulted in a divorce.

B. Results of the Tribunal (Ezra 10:18-19)

The marriage tribunal found 113 cases where foreign wives had been married. Of these, seventeen cases were among priests and ten among Levites and other temple personnel. These pledged themselves (lit. "they gave their hands") to put away their wives. They offered a ram of the flock for their offense. The families affected by these actions were a small percentage of the entire population. What is more alarming, however, is that some 25% of those guilty were religious leaders. Ezra could see where this trend would lead if left unchecked.

Families Affected
Ezra 10:18-44

A. Priestly Sacrifices (Ezra 10:19)

The Book of Ezra concludes with the listing of the names of those who had married foreign wives. Nine of the thirty-three families and town groups that appeared in 2:3-35 are represented here, and two new families appear that were not in the earlier list. The names of priests who had married foreign wives are given first. These priests pledged to send their illegal wives away. Each offered a ram as a guilt offering. As religious leaders the priests were setting an example for the others who were guilty.

B. Purpose of the List

Perhaps the author means to attach infamy to the names of those who had married foreign wives. On the other hand, he may mean to commend them for choosing to follow the difficult path of separation rather than surrender their position among God's people. In any case, the separations ordered by the marriage tribunal must have been painful, especially since in some cases children were also involved. One can assume that the court did everything in its power to see that suitable material support was provided for the women who were put away.

EZRA'S FAILURE
Ezra 4:8-23

In Ezra 4 the author gathered examples of opposition to the postexilic community from several different periods. One of those efforts seems to have involved Ezra.

Official Complaint
Ezra 4:7-16

A. Origin of the Complaint (Ezra 4:7-10)

A letter in the official Aramaic language was sent to Artaxerxes by Rehum *the commander* and Shimshai the scribe. Several groups of lesser leaders joined in support of this official complaint. These men were foreigners—Elamites, Babylonians, et al.)—who had been settled in the Trans-Euphrates province, i.e., west of the Euphrates River, by the great Osnappar, i.e., Ashurbanipal who ruled 669-626 BC.

B. Unauthorized Wall-building (Ezra 4:11-12)

The letter documents how a group of Jews had come to Jerusalem with the permission of Artaxerxes. These Jews were *rebuilding the rebellious and evil city* and were *finishing the walls*. The word *rebellious* was an explosive word in this period, since the Persian kings were facing rebellions from one end of their empire to the other. The only group of Jews known to have come to Jerusalem with the permission of Artaxerxes was that group led by Ezra in 458 BC. Apparently this group had attempted to rebuild the walls of Jerusalem. Since they had no royal building permit, the effort was legally vulnerable. The peoples of the land were swift to exploit that vulnerability.

C. Warnings about the Jews (Ezra 4:13-16)

The letter charged that should the Jews succeed in their building efforts, they would declare their independence and refuse to pay taxes. The Samaritans supported their accusation with two considerations. First, those writing the letter *were in the service of the king,* (lit., "eat the salt of the palace"). They had only the best interest of Artaxerxes at heart. Second, the royal records indicated that the Jews had a history of rebellion against their foreign masters. Indeed, the city was presently in ruins because of such a rebellion. The letter concluded with an exaggeration. Should the construction work at Jerusalem go unchecked, the king will lose the entire Trans-Euphrates province. The insinuation is that the Jerusalem rebellion will spread through the entire province, or more preposterous, that the Jews will attempt to take over the Trans-Euphrates province.

Official Response
Ezra 4:17-22

In his response to the letter, Artaxerxes indicated that he had ordered a search of the royal archives. The records indicated that indeed the accusation was justified. The city in the past had a reputation for rebellion and revolt against foreign kings who tried to impose taxes on the area. For this reason, Artaxerxes directed his local representative in Samaria to issue a decree ordering the reconstruction of Jerusalem to cease until *a decree is made by me.* This left open the possibility of a policy review at some future date.

That was the possibility that Nehemiah will exploit some thirteen years later when he secured permission from this same king to return and build the walls. The king concluded his letter with a warning that his representatives in the region should not be negligent in carrying out this edict.

Tearing Down Walls
Ezra 4:23

Rehum the commander and Shimshai the scribe lost no time in implementing the decree of Artaxerxes. Along with their supporters, they went to Jerusalem and stopped the rebuilding of the walls by force of arms. Rehum and his men actually went beyond the terms of this decree by demolishing and burning what already had been constructed (Nehemiah 1:3).

Conclusion

The people of God had been restored to their land in 538 BC under the leadership of Zerubbabel (Sheshbazzar). The temple had been rebuilt in 515 BC. The threat of the annihilation of the Jews was defeated by the work of Esther and Mordecai in 474-473 BC. Ezra had returned in 458 BC to restore the law to its rightful place among the people of God. Yet to be restored was Jerusalem, the holy city.

42
RECONSTRUCTION
OF THE NATION
Nehemiah 1-13

Chapter Chronology

			423	
	ARTAXERXES			
464				
		445	NEHEMIAH	
	EZRA		Governor 445-432	Governor 430-???
	458			

BUILDING
JERUSALEM'S WALLS
Nehemiah 1-6

Commission of Nehemiah
Nehemiah 1:1-2:9

Just as Esther was providentially placed in the harem of King Xerxes, so Nehemiah also found himself in a position to help his people in a new crisis.

A. Nehemiah's Grief (Nehemiah 1:1-4)

1. A delegation from Jerusalem (1:1-3): In the month of Chislev of the twentieth[88] year of Artaxerxes (Nov/Dec 446 BC) a delegation of Jews arrived in Susa the Persian capital. One of these men was Hanani, the brother (or kinsman) of Nehemiah the cupbearer to the king.

2. Jerusalem's welfare (1:4): The uppermost question in the mind of Nehemiah concerned the welfare of the Jews of the postexilic community. The news was not good. The remnant was in great

---

[88]In the light of Nehemiah 2:1, one would expect the reading in 1:1 to be "nineteenth" year. Either an autumn-to-autumn reckoning of the years of Artaxerxes is being employed here, or the figure in 1:1 is the result of a scribal error. Another possibility is that "twentieth" refers, not to the regnal years of Artaxerxes, but to Nehemiah's years of service in Susa.

distress and reproach as a result of the fact that the wall of Jerusalem was broken down, the gates burned with fire. The description most likely refers to conditions following the time a few years earlier when Rehum went to Jerusalem and by force made the Jews stop rebuilding their walls (Ezra 4:23). A city without a wall was an open shame, not to mention dangerous place to live. Nehemiah was grief-stricken over this news. He fasted and mourned for days.

B. Nehemiah's Prayer (Nehemiah 1:5-11)

1. A great God (1:5): Some nine prayers are attributed to Nehemiah. The prayer in chapter 1 is the longest in the book. It is directed to *Yahweh God of heaven.* To Nehemiah Yahweh was *the great and awesome God.* He faithfully kept his covenant with *those who love him and keep his commandments.* Correct theology inspires bold petition. Nehemiah knew his God was great. He therefore was not afraid to make of him a bold request.

2. A great confession (1:6-7): After the address, the prayer proceeds to confession. The great intercessor included himself among the sinful people for whom he prayed. He confessed that the sons of Israel had acted very corruptly against God. They had disregarded the divine commandments of the Law of Moses.

3. A great commitment (1:8-10): Nehemiah next asked the Lord to remember the word he had revealed through Moses. Yahweh had threatened to scatter Israel among the people of the earth if they were unfaithful to his word. He had also promised to gather those who repented in those distant lands and bring them back to that land where he had chosen to reveal himself (*cause my name to dwell*). Those who returned to the Lord were truly his people, his servants, whom God had redeemed by his *strong arm.* Thus God had shown his favor towards his people. Now Nehemiah was about to make a request that was ultimately to benefit those same people.

4. A great request (1:11): Nehemiah asked God to be attentive to his prayer and the prayers of other faithful servants who were lifting up the postexilic community before the throne of grace. In particular, Nehemiah asked that he might be successful and find favor before *this man.* Not until this point in the book does Nehemiah identify himself and the king he served. He was a cupbearer to King Artaxerxes. His basic duty was to sample the wine served to the king to make sure it had not been poisoned. The position gave him frequent access to the king and made him potentially a man of great influence.

C. Nehemiah's Appointment (Nehemiah 2:1-8)

1. Nehemiah's predicament (2:1-2): In the month of Nisan of the twentieth year of Artaxerxes (Mar/Apr 445 BC), about four months after news arrived from Jerusalem, Nehemiah was scheduled for his duties in the palace. This was his opportunity. Yet Nehemiah's life was also in jeopardy because Persian kings never allowed sadness in their presence. Artaxerxes soon noticed that his cupbearer was exhibiting a sadness of heart unrelated to health. Nehemiah was justifiably afraid when the king inquired about his disposition. Court etiquette would be offended if one who enjoyed the king's presence were to ask leave to depart to another place.

2. Nehemiah's explanation (2:3): Nehemiah made no effort to evade the king's question. He told Artaxerxes that his sadness was justifiable in view of the desolate condition of Jerusalem, *the place of my fathers' tombs* (NASB). The reference to the tombs was a stroke of genius. Persians were paranoid about respect for the dead and proper burial. The phrase evoked immediate sympathy from this monarch who only a few years before had ordered the work of rebuilding Jerusalem to cease.

3. Nehemiah's tact: In a masterpiece of diplomacy, Nehemiah avoided mentioning the word Jerusalem. That name would have reminded the king of his earlier investigation regarding the history of that city (cf. Ezra 4:8-23). Eventually, of course, the king ascertained the name of the city. At the outset of the negotiations, however, expediency dictated that Nehemiah not mention the name of the place.

4. Nehemiah's request (2:4-8): Nehemiah anticipated the next question of the king, *What would you request?* He had prayed long about how he might answer that question. He requested permission to go to Judah to rebuild *the city of my fathers' tombs.* Again the king was moved by the concern of this man for the graves of his ancestors. Artaxerxes was perfectly willing to allow Nehemiah to return to his native land. Only details regarding his time of absence from the royal court needed to be worked out. The *good hand of God* was truly upon Nehemiah. The mention of the queen being with the king suggests 1) this was a private occasion; and 2) that she may have interceded on Nehemiah's behalf.

639

Nehemiah continued to press for concessions. He asked for passport letters which would allow him to travel without provincial interference en route to Judah. He further requested a letter to the overseer of the king's forests in the region (probably in Lebanon) authorizing a grant of timber to be used in reconstructing the gates of the city. Again the king acceded.

Beginning of the Work
Nehemiah 2:9-3:32

The powerful leadership qualities of Nehemiah stand out in the account of how he motivated the Jews to rebuild their walls, and then organized them for this project.

A. Arrival in Jerusalem (Nehemiah 2:9-20)

1. Nehemiah's journey (2:9-10): Nehemiah was accompanied by an armed Persian military escort during his journey. Not only did this provide protection, it guaranteed that Nehemiah arrived in style. The escort also gave credibility to his authority and underscored the change in royal policy. Along the way Nehemiah presented the king's letters to the various governors of the Trans-Euphrates province. Among those governors were Sanballat the Horonite[89] and Tobiah the Ammonite.[90] Tobiah was a Jew who occupied the position of *king's servant* in the region of Ammon. The two officials were very displeased that anyone had come to seek the welfare of the sons of Israel.

2. Nehemiah's night tour (2:11-16): Upon arriving in Jerusalem, Nehemiah rested three days. Then by night he, and a few trusted associates, made a night time circuit of the walls in order to assess their condition. At one point he found it impossible for his mount to pass. The obstruction may have been the huge spill of rubble left from Nebuchadnezzar's assault 140 years earlier. Nehemiah told none of

---

[89]In the Elephantine papyri, dating some thirty-eight years after the events of Nehemiah 2, Sanballat is named as governor of Samaria. *Horonite* is thought by some to be derived from the name of a town in Moab. Others, with more probability, trace the term to Beth-horon, a town in the tribal area of Ephraim which at this time was controlled by the Samaritans.

[90]Tobiah is a Jewish name, not an Ammonite one. This family continued to be a powerful force in Ammon down into the third century. Some trace the hostility of Tobiah back to Ezra 2:59f where the *sons of Tobiah* were not allowed to serve as priests because they could not establish their priestly pedigree.

the local leaders what he was doing. Apparently he did not wish to reveal his intentions until he had formulated a plan by which his mission could be concluded successfully.

3. *Nehemiah's address (2:17-18a):* When he had a clear concept of how the task should be approached, Nehemiah assembled the leaders of the community. First, he called attention to the obvious. Jerusalem was *desolate,* i.e., without walls or gates. The eyes of a stranger may see more clearly what has been made obscure by familiarity. Second, he urged them to rebuild the wall so that God's people no longer were a reproach among the nations. Third, he encouraged them by testifying how God and King Artaxerxes had been favorably disposed to him.

4. *Response of the Jews (2:18b):* Nehemiah must have been a powerful motivator. The people responded, *Let us arise and build.* The work began immediately: *They put their hands to the good work.*

5. *Reaction of enemies (2:19-20):* Sanballat and Tobiah were joined by Geshem the Arab in mocking the initial efforts. In his response to this mockery, Nehemiah did not mention his authority from the king. The enemies already knew about that. He cited higher authority, viz., *the God of heaven.* He identified the Israelites as servants of this God. He calmly reaffirmed the intentions of the Jews to rebuild. They did not need nor want the help of these powerful officials. These antagonists had no *portion, right, or memorial* in Jerusalem, i.e., they had no past, present or future with the people of God. These remarks had important legal ramifications. Jerusalem was the city of the Jews and the enemies had no legal authority over it.

B. Organization of the Effort (Nehemiah 3:1-32)

Nehemiah's plan was for the entire wall to go up simultaneously. He assigned each of some forty segments of the wall to groups of builders. The list is full of heterogeneous groups working side by side for the common good of the community: families, communities, crafts (e.g., goldsmiths, and the perfumer in verse 8), and trades (merchants in verse 31). Nehemiah 3 contains another one of those honor rolls of faith that are characteristic of the postexilic literature. A few notes on this chapter are appropriate.

- Ten gates of the city are mentioned. The story of the wall building focuses on them. In Nehemiah 12:39 two other gates are mentioned which apparently were not in need of repair. Old Jerusalem, then, had twelve gates. So also does the New Jerusalem of Revelation 21:12.

- Among the workers was Eliashib the high priest. He led the other priests in rebuilding the Sheep Gate. Since this area of the wall was near the temple, the priests consecrated this section of the wall (3:1).

- Not everyone in the area supported Nehemiah's effort. The citizens of the village of Tekoa worked in the area of the Fish Gate. *Their nobles,* however, did not *support* (lit., bring their neck to) the work.

- Women may have taken an active part in the construction. One segment of the wall was repaired by *Shallum...and his daughters* (3:12).

- One worker is singled out for special commendation. Baruch *zealously repaired* one segment of the wall (3:20).

- Seven work groups did double duty (verses 11, 19-21, 24, 27, 30). Thank God for those blessed souls who do more than their share of kingdom work!

Hindrances from Without
Nehemiah 4:1-23

As they saw the work going forward, the enemies of the Jews launched an attack to intimidate the workers.

A. Opposition by Mockery (Nehemiah 4:1-6)
1. Pubic ridicule (4:1-3): Sanballat became furious when he heard that the Jews were rebuilding the wall. Before some formal assembly of the wealthy citizens of Samaria he launched a propaganda campaign against the Jews. He used five rhetorical questions to demean the workers and question their perseverance. Tobiah spoke up to mock the quality of the work. A fox could break through their wall by merely leaping on it. Some wall!
2. Nehemiah's response (4:4-5): Nehemiah responded to the mockery with prayer. Undergirding the prayer is the proposition that the work being done was of God. To oppose the work, therefore, was to oppose God. Nehemiah asked that God might take their reproach and hurl it back upon the heads of the mockers, i.e., bring upon them what they had wished for the Jews. He prayed that the enemies be removed from their land, that they lose their wealth and their

642

freedom. He requested the Lord not to forgive, i.e., ignore, the sins of the enemies in deriding the work of God. The prayer was thus not vindictive because the Jews were insulted, but because God's work was ridiculed.

3. *Work progress (4:6):* Even as the Samaritan enemies mocked, the work on the wall was progressing. Soon the walls had reached half their height. Rather than completing a number of separate sections in succession, priority was given to closing the ring at however modest a level. The progress in spite of opposition is explained by the fact that *the people had a mind to work,* lit., "the heart of the people was to do the work"

B. Threat of Open Attack (Nehemiah 4:7-9)

The ranks of the enemies began to swell. Arabs from the south, Ammonites from the east, and Ashdodites from the west joined the Samaritans who lived north of Judea. God's people were encircled by enemies! The anger of these enemies increased as they witnessed the breaches of the walls being filled. A new strategy was devised to thwart the work: a swift raid that would produce disruption within the city. The builders learned of this impending attack and took appropriate precautions. First they prayed. Then they stationed a guard against such an attack night and day. Here again is the partnership between heaven and earth so evident throughout the Book of Nehemiah.

C. Discouraged Workers (Nehemiah 4:10)

The Jewish work force was particularly vulnerable at this point. Because of all the debris that had to be removed and the diminished work force now that some were posted on guard duty, the strength of the burden bearers was waning. Soon everyone in Judah was repeating a couplet that reflected their doubts about the viability of the project. These were not the last builders of Zion to discover that the removal of rubbish (man-made traditions) is a necessary but discouraging work.

D. Threat of Sneak Attack (Nehemiah 4:11-23)

1. *Rumors circulated (4:11-12):* The Jews who lived near the enemies heard the rumors of a massive, all-out attack. Whether they were unwitting purveyors of propaganda or useful informants is difficult to determine. They kept on warning the builders (*ten times*)

that this attack was to come from all directions. Such a prospect generated fear in Jerusalem.

   2. Nehemiah's response (4:13-14): Nehemiah stationed guards in high spots where they could easily be seen over the low walls. This was counter intimidation. He armed all the workers and placed them with their family groups where they would have the greatest incentive to fight manfully. When he saw their fear, Nehemiah reminded the builders that God *is great and awesome.*

   3. Work progress (4:15-20): The Samaritans backed off when they realized the Jews were prepared for an attack. The Jews then returned to the work, but extra precautions were taken.

   • First, Nehemiah had half of his own personal servants and bodyguards assisted with the work. The other half he had ready with weapons to rush to any point where attack threatened. Nehemiah's servants had at their disposal swords, spears and bows that were accurate up to 300 yards. Shields and breastplates are also mentioned. The builders were well armed!
   • Second, the rulers remained behind the workers, both directing and encouraging them.
   • Third, those with the job of loading and carrying materials handled them with one hand, and kept a sword in the other.
   • Fourth, those who had to use both hands in building kept their swords at their sides.
   • Fifth, a trumpeter stood near Nehemiah who could signal the workers where to rally in case of attack.
   • Sixth, Nehemiah kept encouraging his subordinates with assurances that God would fight for them in any showdown with the Samaritans.

   4. Other precautions (4:21-23): By taking these precautions Nehemiah thwarted the sneak attack planned by the enemy. Half of his men were on guard throughout the day. At night he encouraged his men to remain within the city. Throughout this period of danger no man removed *his clothes,* i.e., his military gear. Even during water breaks each man carried his weapon.

Hindrances from Within
Nehemiah 5:1-19

While Nehemiah dealt with a determined foe without, at the same time he had internal problems that threatened to hinder progress on the walls. Serious dissension arose among the workers.

A. Source of the Problem (Nehemiah 5:1-5)

1. Exploitation of the poor (5:1-4): Some of the Jews—especially the farmers—were poverty stricken, and their economic condition was being exploited by their brothers. The poor families cited three reasons for their destitute condition. First, they had big families and they could not produce enough to feed their families. They, therefore, had to buy grain, and for that they had no money. Second, to secure money to buy grain they had to mortgage their real estate—fields, vineyards, even their houses. Third, the farmers had to borrow money to pay the royal tax on their estates. Perhaps these conditions had even been exacerbated by the concentrated work on the walls that pulled laborers away from their normal pursuits. Beneath the surface the cry of the populace seems to have been that the personal cost of the wall building effort was too high.

2. Results of poverty (5:5): The destitute condition of some families led to three unfortunate results. First, poverty stricken families were being forced to sell their sons and daughters into debtors' servitude (cf. Exodus 21:1-11). Second, some of their daughters had been forced into *bondage* (NASB), i.e., the humiliation of undesirable marriages. Third, many of the people felt *helpless* (lit., "there is no power for our hands") because their property was now owned by others.

B. Solution to the Problem (Nehemiah 5:6-13)

1. Private rebuke (5:6-7): Nehemiah was filled with righteous indignation when he heard the complaints of these destitute Jews. The governor met with the wealthy land owners. He accused them of violating the Law of Moses (Leviticus 25:35-37) by exacting usury from their brothers. The lenders were acting like harsh pawnbrokers, not compassionate brothers. The depth of the poverty called for gifts, not loans. When private rebuke failed to solve the problem, Nehemiah called for a great assembly to deal with the guilty nobles.

2. Public rebuke (5:8-9): Nehemiah pointed out to the assembly that efforts had been made to redeem Jewish brothers from debtors' servitude to foreign peoples. Now, however, the nobles were putting their brothers back into economic bondage. To this accusation the nobles had no reply. Nehemiah bluntly stated that what the nobles were doing was not good. In these times when God's people were a reproach among the nations, all Jews should *walk in the fear of the Lord,* i.e., observe the law of God. The law required the release of debtor slaves after six years (cf. Exodus 21:2).

3. *Appeal to the wealthy (5:10-11):* Nehemiah admitted that he and his associates had been guilty of lending the poor money and grain. Thus he himself had contributed to the dissatisfaction among the farmers. He pled with the nobles to join with him in 1) absolving the loans to the poor; 2) returning properties that had been seized for failure of payment; and 3) refunding *the hundredth part of the money,* i.e., the one percent per month charge on the unpaid balance. These actions were designed in effect to cancel the debts.

4. *Response of the nobles (5:12-13):* The nobles agreed to give back property and cancel existing debt. Nehemiah moved immediately to upgrade the commitment from promise to oath. He summoned priests and extracted an oath from these nobles that they would keep their promise. Nehemiah shook out his garment as a symbolic gesture to underscore the penalty that would befall those who reneged on the oath. The folds of garments were like pockets in which personal possessions were kept. Nehemiah emptied the pockets before the people, shaking out everything. This was symbolic of a curse. God would shake them out of their possessions if they broke their word. All the assembly shouted *Amen* in agreement with the actions of Nehemiah and the oath of the nobles. The assembly praised the Lord. Then the nobles did as they had promised.

C. Example of Nehemiah (Nehemiah 5:14-19)

1. *Efforts to break down class envy (5:14-18):* Nehemiah's work in Jerusalem was a labor of love. During his twelve-year tenure (445-432 BC), neither he nor his kinsmen ever ate the governor's food allowance. Former governors laid a burden on the people, requiring of them bread, wine and forty shekels of silver for food allowance. Because he feared Yahweh, Nehemiah refrained from enforcing these regulations. Furthermore, both he and his servants worked on the wall alongside the citizens. Nor did Nehemiah use his considerable wealth to buy up land around Jerusalem. The governor fed at his table and personal expense 150 Jews and officials, not to mention *those who*

came to us from the nations that were around us. Every day an enormous quantity of food was consumed at the governor's house—an ox, six sheep, birds, wine. Yet because the servitude was heavy upon the people Nehemiah did not demand the food allowance to which he was entitled.

2. Nehemiah's prayer (5:19): In all of this Nehemiah sought the praise of God rather than man. He prayed that God would remember all the good that he had done for his people. Thus Nehemiah's actions were religiously motivated, and were not done for purely humanitarian reasons.

Personal Attacks
Nehemiah 6:1-14, 17-19

The walls were now up. Only the doors of the gates remained to be set in place. Those open gateways were the enemy's last hope of regaining the upper hand without actually mounting a siege, which would be out of the question against fellow subjects of Persia. Having failed to intimidate the workers, Sanballat and Geshem now changed their tactics. Their strategy now became to eliminate Nehemiah.

A. Lure of Compromise (Nehemiah 6:1-4)
1. Invitation to Ono (6:1-2): The enemies sent a message to Nehemiah inviting him to meet with them at Chephirim in the plain of Ono, twenty-seven miles northwest of Jerusalem and an equal distance from Samaria. This plain was outside Judean territory. Sanballat's plan was transparent. The plain of Ono bordered on the districts of both Samaria and Ashdod. Since both of these were hostile regions, the plan reeked of treachery.

2. Nehemiah's response (6:3-4): Nehemiah sent word back to them that he could not come down to Ono because *I am doing a great work.* A trip to Ono would only interrupt the work in Jerusalem. Several precious days would be wasted. So *why should the work stop?* Four times the invitations came to Nehemiah, and four times Nehemiah answered them in the same manner.

B. Malicious Slander (Nehemiah 6:5-9)
1. An open letter (6:5-7): Sanballat sent his messenger to Nehemiah a fifth time with an open letter. The letter reported a rumor circulating among surrounding nations, a rumor that was validated by

647

Gashmu (Geshem the Arab). The rumor was that Nehemiah wanted to be king of the Jews, and that he planned to lead a rebellion against the Persians when the walls were rebuilt. Supposedly Nehemiah had authorized prophets to proclaim his kingship in Judea. Sanballat stated that he felt it his duty to inform the king of Persia about this, but wished first to confer with Nehemiah to hear his side of the matter.

2. *Transparent plan:* Again the malicious intentions of Sanballat were transparent. First, he sent an *open* letter, one that could be read by anyone along the way. Normally the correspondence between two governors was sealed. Second, he insisted that Nehemiah meet with him. Had he really believed that Nehemiah was involved in a rebellion against the Persians, he would never have wanted to be associated with him in any manner.

3. *Nehemiah's response (6:8-9):* Nehemiah replied to the slander of Sanballat by simply denying that it was true. First, he exposed the source of the rumors. These rumors were only fabrications of Sanballat's mind. Second, Nehemiah exposed the real motives for such lies. The Samaritans were merely trying to frighten and discourage the wall builders. Their ultimate goal was to stop the work. Faced with this new threat, Nehemiah went again to God in prayer: *Strengthen my hands,* he prayed.

C. False Prophecy (Nehemiah 6:10-14)

1. *Actions of a false prophet (6:10a):* A man of God respects the word of God. Perhaps, the enemies thought, Nehemiah could be goaded into making a wrong move by the word of a prophet. So now the enemies attempted to use Nehemiah's own people against him. Obviously not all the Jews backed the wall project. Prophets, male and female, were hired to predict that Nehemiah was about to be the victim of a nighttime assassination. Nehemiah first heard this prediction in the house of Shemaiah who for some unexplained reason was confined at home. Perhaps his confinement was self-imposed as a kind of symbolic action to dramatize the need for precautions against the supposed assassins. Shemaiah hoped that Nehemiah's visit would be noticed by his coworkers and construed as a search for guidance and a sign of uncertainty.

2. *Words of a false prophet (6:10b):* Having secured his audience with Nehemiah, the prophet presented his proposal in poetic verse, a fact recognized in the Jerusalem Bible translation. Shemaiah

wanted the form of his message to be as compelling as its content. He advised Nehemiah to flee behind the walls of the temple for protection. The intention was to discredit Nehemiah in the eyes of his followers as a terrified leader who urged boldness in others while he took every precaution to save his own life. On the other hand, the intention may have been to lure this layman—and possible eunuch—into an area where only priests were permitted to go. This would cause Nehemiah to lose the support of the priesthood and others who strictly followed the law of God. Nehemiah might even be killed by his own people for desecrating the temple.

3. *Nehemiah's response (6:11-14):* Nehemiah perceived immediately that God had not sent this message. The Lord never encourages cowardly acts. He reasoned that Shemaiah must be the hireling of Tobiah and Sanballat. (Tobiah was named first because he was the main instigator of this plan.) He realized that the enemies were only trying to maneuver him into a wrong move so that they might *reproach* him. Nehemiah prayed for God to remember in judgment these actions of Sanballat and Tobiah as well as those of Noadiah the prophetess and the others who had sold out to the enemy.

D. Threatening Letters (Nehemiah 6:17-19)
During the course of the wall building effort many letters were exchanged between the nobles in Jerusalem and Tobiah the Jewish leader of Ammon. Tobiah was related by marriage to one of the leading families in Jerusalem. Several of the nobles within the city had pledged on oath their loyalty to Tobiah. These oaths were probably trading contracts. They constantly spoke of Tobiah's good deeds before Nehemiah. At the same time, these nobles were a pipeline of information to the enemies concerning every plan and action of Nehemiah. As part of the campaign to discourage and discredit Nehemiah, threatening letters were sent to him from time to time by Tobiah. Working around these fifth columnists within the community must have been very difficult for Nehemiah.

Success of the Work
Nehemiah 6:15-16

A. A Speedy Completion (6:15)
After fifty-two hectic days, on the 25th day of Elul (October 2, 445 BC) the wall was completed. Thus within ten months after he had

heard of the plight of Jerusalem, Nehemiah had finished his commission to rebuild the wall. The speed with which the project was completed can be explained as a result of the following factors:

- The people had a mind to work.
- A large force of workmen, not only from Jerusalem, but from surrounding areas, was engaged in the task.
- The ruins of the previous wall contained large quantities of stone that could be used in the present project.
- God was with the workers supernaturally blessing their efforts.
- In Nehemiah the project had a wise and energetic leader.

B. Response of Enemies (6:16)

When the enemies saw that the wall had been completed in spite of their well orchestrated campaign to prevent it from happening, they *lost their confidence* (NASB), lit., "fell exceedingly in their own eyes." They no longer felt as important as they once did. They were humbled by their inability to stop the work. They recognized that the work could only have been accomplished with the help of God.

The building of Jerusalem's walls was the priority of Nehemiah's first months in Judea. With that task now complete, he turned to an even more formidable one, viz., building a community.

BUILDING
GOD'S COMMUNITY
Nehemiah 7-13

Protecting the City
Nehemiah 7:1-73

The major concerns dominating the Book of Nehemiah can be summarized in two words: community and continuity. Even while Nehemiah took the first steps in building a community that can survive the present and live into the future, he was concerned about demonstrating that community's continuity with the past.

A. Building of Community (Nehemiah 7:1-5)

1. Appointments (7:1-2): After the wall was complete Nehemiah made various appointments of gatekeepers, singers and Levites. That the Levites are prominent in the building of the community should not be thought strange. Jerusalem was a holy city, and worship was its *raison d'être.*

Nehemiah appointed over Jerusalem his brother Hanani and Hananiah, commander of the fortress adjoining the temple. The latter man was one local leader who could be trusted. He was *a faithful man* who *feared God more than many.* Some think these appointments indicate that Nehemiah was contemplating a trip back to the Persian court to report on his progress to the king.

2. Security precautions (7:3-4): Precautions were taken to prevent infiltration of the city by the enemies during early morning or late evening darkness. The gates were to be opened late and closed early. Guards were to be stationed at each gate and at other strategic positions around the city. Residents were to be prepared to defend their own homes. Watchfulness was to be the rule of the day!

3. A census (7:5): Before the walls had been rebuilt few Jews had the courage to build their homes in the city limits of Jerusalem. That the population was too small adequately to defend the city on a continuing basis now became evident. Nehemiah moved decisively again. He took a census of the postexilic community. In the process he found the scroll containing the names of those who had returned to Judea back in 538 BC under Zerubbabel. Nehemiah used that genealogical record to help solve the problem of the under population of Jerusalem.

B. Demonstrating Continuity (Nehemiah 7:6-73)

Nehemiah inserted a copy of the old register in the record at this point. Except for certain slight differences, the balance of Nehemiah 7 is a virtual duplicate of the list in Ezra 2. Ezra's list was prepared in Babylon. It contained a list of those who expected to return to Judea. The list given by Nehemiah contains the names of those who actually did return. This could account for the small differences between the two lists. The incorporation of the list here in Nehemiah accomplishes two purposes. First, it established the city's continuity with the past. These people needed to have a sense of their inheritance and their calling. Second, it became the basis for reorganizing the population of Judea.

651

Celebrating the Feast
Nehemiah 8:1-18

The initial phase of wall building was completed on the 25th day of Elul, the sixth month (6:15). On the first day of the sacred seventh month, all those living in outlying areas gathered *as one man* to Jerusalem. Under the law, this day—New Year's Day on the religious calendar—was regarded as a day of rest sacred to the Lord (cf. Leviticus 23:24).

A. Great Assembly (Nehemiah 8:1-2)
1. Assembly's request (8:1a): No mention has been made of Ezra during the days of Nehemiah's struggle to rebuild the wall. For some thirteen years his godly leadership had been rejected. Now, however, the spirit of revival was sweeping over the people. They wanted to hear again the law of their God. They asked the godly old scribe to read it to them. Waiting to be asked was characteristic of the leadership style of Ezra (cf. Ezra 10:2).
2. Assembly's purpose: What the people wanted to hear, and what Ezra presumably read to them, was ancient *(the book of the Law of Moses)* and authoritative *(which Yahweh had commanded to Israel)*. To represent what transpired here as the earliest canonization of Scripture clearly is in error. The writings of Moses were regarded as Scripture long before Ezra read these documents to the people.
3. Place of Assembly (8:1b): The place of assembly was the square in front of the Water Gate on the east side of the city. Unlike the earlier great assembly (Ezra 3:2-6), the temple court was not chosen either because it was too small, or because of the composition of the assembly. The Water Gate was one of the centers of city life. God's word cries out to be heard in the streets as well as in the sanctuaries of the land (cf. Proverbs 1:20f; 8:1ff).
3. Make-up of assembly (8:2): The congregation consisted of men, women and *all who could listen with understanding.* Mindless superstition is the mark of paganism. Biblical faith requires intelligent interpretation and application of propositional truth! How much of the Pentateuch Ezra read that day is not important. What is stressed throughout the record is not the quantity of what was read, but the quality of the understanding of the auditors.

B. Reading God's Law (Nehemiah 8:3-12)

1. Respected leaders (8:3-4): Ezra brought the scroll before the assembly and read from it from early morning until midday. He read from a platform that elevated him so that all present could see and hear. Beside him stood thirteen men, presumably leaders of the community, possibly priests. Perhaps these men assisted Ezra in the reading of the law. All the people were attentive throughout the five or six hours of reading.

2. Respectful audience (8:5-6): The author delights in narrating the details of that glorious day when the people listened, for the first time in a long time, to the words of God. As Ezra opened the scroll, the people stood up as a gesture of respect for the word of the Lord. The scribe first *blessed Yahweh*. All the people shouted a double *Amen* while lifting up their hands in grateful acknowledgment to the God of heaven. Then they bowed low with faces to the ground to worship the Lord. Presumably returning to a standing position, the people listened as Ezra read the Hebrew words from the scroll.

3. Available teachers (8:5-8): Thirteen Levites assisted Ezra by *causing the people to understand the law*. Whether these men acted as translators or popular expositors is not clear. G. Campbell Morgan suggested that the public reading was followed by a separation of the assembly into groups led by one of the thirteen Levites. They explained and applied the various passages that Ezra had read. Merely reading the word without understanding it has no benefit for God's people.

4. Significance of the day: The significance of this day in Jewish history should not be missed. Hereafter the Jews were known as a people of the book. At the dedication of Solomon's temple the crowds had been overawed by the architectural beauty and supernatural glory. On this occasion attention was riveted to a man on a simple platform reading from a scroll. More specifically, attention was fixed on the words of that scroll.

5. Impact on the people (8:9-12): The people were moved to tears by the hearing of God's word. Nehemiah, Ezra and the Levites, however, kept stressing that this was a day to celebrate, not to mourn. Feasting and sharing with the less fortunate were the appropriate ways to celebrate this holy day. *Do not be grieved, for the joy of Yahweh is your strength!* So the people celebrated that day as a festival, not because the walls had been completed, but because they had understood the word of the Lord.

C. Feast Observed (Nehemiah 8:13-18)

1. Lesson about the feast (8:13-14): On the second day the heads of families gathered to Ezra to receive further instruction from the law of God. This was a more select group than that of the previous day. In the lesson of the second day they learned how they should live in booths during the feast of Tabernacles in the seventh month. This fresh discovery from Scripture seems to have come as a surprise to these students. This feast had been celebrated by the pioneer returnees some nine decades earlier (cf. Ezra 3:4). It seems, however, that the booth-dwelling aspect of the feast which commemorated the wilderness wandering had been disregarded or at least reduced to tokenism.

2. Proclamation about the feast (8:15): A proclamation was circulated instructing the people to go to the nearby hills and cut tree branches to make their booths according to the law. Since the feast did not begin until the fifteenth day of the month, the people had nearly two weeks in which to make their preparations.

3. Observance of the feast (8:16-18): The people complied with the directive of their leaders with enthusiasm. They brought their tree branches to Jerusalem, the proper place for the observance of the feast (cf. Deuteronomy 31:11). They erected their booths in every open place, public and private, which they could find. Some even put their booths on the flat roofs of their homes! The entire assembly lived in booths for the seven days of the feast. Not since the days of Joshua had the feast of Tabernacles been so universally and enthusiastically observed. Great rejoicing filled the land. Each day of the week-long festival Ezra read to the people from the scroll of the law. He thus followed precisely the stipulations of Deuteronomy 31:11.

Confessing Transgression
Nehemiah 9:1-37

Fasting, repentance and confession precede forgiveness and reinstatement for God's people. The joyous festivity of Tabernacles celebration began on the eighth day to move in this direction (cf. Leviticus 23:27; Numbers 29:35).

A. Day of Fasting (Nehemiah 9:1-4)

1. Another assembly (9:1-2): The day after the feast of Tabernacles was a day of fasting. The worshipers wore sackcloth, a coarse rough material made of goat's hair. The wearing of this garb symbolized mourning. Their heads were darkened by the dirt that they had thrown over themselves. The purpose of the assembly was to make a corporate confession of sin and formally pledge to separate themselves from all foreigners. The repeated readings from the law were bearing fruit! That this group confessed the sins of their ancestors as well as their own is striking. They felt their solidarity with previous generations.

2. *Format of the assembly (9:3-4):* The format of the assembly was simple. The people stood while *they* (priests and/or Levites) read from the book of the law for a fourth of the day, i.e., about three hours. For an equal amount of time penitents *confessed and worshiped* God. Eight Levites then led the people in voicing their spiritual distress. A second group of eight Levites led a responsive prayer of praise. Apparently they all recited the prayer in unison, so it must have been written beforehand. Since the language is similar to the prayer in Ezra 9, the great scribe and priest was most likely the author of the prayer.

B. Confession of Faith (Nehemiah 9:5-15)

The Levites' prayer is one of the longest in the Bible. It begins with a confession of God's greatness—his glorious name, his creative works, his covenant with Abraham, and his gift of the Promised Land to Israel. The prayer shows the influence of the Scripture reading of recent weeks. It rehearsed how God brought Israel out of Egypt with signs and wonders, dividing the sea, leading them by fiery cloud. At Sinai he gave Israel his law including the holy Sabbath. Through the wilderness period God provided manna from heaven and water from a rock. Such is the record of Yahweh's faithfulness to his people.

C. Confession of Sin (Nehemiah 9:16-31)

1. *Israel's wilderness experience (9:16-21):* The Israelites, however, proved unfaithful to the gracious God who redeemed them. Within weeks they forgot the wondrous deeds he had done on their behalf. They stubbornly refused to obey his words. They made a calf idol. They appointed a leader to take them back to Egyptian slavery. Even so, God did not forsake his people. He led them with the fiery cloud. He fed them with manna. He instructed them through his Spirit. He gave them water for their thirst. For forty years he provided

655

for them so that *their clothes did not wear out, nor their feet swell* from the long marches.

2. *Israel's inheritance (9:22-25):* When they left the wilderness, the Lord delivered the kingdoms of Sihon and Og into the hands of his people. He brought Israel into the Promised Land. There he enabled them to capture fortified cities and well-furnished houses. Fertile fields, orchards, vineyards and cisterns fell into their hands. Israel *reveled* in the good things that God had placed at their disposal.

3. *Israel's oppressors (9:26-31):* Still Israel failed God. They cast his law behind their back, i.e., put it out of mind. They killed God's prophets and committed great blasphemies. To discipline his people, God delivered them into the power of a series of oppressors. Each time, however, when Israel cried out to the Lord he sent a deliverer to set them free. This cycle of sin, suffering, supplication and salvation was repeated many times during the period of the Judges. Israel never seemed to learn from these experiences. Yet God continued to bear with them. He admonished them by his Spirit through the prophets. Finally God gave them into the hands of the peoples of the land, i.e., the great powers. Even then, however, he did not make a full end of Israel. He showed his compassion yet once more.

D. Appeal for Grace (Nehemiah 9:32-37)

After this summary of the relationship of God and his people, the Levites made the only petition in this long prayer. They asked that God might note all the hardship that Israel had experienced from the days of the kings of Assyria unto that very moment. They hastened to add that their condition in no way impugned the justice of God. Israel deserved all that she had experienced, for the entire nation had not kept God's law. They had not turned from their evil ways. Thus at that moment, even though they were living in the land that God had promised their ancestors, they were slaves to a foreign power. Persian taxes required large portions of their produce and cattle. Thus the people of God were in great distress.

Renewing Commitment
Nehemiah 9:38-10:39

Following the acknowledgment of sin and appeal for grace, the post-Tabernacles solemn assembly began to take a more positive direction.

A. Covenant Document (Nehemiah 9:38-10:27)

The leaders, priests and Levites in the postexilic community agreed in writing to follow the law of God from that day forward. Nehemiah set the example by placing his name at the head of the list. Next is listed the name of a certain Zedekiah who probably assisted Nehemiah in civil authority. Next are listed twenty-one priestly names, of which at least fifteen are the names of families. This may explain why Ezra's name does not appear in the list. He was a member of the Seriah family that heads the list (cf. Ezra 7:1; 1 Chronicles 6:14). Seventeen Levites and forty-four leaders of the people were also signatories. Again these lists contain both family names and individual names.

B. Covenant Oath (Nehemiah 10:28-29)

1. United commitment (10:28): The community was united in its commitment. Everyone, including women and children old enough to understand, joined in the oath of allegiance. The list (priests, Levites, gatekeepers, etc.) points to an ordered community, restored to the traditional organization established centuries earlier. Furthermore, this community was sensitive to its calling to be *separate from the peoples.*

2. Serious commitment (10:29): Following the signing of the document, the next step in renewing the covenant was the ceremony of taking an oath. The rest of the people joined their leaders in taking upon themselves *a curse and an oath* that they would walk by God's law. Failure to abide by the terms of the covenant automatically triggered the implementation of the *curse,* i.e., stipulated penalties for disobedience.

C. Covenant Stipulations (Nehemiah 10:30-39)

Specific obligations were assumed by each of those who entered into the oath to walk by God's law. Seven provisions of the covenant are outlined in the closing verses of Nehemiah 10.

1. Negative stipulations (10:30-31): On the negative side, this covenant involved three obligations. First, they agreed to refrain from intermarrying with the peoples of the land. Second, they will refuse to

657

purchase any items from foreign merchants on the Sabbath or holy days. Purchasing items from foreign merchants violated the spirit if not the letter of the Sabbath law. Third, they will observe the sabbatical year (cf. Exodus 23:10-11; Leviticus 25:2-7) by 1) not planting crops; and 2) by not making exactions on any debt, i.e., requiring payments on debt.

2. *Positive stipulations (10:32-39):* The covenant also involved four positive obligations.

- They will contribute annually one third of a shekel to supply the regular sacrifices for the temple.
- By lot families will assume for a period of time the responsibility for supplying the wood for the altar. Apparently they had discovered that everybody's business was nobody's business.
- They agreed to give the Lord his due viz., the first fruits of ground and tree and the firstborn of sons and livestock.
- They pledged that, no matter what the cost, *we will not neglect the house of our God.*

3. *Significance:* The significance of what is being pledged here must not be missed. For years the Persian kings had taken responsibility for the maintenance of the temple service. Now the Jews were assuming that responsibility. This will be a heavy burden for a relatively small and poor community. The religious zeal triggered by the revival led by Ezra and Nehemiah now was being translated into concrete deeds. A faith that costs nothing is worth nothing.

Registers of Nehemiah's Generation
Nehemiah 11:1-36

Nehemiah again records the names of various individuals and families that figured prominently in the postexilic resettlement. These lists serve 1) to give honor to whom honor is due; 2) to trace the roots of the community to the past; and 3) to stress that the community was organized to carry out its calling to be a kingdom of priests and a holy nation. As detailed as these lists are, they are not complete. Those named come from the tribes of Judah, Benjamin and Levi. According to 1 Chronicles 9 Israelites of other tribes also took up residence in Jerusalem.

A. Residents of Jerusalem (Nehemiah 11:1-24)

1. Lottery (11:1-2): The hint in Nehemiah 7:4-5 that something was done about the sparse population of Jerusalem is now made explicit. The people cast lots to bring one out of ten families to join their leaders living in Jerusalem. All the men who volunteered to be part of this lottery were blessed by the people. The willingness of many to uproot their families to repopulate Jerusalem is another indication of the eagerness to see the community of God's people restored to its former glory.

2. Sub-categories (11:3-24): The register of those who came to live in Jerusalem includes sons of Judah (468), sons of Benjamin (928), priests (822), Levites (284), gatekeepers (172) and others. The temple singers had a special status in the city for they functioned under a direct commandment from King Artaxerxes.

3. Organization: The population of Jerusalem was well organized. Various overseers are mentioned (cf. verses 9, 14, 22). A Benjamite named Judah was *second in command of the city.* Some of the citizens are called *mighty men of valor* (verse 14); others are called *able men* (verse 6). These expressions in Hebrew are ambiguous. They can refer to either men of wealth or men of military skill. Jerusalem is twice called *the holy city* (verses 1, 18). This indicates that the postexilic community saw its mission as reflecting the holiness of God.

4. Choirs (11:25-36): The Persian king had a role in helping to organize the Jerusalem community. He authorized (and probably subsidized) the choirs that performed at stated times in the temple. The interests of the Jews were represented in the royal court by Pethahiah of Judah.

B. Residents of Villages (Nehemiah 11:25-36)

Seventeen villages from Beersheba in the south to the valley of Hinnom in the north were occupied by sons of Judah. Fifteen villages are identified as having been occupied by the sons of Benjamin. Some of these villages (e.g., Kiriath-arba and Beersheba) clearly were outside the territorial limits of the Persian province of Judea. Yet the Jews were permitted by the government to *encamp* (verse 30) in these old ancestral villages. Perhaps the Jewish leaders had in mind

659

someday reclaiming all the former territory that once had belonged to
the kingdom of Judah.

Registers of Priests and Levites
Nehemiah 12:1-26

Again the concern of the author is continuity. The significance of
the present can only be ascertained when its roots in the past are
clearly understood.

A. Original Émigrés (Nehemiah 12:1-11)
1. Priests (12:1-7): In the days of Jeshua the high priest—first
generation of the Restoration—there were twenty-two heads of
priestly families. Apparently two of the original twenty-four priestly
divisions had not yet been restored. Fifteen of those who signed the
covenant of Nehemiah 10 used their family names rather than their
personal names.
2. Levites (12:8-9): Eight heads of Levitical families are named.
This fills out the list found in Ezra 2:40 where only three Levitical
families are mentioned. Some of these names (e.g., Sherebiah)
continued to be used by Levites in Nehemiah's day. In some cases
these men hold the same offices as their namesakes a century earlier
(cf. Nehemiah 8:7; 9:4; 10:12). Members of these families had been
faithful to their ministries over several generations.

B. High Priestly Family (Nehemiah 12:10-11)
Jeshua was the first high priest after the return from captivity
(Ezra 3:2; Haggai 1:1). That the list is probably selective is indicated
by the fact that only one high priest—Joiakim—is named between
Jeshua and Eliashib, the high priest of Nehemiah's day a century
later. Three high priests are named as having followed Eliashib. The
list terminates with those who were active in the days of Darius II
(423-404 BC) during whose reign Nehemiah must have died. The last
name on the list is Jaddua. According to Josephus (*Antiquities* 11.8.4,
5) the name of the high priest who received Alexander the Great (332
BC) was Jaddua.

C. Second Generation (Nehemiah 12:12-21)
Joiakim was the high priest who followed Jeshua. This second
generation of priests contained twenty heads of families. This list

drives home once again the point that the priestly houses held on to their traditional names, not changing them with successive leaders.

D. Levitical Families (Nehemiah 12:22-26)

The list of heads of Levitical families was kept in a book of chronicles (not the biblical book by that name). This list seems to suggest that some singers were also employed as gatekeepers of the temple. The author stresses that the musical prescriptions of David were carefully followed in the postexilic community. Several of the Levitical names here appear in the list of those who signed the covenant document Nehemiah 10.

Dedicating the Walls
Nehemiah 12:27-43

A. Sacrifices (Nehemiah 12:27-30)

For the dedication of the wall all the Levites were assembled so that the event might be celebrated with great vocal and instrumental music. Purification rituals were performed both for these Levites and for the wall and its gates. On the analogy of 2 Chronicles 29:29, this probably was done by offering sin offerings and burnt offerings.

B. Walking the Walls (Nehemiah 12:31-43)

The highlight of the day was the walking on the walls. The leaders of the people and the musicians were divided into two groups. One group was led by Ezra. Nehemiah followed the other. The groups started in opposite directions around the circuit of the wall. The two choirs met and stood together in the house of God and sang praises to the Lord. Sacrifices followed. The city was filled with great joy.

Other Reforms
Nehemiah 12:44-13:3

Certain reforms were instituted on the day Jerusalem's walls were dedicated.

A. Contributions (Nehemiah 12:44-47)

Various officials were appointed that day to oversee the collection of temple contributions, *the portions required by the law for the priests and Levites.* The purification rituals of the Law of

661

Moses were performed as were the musical arrangements dating back to the days of David and Solomon. In the postexilic community from the days of Zerubbabel to the days of Nehemiah the people willingly had been paying their dues to priests and Levites because *they rejoiced over the priests and Levites who served.*

B. Separation (Nehemiah 13:1-3)

On wall dedication day they read aloud the Scriptures. From the book of Moses (cf. Deuteronomy 23:3-5) they learned that no Ammonite or Moabite should ever enter the assembly of God. This judgment went back to the days of Moses when these two peoples failed to aid the Israelites in their migration toward the Promised Land. In fact, the Ammonites and Moabites had attempted to curse Israel through the prophecies of Balaam. God, however, turned their curses into blessings. Having heard the verdict of Scripture, the postexilic community excluded all foreigners from Israel.

Once again the reading of Scripture had driven home to the Jews the obligation to be holy unto Yahweh. The prohibition enjoined was not absolute. It was religious, not ethnic. Those who embraced in faith the God of Israel, like Ruth the Moabitess, could find a very different reception in Israel.

Nehemiah's Second Governorship
Nehemiah 13:4-31

Nehemiah completed his first term as governor in the thirty-second year of Artaxerxes (432 BC). He returned to the Persian court to have his appointment reviewed and renewed. The record does not indicate how long he was absent from Jerusalem. During that absence, the postexilic community relapsed into some old sins. Nehemiah had been back only a short time before he once again clashed with compromise and created a spiritual earthquake.

A. Failure in Sanctity (Nehemiah 13:4-9)

1. Tobiah in the temple (13:4-6): Nehemiah's archenemy Tobiah had ardent supporters in Jerusalem (cf. 6:17-19). Eliashib the high priest, being related to Tobiah by marriage, actually had prepared for Tobiah a room in one of the temple chambers where contributions of the people previously had been stored. What audacity to empty a sacred chamber of what was dedicated to God to create a

662

warehouse for the personal possessions of any person, not to mention an enemy. From the temple, the very nerve-center of Jerusalem, Tobiah could wield his ungodly influence upon all the affairs of the Jewish people.

2. Nehemiah's action (13:7-9): When Nehemiah returned to Jerusalem, he learned about the evil that Eliashib had done in allowing an avowed enemy of the Jews to have a room in the temple. The governor (personally?) threw Tobiah's belongings out of the room. He then gave an order for all the rooms to be cleansed that had been defiled by the presence of this unbeliever. The dedicated utensils, grain offerings and frankincense were then returned to those rooms. For Nehemiah holiness was not negotiable. In this cleansing of the temple he became the forerunner of Christ.

B. Failure in Support (Nehemiah 13:10-14)

1. Problem (13:10): If the Jews before the exile erred in thinking they could bribe God by lavish gifts (e.g., Isaiah 1:11), the fault of the postexilic community was in robbing God of his due (Malachi 3:8). Nehemiah discovered that during his absence the Levites had not been given their due from the harvest. These servants of the Lord had been forced to leave the temple service to work the fields. The lofty commitment not to forsake the house of the God in chapter 10 had now become hollow words. Full-time servants of God cannot feed their families on rhetoric.

2. Nehemiah's action (13:11-14): Nehemiah reprimanded the officials for allowing this situation to exist. He then restored the Levites to their posts. A committee of four reliable priests and Levites was appointed to distribute the tithes and offerings among their kinsmen. Nehemiah then prayed that God might remember these actions taken on behalf of his house.

C. Sabbath Observance (Nehemiah 13:15-22)

1. Problem (13:15-18): Sabbath abuse was another problem that Nehemiah dealt with decisively. Some Jews were treating the Sabbath as an ordinary work day. Farmers were treading the grapes in the winepresses; others were hauling wine, grapes and figs into the city to put on sale. Nehemiah *admonished* these Jews. Foreign merchants were peddling their wares in Jerusalem on the Sabbath. The nobles were reprimanded for allowing such abuse of the holy day. Nehemiah pointed out to them that this was the same sin that got their fathers in trouble with the Lord. By profaning the Sabbath they were adding to the wrath on Israel (cf. Jeremiah 17:27).

2. Nehemiah's action (13:19-22): Nehemiah ordered the gates of the city closed just before dark on the Sabbath. He ordered that the gates not be reopened until after the Sabbath. He stationed temporarily some of his own servants at the gates to prevent any load from entering the city on the holy day. Once or twice the foreign merchants camped outside the walls of Jerusalem on the Sabbath. They may have been trying to do business with people on the wall. Nehemiah warned these merchants that if they continued to camp in front of the wall on the Sabbath he would use force against them. He also appointed Levites to be Sabbath gatekeepers so that the holy day might be properly observed within the city. Nehemiah prayed that God would remember such good deeds and have compassion on him.

D. Failure in Separation (Nehemiah 13:23-29)

1. Problem (13:23-24): During Nehemiah's absence from Jerusalem, Jews had intermarried with women from Ashdod, Ammon and Moab. Children were growing up in these homes that were unable to speak the language of Judah. Nehemiah saw clearly that religious intermarriage corrupts the second generation as well as the first. The confusion of tongues among the children signaled the erosion of Israelite identity. Nehemiah could not allow the compromise of his generation to undo the work of centuries. The situation was desperate.

2. Nehemiah's actions (13:25-27): Nehemiah contended with the men who had married these wives. He *cursed them,* i.e., placed a religious curse on them. He struck some of them and pulled out their hair. These were punishments that no doubt were part of the stipulated penalties in the oaths these men had taken some years before (cf. 10:30). He then made them renew their oath not to be involved in any way in intermarriage with the peoples of the land. Nehemiah pointed out that it was marriage to foreign wives that caused Solomon, a man greatly blessed and beloved by God, to sin. In the light of the historical record of the damage done by religious intermarriage, Nehemiah expressed shock that these men had acted unfaithfully against their God in this matter.

3. High profile case (13:28-29): In the process of his investigation, Nehemiah discovered that the grandson of the high priest had married the daughter of Sanballat the Horonite, that bitter enemy who had resisted so resolutely the building of the wall.

664

Nehemiah *drove him from me,* i.e. the grandson was expelled from Jerusalem. Nehemiah called upon God to remember those who so grievously had defiled the priesthood. After doing what he could do to solve the problem, Nehemiah simply committed the whole matter to the Lord.

E. Other Reforms (Nehemiah 13:30-31)

Other measures taken by Nehemiah upon his return included 1) purifying the people from everything foreign; 2) appointing specific duties for priests and Levites; 3) arranging for the wood supply for the temple; 4) arranging for the first fruits to be collected and distributed. For these reforms Nehemiah prayed that God might remember him for good. The inclusion of Nehemiah's memoirs in the sacred canon was one way Heaven answered this concluding prayer.

Conclusion

The final chapter of Nehemiah underscores the impression about this man already created by the earlier chapters. He was fervent in zeal for Yahweh. He possessed a holy boldness that made him brutally blunt with both friend and foe. Nehemiah was a masterful organizer and motivator. He was also a man of action. Even more important, he was a man of the Scriptures and a man of prayer. A man who approaches God on his knees will stand tall in any generation.

END OF THE PERSIAN PERIOD

We have now completed 1000 years of biblical history

OTHER BOOKS BY THE AUTHOR

Printed in Great Britain
by Amazon.co.uk, Ltd.,
Marston Gate.